제7판

교원임용고시
일반영어 필독서

임용영어 수험생 대다수가 선택하는

전공영어의 보통명사

유희태 일반영어

2S2R ③ 기출

- 교원임용고시 전공영어 독보적 전국 1위
  (2025년 예스24 전공영어 부문 박문각 누적 판매량 1위)
- 미국 버클리대학 유희태 박사의 독창적 방법론을 통한 기출분석
- 1997~2026학년도 모든 기출문제와 답안 수록
- 2016~2026학년도 기출문제의 섬세한 분석 제공

LSI 영어연구소 유희태 박사 편저

박문각 임용 동영상강의 www.pmg.co.kr

PREFACE

2026년 《2S2R 기출》 7판을 내며

2010년 4월 초판이 출간된 지 16년, 6판이 나온 지 3년이 지났다. 그 기간 노량진에서 강의하면서 이 교재의 장단점에 대해 수험생들과 의견을 교환할 기회가 있었다. 이 7판은 그 대화의 산물이다. 하지만 6판의 문제의식이나 방향성은 그대로 유지했다. 2016학년도에 임용시험 유형이 일부 바뀐 이후 (예를 들면 그 이전에 있던 논술형 10점짜리 문제가 없어졌다) 현재까지 제도의 변화가 없었기 때문이다.

이 7판 교재는 《유희태 일반영어 시리즈 ① - 2S2R 기본》, 《유희태 일반영어 시리즈 ② - 2S2R 유형》, 《유희태 일반영어 시리즈 ④ - 1 - 2S2R 문제은행》, 《유희태 일반영어 시리즈 ④ - 2 - 2S2R 문제은행》, 《유희태 일반영어 시리즈 ⑤ - 기출 VOCA 30days》와 함께 하나의 시리즈를 이룬다. 이 교재는 시리즈 ①, ② 그리고 ⑤를 통해 길러진 일반영어에 대한 이론과 유형, 어휘를 기출문제에 적용해 보도록 짜여있다. 이 시리즈를 통해 공부한다면 임용시험의 기본 과목인 일반영어를 충분히 정복할 수 있으리라 믿는다.

『유희태 2S2R 시리즈』를 효과적으로 활용하는 방법은, 대학 1~2학년 때 《2S2R 기본》을 최소 3회독, 평균 5회독하여 일반영어 기본이론을 확실하게 다진 뒤, 2~3학년 때 《2S2R 유형》을 최소 3회독하여 임용 유형에 기본이론을 확장 적용하는 훈련을 하고, 3학년 때 《2S2R 기출》을 2회독한 다음, 처음으로 임용시험을 치르는 4학년 때 《2S2R 문제은행》을 가지고 공부하는 것이다. 이 과정에서 《기출 VOCA 30days》는 1~2학년 때부터 주 6회 매일 20분씩 꾸준히 공부하기를 추천한다.

이 7판 작업을 하면서 많은 분의 도움을 받았다. 원고를 보기 좋은 최종 결과물로 만들어준 박문각의 문석희 편집자와 박용 회장님께 고마움을 전한다. 이 교재가 출간되는 과정에서 묵묵히 최선을 다해주신 모든 인쇄 출판 노동자들께도 감사의 말씀을 전하고 싶다. 아무쪼록 이 《2S2R 기출》 7판 교재가 예비 교사 여러분의 합격에 도움이 되기를 진심으로 바란다.

2026년 새해를 앞두고 LSI 영어연구소에서

유희태

GUIDE

01 2026~2016학년도 일반영어 기출분석

2026학년도

2026학년도 일반영어는 총 3문항 12점(15%)이 출제되어 작년과 동일했다. A형에서 서술형 1문항(4점), B형에서 서술형 2문항(8점)이 출제된 것 역시 작년과 같았다. 6년 연속 3문항만 출제되고 있다. 난이도 면에서 올해 일반영어는 작년과 유사했다는 것이 중론이다. 작년과 마찬가지로 올해 문제도 정답이 명확하게 도출되는 문제가 대부분이었다. 서술형에서는 최근의 경향이었던 비유적 언어의 의미를 묻는 문제 대신 개념 설명형 문제가 출제되었다. 수능형 내용 확인 문제가 아니라 전문적 독해력과 설명력을 요구하는 문제였다. 정답을 정확히 서술하기 위해서는 텍스트의 추상적 핵심 개념 추출 능력, 논리적 연결성을 기반으로 한 어휘 선택 능력, 그리고 철학적 설명을 명확히 재진술하는 능력 등이 요구되었다. 상당히 고난도의 문제라 할 수 있다. 빈칸추론 문제는 2문항이 출제되었는데, A형은 평이했지만 B형은 상당히 까다로웠다. B형의 Summary 문제는 이전 문제들과 마찬가지로 가장 기본적인 series 패턴이 출제되어, 2S2R로 공부한 수험생이라면 매우 쉽게 풀 수 있었다는 것이 중론이었다.

문제 유형 면에서는 작년과 마찬가지로 기입형 2점 문항은 출제되지 않았고, 3문항 모두 서술형이었다. A형 1문항과 B형 2문항이었으며, 요약 문항을 제외한 나머지 두 문항에는 모두 빈칸추론 유형의 문제가 포함되었다. 지문 내용 면에서는 A형과 B형 모두 작년보다 약간 어려웠다. 지문 길이 면에서는 A형 11번이 440자로 작년 400자보다 40자 정도 늘었고, B형 7번은 460자로 작년 345자보다 115자 늘었다. B형 10번 요약 문제는 317자로 작년 282자보다 35자 늘었다. 전체적으로 일반영어 지문의 길이가 상당히 길어져 수험생들이 느끼는 체감 난도는 더 높았을 것으로 보인다.

한마디로, 2026학년도 일반영어는 글의 논리를 정확하게 파악해야만 정답을 도출할 수 있는 문제 중심이었다. 서술형 문제와 빈칸추론 문제 모두 결국 글의 내적 논리를 정확히 파악해야만 정답이 나오기 때문이다. 빈칸추론 문제에서 지문 전체 구조를 연결하는 핵심 연결어를 고르는 문제는 임용시험의 단골 유형인데, 올해도 예외는 아니었다. 항상 강조하지만, 평소에 논리적 지문 분석 방법을 꼼꼼하고 구조적으로 철저히 연습한 수험생이라면 좋은 결과를 얻을 수 있었을 것이다.

2025학년도

2025학년도 일반영어는 총 3문항 12점(15%)이 출제되어, 작년과 변화가 없었다. A형에서 서술형 1문항(4점), B형에선 서술형 2문항(8점)이 출제된 것도 작년과 같았다. 5년 연속 3문항밖에 출제되지 않았다. 난이도에 있어서, 올해 일반영어는 작년과 유사했다는 것이 중론이다. 작년과 마찬가지로 올해 문제도 정답이 딱 떨어지는 문제가 대부분이었다. 서술형에선 최근의 흐름인 일반영어에서 문학의 비유적 언어의 의미를 물어보는 문제가 올해도 출제되었다. 문제 유형에 있어서는, 작년과 마찬가지로 A형 서술형 1문항과 B형 서술형 1문항 모두 빈칸추론 유형의 문제가 포함되었는데, 빈칸에 들어갈 단어를 찾기가 그렇게 쉽지만은 않았다. B형의 Summary 문제는 그 이전 문제들과 마찬가지로 가장 기본적인 series 패턴이 출제되어 2S2R로 공부한 수험생이라면 매우 쉽게 풀 수 있었다는 것이 수험생들의 중론이었다. 지문의 내용 면에서는 A형은 쉬웠던 반면, B형은 어려웠다. 지문의 길이 측면에서는, A형 10번은 400자로 작년 404자와 유사하였고, B형 8번은 345자로 작년 373자보다 28자 줄어들었다. B형 9번 Summary 문제는 282자로 작년 269자보다 13자 늘어났다.

한마디로, 2025학년도 일반영어는 예년과 마찬가지로, 글의 논리를 정확하게 파악해야만 답을 올바르게 찾을 수 있는 문제 중심이었다. 빈칸추론은 결국 글의 내적 논리를 정확히 알아야만 정답이 정확하게 나오기 때문이다. 다행히 A형과 B형의 빈칸추론 문제에서 작년과 마찬가지로 명확한 답안 추론이 가능하였기에, 수험생이 쓸데없이 고민하지 않을 수 있었다. 항상 강조하지만, 평소에 지문분석 방법을 논리적으로 꼼꼼히 그리고 구조적으로 철저히 연습한 수험생이라면 좋은 결과가 나올 수 있었을 것이다.

2024학년도

2024학년도 일반영어는 총 3문항 12점(15%)이 출제되어, 작년과 변화가 없었다. A형에서 서술형 1문항(4점), B형에선 서술형 2문항(8점)이 출제가 된 것도 작년과 같았다. 4년 연속 3문항밖에 출제되지 않았는데, 일반영어는 3문항(12점)으로 고정되는 느낌이다. 난이도에 있어서, 올해 일반영어는 작년과 유사했지만, 지문의 길이가 작년보다 훨씬 짧아졌기에 체감적으로는 덜 어려웠다. 또한 작년과 마찬가지로 올해 문제도 정답이 딱 떨어지는 문제가 대부분이었다. 문제 유형에 있어서는, 작년과 마찬가지로 A형 서술형 1문항과 B형 서술형 1문항 모두 빈칸추론 유형의 문제가 포함되었는데, 빈칸에 들어갈 단어를 찾는 게 그렇게 쉽지는 않았다. 또한

GUIDE

서술형 답안쓰기도 교수법에서 시간을 많이 빼앗긴 바람에 시간이 부족했다. 하지만, B형의 Summary 문제는 그 이전 문제들과 마찬가지로 가장 기본적 패턴인 series와 contrast 패턴으로 출제되어 2S2R로 공부한 수험생이라면 매우 쉽게 풀 수 있었다는 것이 수험생들의 중론이었다. 지문의 내용 면에서는 A형은 쉬웠던 반면, B형은 어려웠다. 지문의 길이 측면에서는, A형 10번은 330자로 작년 404자보다 74자 짧아졌고, B형 9번도 373자로 작년 468자에서 95자 줄었다. B형 8번 Summary 문제도 269자로 작년 297자에서 28자 줄어들었다. 한마디로, 2024학년도 일반영어는 예년과 마찬가지로, 글의 논리를 정확하게 파악해야만 답을 올바르게 찾을 수 있는 문제 중심이었다. 빈칸추론은 결국 글의 내적 논리를 정확히 알아야만 정답이 정확하게 나오기 때문이다. 다행히 A형과 B형의 빈칸추론 문제에서 작년과 마찬가지로 명확한 답안 추론이 가능하였기에, 수험생이 쓸데없는 고민은 하지 않을 수 있었다. 항상 강조하지만, 평소에 지문분석 방법을 논리적으로 꼼꼼히 그리고 구조적으로 철저히 연습한 수험생이라면 좋은 결과가 나올 수 있었을 것이다.

2023학년도

2023학년도 일반영어는 총 3문항 12점(15%)이 출제되어, 작년과 변화가 없었다. A형에서 서술형 1문항(4점), B형에서 서술형 2문항(8점)이 출제된 것도 작년과 같았다. 3년 연속 3문항밖에 출제되지 않았는데, 일반영어는 3문항(12점)으로 고정되는 느낌이다. 난이도에 있어서, 올해 일반영어는 작년보다는 쉬웠다는 것이 중평이다. 체감적 난이도는 작년과 유사했지만, 복수의 답도 가능할 정도로 설득력이 떨어졌던 작년 문제에 비해서, 올해 문제는 정답이 딱 떨어지는 문제가 대부분이었기에, 실제 답을 쓰기는 그렇게 어렵지 않았다. 문제 유형에 있어서는, 작년과 마찬가지로 A형 서술형 1문항과 B형 서술형 1문항 모두 빈칸추론 유형의 문제가 포함되었는데, 빈칸에 들어갈 단어를 찾기가 그렇게 어렵지 않았다. 오히려 상대적으로 서술형 답안쓰기가 더 어렵게 느껴졌다는 것이 수험생들의 중론이었다. B형의 Summary 문제는 그 이전 문제들과 마찬가지로 가장 기본적 패턴인 series 패턴이 출제되어 2S2R로 공부한 수험생이라면 매우 쉽게 풀 수 있었던 문제였다. 지문의 내용면에서는, 수험생들이 어려워하는 미학과 자연과학에 관련된 내용이 출제되었던 작년과는 다르게, 상대적으로 익숙한 '2개 국어를 말하는 능력(bilingualism)'과 자동화와 관련된 내용이 출제되어 체감 난이도는 높지 않았다. 지문의 길이는 A형 11번은 404자로 작년보다 70자 정도 길어졌고, B형 9번도 468자로 작년보다 86자 늘었다. 반면 B형 8번 Summary 문제는 297자로 12자 줄어들었다. 전체적으로 지문의 길이가 약간씩 늘어났기에 시간 배분을 잘하는 것도 중요한 일이었다. 특히 B형은 그 어느 때보다 길이가 긴 지문이 나와서 시간이 많이 요구되는 문제였다.

한마디로 정리하면, 2023학년도 올해 일반영어는 예년과 마찬가지로, 글의 논리를 정확하게 파악해야만 답을 올바르게 찾을 수 있는 문제 중심이었다. 빈칸추론은 결국 글의 내적 논리를 정확히 알아야만 정답이 정확하게 나오기 때문이다. 다행히 A형과 B형의 빈칸추론 문제에서 작년보다는 명확한 답안 추론이 가능하였기에, 수험생이 쓸데없는 고민을 하지는 않을 수 있었다. 항상 강조하지만, 평소에 논리적으로 지문분석 방법을 꼼꼼히 그리고 구조적으로 철저히 연습한 수험생이라면 좋은 결과가 나올 수 있었을 것이다.

2022학년도

2022학년도 일반영어는 총 3문항 12점(15%)이 출제되어, 작년과 변화가 없었다. A형에서 서술형 1문항(4점), B형에서 서술형 2문항(8점)이 출제되었다. 난이도에 있어서, 올해 일반영어는 작년과 유사하게, 체감적으로는 쉽게 느껴졌지만, 실제 답을 쓰기는 만만치 않았다. 문제 유형에 있어서는, 작년과 마찬가지로 A형 서술형 1문항과 B형 서술형 1문항 모두 빈칸추론 유형의 문제가 포함되었는데, 빈칸에 들어갈 단어를 찾기가 만만치 않았다. 상대적으로 서술형 답안쓰기는 빈칸추론보다는 평이하게 느껴졌지만, 그럼에도 쉽게 풀 수 있는 문제들은 아니었다. 특히 B형 8번 문제는 꽤 까다로웠다. Summary는 series 패턴의 유형으로 2S2R로 공부한 수험생이라면 매우 쉽게 풀 수 있었던 문제였다. 심지어 doublespeak를 다루는 지문이 예전 모의고사에 출제된 적도 있었던 만큼 매우 편하게 풀 수 있었다. 지문의 내용면에서는, 자연과학에서 1개, 예술(미학)에서 1개, 정치적 이중 언어(doublespeak)에서 1개가 출제되었다. 대다수 수험생들이 예술지문을 가장 어렵게 느꼈고, 실제로도 어려웠다. 그럼에도 평소 미학적 글에 익숙한 수험생들은 상대적으로 쉽게 풀 수 있었던 문제였다. 지문의 길이는 A형 11번은 338자로 작년보다 38자 길어졌고, B형 8번도 382자로 작년보다 32자 늘었다. 그리고 B형 9번 Summary 문제도 310자로 12자 늘어났다. 전체적으로 지문의 길이가 약간씩 늘어났기에 시간 배분을 잘하는 것도 중요한 일이었다.
한마디로 정리하면, 2022학년도 올해 일반영어는 예년과 마찬가지로, 글의 논리를 정확하게 파악해야만 답을 올바르게 찾을 수 있는 문제 중심이었다. 빈칸추론은 결국 글의 내적 논리를 정확히 알아야만 정답이 정확하게 나오기 때문이다. A형과 B형 문제 모두 빈칸추론 문제는 쉽지는 않았지만, 평소에 논리적으로 지문분석 방법을 꼼꼼히 그리고 구조적으로 철저히 연습한 수험생이라면 상대적으로 잘 풀 수 있는 문제였다. 다시 한번 강조하지만 영어 독해의 기본을 튼튼하게 공부하는 것이 임용 일반영어에서 고득점을 받을 수 있는 지름길임을 명심하자.

GUIDE

2021학년도

2021학년도 일반영어는 총 3문항 12점(15%)이 출제되어, 문항 수에 있어서 총 6문항 22점(27%)이 출제되었던 작년보다 문항수와 더불어 출제 비중도 대폭 줄었다. A형에서 서술형 1문항(4점), B형에서 서술형 2문항(8점)이 출제되었다. 올해 일반영어는 작년과 비교하여 체감적으로는 매우 쉽게 느껴졌지만, 실제 답을 쓰기는 꽤 까다롭게 출제되었다. 문제 유형에 있어서는, 작년과 마찬가지로 A형 서술형 1문항과 B형 서술형 1문항 모두 빈칸추론 유형의 문제가 포함되었는데, 빈칸에 들어갈 한 단어를 찾기가 만만치 않았고, 서술형 답안쓰기 문제도 꽤 까다로웠다. 지문의 내용면에서는, 예년과 다르게 두 지문 모두 예술(미학)과 관련된 것이 출제되어, 평소 미학적 글에 익숙하지 않은 수험생들은 매우 어려울수 밖에 없었다. 지문의 길이는 A형 11번은 300자, B형 10번은 350자, B형 11번 Summary문제는 298자로, 예년보다 상대적으로 짧았다.
한마디로 정리하면, 2021학년도 올해 일반영어는 예년과 유사하게, 글의 논리를 정확하게 파악해야만 답을 정확하게 찾을 수 있는 문제 중심이었다. 빈칸추론은 결국 글의 내적 논리를 정확히 알아야만 정답이 정확하게 나오기 때문이다. A형과 B형 문제 모두 빈칸추론 문제는 쉽지는 않았지만, 평소에 논리적으로 지문분석 방법을 꼼꼼히 그리고 구조적으로 철저히 연습한 수험생이라면 상대적으로 잘 풀 수 있는 문제였다. B형 서술형 11번 Summary 문제는 예년과 난이도에 있어서 큰 차이가 없었던 문제로 2S2R로 공부한 수험생이라면 무난히 풀 수 있는 문제였다.

2020학년도

2020학년도 일반영어는 총 5문항 20점(25%)이 출제되어, 문항 수에 있어서 총 4문항 15점(19%)이 출제되었던 작년보다 문항 수와 더불어 출제 비중도 늘어났다. A형에서 서술형 4문항(16점), B형에선 서술형 1문항(Summary)이 출제되었다. 올해 일반영어는 예년과 다른 유형이 출제되어 체감적으로 어렵게 느껴졌고, 실제로도 답을 구하기 까다롭게 출제되었다. 난이도의 측면에서 보면, 작년보다는 2018학년도와 유사하여 매우 까다로웠다. A형 서술형 4문항 모두 빈칸추론 문제가 포함되었는데, 빈칸에 들어갈 한 단어를 찾기가 수월하지 않았다. 반면, 서술형 답안쓰기는 상대적으로 무난한 편이었다. 내용적으로는 예년과 유사하게 다양한 영역에서 출제되었다. A형 8번(441자)은 경제, 9번(381자)은 문화사회학, 11번(368자)은 역사, 12번(344자)은 의학, B형 9번 Summary 문제(366자)는 교육에 관련된 문제가 출제되었다.

한마디로 정리하면, 글의 논리를 정확하게 파악했는지 아닌지를 물어보는 문제가 대다수였다. 빈칸추론 문제는 결국 글의 내적 논리를 정확히 알아야만 정확하게 정답이 나오기 때문이다. A형 빈칸추론 문제는 쉽지는 않았지만, 평소에 논리적으로 지문분석 방법을 꼼꼼하고 철저히 연습한 수험생이라면 상대적으로 잘 풀 수 있는 문제였다. B형 서술형 9번 Summary 문제는 예년과 난이도에 있어서 큰 차이가 없어서 2S2R로 공부한 수험생이라면 무난히 풀 수 있는 문제였다.

2019학년도

2019학년도 일반영어는 총 4문항 15점(19%)이 출제되어, 문항 수에 있어서 총 4문항 15점(19%)이 출제되었던 작년과 동일하였다. 일반영어는 예년에 비해 지문의 길이가 길어 체감적으로는 어렵게 느껴질 수도 있었지만, 전체적으로는 작년보다 어렵지 않았다는 것이 수험생들의 중론이다. A형 기입형 8번 문제는 서로 다른 문화에 대한 이해를 묻는 문제였는데 매우 평이한 문제였다. A형 서술형 13번 문제는 지문의 길이가 꽤 길어 시간이 좀 걸리는 문제였지만, 평소에 과학과 실험에 대한 준비를 많이 한 수험생이라면 어렵지 않게 풀어낼 수 있는 문제였다. B형 5번 서술형 문항은 일반영어 문제 가운데 가장 어렵게 느껴졌던 문제였다. 우선 지문의 길이가 450자로 매우 길었고, 빈칸추론도 그렇게 쉽지만은 않았다. 하지만 평소에 논리적으로 지문분석을 연습한 수험생이라면 무난히 풀 수 있는 문제였다. B형 서술형 7번 Summary 문제는 예년과 난이도에 있어서 큰 차이가 없어서 2S2R로 공부한 수험생이라면 매우 쉽게 답을 쓸 수 있는 문제였다. 지문의 내용은 작년과 유사하게 사회학, 실험, 인문학 등 골고루 출제되었다.

2018학년도

2018학년도 일반영어는 총 4문항 15점(19%)이 출제되어, 문항 수에 있어서는 3문항 11점(13%)이 출제되었던 작년보다 서술형 1문항이 더 늘어났다. 특히 예년과 마찬가지로 수험생들이 꽤 부담을 가지고 풀었던 문제가 많았다. A형 기입형 2번 빈칸추론 문제는 평이하게 출제되어 큰 어려움이 없었고, B형 서술형 7번 Summary 문제는 예년과 난이도에 있어서 큰 차이가 없었던 문제로 2S2R로 공부한 수험생이라면 충분히 답을 쓸 수 있는 문제였다. A형 서술형 14번 문제는 지문 번역은 어렵지 않았지만 출제자가 요구하는 답을 정확하게 서술한 수험생들이 많지 않았던 꽤 까다로운 문제였다. B형 서술형 3번 dowsing에 관련된 문제는 지문도 어려웠고, 답을 서술하는 것도 어려워서 2018학년도 시험에서 가장 어려웠던 문제 가운데 하나라는 것이 중론이다. 지문의 내용은 주로 경제 중심의 지문이 출제되었던 작년과는 다르게 교육, 사회학, 실험, 인문학 등 골고루 출제되었다.

GUIDE

2017학년도

2017학년도 일반영어는 총 3문항 11점(13%)이 출제되어, 문항 수에 있어서는 2016학년도와 동일하였다. 하지만 3문항 13점(16%)이 출제되었던 2016학년도에 비하면 배점이 약간 줄었다. 2015학년도에는 3문항 17점(21%)이었고, 2014학년도에는 4문항 20점(25%)이었다. 즉, 전체적인 흐름을 보면 일반영어의 비중은 2014학년도 이후에 계속 줄어들고 있다. 점수의 비중이 줄어든 결정적 원인은 2016학년도와 2017학년도엔 그 전년들과는 다르게 논술형 10점짜리가 출제되지 않았기 때문이다. 그렇기에 절대적인 점수 비중이 줄어들었음에도 불구하고 많은 수험생들이 여전히 일반영어에 대한 큰 부담감을 가지고 있음을 부정할 수 없다. 논술형으로 출제된 일반영어는 상대적으로 쉽게 느껴졌기 때문이다. 지문의 내용은 과학, 환경, 사회 등 다양한 지문이 출제되었던 그 이전 시험과는 다르게 주로 경제 중심의 지문이 출제되었다.

2016학년도

2016학년도 일반영어는 총 3문항 13점(16%)이 출제되어, 3문항 17점(21%)이 출제되었던 2015학년도와 4문항, 20점(25%)이 출제되었던 2014학년도에 비해 배점은 많이 줄어들었다. 하지만 2016학년도 수험생들이 느꼈던 체감 난이도 때문에 일반영어는 문항 비중과는 관계없이 두려움의 대상이 되어버렸다. 실제로 2016학년도 시험에서 합격을 좌우할 문제로 대다수 수험생들은 A형 서술형 14번 문학문제와 함께 B형 일반영어 4번 문제를 지목하였다. 이 두 문항에 출제된 지문은 모두 20세기 상반기에 쓰인 글답게 비유적 언어가 많이 사용되어, 직설적 화법에 익숙한 현대인들이 읽고 이해하기에는 만만치 않은 것이 사실이다. 특히 20세기 상반기에 필명을 날리던 Darrell Huff의 유명한 에세이 「How to Lie with Statistics」에서 발췌된 지문은, 소위 '일반영어 독해'만 가지고는 풀리지 않는다는 게 수험생들의 애로 사항이 있었다. 밑줄 친 부분 "little dash of powder, little pot of paint"가 가리키는 것을 찾는 문제였는데, 철저히 논리에 기반해야 정답이 나올 수 있는 아주 좋은 문제였다. 이 문제가 2016학년도 영어 임용시험에서 최고의 논란거리가 된 데에는 노량진에서 일반영어를 강의하는 각 학원의 선생님들의 답안이 모두 달라 수험생들을 더욱 혼란스럽게 했기 때문이다. A형 11번 서술형 문제는 지문을 ≪Newsweek≫(Aug 15, 2009)에서 뽑았다. 이슈가 된 환경문제를 다룬 것으로 시의적절한 면이 있다고 생각된다. 이 문제도 서술형 문제보다는 빈칸추론이 더 어려운 문제였다. 이 문제도 '독해'가 된다고 해서 답이 나오는 것이 아니라, 철저히 논리에 기반하여 풀어야만 답이 나올 수 있는 문제로, 수험생들이 어려움을 느꼈던 문제 가운데 하나였다. 지금까지 단 한 번도 빠지지 않고 논술형 10점짜리로 출제되었던 일반영어가 2016학년도엔 5점짜리 서술형 문제로 축소되어 출제되었다. Summary 문제였으며, 그리 어렵지는 않았다. 2S2R을 열심히 한 수험생들은 모두 맞출 수 있는 문제였기 때문이다.

02 일반영어 대비전략

임용고시에서 일반영어는 중요하다. 일반영어에서 고득점을 받지 못하면 합격이 쉽지 않기 때문이다. 수험생들이 가장 많은 시간을 들이고도 효과를 가장 적게 보는 과목이 일반영어이다. 항상 하는 말이지만, 시험이란 것은 문제가 쉬운 해도 있고 어려운 해도 있다. 예전에도 2010학년도와 2012학년도에는 어려웠고, 2011학년도와 2013학년도는 상대적으로 쉬웠다. 그 이후에도, 2016학년도는 매우 어려웠는데, 다음해인 2017학년도엔 상대적으로 평이하게 출제되었다. 2018학년도에도 매우 어려웠다가 2019학년도에는 다시 쉽게 출제되었다. 그러다가 2020학년도는 역대 가장 어려웠다는 평가를 받았고, 2021학년도에선, 예전과는 다르게, 문항 수는 줄었지만 문제 자체는 어려웠다. 따라서 일반영어 시험의 경향이 이렇기 때문에, 시험 준비를 할 때는 원칙에 충실해 기본을 튼튼히 하는 것이 가장 중요하다. 수박 겉 핥기식 독해 공부는 실전에 별 도움이 되지 않는다. 다시 강조하지만 '시험은 문제가 쉬운 해도 있고 어려운 해도 있다'는 것을 항상 명심하여 그 어떠한 문제가 나오더라도 다 맞출 수 있는 실력 그 자체를 키우는 것 외에는 정답이 있을 수 없다. 이리 뛰고 저리 뛰는 캥거루식 공부는 지양하고, 묵묵히 무소의 뿔처럼 홀로 힘차게 나아가는 지혜가 필요하다.

일반영어를 대비하는 다음의 10가지 방법을 명심하기 바란다.

1. 논리적 사고력이 없으면, 일반영어 고득점은 절대 불가능하다는 점을 명심하자.

   Summary나 빈칸추론 등을 묻는 문제는 거의 매년 출제되므로 평소에 철저하게 많이 준비하는 것이 필수적이다. 선택이 아니라 필수라는 점을 염두에 두자. 이런 문제들은 번역이 된다고 해서 풀리지 않는다. 즉, 여러분이 교사가 되어 학생들을 가르칠 때 얼마나 논리정연하게 가르칠 것인가를 미리 테스트하는 문제이다. 평소에 이런 문제에 대비해 논리·구조·대화적으로 글을 읽는 연습을 심도 있게 하는 것이 가장 중요하다.

2. 체계 없이 무작정 많이 읽고 보는 식의 독해 방법을 지양하자.

   시간이 많이 걸릴뿐더러 문장을 해석하고 난 후에도 지문을 제대로 이해하지 못하거나 글쓴이의 생각을 제대로 파악하지 못해 결국 오답을 고르는 우를 범하기 때문이다. 따라서 빠른 시간 내에 효율적으로 독해를 하고, 글쓴이의 마음속을 꿰뚫어 볼 수 있는 영문독해 방법이 요구된다. Pattern 중심의 읽기 방법론을 권한다.

3. 10권의 책을 1번 보는 것보다 1권의 책을 10번 반복해 보는 것이 효과적이다.

   반복적인 학습 과정에서 구문과 글의 구조가 부지불식간에 여러분의 것으로 되어 있을 것이기 때문이다. 일반영어를 위해 이것저것 많은 교재를 공부하지 말고 임용에 포커스를 둔 교재들을 반복해서 공부하기 바란다.

4. 최상의 시험전략은 틀린 문제를 두 번 다시 틀리지 않는 것이다.

강의를 듣기 전에 정해놓은 분량을 풀고, 채점한 다음 강의를 듣고, 틀린 부분을 확인하는 식으로 한 권을 다 풀고 난 후 취약한 부분, 틀린 문제들을 다시 반복하자. 그리고 가능하면, 오답노트를 만들기 바란다. 일반적으로 틀리는 것을 자꾸 틀리는 경향이 있는 데다 시험장에서도 마찬가지이기 때문이다. 처음엔 틀리는 문제가 너무 많아서 오답노트 만들기가 힘들겠지만, 점점 그 양이 줄어들게 되므로 너무 걱정하지 않아도 된다. 오답노트에는 단어, 어휘, 문장뿐 아니라 문제 유형 그리고 글의 구문이나 구조 등이 들어가 있으면 좋다.

주의사항 오답노트의 진가는 형식이 아닌 정신에 있다는 것을 명심하자. 틀린 것을 겸허히 받아들이고, 절대 두 번 다시 틀리지 않겠다는 마음가짐이 필요하다. 예쁜 오답노트가 항상 좋은 것만은 아니다. 단지 본인의 만족감만을 높여주는 것은 의미가 없다.

5. 매일 20분 동안 단어를 공부하자(주 6일).

외울 땐 동의어 한 개 정도는 같이 반복하자. 같은 단어를 16일 동안 반복하자.

6. 어려운 구문과 비유적 언어가 많이 쓰인 고급지문을 많이 읽자.

짧은 영미 단편소설을 1~2주에 하나 정도 읽어주자.

7. 평소에 시간 관리를 위해 시계를 항상 곁에 놓는 것도 권할 만하다.

빠르게 읽고 푸는 연습을 하는 데 좋은 방법이 될 수 있기 때문이다. 연습도 항상 실전이라는 마음가짐으로 준비하는 것이 필요하다.

8. 나 자신에게 냉정해지자.

우리는 본성상 자신에게 너그러울 수밖에 없다. 예를 들어, 3분 안에 풀어야 할 문제를 10분 안에 풀고 맞았다고 안도하지 말라는 것이다. 이미 그것은 틀린 것이다. '시간의 검증'을 통과하지 못했기 때문이다. 자신의 현 위치를 냉엄하게 판단하고 그 출발점에서 현재의 '가능성'을 미래의 '현실성'으로 바꾸어 나가는 지혜가 필요함을 잊지 말자.

9. Self-handicapping(스스로에게 핸디캡 주기)는 이제 그만!

Self-handicapping이란 자신이 행한 결과가 좋지 않을 것을 미리 준비해서, 사전에 그것을 합리화하기 위한 행동을 말한다. 우리는 모두 이런 경험들을 가지고 있다. 시험 날인데, 친구들에게 물어보면, 하나같이 전날 시험 준비를 잘 못했다고 말한다. 스스로 단점이나 결점을 만드는 것인데, 이것은 결국 시험을 못 봤을 때를 대비하고자 미리 변명거리를 만들어놓은 것에 불과하다. 하지만 이것의 속뜻은 '나는 원래 이 정도로 못하는 사람은 아니야'

라는 자기 우월감도 동시에 있는 것이기도 하다. 이런 일이 발생하는 근본 원인은 '남들의 평가를 지나치게 의식하기 때문'이다. 시험을 준비할 때 우리가 명심해야 할 것은 '남들의 평가'가 아니라 '나 자신의 자신감'임을 명심하자. 모든 공부는 여기서 시작되어야 한다. 나에 대한 자신감, 즉, 나를 속이지 않는 마음이 모든 것의 시작임을 명심하자.

10. 기억력 비중의 원리를 잘 활용하자.

다음 <그림>은 우리가 하는 행동에 따라서 기억이 얼마나 오래 남느냐는 것을 보여준다. 단지 읽는 것만으로는 10%만 기억하게 되고, 듣는 것은 20%, 보는 것는 30%를 기억하게 되며, 그것이 혼합된 영상 등은 50%를 기억하게 된다. 하지만 능동적으로 학습하게 되면, 즉 토론을 하거나 모의역할을 하게 된다면 70% 이상을 기억하게 된다. 따라서 수업시간에 멍하니 앉아 있으면 안 된다. 끊임없이 선생님들과 속으로 대화하면서 수업을 들어야 한다.3. 10권의 책을 1번 보는 것보다 1권의 책을 10번 반복해 보는 것이 효과적이다. 게 된다. 하지만 능동적으로 학습하게 되면, 즉 토론을 하거나 모의역할을 하게 된다면 70% 이상을 기억하게 된다. 따라서 수업시간에 멍하니 앉아 있으면 안 된다. 끊임없이 선생님들과 속으로 대화하면서 수업을 들어야 한다.

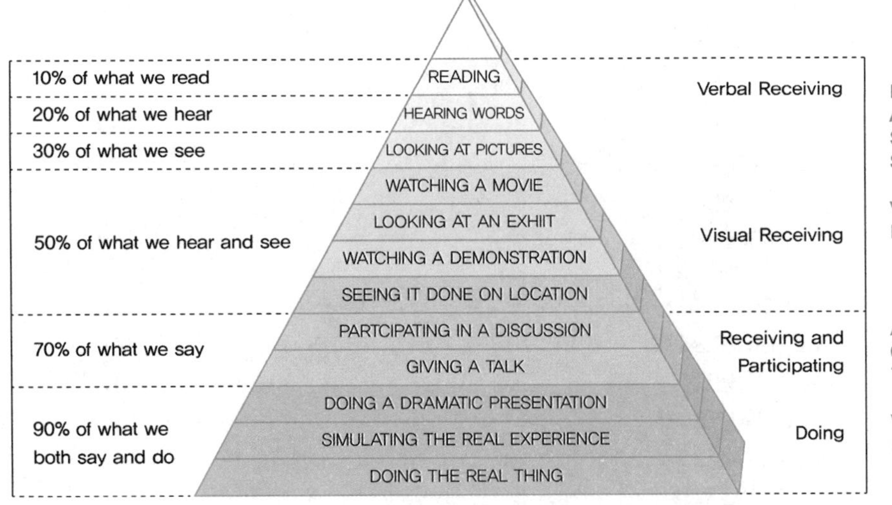

CONTENTS

PART 01 Applying 2S2R

2025~1997학년도 기출문제 ········ 018

PART 02 2026~1997학년도 기출문제

Chapter 01 2026~2014학년도 기출문제

2026학년도 ········ 218
2025학년도 ········ 224
2024학년도 ········ 230
2023학년도 ········ 236
2022학년도 ········ 242
2021학년도 ········ 248
2020학년도 ········ 254
2019학년도 ········ 266
2018학년도 ········ 274
2017학년도 ········ 282
2016학년도 ········ 288
2015학년도 ········ 293
2014학년도 ········ 298

Chapter 02 2013~2009학년도 기출문제

2013학년도 1차 ········ 306
2013학년도 2차 ········ 312
2012학년도 1차 ········ 314
2012학년도 2차 ········ 320
2011학년도 1차 ········ 322
2011학년도 2차 ········ 328

2010학년도 1차 ······ 330
2010학년도 2차 ······ 336
2009학년도 1차 ······ 338
2009학년도 2차 ······ 343
2009학년도 6월 모의평가 ······ 344

Chapter 03 2008~1997학년도 기출문제

2008학년도 서울·인천 ······ 350
2008학년도 전국 ······ 356
2007학년도 서울·인천 ······ 361
2007학년도 전국 ······ 365
2006학년도 서울·인천 ······ 369
2006학년도 전국 ······ 373
2005학년도 서울·인천 ······ 377
2005학년도 전국 ······ 382
2004학년도 서울·인천 ······ 386
2004학년도 전국 ······ 396
2003학년도 서울 ······ 406
2003학년도 전국 ······ 412
2002학년도 서울 ······ 419
2002학년도 전국 ······ 426
2001학년도 ······ 431
2000학년도 추가 ······ 440
2000학년도 ······ 446
1999학년도 ······ 451
1998학년도 ······ 462
1997학년도 ······ 472

2S2R

유희태 일반영어

③ 기출

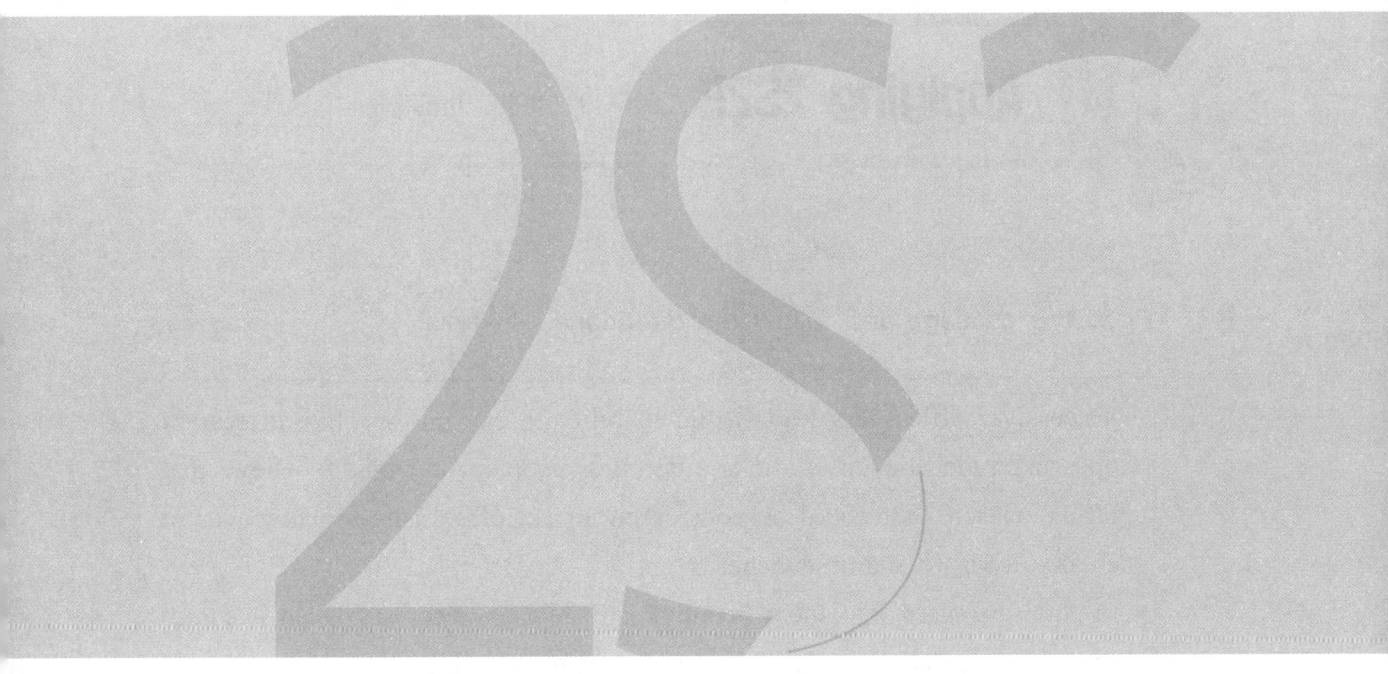

PART 01

Applying 2S2R

Part 01

Applying 2S2R _ 2025~1997학년도 기출문제

01 **Read the passage and follow the directions.** [4 points] 2025학년도

Excessive selflessness leads to an inability to say no. We live in fear of appearing rude and upsetting or offending people. One might believe that putting oneself first could be considered an act of selfishness—however, it actually leads to multiple benefits.

A total disregard for others' feelings isn't always necessary when it comes to putting yourself first. For example, a friend asks you to go shopping and you say yes because you don't want to let her down. Consequently, you're stressed before you've even stepped foot inside a shop; you spend the entire trip stressed for being dragged along. What would the outcome have been if you'd said no? She might initially feel somewhat put out, but she wouldn't have to put up with a grumpy, stressed-out shopping companion!

Putting yourself first can also lead to happiness all around. A growing body of research suggests that when people put themselves first they feel happier than when they prioritize others' needs. In turn, they are able to share that happiness with others. Taking time out from the kids might feel like an indulgence but if a one-hour bubble bath is what you want, your kids are going to be much happier with a relaxed parent than one who is trying to do everything for everyone, and not giving themselves a well-earned break.

If you don't start putting yourself first, you may ultimately become a negative force both for yourself and for others. In the long run, putting yourself first can often benefit everyone involved. In that sense, selfishness may—in many cases—also become an act of selflessness. Therefore, don't be afraid to just say no the next time you're asked to do something difficult.

Write a summary following the guidelines below.

Guidelines

- Summarize the passage above in one paragraph.
- Provide a topic sentence, two supporting ideas, and a concluding sentence based on the passage.
- Do NOT copy more than FOUR consecutive words from the passage.

NOTE

Step 1	Ⓢurvey
Key Words	
Signal Words	
Step 2	**Ⓡeading**
Purpose	
Pattern of Organization	
Tone	
Main Idea	
Step 3	**Ⓢummary**
지문 요약하기 (Paraphrasing)	
Step 4	**Ⓡecite**
요약문 말로 설명하기	

Answer Key

Excessive selflessness leads to an inability to say no. We live in fear of appearing rude and upsetting or offending people. One might believe that **putting oneself first** could be considered an act of selfishness—however, it actually leads to multiple benefits.

A total disregard for others' feelings isn't always necessary when it comes to **putting yourself first**. For example, a friend asks you to go shopping and you say yes because you don't want to let her down. Consequently, you're **stressed** before you've even stepped foot inside a shop; you spend the entire trip **stressed** for being dragged along. What would the outcome have been if you'd said no? She might initially feel somewhat put out, but she wouldn't have to put up with a grumpy, **stressed-out** shopping companion!

Putting yourself first can also lead to **happiness** all around. A growing body of research suggests that when people put themselves first they feel happier than when they prioritize others' needs. In turn, they are able to share that happiness with others. Taking time out from the kids might feel like an indulgence but if a one-hour bubble bath is what you want, your kids are going to be much happier with a relaxed parent than one who is trying to do everything for everyone, and not giving themselves a well-earned break.

If you don't start **putting yourself first**, you may ultimately become a negative force both for yourself and for others. In the long run, **putting yourself first** can often **benefit** everyone involved. In that sense, selfishness may—in many cases—also become an act of selflessness. Therefore, don't be afraid to just say no the next time you're asked to do something difficult.

→ key words

→ key words

→ key word

→ key words

→ key word

모범답안 Putting oneself first can offer several advantages, not only for individuals but also for those around them. First, declining unwanted requests, such as avoiding shopping trip where both people might end up feeling unhappy, can reduce stress and improve relationships. Second, prioritizing personal well-being increases happiness, which can positively impact those around us, such as children benefiting from a relaxed parent. In conclusion, it is important to have the confidence to decline requests that feel overly demanding.

한글번역

지나친 이타심은 '거절하지 못하는 것'으로 이어진다. 우리는 무례하게 보이거나, 사람들을 불쾌하게 하거나, 기분 상하게 할까 봐 두려움 속에 살아간다. 어떤 사람은 자신을 먼저 생각하는 것이 이기적인 행동이라고 믿을 수도 있다. 그러나 자신을 먼저 생각하는 것은 실제로 여러 가지 이점을 가져온다.

자신을 우선시한다고 해서 항상 다른 사람의 감정을 완전히 무시할 필요는 없다. 예를 들어, 친구가 당신에게 쇼핑하러 가자고 요청했고, 당신은 그녀를 실망시키고 싶지 않아서 "예스"라고 대답했다. 결과적으로, 당신은 가게에 들어서기도 전에 스트레스를 받게 된다. 그리고 당신은 억지로 따라간 그 쇼핑 내내 스트레스를 받는다. 만약 당신이 "아니"라고 말했다면 결과는 어땠을까? 그녀는 처음에는 다소 섭섭하게 느낄 수 있었겠지만, 짜증 나고 스트레스받은 쇼핑 친구를 참을 필요는 없었을 것이다!

또한, 자신을 우선시하는 것은 주변 사람들의 행복에도 기여할 수 있다. 점점 더 많은 연구들이 사람들이 다른 사람의 필요를 우선시할 때보다 자신을 우선시할 때 더 행복하다고 제시하고 있다. 결과적으로, 그들은 그 행복을 다른 사람들과 나눌 수 있다. 아이들과 시간을 보내는 것이 사치처럼 느껴질 수 있지만, 만약 한 시간의 거품 목욕이 당신이 원하는 것이라면, 아이들은 모든 사람을 위해 무언가를 하려고 애쓰며 자신에게 제대로 된 휴식조차 주지 않는 부모보다 휴식을 취한 부모와 함께 있을 때 훨씬 더 행복할 것이다.

자신을 우선시하지 않으면 결국 자신과 다른 사람들에게 모두 부정적인 힘이 될 수 있다. 장기적으로, 자신을 우선시하는 것은 종종 관련된 모두에게 이익이 된다. 이런 의미에서, 이기심(자신을 우선시하는 것)은—많은 경우—이타적인 행동이 될 수도 있다(while putting yourself first may seem like an act of selfishness, in the long run, it can actually lead to greater benefits for others, making it an act of selflessness). 그러므로, 다음에, 어려운 일을 부탁받을 때 '아니오'라고 말하는 것을 두려워하지 마라.

NOTE

Step 1	Survey
Key Words	Putting oneself first; benefits; stressed; happiness
Signal Words	Multiple; For example; also; leads to
Step 2	**Reading**
Purpose	To show why "putting oneself first" is crucial
Pattern of Organization	Series; cause/effect
Tone	Persuasive
Main Idea	Putting oneself first can offer several advantages, not only for individuals but also for those around them.
Step 3	**Summary**
지문 요약하기 (Paraphrasing)	Putting oneself first can offer several advantages, not only for individuals but also for those around them. First, declining unwanted requests, such as avoiding shopping trip where both people might end up feeling unhappy, can reduce stress and improve relationships. Second, prioritizing personal well-being increases happiness, which can positively impact those around us, such as children benefiting from a relaxed parent. In conclusion, it is important to have the confidence to decline requests that feel overly demanding.
Step 4	**Recite**
요약문 말로 설명하기	

02 Read the passage and follow the directions. [4 points]

2024학년도

When we paint on canvas we create a purely physical representation. When we take a selfie on our cell phone, however, the phone produces a digital representation—that is, a recording of an object using a finite set of symbols. The phone's camera divides our face into a numerical grid of tiny cells each of which is given a number. It is these numbers that make up the essence of our digital image. This digital representation offers many benefits over a more traditional physical representation.

Digital representations can be stored for long periods of time without erosion of information. After converting our face to a series of numbers, this numerical version can be maintained and transmitted with no further loss of quality. Unlike our parent's analog photos which have degraded over time, that image of our face will remain the same for a long period.

Rather than being something static, this digital representation can be manipulated. The digital representation can be brightened and sharpened by adding visual effects. On computer programs a smile can be added, a tree in the background erased, and it would even be possible to change the color of our eyes. This is certainly something that never would have been possible for analog photos in the past.

Digital representations are storable and easy to manipulate. While these two essential qualities offer benefits, it also means that we could be victims of digital representations. The digital representations of each of us encoded by algorithms can float around online even when we do not want them to. Therefore, caution should be exercised when we upload digital representations online.

Write a summary following the guidelines below.

Guidelines

- Summarize the above passage in one paragraph.
- Provide a topic sentence, two supporting ideas, and a concluding sentence based on the passage.
- Do NOT copy more than FOUR consecutive words from the passage.

NOTE

Step 1	Ⓢurvey
Key Words	
Signal Words	
Step 2	**Ⓡeading**
Purpose	
Pattern of Organization	
Tone	
Main Idea	
Step 3	**Ⓢummary**
지문 요약하기 (Paraphrasing)	
Step 4	**Ⓡecite**
	요약문 말로 설명하기

01

Answer Key

When we paint on canvas we create a purely **physical representation**. When we take a selfie on our cell phone, however, the phone produces a **digital representation**—that is, a recording of an object using a finite set of symbols. The phone's camera divides our face into a numerical grid of tiny cells each of which is given a number. It is these numbers that make up the essence of our digital image. This **digital representation** offers many benefits over a more traditional **physical representation**.

Digital representations can **be stored for long periods of time** without erosion of information. After converting our face to a series of numbers, this numerical version can be maintained and transmitted with no further loss of quality. Unlike our parent's analog photos which have degraded over time, that image of our face will remain the same for a long period.

Rather than being something static, this **digital representation** can be **manipulated**. The digital representation can be brightened and sharpened by adding visual effects. On computer programs a smile can be added, a tree in the background erased, and it would even be possible to change the color of our eyes. This is certainly something that never would have been possible for analog photos in the past.

Digital representations are **storable** and **easy to manipulate**. While these two essential qualities offer benefits, it also means that we could be victims of digital representations. The digital representations of each of us encoded by algorithms can float around online even when we do not want them to. Therefore, **caution should be exercised when we upload digital representations online**.

key words

key words

signal words

①

signal word

signal words

②

conclusion

모범답안 A digital representation offers two advantages over a physical representation. First, digital representations, unlike traditional representations, can be stored and maintained without information damage for an extended period, since they are a series of numbers. Second, unlike the static analog images of the past, digital images are easy to manipulate, incorporating visual effects with computer programs. In conclusion, while digital representations present advantages, caution is necessary in their use and online sharing.

한글번역

캔버스에 그림을 그릴 때 우리는 순전히 물리적 재현을 창조해낸다. 그러나 휴대폰으로 셀카를 찍을 때, 휴대폰은 디지털 재현을 만들어낸다—즉, 유한한 기호 집합을 사용해 물체를 기록하는 것이다. 휴대폰의 카메라는 우리 얼굴을 작은 셀의 수치적 그리드로 나누고 각각에 숫자를 부여한다. 이 숫자들이 우리 디지털 이미지의 본질을 구성한다. 이 디지털 재현은 더 전통적인 물리적 재현보다 많은 이점을 제공한다.

디지털 표현은 정보의 훼손 없이 오랫동안 저장될 수 있다. 우리의 얼굴을 일련의 숫자로 변환한 후, 이 수치적 버전은 더 이상의 품질 손실 없이 유지되고 전송될 수 있다. 시간이 지남에 따라 품질이 저하되는 부모님의 아날로그 사진들과 달리, 우리 얼굴의 그 이미지는 오랜 기간 동안 동일하게 유지될 것이다.

정적인 것이 아니라, 이 디지털 재현은 조작될 수 있다. 디지털 표현은 시각적 효과를 추가함으로써 밝게 하고 선명하게 할 수 있다. 컴퓨터 프로그램에서는 미소를 추가하거나, 배경의 나무를 지우거나, 심지어 우리 눈의 색을 바꾸는 것도 가능하다. 이것은 확실히 과거의 아날로그 사진에서는 절대 가능하지 않았을 것이다.

디지털 표현은 저장할 수 있고 조작하기 쉽다. 이 두 가지 필수적인 특성이 이점을 제공하는 반면, 그것은 또한 우리가 디지털 재현의 피해자가 될 수도 있다는 것을 의미한다. 알고리즘에 의해 인코딩된 우리 각자의 디지털 재현은 우리가 원하지 않을 때도 온라인에서 떠돌 수 있다. 따라서, 우리가 디지털로 재현된 것을 온라인에 업로드할 때는 주의를 기울여야 한다.

Step 1	Survey
Key Words	Physical representation; digital representation
Signal Words	Many benefits; over; Unlike; Rather than; Therefore
Step 2	**Reading**
Purpose	To show advantages of a digital representation
Pattern of Organization	Series; contrast
Tone	Informative
Main Idea	A digital representation offers two advantages over a physical representation.
Step 3	**Summary**
지문 요약하기 (Paraphrasing)	A digital representation offers two advantages over a physical representation. First, digital representations, unlike traditional representations, can be stored and maintained without information damage for an extended period, since they are a series of numbers. Second, unlike the static analog images of the past, digital images are easy to manipulate, incorporating visual effects with computer programs. In conclusion, while digital representations present advantages, caution is necessary in their use and online sharing.
Step 4	**Recite**
요약문 말로 설명하기	

03 Read the passage and follow the directions. [4 points]

2023학년도

Tunnel vision is an experience common to almost everyone. While experiencing tunnel vision, the world seems to shrink and the field of vision narrows, as if the person is looking through a tube or pipe. Attention focuses on one or two small details, context is lost, and understanding becomes very difficult. This is the consequence of the brain's limited ability to process visual stimuli. Tunnel vision occurs when your mind receives too many bits of visual information that do not make sense as part of a larger system. There are two main causes of tunnel vision as follows.

A general lack of background and/or contextual knowledge is the first major cause of tunnel vision. Learners with a weakness in art or physical education might suffer from tunnel vision when they attempt to paint or remember the rules of baseball. Their lack of background knowledge in painting and baseball might cause them to lose track of the larger flow of a game or piece of art, even if they are otherwise effective learners.

Poor reading habits are the second major cause of tunnel vision. Slow reading is one such bad habit. Many people read slowly because they are afraid they will not comprehend everything if they speed up. Reading too slowly encourages the brain to obsess over each little feature of a text and creates a perfect situation for tunnel vision to arise. It clogs up the visual system with too many individual letters and words.

As mentioned above, tunnel vision is most likely to occur due to a general lack of background information and/or poor reading habits. If there is a lack of contextual knowledge, then the learner must seek elsewhere to acquire it. When you struggle as a reader, speeding up might cure your tunnel vision.

Write a summary following the guidelines below.

Guidelines

- Summarize the above passage in one paragraph.
- Provide a topic sentence, two supporting ideas, and a concluding sentence based on the passage.
- Do NOT copy more than FIVE consecutive words from the passage.

NOTE

Step 1	Survey
Key Words	
Signal Words	
Step 2	**Reading**
Purpose	
Pattern of Organization	
Tone	
Main Idea	
Step 3	**Summary**
지문 요약하기 (Paraphrasing)	
Step 4	**Recite**
요약문 말로 설명하기	

Answer Key

Tunnel vision is an experience common to almost everyone. While experiencing tunnel vision, **the world seems to shrink and the field of vision narrows**, as if the person is looking through a tube or pipe. Attention focuses on one or two small details, context is lost, and understanding becomes very difficult. This is the consequence of the brain's limited ability to process visual stimuli. **Tunnel vision** occurs when your mind receives too many bits of visual information that do not make sense as part of a larger system. There are two main causes of **tunnel vision** as follows.

A general lack of background and/or contextual knowledge is the first major cause of **tunnel vision**. Learners with a weakness in art or physical education might suffer from tunnel vision when they attempt to paint or remember the rules of baseball. Their lack of background knowledge in painting and baseball might cause them to **lose track of the larger flow of a game or piece of art**, even if they are otherwise effective learners.

Poor reading habits are the second major cause of **tunnel vision. Slow reading** is one such bad habit. Many people read slowly because they are afraid they will not comprehend everything if they speed up. **Reading too slowly** encourages the brain to obsess over each little feature of a text and creates a perfect situation for tunnel vision to arise. It clogs up the visual system with too many individual letters and words.

As mentioned above, **tunnel vision** is most likely to occur due to a **general lack of background information** and/or **poor reading habits**. If there is a lack of contextual knowledge, then the learner must seek elsewhere to acquire it. When you struggle as a reader, **speeding up might cure your tunnel vision.**

→ key words
definition
→ signal words
→ signal words
→ signal words
→ signal words
→ key words
→ signal words
conclusion

모범답안 Tunnel vision, which is a common experience where a person's field of vision shrinks as if looking through a tube, has two major causes. First, lacking background knowledge can make learners lose track of the bigger picture. Second, poor reading habits, especially reading too slowly, lead to excessive focus on individual details rather than the whole text. In conclusion, building contextual knowledge and increasing reading speed can effectively cure tunnel vision.

한글번역

터널 비전(앞이 똑바르지 않아 잘 보이지 않는 것; 좁은 시야)은 거의 모든 사람들에게 공통적인 경험이다. 터널 비전을 경험하는 동안, 마치 사람이 튜브나 파이프를 통해 보는 것처럼 세상이 축소되고 시야가 좁아지는 것처럼 보인다. 주의는 한두 개의 작은 세부 사항에 집중되고, 맥락은 사라지고, 이해는 매우 어려워진다. 이것은 시각적 자극을 처리하는 뇌의 제한된 능력의 결과이다. 터널 비전은 당신의 마음이 더 큰 시스템의 일부로서 의미가 없는 시각적 정보를 너무 많이 수신할 때 발생한다. 터널비전의 주요 원인은 다음과 같이 두 가지이다.

일반적인 배경 및 맥락 지식의 부족은 터널 비전의 첫 번째 주요 원인이다. 예체능에 약한 학습자들은 그림을 그리거나 야구 규칙을 기억하려고 할 때 터널 비전에 시달릴 수 있다. 그들의 그림과 야구에 대한 배경지식의 부족은 비록 그들이 효과적인 학습자일지라도 게임이나 예술 작품의 더 큰 흐름을 놓치게 할 수 있다.

나쁜 독서 습관은 터널 비전의 두 번째 주요 원인이다. 느린 독서는 그러한 나쁜 습관 중 하나다. 속도를 내면 다 이해하지 못할까 봐 천천히 읽는 사람들이 많다. 너무 느리게 읽는 것은 뇌가 텍스트의 각각의 작은 특징에 집착하도록 장려하고 터널 비전이 발생하기에 완벽한 상황을 만든다. 그것은 너무 많은 개별 문자와 단어들로 시각 체계를 막는다.

위에서 언급한 바와 같이, 터널 비전은 일반적인 배경 정보 부족 및 잘못된 독서 습관으로 인해 발생할 가능성이 가장 높다. 문맥적 지식이 부족하다면, 학습자는 다른 곳에서라도 지식을 얻어와야 한다. 읽기가 잘 안된다면, 속도를 높이는 것이 당신의 터널 비전을 고쳐줄 수도 있다.

NOTE

Step 1	Ⓢurvey
Key Words	Tunnel vision; Slow reading
Signal Words	Two main causes; first; major cause; cause … to; second; major cause; due to
Step 2	**Ⓡeading**
Purpose	To explain why tunnel vision comes to pass
Pattern of Organization	Series; cause/effect; definition
Tone	Informative
Main Idea	Tunnel vision, which is a common experience where a person's field of vision shrinks as if looking through a tube, has two major causes.
Step 3	**Ⓢummary**
지문 요약하기 (Paraphrasing)	Tunnel vision, which is a common experience where a person's field of vision shrinks as if looking through a tube, has two major causes. First, lacking background knowledge can make learners lose track of the bigger picture. Second, poor reading habits, especially reading too slowly, lead to excessive focus on individual details rather than the whole text. In conclusion, building contextual knowledge and increasing reading speed can effectively cure tunnel vision.
Step 4	**Ⓡecite**
요약문 말로 설명하기	

04 **Read the passage and follow the directions.** [4 points] 2022학년도

What did a presidential administration mean when they proposed "revenue enhancement" through "user fees"? Translated, "revenue enhancement" through "user fees" is taxes paid by citizens. This is an example of doublespeak. Doublespeak is carefully designed and constructed language used to make things seem different from what they are, and it comes in several forms.

One form of doublespeak is inflated language. Inflated language is designed to make the ordinary seem extraordinary. Cheap material used to make a purse could be described as "genuine imitation leather" or a glass stone in a piece of jewelry as a "real counterfeit diamond." These types of descriptions can also be used to describe situations. A guide telling a group of French tourists that their visit to the Eifel Tower is a "once in a lifetime opportunity" is almost certainly using doublespeak, especially as the attraction is not far from home. This type of language gives a perception of importance to situations and things that would not normally be considered important.

Another form of doublespeak is jargon. Jargon as doublespeak occurs when professional language is used with people not "in-the-know." The use of jargon can be an efficient way of communicating within a specialized group. But when used with those not in-the-know, the intention may be to give an air of profundity, authority, and prestige. If a computer technician tells a novice computer user with an internet connection problem to "power-cycle" their router rather than saying "you need to unplug the router and plug it back in," the technician might be using doublespeak.

Doublespeak is language used to make the bad seem good and the basic profound. As shown in the examples above, it is present in many aspects of our lives. Keeping awareness of the definition and forms of doublespeak can help us discriminate between what someone wants us to believe and the reality.

Write a summary following the guidelines below.

Guidelines

- Summarize the above passage in one paragraph.
- Based on the passage, provide a topic sentence, two supporting details, and a concluding sentence.
- Do NOT copy more than FIVE consecutive words from the passage.

NOTE

Step 1	Ⓢurvey
Key Words	
Signal Words	
Step 2	**Ⓡeading**
Purpose	
Pattern of Organization	
Tone	
Main Idea	
Step 3	**Ⓢummary**
지문 요약하기 (Paraphrasing)	
Step 4	**Ⓡecite**
요약문 말로 설명하기	

Answer Key

What did a presidential administration mean when they proposed "revenue enhancement" through "user fees"? Translated, "revenue enhancement" through "user fees" is taxes paid by citizens. This is an example of **doublespeak. Doublespeak** is **carefully designed and constructed language used to make things seem different from what they are**, and it comes in several forms.

One form of **doublespeak** is **inflated language. Inflated language** is **designed to make the ordinary seem extraordinary**. Cheap material used to make a purse could be described as "genuine imitation leather" or a glass stone in a piece of jewelry as a "real counterfeit diamond." These types of descriptions can also be used to describe situations. A guide telling a group of French tourists that their visit to the Eifel Tower is a "once in a lifetime opportunity" is almost certainly using doublespeak, especially as the attraction is not far from home. **This type** of **language gives a perception of importance to situations and things that would not normally be considered** important.

Another form of **doublespeak** is **jargon. Jargon** as **doublespeak** occurs **when professional language is used with people not "in-the-know**." The use of **jargon** can be an efficient way of communicating within a specialized group. But when used with those not in-the-know, the intention may be to give an air of profundity, authority, and prestige. If a computer technician tells a novice computer user with an internet connection problem to "power-cycle" their router rather than saying "you need to unplug the router and plug it back in," the technician might be using **doublespeak.**

Doublespeak is **language used to make the bad seem good and the basic profound**. As shown in the examples above, it is present in many aspects of our lives. **Keeping awareness of the definition and forms of doublespeak** can help us discriminate between what someone wants us to believe and the reality.

key word
definition
signal words
signal words
signal words
conclusion

모범답안 Doublespeak, which is language used to misrepresent things intentionally, has several forms. The first of doublespeak's forms comes from inflated language. Inflated language occurs when ordinary things and situations are given importance they don't deserve. The second form of doublespeak is jargon. It comes to pass when professional language is used with those outside of a specialized group to add prestige to one's expression. In conclusion, since doublespeak is a common tool used to distort reality, we, thus, should be aware of various forms of doublespeak.

한글번역

대통령의 행정부가 "사용자 수수료"를 통한 "수입 확대"를 제안했을 때 무슨 의미였는가? 번역하자면, "사용자 수수료"를 통한 "수입 확대"는 시민들이 내는 세금을 말하는 것이다. 이것은 이중어법의 예시다. 이중어법은 사물이 실제와 다르게 보이도록 신중하게 설계되고 구성된 언어이며, 여러 형태로 나타난다.

이중어법의 한 형태는 과장된 언어다. 과장된 언어는 평범한 것을 특별하게 보이도록 설계됐다. 가방 제작에 사용된 저렴한 재료는 "정품 모조 가죽"으로, 장신구의 유리 돌은 "진짜 모조 다이아몬드"로 묘사될 수 있다. 이런 종류의 묘사는, 상황을 설명하기 위해서도 사용될 수 있다. 한 무리의 프랑스 관광객에게 에펠탑 방문이 "일생에 단 한 번뿐인 기회"라고 말하는 가이드는 거의 확실히 이중어법을 사용하고 있다, 특히 그 명소가 집에서 멀지 않을 때는 더욱 그렇다. 이런 유형의 언어는 일반적으로 중요하다고 여겨지지 않는 상황과 사물을 마치 중요한 것처럼 인식하도록 해준다.

이중어법의 또 다른 형태는 전문용어다. 전문용어가 이중어법으로 사용되는 경우는 "내부자"가 아닌 사람들에게 전문적인 언어가 사용될 때다. 전문용어의 사용은 특수 집단 내에서 효율적인 의사소통 방법일 수 있다. 그러나 내부자가 아닌 사람들에게 사용될 때, 그 의도는 심오함, 권위, 위신을 부여하기 위한 것일 수 있다. 컴퓨터 기술자가 인터넷 연결 문제가 있는 초보 컴퓨터 사용자에게 "라우터 플러그를 뽑았다가 다시 꽂으세요"라고 말하는 대신 "라우터를 전원 주기해보세요"라고 말하면, 그 기술자는 이중어법을 사용하고 있을 수 있다.

이중어법은 나쁜 것을 좋게, 기본적인 것을 심오하게 만드는 언어다. 위의 예에서 볼 수 있듯이, 이중어법은 우리 삶의 많은 측면에 존재한다. 이중어법의 정의와 형태에 대한 인식을 유지하는 것은 누군가가 우리에게 믿게 하려는 것과 현실 사이를 구별하는 데 도움이 될 수 있다.

NOTE

Step 1	Ⓢurvey
Key Words	Doublespeak
Signal Words	Several forms; One form; Another form
Step 2	**Ⓡeading**
Purpose	To explain several forms of doublespeak
Pattern of Organization	Series; definition
Tone	Critical
Main Idea	Doublespeak, which is language used to misrepresent things intentionally, has several forms.
Step 3	**Ⓢummary**
지문 요약하기 (Paraphrasing)	Doublespeak, which is language used to misrepresent things intentionally, has several forms. The first of doublespeak's forms comes from inflated language. Inflated language occurs when ordinary things and situations are given importance they don't deserve. The second form of doublespeak is jargon. It comes to pass when professional language is used with those outside of a specialized group to add prestige to one's expression. In conclusion, since doublespeak is a common tool used to distort reality, we, thus, should be aware of various forms of doublespeak.
Step 4	**Ⓡecite**
요약문 말로 설명하기	

05 Read the passage and follow the directions. [4 points]

2021학년도

In the classroom today, there are a growing number of children who are being raised outside their parents' home cultures after moving across geographic boundaries because of their parents' employment. Children in this situation are called "Third Culture Kids" (TCKs). To be categorized as a TCK, a child must spend more than three years outside their passport country during the developmental years, from birth to eighteen years old. Living as a TCK can provide benefits as well as undeniable challenges.

Growing up internationally, TCKs are able to become speakers of multiple languages. Learning a language can be easier if you have daily exposure to it. TCKs attend schools taught in the target language and encounter the language in everyday life. This can help them learn the language more quickly, especially during their formative years. Depending on how much time is spent in a country, the level of fluency can vary, but it would not be unlikely for a TCK to be capable of speaking three or more languages by the end of high school.

Despite this benefit, there is an undeniable challenge that comes along with being a TCK. The multiple shifts in location can lead to a sense of isolation for these children. Having to repeat the process of moving and adjusting to new life circumstances can take a serious toll. Such changes can prevent children from maintaining relationships with those outside their immediate family. Hence, isolation becomes the most common challenge for TCKs.

Given the modern context in which the migration and transnational flow is increasing, understanding TCKs' lives will be a valuable resource for international and global education. It is important that educators support this growing community by maximizing the potential benefits of cross-cultural experiences while helping them navigate the challenges that arise.

Write a summary following the guidelines below.

Guidelines

- Summarize the above passage in one paragraph.
- Provide a topic sentence, two supporting ideas, and a concluding sentence based on the passage.
- Do NOT copy more than FIVE consecutive words from the passage.

NOTE

Step 1	Survey
Key Words	
Signal Words	
Step 2	**Reading**
Purpose	
Pattern of Organization	
Tone	
Main Idea	
Step 3	**Summary**
지문 요약하기 (Paraphrasing)	
Step 4	**Recite**
요약문 말로 설명하기	

Answer Key

In the classroom today, there are a growing number of children who are being raised outside their parents' home cultures after moving across geographic boundaries because of their parents' employment. Children in this situation are called **"Third Culture Kids" (TCKs)**. To be categorized as a **TCK**, a child must spend more than three years outside their passport country during the developmental years, from birth to eighteen years old. Living as a **TCK** can provide benefits as well as undeniable challenges.

Growing up internationally, **TCKs** are able to become speakers of multiple languages. Learning a language can be easier if you have daily exposure to it. TCKs attend schools taught in the target language and encounter the language in everyday life. This can help them learn the language more quickly, especially during their formative years. Depending on how much time is spent in a country, the level of fluency can vary, but it would not be unlikely for a TCK to be capable of speaking three or more languages by the end of high school.

Despite **this benefit**, there is an **undeniable challenge** that comes along with being a TCK. The multiple shifts in location can lead to a sense of isolation for these children. Having to repeat the process of moving and adjusting to new life circumstances can take a serious toll. Such changes can prevent children from maintaining relationships with those outside their immediate family. Hence, isolation becomes the most common challenge for TCKs.

Given the modern context in which the migration and transnational flow is increasing, understanding TCKs' lives will be a valuable resource for international and global education. It is important that educators support this growing community by maximizing the potential benefits of cross-cultural experiences while helping them navigate the challenges that arise.

key words

benefit

key words

key words

difficulty

모범답안 Third Culture Kids (TCKs) face their own benefits(advantages) and disadvantages. Regarding the former, TCKs can acquire more languages through daily exposure in their formative, everyday lives with new languages. On the other hand, the moving can create isolation and problems in maintaining relationships. In conclusion, these issues should be accommodated by educators to reap the benefits of their cross-cultural lives with less harm.

한글번역

오늘날 학교에는, 부모님의 직업으로 인해 지리적 경계를 넘어 이사한 후 부모님의 가정문화 밖에서 길러지는 학생들 수가 늘어나고 있다. 이러한 환경 속에 있는 아이들을 "제3문화 아이들"(TCKs)이라고 부른다. TCK로 분류하려면 아이는 출생 후 18세 이전까지의 발달단계 동안 모국 밖에서 3년 이상을 보내야 한다. TCK로 산다는 것은 부인할 수 없는 어려움도 분명 있지만 장점도 있다.

국제적으로 자라나기 때문에, 이들은 다양한 언어를 사용할 수 있다. 일상 속에서 목표 언어에 노출이 된다면, 언어를 배우는 것 또한 쉬울 것이다. 이들은 목표 언어를 사용하는 학교에 다니고 일상생활에서 그 언어를 접한다. 이것은 이들이 언어를 더 빠르게 습득할 수 있도록 도와주는데, 특히 형성기에 그렇다. 해당 국가에서 얼마나 많은 시간을 보냈는가에 따라 유창성 정도는 다양하지만 고등학교 졸업 전까지는 적어도 3가지 이상의 언어를 습득할 수 있을 것이다.

이러한 장점에도 불구하고, TCK로서 부인할 수 없는 어려움 또한 존재한다. 많은 거주 변화는 이러한 아이들이 고립감을 느끼게 한다. 새로운 삶의 상황에 적응하고 옮기는 과정을 반복하는 것은 심각한 고통을 수반한다. 이러한 변화는 아이들이 그들의 직계가족 외에 다른 사람들과 관계를 유지하는 것을 어렵게 한다. 그러므로 고립감은 TCK들에게 가장 흔한 어려움이다.

이민과 초국가적인 유입이 증가하는 현대 상황을 고려했을 때, TCK의 삶을 이해하는 것은 국제 교육을 위한 가치 있는 자원이 될 것이다. 교육자들은 이들의 다양한 문화 경험의 잠재적인 이점들을 극대화함과 동시에 발생하는 어려움들을 헤쳐나갈 수 있도록 도와줌으로써 이러한 증가하는 지역공동체를 지원할 필요가 있다.

NOTE

Step 1	Ⓢurvey
Key Words	Third Culture Kids; educators; isolation; benefit; challenge
Signal Words	Despite this benefit; Given the modern context
Step 2	**Ⓡeading**
Purpose	To show the benefits and challenges Third Culture Kids face
Pattern of Organization	Series
Tone	Informative
Main Idea	Third Culture Kids (TCKs) face their own benefits(advantages) and disadvantages.
Step 3	**Ⓢummary**
지문 요약하기 (Paraphrasing)	Third Culture Kids (TCKs) face their own benefits(advantages) and disadvantages. Regarding the former, TCKs can acquire more languages through daily exposure in their formative, everyday lives with new languages. On the other hand, the moving can create isolation and problems in maintaining relationships. In conclusion, these issues should be accommodated by educators to reap the benefits of their cross-cultural lives with less harm.
Step 4	**Ⓡecite**
요약문 말로 설명하기	

06 Read the passage and follow the directions. [4 points] 2020학년도

Included in the possible outcomes of culture learning are several not always desirable results, such as alienation from the native culture and marginality. Marginality refers to a situation in which a person, for a variety of reasons (such as race or religion) remains on the outskirts of a social or cultural group. Marginal individuals or groups are isolated, and, in the words of John Lum, their actions "do not reflect well any one culture." Marginality is not necessarily always a(n) __________ factor. It plays a part in all cultural change; it is part of the lives of children whose parents remain monocultural while they become bicultural. Richard Rodriguez' poignant book *Hunger of Memory* recounts the pains of cultural transition and the agonies of the loss of cultural identity. In anthropology, the marginal person has often been seen as the one most likely to accept change and to be willing to deal with the foreigner (e.g., the anthropologist) who comes along and asks such seemingly stupid questions.

That marginality and mediation are lonely states is also beautifully expressed in an often-quoted passage from the autobiography of Nehru:

I have become a queer mixture of the East and the West, out of place everywhere, at home nowhere. Perhaps my thoughts and approach to life are more akin to what is called Western than Eastern, but India clings to me, as she does to all her children, in innumerable ways; and behind me lie, somewhere in the subconscious, racial memories of a hundred, or whatever the number may be, generations of Brahmans. I cannot get rid of either that past inheritance or my recent acquisitions. They are both part of me, and, though they help me in both the East and the West, they also create in me a negative feeling of spiritual loneliness not only in public activities but in life itself. I am a stranger and alien in the West. I cannot be of it. But in my own country also, sometimes, I have an exile's feeling.

Lum concludes that "marginal people who fall may be rootless or alienated; those who rise may be synthesizers." They may become marginal in all cultures, belonging wholly to none and without cultural identity. On the other hand, they may cross cultural boundaries and leap cultural chasms.

Fill in the blank with the ONE most appropriate word from the passage. Then, explain what the underlined part means. Do NOT copy more than FOUR consecutive words from the passage.

NOTE

Step 1	Ⓢurvey
Key Words	
Signal Words	
Step 2	**Ⓡeading**
Purpose	
Pattern of Organization	
Tone	
Main Idea	
Step 3	**Ⓢummary**
지문 요약하기 (Paraphrasing)	
Step 4	**Ⓡecite**
요약문 말로 설명하기	

Answer Key

Included in the possible outcomes of culture learning are several not always desirable results, such as **alienation from the native culture** and **marginality**. **Marginality** refers to a situation in which a person, for a variety of reasons (such as race or religion) remains on the outskirts of a social or cultural group. Marginal individuals or groups are isolated, and, in the words of John Lum, their actions "do not reflect well any one culture." **Marginality** is not necessarily always a negative factor. It plays a part in all **cultural change**; it is part of the lives of children whose parents remain monocultural while they become bicultural. Richard Rodriguez' poignant book *Hunger of Memory* recounts the pains of cultural transition and the agonies of the loss of cultural identity. In anthropology, **the marginal person** has often been seen as the one most likely to accept change and to be willing to deal with the foreigner (e.g., the anthropologist) who comes along and asks such seemingly stupid questions.

→ key words (alienation from the native culture)

→ key word (Marginality)

→ key words (cultural change)

That **marginality** and **mediation** are lonely states is also beautifully expressed in an often-quoted passage from the autobiography of Nehru:

I have become a queer mixture of the East and the West, out of place everywhere, at home nowhere. Perhaps my thoughts and approach to life are more akin to what is called Western than Eastern, but India clings to me, as she does to all her children, in innumerable ways; and behind me lie, somewhere in the subconscious, racial memories of a hundred, or whatever the number may be, generations of Brahmans. I cannot get rid of either that past inheritance or my recent acquisitions. They are both part of me, and, though they help me in both the East and the West, they also create in me a negative feeling of spiritual loneliness not only in public activities but in life itself. I am a stranger and alien in the West. I cannot be of it. But in my own country also, sometimes, I have an exile's feeling.

Lum concludes that "marginal people who fall may be rootless or alienated; those who rise may be **synthesizers**." They may become marginal in all cultures, belonging wholly to none and without cultural identity. On the other hand, they may cross cultural boundaries and leap cultural chasms.

→ key word (synthesizers)

모범답안 The best word for the blank is "negative". Second, the underlined part means marginal people belonging to no one culture and benefiting from being free of cultural impediments. (또는 Second, the meaning of the underlined "synthesizers" is marginal people who cross-cultural boundaries without suffering from cultural impediments.)

한글번역

문화 학습에서 일어날 수 있는 결과에 포함된 몇몇 결과가 항상 바람직한 것만은 아닌데, 이를테면 토박이 문화로부터의 소외나 주변성과 같은 것이다. 주변성이란 어떤 사람이 (인종이나 종교와 같은) 다양한 이유 때문에 사회적 혹은 문화적 집단의 주변에만 머물게 되는 상황을 일컫는다. 주변적인 개인이나 집단들은 소외되며, 존 럼의 말을 빌리자면, 그들의 행위는 "어떠한 하나의 문화도 제대로 반영하지 않는다." 주변성이 항상 부정적인 요소만은 아니다. 주변성은 모든 문화적 변화에서 일정 역할을 담당한다. 주변성은 자신들이 이중 문화적 특성을 가지는 동안 부모는 단일 문화에 남아 있는 아이들의 삶의 일부이다. 리차드 로드리게스의 감동적인 책 ≪기억의 기아≫는 문화 변동에서 발생하는 고통과 문화적 정체성의 상실에서 나오는 고뇌를 말해준다. 인류학에서, 주변인은 종종 변화를 매우 잘 받아들이고, 외지인들과 기꺼이 접촉할 가능성이 높은 사람들이다. 이때, 외지인들(예를 들면 인류학자)은 그 주변인들을 따라온 뒤, 외관상으로 볼 때 바보 같은 질문을 하는 사람들이다.

주변성과 매개가 외로운 특성이라는 것은, 네루의 자서전에서 자주 인용되는 구절에 아름답게 묘사돼있다:

나는 모든 곳으로부터 왔으나, 그 어디도 고향이 아닌, 동양과 서양의 이상한 혼합이 됐다. 아마도 삶에 대한 나의 생각들과 접근은 동양보다는 서양이라고 불리는 곳과 더 유사할 것이나, 인도가 그 모든 자손들에게 그러하듯 나에게도 수많은 방식으로 고착돼 있다. 그리고 내 뒤에, 백 개의, 혹은 몇 개가 됐든 브라만의 세대들이 가지고 있는 잠재의식적이고, 인종과 관련된 기억들의 그 어딘가에 인도가 놓여 있다. 나는 과거의 유산이든 내가 최근에 습득한 것들이든 그 어떤 것도 버릴 수 없다. 이들은 둘 다 나의 일부이며, 비록 이들이 동양에서도 서양에서도 나를 돕지만, 공적인 활동뿐 아니라 삶 그 자체 안에서 영적인 외로움이라는 부정적인 감정 또한 만들어낸다. 나는 서양에서 이방인이자 외지인이다. 나는 서양의 일부가 될 수 없다. 그러나 나의 본국에서 또한, 가끔, 나는 망명인의 기분을 느낀다.

럼은 "추락해버린 주변적 인간은 뿌리가 없고 소외될 수도 있지만; 상승하는 주변적 인간은 여러 가지 것을 합성하는 자가 될 수도 있다."고 결론 내렸다. 주변적 인간들은 모든 문화에서 주변적이 돼, 어떤 문화에도 온전히 속하지 못하고 문화적 정체성이 없게 될 수도 있다. 반면에, 주변적 인간들은 문화적 경계를 넘어서고 문화적 간극을 뛰어넘을 수도 있다.

01

NOTE

Step 1	Ⓢurvey
Key Words	Marginality; alienation; mediation; cultural change; synthesizers
Signal Words	Not clear
Step 2	**Ⓡeading**
Purpose	To explain the lonely marginality that is experienced on the outskirts of a social group
Pattern of Organization	Cause/effect
Tone	Concerned; sorrow
Main Idea	The marginal people in a social or cultural group suffer from loneliness but might benefit in becoming synthesizers.
Step 3	**Ⓢummary**
지문 요약하기 (Paraphrasing)	In the marginal position of cultural learning there are some benefits and drawbacks to understand. Cultural learning can create isolation, when individuals are marginalized or children who become bicultural while their parents remain monocultural. They can also benefit from being synthesizers and crossing boundaries and cultural gaps.
Step 4	**Ⓡecite**
요약문 말로 설명하기	

07 Read the passage and follow the directions. [4 points]

2020학년도

Many contemporary tourists avoid encountering reality directly but thrive on pseudo-events in their tourism experiences thus affecting tourism entrepreneurs and indigenous populations. For one, many tourists prefer to stay in comfortable accomodations, thereby separating themselves from the local people and environment. For instance, sleeping in a hotel filled with the comforts of home may insulate them from the fact that they are in a foreign land. In addition, much of the tourism industry is bolstered by the use of tourist-focused institutions such as museums and shopping centers. The needs of the contemporary tourists have induced entrepreneurs to build tourist attractions for the sole purpose of entertaining visitors. This detracts from the colorful local culture and presents a false view of the indigenous cultures. The other group affected by modern tourism is the local population. These people find themselves learning languages in a contrived way based on the changing tides of tourist groups solely for marketing purposes. Furthermore, when curious visitors do venture outside their cultural bubbles, they enjoy, albeit intrusively, watching locals doing their daily tasks, thereby making them the subject of the tourist gaze. In sum, while tourism is on the rise, the trend is to maintain a distance from the real environment rather than to see the locations for their own values, and this negatively affects tourism entrepreneurs and local people.

Complete the topic sentence in the handout. Do NOT copy more than FOUR consecutive words from the passage.

Handout

Topic sentence : Modern tourists' demands ______________________

____

A. Effects on tourism entrepreneurs
- Provide comfortable accommodations
- Create tourist-focused entertainment attractions

B. Effects on local populations
- Learn tourists' languages
- Become the objects of the tourist gaze

____

NOTE

Step 1	Ⓢurvey
Key Words	
Signal Words	
Step 2	**Ⓡeading**
Purpose	
Pattern of Organization	
Tone	
Main Idea	
Step 3	**Ⓢummary**
지문 요약하기 (Paraphrasing)	
Step 4	**Ⓡecite**
요약문 말로 설명하기	

Answer Key

Many **contemporary tourists** avoid encountering reality directly but thrive on pseudo-events in their tourism experiences thus affecting **tourism entrepreneurs** and indigenous populations. For one, many tourists prefer to stay in comfortable accomodations, thereby separating themselves from **the local people** and **environment**. For instance, sleeping in a hotel filled with the comforts of home may insulate them from the fact that they are in a foreign land. In addition, much of the **tourism industry** is bolstered by the use of tourist-focused institutions such as museums and shopping centers. The needs of the contemporary tourists have induced entrepreneurs to build tourist attractions for the sole purpose of entertaining visitors. This detracts from the colorful local culture and presents a false view of the indigenous cultures. The other group **affected** by **modern tourism** is **the local population**. These people find themselves learning languages in a contrived way based on the changing tides of tourist groups solely for marketing purposes. Furthermore, when curious visitors do venture outside their cultural bubbles, they enjoy, albeit intrusively, watching locals doing their daily tasks, thereby making them the subject of the tourist gaze. In sum, while tourism is on the rise, the trend is to maintain a distance from the real environment rather than to see the locations for their own values, and this negatively affects tourism entrepreneurs and local people.

→ key words

→ key words

→ key words

→ key words

→ key words

Main idea

모범답안 have a negative effect on tourism entrepreneurs and the local population.

한글번역

동시대의 많은 여행자들은 현실을 직면하는 것을 피하고, 그 대신 그들의 여행 경험 속에서 가짜 사건들을 즐김으로써 여행 기업과 토속 주민들에 영향을 끼치고 있다. 우선, 많은 여행자들은 편안한 숙소에 머무르는 것을 선호하며, 그럼으로써 지역 사람들과 환경으로부터 자신들을 분리시킨다. 예를 들어, 가정의 편의용품들로 채워진 호텔에서 자는 것은 그들이 이국 땅에 있다는 사실로부터 그들을 절연시킨다. 게다가, 많은 여행산업은 박물관과 쇼핑센터와 같은 관광객 중심 시설의 사용에 의해 더 강화된다. 우리 시대 여행객들의 요구는 기업들이 방문객을 즐겁게 하려는 목적 하나만을 가지고 관광객을 이끌 명소를 짓도록 유도해왔다. 이는 다채로운 지역 문화를 격하시키며 토속 문화에 대한 잘못된 시각을 보여준다. 현대적 관광에 영향을 받는 다른 집단은 지역 주민들이다. 지역 주민들은 오직 시장적 목적만을 위해서 관광객 집단의 경향의 변화에 따라 부자연스러운 방식으로 언어를 배우고 있음을 발견하게 된다. 더불어, 호기심 많은 방문객들이 그들의 문화적 보호막 밖으로 모험을 감행할 때, 그들은, 비록 그것이 방해가 될지라도, 지역민들이 일상생활을 영위하는 것을 구경하는 것을 즐김으로써 지역민들을 관광객들의 시선으로 대상화하게 된다. 요약하자면, 관광이 상승세인 반면, 그 추세는 지역을 그 고유 가치를 가지고 보기 보다는 실제 환경과 거리를 유지하는 것이며, 이것은 여행 기업과 지역 주민들에게 부정적으로 영향을 미칠 수 있다.

Step 1	Survey
Key Words	Contemporary tourists; tourism entrepreneurs; accomodations; local culture
Signal Words	Affected; For one; for instance; The other group affected; Furthermore; In sum
Step 2	**Reading**
Purpose	To show how modern tourists negatively impacts local businesses and culture
Pattern of Organization	Cause/effect; series
Tone	Critical; concerned
Main Idea	Modern tourists' demands have a negative effect on tourism entrepreneurs and the local population.
Step 3	**Summary**
지문 요약하기 (Paraphrasing)	Modern tourists' demands have a negative effect on tourism entrepreneurs and the local population. They stay in comfortable accommodations separated from locals and promote institutions meant for their sole benefit. Consequently, this influences the learning of languages by locals and places them under the tourists' gaze.
Step 4	**Recite**
요약문 말로 설명하기	

08 Read the passage and follow the directions. [4 points] 2020학년도

We've come to assume that just about any bug we're saddled with—from strep to staph—can be wiped out with a quick round of antibiotics. But in the U.S. alone, roughly 2 million people every year get infections that can't be treated with antibiotics, and 23,000 of them die as a result. The bacteria to blame are now present in every corner of the planet, according to a landmark report from the World Health Organization (WHO). In some countries, about 50% of people infected with *K. pneumoniae* or *E. coli* bacteria won't respond to our most powerful antibiotics, say global health experts. That suggests doctors are increasingly running out of (1) <u>the ammunition</u> they rely on to fight these harmful microbes.

Bacteria have been evolving to resist the drugs designed to kill them since the first antibiotic was discovered in 1928. But our overuse of antibiotics in farming, prescription drugs and antibacterial soaps has supercharged (2) <u>the process</u>. The WHO report was a sober warning of a dire future, but globally, progress is slowly being made.

France used to have the highest rate of antibiotic prescription in Europe, but a government mandate helped lower the number of doctor-issued Rxs by 26% in six years.

In Sweden, regulations to phase out preventive use of antibiotics in agriculture—in which low doses are given to keep animals healthy and plump—cut sales of the drugs for farming by 67% since 1986. The Netherlands and Denmark have also restricted antibiotic use on livestock.

Progress in the U.S. has been slower. The Food and Drug Administration recently tried to encourage farmers to voluntarily reduce antibiotics in farming. The agency is also taking steps to curb use of antibacterials in some consumer goods, requiring manufacturers to prove that antibacterials are better than simple soap and water in keeping germs at bay.

Before antibiotics, something as minor as a cut or a sore throat could be a death sentence. While some ________ has recently been made in the right direction, some might say that much more needs to be done.

Fill in the blank with the ONE most appropriate word from the passage. Then, specify what the underlined parts (1) and (2) refer to, respectively. Do NOT copy more than THREE consecutive words from the passage.

NOTE

Step 1	Survey
Key Words	
Signal Words	
Step 2	Reading
Purpose	
Pattern of Organization	
Tone	
Main Idea	
Step 3	Summary
지문 요약하기 (Paraphrasing)	
Step 4	Recite
요약문 말로 설명하기	

Answer Key

We've come to assume that just about any bug we're saddled with—from strep to staph—can be wiped out with a quick round of **antibiotics**. But in the U.S. alone, roughly 2 million people every year get infections that can't be treated with **antibiotics**, and 23,000 of them die as a result. **The bacteria** to blame are now present in every corner of the planet, according to a landmark report from the World Health Organization (WHO). In some countries, about 50% of people infected with *K. pneumoniae* or *E. coli* bacteria won't respond to our most powerful antibiotics, say global health experts. That suggests doctors are increasingly running out of the ammunition they rely on to fight these harmful microbes.

→ key word
→ key word
→ key word

Bacteria have been evolving to resist the drugs designed to kill them since the first antibiotic was discovered in 1928. But our **overuse** of antibiotics in farming, prescription drugs and antibacterial soaps has supercharged the process. The WHO report was a sober warning of a dire future, but globally, progress is slowly being made.

→ key word

France used to have the highest rate of antibiotic prescription in Europe, but a government mandate helped lower the number of doctor-issued Rxs by 26% in six years.

<examples>

In **Sweden**, regulations to **phase out preventive use of antibiotics** in agriculture—in which low doses are given to keep animals healthy and plump—cut sales of the drugs for farming by 67% since 1986. **The Netherlands** and **Denmark** have also restricted antibiotic use on livestock.

→ key words

Progress in the U.S. has been slower. The Food and Drug Administration recently tried to encourage farmers to voluntarily **reduce antibiotics** in farming. The agency is also taking steps to **curb use of antibacterials** in some consumer goods, requiring manufacturers to prove that antibacterials are better than simple soap and water in keeping germs at bay.

→ key words
→ key words
→ key words

Before antibiotics, something as minor as a cut or a sore throat could be a death sentence. While some **progress** has recently been made in the right direction, some might say that much more needs to be done.

→ key word

conclusion

모범답안 The word that best completes the blank is "progress". Second, the underlined in (1) and (2) refer to "antibiotics" and "bacteria evolving against antibiotics", respectively.

한글번역

우리는 연쇄상구균에서 포도상구균에 이르기까지 우리가 다루기 어려워하는 거의 모든 어떤 종류의 병균이라도 항생제의 신속한 투약으로 제거할 수 있다고 가정하기에 이르렀다. 그러나 미국에서만 매년 약 2백만 명의 사람들에게 항생제로 처치될 수 없는 감염이 생기며, 그들 중 2만 3천 명이 그 결과 사망한다. 세계보건기구(WHO)의 획기적인 한 보고서에 따르면, 문제의 박테리아는 현재 지구 모든 곳곳에서 나타난다. 일부 국가들에서, 폐렴간균이나 대장균에 감염된 사람들 중 약 50%가 우리가 가진 가장 강력한 항생제에 반응하지 않을 것이라고 세계의 여러 보건 전문가들은 말한다. 이것이 시사하는 점은 의사들이 이런 해로운 미생물과 싸우기 위해 의존하는 탄약이 점점 더 부족해지고 있다는 점이다.

박테리아는 1928년에 첫 항생제가 발견된 이후로 그들을 죽이도록 설계된 약에 저항하도록 진화해왔다. 그러나 우리가 농장, 처방약과 항균비누 따위에서 항생제를 과용하는 것은 (박테리아가 진화하는) 그 과정을 더 가속시켰다. WHO 보고서는 심각한 미래에 대한 진지한 경고였지만, 세계적으로, 진전은 느리게 되고 있다.

프랑스는 과거에 유럽에서 가장 높은 항생제 처방 비율을 가지고 있었으나, 정부의 명령이 의사 발행 처방전의 수를 6년 동안 26%만큼 줄이는 것을 가능케 했다.

스웨덴에서는, 농업에 있어 동물을 건강하고 살찌게 만들기 위해 저용량을 투여하는 예방적인 항생제 사용을 단계적으로 폐지하는 규제가 시행돼, 1986년 이후 농업용 항생제 판매량을 67% 감소시켰다. 네덜란드와 덴마크 역시 가축에게 사용되는 항생제를 규제해왔다.

미국 내에서 진전은 (다른 나라들보다는) 더 느리다. FDA(미국 식약처)는 최근에 농부들이 농업에서 자발적으로 항생제를 줄이도록 독려하려고 노력했다. 해당 기관은 또한 제조자들이 항균제가 단순 비누와 물에 비해 세균을 방지하는 데 더 좋다는 것을 증명하도록 요구함으로써, 일부 소비재에 항균제품을 사용하는 것을 억제하기 위한 조치를 취하고 있다.

항생제가 발견되기 전에는, 창상이나 인후통과 같은 사소한 것이 사형 선고가 될 수도 있었다. 일부 진전은 최근 옳은 방향으로 되고 있는 반면에, 누군가는 훨씬 더 많은 진보가 이뤄질 필요가 있다고 말할 수도 있다.

NOTE

Step 1	Ⓢurvey
Key Words	Antibiotics; bacteria; overuse; progress
Signal Words	But in the U.S. alone; France used; In Sweden; Before antibiotics
Step 2	Ⓡeading
Purpose	To outline the negative effects of antibiotics overuse
Pattern of Organization	Series; cause/effect
Tone	Concerned; alarmed
Main Idea	Bacteria has been evolving at a dangerous rate due to the overuse of antibiotics.
Step 3	Ⓢummary
지문 요약하기 (Paraphrasing)	Overuse of antibiotics is evolving bacteria to become too strong to fight against. This overuse in farming, prescription drugs and soap is accelerating the process of this evolution. To fight this, several European nations have taken efforts to regulate and reduce antibiotic usage. Though in the U.S. there has been slower progress made, there has been a decrease in the usage of antibiotics especially in farming and consumer products. In conclusion, despite some progress in the proper direction, there is a need for more change to be conducted *(or more action to be taken)*.
Step 4	Ⓡecite
	요약문 말로 설명하기

09 Read the passage and follow the directions. [4 points] 2020학년도

What could be better than studying physics under Albert Einstein? A lot, it turns out. While geniuses have done much to help society progress and flourish, perhaps they don't belong in front of the classroom. While logic dictates that the best teachers would be the most capable and accomplished people, there are two other qualities that are more vital than intelligence.

The first quality of effective teachers is that they had to put forth a lot of effort into their studies. While this may seem counterintuitive, it is probably more helpful to be guided by a person who had to work daily to master difficult concepts than by someone for whom learning was a breeze. Students often gravitate toward prodigies like Einstein because their expertise seems so effortless, but that's a mistake. It makes more sense to study under people who had to struggle to become experts because they've gone through the process of building their knowledge one concept at a time.

The next quality is a little more obvious but is often overlooked: being able to explain content clearly. A teacher who has a long list of publications probably isn't going to remember how to methodically explain the basics. In the first university course he taught, Einstein wasn't able to attract much interest in the esoteric subject of thermodynamics: Just three students signed up, and they were all friends of his. The next semester he had to cancel the class after only one student enrolled. This example shows how someone who has inborn genius may not be able to relate to students' ignorance to help them understand abstract concepts.

It's often said that those who can't do teach, yet the reality is that the best doers are often the worst teachers. So, teachers' most important qualities are having had the experience of building their knowledge and having the ability to make content easy to grasp. Being a great physicist doesn't make one a great physics teacher. Rather than taking an introduction to physics class with Einstein, it would be more valuable to learn from his protégé who spent years figuring out how to explain what it would be like to chase a beam of light.

Write a summary following the guidelines below.

Guidelines

- Summarize the above passage in one paragraph.
- Provide a topic sentence, two supporting ideas, and a concluding sentence based on the passage.
- Do NOT copy more than FIVE consecutive words from the passage.

NOTE

Step 1	Ⓢurvey
Key Words	
Signal Words	
Step 2	**Ⓡeading**
Purpose	
Pattern of Organization	
Tone	
Main Idea	
Step 3	**Ⓢummary**
지문 요약하기 (Paraphrasing)	
Step 4	**Ⓡecite**
요약문 말로 설명하기	

Answer Key

What could be better than studying physics under **Albert Einstein**? A lot, it turns out. While **geniuses** have done much to help society progress and flourish, perhaps they don't belong in front of the classroom. While logic dictates that the **best teachers** would be the most capable and accomplished people, there are two other qualities that are more vital than intelligence.

The first quality of **effective teachers** is that they had to put forth a **lot of effort into their studies**. While this may seem counterintuitive, it is probably more helpful to be guided by a person who had to work daily to master difficult concepts than by someone for whom learning was a breeze. Students often gravitate toward prodigies like Einstein because their expertise seems so effortless, but that's a mistake. It makes more sense to study under people who had to struggle to become experts because they've gone through the process of building their knowledge one concept at a time.

The next quality is a little more obvious but is often overlooked: **being able to explain content clearly. A teacher who has a long list of publications** probably isn't going to remember how to methodically explain the basics. In the first university course he taught, **Einstein** wasn't able to attract much interest in the esoteric subject of thermodynamics: Just three students signed up, and they were all friends of his. The next semester he had to cancel the class after only one student enrolled. This example shows how **someone who has inborn genius may not be able to relate to students' ignorance to help them understand abstract concepts.**

It's often said that those who can't do teach, yet the reality is that **the best doers are often the worst teachers.** So, **teachers' most important qualities** are having had the experience of building their knowledge and having the ability to make content easy to grasp. Being a great physicist doesn't make one a great physics teacher. Rather than taking an introduction to physics class with Einstein, **it would be more valuable to learn from his protégé who spent years figuring out how to explain what it would be like to chase a beam of light.**

<Introduction>
key word
key word(s)
signal words
key words
episode(example)
key words
conclusion
– 제안, 권고

모범답안 Geniuses such as Einstein do not necessarily make great teachers due to two important qualities. *(There are two important qualities great teachers have that geniuses such as Einstein may not have.)* The first quality is that non-geniuses have made a lot of effort *(or have struggled)*, unlike geniuses, to build their knowledge and thus are familiar with learning concepts one at a time. Second, effective teachers can explain difficult content clearly as opposed to geniuses, who may not relate enough to the ignorance of students to communicate well, as in Einstein's sparsely-attended lectures. To sum up, looking for a great teacher rather than a genius is recommended.

한글번역

앨버트 아인슈타인 아래에서 물리학을 공부하는 것보다 더 나은 것이 있을 수 있을까? 실제로는, 아주 많은 것들이 있을 수 있다. 천재들이 사회가 진보하고 번영하는 데 도움이 되는 많은 것을 해 온 것은 사실이지만, 아마도 교단 앞은 그 천재들이 속할 곳은 아니다. 논리에 따르자면 최고의 선생님이란 가장 유능하고 성공한 사람일 수도 있겠지만, 사실, 지능보다 더 중대한 두 가지 다른 자질이 있다.

효과적인 교사의 첫 번째 자질은 교사가 자신의 공부에 정말 많은 노력을 했다는 점이다. 이것은 직관에 어긋나 보이지만, 배우는 것이 식은 죽 먹기였던 사람보다는 어려운 개념을 숙달하기 위해 매일같이 노력해야 했던 사람에게 지도를 받는 것이 아마 더 도움이 될 수 있다. 학생들이 종종 아인슈타인과 같은 영재에게 끌리는 이유는 그 영재들의 전문성이 너무도 수월해 보이기 때문인데, 그러나 그것은 오해이다. 전문가가 되기 위해 분투해야 했던 사람 문하에서 공부하는 것이 더 이치에 맞는데, 이는 그러한 사람들이 그들의 지식을 한 번에 한 개념씩 구축해오는 과정을 거쳐 왔기 때문이다.

다음의 자질은, 조금 더 명백하지만 종종 경시되는 것인데, 내용을 명확하게 설명할 수 있는 것이다. (자신의) 출판물의 긴 목록을 가지고 있는 교사는 기초를 어떻게 방법론적으로 설명해야 할지 기억해내지 못할 수도 있다. 아인슈타인은 그가 가르친 첫 번째 대학 강의에서, 열역학의 난해한 주제에 많은 관심을 끌어올 수 없었다: 단지 세 학생만이 등록했고, 그들은 모두 아인슈타인의 친구였다. 그 다음 학기에 오직 한 학생만이 등록한 후 아인슈타인은 수업을 취소해야 했다. 이 예시가 보여주는 것은 선천적으로 천재성을 가진 자가 어떻게 학생들의 무지를 이해하지 못해 학생들이 추상적인 개념을 이해할 수 있도록 돕지 못할 수도 있는가이다.

할 수 없는(능력 없는) 자가 가르친다고 종종 일컬어지지만, 현실은 최고로 잘 하는 사람들이 최악의 교사인 경우가 자주 있다. 따라서, 교사의 가장 중요한 자질들은 그들의 지식을 구축하는 경험을 가지고 있는 것과 내용을 파악하기 쉽게 만드는 능력을 가지고 있는 것이다. 위대한 물리학자가 되는 것이 위대한 물리 교사를 만들어 주는 것은 아니다. 아인슈타인에게 물리학 개론 수업을 듣는 것보다는, 광선을 쫓아가는 것이 무엇과 같을지를 어떻게 설명할지 알아내느라 수년을 쓴 아인슈타인의 제자에게 배우는 것이 더 가치 있을 것이다.

NOTE

Step 1	Survey
Key Words	Einstein; geniuses; effective teachers
Signal Words	The first quality; The next quality
Step 2	**Reading**
Purpose	To show that teaching requires specific insight
Pattern of Organization	Series
Tone	Subjective
Main Idea	Teaching requires specific insight that geniuses might lack.
Step 3	**Summary**
지문 요약하기 (Paraphrasing)	Geniuses such as Einstein do not necessarily make great teachers due to two important qualities. *(There are two important qualities great teachers have that geniuses such as Einstein may not have.)* The first quality is that non-geniuses have made a lot of effort *(or have struggled)*, unlike geniuses, to build their knowledge and thus are familiar with learning concepts one at a time. Second, effective teachers can explain difficult content clearly as opposed to geniuses, who may not relate enough to the ignorance of students to communicate well, as in Einstein's sparsely-attended lectures. To sum up, looking for a great teacher rather than a genius is recommended.
Step 4	**Recite**
요약문 말로 설명하기	

10 Read the passage and follow the directions. [2 points]

2019학년도

Ancient Easterners saw the world as consisting of continuous substances while ancient Westerners tended to see the world as being composed of discrete objects or separate atoms. Remarkably, it is still the same in the modern era.

In a survey of the values of middle managers, Hampden-Turner and Trompenaars examined whether respondents from both Eastern and Western cultures thought of a company as a system to organize tasks or as an organism coordinating people working together. They asked respondents to choose between the following definitions:

(a) A company is a system designed to perform functions and tasks in an efficient way. People are hired to fulfill these functions with the help of machines and other equipment. They are paid for the tasks they perform.

(b) A company is a group of people working together. The people have social relations with other people and with the organization. The functioning is dependent on these relations.

About 75 percent of Americans chose the first definition, and more than 50 percent of Canadians, Australians, British, Dutch, and Swedes chose that definition. About a third of a group of Japanese and Singaporeans chose it. Thus for the Westerners, especially the Americans and the other people of primarily northern European culture, a company is an atomistic, modular place where people perform their distinctive functions. For the Easterners, a company is an organism where the social relations are an integral part of what holds things together.

Fill in the blank with the ONE most appropriate word from the passage.

Research shows that people from Western cultures tend to see the world in a more atomistic way. This view leads them to see a social institution like a workplace as a system to perform distinctive functions. On the other hand, according to the Easterners' perspective, a company is seen as an interdependent organism. Its function is made possible by ____________ among its members as well as between the members and the organization. Knowledge of such differences can be helpful for intercultural understanding.

____

NOTE

Step 1	Ⓢurvey
Key Words	
Signal Words	
Step 2	**Ⓡeading**
Purpose	
Pattern of Organization	
Tone	
Main Idea	
Step 3	**Ⓢummary**
지문 요약하기 (Paraphrasing)	
Step 4	**Ⓡecite**
요약문 말로 설명하기	

Answer Key

Ancient Easterners saw the world as consisting of continuous substances while **ancient Westerners** tended to see the world as being composed of discrete objects or separate atoms. Remarkably, **it is still the same** in the modern era.

In a survey of the values of middle managers, Hampden-Turner and Trompenaars examined whether respondents from both Eastern and Western cultures thought of a company as a system to organize tasks or as an organism coordinating people working together. They asked respondents to choose between the following definitions:

(a) A company is a system designed to perform functions and tasks in an efficient way. People are hired to fulfill these functions with the help of machines and other equipment. They are paid for the tasks they perform.

(b) A company is a group of people working together. The people have social relations with other people and with the organization. The functioning is dependent on these relations.

About 75 percent of Americans chose the first definition, and more than 50 percent of Canadians, Australians, British, Dutch, and Swedes chose that definition. About a third of a group of Japanese and Singaporeans chose it. Thus for the Westerners, especially the Americans and the other people of primarily northern European culture, a company is an atomistic, modular place where people perform their distinctive functions. For the Easterners, a company is an organism where **the social relations** are an integral part of what holds things together.

key words

key words

<contrast>

<contrast>

key words

모범답안 relations

한글번역

고대 동양인들은 세계를 연속적인 물질로 구성돼있다고 보는 반면, 고대 서양인들은 세계를 별개의 물체나 분리된 원자로 구성돼있다고 보는 경향이 있었다. 놀랍게도, 그것은 현대에서도 여전히 똑같다.

중간 관리자들의 가치관에 대한 조사에서, 햄든-터너와 트롬펜나르스는 동양과 서양 문화권의 응답자들이 회사를 업무를 조직하는 시스템으로 생각하는지 아니면 함께 일하는 사람들을 조정하는 유기체로 생각하는지 조사했다. 그들은 응답자들에게 다음 정의 중 하나를 선택하도록 요청했다.

(a) 회사는 효율적인 방법으로 기능과 업무를 수행하도록 설계된 시스템이다. 사람들은 기계와 다른 장비들의 도움으로 이러한 기능을 수행하기 위해 고용된다. 그들은 그들이 수행하는 업무에 대해 보수를 받는다.
(b) 회사는 함께 일하는 일군의 사람들이다. 사람들은 다른 사람들과 그리고 조직과 사회적 관계를 가진다. 이러한 관계에 따라 회사의 기능은 달라진다.

미국인의 약 75%가 첫 번째 정의를 선택했고 캐나다인, 호주인, 영국인, 네덜란드인, 스웨덴인 중 50퍼센트 이상이 첫 번째 정의를 선택했다. 일본인과 싱가포르인 중 약 3분의 1이 그 정의를 선택했다. 그러므로 서양인들, 특히 미국인과 주로 북유럽 문화의 다른 사람들에게 회사는 사람들이 그들의 독특한 기능을 수행하는 원자적이고 조립식인 장소이다. 동양인에게 회사는 사회적 관계가 여러 상황들을 하나로 묶어주는 것의 필수적인 부분인 유기체이다.

NOTE

Step 1	Ⓢurvey
Key Words	Easterners; Westerners; company; coordinating; social relations
Signal Words	While; Thus for the Westerners
Step 2	**Ⓡeading**
Purpose	To show differences in the differing views of the work place between Eastern and Western cultures
Pattern of Organization	Compare/contrast
Tone	Neutral
Main Idea	Western cultures view a company in a more atomistic way, while Eastern cultures view one as an interdependent organism.
Step 3	**Ⓢummary**
지문 요약하기 (Paraphrasing)	Research shows that people from Western cultures tend to see the world in a more atomistic way. This view leads them to see a social institution like a workplace as a system to perform distinctive functions. On the other hand, according to the Easterners' perspective, a company is seen as an interdependent organism. Its function is made possible by relations among its members as well as between the members and the organization. Knowledge of such differences can be helpful for intercultural understanding.
Step 4	**Ⓡecite**
요약문 말로 설명하기	

11 Read the passage and follow the directions. [4 points] 2019학년도

Inanimate objects are classified scientifically into three major categories. The goal of all inanimate objects is to resist man and ultimately to defeat him, and the three major classifications are based on the method each object uses to achieve its purpose.

As a general rule, any object capable of breaking down at the moment when it is almost needed will do so. The automobile is typical of the category. With the cunning typical of its breed, the automobile never breaks down while entering a filling station. It waits until it reaches a downtown intersection in the middle of the rush hour. Thus it creates maximum inconvenience, frustration and irritability among its human cargo, thereby reducing its owner's life span.

Many inanimate objects, of course, find it extremely difficult to break down. Keys, for example, are almost totally incapable of breaking down. Therefore, they have had to evolve a different technique for resisting man. They get lost. Science has still not solved the mystery of how they do it, and no man has ever caught one of them in the act of getting lost. The most plausible theory is that they have developed a secret method of locomotion which they are able to conceal the instant a human eye falls upon them.

Scientists have been struck by the fact that things that break down virtually never get lost, while things that get lost hardly ever break down. A furnace, for example, will invariably break down at the depth of the first winter cold wave, but it will never get lost. A woman's purse, which after all does have some inherent capacity for breaking down, hardly ever does. Some persons believe this constitutes evidence that inanimate objects are not entirely hostile to man, and that a negotiated peace is possible.

The third class of objects is the most curious of all. These include such objects as cigarette lighters and flashlights. It is inaccurate, of course, to say that they never work. They work once, usually for the first few hours after being brought home, and then quit. Thereafter, they never work again.

In fact, it is widely assumed that they are built for the purpose of not working.

They have truly defeated man by training him never to expect anything of them, and in return they have given man the only peace he receives from inanimate society. He does not expect his cigarette lighter to light or his flashlight to illuminate, and when they don't it does not raise his blood pressure. He cannot attain that ______________ with furnaces and keys, and cars and women's purses as long as he demands that they work for their keep.

Fill in the blank with the ONE most appropriate word from the passage. Then, state THREE methods that inanimate objects use to resist man.

____

____

____

____

____

NOTE

Step 1	Survey
Key Words	
Signal Words	
Step 2	**Reading**
Purpose	
Pattern of Organization	
Tone	
Main Idea	
Step 3	**Summary**
지문 요약하기 (Paraphrasing)	
Step 4	**Recite**
요약문 말로 설명하기	

Answer Key

Inanimate objects are classified scientifically into three major categories. The goal of all inanimate objects is to resist man and ultimately to defeat him, and the three major classifications are based on the method each object uses to achieve its purpose.

→ key words

As a general rule, any object capable of **breaking down** at the moment when it is almost needed will do so. **The automobile** is typical of the category. With the cunning typical of its breed, the automobile never breaks down while entering a filling station. It waits until it reaches a downtown intersection in the middle of the rush hour. Thus it creates maximum inconvenience, frustration and irritability among its human cargo, thereby reducing its owner's life span.

example 1
– automobile

Many inanimate objects, of course, find it extremely difficult to break down. **Keys**, for example, are almost totally incapable of breaking down. Therefore, they have had to evolve a different technique for resisting man. They **get lost**. Science has still not solved the mystery of how they do it, and no man has ever caught one of them in the act of **getting lost**. The most plausible theory is that they have developed a secret method of locomotion which they are able to conceal the instant a human eye falls upon them.

example 2-1
– Keys

Scientists have been struck by the fact that things that break down virtually never get lost, while things that get lost hardly ever break down. **A furnace**, for example, will invariably break down at the depth of the first winter cold wave, but it will never get lost. **A woman's purse**, which after all does have some inherent capacity for breaking down, hardly ever does. Some persons believe this constitutes evidence that inanimate objects are not entirely hostile to man, and that a negotiated peace is possible.

example 2-2
– furnace, purse

The third class of objects is the most curious of all. These include such objects as **cigarette lighters and flashlights**. It is inaccurate, of course, to say that they never work. They work once, usually for the first few hours after being brought home, and then quit. Thereafter, they never work again. In fact, it is widely assumed that they are built for the purpose of not working.

example 3
– cigarette lighters
and flashlights

They have truly defeated man by training him never to expect anything of them, and in return they have given man the only peace he receives from inanimate society. He does not expect his cigarette lighter to light or his flashlight to illuminate, and when they don't it does not raise his blood pressure. He cannot attain that peace with furnaces and keys, and cars and women's purses as long as he demands that they work for their keep.

<conclusion>

모범답안 The word for the blank is "peace". Next, the three methods that inanimate objects use to resist man are breaking down when needed, getting lost, and working for just the first few hours.

한글번역

무생물들은 과학적으로 크게 세 가지 범주로 분류된다. 모든 무생물체들의 목표는 인간에게 저항하고 궁극적으로 인간을 굴복시키는 것이다. 그리고 세 가지 주된 분류체계는 각 물체들이 목적을 달성하기 위해 사용하는 방법에 근거를 둔다.

일반적으로, 필요할 때 고장 날 수 있는 모든 물체는, 우리 인간이 필요로 하는 그 순간 바로 고장 나는 경향이 있다. 자동차가 이런 범주의 전형적인 부류이다. 그런 교활한 전형적 종자인, 자동차는 주유소에 들어가는 동안에는 절대 고장 나지 않는다. 자동차는 러시아워 중에 시내 교차로에 들어설 때까지 기다린다. 이런 식으로 자동차는 운전자들에게 극도의 불편함과 좌절 그리고 짜증을 야기해 자신의 주인의 생명을 단축시킨다.

물론 많은 무생물체들은 고장 나는 것이 극도로 어렵다는 것을 알게 된다. 예를 들어, 열쇠들이 완전히 고장 나는 것은 거의 불가능하다. 따라서 그들은 인간에게 저항하기 위한 다른 기술을 진화시켜야만 했다. 그것들은 분실된다. 과학은 여전히 어떻게 그것들이 그렇게 분실되는지에 대한 미스터리를 풀지 못했다. 그리고 어떤 인간도 분실되는 행동 중에 그것들을 발견하지 못했다. 가장 그럴듯한 이론은 그것들이 인간의 눈이 자기들에게로 향하자마자, 스스로를 은폐할 수 있는 비밀스러운 이동방법을 개발했다는 것이다.

과학자들은 고장 나는 것들은 사실상 결코 잃어버려지지 않는 반면에 분실되는 것들은 거의 고장 나지 않는다는 사실을 깨닫게 됐다. 예를 들면, 용광로는 첫 겨울 한파가 절정인 때 항상 고장 나곤 하지만, 결코 분실되지는 않는 경향이 있다. 여성용 지갑은 결국 고장 나는 어떤 내재적인 능력을 갖고 있지만, 거의 그러지는 않는다. 어떤 사람들은 이것이 무생물체들이 인간에게 완전히 적대적이지는 않다는 증거가 된다고 생각하면서, 협상된 평화가 가능하다고 믿는다.

세 번째 부류의 물체들은 모든 것 가운데 가장 별난 것이다. 이것들은 담배 라이터와 손전등과 같은 것을 포함한다. 물론 이것들이 결코 작동하지 않는다고 말하는 것은 부정확하다. 그것들은 한 번은 작동하는데, 대체로 집으로 데려온 지 첫 몇 시간 동안이다. 그리고는 멈춘다. 그러고는 절대로 다시는 작동하지 않는다. 사실, 널리 가정되는 바로는 그것들이 작동하지 않기 위해서 만들어졌다는 것이다.

이런 물건들은 인간이 자신들에게 어떤 기대도 하지 않도록 사람을 훈련시키는 것으로 굴복시킨다. 그리고 그에 대한 보답으로 이 물건들은 자신들의 사회로부터 인간이 받을 수 있는 유일한 평화를 준다. 인간은 자신의 담배 라이터가 불을 붙이거나 손전등이 빛을 비출 거라고 기대하지 않고, 그것들이 그렇게 하지 않을 때, 인간은 자신의 혈압을 올리지 않는다. 그가 그것들을 보유하기 위해 그것들로 하여금 작동하도록 요구하는 한, 인간은 용광로, 열쇠, 자동차 그리고 여성용 지갑으로부터 그런 평화를 얻을 수 없다.

NOTE

Step 1	Ⓢurvey
Key Words	Inanimate objects; resist; break down; lost; stop working
Signal Words	Three major categories; As a general rule; is typical of the category; for example; The third class of objects
Step 2	**Ⓡeading**
Purpose	To outline some of the frustrations with having things lost or broken
Pattern of Organization	Series
Tone	Humorous
Main Idea	Inanimate objects all fail by breaking, getting lost, or working just once.
Step 3	**Ⓢummary**
지문 요약하기 (Paraphrasing)	Inanimate objects resist mankind in three ways. First, there are those that breakdown at the worst times. Next are those that get themselves lost. However, it has been noted that things that break down hardly become lost, showing some possible relationships between objects and mankind. Finally, there are objects that quit working quickly. By accepting this resistance, a man can find peace without relying on objects.
Step 4	**Ⓡecite**
요약문 말로 설명하기	

12 Read the passage and follow the directions. [5 points]

2019학년도

Melatonin—a hormone naturally produced by the pineal gland—is released when darkness falls, signaling to the body that it is time to rest. While it is well known for its sleep-inducing properties, now, as a result of growing research, scientists know that the substance not only induces sleep but also keeps the brain in order.

One way it does so is as an antidepressant. Seasonal affective disorder is a form of depression common during winter months, thought to be the effect of a mismatch between one's normal sleep cycle and the shifting light-dark cycle. For some people this rhythm mismatch depresses mood. However, this disorder can be readily treated with melatonin. Research has shown that low doses of melatonin along with bright light therapy can realign the sleep-wake cycle and alleviate symptoms of seasonal affective disorder.

Another way it keeps the brain in order is by slowing the cognitive impairment associated with age-related diseases such as Alzheimer's. Amyloid beta and tau proteins are toxic and they build up in patients with this disease, leading to cognitive decline. Melatonin helps to offset the toxic effects of these proteins, but people with Alzheimer's disease produce one fifth the amount of melatonin as healthy young adults. Therefore, melatonin supplements can improve cognitive function in these patients by countering the toxic influence of these two harmful proteins.

These promising newly found effects of this hormone have attracted much attention and have stimulated further research to make humans healthier and happier. What is clear is that melatonin is no longer just an alternative to counting sheep.

Write a summary following the guidelines below.

Guidelines

- Summarize the above passage in one paragraph.
- Provide a topic sentence, two supporting ideas, and a concluding sentence based on the passage.
- Do NOT copy more than FIVE consecutive words from the passage.

NOTE

Step 1	Ⓢurvey
Key Words	
Signal Words	
Step 2	**Ⓡeading**
Purpose	
Pattern of Organization	
Tone	
Main Idea	
Step 3	**Ⓢummary**
지문 요약하기 (Paraphrasing)	
Step 4	**Ⓡecite**
요약문 말로 설명하기	

Answer Key

Melatonin—a hormone naturally produced by the pineal gland—is released when darkness falls, signaling to the body that it is time to rest. While it is well known for its sleep-inducing properties, now, as a result of growing research, scientists know that the substance not only induces sleep but also keeps the brain in order.

One way it does so is as **an antidepressant**. Seasonal affective disorder is a form of depression common during winter months, thought to be the effect of a mismatch between one's normal sleep cycle and the shifting light-dark cycle. For some people this rhythm mismatch depresses mood. However, this disorder can be readily treated with melatonin. Research has shown that **low doses of melatonin** along with bright light therapy can realign the sleep-wake cycle and alleviate symptoms of seasonal affective disorder.

Another way it keeps the brain in order is by **slowing the cognitive impairment** associated with age-related diseases such as Alzheimer's. Amyloid beta and tau proteins are toxic and they build up in patients with this disease, leading to cognitive decline. **Melatonin helps** to offset the toxic effects of these proteins, but people with Alzheimer's disease produce one fifth the amount of melatonin as healthy young adults. Therefore, melatonin supplements can improve **cognitive function** in these patients by countering the toxic influence of these two harmful proteins.

These promising newly found effects of this hormone have attracted much attention and have stimulated further research to make humans healthier and happier. What is clear is that melatonin is no longer just an alternative to counting sheep.

→ key word

→ key words

→ key words

→ key words

→ conclusion : 전망

모범답안 Melatonin has important benefits for the brain's health as well as inducing sleep. First, it acts as an antidepressant, helping to combat seasonal affective disorder, which is a kind of depression, when given along with light therapy. Also, melatonin can aid in countering the effects of mental decline in Alzheimer's patients by offsetting toxins caused by harmful proteins such as amyloid beta and tau. In conclusion, given these promising effects, further research on melatonin's other health benefits has been stimulated.

한글번역

송과샘(좌우 대뇌 반구 사이 제3뇌실에 있는 내분비 기관)에 의해 자연적으로 생성되는 호르몬인 멜라토닌은 어둠이 내려올 때 몸에 쉴 시간이라고 신호를 보내주며 분출된다. 이것은 잠을 유도하는 특성으로 잘 알려져 있지만, 연구가 늘어나면서 지금은 과학자들이 멜라토닌이 잠을 유도하는 것뿐 아니라 두뇌를 잘 유지시키는 데 도움이 된다는 것을 알고 있다.

멜라토닌이 두뇌를 잘 유지하는 한 가지 방법은 항우울제로서다. 계절성 정서 장애는 보통의 수면 주기와 바뀌는 낮과 밤의 주기 간에 부조화의 영향으로 여겨지는 겨울 동안 흔한 우울증의 한 형태이다. 이러한 주기의 부조화는 몇몇의 사람들을 우울하게 하기도 한다. 하지만, 이러한 장애는 멜라토닌으로 손쉽게 치료될 수 있다. 연구는 밝은 광 치료와 함께 소량의 멜라토닌이 수면 및 각성 주기를 재편성하고 계절성 정서 장애의 증상을 완화할 수 있다고 보여주고 있다.

멜라토닌이 두뇌를 잘 유지시키는 다른 방법은 알츠하이머와 같이 나이와 관련된 질병과 연관돼있는 인지 손상을 둔화시킴으로써다. 아밀로이드 베타와 T단백질은 독성이 있는데, 이것들은 이러한 질병을 가지고 있는 환자들 안에서 쌓이고, 인지능력 감소를 초래한다. 멜라토닌은 이러한 단백질의 유해한 효과를 상쇄시키는 것을 돕지만, 알츠하이머 질병을 지닌 사람들은 건강하고 젊은 사람들이 생성하는 멜라토닌의 양의 5분의 1만을 생성한다. 그래서 멜라토닌 공급은 이러한 두 가지의 해로운 단백질의 독소적 영향을 상쇄시킴으로써 알츠하이머 환자들의 인지 기능을 증진시킬 수 있다.

멜라토닌의 이러한 새롭게 발견된 유망한 효과들은 많은 주목을 받고 있고, 사람들을 더욱 건강하고 행복하게 만들기 위한 추가 연구를 자극하고 있다. 확실한 것은 멜라토닌이 더 이상 단순히 양을 세는 것(주-서양에선 잠이 안 올 때 머릿속으로 양을 셈으로써 잠을 자려 노력함)의 대안은 아니라는 것이다.

Step 1	Ⓢurvey
Key Words	Melatonin; sleep; antidepressant; cognitive function
Signal Words	One way; another way
Step 2	**Ⓡeading**
Purpose	To explain the benefits of melatonin
Pattern of Organization	Series
Tone	Neutral
Main Idea	Melatonin has important benefits for health and happiness.
Step 3	**Ⓢummary**
지문 요약하기 (Paraphrasing)	Melatonin has important benefits for the brain's health as well as inducing sleep. First, it acts as an antidepressant, helping to combat seasonal affective disorder, which is a kind of depression, when given along with light therapy. Also, melatonin can aid in countering the effects of mental decline in Alzheimer's patients by offsetting toxins caused by harmful proteins such as amyloid beta and tau. In conclusion, given these promising effects, further research on melatonin's other health benefits has been stimulated.
Step 4	**Ⓡecite**
요약문 말로 설명하기	

13 Read the passage and follow the directions. [2 points]

2018학년도

From the very beginning of school we make books and reading a constant source of possible failure and public humiliation. When children are little we make them read aloud, before the teacher and other children, so that we can be sure they "know" all the words they are reading. This means that when they don't know a word, they are going to make a mistake, right in front of the whole class. Instantly they are made to realize that they have done something wrong. Perhaps some of the other children will begin to wave their hands and say, "Ooooh! O-o-o-oh!" Perhaps they will just giggle, or nudge each other, or make a face. Perhaps the teacher will say, "Are you sure?" or ask someone else what he thinks. Or perhaps, if the teacher is kind, she will just smile a sweet, sad smile—often one of the most painful punishments a child can suffer in school. In any case, the child who has made the mistake knows he has made it, and feels foolish, stupid, and ashamed, just as any of us would in his shoes.

Before long many children associate books and reading with mistakes, real or feared, and penalties and humiliation. This may not seem sensible, but it is natural. Mark Twain once said that a cat that sat on a hot stove lid would never sit on one again—but it would never sit on a cold one either. As true of ________________ as of cats. If they, so to speak, sit on a hot book a few times, if books cause them humiliation and pain, they are likely to decide that the safest thing to do is to leave all books alone.

Fill in the blank with the ONE most appropriate word from the passage.

____

NOTE

Step 1	Survey
Key Words	
Signal Words	
Step 2	**Reading**
Purpose	
Pattern of Organization	
Tone	
Main Idea	
Step 3	**Summary**
지문 요약하기 (Paraphrasing)	
Step 4	**Recite**
요약문 말로 설명하기	

Answer Key

From the very beginning of school we make **books and reading** a constant **source** of possible **failure and public humiliation**. When **children** are little we make them **read aloud**, before the teacher and other children, so that we can be sure they "know" all the words they are reading. This means that when they don't know a word, they are going to make a mistake, right in front of the whole class. Instantly they are made to realize that they have done something wrong. Perhaps some of the other children will begin to wave their hands and say, "Ooooh! O-o-o-oh!" Perhaps they will just giggle, or nudge each other, or make a face. Perhaps the teacher will say, "Are you sure?" or ask someone else what he thinks. Or perhaps, if the teacher is kind, she will just smile a sweet, sad smile—often one of the most painful punishments a child can suffer in school. In any case, the child who has made the mistake knows he has made it, and feels foolish, stupid, and ashamed, just as any of us would in his shoes.

Before long many **children** associate **books and reading** with **mistakes, real or feared, and penalties and humiliation**. This may not seem sensible, but it is natural. Mark Twain once said that a cat that sat on a hot stove lid would never sit on one again—but it would never sit on a cold one either. As true of children as of cats. If they, so to speak, sit on a hot book a few times, if books cause them humiliation and pain, they are likely to decide that the safest thing to do is to leave all books alone.

→ key words
→ key words
→ key word
→ key words
→ result

모범답안 children

한글번역

우리는 아주 이른 학창 시절에서부터 책과 독서를 끊임없는 실패와 남들 앞에서 창피를 당하게 만드는 것이 되도록 만든다. 아이들이 어릴 때, 우리는 읽는 단어를 전부 알고 있는지 확인하기 위해 교사와 다른 아이들 앞에서 그 아이들에게 소리 내서 책을 읽게 한다. 이는 아이들이 한 단어라도 모르면 학급의 모든 아이들이 지켜보고 있는 가운데 실수를 할 것임을 의미한다. 이렇게 되면 즉시 그 아이들은 자신이 무언가를 잘못했다는 것을 깨닫는다. 어떤 아이들은 손을 흔들며 야유를 할 것이고, 다른 어떤 아이들은 단순히 낄낄거리거나, 서로를 툭툭 치거나, 얼굴을 찌푸릴 것이다. 어쩌면 교사는 "너 그것 확신하니?"라고 묻거나 다른 아이에게 어떻게 생각하는지 다시 질문을 할 것이다. 혹은 그 선생이 괜찮은 사람이라면, 그녀는 부드럽고도 슬픈 미소만을 지을 것이다. 이것은 학생이 학교에서 겪을 수 있는 처벌 중에 가장 고통스러운 처벌일 것이다. 어찌됐든, 실수를 저지른 학생은 자신이 실수를 했다는 것을 알 것이며, 누구든 그의 입장이 되면 그렇겠듯이 자신이 바보 같고 어리석고 부끄러울 것이다.

곧 많은 아이들이 책과 독서를, 실제로 그렇든 아니면 무서워서든, 실수나 처벌, 그리고 창피함과 연관 짓는다. 이는 합리적이라고 말하기는 어렵지만 자연스러운 일이다. 마크 트웨인은 뜨거운 솥뚜껑 위에 앉아 본 고양이는 다시는 그 위에 앉지 않지만, 또한 차가운 솥뚜껑 위에도 앉지 않는다고 말한 적이 있다. 고양이에게 적용되듯이 아이들에게도 그러하다. 말하자면, 아이들이 뜨거운 책 위에 몇 번 앉아 있다면, 책이 그들에게 창피함과 고통을 안겨준다면, 그들은 책을 멀리하는 것이 가장 좋다는 결론에 다다를 것이다.

NOTE

Step 1	Ⓢurvey
Key Words	Books and reading; read aloud; children
Signal Words	Make; source; cause; From the very beginning of school; Before long
Step 2	**Ⓡeading**
Purpose	To criticize the tendency to make students read aloud, which can cause them to leave books and reading alone
Pattern of Organization	Cause/effect
Tone	Critical
Main Idea	The practice of students reading aloud can lead them to abandon books and reading.
Step 3	**Ⓢummary**
지문 요약하기 (Paraphrasing)	The practice of students reading aloud can lead them to abandon books and reading. The humiliation felt when they make mistakes while reading aloud is real suffering. This creates negative associations with books that make students likely to leave them alone.
Step 4	**Ⓡecite**
요약문 말로 설명하기	

14 Read the passage and follow the directions. [4 points]

2018학년도

For at least 10,000 years, humans have been manipulating their own brains by drinking alcohol. And for at least the last few decades, researchers have wondered whether alcohol had a positive effect on physical health. Study after study seemed to suggest that people who imbibed one alcoholic beverage per day—a 12-ounce beer, a 6-ounce glass of wine, or a 1.5-ounce shot of spirits—had healthier hearts than did people who abstained from drinking altogether. A drink a day, it seemed, kept the cardiologist away.

Yet the methods in these studies may be flawed. When Kaye Fillmore, a researcher at the University of California, San Francisco, and her team analyzed 54 published studies on how moderate drinking affects the heart, they found that most of the drink-a-day studies had not used random assignment. In studies with random assignment, researchers used coin tosses or the like to decide into which condition—the control group or various experimental groups—each study participant should go. By letting chance dictate who goes into which group, researchers are more likely to end up with truly comparable groups.

Instead of randomly assigning participants to drinking and non-drinking groups, though, 47 of the 54 studies compared people who were already having one drink daily to people who were already teetotaling. Why is this design method a problem? In the United States, where most of these studies took place, many people have a drink once in a while. Usually, people who never drink abstain for a reason, such as religious prohibitions or medical concerns.

In fact, Fillmore and her team found that many of the nondrinkers in these studies were abstaining from alcohol for medical reasons, including advanced age or a history of alcoholism. In other words, the nondrinking groups in most of the studies included more unhealthy people to begin with, compared to the drinking groups. As a result, these studies didn't show that drinking alcohol led to better health. Instead, they showed that better health often leads to a level of alcohol consumption that is moderate.

First, describe the characteristics of the participants in the two groups in 47 of the 54 studies. Second, explain why those 47 studies were flawed in design.

NOTE

Step 1	Survey
Key Words	
Signal Words	
Step 2	**Reading**
Purpose	
Pattern of Organization	
Tone	
Main Idea	
Step 3	**Summary**
지문 요약하기 (Paraphrasing)	
Step 4	**Recite**
요약문 말로 설명하기	

Answer Key

For at least 10,000 years, humans have been manipulating their own brains by drinking alcohol. And for at least the last few decades, researchers have wondered **whether alcohol had a positive effect on physical health**. Study after study seemed to suggest that people who imbibed one alcoholic beverage per day—a 12-ounce beer, a 6-ounce glass of wine, or a 1.5-ounce shot of spirits—had healthier hearts than did people who abstained from drinking altogether. A drink a day, it seemed, kept the cardiologist away.

Yet the methods in these studies may be flawed. When Kaye Fillmore, a researcher at the University of California, San Francisco, and her team analyzed 54 published studies on how moderate drinking affects the heart, they found that most of the drink-a-day studies had not used **random assignment**. **In studies with random assignment**, researchers used coin tosses or the like to decide into which condition—the control group or various experimental groups—each study participant should go. By letting chance dictate who goes into which group, researchers are more likely to end up with truly comparable groups.

Instead of randomly assigning participants to drinking and non-drinking groups, though, 47 of the 54 studies compared people who were already having one drink daily to people who were already teetotaling. **Why is this design method a problem?** In the United States, where most of these studies took place, many people have a drink once in a while. Usually, people who never drink abstain for a reason, such as religious prohibitions or medical concerns.

In fact, **Fillmore and her team** found that many of the nondrinkers in these studies were abstaining from alcohol for medical reasons, including advanced age or a history of alcoholism. **In other words**, the nondrinking groups in most of the studies included more unhealthy people to begin with, compared to the drinking groups. **As a result**, these studies didn't show that drinking alcohol led to better health. Instead, they showed that better health often **leads to** a level of alcohol consumption that is moderate.

기존 연구의 핵심적 내용

random assignment 방법

핵심적 발견

모범답안 The characteristics of the two groups in 47 of the 54 studies are that one group already imbibed*(had)* a drink a day and the other already abstained before the studies began, without being randomly assigned to do so. Second, these studies are problematic*(flawed; imperfect)* because the latter group wasn't randomly-selected and were often already abstaining because of medical conditions, meaning that those non-drinkers were in poor health from the start (and not because of their non-drinking during the course of the given study).

한글번역

적어도 지난 10,000년 동안, 인간은 음주를 통해 그들 자신의 뇌를 조작해왔다. 그리고 적어도 지난 수십 년 동안, 연구원들은 술이 인간의 육체 건강에 긍정적인 영향을 끼칠지에 대해 연구해왔다. 여러 연구들에 따르면, 하루에 술 한 잔, 즉 맥주 12온스, 와인 6온스, 혹은 1.5온스의 증류주 한 잔을 마시는 사람들이 완전히 술을 절제하고 있는 사람들보다 더 건강한 심장을 가지고 있을 수 있다고 암시하는 것처럼 보인다. 하루에 한 잔의 술을 마시면 심장병 전문의를 만날 일이 없다는 것이다.

하지만 이런 연구원들의 접근 방식은 틀렸을 수 있다. 샌프란시스코 캘리포니아 대학교의 연구원인 캐이 필모어와 그녀의 팀은 적절한 음주가 심장에 미치는 영향을 다룬 54개의 출간된 논문을 분석했는데, 그들은 그 논문들 중 대부분이 무작위할당(무선할당) 방법을 사용하지 않았다는 사실을 밝혀냈다. 무선할당 방법이 사용된 연구에서는 연구자들이 동전을 던지거나 참가자가 통제집단과 실험집단 중 어떤 쪽에 배속될지 고르게 하는 식의 방법을 썼다. 누가 어떤 집단에 들어갈지를 우연에 맡김으로써 연구자들은 진정한 비교 가능한 집단을 만들어 낼 수 있었던 것이다.

참가자들을 음주 집단과 비음주 집단으로 임의로 배정하는 대신, 54개 중 47개의 연구는 음주를 전혀 하지 않는 사람들과 하루에 한 잔의 음주를 하는 사람들을 비교했다. 왜 이런 연구 설계가 문제가 되는가? 이러한 연구의 대부분이 이루어지는 미국에서는 많은 사람들이 어쩌다 한 번씩 술을 먹는 것은 흔한 일이다. 보통 술을 절대 마시지 않는 사람들은 종교적인 금기나 건강상의 염려와 같은 이유 때문에 술을 마시지 않는다.

필모어와 그녀의 팀은 이런 연구들에서 비음주 그룹 중 대부분은 고령이나 알코올 중독 이력 등의 의학적인 문제 때문에 음주를 멀리하고 있다는 사실을 발견했다. 즉, 대부분의 연구 안의 비음주 그룹은 음주 그룹에 비해 원래부터 건강이 좋지 않았던 사람들을 포함했던 것이다. 결과적으로 이 연구들은 음주가 건강에 도움이 되는지를 밝혀내지 못했다. 대신에 필모어와 그녀의 팀은 더 나은 건강상태가 자주 적절한 음주로 이어진다는 사실을 밝혀냈다.

NOTE

Step 1	Ⓢurvey
Key Words	47 published studies; design method; drinking alcohol; Fillmore study
Signal Words	Yet the methods; in studies with random assignment; In fact
Step 2	**Ⓡeading**
Purpose	To show the problems in previous studies on alcohol's positive effects
Pattern of Organization	Compare/contrast
Tone	Informative
Main Idea	Earlier research on drinking showed that it had a positive effect on health, but the current research has been proven as inaccurate.
Step 3	**Ⓢummary**
지문 요약하기 (Paraphrasing)	Earlier research on drinking showed that it had a positive effect on health, but the research has been proven as inaccurate. That previous research was shown to have not used random assignment, which produced inaccurate results. Instead, it was proven that better health often led to a moderate level of consumption.
Step 4	**Ⓡecite**
요약문 말로 설명하기	

15 Read the passage and follow the directions. [5 points]

2018학년도

As children, many of us were taken to museums. In most cases this was probably with a group of fellow students from our school on a field trip. We were there to learn. The displays were static and the importance of the so-called great works escaped many in attendance. As a result, many adults rarely revisited museums. Museums were only seen as cultural repositories. In the last few decades, however, they have changed their purpose and role in society.

Throughout human history, museums collected the extraordinary as evidence of the past. More recently, they have reevaluated the purpose of their collections and put much more effort into collecting the ordinary and everyday, in recognition of the fact that it is this material which best represents the lives of most people. Such a change in their collections enables museums to show their relevance to people who previously were underrepresented, and thus uninterested in museums.

Museums have started to play a new role in society through their partnerships, as well. It is no longer an option for a museum to remain isolated and aloof. Museums are social constructs and have assumed their place in mainstream contemporary life. They are now networking their value to all sectors of society, not just with traditional allies like the education sector. Political associations and business and community sectors are now included.

In these ways, the institutions that once were just hallowed halls of important objects are now quickly adapting with new attitudes towards what they collect. They also have evolved to interact and work with a variety of members within their communities. Modern museums are reinventing themselves as the center of contemporary culture.

Write a summary following the guidelines below.

Guidelines

- Summarize the above passage in one paragraph.
- Provide a topic sentence, two supporting ideas, and a concluding sentence based on the passage.
- Do NOT copy more than FIVE consecutive words from the passage.

NOTE

Step 1	Ⓢurvey
Key Words	
Signal Words	
Step 2	Ⓡeading
Purpose	
Pattern of Organization	
Tone	
Main Idea	
Step 3	Ⓢummary
지문 요약하기 (Paraphrasing)	
Step 4	Ⓡecite
요약문 말로 설명하기	

Answer Key

As children, many of us were taken to **museums**. In most cases this was probably with a group of fellow students from our school on a field trip. We were there to learn. The displays were static and the importance of the so-called great works escaped many in attendance. As a result, many adults rarely revisited museums. Museums were only seen as **cultural repositories**. In the last few decades, however, they **have changed their purpose and role in society**.

Throughout human history, museums collected the extraordinary as evidence of the past. More recently, they have reevaluated the purpose of their collections and put much more effort into collecting **the ordinary and everyday**, in recognition of the fact that it is this material which best represents the lives of most people. Such **a change in their collections** enables museums to show their relevance to people who previously were underrepresented, and thus uninterested in museums.

Museums have started to play a new role in society through their partnerships, as well. It is no longer an option for a museum to remain isolated and aloof. Museums are social constructs and have assumed their place in mainstream contemporary life. They are now **networking** their value to all sectors of society, not just with traditional allies like the education sector. Political associations and business and community sectors are now included.

In these ways, **the institutions** that once were just hallowed halls of important objects are now quickly adapting with **new attitudes towards what they collect. They also have evolved to interact and work with a variety of members within their communities**. Modern museums are reinventing themselves as the center of contemporary culture.

key word
<Introduction>

key words

key words

① collection에서의 변화

key words

② role에서의 변화

key words

<conclusion>

모범답안 Museums have recently transformed their aims and functions in society. First, museums now collect more ordinary objects instead of special or rare items to better portray common living in the past. In addition to this, museums have begun to partner with allies*(sectors)* beyond the narrow educational sphere, reaching out to political, business, and community institutes. Through these changes, modern museums have adapted themselves to be a crucial part of contemporary culture.

한글번역

우리는 어린 시절에 박물관에 가 보게 된다. 대부분의 경우 이런 경험은 학교에서 또래 친구들과 같이 현장 학습을 가는 경우일 것이다. 우리는 그곳에 배움을 위해 갔다. 전시품들은 정적이었고 소위 말하는 위대한 작품들의 중요성은 많은 이들의 이목에서 벗어났다. 결과적으로, 많은 성인들은 거의 박물관에 재방문하지 않았다. 그저 박물관들은 문화 저장소로 여겨졌다. 그러나 최근 몇십 년 동안 박물관은 사회에서의 그들의 목적과 역할을 바꿔오고 있다.

인류의 역사 속에서 박물관들은 과거를 보여주는 증거로서 예외적인 것들을 수집해왔다. 최근 들어서 박물관들은 그들이 수집하는 작품들의 목적에 대해 다시 평가하고, 평범하고 일상적인 것들을 모으는 것에 더 많은 노력을 쏟고 있다. 이렇게 하는 것은 대다수의 사람들의 삶을 가장 잘 드러내 보여주는 것이 바로 이런 수집품들이라는 것을 인식했기 때문이다. 이러한 수집품에 대한 변화는 전에는 과소평가됐던 사람들, 따라서 박물관에 별 관심이 없던 사람들과의 연관성을 보여주게 한다.

박물관은 협업을 통해 사회에서 새로운 역할을 하기도 한다. 박물관의 입장에서는 홀로 고립되는 것은 더 이상 선택지에 없다. 박물관은 사회 구조의 일부분이고 현대인의 삶의 주류에 자신을 위치시켰다. 그들은 자신의 가치를 교육 분야와 같이 전통적인 영역뿐 아니라 사회 전 영역과 연결시키고 있는 것이다. 이제는 정치적 연계와 기업과 지역의 분야도 포함돼있는 것이다.

이러한 방식으로, 한때 단지 중요한 물건들이 있는 텅 빈 복도였던 기관(박물관)이 이제는 그들이 수집한 것들에 맞춰 새로운 자세로 적응하고 있다. 박물관은 또한 공동체 안에서 다양한 구성원들과 상호 교류하고 작업하기 위해 진화해왔다. 현대 박물관들은 현대 문화의 중심으로 스스로를 재창조하고 있는 중이다.

Step 1	Ⓢurvey
Key Words	Museums; cultural repositories; collections; the ordinary and everyday; purpose and role in society; communities; hallowed halls of important objects; center of contemporary culture
Signal Words	As children; In the last few decades; however; have changed; More recently; have started; now; now; once; new
Step 2	**Ⓡeading**
Purpose	To explain the way museums have changed their purpose and role in society
Pattern of Organization	Time order
Tone	Subjective; persuasive
Main Idea	Museums have recently transformed their aims and functions in society.
Step 3	**Ⓢummary**
지문 요약하기 (Paraphrasing)	Museums have recently transformed their aims and functions in society. First, museums now collect more ordinary objects instead of special or rare items to better portray common living in the past. In addition to this, museums have begun to partner with allies*(sectors)* beyond the narrow educational sphere, reaching out to political, business, and community institutes. Through these changes, modern museums have adapted themselves to be a crucial part of contemporary culture.
Step 4	**Ⓡecite**
요약문 말로 설명하기	

16 Read the passage and follow the directions. [2 points] 2017학년도

M. Ringelmann, a French agricultural engineer, was one of the first researchers to study the relationship between process loss and group productivity. Ringelmann's questions were practical ones: How many oxen should be yoked in one team? Should you plow a field with two horses or three? Can five men turn a mill crank faster than four? Instead of speculating about the answers to these questions, Ringelmann set up teams of varying sizes and measured their collective power.

Ringelmann's most startling discovery was that workers—including horses, oxen, and men—all become less productive in groups. A group of five writers developing funny skits can easily outperform a single person, just as a team pulling a rope is stronger than a single opponent. But even though a group outperforms an individual, the group does not usually work at maximum efficiency. When Ringelmann had individuals and groups pull on a rope attached to a pressure gauge, groups performed below their theoretical capabilities. If person A and person B could each pull 100 units when they worked alone, could they pull 200 units when they pooled their efforts? No, their output reached only 186. A three-person group did not produce 300 units, but only 255. An eight-person group managed only 392, not 800. Groups certainly outperformed individuals—but as more and more people were added, the group became increasingly inefficient. To honor its discoverer, this tendency is now known as the Ringelmann effect.

Ringelmann identified two key sources of process losses when people worked together. First, Ringelmann believed some of the decline in productivity was caused by motivation losses: People may not work so hard when they are in groups. Second, coordination losses, caused by "the lack of simultaneity of their efforts," also interfere with performance. Even on a simple task, such as rope pulling, people tend to pull and pause at different times, resulting in a failure to reach their full productive potential.

Complete the main idea by filling in the blank with the ONE most appropriate word from the passage.

Groups were found to become more ____________ as group size increased because the potential output that each member could contribute individually was not realized when they participated in groups.

NOTE

Step 1	Ⓢurvey
Key Words	
Signal Words	
Step 2	**Ⓡeading**
Purpose	
Pattern of Organization	
Tone	
Main Idea	
Step 3	**Ⓢummary**
지문 요약하기 (Paraphrasing)	
Step 4	**Ⓡecite**
요약문 말로 설명하기	

01

Answer Key

M. Ringelmann, a French agricultural engineer, was one of the first researchers to study **the relationship between process loss and group productivity**. Ringelmann's questions were practical ones: How many oxen should be yoked in one team? Should you plow a field with two horses or three? Can five men turn a mill crank faster than four? Instead of speculating about the answers to these questions, Ringelmann set up teams of varying sizes and measured their collective power.

Ringelmann's most startling discovery was that workers—including horses, oxen, and men—all become **less productive in groups**. A group of five writers developing funny skits can easily outperform a single person, just as a team pulling a rope is stronger than a single opponent. But even though a group outperforms an individual, the group does not usually work at maximum efficiency. When Ringelmann had individuals and groups pull on a rope attached to a pressure gauge, groups performed below their theoretical capabilities. If person A and person B could each pull 100 units when they worked alone, could they pull 200 units when they pooled their efforts? No, their output reached only 186. A three-person group did not produce 300 units, but only 255. An eight-person group managed only 392, not 800. Groups certainly outperformed individuals—but as more and more people were added, **the group became increasingly inefficient**. To honor its discoverer, this tendency is now known as the Ringelmann effect.

Ringelmann identified **two key sources of process losses** when people worked together. First, Ringelmann believed some of the decline in productivity was caused by motivation losses: People may not work so hard when they are in groups. Second, coordination losses, caused by "the lack of simultaneity of their efforts," also interfere with performance. Even on a simple task, such as rope pulling, people tend to pull and pause at different times, resulting in a failure to reach their full productive potential.

key word
key words
R's questions
R's discovery
example ①
example ②
key words

모범답안 inefficient

한글번역

프랑스의 농업 기술자인 M. 링겔만은 과정에서의 손실과 그룹(집단)의 생산성 간의 관계를 연구한 최초의 연구원들 중 한 사람이다. 링겔만의 의문은 실용적인 것들이었는데 다음과 같은 것들이었다. 한 팀에 몇 마리의 소에게 멍에를 씌워야 하는가? 두 마리 혹은 세 마리의 말로 밭을 갈아야 하는가? 다섯 명의 남자가 네 명의 남자보다 방앗간 크랭크를 더 빨리 돌릴 수 있을까? 질문들에 대한 답을 (단순히 머릿속에서) 추측하는 것 대신에 링겔만은 다양한 크기의 팀을 만들었고 그들의 집단적 힘을 측정했다.

링겔만의 가장 놀라운 발견은 말, 소 그리고 사람을 포함한 모든 일꾼들이 집단으로는 효과가 덜하다는 것이었다. 재미있는 촌극을 개발한 다섯 명의 작가로 이루어진 집단은 한 작가가 한 것보다 더 뛰어난 성취를 보였는데, 이것은 밧줄을 잡아당기는 집단이 단 한 명의 상대보다 강한 것과 마찬가지 이치이다. 하지만, 집단이 개인을 능가함에도 불구하고 집단은 최고로 효율적으로 일하지는 않는다. 링겔만이 개인과 집단이 압력 게이지에 부착된 줄을 당기도록 했을 때, 집단은 그들이 이론적으로 가능한 능력보다 부족하게 일을 했다. 만약 A라는 사람과 B라는 사람이 혼자서 일할 때 각각 100단위를 잡아당길 수 있다면, 그들이 그들의 노력을 모았을 때 200단위를 잡아당길 수 있을까? 그들의 생산량은 겨우 186단위밖에 되지 않았다. 세 명으로 구성된 집단은 300단위를 산출하지 못했고 단지 255단위만을 산출했다. 여덟 명으로 구성된 집단은 800단위가 아닌 단 392단위만 해냈다. 확실히 집단은 개인을 능가하지만, 사람이 추가되면 될수록 집단은 상당히 비효율적이게 된다. 이것의 발견자를 기리기 위해 이 경향은 지금 링겔만 효과로 알려져있다.

링겔만은 사람들이 함께 일을 할 때 일어나는 과정에서의 손실의 두 가지 중요한 원천을 알아봤다. 첫째로, 링겔만은 생산성의 저하 중 일부는 동기 손실로 인해 발생한다고 믿었다. 즉, 사람들은 집단 내에 있을 때 일을 매우 열심히는 하지 않을 가능성이 있다는 것이다. 둘째로, 노력의 동시성 부족에서 기인한 협동 손실은 수행에 방해가 된다. 심지어 줄 잡아당기기와 같은 단순한 과제에 있어서도 사람들은 서로 다른 타이밍에 잡아당기고 멈추는 경향이 있어서 최대로 끌어낼 수 있는 잠재적 생산성에 도달하는 데 실패한다는 것이다.

NOTE

Step 1	Ⓢurvey
Key Words	Ringelmann; collective power; efficiency; process losses; motivation losses; coordination losses
Signal Words	Even on a simple task; Ringelmann's most startling discovery was...; Ringelmann identified two...; First; Second
Step 2	**Ⓡeading**
Purpose	To illustrate how individuals perform less efficiently in groups
Pattern of Organization	Series; cause/effect
Tone	Neutral (informative)
Main Idea	M. Ringelmann discovered groups were found to become more inefficient as group size increased because the potential output that each member could contribute individually was not realized when they participated in groups.
Step 3	**Ⓢummary**
지문 요약하기 (Paraphrasing)	M. Ringelmann discovered groups were found to become more inefficient as group size increased because the potential output that each member could contribute individually was not realized when they participated in groups. His study showed that groups suffered greater process losses as they increased with the number of members. The two sources of this problem were identified as motivation losses and coordination losses.
Step 4	**Ⓡecite**
요약문 말로 설명하기	

17 Read the passage and follow the directions. [5 points] 2017학년도

Have you ever felt overwhelmed trying to do too many things at once? In modern times, hurry, bustle, and agitation have become a regular way of life for many people—so much so that we have embraced a word to describe our efforts to respond to the many pressing demands of our time: multitasking. Used for decades to describe the parallel processing abilities of computers, in the 1990s the term multitasking became shorthand for the human attempt to simultaneously do as many things as possible, as quickly as possible, and with the help of new technologies.

It was originally assumed that multitasking was a useful strategy for increasing productivity. More recently, however, challenges to the presumed advantages of multitasking began to emerge. For example, numerous studies have addressed the sometimes fatal danger of driving and using cell phones or other electronic devices at the same time. As a result, several countries have now made that particular form of multitasking illegal. Researchers have also found that multitasking in the workplace can actually decrease productivity because the constant attention paid to emails, messaging apps, and phone calls temporarily impairs our ability to solve complex problems. Moreover, multitasking may negatively influence how we learn. Even if we learn while multitasking, that learning is likely to be less flexible and more fragmented, so we cannot recall the information as easily. As the research on multitasking implies, perhaps it is time to challenge the assumption that doing more is better.

Write a summary following the guidelines below.

Guidelines

- Summarize the above passage in ONE paragraph.
- Provide a topic sentence, supporting ideas from the passage, and a concluding sentence.
- Do NOT copy more than FIVE consecutive words from the passage.

NOTE

Step 1	Ⓢurvey
Key Words	
Signal Words	
Step 2	**Ⓡeading**
Purpose	
Pattern of Organization	
Tone	
Main Idea	
Step 3	**Ⓢummary**
지문 요약하기 (Paraphrasing)	
Step 4	**Ⓡecite**
요약문 말로 설명하기	

Answer Key

Have you ever felt overwhelmed trying to do **too many things** at once? In modern times, hurry, bustle, and agitation have become a regular way of life for many people—so much so that we have embraced a word to describe our efforts to respond to the many pressing demands of our time: **multitasking**. Used for decades to describe the parallel processing abilities of computers, in the 1990s the term multitasking became shorthand for **the human attempt to simultaneously do as many things as possible, as quickly as possible, and with the help of new technologies.**

It was originally assumed that multitasking was a useful strategy for increasing productivity. More recently, however, **challenges** to the presumed advantages of multitasking began to emerge. For example, numerous studies have addressed the sometimes **fatal danger** of driving and using cell phones or other electronic devices at the same time. As a result, several countries have now made that particular form of multitasking illegal. Researchers have also found that multitasking in the workplace can actually **decrease productivity** because the constant attention paid to emails, messaging apps, and phone calls temporarily impairs our ability to solve complex problems. Moreover, multitasking may negatively influence how we learn. Even if we learn while multitasking, that learning is likely to be less flexible and more fragmented, so we cannot recall the information as easily. **As the research on multitasking implies, perhaps it is time to challenge the assumption that doing more is better.**

key word

definition

key word

<challenges>

① safety 문제

② productivity 문제

③ learning 문제

conclusion

모범답안 Multitasking is not as beneficial as people originally thought. Multitasking, which is motivated by the desire to fulfill many demands simultaneously, has been shown to (be ineffective and) have many problems (as opposed to conventional thinking). It increases the danger in driving, reduces productivity in the workplace, and has a negative effect on the way people learn. Given these negative factors, multitasking should not be recommended.

한글번역

한 번에 너무 많은 일을 동시에 해보려고 시도하다가 압도당한 느낌을 받은 적이 있는가? 현대에는 서두름, 부산스러움, 그리고 동요가 많은 사람들에게 삶의 일상적 방식이 돼왔다. 그런데 그런 것이 많은 사람들에게 너무나 삶의 일상적 방식이 돼서, 우리 시대의 많은 거절할 수 없는 요구사항들에 대응하기 위해 우리는 하나의 용어를 받아들였는데, 그것은 다중작업이다. 컴퓨터의 병행처리 능력을 묘사하기 위해 수십 년 동안 사용되던 다중작업이라는 용어는 1990년대 동시적으로 가능한 많은 것들을, 가능한 빠르게, 그리고 새로운 기술의 도움으로 하려는 인간의 시도를 일컫는 약칭이 됐다.

다중작업은 원래는 생산성을 향상시키는 데 유용한 전략으로 추정됐다. 그러나 보다 최근에 들어서는 다중작업에 대해 당연하게 여겨지는 장점들에 대한 이의 제기가 생겨나기 시작했다. 예를 들어, 많은 연구들은 운전 중 핸드폰이나 다른 전자기기들을 동시에 사용하는 것의 치명적인 위험성에 대해 말해왔다. 그 결과, 몇몇 국가에서는 다중작업의 특정한 형태를 불법화했다. 연구자들은 또한 직장에서의 다중작업이 실제로 생산성을 감소시킨다는 것을 발견했는데, 그 이유는 이메일, 전자통신 앱, 전화에 기울여지는 끊임없는 주의가 복잡한 문제를 해결하기 위한 우리의 능력을 손상시키기 때문이다. 게다가, 다중작업은 우리가 어떻게 배우는지에 대해 부정적으로 영향을 끼칠지도 모른다. 우리가 다중작업 중에 무언가 배울지라도, 그 학습은 덜 유연하고 더 파편적일 것으로 예상되고, 그렇기 때문에 우리는 그 정보를 쉽게 기억해 낼 수 없다. 다중작업에 관한 연구가 암시해주는 것처럼, 아마도 이제는 더 많이 하는 것이 더 좋다는 가정에 이의를 제기할 때가 아닌가 싶다.

NOTE

Step 1	Ⓢurvey
Key Words	Multitasking; fatal danger; productivity; learning
Signal Words	For decades; In the 1990s; originally; More recently; For example; As a result; because; also; Moreover
Step 2	**Ⓡeading**
Purpose	To show the negative consequences of multitasking
Pattern of Organization	Definition; time order; cause/effect; series
Tone	Critical
Main Idea	Multitasking is not as beneficial as people originally thought.
Step 3	**Ⓢummary**
지문 요약하기 (Paraphrasing)	Multitasking is not as beneficial as people originally thought. Multitasking, which is motivated by the desire to fulfill many demands simultaneously, has been shown to (be ineffective and) have many problems (as opposed to conventional thinking). It increases the danger in driving, reduces productivity in the workplace, and has a negative effect on the way people learn. Given these negative factors, multitasking should not be recommended.
Step 4	**Ⓡecite**
요약문 말로 설명하기	

18 Read the passage and follow the directions. [4 points] 2016학년도

A paragraph in the papers of last week recorded the unusual action of a gentleman called Smith (or some such name) who had refused for reasons of conscience to be made a justice of the peace. Smith's case was that the commission was offered to him as a reward for political services, and that this was a method of selecting magistrates of which he did not approve. So he showed his contempt for the system by refusing an honour which most people covet, and earned by this such notoriety as the papers can give. "Portrait of a gentleman who has refused something!" He takes his place in (1) <u>the gallery of the odd</u>.

The subject for essay has frequently been given, "If a million pounds were left to you, how could you do most good with it?" Some say they would endow hospitals, some that they would establish almshouses; there may even be some who would go as far as to build half a Dreadnought. But there would be a more decisive way of doing good than any of these. You might refuse the million pounds. That would be a shock to the systems of the comfortable—a blow struck at the great Money God which would make it totter; a thrust in defence of pride and freedom such as had not been seen before. That would be a moral tonic more needed than all the draughts of your newly endowed hospitals. (2) <u>Will it ever be administered</u>? Well, perhaps when the Declined-with-Thanks club has grown a little stronger.

Write TWO consecutive words from the passage that correspond to the meaning of the underlined words in (1). Then explain the implication of the underlined words in (2).

NOTE

Step 1	Survey
Key Words	
Signal Words	
Step 2	**Reading**
Purpose	
Pattern of Organization	
Tone	
Main Idea	
Step 3	**Summary**
지문 요약하기 (Paraphrasing)	
Step 4	**Recite**
요약문 말로 설명하기	

Answer Key

A paragraph in the papers of last week recorded the unusual action of a gentleman called Smith (or some such name) who had **refused** for reasons of conscience to be made a justice of the peace. **Smith's case** was that the commission was offered to him as a reward for political services, and that this was a method of selecting magistrates of which he did not approve. So he showed his contempt for the system by **refusing** an honour which most people covet, and earned by this such notoriety as the papers can give. "Portrait of a gentleman who has **refused** something!" He takes his place in the gallery of the odd.

The subject for essay has frequently been given, "If a million pounds were left to you, how could you do most good with it?" Some say they would endow hospitals, some that they would establish almshouses; there may even be some who would go as far as to build half a Dreadnought. But **there would be a more decisive way of doing good than any of these.** You might **refuse** the million pounds. That would be a shock to the systems of the comfortable—**a blow struck at the great Money God** which would make **it** totter; a thrust in defence of **pride and freedom** such as had not been seen before. That would be a moral tonic more needed than all the draughts of your newly endowed hospitals. Will it ever be administered? Well, perhaps when **the Declined-with-Thanks club** has grown a little stronger.

episode : smith's case
tone : casual
→ key word
→ key word
→ key word
writer's opinion
→ key word
tone : critical/cynical
→ key word
skeptical

모범답안 The corresponding two words are "Declined-with-Thanks club". Second, the implication of the underlined words is that these surprising refusals to participate in gifted money or power would give a spiritual cure to the system that is more helpful than the medical cure of a newly-created hospital. However, the writer is skeptical of the possibility that people would refuse such rewards.

한글번역

지난주 신문들의 한 단락은 스미스라던가 혹은 그와 유사한 이름의 한 신사가 양심상의 이유로 치안판사 직을 거절한 흔하지 않은 행위에 대해 보도했다. 스미스의 경우는, 그 직위가 정치적으로 봉사한 것에 대한 보상으로 그에게 주어졌는데, 이런 식으로 치안판사가 뽑히는 방식은 그가 용납할 수 없는 방식이었다. 그래서 그는 대부분의 사람들이 갈망하는 명예를 거절함으로써 그런 시스템에 대한 경멸을 드러냈고, 그는 신문기사가 줄 수 있는 악명을 얻게 됐다. '어마어마한 것을 거절한 신사의 초상'이라는. 그는 괴짜들의 모임 안에서 자신의 자리를 잡게 됐다.

"만약 네게 백만 파운드가 상속된다면 그 돈을 가지고 가장 좋은 일을 어떻게 할 것 같니?"라는 에세이의 주제는 빈번하게 제시돼왔다. 몇몇 사람들은 병원에 그 돈을 기증한다고 말하거나 또한 몇몇은 빈민 구호소를 설립할 것이라고 말한다. 심지어 일종의 드레드노트(전함)의 절반 정도를 만들기까지 한다는 사람도 몇몇 있다. 그러나 위에 제시된 어느 것들보다도, 좋은 일을 할 수 있는 훨씬 결단력이 있는 방법이 있다. 바로 그것은 백만 달러 상속을 포기하는 것이다. 그것은 편안함을 추구하는 시스템에 대한 충격을 가하는 것이고, 그 충격은 위대한 돈의 신을 강타해서 휘청거리게 만들 수 있는 것이고, 이전에는 볼 수 없었던 형태의 자긍심과 자유를 방어하는 타격이다. 그것은 최근에 기증한 병원에서 나오는 모든 약들보다도 더욱 필요한 우리 사회의 도덕적인 강장제가 될 가능성이 있다. 과연 그것(도덕적인 강장제)이 주어질 수 있을까? 글쎄, 아마도 '고맙다고 말하면서 (돈을) 거절하는 모임'이 점점 더 힘을 얻게 될 때 가능할 것 같다.

NOTE

Step 1	Ⓢurvey
Key Words	Unusual action; Smith's case; refused; moral tonic; the Declined-with-Thanks Club
Signal Words	Not clear
Step 2	**Ⓡeading**
Purpose	To encourage the practice of refusing honors and grants
Pattern of Organization	Not clear
Tone	Cynical
Main Idea	The refusal of rewards can be more potent than their usage.
Step 3	**Ⓢummary**
지문 요약하기 (Paraphrasing)	The refusal of rewards can be more potent than their usage. For example, the gentleman Smith who refused an official appointment with moral justification made a strong impact. Similarly, if one were endowed with a million pounds and refused, it would have a greater effect than any charitable spending would.
Step 4	**Ⓡecite**
요약문 말로 설명하기	

19 **Read the passage and follow the directions.** [4 points] 2016학년도

When it comes to climate, what counts is not only what humans do to reduce the buildup of greenhouse gases, but also how the earth responds. Currently half the carbon we release into the atmosphere gets absorbed by land and sea—much of it by plants, which take in carbon dioxide in the process of photosynthesis.

This cycle has the potential to change at any time. At issue is the balance between two natural phenomena. One is beneficial: as carbon-dioxide levels in the air rise, plants grow more quickly, absorbing more carbon in return. Scientists can measure this in the lab, but they don't know how much more fertile the new, carbon-enhanced environment will be for plants. The other is that as temperatures rise, permafrost, which holds an enormous amount of carbon from long-dead plants, tends to dry out, allowing decay and a release of carbon into the atmosphere. If this phenomenon, called "outgassing," were to kick in, it could inundate the atmosphere with carbon dioxide, perhaps doubling or tripling the effect of the past century of human industry.

Nobody knows for sure what might trigger outgassing, but preventing a global temperature increase of more than 2 degrees Celsius is considered essential. To stay below that limit, the consensus is that we should establish a maximum level of carbon in the atmosphere and do whatever is necessary to stay below it. A few years ago, scientists thought that a doubling of carbon concentrations over preindustrial times, to 550 parts per million, was a reasonable line in the sand; in recent years they've revised that figure downward, to 450 ppm. But reaching that would require a drastic 80 percent cut in emissions by midcentury.

Meanwhile, observations, though not conclusive, have been pointing in the wrong direction: temperatures are rising quickly at the poles, the north polar ice cap is in retreat, permafrost is showing troubling signs of change, and ocean currents may be weakening the uptake of carbon. As we feel good about driving hybrids and using fluorescent bulbs, our fate may be riding on an obscure contest between ________________ and permafrost.

Fill in the blank with ONE word from the passage. Then explain what would happen to the permafrost if global temperature rises by more than 2 degrees Celsius.

NOTE

Step 1	Ⓢurvey
Key Words	
Signal Words	
Step 2	**Ⓡeading**
Purpose	
Pattern of Organization	
Tone	
Main Idea	
Step 3	**Ⓢummary**
지문 요약하기 (Paraphrasing)	
Step 4	**Ⓡecite**
요약문 말로 설명하기	

Answer Key

When it comes to **climate**, what counts is not only what humans do to reduce the buildup of greenhouse gases, but also **how the earth responds**. Currently half the carbon we release into the atmosphere gets absorbed by land and sea—much of it by **plants**, which take in carbon dioxide in the process of photosynthesis.

key word

key word

This cycle has the potential to change at any time. At issue is **the balance between two natural phenomena**. One is beneficial: as carbon-dioxide levels in the air rise, plants grow more quickly, absorbing more carbon in return. Scientists can measure this in the lab, but they don't know how much more fertile the new, carbon-enhanced environment will be for plants. The other is that as temperatures rise, **permafrost**, which holds an enormous amount of carbon from long-dead plants, tends to dry out, allowing decay and a release of carbon into the atmosphere. If this phenomenon, called "**outgassing**," were to kick in, it could inundate the atmosphere with carbon dioxide, perhaps doubling or tripling the effect of the past century of human industry.

key word

key word

Nobody knows for sure what might trigger **outgassing**, but preventing **a global temperature increase** of more than 2 degrees Celsius is considered essential. To stay below that limit, the consensus is that we should establish a maximum level of carbon in the atmosphere and do whatever is necessary to stay below it. A few years ago, scientists thought that a doubling of carbon concentrations over preindustrial times, to 550 parts per million, was a reasonable line in the sand; in recent years they've revised that figure downward, to 450 ppm. But reaching that would require a drastic 80 percent cut in emissions by midcentury.

Meanwhile, observations, though not conclusive, have been **pointing in the wrong direction**: temperatures are rising quickly at the poles, the north polar ice cap is in retreat, **permafrost** is showing troubling signs of change, and ocean currents may be weakening the uptake of carbon. As we feel good about driving hybrids and using fluorescent bulbs, our fate may be riding on an obscure contest between **plant** and **permafrost**.

tone : critical

모범답안 The proper word for the blank is “plants”. A rise of 2 degrees in global temperatures is predicted to cause permafrost to dry out and release carbon emissions in a process called “outgassing”.

한글번역

기후에 관해 볼 때, 인간이 온실가스가 축적되는 것을 줄이기 위해 하는 일뿐만 아니라, 어떻게 지구가 반응하는지도 중요한 점이다. 현재, 우리가 대기로 배출하는 탄소의 절반은 대지와 바다, 주로 광합성 과정에 이산화탄소를 흡수하는 식물들에 의해 흡수된다.

이러한 주기는 언제든지 바뀔 수 있다는 잠재성을 지니고 있다. 쟁점은 두 자연적 현상 간의 균형이다. 한 가지는 이롭다. 공기 중의 이산화탄소 수준이 높아짐에 따라, 식물은 더 많은 이산화탄소를 흡수하면서 더 빠르게 자라게 된다. 과학자들은 이것을 실험실에서 확인할 수 있지만, 그들은 새롭고, 탄소가 증가된 환경이 식물에 얼마나 더 비옥할지 모른다. 나머지 하나는 온도가 올라감에 따라, 오래전에 죽은 식물로부터 상당한 양의 탄소를 지니고 있는 영구동토층이 부패한 것들과 대기로의 탄소를 방출하는 것을 허락하면서 고갈되는 경향이 있다. ‘가스분출’이라 불리는 이러한 현상이 시작되면, 이는 감당하지 못할 정도로, 아마도 인간 산업사회 전(前) 세기의 영향의 2배, 3배의 영향을 주면서, 대기에 탄소를 방출하게 될 수도 있다.

아무도 무엇이 가스분출을 촉발시키는지 확실히 알지 못하지만, 섭씨 2도 이상으로 지구 기온의 증가를 막는 것은 필수적이라고 여겨진다. 그 한계 아래에 머물기 위해서, 합의안은 우리가 대기 중에 있는 탄소의 최대 수위를 설정하고, 그 아래로 유지하기 위해 필요한 어떠한 것이든 해야 한다는 것이다. 몇 년 전, 과학자들은 산업화 시기 이전보다 탄소 농도를 두 배로 만드는 것인, 550ppm까지 정도가 상황을 유지시키는 타당한 수준이라 생각했다. 최근에 그들은 450ppm까지 그 수치를 아래로 조정했다. 그러나 그 목표치에 도달하려면 금세기 중반까지 방출량의 80%나 되는 대폭적인 삭감이 필요할 것이다.

한편, 관측기록은 비록 결정적이진 않지만, 틀린 방향을 가리켜왔다. 극지방에서 기온은 급격하게 올라가고 있고, 북극의 만년설이 후퇴 중이고(사라지는 중이고), 영구동토층은 변화의 골치 아픈 신호를 보여주고 있으며, 해류는 탄소의 흡수를 약하게 만들고 있을지 모른다는 것이다. 우리가 하이브리드 자동차를 타는 것과 형광 전구를 사용하는 것에 대해 기분이 좋음에도 불구하고, 우리의 운명은 식물과 영구동토층 간의 모호한 경쟁에 달려 있을지 모른다.

01

NOTE

Step 1	Ⓢurvey
Key Words	Carbon dioxide; outgassing; plants; permafrost
Signal Words	When it comes to climate; currently; One is...; The other is...; If this phenomenon...; were to kick in; Meanwhile
Step 2	Ⓡeading
Purpose	To warn that the possible effects of outgassing, which can cause a dramatic shift in carbon levels
Pattern of Organization	Series; cause/effect
Tone	Cynical; pessimistic
Main Idea	The effects of outgassing can cause a dramatic shift in carbon levels and are of high concern.
Step 3	Ⓢummary
지문 요약하기 (Paraphrasing)	The effects of outgassing can cause a dramatic shift in carbon levels and are of high concern. While plants are able to absorb part of the carbon in the air, when temperature rises, permafrost releases large amounts of carbon in the aforementioned "outgassing". It is believed that rising temperature can cause this and thus carbon should be dramatically reduced soon. However, it appears that the opposite is happening.
Step 4	Ⓡecite
요약문 말로 설명하기	

20 **Read the passage and fill in the blank with ONE word from the passage.** [2 points] 2015학년도

A psychology professor spent several decades studying the "fixed mindset entity theory." She refers to people who view talent as a quality they either possess or lack as having a "fixed mindset." People with a "growth mindset," in contrast, enjoy challenges, strive to learn, and consistently see potential to develop new skills.

Now Carol Dweck, the psychology professor, is extending her work on mindset beyond individuals. Can an organization, like an individual, have a fixed or a growth mindset? If so, how can managers help organizations embrace a growth mindset? To explore this issue, she conducted surveys and found that often top management must drive the change; for instance, a new CEO might focus on maximizing employees' potential. Dweck points to one emblematic growth mindset CEO who hired according to "runway," not pedigree, preferring big state university graduates and military veterans to Ivy Leaguers, and spent thousands of hours grooming and coaching employees on his executive team.

As this CEO's example shows, one area in which mindset is especially important is hiring. Fixed mindset organizations reflexively look outside their companies, while growth mindset organizations are likely to hire from within their ranks. "Focusing on ________________ is not as effective as looking for people who love challenges, who want to grow, and who want to collaborate," Dweck says. Some companies appear to be making such a shift; these companies have recently begun hiring more people who have proven that they are capable independent learners.

Despite the survey results, not all employees will be happier in growth mindset organizations, Dweck acknowledges. In general, though, the early evidence suggests that organizations focused on employees' capacity for growth will experience significant advantages.

NOTE

Step 1	Survey
Key Words	
Signal Words	
Step 2	**Reading**
Purpose	
Pattern of Organization	
Tone	
Main Idea	
Step 3	**Summary**
지문 요약하기 (Paraphrasing)	
Step 4	**Recite**
요약문 말로 설명하기	

Answer Key

A psychology professor spent several decades studying **the "fixed mindset entity theory**." She refers to people who view **talent** as a quality they either possess or lack as having a "**fixed mindset**." People with a "**growth mindset**," in contrast, enjoy challenges, strive to learn, and consistently see potential to develop new skills.

Now Carol Dweck, the psychology professor, is extending her work on mindset beyond individuals. Can an **organization**, like an **individual**, have **a fixed** or **a growth mindset**? If so, how can managers help organizations embrace a growth mindset? To explore this issue, she conducted surveys and found that often top management must drive the change; for instance, a new CEO might focus on maximizing employees' potential. Dweck points to one emblematic growth mindset CEO who **hired** according to "**runway**," not **pedigree**, preferring big state university graduates and military veterans to Ivy Leaguers, and spent thousands of hours grooming and coaching employees on his executive team.

As this CEO's example shows, one area in which mindset is especially important is **hiring. Fixed mindset organizations** reflexively look outside their companies, while **growth mindset organizations** are likely to hire from within their ranks. "**Focusing on pedigree** is not as effective as looking for **people who love challenges, who want to grow, and who want to collaborate,**" Dweck says. Some companies appear to be making such a shift; these companies have recently begun hiring more people who have proven that they are capable independent learners.

Despite the survey results, not all employees will be happier in growth mindset organizations, Dweck acknowledges. In general, though, the early evidence suggests that organizations focused on employees' capacity for growth will experience significant advantages.

key words
key words
key word
key word
key words

모범답안 pedigree

한글번역

한 심리학 교수가 '고정된 사고방식 이론'을 연구하는 데 수십 년을 보냈다. 그녀는 재능을 그들이 가지거나 부족한 자질로 보는 사람들을 고정된 사고방식을 가진 것으로 간주한다. '성장적 사고방식'을 갖춘 사람들은 대조적으로 도전을 즐기고, 배우려고 노력하고, 계속적으로 새로운 기술을 발전시킬 잠재력을 찾는다.

그 심리학 교수인 캐럴 드웩은 그녀의 사고방식에 대한 연구를 개인들을 넘어 확장시키고 있다. 개인과 마찬가지로 조직도 고정된 혹은 성장적 사고방식을 가질 수 있을까? 만약 그렇다면 어떻게 하면 관리자들은 자신들의 조직이 성장적 사고방식을 수용하도록 할 수 있을까? 이 문제를 탐구하기 위해 그녀는 설문조사를 수행했고, 최고경영자가 자주 변화를 이끌어야 한다는 것을 발견했다. 예를 들어, 새로운 회사 대표는 노동자들의 잠재력을 극대화하는 문제에 집중할 수도 있다. 드웩은 성장적 사고방식을 지닌 최고경영자로 상징성이 있는 한 인물에 주목했다. 이 최고경영자는 규모가 큰 주립대학 졸업생이나 참전 군인을 아이비리그 출신들보다 더 선호해 채용했는데, 이것은 혈통이 아닌 능력에 따른 것이었다. 또한 그는 수천 시간을 임원진 내에 있는 직원들을 훈련시키고 지도하는 데 사용했다.

이 최고경영자의 사례가 보여주듯이, 사고방식이 특히나 중요한 한 분야는 채용 부문이다. 고정된 사고방식을 지닌 조직들은 자동적으로 그들의 회사 바깥을 본다. 반면에 성장적 사고방식을 지닌 조직들은 그들의 회사 내에 있는 구성원들 안에서 채용한다. 드웩은 말한다. "혈통에 집중하는 것은 도전을 사랑하고, 성장하기 원하고, 협력하기 원하는 사람을 찾는 데 효과적이지 못하다." 몇몇 회사는 이와 같은 변혁을 진행 중인 것으로 보인다. 이러한 회사들은 최근에 유능하고 독립적인 학습자라 판명된 사람들을 더 고용하기 시작했다.

조사 결과에도 불구하고, 모든 노동자들이 성장적 사고방식을 지향하는 조직에서 더 행복한 것은 아니라고 드웩은 인정한다. 하지만, 일반적으로, 앞선 증거는 성장을 위한 노동자들의 능력에 초점을 둔 조직들이 상당한 이점을 경험할 것이라는 점을 시사해준다.

NOTE

Step 1	Ⓢurvey
Key Words	Fixed mindset; growth mindset; Fixed mindset organizations; growth mindset organizations; hiring; runway; pedigree
Signal Words	In contrast; not A; while; not as … as
Step 2	**Ⓡeading**
Purpose	To show the benefits of a growth mindset for companies
Pattern of Organization	Comparison/contrast
Tone	Informative
Main Idea	Companies with a growth mindset will experience significant advantages.
Step 3	**Ⓢummary**
지문 요약하기 (Paraphrasing)	Companies with a growth mindset will experience significant advantages. On the other hand, fixed mindset companies will focus less on grooming their own employees, instead focus on pedigree. Hiring with a growth mindset will encourage growth from within proven people. Though not all employees will be happy, overall it will be better.
Step 4	**Ⓡecite**
요약문 말로 설명하기	

21 Read the passage and follow the directions. [3 points]

2014학년도

If there is a single most important flaw in the current news style, it is the overwhelming tendency to downplay the big social, economic, or political picture in favor of the human trials, tragedies, and triumphs that sit at the surface of events. For example, instead of focusing on power and process, the media concentrate on the people engaged in political combat over the issues. The reasons for this are numerous, from the journalist's fear that probing analysis will turn off audiences to the relative ease of telling the human-interest side of a story as opposed to explaining deeper causes and effects.

When people are invited to take the news personally, they can find a wide range of private, emotional meanings in it. However, the meanings inspired by personalized news may not add up to the shared critical understandings on which healthy citizen involvement thrives. The focus on personalities encourages a passive spectator attitude among the public. Whether the focus is on sympathetic heroes and victims or hateful scoundrels and culprits, the media preference for personalized human-interest news creates a "can't-see-the-forest-for-the-trees" information bias that makes it difficult to see the big picture that lies beyond the many actors crowding center stage who are caught in the eye of the news camera.

The tendency to personalize the news would be less worrisome if human-interest angles were used to hook audiences into more serious analysis of issues and problems. Almost all great literature and theater, from the Greek dramas to the modern day, use strong characters to promote audience identifications and reactions in order to draw people into thinking about larger moral and social issues. News often stops at the character development stage, however, and leaves the larger lessons and social significance, if there is any, to the imagination of the audience. As a result, the main problem with personalized news is that the focus on personal concerns is seldom linked to more in-depth analysis. What often passes for analysis are opaque news formulas such as "He/She was a reflection of us," a line that was used in the media frenzies that followed the deaths of Britain's Princess Diana and America's John Kennedy, Jr. Even when large portions of the public reject personalized news formulas, the personalization never stops. This systematic tendency to personalize situations is one of the defining biases of news.

Describe the defining characteristic of the current news style, and explain how it differs from the common characteristic of great literature and theater. Do NOT copy more than FIVE consecutive words from the passage.

NOTE

Step 1	Ⓢurvey
Key Words	
Signal Words	
Step 2	**Ⓡeading**
Purpose	
Pattern of Organization	
Tone	
Main Idea	
Step 3	**Ⓢummary**
지문 요약하기 (Paraphrasing)	
Step 4	**Ⓡecite**
요약문 말로 설명하기	

Answer Key

If there is **a single most important flaw in the current news style**, it is the overwhelming tendency to downplay **the big social, economic, or political picture** in favor of the **human trials, tragedies, and triumphs** that sit at the surface of events. For example, instead of focusing on **power and process**, the media concentrate on **the people engaged in political combat over the issues**. The reasons for this are numerous, from the journalist's fear that probing analysis will turn off audiences to the relative ease of telling the human-interest side of a story as opposed to **explaining deeper causes and effects**.

When people are invited to take the news **personally**, they can find a wide range of private, emotional meanings in it. However, the meanings inspired by **personalized news** may not add up to the shared critical understandings on which healthy citizen involvement thrives. The focus on **personalities** encourages a passive spectator attitude among the public. Whether the focus is on sympathetic heroes and victims or hateful scoundrels and culprits, the media preference for **personalized human-interest** news creates a **"can't-see-the-forest-for-the-trees" information bias** that makes it difficult to see **the big picture** that lies beyond the many actors crowding center stage who are caught in the eye of the news camera.

The tendency to personalize the news would be less worrisome if human-interest angles were used to hook audiences into **more serious analysis of issues and problems**. Almost all great literature and theater, from the Greek dramas to the modern day, use strong characters to promote audience identifications and reactions in order to draw people into thinking about larger moral and social issues. News often stops at the character development stage, however, and leaves the larger lessons and social significance, if there is any, to the imagination of the audience. As a result, the **main problem with personalized news** is that the **focus on personal concerns** is seldom linked to more in-depth analysis. What often passes for analysis are opaque news formulas such as "He/She was a reflection of us," a line that was used in the media frenzies that followed the deaths of Britain's Princess Diana and America's John Kennedy, Jr. Even when large portions of the public reject personalized news formulas, the **personalization** never stops. **This systematic tendency to personalize situations** is one of the **defining biases of news**.

key words

key words

key word

key words

key word

모범답안 The current news tends to neglect the big institutional aspects and to personalize serious issues and problems. Second, the current news style is different from great literature and theater in that the latter employs strong characters to make audience think about larger moral and social situations in critical terms whereas the former rarely makes people engage in serious social issues because of its systematic tendency to personalize social, economic, and political situations.

한글번역

최근 뉴스 형태에서 단 하나 가장 중요한 결점이 있다면 그것은 사건들의 표면에 있는 인간의 재판, 비극 그리고 대성공을 선호해, 큰 사회적, 경제적, 그리고 정치적 상황을 경시하는 압도적인 경향성이다. 예를 들면, 권력과 과정에 초점을 맞추는 대신 매체는 그 이슈에 관해 정치적 싸움에 연루된 사람들에게 집중한다. 이에 대한 이유들은 무수히 많은데, 면밀한 분석이 청중들의 관심을 끄게 만들 거라는 기자의 공포감부터 시작해, 심오한 원인과 결과를 설명하는 것과는 반대로 어떤 이야기의 흥미를 불러일으키는 면을 말하는 것이 상대적으로 편하기 때문이다.

사람들이 뉴스를 개인적으로 받아들이도록 요청됐을 때, 그들은 넓은 범위의 사적이고, 감정적인 의미들을 그 뉴스 안에서 찾을 수 있다. 하지만, 개인화된 뉴스에서 영감을 받은 의미들은 건강한 시민들의 참여가 넘쳐나게 하는 공유되는 비판적 이해에 도움이 되지 않는다. 인물에 대한 초점은 대중들 사이에서 수동적인 방관자 태도를 부추긴다. 그 초점이 동정어린 주인공들과 희생자들에 있든지 아니면 혐오스러운 악당들과 범죄자들에 있든지 간에, 개인화된 흥미를 불러일으킬 만한 뉴스에 대한 매체의 선호도는 "나무들 때문에 숲을 보지 못하는" 정보 편파를 만들고, 이것은 뉴스 카메라의 시선에 잡힌 무대 중앙에 북적거리는 많은 배우들 너머에 있는 큰 그림을 보기 어렵게 만든다.

만약 독자의 흥미를 불러일으키는 관점이 독자들로 하여금 이슈와 문제들에 대한 더 진중한 분석을 요구하도록 사용된다면 뉴스를 개인화하는 추세가 덜 우려될 것이다. 고대 그리스 희곡부터 현재까지 대부분의 위대한 문학과 연극은 사람들이 더욱 큰 도덕적이고 사회적인 문제들에 대해 생각하도록 이끌기 위해 청중의 인지 발견과 반응을 촉진하는 강한 캐릭터를 사용한다. 하지만, 뉴스는 종종 캐릭터 개발 단계에서 멈추고, 더 큰 교훈과 사회적 의의를—(별로 없을 것 같지만) 만약 그것이 있다고 한다면—청중들의 상상에 남겨둔다. 결과적으로, 개인화시킨 뉴스의 주요 문제는 개인 문제에 대한 초점이 결코 더 심도 있는 분석으로 연결되지 않는다는 점이다. 종종 분석으로 여겨지는 것은 불분명한 판에 박힌 뉴스 문구들인데, "그/그녀는 우리의 반영이었다"와 같은 것들이다. 이 말은 영국 왕자빈이었던 다이애나와 미국의 존 케네디 주니어의 죽음 뒤에 나온 매체들의 광란에서 사용됐다. 심지어 다수의 대중이 개인화된 뉴스의 판에 박힌 공식을 거부했을 때도, 개인화는 결코 멈추지 않는다. 객관적 상황을 개인화하려는 이 조직적인 경향성은 뉴스의 결정적인 편향 중 하나다.

NOTE

Step 1	Ⓢurvey
Key Words	Flaw in the current news style; personalization; big picture
Signal Words	For example; The reasons for; However; As a result
Step 2	Ⓡeading
Purpose	To criticize the personalization of news
Pattern of Organization	Cause/effect; definition
Tone	Critical
Main Idea	The personalization of the current news is a major problem.
Step 3	Ⓢummary
지문 요약하기 (Paraphrasing)	The personalization of the current news is a major problem. By focusing on people engaged in issues and not on the larger issues themselves, the news stays much more popular and interesting. However, this focus leaves out the big picture and analysis. Unlike literature, which links character development to thinking on larger issues, the current news doesn't link well to in-depth analysis.
Step 4	Ⓡecite
요약문 말로 설명하기	

22 Read the passage and answer the question.

2012학년도

Although he availed himself of the results of the labours of preceding artists, William Turner nevertheless, from his earliest youth, received his sole inspiration from nature. And yet his art did not lie in the literal transcription of nature. His was not the skill to count the blades of grass, and reproduce, without variation, the exact aspect of the scene before him. Every scene that he has represented is bathed, so to speak, in the mystic poetry of his own imagination. He painted his portrait of the earth not merely as it appeared to him at any one given moment, but with a true comprehension of all its past history, of the earthquakes that had shaken it, the storm-winds that had swept over it, and the loveliness that still clung to it. He has revealed to us this loveliness in all its varying aspects—in its joy and in its sadness, in its brightness and its gloom, in its pensive mood and in its fierce madness, in its love and in its hate, but the portrait, although true in the highest sense, is never directly copied from nature for he painted, like Raphael and all great idealists, from an image or ideal in his own mind. But this ideal was founded on the closest observation and study of the real.

What is the title of the passage? Write your answer by filling in the blank below with the ONE most appropriate word from the passage. [3 points]

William Turner : A Painter of Idealized Reality of ________________

NOTE

Step 1	Ⓢurvey
Key Words	
Signal Words	
Step 2	**Ⓡeading**
Purpose	
Pattern of Organization	
Tone	
Main Idea	
Step 3	**Ⓢummary**
지문 요약하기 (Paraphrasing)	
Step 4	**Ⓡecite**
요약문 말로 설명하기	

Answer Key

Although he availed himself of the results of the labours of preceding artists, **William Turner** nevertheless, from his earliest youth, received his sole inspiration from **nature**. And yet his art did not lie in the literal transcription of **nature**. His was not the skill to count the blades of grass, and reproduce, without variation, the exact aspect of the scene before him. Every scene that he has represented is bathed, so to speak, in the mystic poetry of **his own imagination**. He painted his portrait of the earth not merely as it appeared to him at any one given moment, but with a true comprehension of all its past history, of the earthquakes that had shaken it, the storm-winds that had swept over it, and the loveliness that still clung to it. He has revealed to us this loveliness in all its varying aspects—in its joy and in its sadness, in its brightness and its gloom, in its pensive mood and in its fierce madness, in its love and in its hate, but the portrait, although true in the highest sense, is never directly copied from nature for he painted, like Raphael and all great idealists, from an **image or ideal in his own mind**. But this ideal was founded on the closest observation and study of **the real**.

key word 1
key word 2
key word 2
key word 3
<example>
<Main idea>
key word 3′
key word 4

모범답안 Nature

한글번역

비록 그는 앞선 예술가들의 노동의 결과물들을 활용했지만, 그럼에도 불구하고 윌리엄 터너는 그의 유년 시절부터 자연으로부터 자신의 유일한 영감을 얻었다. 하지만 그의 예술은 자연을 있는 그대로 옮기는 것에 있지 않았다. 그의 예술은 풀잎의 개수를 센다던가, 변형 없이 자신의 앞에 놓인 장면의 정확한 양상을 재현하는 기술에 있지 않았다. 그가 재현했던 모든 장면들은, 말하자면, 그의 고유한 상상의 신비로운 시에 휩싸여 있다. 그는 대지를 묘사할 때 그 대지가 어떤 주어진 한 순간에 보이는 대로만 그리는 것이 아니라, 그 대지의 지나간 과거 역사와 그 대지를 흔들어대던 지진, 대지를 압도했던 폭풍우, 그리고 여전히 대지에 있는 사랑스러움 등에 대한 진실한 이해를 가지고 그렸다. 그는 우리에게 즐거움과 슬픔, 밝음과 어둠, 수심어린 분위기와 강렬한 광기, 사랑과 미움과 같은 모든 다양한 측면에서의 사랑스러움을 드러내왔다. 하지만 그의 묘사가 최고조로 사실적이었지만, 그의 그림은 자연으로부터 그대로 복사된 것이 아니었는데, 그것은 그가, 라파엘로와 모든 위대한 이상주의자들이 그랬던 것처럼, 그 자신의 마음속 이미지나 이상으로부터 온 것이었기 때문이다. 하지만, 이러한 이상은 가장 면밀한 관찰과 실제에 대한 탐구에 기반을 두고 있다.

NOTE

Step 1	Ⓢurvey
Key Words	William Turner; nature; his own imagination; image or ideal in his own mind; the real
Signal Words	Not clear
Step 2	**Ⓡeading**
Purpose	To explain William Turner's art
Pattern of Organization	Not clear
Tone	Informative
Main Idea	William Turner portrayed nature from the ideal in his own mind as well as the real.
Step 3	**Ⓢummary**
지문 요약하기 (Paraphrasing)	William Turner portrayed nature from the ideal in his own mind as well as the real. He portrayed every scene of nature from his own imagination but at the same time, his ideal was founded on the real.
Step 4	**Ⓡecite**
요약문 말로 설명하기	

23 **Read the passage and answer the question.** [1.5 points] 2011학년도

A person usually has two reasons for doing a thing: one that sounds good and a real one. The person himself will think of the real reason. You don't need to emphasize that. But all of us, being idealists at heart, like to think of motives that sound good. When the late Lord Northcliffe found a newspaper using a picture of him which he didn't want published, he wrote the editor a letter. But did he say, "Please do not publish that picture of me anymore; I don't like it?" No, he appealed to a nobler motive. He appealed to the respect and love that all of us have for motherhood. He wrote, "Please do not publish that picture of me anymore. My mother doesn't like it." When John D. Rockefeller Jr. wished to stop newspaper photographers from snapping pictures of his children, he too appealed to the nobler motive. He didn't say, "I don't want their pictures published." No, he appealed to the desire, deep in all of us, to refrain from harming children. He said, "You know how it is, boys. You've got children yourselves, some of you. And you know it's not good for youngsters to get too much publicity."

What is the title of the passage? Write your answer in TWO words.

An Appeal to a ______________________

NOTE

Step 1	Survey
Key Words	
Signal Words	
Step 2	**Reading**
Purpose	
Pattern of Organization	
Tone	
Main Idea	
Step 3	**Summary**
지문 요약하기 (Paraphrasing)	
Step 4	**Recite**
요약문 말로 설명하기	

Answer Key

A person usually has two reasons for doing a thing: one that **sounds good** and a real one. The person himself will think of the real **reason**. You don't need to emphasize that. But all of us, being idealists at heart, like to think **of motives** that **sound good**. When the late Lord Northcliffe found a newspaper using a picture of him which he didn't want published, he wrote the editor a letter. But did he say, "Please do not publish that picture of me anymore; I don't like it"? No, he appealed to a **nobler motive**. He appealed to the respect and love that all of us have for motherhood. He wrote, "Please do not publish that picture of me anymore. My mother doesn't like it." When John D. Rockefeller Jr. wished to stop newspaper photographers from snapping pictures of his children, he too appealed to **the nobler motive**. He didn't say, "I don't want their pictures published." No, he appealed to the desire, deep in all of us, to refrain from harming children. He said, "You know how it is, boys. You've got children yourselves, some of you. And you know it's not good for youngsters to get too much publicity."

→ key word 1
→ key word 2
→ key word 2′
→ key word 1
<example>
<Main idea>
→ key word 1′
→ key word 1′

모범답안 Nobler Motive

한글번역

한 사람이 어떤 일을 하는 데는 보통 두 가지 이유가 있다. 바로 듣기 좋은 이유와 진짜 이유이다. 그 사람 스스로는 진짜 이유를 머리에 떠올릴 것이다. 당신은 그것을 굳이 강조할 필요가 없다. 그러나 내심 이상주의자로서 우리 모두는 듣기 좋은 이유들을 생각하고 싶어 한다. 고인이 된 노스클리프 경은 그가 게재되지 않길 원했던 그의 사진을 사용하는 신문을 발견했을 때, 편집장에게 편지를 썼다. 허나 그가 "제발 나의 사진을 더 이상 싣지 마시오, 나는 그 사진을 좋아하지 않소."라고 말했을까? 아니다, 그는 더 숭고한 이유에 호소했다. 그는 누구나 가지고 있는 어머니에 대한 존경과 사랑에 호소했다. 그는 "제발 나의 사진을 더 이상 싣지 마시오. 나의 어머니가 그 사진을 좋아하지 않소."라고 편지를 썼다. 존 록펠러 주니어는 신문 사진기자들이 그의 아이들의 사진을 찍는 것을 막고 싶었을 때, "아이들의 사진이 게재되는 것을 바라지 않습니다."라고 말하지 않았다. 그는 아이들이 다치지 않길 바라는 우리 모두에게 내재된 강렬한 소망에 호소했다. 그는 "당신들도 어떠할지 알 겁니다. 당신들 중 누군가도 아이들이 있을 거예요. 그리고 아이들에게 너무 많은 매스컴의 관심이 좋지 않다는 것도 아실 겁니다."라고 말했다.

Step 1	Ⓢurvey
Key Words	Motives; sound good; nobler motive
Signal Words	Reasons; But; when
Step 2	**Ⓡeading**
Purpose	To show how people appeal to a nobler motive to make his(her) cause sound good
Pattern of Organization	Series; cause/effect
Tone	Neutral
Main Idea	People appeal to a nobler motive to make their cause sound good.
Step 3	**Ⓢummary**
지문 요약하기 (Paraphrasing)	People usually have two reasons, one that sounds good and a real one, for doing a thing. However, they appeal to a nobler motive to make their causes sound good.
Step 4	**Ⓡecite**
요약문 말로 설명하기	

24 Read the passage and answer the question.

2010학년도

Like the corporate pursuit of computer technology, profit-motivated biotechnology creates several concerns. First is the concern that only the rich will have access to such life-saving technologies as genetic screening and cloned organs. Such fears are justified, considering that companies have been patenting human life. The obesity gene, the premature aging gene, and the breast cancer gene, for example, have already been patented. These patents result in gene monopolies, which could lead to astronomical patient costs for genetic screening and treatment. A biotechnology industry argues that such patents are the only way to recoup research costs that, in turn, lead to further innovations. The commercialization of technology causes several other concerns, including issues of quality control and the tendency for discoveries to remain closely guarded secrets rather than collaborative efforts. In addition, industry involvement has made government control more difficult because researchers depend less and less on federal funding. Finally, although there is little doubt that profit acts as a catalyst for some scientific discoveries, other less commercially profitable but equally important projects may be ignored.

24-1 What is the main idea of the passage? [2 points]

____

24-2 What are the specific concerns of the author? [3 points]

① ______________________________

② ______________________________

③ ______________________________

④ ______________________________

⑤ ______________________________

NOTE

Step 1	Survey
Key Words	
Signal Words	
Step 2	**Reading**
Purpose	
Pattern of Organization	
Tone	
Main Idea	
Step 3	**Summary**
지문 요약하기 (Paraphrasing)	
Step 4	**Recite**
요약문 말로 설명하기	

Answer Key

Like the corporate pursuit of computer technology, **profit-motivated biotechnology** creates several **concerns**. First is the concern that only the rich will have access to such life-saving technologies as genetic screening and cloned organs. Such **fears** are justified, considering that companies have been patenting human life. The obesity gene, the premature aging gene, and the breast cancer gene, for example, have already been patented. These patents result in gene monopolies, which could lead to astronomical patient costs for genetic screening and treatment. A **biotechnology industry** argues that such patents are the only way to recoup research costs that, in turn, lead to further innovations. **The commercialization of technology** causes several other **concerns**, including issues of quality control and the tendency for discoveries to remain closely guarded secrets rather than collaborative efforts. In addition, industry involvement has made government control more difficult because researchers depend less and less on federal funding. Finally, although there is little doubt that profit acts as a catalyst for some scientific discoveries, other less commercially profitable but equally important projects may be ignored.

key word 1
<Main idea>
key word 2
key word 2′
key word 1′
key word 1″
key word 2″
<series & example>

모범답안

24-1 Profit-motivated biotechnology involves many problems and concerns.

24-2 ① Only the rich will be able to access those biotechnologies.
② The quality control is an issue under commercialized bio-industry.
③ The new discovery would remain secret rather than be shared.
④ Goverment control would get more difficult when the researchers are under private companies.
⑤ Less commercially profitable project would be ignored.

한글번역

컴퓨터 기술에 대한 기업의 추구처럼, 이익에 고무된 생명공학은 여러 우려를 만든다. 첫 번째 우려는, 오직 부자만이 유전자 검사나 복제 장기 등과 같은 사람의 생명을 살릴 수 있는 기술에 접근할 수 있다는 점이다. 기업들이 인간의 생명을 특허내고 있는 것을 고려하면, 그런 두려움은 정당화된다. 예를 들어, 비만 유전자, 조숙한 노화 유전자와 유방암 유전자는 이미 특허가 됐다. 이들 특허는 유전자 검사와 처방을 위한 천문학적인 환자 비용을 야기시킬 수 있는 유전자 독점으로 귀착된다. 생명공학 산업은 그와 같은 특허가 보다 더 나아간 혁신을 이끌어내는 연구 비용을 메우는 유일한 방법이라고 주장한다. 기술의 상업화는 품질 관리라는 문제와, 협조적인 노력보다는 오히려 발견들을 철저히 비밀에 부치려는 경향성을 포함한 여러 다른 우려들을 일으킨다. 게다가, 기업의 개입은 연구원들이 연방 자금 조달에 점점 더 적게 의존하기 때문에 정부 통제를 더욱 어렵게 했다. 마지막으로, 이익이 몇 가지 과학적인 발견을 위한 촉매로 작동하는 것이 거의 확실할지라도, 상업적으로 돈이 덜 되기는 하지만 마찬가지로 중요한 다른 프로젝트는 묵살될 가능성이 있다.

NOTE

Step 1	Survey
Key Words	Profit-motivated biotechnology; biotechnology industry; commercialization of technology; concerns; fears
Signal Words	Several concerns; First; for example; several other; In addition; Finally; creates; result in; lead to; has made; because
Step 2	Reading
Purpose	To argue the problems of commercialized biotechnology industry
Pattern of Organization	Series; cause/effect
Tone	Critical
Main Idea	Profit-oriented biotechnology causes many problems and concerns.
Step 3	Summary
지문 요약하기 (Paraphrasing)	The commercialization of technology causes many problems and concerns. First, only the rich will be able to access those biotechnologies. Second, quality control is an issue under commercialized bio-industry. Third, new discovery would remain secret rather than be shared. Fourth, government control would become more difficult when the researchers are under private companies. Lastly, less commercially profitable project would be dismissed.
Step 4	Recite
요약문 말로 설명하기	

25 **Read the passage and answer the question.** 2008학년도 서울 · 인천

Is it better to be loved than feared, or vice versa? I don't doubt that every prince would like to be both; but since it is hard to accommodate these qualities, if you have to make a choice, to be feared is much safer than to be loved. For it is a good general rule about men, that they are ungrateful, fickle, liars and deceivers, fearful of danger and greedy for gain. While you serve their welfare, they are all yours, offering their blood, their belongings, their lives, and their children's lives—so long as the danger is remote. But when the danger is close at hand, they turn against you. Then, any prince who has relied on their words and has made no other preparations will come to grief; because people are less concerned with offending a man who makes himself loved than one who makes himself feared. The reason is that love is a link of obligation which men, because they are rotten, will break any time they think doing so serves their advantage; but fear involves dread of punishment, from which they can never escape. Still, a prince should make himself feared in such a way that, even if he gets no love, he gets no hate either.

What is the main idea of the passage? Write your answer in one sentence.
[3 points]

NOTE

Step 1	Ⓢurvey
Key Words	
Signal Words	
Step 2	**Ⓡeading**
Purpose	
Pattern of Organization	
Tone	
Main Idea	
Step 3	**Ⓢummary**
지문 요약하기 (Paraphrasing)	
Step 4	**Ⓡecite**
요약문 말로 설명하기	

Answer Key

Is it better to **be loved** than **feared**, or vice versa? I don't doubt that every **prince** would like to be both; (but) since it is hard to accommodate these qualities, if you have to make a choice, to be **feared** is much safer than to be loved. (For) it is a good general rule about men, that they are ungrateful, fickle, liars and deceivers, fearful of danger and greedy for gain. While you serve their welfare, they are all yours, offering their blood, their belongings, their lives, and their children's lives—so long as the danger is remote. But when the danger is close at hand, they turn against you. Then, any **prince** who has relied on their words and has made no other preparations will come to grief; because people are less concerned with offending a man who makes himself loved than one who makes himself feared. The reason is that love is a link of obligation which men, because they are rotten, will break any time they think doing so serves their advantage; but fear involves dread of punishment, from which they can never escape. (Still,) a **prince** (should) make himself feared in such a way that, even if he gets no love, he gets no hate either.

key word 2
key word 1
key word 3
<Main idea>
key word 2
<examples>
key word 3
key word 3
<Main idea>

모범답안 A prince should be feared rather than loved (but he should escape being hated).

한글번역

사랑을 받는 대상이 되는 것이 두려움의 대상이 되는 것보다 나을까 아니면 그 반대일까? 나는 모든 군주들이 두 가지 모두 되고 싶어 할 거라 생각한다. 하지만, 이 가치들을 모두 받아들이는 것은 힘들기 때문에 만약 당신이 둘 중 하나를 선택해야 한다면, 두려움을 받는 것이 사랑을 받는 것보다 훨씬 안전하다. 왜냐하면 사람이 은혜를 모르고, 변덕이 심하며, 거짓말쟁이이고 사기꾼이며 위험을 무서워하고 이익에 대한 욕심이 많다는 것은 매우 타당한 일반원칙이기 때문이다. 당신이 그들의 복지에 기여하는 동안에는, 그들은 모두 당신의 것이고, 그들의 피와 소유물, 그들의 생명과 그 아이들의 생명까지도 바칠 것이다. 단 위험이 멀리 있는 한에만 그렇다. 하지만 위험이 가까이 오게 되면, 그들은 당신에게서 등을 돌린다. 그러면 그들의 약속에만 의존했고 다른 준비는 전혀 해두지 않았던 왕들은 슬픔에 빠지게 된다. 왜냐하면 사람들은 두려움의 대상이 되도록 자기 자신을 만드는 사람보다 사랑받도록 자기 자신을 만드는 사람을 불쾌하게 만드는 것을 더 개의치 않아 하기 때문이다. 그 이유는 사랑이란 사람들이 타락해, 의무를 깨버리는 것이 그들에게 이익을 가져다 줄 것이라 판단하는 순간 언제든 깨버릴 의무의 연결고리이기 때문이다. 하지만 두려움은 그들이 절대 벗어날 수 없는 처벌의 두려움을 포함한다. 그러나 왕은 다음과 같은 방식으로 스스로가 두려운 존재가 돼야 한다. 사랑은 받지 못하더라도 증오도 받지 않는 방식으로 말이다.

NOTE

Step 1	Ⓢurvey
Key Words	To be loved; to be feared; prince
Signal Words	Not clear
Step 2	**Ⓡeading**
Purpose	To argue that, for a prince, to be feared is much safer than to be loved
Pattern of Organization	Not clear
Tone	Argumentative
Main Idea	A prince should be feared rather than loved, but he should escape being hated.
Step 3	**Ⓢummary**
지문 요약하기 (Paraphrasing)	A prince should be feared rather than loved, but he should escape being hated. Love is easy to be broken by people when necessary whereas fear can never let them go due to their fear of punishment. Thus, it is safer to be feared. However, it is necessary to get no hate from people either.
Step 4	**Ⓡecite**
요약문 말로 설명하기	

26 Read the passage and answer the question.

2005학년도 서울 · 인천

Good writers assume, with a pessimism born of experience, that whatever isn't plainly stated, the reader will invariably misconstrue. They keep in mind that she is, after all, a perfect stranger to their garden of ingenious ideas. In fact, to her, that garden may initially resemble a tangled thicket, if not a tropical rain forest. This being so, their job as a writer is to guide her through, step by step, so that the experience will be quick and memorable. This involves alertly anticipating her moments of confusion and periodically giving her an explanation of where she's headed. The writer's golden rule is the same as the moralists: Do unto others as you would have them do unto you.

Complete the main idea of the passage by filling in the blank with about 10 words. [3 points]

A good writer's duty ______________________________.

NOTE

Step 1	Ⓢurvey
Key Words	
Signal Words	
Step 2	**Ⓡeading**
Purpose	
Pattern of Organization	
Tone	
Main Idea	
Step 3	**Ⓢummary**
지문 요약하기 (Paraphrasing)	
Step 4	**Ⓡecite**
요약문 말로 설명하기	

Answer Key

Good **writers** assume, with a pessimism born of experience, that whatever isn't plainly stated, **the reader** will invariably **misconstrue**. They keep in mind that she is, after all, a perfect **stranger** to their garden of ingenious ideas. In fact, to her, that garden may initially resemble a tangled thicket, if not a tropical rain forest. This being so, their job as a writer is to **guide** her through, step by step, so that the experience will be quick and memorable. This involves alertly anticipating her moments of **confusion** and periodically giving her **an explanation of** where she's headed. The writer's golden rule is the same as the moralists: Do unto others as you would have them do unto you.

<Main idea>
key word 1
key word 2
key word 3
key word 3′
key word 4
<comparison : use of figurative language>
key word 3″
key word 4
Main idea

모범답안 is to give readers an explanation of where they are headed. (또는 is to state his ideas plainly to readers)

한글번역

훌륭한 작가들은, 경험에서 생긴 염세주의로 인해, 분명하게 명시되지 않은 것은 무엇이든지 독자가 분명히 오해할 것이라 가정한다. 그들은 결국 그녀(독자)가 그들의 독창적 생각이란 정원에 완전한 이방인이란 사실을 염두에 두고 있다. 사실 그녀에게 그 정원은 처음에는 얼기설기 얽힌 잡목 숲 같은 것이다. 열대 우림은 아니라도 말이다. 이러하기에 작가로서 그들의 일은 그녀를 한 걸음씩 인도해 그 경험이 이해가 쉽고, 기억할 만한 것이 되게 하는 것이다. 이는 기민하게 그녀가 혼란스러워하는 순간을 예상하고 그녀가 향하는 곳에 대한 설명을 주기적으로 해주는 것과 관계있다. 작가의 황금률은 윤리주의자의 그것과 같다. 다른 사람이 당신에게 하기 원하는 대로 그 사람에게 하라.

NOTE

Step 1	Ⓢurvey
Key Words	Writer; reader; misconstrue; stranger; confusion; guide; explain
Signal Words	Not clear
Step 2	Ⓡeading
Purpose	To explain a good writer's approach to a reader
Pattern of Organization	Definition
Tone	Subjective
Main Idea	A good writer is to state his ideas plainly to readers.
Step 3	Ⓢummary
지문 요약하기 (Paraphrasing)	A good writer is to state his ideas plainly to readers. A good writer should guide the readers in order to help them understand his idea clearly and memorably.
Step 4	Ⓡecite
요약문 말로 설명하기	

27 Read the passage and answer the question.

2005학년도 전국

In the United States, it is important to be on time for an appointment, a class, etc. However, this may not be true in all countries. An American professor discovered this difference in a Brazilian university. His first two-hour class was scheduled to begin at 10 a.m. and end at 12 p.m. On the first day, when the professor arrived on time, no one was in the classroom. Many students came after 10 a.m. Several arrived after 10:30 a.m. Two students came after 11 a.m. These students greeted the professor and few apologized for their lateness. Were these students being rude? He decided to study the students' behavior.

The professor talked to American and Brazilian students about lateness in both an informal and formal situation: lunch with a friend and attendance in a university class, respectively. He gave them an example and asked them how they would react. If they had a lunch appointment with a friend, the average American student defined lateness as 9 minutes after the agreed time. On the other hand, the average Brazilian students felt the friend was late after 33 minutes.

Unlike students in an American university, neither the teacher nor the students always arrive at the university at the appointed hour in Brazil. Classes begin and end at the scheduled time in the United States. In the Brazilian class, however, few students left the class at noon and many students remained past 12:30 p.m. to discuss the class and asked more questions. The explanation for these differences is complicated. In Brazil, the students believe that a person who usually arrives late is probably successful than a person who is always on time. In fact, Brazilians expect a person with status or prestige to arrive late, while in the United States lateness is usually considered to be disrespectful and unacceptable. Consequently, if a Brazilian is late for an appointment with a North American, the American may misinterpret the reason for the lateness and become angry.

What is the main idea of the passage? Write your answer using ALL and ONLY the words given in the box below. [3 points]

보기

among, punctual, towards, being, attitudes, differ, cultures

People's ______________________________.

NOTE

Step 1	Ⓢurvey
Key Words	
Signal Words	
Step 2	**Ⓡeading**
Purpose	
Pattern of Organization	
Tone	
Main Idea	
Step 3	**Ⓢummary**
지문 요약하기 (Paraphrasing)	
Step 4	**Ⓡecite**
요약문 말로 설명하기	

Answer Key

In the United States, it is important to be **on time** for an appointment, a class, etc. However, this may not be true in all countries. An **American** professor discovered this difference in a **Brazilian university**. His first two-hour class was scheduled to begin at 10 a.m. and end at 12 p.m. On the first day, when the professor arrived on time, no one was in the classroom. Many students came after 10 a .m. Several arrived after 10:30 a.m. Two students came after 11 a.m. These students greeted the professor and few apologized for their **lateness**. Were these students being rude? He decided to study the students' behavior.

The professor talked to **American** and Brazilian students about **lateness** in both an informal and formal situation: lunch with a friend and attendance in a university class, respectively. He gave them an example and asked them how they would react. If they had a lunch appointment with a friend, the average American student defined lateness as 9 minutes after the agreed time. On the other hand, the average Brazilian students felt the friend was late after 33 minutes. Unlike students in an American university, neither the teacher nor the students always arrive at the university, at the appointed hour in **Brazil**. Classes begin and end at the scheduled time in the United States. In the Brazilian class, however, few students left the class at noon and many students remained past 12:30 p.m. to discuss the class and asked more questions. The explanation for these differences is complicated. In Brazil, the students believe that a person who usually arrives late is probably successful than a person who is always on time. In fact, Brazilians expect a person with status or prestige to arrive late, while in the United States lateness is usually considered to be disrespectful and unacceptable. Consequently, if a Brazilian is late for an appointment with a North American, the American may misinterpret the reason for the lateness and become angry.

key word 1
key word 2
key word 3
key word 1′
key word 2
<comparison and contrast>
key word 3
<conclusion>

모범답안 attitudes towards being punctual differ among cultures

한글번역

미국에서 약속, 수업 시간 등을 지키는 것은 중요하다. 그러나 이것은 모든 나라에서 다 그런 것은 아니다. 한 미국인 교수는 브라질의 한 대학에서 이 차이를 발견했다. 그의 첫 2시간 수업은 10시에 시작해 12시에 끝나는 것으로 정해졌다. 첫날, 교수가 시간에 맞춰 도착했을 때 교실에는 아무도 없었다. 많은 학생들은 10시가 넘어서 들어왔다. 몇몇은 10시 30분이 지나서야 도착했다. 두 학생은 11시 이후에 들어왔다. 이 학생들은 교수에게 인사했지만, 지각에 대해 사과하는 학생은 거의 없었다. 이 학생들은 무례했던 것인가? 그는 이 학생들의 행태를 연구하기로 했다.

이 교수는 공적인 상황과 그렇지 않은 상황 모두에서 지각하는 것에 대해 미국인 학생과 브라질 학생에게 이야기해봤다. 즉 대학 수업에 출석할 때와 친구와 식사할 때 각각의 경우에 대해서 말이다. 그는 학생들에게 예를 주고 어떻게 반응하는지 물었다. 그들이 친구와 점심 약속이 있다면, 보통 미국인 학생은 동의한 시간보다 9분 정도 늦는 것을 지각으로 정의했다. 한편 평균적인 브라질 학생은 33분이 늦으면 지각했다고 느꼈다.

미국의 대학생들과 달리, 브라질에서는 선생이나 학생들 중 그 누구도 약속된 시간에 늘 나타나지는 않는다. 미국에서 수업은 계획된 대로 시작하고 끝난다. 하지만 브라질의 교실에서는, 정오에 교실을 떠나는 학생은 거의 없고 12시 30분이 지나도 많은 학생들이 남아 수업에 대해 토론하고 더 많은 질문을 한다. 이러한 차이에 대해 설명하는 것은 복잡하다. 브라질에서, 학생들은 보통 늦게 도착하는 사람은 아마도 항상 시간을 지키는 사람보다 더 성공적일 것이라 믿는다. 사실 브라질 사람들은 지위와 명성을 가진 사람이 늦게 도착할 것이라 기대한다. 반면에 미국에서는 지각이 대체로 예의 없고 받아들일 수 없는 것으로 간주된다. 결과적으로 브라질 사람들이 북미인과의 약속에 늦는다면 미국인은 지각의 이유를 잘못 해석해 화를 낼 수도 있다.

NOTE

Step 1	Ⓢurvey
Key Words	On time; American; Brazilian; lateness
Signal Words	However; On the other hand; Unlike; In fact
Step 2	**Ⓡeading**
Purpose	To show difference of time concept in different countries (cultures)
Pattern of Organization	Comparison/contrast
Tone	Informative
Main Idea	People's attitudes towards being punctual differ among cultures.
Step 3	**Ⓢummary**
지문 요약하기 (Paraphrasing)	People's attitudes towards being punctual differ among cultures. In the United States, it is rude and disrespectful to be tardy for an appointment. On the other hand, in Brazil, lateness is regarded as high status and success. People's attitude towards punctuality differs among cultures.
Step 4	**Ⓡecite**
요약문 말로 설명하기	

28 Read the passage and follow the directions.

2000학년도

A thorough analysis of utopia would involve showing first that it is rooted in the nature of man himself, for it is impossible to understand what it means for man "to have utopia" apart from this fundamental fact.

Any evaluation of utopia must begin with its positive meaning, and the first positive characteristic to be pointed out is its truth—utopia is truth. Why is it truth? Because it expresses man's essence, the inner aim of his existence. Utopia shows what man is essentially and what he should have as telos* of his existence. Every utopia is but one manifestation of what man has as inner aim and what he must have for fulfillment as a person. This definition stresses the social as much as the personal, for it is impossible to understand the one apart from the other. A socially defined utopia loses its truth if it does not at the same time fulfill the person, just as the individually defined utopia loses its truth if it does not at the same time bring fulfillment to society.

** telos : final purpose*

What is the main idea of the passage? Write your answer in about 20 words.

[3 points]

NOTE

Step 1	Survey
Key Words	
Signal Words	
Step 2	**Reading**
Purpose	
Pattern of Organization	
Tone	
Main Idea	
Step 3	**Summary**
지문 요약하기 (Paraphrasing)	
Step 4	**Recite**
요약문 말로 설명하기	

Answer Key

A thorough **analysis of utopia** would involve showing first that it is rooted in **the nature of man** himself, for it is impossible to understand what it means for man "to have **utopia**" apart from this fundamental fact.

Any **evaluation of utopia** must begin with its positive meaning, and the first positive characteristic to be pointed out is its truth—utopia is truth. Why is it truth? Because it expresses **man's essence**, the inner aim of his existence. Utopia shows what man is essentially and what he should have as telos* of his existence. Every utopia is but one manifestation of what **man has as inner aim** and what he must have for fulfillment as a person. This **definition** stresses **the social** as much as **the personal**, for it is impossible to understand the one apart from the other. **A socially defined utopia** loses its truth if it does not at the same time fulfill **the person**, just as **the individually defined utopia** loses its truth if it does not at the same time bring fulfillment to **society**.

** telos : final purpose*

→ key word 1
→ key word 2
→ key word 1
→ key word 2′ <Definition>
→ key word 2″
→ key word 3

모범답안

Utopia, which expresses a human being's essence, can be truth only when it emphasizes not only the personal but also the social.

한글번역

유토피아를 철저하게 분석하게 되면 유토피아가 인간 자체의 본성에 깊이 관여하고 있다는 사실을 알게 될 것이다. 왜냐하면, 이러한 기본적인 사실을 별개로 '인간이 유토피아를 갖는다'는 게 무엇인지 이해하는 것은 불가능하기 때문이다.

유토피아를 평가하는 것이 무엇이 됐든 그것은 유토피아에 대한 긍정적인 의미로 시작할 것임에 틀림없다. 또 지적해야 할 그 첫 번째 긍정적인 특징은 그것이 진리라는 것이다. 즉, 유토피아는 진리라는 사실이다. 왜 그것이 진리인가? 유토피아는 인간의 본질 즉, 그의 존재의 내적인 목적을 표현하기 때문이다. 유토피아는 인간이 본질적으로 무엇인지 또 인간이 그 존재의 궁극적 목적으로 무엇을 가져야 하는지를 보여준다. 모든 유토피아는 단지 인간이 내적인 목적으로 무엇을 가져야 하는지 그리고 인간으로서의 성취를 위해 무엇을 가져야 하는지를 단 한 가지로 보여주고 있다. 이러한 정의는 개인적인 것은 물론이려니와 사회적인 것을 강조하고 있다. 왜냐하면, 사회적인 것을 개인적인 것과 별개로 해서 이해한다는 것은 불가능하기 때문이다. 개인적으로 정의된 유토피아가 만약 사회에 만족감을 가져올 수 없으면 진리를 상실하듯이, 사회적으로 정의된 유토피아가 만약 개인을 만족시키지 못하면 진리를 상실하게 된다.

NOTE

Step 1	Ⓢurvey
Key Words	Analysis of utopia; evaluation of utopia; the nature of man; man's essence; man has an inner aim
Signal Words	What it means; the social; the personal definition; socially defined; individually defined
Step 2	**Ⓡeading**
Purpose	To tell what the true nature of utopia is
Pattern of Organization	Definition
Tone	Persuasive
Main Idea	Utopia can be truth when it shows a man's inner aim as well as its social fulfillment.
Step 3	**Ⓢummary**
지문 요약하기 (Paraphrasing)	Utopia, which expresses a human being's essence, can be truth only when it emphasizes not only the personal but also the social.
Step 4	**Ⓡecite**
요약문 말로 설명하기	

29 Read the passage and follow the directions.

2000학년도

> There are a number of reasons why there should not be dress-down days at work. First of all, workplace need to maintain a conscious distinction between the professional and the casual. This distinction is maintained largely by dress. When this distinction vanishes, workers might begin to be more casual with each other, making it difficult to maintain a professional atmosphere. More importantly, casual wear destroys company hierarchy. When the president of the company comes to work wearing khaki pants and a polo shirt, employes are likely to say, "why, he's just one of us." While in "real life" he may indeed be their equal, in the workplace he is not. But the most important reason employees should not be allowed to come to work dressed casually is because it drastically decreases productivity. When people are dressed in their work clothes, they work; when they are dressed casually, the temptation to be casual about getting work done is too great. Employees spend a great deal of time milling about and have a great tendency to cut corners; "Oh, I don't need to proofread again. It's good enough." This attitude in the workplace can not only be dangerous to a company's welfare—it can be deadly.

Explain the THREE reasons why there should not be dress-down days at work. [3 points]

ⓐ To maintain ______________________________

ⓑ To keep ______________________________

ⓒ To increase ______________________________

NOTE

Step 1	Ⓢurvey
Key Words	
Signal Words	
Step 2	**Ⓡeading**
Purpose	
Pattern of Organization	
Tone	
Main Idea	
Step 3	**Ⓢummary**
지문 요약하기 (Paraphrasing)	
Step 4	**Ⓡecite**
요약문 말로 설명하기	

Answer Key

There are a number of reasons why there should not be dress-down days at work. First of all, **workplace** need to maintain a conscious **distinction** between the professional and the casual. This distinction is maintained largely by **dress**. When this distinction vanishes, workers might begin to be more casual with each other, making it difficult to maintain a professional atmosphere. **More importantly, casual wear** destroys company hierarchy. When the president of the company comes to work wearing khaki pants and a polo shirt, employes are likely to say, "why, he's just one of us." While in "real life" he may indeed be their equal, in the **workplace** he is not. But the most important reason employees should not be allowed to come to work dressed casually is **because** it drastically decreases productivity. When people are dressed in their work clothes, they work; when they are dressed casually, the temptation to be casual about getting work done is too great. Employees spend a great deal of time milling about and have a great tendency to cut corners; "Oh, I don't need to proofread again. It's good enough." This attitude in the workplace can not only be dangerous to a company's welfare—it can be deadly.

Main idea
key word 1
key word 2
key word 3
key word 3′
<cause-effect>
key word 1
<cause-effect>
<series : examples>

모범답안 ⓐ a conscious distinction between the professional and the casual; or professional atmosphere
ⓑ company hierarchy
ⓒ productivity

한글번역

직장에서 간편복을 입어서는 안 되는 많은 이유가 있다. 우선, 직장에서는 직업적인 것과 일상적인 것 사이를 의식적으로 구별할 필요가 있다. 이러한 구별은 주로 복장에 의해 유지된다. 이러한 구별이 사라지게 되면, 노동자들은 서로서로에게 더욱 태평스럽게 대하게 될 수 있고, 이런 태도는 직업적 분위기를 유지하는 것을 어렵게 만들 수 있다. 이보다 더 중요한 문제는, 일상복은 회사의 위계질서를 해친다. 회사의 회장이 카키 바지와 폴로셔츠를 입고 일하러 오게 되면 노동자들은 다음과 같이 말할 것이다: "음, 회장도 단지 우리 가운데 하나일 뿐이야". 물론, '실생활'에서는 회장도 노동자들과 동등한 한 인간이지만, 직장에서는 그렇지 않다. 하지만 종업원들이 직장에서 일상복으로 작업하는 것이 허용돼서는 안 되는 가장 중요한 이유는 그것이 생산성을 철저하게 떨어뜨리기 때문이다. 사람들이 작업복을 입을 때, 그들은 일을 한다. 반면 사람들이 일상복을 입고 일할 때, 일도 대충 끝내려고 하는 유혹을 매우 강하게 받게 된다. 종업원들은 상당한 시간을 어영부영 보내며, 절차를 무시하려는 경향을 강하게 보인다. "아, 나는 다시 점검할 필요가 없어. 그것이면 충분해"라고 생각하면서. 직장에서의 이러한 태도는 회사의 안녕에 위험이 될 뿐만 아니라 치명적일 수도 있다.

NOTE

Step 1	Ⓢurvey
Key Words	Workplace; distinction; dress; professional; casual wear; professional atmosphere; hierarchy; productivity
Signal Words	More importantly; But; ;(semi-colon); the most important reason; because
Step 2	**Ⓡeading**
Purpose	To argue the importance of professional wear in workplace
Pattern of Organization	Cause/effect; series(examples)
Tone	Argumentative
Main Idea	There are several reasons why professional wear is needed in workplace.
Step 3	**Ⓢummary**
지문 요약하기 (Paraphrasing)	Workers should put on professional dress in workplace for professional atmosphere, company hierarchy, and productive work environments.
Step 4	**Ⓡecite**
요약문 말로 설명하기	

30 Read the passage and follow the directions.

2000학년도

The whole subject of happiness has, in my opinion, been treated too solemnly. It had been thought that man cannot be happy without a theory of life. Perhaps those who have been rendered unhappy by a bad theory may need a better theory to help them to recovery, just as you may need a tonic when you have been ill. But when things are normal, a man should be healthy without a tonic and happy without a theory. If a man delights in his wife and children, and finds pleasure in the alternation of day and night, he will be happy whatever his philosophy may be. If, on the other hand, he finds his wife hateful, his children's noise unendurable; if in the daytime he longs for night, and at night sighs for the light of day, then ______ⓐ______.

Man is an animal, and his happiness depends on his physiology more than he likes to think. This is a humble conclusion, but I cannot make myself disbelieve it. Unhappy businessmen would increase their happiness more by walking six miles every day than by any conceivable change of philosophy. This, incidentally, was the opinion of Jefferson, who on this ground deplored the horse. ⓑ Language would have failed him if he could have foreseen the motor-car.

30-1 Fill in the blank ⓐ using ONLY and ALL the words given in the box below. [2 points]

is not, what, a new philosophy, a new exercise, he, but, needs

____

30-2 Translate the underlined ⓑ into Korean. Also, explain the reason the writer says like that. [3 points]

____

____

NOTE

Step 1	Ⓢurvey
Key Words	
Signal Words	
Step 2	**Ⓡeading**
Purpose	
Pattern of Organization	
Tone	
Main Idea	
Step 3	**Ⓢummary**
지문 요약하기 (Paraphrasing)	
Step 4	**Ⓡecite**
요약문 말로 설명하기	

Answer Key

The whole subject of **happiness** has, in my opinion, been treated too solemnly. It had been thought that man cannot be happy without a **theory of life**. Perhaps those who have been rende red unhappy by a bad **theory** may need a better theory to help them to recovery, just as you may need a tonic when you have been ill. But when things are normal, a man should be healthy without a tonic and happy without a theory. If a man delights in his wife and children, and finds pleasure in the alternation of day and night, he will be happy whatever his **philosophy** may be. If, on the other hand, he finds his wife hateful, his children's noise unendurable; if in the daytime he longs for night, and at night sighs for the light of day, then what he needs is not a new philosophy but a new exercise.

Man is an animal, and his happiness depends on his **physiology** more than he likes to think. This is a humble conclusion, but I cannot make myself disbelieve it. Unhappy businessmen would increase their happpiness more by **walking six miles** every day than by any conceivable change of **philosophy**. This, incidentally, was the opinion of Jefferson, who on this ground deplored the horse. Language would have failed him if he could have foreseen the motor-car.

key word 1
key word 2
<Main idea : opinion>
<comparison>
key word 3
<examples>
key word 2
<Main idea : opinion>
key word 2′
key word 3

모범답안

30-1 what he needs is not a new philosophy but a new exercise

30-2 Jefferson, who deplored the horse on the grounds that people did not walk (exercise) because of the animal, would have been struck dumb with amazement. (be struck dumb with amazement = 기가 차서 말문이 막히다)

한글번역

행복이라는 전체 주제는 내가 보기엔, 지나치게 거창하게 취급돼왔다. 인간은 생에 관한 이론이 없으면 행복할 수 없는 것으로 생각돼왔다. 아마도 나쁜 이론에 의해 불행하게 된 사람들은 그들이 회복하는 데 도움을 줄 더 나은 이론을 필요로 할지 모른다. 마치 당신이 아플 때는 강장제를 필요로 하듯이 말이다. 모든 게 정상일 때, 인간은 강장제 없이도 건강할 수 있으며 이론이 없이도 행복할 수 있다. 만일 누군가가 아내와 아이들을 보고 즐거워한다면, 또 밤낮이 바뀌는 데서 즐거움을 발견한다면 그는 그의 철학이 무엇이든지 간에 행복할 것이다. 한편으로는, 만일 그가 자신의 아내가 밉다는 사실을 발견하거나 아이들의 시끄러운 소리를 견딜 수 없다는 것을 확인하게 되면, 또 낮에는 밤을 그리워하고 밤에는 낮의 햇빛을 한숨지으며 그리워한다면, 그러면 그는 새로운 철학이 필요한 것이 아니라 새로운 운동이 필요한 것이다.

인간은 동물이므로 그의 행복은 자기가 생각하는 것 이상으로 생리학에 달려 있다. 이것은 보잘것없는 결론이지만 나는 그것을 믿지 않을 수 없다. 불행한 사무직 종사자들은 철학의 변화를 생각하기보다는 날마다 6마일을 걷게 되면 더 행복할 것이다. 우연히도 이것은 제퍼슨의 생각이기도 했는데, 그는 이러한 사실에 근거해 그 말을 한탄했던 것이다. 그가 만일 자동차를 예견했더라면 할 말을 잃었을 것이다.

NOTE

Step 1	Ⓢurvey
Key Words	Happiness; theory; philosophy; physiology; walking six miles
Signal Words	Not clear
Step 2	**Ⓡeading**
Purpose	To tell how one becomes happy
Pattern of Organization	Not clear
Tone	Persuasive
Main Idea	Man does not need to have a theory of happiness in order to be happy; rather one's physical condition is more important to make one happy.
Step 3	**Ⓢummary**
지문 요약하기 (Paraphrasing)	Man does not need to have a theory of happiness in order to be happy; rather one's physical condition is more important to make one happy. Therefore, if a person feels unhappy, he had better do physical activities such as walking to make him feel happy.
Step 4	**Ⓡecite**
요약문 말로 설명하기	

31 Read the passage and follow the directions.

1999학년도

FARMERS NO LONGER HAVE COWS, PIGS, CHICKENS, or other animals on their farms; according to the U. S. Department of Agriculture, farmers have "grain-consuming animal units" (which, according to the Tax Reform Act of 1986, are kept in "single-purpose agricultural structures," not pig pens and chicken coops). Attentive observers of the English language also learned recently that the multibillion dollar stock market crash of 1987 was simply a "fourth quarter equity retreat"; that (a) <u>airplanes don't crash,</u> they just have "uncontrolled contact with the ground"; that (b) <u>janitors are really "environmental technicians</u>"; that it was a "diagnostic misadventure of high magnitude" which cause the death of a patient in Philadelphia hospital, not medical malpractice; and that President Reagan wasn't really unconscious while he underwent minor surgery, he was just in a "non-decision-making form." In other words, doublespeak continues to spread as the official language of the public discourse. Doublespeak is a blanket term for language which pretends to communicate but doesn't, language which makes the bad seem good, the negative appear positive, the unpleasant attractive, or at least tolerable. It is language which avoids, shifts, or denies responsibility, language which is at variance with its real or its purported meaning. It is language which conceals or prevents thought. Basic to doublespeak is incongruity, the incongruity between what is said, or left unsaid, and what really is: between the word and the referent, between seem and be, between the essential function of language, communication, and what doublespeak does—mislead, distort, deceive, inflate, circumvent, obfuscate.

31-1 **Answer the following question with "yes" or "no": In (a), does the author mean that airplanes don't crash? Then give a reason for your answer according to the passage given.** [2 points]

____

____

31-2 **In (b), why are "janitors" named as "environmental technicians"? Write your answer in one sentence.** [1 point]

It is because ______________________________________

____

NOTE

Step 1	Ⓢurvey
Key Words	
Signal Words	
Step 2	**Ⓡeading**
Purpose	
Pattern of Organization	
Tone	
Main Idea	
Step 3	**Ⓢummary**
지문 요약하기 (Paraphrasing)	
Step 4	**Ⓡecite**
요약문 말로 설명하기	

Answer Key

FARMERS NO LONGER HAVE COWS, PIGS, CHICKENS, or other animals on their farms; according to the U. S. Department of Agriculture, farmers have "grain-consuming animal units" (which, according to the Tax Reform Act of 1986, are kept in "single-purpose agricultural structures," not pig pens and chicken coops). Attentive observers of the **English language** also learned recently that the multibillion dollar stock market crash of 1987 was simply a "fourth quarter equity retreat"; that airplanes don't crash, they just have "uncontrolled contact with the ground"; that janitors are really "environmental technicians"; that it was a "diagnostic misadventure of high magnitude" which cause the death of a patient in Philadelphia hospital, not medical malpractice; and that President Reagan wasn't really unconscious while he underwent minor surgery, he was just in a "non-decision-making form." In other words, **doublespeak** continues to spread as the official language of the public discourse. **Doublespeak** is a blanket term for language which pretends to communicate but doesn't, language which makes the bad seem good, the negative appear positive, the unpleasant attractive, or at least tolerable. It is language which avoids, shifts, or denies responsibility, language which is at variance with its real or its purported meaning. It is language which conceals or prevents thought. Basic to **doublespeak is incongruity**, the incongruity between what is said, or left unsaid, and what really is: between the word and the referent, between seem and be, between the essential function of language, communication, and what doublespeak does—mislead, distort, deceive, inflate, circumvent, obfuscate.

key word 1
Series(examples)

key word 2
<Definition>

key word 2

key word 3

Main idea

모범답안

31-1 No. The comment is a doublespeak which distorts the truth and makes the disastrous situation acceptable.

31-2 The term "environment technicians" makes the janitorial job appear to be more positive and attractive than it actually is.

한글번역

농장에는 더 이상 소나 돼지, 닭 또는 다른 동물이 없다. 미국 농무부에 따르면, 농부들은 '곡식을 소비하는 동물 단위들'을 가지고 있다(1986년 세제 개혁법에 따르면 그 단위들은 돼지 축사나 닭장이 아닌 '단일 목적의 농업용 구조물'에서만 길러야 되는 것들이다). 영어를 주의 깊게 관찰하는 사람들은 최근에, 1987년의 수십억 달러의 주식시장 붕괴가 단순히 '4/4분기의 주가 하락'이라는 사실을 알게 됐다. 또 비행기는 추락하지 않았다. 비행기가 다만 '지상과 통제를 벗어난 접촉'을 했을 뿐이라는 사실도 듣게 됐다. 또 '문지기야말로 진정으로 환경 기술자들이다', 필라델피아 병원에서 환자 사망의 원인은 진료 과실이 아니라 '매우 중대한 진단 사고'이다. 레이건 대통령이 간단한 수술을 받는 중에 정말로 의식을 잃은 것은 아니며, 다만 '결정을 내리지 못하는 상태'에 있는 것이다 등등의 말을 듣게 됐다. 달리 말하면, 이중화법은 공공 담화라는 공식적인 언어로 계속 확산되고 있다. 이중화법은 의사전달을 하는 것 같아 보이지만 의사전달을 하지 않는 언어에 대한 포괄적인 용어다. 다시 말해, 나쁜 것을 좋게 보이도록 하는 언어이며, 부정적인 것을 긍정적인 것으로, 싫어하는 것을 매력적인 것으로 또는 적어도 견딜 만한 것으로 만드는 언어를 말한다. 그것은 책임을 회피하고 바꾸며 부인하는 언어이다. 즉, 실제 의미나 의도된 의미와 일치하지 않는 언어이다. 그것은 생각을 감추거나 가로막는 언어이다. 이중화법의 기본은 불일치다. 말한 것 또는 말하지 않은 것과 실제로 말한 것 사이의 불일치가 기본인 것이다. 또 단어와 지시 대상, 보이는 것과 실제로 그런 것, 언어의 본질적 기능인 의사소통과 이중화법이 전달하는 것과의 불일치가 그것이다. 이중화법이 전달하는 것이란, 오도, 왜곡, 기만, 과장, 우회 표현, 판단을 흐리게 하기 등이다.

NOTE

Step 1	ⓢSurvey
Key Words	Doublespeak
Signal Words	In other words; is
Step 2	**ⓡReading**
Purpose	To explain(or define) doublespeak
Pattern of Organization	Definition; series
Tone	Critical
Main Idea	Doublespeak, a blanket term for language which pretends to communicate but doesn't, has continuously been used as the official language of the public discourse to distort or conceal truth and reality.
Step 3	**ⓢSummary**
지문 요약하기 (Paraphrasing)	Doublespeak, a blanket term for language which pretends to communicate but doesn't, has continuously been used as the official language of the public discourse to distort or conceal truth and reality.
Step 4	**ⓡRecite**
요약문 말로 설명하기	

32 Read the passage and follow the directions.

1999학년도

Brenda Linson never goes anywhere without an empty spectacles case. It is as vital to her as her purse. Yet, she doesn't wear glasses. The reason she can't do without it is because she can't read and she can't write. If ever she gets into any situation where she might be expected to do either of these things, she fishes around in her bag for the specs case, finds it's empty, and asks the person concerned to do the reading for her. Brenda is now in her late thirties. She's capable and articulate and a few months ago hardly anybody knew she was illiterate. Her husband didn't know and her children didn't know. The children still don't.

She had any number of tactics for concealing <u>her difficulty</u>—for example, never lingering near a phone at work, in case she had to answer it and might be required to write something down. But, in fact, it is easier for illiterates to conceal the truth than the rest of us might imagine. Literacy is so much taken for granted that people simply don't spot the giveaway signs.

It has never been occurred to the children that their mother cannot read. She doesn't read them stories, but then their father doesn't either, so they find nothing surprising in the fact. Similarly they just accept that Dad is the one who writes the sick notes and reads the school reports. Now that the elder boy Tom is quite a proficient reader, Brenda can skillfully get him to read any notes brought home from school simply by asking, "What's that all about, then?"

Brenda's husband never guessed the truth in 10 years of marriage. For one thing he insists on handling all domestic correspondence and bills himself. An importer of Persian carpets, he travels a great deal and so is not around so much to spot the truth. While he's away Brenda copes with any situations, by explaining that she can't do anything until she's discussed it with her husband.

Brenda was very successful in her job until recently. For the last five years she had worked as waitress at an exclusive private club, and had eventually been promoted to head waitress. She kept the thing a secret there too, and got over the practical difficulties somehow.

32-1 **Explain the underlined "her difficulty" in one English sentence.** [1 point]

____

32-2 **The following is part of the summary of the passage. Complete the summary in less than 50 English words.** [3 points]

This article describes the case of Brenda, ______________________________

____

____

____

NOTE

Step 1	Survey
Key Words	
Signal Words	
Step 2	**Reading**
Purpose	
Pattern of Organization	
Tone	
Main Idea	
Step 3	**Summary**
지문 요약하기 (Paraphrasing)	
Step 4	**Recite**
요약문 말로 설명하기	

Answer Key

Brenda Linson never goes anywhere without an empty spectacles case. It is as vital to her as her purse. Yet, she doesn't wear glasses. The reason she can't do without it is because she **can't read and she can't write**. If ever she gets into any situation where she might be expected to do either of these things, she fishes around in her bag for the specs case, finds it's empty, and asks the person concerned to do the reading for her. Brenda is now in her late thirties. She's capable and articulate and a few months ago **hardly anybody knew** she was **illiterate**. Her husband didn't know and her children **didn't know**. The children still don't.

She had any number of **tactics** for concealing **her difficulty**—for example, never lingering near a phone at work, in case she had to answer it and might be required to write something down. But, in fact, it is easier for illiterates to conceal the truth than the rest of us might imagine. Literacy is so much taken for granted that people simply don't spot the giveaway signs.

It has never been occurred to **the children** that their mother cannot read. She doesn't read them stories, but then their father doesn't either, so they find nothing surprising in the fact. Similarly they just accept that Dad is the one who writes the sick notes and reads the school reports. Now that the elder boy Tom is quite a proficient reader, Brenda can skillfully get him to read any notes brought home from school simply by asking, "What's that all about, then?"

Brenda's **husband** never guessed **the truth** in 10 years of marriage. For one thing he insists on handling all domestic correspondence and bills himself. An importer of Persian carpets, he travels a great deal and so is not around so much to spot the truth. While he's away Brenda copes with any situations, by explaining that she can't do anything until she's discussed it with her husband.

Brenda was very successful in **her job** until recently. For the last five years she had worked as waitress at an exclusive private club, and had eventually been promoted to head waitress. She kept the thing a secret there too, and got over the practical difficulties somehow.

→ key word 1
→ key word 1′
→ key word 2
→ key word 2′
→ key word 1″
→ key word 3
<narrative>
① children
→ key word 2
② husband
③ job

모범답안

32-1 She is illiterate. (또는 She cannot read and write.)

32-2 a married woman in her late thirties who cannot read and write. By employing a number of tactics, she has so far managed to hide her difficulty from the people she works with and even from her children and husband.

한글번역

브렌다 린슨은 안경이 없는 빈 안경집 없이는 어디도 가지 않는다. 안경집은 그녀에게 지갑만큼 중요하다. 하지만 그녀는 안경을 끼지 않는다. 그녀가 안경 없이 지낼 수 없는 이유는 그녀가 읽고 쓸 수 없기 때문이다. 만일 그녀가 읽거나 쓰거나 하는 일이 예상되는 어떤 상황에 빠진다면 안경집을 찾아 가방을 뒤진다. 안경이 없을 경우, 그녀는 관계된 사람에게 그녀를 위해 읽어달라고 요청한다. 브렌다는 이제 30대 후반이다. 그녀는 능력이 있으며, 매사에 분명하다. 또 몇 달 전까지 그녀가 읽고 쓰는 능력이 없다는 사실을 안 사람은 거의 없었다. 그녀의 남편도 몰랐고 아이들도 몰랐다. 아이들은 지금도 모른다.

그녀는 자신의 어려움을 숨기기 위한 꽤 많은 방안을 갖고 있다. 예를 들면, 무언가에 대답을 하고 그것을 받아 적어야 하는 경우가 있을라치면, 작업 시간에 전화기 주변을 맴도는 일을 아예 하지 않는다든가 하는 등이다. 하지만, 사실 글을 읽지 못하는 사람이 그것을 감추는 것은 우리가 생각하는 것보다 더 쉽다. 글 읽는 능력이 있다는 것은 아주 당연한 것으로 여겨지기 때문에 사람들은 그것을 드러내는 징후를 발견하지 못한다.

어머니가 읽을 수 없다는 사실을 아이들은 꿈에도 생각하지 않았다. 그녀는 아이들에게 책을 읽어주지 않는다. 하지만 그 경우 아버지 또한 그렇게 읽어주지 않는다. 그래서 아이들은 그 사실(어머니가 책을 읽어주지 않는 사실)이 전혀 놀랍지 않은 것이다. 마찬가지로 그 아이들은 병결증명서를 쓰고 성적표를 읽는 사람은 아버지임을 받아들인다. 큰 아이 톰은 글을 아주 능숙하게 읽으므로 브렌다는 교묘하게 그로 하여금 학교에서 집으로 오는 모든 통지문을 읽게 한다. 단순히 "근데 그거 뭐에 관한 거니?"라고 물음으로써 읽게 하는 것이다.

브렌다의 남편은 결혼한 지 10년이 지났지만 그 사실을 전혀 모른다. 한 가지 이유는 그는 모든 집안의 서신과 계산서 등을 자신이 직접 다뤄야 한다고 주장하기 때문이다. 페르시아 카펫 수입업자인 그는 여행을 아주 많이 한다. 그래서 그 사실을 발견할 가망은 별로 없다. 남편이 떠나 있는 동안에 브렌다는 그 어떤 상황이라도 헤쳐 나간다. 다음과 같이 설명함으로써 그렇게 한다. 즉, 남편과 상의할 때까지는 어떤 것도 할 수 없다고 설명해 그 상황을 극복하는 것이다.

브렌다는 최근까지 그녀의 일에 성공적이었다. 지난 5년 동안 그녀는 한 고급 개인 클럽에서 점원으로 일했다. 그리고 마침내 급사장으로까지 승진했다. 그녀는 그 일을 그곳에서도 여전히 비밀로 했으며, 어떻게든 현실에서 겪는 어려움을 극복했다.

NOTE

Step 1	Ⓢurvey
Key Words	Can't read and can't write; illiterate; tactics; her difficulty
Signal Words	Not clear
Step 2	**Ⓡeading**
Purpose	To narrate a woman's situation who is illiterate
Pattern of Organization	Narrative (time order)
Tone	Neutral
Main Idea	Brenda, who is illiterate, has managed to hide this difficulty from the people around her by using many tactics.
Step 3	**Ⓢummary**
지문 요약하기 (Paraphrasing)	Brenda is a married woman in her late thirties who cannot read and write. By employing a number of tactics, she has managed to hide this difficulty from the people who she works with and even from her children and husband.
Step 4	**Ⓡecite**
요약문 말로 설명하기	

33 Read the passage and follow the directions. 1999학년도

The technological revolution that will prevail for the remainder of this century will create jobs and professions that as little as five years ago were nonexistent. These newly developed markets will demand of workers an understanding of sophisticated technical communications systems as well as an increased technical expertise. By the year 2001 basic skills that once were vital to business will be rendered obsolete. The spot welder on the automobile production line and the field worker on a farm will go the way of the steamboat pilot and the blacksmith. The most significant trend in years to come will be the demise of the blue-collar worker. The American economy will witness the demise as automation and robotics become more prevalent, heralding the rise of <u>the steel-collar worker</u>. Such traditional blue-collar employers as automobile companies have already begun to automate their factories. By contrast, office and service jobs will be abundant, but only for those prepared to improve their technical skills. Again it will be automation that will displace many of the low-skilled and semiskilled workers in the present economy. In fact, the era of the paperless office has already begun. It has been promoted by two principal developments: computers and the explosive growth of telecommunications systems. This office revolution not only has changed how work is done and information is handled but has redefined the function of everyone who works in an office, from the corporate executive down to the lowliest clerk. For the job hunter of 2020, scanning classified ads will be a quick education in how drastically the workplace will have changed. He or she is likely to see openings for such positions as biological historians, biofarming experts, robot trainers, teleconferencing coordinators, to cite but a few.

33-1 **What is the main idea of this passage? Write your answer in ONE sentence.** [3 points]

33-2 **What does the underlined "the steel-collar worker" refer to? Write your answer in one or two word(s).** [2 points]

NOTE

Step 1	Survey
Key Words	
Signal Words	
Step 2	**Reading**
Purpose	
Pattern of Organization	
Tone	
Main Idea	
Step 3	**Summary**
지문 요약하기 (Paraphrasing)	
Step 4	**Recite**
요약문 말로 설명하기	

Answer Key

The technological revolution that will prevail for the remainder of this century will create **jobs and professions** that as little as five years ago were nonexistent. These newly developed markets will demand of workers an understanding of sophisticated **technical** communications systems as well as an increased **technical** expertise. By the year 2001 basic skills that once were vital to business will be rendered obsolete. The spot welder on the automobile production line and the field **worker** on a farm will go the way of the steamboat pilot and the blacksmith. The most significant trend in years to come will be the demise of the blue-collar worker. The American economy will witness the demise as **automation** and robotics become more prevalent, heralding the rise of the steel-collar worker. Such traditional blue-collar employers as automobile companies have already begun to automate their factories. By contrast, office and service jobs will be abundant, but only for those prepared to improve their technical skills. Again it will be **automation** that will displace many of the low-skilled and semiskilled **workers** in the present economy. In fact, the era of the paperless office has already begun. It has been promoted by two principal developments: computers and the explosive growth of telecommunications systems. This office revolution not only has changed how work is done and information is handled but has redefined the function of everyone who works in an office, from the corporate executive down to the lowliest clerk. For the job hunter of 2020, scanning classified ads will be a quick education in how drastically the workplace will have changed. He or she is likely to see openings for such positions as biological historians, biofarming experts, robot trainers, teleconferencing coordinators, to cite but a few.

→ key word 1
→ key word 2
→ key word 1
<time order>
→ key word 2′
→ key word 3
<contrast>
→ key word 3
→ key word 2′
<series>

모범답안

33-1 The technical revolution will cause unexpected changes in jobs in the future, and therefore we have to make full preparations for getting new jobs.

33-2 robots; the robot

한글번역

남은 금세기 동안 확산될 기술 혁명은 5년 전까지만 해도 존재하지 않던 직업을 만들어 낼 것이다. 이 새롭게 발달된 시장은 노동자들에게 늘어만 가는 전문기술뿐만 아니라 복잡한 기술 커뮤니케이션 시스템을 이해할 것을 요구하고 있다. 2001년경에는 한때 산업에 중요했던 기본 기술들이 쓸모없는 것이 되고 말 것이다. 자동차 생산라인의 점용접공들과 농장의 현장 노동자들은 기선의 도선사들과 대장장이의 전철을 밟을 것이다. 가까운 미래에 가장 중요한 경향은 현장 근로자(블루칼라)의 몰락이 될 것이다. 따라서 미국 경제는 자동화와 로봇학이 확산됨에 따라 그러한 몰락을 목격하게 될 것이다. 이는 스틸칼라 노동자의 등장을 예고하는 것이다. 자동차 회사처럼 전통적 현장 근로자를 고용했던 회사들은 이미 공장을 자동화하기 시작했다. 이와는 달리, 사무직과 서비스직은 더 늘어날 것이다. 하지만 그것도 자신들의 기술을 향상시키기 위해 준비하는 사람들에게만 해당될 것이다. 다시 말해, 현재 경제구조에서 많은 비숙련 및 준숙련 근로자들을 대체시키게 될 것은 바로 자동화가 될 것이다. 사실, 종이 없는 사무실의 시대가 이미 시작됐다. 그것은 두 가지 주요한 발달에 의해 촉진되고 있는데, 바로 컴퓨터와 급격하게 성장하는 원거리 통신 시스템이 그 촉진역을 맡고 있다. 이러한 사무실 혁명은 작업 방식과 정보 처리 방식을 변화시켰을 뿐만 아니라, 위로는 기업의 중역에서 아래로는 최하층의 점원에 이르기까지 사무실 직원의 기능도 재편해왔다. 2020년에 직업을 구하려는 사람에게 구인구직 광고를 살피는 것은 작업장이 얼마나 철저히 변화될 것인지에 대해 빠른 교육이 될 것이다. 조금만 열거하자면, 그 사람은 생물 역사학자, 생명농업 전문가, 로봇 훈련사, 원거리회의 코디네이터 등과 같은 직업에 대한 기회를 발견할 수 있을 것이다.

Step 1	Survey
Key Words	Technological revolution; technical; jobs and professions; worker; automation; automate
Signal Words	By the year 2001; By contrast; In fact; 2020
Step 2	**Reading**
Purpose	To explain how the technical revolution will change the jobs and professions
Pattern of Organization	Cause/effect; time order
Tone	Neutral
Main Idea	The technological revolution will cause unexpected changes in jobs in the future, and therefore we have to make full preparations for getting new jobs.
Step 3	**Summary**
지문 요약하기 (Paraphrasing)	The technological revolution will bring a lot of changes to the workplace. Many current blue-collar and low-skilled workers will be replaced by automation and robots while office and service jobs will be abundant for those who have technical expertise. Therefore, people need to understand how drastically the workplace will have changed and to make full preparations for getting future jobs.
Step 4	**Recite**
요약문 말로 설명하기	

34 **Read the passage and answer the question.** [5 points] 1998학년도

The other complaint wives make about their husbands is "He doesn't listen to me anymore." The wives may be right that their husbands aren't listening, if they don't value their wives' telling of problems and secrets to establish rapport. But some of the time men feel unjustly accused: "I was listening." And some of the time, they're right. <u>They were</u>. Whether or not someone is listening only that person can really know. But we judge whether or not we think others are listening by signals we can see—not only their verbal responses but also their eye contact and little listening noises like "mhm," "uh-huh," and "yeah." These listening noises give the go-ahead for talk; if they are misplaced along the track, they can quickly derail a chugging conversation. Maltz and Borker also report that women and men have different ways of showing that they're listening. In the listening role, women make—and expect—more of these noises. So when men are listening to women, they are likely to make too few such noises for the women to feel the men are really listening. And when women are listening to men, making more such listening noises than men expect may give the impression they're impatient or exaggerating their show of interest.

34-1 **Why do the wives feel that their husbands do not "listen to" them? Write your answer using the given words below.** [3 points]

husbands, enough signals, such as, listening noises

It is because ______________________________

____

34-2 **In the underlined part, ONE word is omitted. What is the word?** [2 points]

____

NOTE

Step 1	Ⓢurvey
Key Words	
Signal Words	
Step 2	**Ⓡeading**
Purpose	
Pattern of Organization	
Tone	
Main Idea	
Step 3	**Ⓢummary**
지문 요약하기 (Paraphrasing)	
Step 4	**Ⓡecite**
요약문 말로 설명하기	

Answer Key

The other complaint wives make about their husbands is "He doesn't **listen** to me anymore." The wives may be right that their husbands aren't **listening**, if they don't value their wives' telling of problems and secrets to establish rapport. But some of the time men feel unjustly accused: "I was listening." And some of the time, they're right. They were. Whether or not someone is listening only that person can really know. But we judge whether or not we think others are **listening** by signals we can see—not only their verbal responses but also their eye contact and little **listening noises** like "mhm," "uh-huh," and "yeah." These listening noises give the go-ahead for talk; if they are misplaced along the track, they can quickly derail a chugging conversation. Maltz and Borker also report that **women and men** have different ways of showing that they're listening. In the listening role, women make—and expect—more of **these noises.** So when men are listening to women, they are likely to make too few such noises for the women to feel the men are really listening. And when women are listening to men, making more such **listening noises** than men expect may give the impression they're impatient or exaggerating their show of interest.

key word 1
key word 1
key word 1
key word 2
<series>
Main idea
key word 3
key word 2
<contrast>
key word 2

모범답안

34-1 their husbands do not send enough signals such as listening noises which make wives feel that they are really listening.

34-2 listening

한글번역

아내들이 남편들에 대해 하는 다른 불평은, "그가 내 말을 도무지 듣고 있지 않다"는 것이다. 남편들이 친밀한 관계를 쌓기 위해 문제나 비밀을 털어놓는 아내를 무시한다면 아내들의 말이 맞을 것이다. 하지만 어떤 경우에는 남편들은 부당하게 비난받고 있다는 느낌을 가질 것이다. 실제로 "그는 듣고 있었기" 때문이다. 그래서 어떤 때는 그 남편들이 옳다. 그들은 듣고 있었다. 누군가가 듣고 있는지 아닌지는 그 사람만 알 수 있다. 하지만 우리 생각에 다른 사람이 듣고 있는지 아닌지는 우리가 보는 신호에 의해 확인된다. 그 신호는 언어적 반응일 수도 있고 또한 시선 접촉이나 "음"이나 "어" 또는 "응"과 같은 작은 소음일 수도 있다. 이러한 듣기 반응 소리(listening noises)는 대화를 위한 활력을 준다. 그런데 그 소리들을 잘못 내게 되면 진행되는 대화를 즉각 방해할 수 있다. 몰츠와 보커는 또한 여성과 남성이 듣고 있다는 것을 나타내는 방식이 다름을 보고하고 있다. 듣기 역할에서, 여성은 더 많은 소리를 내고 또 기대한다. 그래서 남성들이 여성들의 말을 들을 때, 남성들은 소리를 너무 적게 내 여성들이 느끼기에는 남성들이 실제로 듣고 있지 않는 것처럼 보일 수 있을 것 같다. 또 여성들이 남성들의 말을 들을 때, 여성들은 남성들이 생각하는 것보다 더 많은 소리를 내게 되므로 남성들에게 자신들이 조급하거나 과장되게 관심을 보여준다는 인상을 줄 수도 있다.

NOTE

Step 1	Ⓢurvey
Key Words	Listening; listening noise; men and women
Signal Words	Different; more; more … than
Step 2	**Ⓡeading**
Purpose	To explain the different listening roles and signals between men and women
Pattern of Organization	Comparison/contrast; cause/effect
Tone	Neutral
Main Idea	Men and women have different expectations, roles and ways of showing in their listening.
Step 3	**Ⓢummary**
지문 요약하기 (Paraphrasing)	Men and women have different expectations, roles and ways of showing in their listening. Many wives complain about their husbands' not listening to them. They feel that way because men do not send signals. Unlike women who expect more listening signals, men consider the signals as inappropriate.
Step 4	**Ⓡecite**
요약문 말로 설명하기	

35 Read the passage and answer the questions.

1998학년도

[1] Science and technology are getting a bad press these days. Increasingly scornful of the materialism of our culture, young people speak about returning to a simpler, preindustrial, pre-scientific day. They fail to realize that the "good old days" were really the horribly bad old days of ignorance, disease, slavery and death. They fancy themselves in Athens, talking to Socrates, listening to the latest play by Sophocles—never as a slave brutalized in the Athenian silver mines. They imagine themselves as medieval knights on armored chargers—never as starving peasants.

[2] Yet, right down to modern times, the wealth and prosperity of a relative few have been built on the animal-like labor and wretched existence of many—peasants, serfs and slaves. What's more, nothing could be done about it. Slavery and peonage were taken for granted. Not until science became prominent did slavery come to be recognized as a dreadful wrong, to be abolished. It was the scientist, supposedly cold and concerned with things rather than ideals, who brought this about. His investigations made possible the harnessing of the energy of the inanimate world. With steam, electricity and radio beams to do our work for us, there was less need for the comparatively weak and fumbling human muscle—and slavery began to vanish.

[3] Yet, science has helped create problems, too—serious ones. And we must labor to solve them—in the only way history tells us problems have been solved; by science. If we were to turn away now, if a noble young generation abandoned the materialism of an industry, what would happen? Without the machinery of that industry, we would inevitably drift back to slavery.

35-1 **What is the main idea of the first paragraph? Write your answer using the given words.** [2 points]

Young people ________________________________.

tend, think, wrongly, preindustrial, better

35-2 **What is the main idea of the second paragraph? Write your answer using the given words.** [2 points]

Advances in science ________________________________.

possible, free, human beings

35-3 **What is the main idea of the third paragraph? Write your answer using the given words.** [2 points]

We have no choice but to solve the problems ____________________.

created, science, help, science

NOTE

Step 1	Ⓢurvey
Key Words	
Signal Words	
Step 2	**Ⓡeading**
Purpose	
Pattern of Organization	
Tone	
Main Idea	
Step 3	**Ⓢummary**
지문 요약하기 (Paraphrasing)	
Step 4	**Ⓡecite**
요약문 말로 설명하기	

Answer Key

Science and technology are getting a bad press these days. Increasingly scornful of the materialism of our culture, young people speak about returning to a simpler, preindustrial, pre-scientific day. They fail to realize that the "good old days" were really the horribly bad old days of ignorance, disease, **slavery** and death. They fancy themselves in Athens, talking to Socrates, listening to the latest play by Sophocles—never as a **slave** brutalized in the Athenian silver mines. They imagine themselves as medieval knights on armored chargers—never as starving peasants.

Yet, right down to modern times, the wealth and prosperity of a relative few have been built on the **animal-like labor** and wretched existence of many—peasants, serfs and slaves. What's more, nothing could be done about it. Slavery and peonage were taken for granted. Not until **science** became prominent did slavery come to be recognized as a dreadful wrong, to be abolished. It was the scientist, supposedly cold and concerned with things rather than ideals, who brought this about. His investigations made possible the harnessing of the energy of the inanimate world. With steam, electricity and radio beams to do our work for us, there was less need for the comparatively weak and fumbling human muscle—and **slavery** began to vanish.

Yet, science has helped create problems, too—serious ones. And we must labor to solved them—in the only way history tells us problems have been solved; by science. If we were to turn away now, if a noble young generation abandoned the materialism of an industry, what would happen? Without the machinery of that industry, we would inevitably drift back to slavery.

→ key word 1
→ key word 2
→ key word 2
→ key word 2′
→ key word 1
<cause-effect>
→ key word 2
<Main idea : opinion>

모범답안

35-1 tend to think wrongly that preindustrial days were better than today

35-2 made it possible to free human beings from slavery

35-3 created by science with the help of science

한글번역

[1] 오늘날 과학과 기술은 부당한 평가를 받고 있다. 젊은이들은 점점 우리 문화가 물질주의적이라고 비웃으면서, 더 단순하고 산업이전 및 과학이전인 시대로 돌아갈 것을 주장하고 있다. 하지만 그들은 그 '좋은 옛날'이 무지와 질병과 노예와 죽음이라는 끔찍하도록 나쁜 과거였다는 것을 깨닫지 못하고 있다. 그들은 자신들이 아테네에 있다고 상상하는데, 소크라테스에게 말을 걸며, 소포클레스의 최신 희곡을 들으면서 말이다. 그들은 자신들이 아테네 은광에서 짐승처럼 된 노예라고는 전혀 상상도 하지 않고 있는 것이다. 또 그들은 자신들을 중세의 중무장한 군마에 올라탄 기사라고 생각할지언정 굶주린 소작농이라고는 조금도 생각하지 않는다.

[2] 그런데, 근대로 내려오면서, 상대적 소수의 부와 번영은 많은 사람들(농민, 농노 및 노예)의 동물 같은 노동과 비참한 생활에 바탕을 두고 이뤄졌다. 더욱이, 그러한 노동과 생존에 관한 어떤 것도 이뤄질 수 없었다. 노예제도는 당연한 것으로 여겨졌다. 과학이 부각되고 나서야 비로소 노예제도가 아주 잘못된 것으로 간주돼 폐지되기에 이르렀다. 추정컨대 냉철하고, 이상보다는 현실적인 것에 관심을 가졌던 그 과학자야말로 이러한 결과(노예제 폐지)를 가져온 사람들이었다. 다시 말해, 과학자의 연구에 힘입어 무생물 세계(즉, 기계)의 에너지를 이용할 수 있게 됐다. 증기와 증기 및 방사선이 인간을 대신해 일을 하게 됨으로써, 비교적 약하고 어설픈 인간의 근육이 그다지 필요치 않게 됐고 이에 노예제도가 사라지게 됐다.

[3] 하지만, 과학은 또한 문제들, 아주 심각한 문제들을 야기하는 데 일조했다. 그래서 우리는 그 문제들을 해결하기 위해 노력을 해야 하는데, 그것은 역사가 우리에게 보여줬던 문제 해결의 방식이어야 한다. 즉, (과학에 의해 야기된 문제이므로) 과학에 의해야 한다. 우리가 다시 옛날로 돌아가려고 한다면, 또 고귀한 젊은이 세대가 산업의 물질주의를 포기한다면, 어떻게 될 것인가? 그 산업의 기계가 없다면 우리는 불가피하게 노예 상태로 떠밀려 되돌아가게 될 것이다.

NOTE

Step 1	Ⓢurvey
Key Words	Science and technology; slavery; animal-like labor
Signal Words	Not clear
Step 2	**Ⓡeading**
Purpose	To persuade the youth the importance of science
Pattern of Organization	Cause/effect
Tone	Critical
Main Idea	Science and technology made it possible to free human beings from slavery and peonage.
Step 3	**Ⓢummary**
지문 요약하기 (Paraphrasing)	Current young people's thought that preindustrial days, when science and technology were not prevalent, were better than today is wrong, because advance in science and technology made it possible to free human beings from slavery and peonage. In addition, without the help of science, we cannot solve our current problems, which have been caused by science.
Step 4	**Ⓡecite**
요약문 말로 설명하기	

36 Read the passage and answer the question. [3 points] 1997학년도

The greatest enrichment the scientific culture could give us is a moral one. Among scientists, deep-natured men know that the individual human condition is tragic; for all its triumphs and joys, the essence of it is loneliness and the end death. But what they will not admit is that, because the individual condition is tragic, therefore the social condition must be tragic, too. Because a man must die, that is no excuse for his dying before his time and after a servile life. The impulse behind the scientists drives them to limit the area of tragedy, to take nothing as tragic that can conceivably lie within men's will. The scientists have nothing but contempt for those representatives of the traditional culture who use a deep insight into man's fate to obscure the social truth, just to hang on to a few perks. Dostoevsky sucking up to the Chancellor Pobedonostsev, who thought the only thing wrong with slavery was that there was not enough of it; Ezra Pound broadcasting for the Fascists; Faulkner giving sentimental reasons for treating Negroes as a different species. They are all symptoms of the deepest temptation of the clerks—which is to say: "Because man's condition is tragic, everyone ought to stay in their place, with mine as it happens somewhere near the top." From that particular temptation, made up of defeat, self-indulgence, and moral vanity, the scientific culture is almost totally immune. It is that kind of moral health of the scientists which, in the last few years, the rest of us have needed most.

Write the main idea of the passage in about 20 words.

____

____

____

NOTE

Step 1	Ⓢurvey
Key Words	
Signal Words	
Step 2	**Ⓡeading**
Purpose	
Pattern of Organization	
Tone	
Main Idea	
Step 3	**Ⓢummary**
지문 요약하기 (Paraphrasing)	
Step 4	**Ⓡecite**
요약문 말로 설명하기	

Answer Key

The greatest enrichment the **scientific culture** could give us is a **moral** one. Among **scientists**, deep-natured men know that the individual human condition is tragic; for all its triumphs and joys, the essence of it is loneliness and the end death. But what they will not admit is that, because the individual condition is tragic, therefore the social condition must be tragic, too. Because a man must die, that is no excuse for his dying before his time and after a servile life. The impulse behind the scientists drives them to limit the area of tragedy, to take nothing as tragic that can conceivably lie within men's will. **The scientists** have nothing but contempt for those representatives of the traditional culture who use a deep insight into man's fate to obscure the social truth, just to hang on to a few perks. Dostoevsky sucking up to the Chancellor Pobedonostsev, who thought the only thing wrong with slavery was that there was not enough of it; Ezra Pound broadcasting for the Fascists; Faulkner giving sentimental reasons for treating Negroes as a different species. They are all symptoms of the deepest temptation of the clerks—which is to say: "Because man's condition is tragic, everyone ought to stay in their place, with mine as it happens somewhere near the top." From that particular temptation, made up of defeat, self-indulgence, and moral vanity, **the scientific culture** is almost totally immune. It is that kind of **moral** health of the scientists which, in the last few years, the rest of us have needed most.

Main idea 1
→ key word 1
→ key word 1′
→ key word 2

→ key word 1′
Main idea 1′

<Series of examples>

<contrast>
→ key word 1

→ key word 2

모범답안 The scientific culture(or The scientists), as opposed to (people who represent) the traditional culture that obscure(s) the social and moral truth, possess(es) a special kind of moral authority.

한글번역

과학 문명이 우리에게 제공할 수 있는 최대의 풍요로움은 도덕적 풍요로움이다. 과학자들 중 사려 깊은 사람들은 개인의 조건이 비극적이라는 것을 알고 있다. 즉, 그러한 조건이 화려하고 즐거운 것이라고 하더라도, 그것의 본질은 외로움이며 최종적으로는 죽음이다. 하지만, 그 과학자들은 개인의 조건이 비극적이라고 해서 사회적 조건 역시 그래야 한다는 사실은 인정하려 들지 않는다. 또 인간이 반드시 죽어야 한다고 해서, 그러한 사실이 그가 때가 되기 전에 죽는다거나 또는 노예 같은 삶을 살다가 죽어야 한다는 것에 대한 구실은 되지 못한다. 과학자들의 심리 기저에 있는 그러한 (현실을 방관하지 않으려는) 충동이 과학자들로 하여금 그 비극의 영역을 줄이도록 하고 있다. 즉, 생각하기에 따라 인간의 의지 안에 놓여 있을 수 있는 그 어떤 것도 비극적인 것으로 간주하지 않도록 하고 있다. 그 과학자들은 이러한 사회적 진실을 흐리기 위해 인간에 대한 깊은 통찰력을 이용하거나 적은 이익에 매달렸던 전통 문화의 대표자들을 경멸한다. 가령, 도스토예프스키는 대법관인 포브도노체브에게 아부를 했는데, 그는 노예제도에 유일한 잘못된 것이 있다면 그것이 충분하지 않다는 사실에 있다고 생각한 사람이었다. 또 에즈라 파운드는 파시즘 정권을 위해 방송을 했고, 포크너는 흑인들을 다른 종으로 대우하는 것에 대한 구실을 제공했다. 이러한 사실 모두는 성직자들의 가장 뿌리 깊은 유혹의 징후인 것이다. 말인즉, "인간의 조건이 비극적이기 때문에, 모든 사람은 자신의 자리에 있어야 한다. 어쩌다 보니 내 자리가 꼭대기에 가까운 어딘가에 있듯이." 하지만 과학 문명은 패배와 방종 및 도덕적 공허에서 비롯된 그 특별한 유혹으로부터 거의 완전히 자유롭다. 최근 몇 년 동안 나머지 우리가 가장 필요로 하는 것은 다름 아닌 바로 그러한 종류의 과학자들의 도덕적 건강성이다.

NOTE

Step 1	**S**urvey
Key Words	The scientific culture; scientist; moral; the traditional culture
Signal Words	;(semi-colon); is
Step 2	**R**eading
Purpose	To explain the virtue of the scientific culture
Pattern of Organization	Contrast; series
Tone	Argumentative
Main Idea	The scientific culture keeps particular moral health unlike the traditional culture.
Step 3	**S**ummary
지문 요약하기 (Paraphrasing)	The scientific culture keeps particular moral health unlike the traditional culture. As opposed to such famous representatives of the traditional culture as Dostoevsky, Pound, and Faulkner who supported the unjust system by obscuring the social and moral truth, the scientists possess a special kind of moral authority.
Step 4	**R**ecite
요약문 말로 설명하기	

37 **Read the passage and answer the questions.** [6 points] 1997학년도

The Eskimos can speak about snow with a great deal more precision and subtlety than we can in English, but this is not because the Eskimo language (one of those sometimes mis-called 'primitive') is inherently more precise and subtle than English. This does not bring to light a defect in English, a show of unexpected 'primitiveness'. The position is simply and obviously that the Eskimos and the English live in different ________. The English language would be just as rich in terms for different kinds of snow, presumably, if the environments in which English was habitually used made such distinction important. Similarly, we have no reason to doubt that the Eskimo language could be as precise and subtle on the subject of motor manufacture or cricket if these topics formed part of the Eskimos' life. For obvious historical reasons, Englishmen in the nineteenth century could not talk about motorcars with the minute discrimination which is possible today; cars were not a part of their culture. But they had a host of terms for horse-drawn vehicles which send us, puzzled, to a historical dictionary when we are reading Scott or Dickens. How many of us could distinguish between a chaise, a landau, a victoria, a brougham, a coupe, a gig, a diligence, a whisky, a calash, a tilbury, a carriole, a phaeton, and a clarence?

37-1 **Fill in the blank with a suitable word used in the text.** [1 point]

____

37-2 **The modern readers of Scott or Dickens often have to consult a historical dictionary, because** ______________________________

______________________________. [2 points]

37-3 **Write down the main idea of the passage in 20-30 words.** [3 points]

____

NOTE

Step 1	Survey
Key Words	
Signal Words	
Step 2	**Reading**
Purpose	
Pattern of Organization	
Tone	
Main Idea	
Step 3	**Summary**
지문 요약하기 (Paraphrasing)	
Step 4	**Recite**
요약문 말로 설명하기	

Answer Key

The Eskimos can speak about snow with a great deal more precision and subtlety than we can in English, but this is not because **the Eskimo language** (one of those sometimes mis-called 'primitive') is inherently more precise and subtle than **English**. This does not bring to light a defect in **English**, a show of unexpected 'primitiveness'. **The position is simply and obviously that the Eskimos and the English live in different environments. The English language would be just as rich in terms for different kinds of snow, presumably, if the environments in which English was habitually used made such distinction important.** Similarly, we have no reason to doubt that the Eskimo language could be as precise and subtle on the subject of motor manufacture or cricket if these topics formed part of the Eskimos' life. For obvious historical reasons, Englishmen in the nineteenth century could not talk about motorcars with the minute discrimination which is possible today; cars were not a part of their culture. But they had a host of terms for horse-drawn vehicles which send us, puzzled, to a historical dictionary when we are reading Scott or Dickens. How many of us could distinguish between a chaise, a landau, a victoria, a brougham, a coupe, a gig, a diligence, a whisky, a calash, a tilbury, a carriole, a phaeton, and a clarence?

→ key word 1
→ key word 2
→ key word 2
→ key word 2
Main idea
→ signal word

모범답안

37-1 environments

37-2 they can't understand many words of horse-drawn vehicles unlike Englishmen in the 19th century whose culture or environments was closely related to them (또는 they have no share of culture, or environment with the people back then 또는 horse-drawn vehicles are not a part of their culture)

37-3 All human languages are equally complete and perfect as instruments of communication because language is influenced by the concrete culture or environments in which the language is used.

한글번역

에스키모어는 눈에 대해 우리가 영어로 할 수 있는 것보다 아주 더 정밀하고 더 섬세하게 말할 수 있다. 하지만, 이러한 사실은 에스키모어(때때로는 '원시적'이라고 불리는 것들 가운데 하나인데)가 내재적으로 영어보다 더 정밀하고 더 섬세하기 때문이 아니다. 또, 이러한 사실이 영어에 결점이 있다는 것을 보여주거나 예기치 않은 '원시성'을 보여주는 것은 아니다. 그러한 입장은 단순하고 분명하게도 에스키모 사람들과 영국사람들이 다른 환경에서 살고 있다는 사실을 보여준다. 짐작건대, 만일 영어가 일상적으로 사용됐던 환경에서 (눈에 대한) 그러한 구별이 중요한 것이라면, 영어는 다른 종류의 눈에 대한 용어(어휘)에서 에스키모어와 마찬가지로 풍부할 것이다. 마찬가지로, 자동차 생산이나 크리켓 등의 주제가 에스키모인의 생활의 일부가 됐다고 가정해보면, 에스키모어 역시 그러한 것들에 대한 주제에 관해 (영어만큼) 정밀하고 섬세할 수 있다고 상상하는 것은 당연하다. 몇 가지 분명한 역사적 이유로 인해, 19세기 영국인들은 자동차에 대해, 오늘날 우리가 하는 세세한 구별을 하면서 말을 할 수 없었다. 왜냐하면 자동차가 그들 문화의 일부가 아니었기 때문이다. 하지만 그들은 말이 끄는 탈것에 대해서는 많은 용어가 있었다. 우리가 스코트나 디킨슨의 책을 읽다가 그 '말이 끄는 탈것'이라는 단어들을 만나면, 우리는 당황하면서 역사 사전을 뒤지러 갈 것이다. 우리들 가운데 얼마나 많은 사람들이 마차, 랜도 마차, 빅토리아 마차, 사륜마차, 쿠페형 마차, 이륜마차, 승합 마차, 경이륜마차, 이륜 포장마차, 지붕 없는 이륜마차, 썰매, 쌍두 사륜마차, 4인승 사륜마차를 구별할 수 있겠는가?

NOTE

Step 1	Ⓢurvey
Key Words	The Eskimo language; English; environments; culture
Signal Words	Similarly; reasons
Step 2	**Ⓡeading**
Purpose	To explain languages in different culture and environments
Pattern of Organization	Cause/effect; comparison/contrast
Tone	Persuasive
Main Idea	All human languages are equally complete and perfect as instruments of communication because (the usage of) language is influenced by the concrete culture or environments in which the language is used.
Step 3	**Ⓢummary**
지문 요약하기 (Paraphrasing)	All human languages are equally complete and perfect as instruments of communication because (the usage of) language is influenced by the concrete culture or environments in which the language is used. The Eskimo language can express snow more precisely than English because Eskimo's culture is more related to snow whereas English is more precise on the subject of motor manufacture.
Step 4	**Ⓡecite**
요약문 말로 설명하기	

MEMO

2S2R

유희태 일반영어

③ 기출

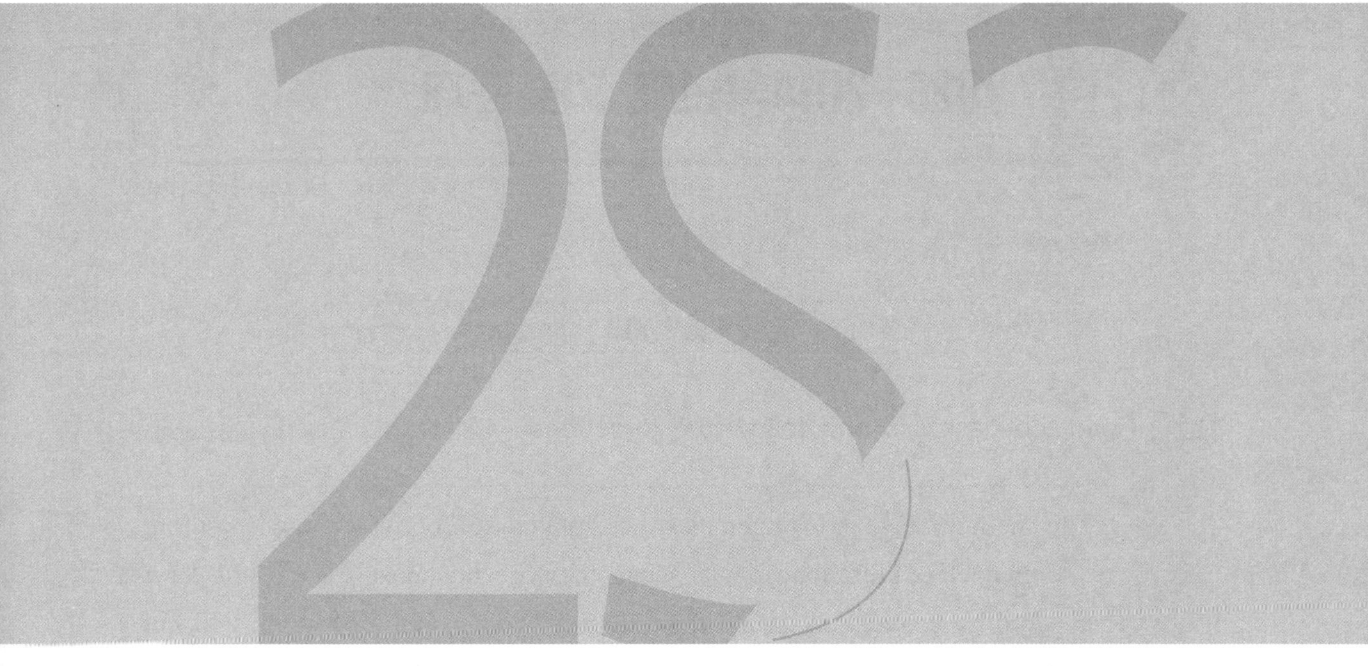

PART 02

2026~1997학년도 기출문제

Chapter 01 2026~2014학년도 기출문제

모범답안 및 번역 p.2

2026학년도

01 **Read the passage, and follow the directions.** [4 points] 전공A 서술형 11번

The modern stage no longer uses the spoken soliloquy, although without it the characters are silenced just when they are the most sincere, the least hampered by convention: when they are alone. The public of today will not tolerate the spoken soliloquy, allegedly because it is "unnatural." Now the film has brought us the silent soliloquy, in which a face can speak with the subtlest shades of meaning without appearing unnatural and arousing the distaste of the spectators. In this silent monologue the solitary human soul can find a tongue more candid and uninhibited than in any spoken soliloquy, for it speaks instinctively, subconsciously. The language of the face cannot be suppressed or controlled. However disciplined and practisedly hypocritical a face may be, in the enlarging ______________ we see even that it is concealing something, that is looking a lie. For such things have their own specific expressions superimposed on the feigned one. It is much easier to lie in words than with the face and the film has proved it beyond doubt.

In the film the mute soliloquy of the face speaks even when the hero is not alone, and herein lies a new great opportunity for depicting man. The poetic significance of the soliloquy is that it is a manifestation of mental, not physical, loneliness. Nevertheless, on the stage a character can speak a monologue only when there is no one else there, even though a character might feel a thousand times more lonely if alone among a large crowd. The monologue of loneliness may raise its voice within him a hundred times even while he is audibly talking to someone. Hence the most deep-felt human soliloquies could not find such expression, for the close-up can lift a character out of the heart of the greatest crowd and show how solitary it is in reality and what it feels in this crowded solitude.

The film, especially the sound film, can separate the words of a character talking to others from the mute play of features by means of which, in the middle of such a conversation, we are made to overhear a mute soliloquy and realize the difference between this soliloquy and the audible conversation. What a flesh-and-blood actor can show on the real stage is at most that his words are insincere and it is a mere convention that the partner in such a conversation is blinded to what every spectator can see. But in the isolated close-up of the film we can see to the bottom of a soul by means of such tiny movements of facial muscles which even the most observant partner would never perceive.

Fill in the blank with the ONE most appropriate word from the passage. Then explain what the underlined part means in the context of the passage. Do NOT copy more than FOUR consecutive words from the passage.

02 **Read the passage, and follow the directions.** [4 points] 전공B 서술형 7번

Science is a rich source of powerful explanatory stories. For example, Newton explained how a force causes a mass to accelerate. This gives us a story of how an apple drops from a tree and a planet circles the sun. It allows us to decide how hard the rocket engine needs to push to get it to the moon. Models of causation let us design complex machines, like factories and computers, that have fabulously long chains of causes and effects. They convert inputs into the outputs we want.

It's tempting to believe that our stories of causes and effects are how the world works. Actually, they're just a framework we use to manipulate the world and construct explanations for the convenience of our own understanding. For example, Newton's equation $F = ma$ doesn't really say that force causes acceleration, any more than it says that mass causes force. We tend to think of force as ______________, because we often have the choice as to whether to apply it or not. On the other hand, we tend to think of mass as not being under our control. Thus, we personify nature, imagining it almost as if natural forces were deciding to push on masses. It's much harder for us to imagine accelerations deciding to cause mass, so we tell the story a certain way. We credit gravitational force for keeping the planets orbiting the sun and blame it for pulling the apple down from the tree.

This convenient personification of nature helps us use our mental storytelling machinery to explain the natural world. The cause-and-effect paradigm works particularly well when science is used for engineering, to arrange the world for our convenience. In this case, we can often set things up so that the illusion of cause-and-effect is almost a reality. The computer is a perfect example. The key to what makes a computer work is that the inputs affect the outputs but not vice versa. The components used to construct the computer are constructed to create that same one-way relationship. These components, such as logic gates, are specifically designed to convert contingent inputs into predictable outputs. In other words, the logic gates of the computer are constructed to be atomic building blocks of cause and effect.

The notion of cause and effect breaks down when the parts we would like to think of as outputs affect the parts we would prefer to think of as inputs. The paradoxes of quantum mechanics are a perfect example of this, where our mere observation of a particle can "cause" a distant particle to be in a different state. Of course there's no real paradox here, there's just a problem with trying to apply our storytelling framework to a situation where it doesn't match.

Fill in the blank with the ONE most appropriate word from the passage. Then explain what the underlined part means in the context of the passage. Do NOT copy more than FOUR consecutive words from the passage.

____

____

____

____

____

03 Read the passage, and follow the directions. [4 points]

전공B 서술형 10번

From children kicking a ball on a playground to the stars at a basketball court, sport is ubiquitous. Regardless of one's age, gender, or background, it is an important activity that not only improves physical health but also provides a recreational outlet for many people. Despite these advantages, the field of sport is under pressure due to its negative impacts on the environment.

The sport event itself is seen as environmentally challenging. The artificialization of the sport environment has an adverse effect on nature and the landscape in many ways. For instance, the rapid spread of golf courses into the green belts that encircle the major cities of the world increases many concerns. While many people, especially golfers, consider a well-manicured course a thing of beauty, its development has an environmental cost. Part of the natural landscape is destroyed, as the courses are built. In addition, huge amounts of chemical fertilizer are put into the soil to develop and then maintain the course.

It is not solely sporting pursuits that have an impact on the environment. Major spectator sports and the associated stadia create problems in the adjacent area. Hundreds and thousands of plastic waste from bottles and food containers are generated in the stadium from crowd consumption and the concession stands nearby. Furthermore, noise emission from the arrival and departure of spectators puts a lot of strain in the area. In the case of football and rugby, the excessive cheering from the spectators and the loud music from the amplified speakers make an enormous amount of noise which lowers the environmental quality of the sport facilities in public spaces.

Collectively, these issues raise concerns in maintaining a sustainable environment in the world of sport. Sport organizations should be more proactive to overcome these difficulties by pursuing policies to reduce the side effects on the environment. This will protect the long term viability and sustainability of sport.

Write a summary following the guidelines below.

Guidelines

- Summarize the passage above in one paragraph.
- Provide a topic sentence, two supporting ideas, and a concluding sentence based on the passage.
- Do NOT copy more than FOUR consecutive words from the passage.

2025학년도

01 **Read the passage and follow the directions.** [4 points] 전공A 서술형 10번

"Telling stories is as basic to human beings as eating," writes Richard Kearney. "More so, in fact, for while food makes us live, stories are what make our lives worth living." Or not worth living. When one lives on the edge of the abyss, as we do, the answer to the fundamental question about the worthiness and meaning of existence depends heavily on the story one tells oneself. And since failure lies at the core of who we are, the most important stories we tell about ourselves, as well as those we read about others, are primarily tales of failing. Indeed, from the Greek tragedies to the latest news reports, there has never been a good story without some degree of failure in it. Such are the narratives that fascinate us. Why would we want to read about the inner life of robots? Failure and storytelling are intimate friends, always working in cahoots.

That's why the observation that our life has been "a complete failure," has "no meaning," or "is not worth the pain" is one many of us may make in the course of our existence. Yet few of us choose to end it right then and there in response. This is not because we lack courage (when one wants to die, one finds the courage), but because we feel that the story, failure-filled though it may be, has not run its course. We want to wait and see. And that is telling.

At any given moment, we may find our life to be less fulfilling and our existence without significance, but we know, at some deeper level, that we are not done yet. Our story is just not over, and it's frustrating—profoundly, viscerally so—to quit a story before the end, whether it's a book, a film, or your own life. Once we have reached that point, we may decide that there is nothing left to tell, but quitting the story while it is still being told is a violation not just of narrative but of nature. The longed-for meaning may be revealed at the very end, and we will no longer be there to receive the revelation. It is written, after all, that the "pearl" we are supposed to retrieve can only be found at the story's end.

Can a story save my life, then? Yes, it can. The truth is, only a story can redeem our lives. And not just our lives, but life itself. That's the reason why there are so many stories in life. Without stories, we would be ______________.

Fill in the blank with the ONE most appropriate word from the passage. Then, explain what the underlined part means in the context of the passage. Do NOT copy more than FOUR consecutive words from the passage.

02 Read the passage and follow the directions. [4 points]

전공B 서술형 8번

Science teaches us that every pleasure exacts a price, and the pain that follows is longer lasting and more intense than the pleasure that gave rise to it.

With prolonged and repeated exposure to pleasurable stimuli, our capacity to tolerate pain decreases, and our threshold for experiencing pleasure increases.

By imprinting instant and permanent memory, we are unable to forget the lessons of pleasure and pain even when we want to: hippocampal tattoos to last a lifetime.

The phylogenetically uber-ancient neurological machinery for processing pleasure and pain has remained largely intact throughout evolution and across species. It is perfectly adapted for a world of ____________. Without pleasure we wouldn't eat, drink, or reproduce. Without pain we wouldn't protect ourselves from injury and death. By raising our neural set point with repeated pleasures, we become endless strivers, never satisfied with what we have, always looking for more.

But herein lies the problem. Human beings, the ultimate seekers, have responded too well to the challenge of pursuing pleasure and avoiding pain. As a result, we've transformed the world from a place of scarcity to a place of overwhelming abundance.

Our brains are not evolved for this world of plenty. As Dr. Tom Finucane, who studies diabetes in the setting of chronic sedentary feeding, said, "<u>We are cacti in the rain forest</u>."

The net effect is that we now need more reward to feel pleasure, and less injury to feel pain. This recalibration is occurring not just at the level of the individual but also at the level of nations. Which invites the question: How do we survive and thrive in this new ecosystem? How do we raise our children? What new ways of thinking and acting will be required of us as denizens of the twenty-first century?

Who better to teach us how to avoid compulsive overconsumption than those most vulnerable to it: those struggling with addiction. Shunned for millennia across cultures as reprobates, parasites, pariahs, and purveyors of moral turpitude, people with addiction have evolved a wisdom perfectly suited to the age we live in now.

Fill in the blank with the ONE most appropriate word from the passage. Then, explain what the underlined part means in the context of the passage. Do NOT copy more than FOUR consecutive words from the passage.

03 Read the passage and follow the directions. [4 points]

전공B 서술형 9번

Excessive selflessness leads to an inability to say no. We live in fear of appearing rude and upsetting or offending people. One might believe that putting oneself first could be considered an act of selfishness—however, it actually leads to multiple benefits.

A total disregard for others' feelings isn't always necessary when it comes to putting yourself first. For example, a friend asks you to go shopping and you say yes because you don't want to let her down. Consequently, you're stressed before you've even stepped foot inside a shop; you spend the entire trip stressed for being dragged along. What would the outcome have been if you'd said no? She might initially feel somewhat put out, but she wouldn't have to put up with a grumpy, stressed-out shopping companion!

Putting yourself first can also lead to happiness all around. A growing body of research suggests that when people put themselves first they feel happier than when they prioritize others' needs. In turn, they are able to share that happiness with others. Taking time out from the kids might feel like an indulgence but if a one-hour bubble bath is what you want, your kids are going to be much happier with a relaxed parent than one who is trying to do everything for everyone, and not giving themselves a well-earned break.

If you don't start putting yourself first, you may ultimately become a negative force both for yourself and for others. In the long run, putting yourself first can often benefit everyone involved. In that sense, selfishness may—in many cases—also become an act of selflessness. Therefore, don't be afraid to just say no the next time you're asked to do something difficult.

02

Write a summary following the guidelines below.

Guidelines

- Summarize the passage above in one paragraph.
- Provide a topic sentence, two supporting ideas, and a concluding sentence based on the passage.
- Do NOT copy more than FOUR consecutive words from the passage.

2024학년도

01 **Read the passage and follow the directions.** [4 points] 전공A 서술형 10번

While tourism research has begun to flourish, the studies dealing with tourism and expressive culture are relatively sparse. It is noted that the anthropology of tourism and semiotics overemphasize the role of image consumers at the expense of the process of image creation that is a by-product of the tourist industry. In other words, while host societies have been studied, it is not frequently in terms of their own expressive culture but more often in terms of their ______________ to tourist pressures. In her work with tourist art, Jules-Rosette found that the longer an artisan was in the business of producing "tourist art," the more he developed an aesthetic that satisfied his own cultural identity. In the complex interplay of market, audience, and performers, the artisans eventually appropriated an externally imposed notion of authenticity.

The tourist, according to Dean MacCannell, is continually in search of authentic experience. In response the tourist industry caters to this craving by using evermore ingenious ways to let the tourist gaze at life as it is really lived in the host society. Yet no matter how far into the everyday domain a tourist is allowed to peek, the authenticity remains staged by the very fact that the tourist is looking at it. But if authenticity in the realm of culture is difficult for the tourist to find, what kind of experience is possible? In Interlaken, in the Bernese Oberland, it is the grandiose physical environment of the Alps. The landscape—unlike culture—cannot be staged, and most tourists prefer not to think about the numerous human intrusions—the carefully tended fields, the rebuilt streams, the many ski lifts and cog railways—for it is only with the aid of some of these that they can get close enough to experience the grandeur. The natural beauty is too large to spoil the impression of an authentic experience, and there would probably be no tourists in Interlaken if it were not for the village's unique geographic location between lakes and peaks.

Fill in the blank with the ONE most appropriate word from the passage. Then explain why the Alps can be attractive to tourists who want to experience authenticity. Do NOT copy more than FOUR consecutive words from the passage.

02 **Read the passage and follow the directions.** [4 points] 전공B 서술형 8번

A signal is a behavior or structure that alters the actions of other organisms, commonly referred to as receivers. Krebs and Dawkins describe animal signaling as an arms race between "manipulators" (signalers) and "mind-readers" (receivers). A signaler has private information about some aspect of its ability or intention and selects a signal to send to a receiver. The receiver responds by selecting an action and the benefit (or cost) depends upon the actions of both individuals. Signals can be acoustic, visual, or chemical, and they portray resource requirements to parents, fighting ability to competitors, or genetic ability to mates.

A central tenet of signaling theory is that, at an evolutionary equilibrium, both signalers and receivers must benefit from the exchange of information. If receivers did not benefit from their responses, selection would favor receivers that ignore the signal. This requirement implies that signals must convey ______________ information. This idea has been the source of controversy surrounding theoretical and empirical studies of animal communication. To understand this controversy, we must define what we mean by dishonest signaling. Searcy and Nowicki provided a formal definition of dishonest signaling. Dishonesty occurs when a receiver registers X from a signaler and responds in a way that not only benefits the signaler but would also benefit the receiver if X means Y, however, Y is false. In other words, dishonest communication occurs when a signal becomes disassociated from the signaler's ability or need. This definition highlights the benefit of dishonesty to the signaler and begs a fundamental question: <u>Why would any organism signal honestly to their opponents when dishonesty potentially delivers notable rewards?</u> If a weak individual signaled as if it was strong, then this weak individual might convince other weak individuals and some strong individuals to yield resources. Because of this benefit, the dishonest signaler's genes might spread within the population. Ultimately, the success of dishonest individuals would destroy

02

the entire system of communication. As the rate of dishonest signaling increased, natural selection would begin to favor receivers that ignored signals of strength over those that noticed them. Once receivers ignored the signal, natural selection would no longer favor the structure or behavior required for signaling. As the population approached an evolutionary equilibrium, reliable signaling would disappear altogether.

Fill in the blank with the ONE most appropriate word from the passage. Then, based on the passage, provide an answer to the question in the underlined part. Do NOT copy more than FOUR consecutive words from the passage.

03 Read the passage and follow the directions. [4 points]

전공B 서술형 9번

When we paint on canvas we create a purely physical representation. When we take a selfie on our cell phone, however, the phone produces a digital representation—that is, a recording of an object using a finite set of symbols. The phone's camera divides our face into a numerical grid of tiny cells each of which is given a number. It is these numbers that make up the essence of our digital image. This digital representation offers many benefits over a more traditional physical representation.

Digital representations can be stored for long periods of time without erosion of information. After converting our face to a series of numbers, this numerical version can be maintained and transmitted with no further loss of quality. Unlike our parent's analog photos which have degraded over time, that image of our face will remain the same for a long period.

Rather than being something static, this digital representation can be manipulated. The digital representation can be brightened and sharpened by adding visual effects. On computer programs a smile can be added, a tree in the background erased, and it would even be possible to change the color of our eyes. This is certainly something that never would have been possible for analog photos in the past.

Digital representations are storable and easy to manipulate. While these two essential qualities offer benefits, it also means that we could be victims of digital representations. The digital representations of each of us encoded by algorithms can float around online even when we do not want them to. Therefore, caution should be exercised when we upload digital representations online.

Write a summary following the guidelines below.

Guidelines

- Summarize the above passage in one paragraph.
- Provide a topic sentence, two supporting ideas, and a concluding sentence based on the passage.
- Do NOT copy more than FOUR consecutive words from the passage.

2023학년도

01 **Read the passage and follow the directions.** [4 points]

Language consumes a large proportion of time within a day while activating regions across the entire brain. Ellen Bialystok and her team tested the theory that bilingualism can increase cognitive reserve and thus delay the age of onset of Alzheimer's disease symptoms in elderly patients. Their study investigates conversion times from mild cognitive impairment to Alzheimer's disease in monolingual and bilingual patients. Although bilingualism delays the onset of symptoms, Bialystok says, once diagnosed, the decline to full-blown Alzheimer's disease is much faster in bilingual people than in monolingual people because the disease is more severe.

Imagine sandbags holding back the floodgates of a river. At some point the river is going to win. <u>The sturdiness of the sandbag barrier is holding back the flood</u> and at the point when they are diagnosed with mild cognitive impairment they already have severe pathology but there has been no evidence of it because they have been able to function thanks to their high cognitive reserve. Even the most resilient people have their limits. When they can no longer resist, the floodgates get completely washed out. As a result, they crash faster.

In the five-year study, researchers followed 158 patients who had been diagnosed with mild cognitive impairment. For the study, they classified bilingual people as having high cognitive reserve and monolingual people as having low cognitive reserve. Patients were matched on age, education, and cognitive level at the time of their diagnosis of mild cognitive impairment. The researchers followed their six-month interval appointments at a hospital memory clinic to see the point at which diagnoses changed from mild cognitive impairment to Alzheimer's disease. The conversion time for bilinguals, 1.8 years after initial diagnosis, was significantly faster than it was for monolinguals, who took 2.6 years to convert to Alzheimer's disease. This difference suggests that bilingual patients had more severe neuropathology at the time they were diagnosed with mild cognitive impairment than the monolinguals, even though they showed the same level of cognitive function.

These results contribute to the growing body of evidence demonstrating that bilinguals are more ______________ in dealing with neurodegeneration than monolinguals. They operate at a higher level of cognition because of their cognitive reserves, which means that many of these individuals will withstand the neuropathology longer. This study adds new evidence by showing that the decline is steeper once a clinical threshold has been crossed, presumably because there is more disease already in the brain.

Fill in the blank with the ONE most appropriate word from the passage. Then, explain what the underlined part means. Do NOT copy more than FOUR consecutive words from the passage.

02 Read the passage and follow the directions. [4 points]

Tunnel vision is an experience common to almost everyone. While experiencing tunnel vision, the world seems to shrink and the field of vision narrows, as if the person is looking through a tube or pipe. Attention focuses on one or two small details, context is lost, and understanding becomes very difficult. This is the consequence of the brain's limited ability to process visual stimuli. Tunnel vision occurs when your mind receives too many bits of visual information that do not make sense as part of a larger system. There are two main causes of tunnel vision as follows.

A general lack of background and/or contextual knowledge is the first major cause of tunnel vision. Learners with a weakness in art or physical education might suffer from tunnel vision when they attempt to paint or remember the rules of baseball. Their lack of background knowledge in painting and baseball might cause them to lose track of the larger flow of a game or piece of art, even if they are otherwise effective learners.

Poor reading habits are the second major cause of tunnel vision. Slow reading is one such bad habit. Many people read slowly because they are afraid they will not comprehend everything if they speed up. Reading too slowly encourages the brain to obsess over each little feature of a text and creates a perfect situation for tunnel vision to arise. It clogs up the visual system with too many individual letters and words.

As mentioned above, tunnel vision is most likely to occur due to a general lack of background information and/or poor reading habits. If there is a lack of contextual knowledge, then the learner must seek elsewhere to acquire it. When you struggle as a reader, speeding up might cure your tunnel vision.

Write a summary following the guildelines below.

Guidelines

- Summarize the above passage in one paragraph.
- Provide a topic sentence, two supporting ideas, and a concluding sentence based on the passage.
- Do NOT copy more than FIVE consecutive words from the passage.

03 **Read the passage and follow the directions.** [4 points]

Automation fundamentally alters the way we behave or think. When we work with computers, we often fall victim to two cognitive ailments—complacency and bias—that can make us error-prone. Automation complacency occurs when a computer lulls us into a delusion of security. Confident that the machine will work flawlessly and handle any problem that crops up, we become inattentive. We become disengaged from our work, and the things going on around us fade into the background. Automation bias occurs when we place too much faith in the accuracy of the information coming through our monitors. Our trust in the software becomes so strong that we ignore or discount other information sources, including our own eyes and ears. When a computer provides incorrect or insufficient data, we remain oblivious to the error. Indeed, automation turns us from actors into observers. That shift may make our lives easier, but it can also inhibit the development of ______________.

In the small island of Igloolik located in northern Canada, Inuit hunters have for some 4,000 years ventured out from their homes and traveled across miles of ice and tundra to search for game. The hunters have navigated vast stretches of the barren Arctic terrain, where landmarks are few, snow formations are in constant flux, and trails disappear overnight. The extraordinary way the Inuit can discover the best paths is born of their prolonged struggles with winds, snowdrift patterns, stars, and tides. Inuit culture, however, is changing now. The Igloolik hunters have begun to rely on computer-generated maps to get around, but reports of serious accidents during hunts have spread. A hunter who hasn't developed an independent means of finding his way can easily become lost, particularly if his GPS receiver fails. The routes so meticulously plotted on satellite maps can also lead them onto thin ice or into other hazards a skilled navigator would avoid. The GPS has already brought a deterioration in how they intuitively adjust for changing conditions.

To know demands action: each time we collide with the real, we deepen our knowledge of the world and become more fully part of it. While we're wrestling with a difficult task, we may be motivated by an anticipation of the ends of our labors, but it's the work itself—the means—that makes us who we are. Computer automation severs the ends from the means. It makes getting what we want easier, but it divorces us from the very struggles that make our desires meaningful. As we transform ourselves into creatures who <u>watch the screen rather than manipulate the yoke,</u> we face an existential question: Does our essence still lie in what we know, or are we now content to be defined by what we want? If we don't grapple with that question ourselves, our gadgets will be happy to answer it for us.

Fill in the blank with the ONE most appropriate word from the passage. Then, explain what the underlined part means. Do NOT copy more than FOUR consecutive words from the passage.

2022학년도

01 **Read the passage and follow the directions.** [4 points] 전공A 서술형 11번

Many species of octopus and squid are known to exhibit a particularly effective behavior that enables them to escape from predators. In the region of their intestines the animals have a special sac-like organ. In the wall of this sac there is a gland which secretes a brown or black liquid rich in the pigment melanin, this is ink. When threatened the animal has the ability to compress the ink sac and squirt a jet of the liquid from its anus. It is thought that the cloud of ink hanging in the water forms a dummy squid termed a pseudomorph, which attracts and holds the attention of the predator allowing the animal to dart away to safety. The ______________ is made all the more effective because long thin species produce long thin pseudomorphs and more round species produce rounder clouds of ink.

Squid and octopus are molluscs, taxonomic relatives of the garden slug and snail. Can you imagine a slug squirting out ink to leave a pseudomorph hanging in the air to decoy a bird predator while the slug made its escape? Of course you can't, for the simple reason that this behavioral strategy can only work when the animal is surrounded by a medium that will support the ink cloud for a sufficient period to allow the escape. In water this works, but in the less dense medium of air it would not.

Some species of octopus and squid are inhabitants of the ocean depths. Here light penetration from the surface is minimal or zero and the seawater is a constant inky black. Obviously the ink-dummy strategy would be no more effective here than it would be in air. The pseudomorph would hang in the water column, but it is unlikely that such deception would be successful against the inky-black backdrop. In this situation species such as the deep-water squid Heteroteuthis secrete a luminescent ink, creating a brief flash of light which is thought to confuse a potential predator just long enough for an escape to be affected.

Fill in the blank with the ONE most appropriate word from the passage. Then, using evidence from the passage, explain why the ink-dummy tactic would not likely succeed in the air and the deep sea, respectively. Do NOT copy more than FOUR consecutive words from the passage.

02 **Read the passage and follow the directions.** [4 points] 전공B 서술형 8번

Fashion criticism should be rigorous, clearly stated, and historically informed. It should neither oversimplify (as current fashion criticism often does) nor be unnecessarily obscure (as current art criticism often is). It should look for vitality and boldness, and distinguish the original from the derivative. It should track a designer's development—or point out standstill or regression—and attempt to figure out what led the designer to make these specific aesthetic choices, elaborate on the techniques and materials that have been used—and finally pass judgment. As already mentioned, a proper judgment is something more than mere opinion—it is a *reasoned* or *justified* opinion which aims for broader validity. Criticism can never be completely objective. It must necessarily to a great extent be subjective, saying as much about the critic as about the object under scrutiny. Which is why writing criticism necessarily means exposing yourself. Writing criticism is about struggling to come to terms with what you do not yet know exactly how to deal with, to pass judgment, to expose yourself, knowing that you expose yourself, putting your prestige and your very identity at risk. As Pierre Bourdieu formulated it: "Taste classifies, and it classifies the classifier." This is a truth that holds for all of us, but it is especially acute in the case of the critic, whose judgment is at the greatest public scrutiny. Writing real criticism is about putting yourself on the line every single time.

What about disagreements between critics? They should be welcomed. It is never a good sign when too many people are in agreement about too much. It almost always means that we are thinking too little. There should be disagreements between critics. Two critics can certainly disagree about the relative merits of two designers, such as for instance Alexandre Herchcovitch and Phoebe Philo. However, one should also note that there will usually be a high degree of convergence between critics in their judgments. One might prefer Herchcovitch and the other Philo, and even find a certain collection plain tasteless, but it would be highly surprising if one of them argued that Herchcovitch or Philo is a designer with virtually no aesthetic merit. Would a serious critic pass such a judgment? There will be disagreements, but disagreements are possible only against a much larger background of ______________.

Fill in the blank with the ONE most appropriate word from the passage. Then, explain what the underlined part means in the context of criticism. Do NOT copy more than FOUR consecutive words from the passage.

03 Read the passage and follow the directions. [4 points] 전공B 서술형 9번

What did a presidential administration mean when they proposed "revenue enhancement" through "user fees"? Translated, "revenue enhancement" through "user fees" is taxes paid by citizens. This is an example of doublespeak. Doublespeak is carefully designed and constructed language used to make things seem different from what they are, and it comes in several forms.

One form of doublespeak is inflated language. Inflated language is designed to make the ordinary seem extraordinary. Cheap material used to make a purse could be described as "genuine imitation leather" or a glass stone in a piece of jewelry as a "real counterfeit diamond." These types of descriptions can also be used to describe situations. A guide telling a group of French tourists that their visit to the Eifel Tower is a "once in a lifetime opportunity" is almost certainly using doublespeak, especially as the attraction is not far from home. This type of language gives a perception of importance to situations and things that would not normally be considered important.

Another form of doublespeak is jargon. Jargon as doublespeak occurs when professional language is used with people not "in-the-know." The use of jargon can be an efficient way of communicating within a specialized group. But when used with those not in-the-know, the intention may be to give an air of profundity, authority, and prestige. If a computer technician tells a novice computer user with an internet connection problem to "power-cycle" their router rather than saying "you need to unplug the router and plug it back in," the technician might be using doublespeak.

Doublespeak is language used to make the bad seem good and the basic profound. As shown in the examples above, it is present in many aspects of our lives. Keeping awareness of the definition and forms of doublespeak can help us discriminate between what someone wants us to believe and the reality.

Write a summary following the guidelines below.

Guidelines

- Summarize the above passage in one paragraph.
- Based on the passage, provide a topic sentence, two supporting details, and a concluding sentence.
- Do NOT copy more than FIVE consecutive words from the passage.

2021학년도

01 **Read the passage and follow the directions.** [4 points] 전공A 서술형 11번

"Palette" is a homophone for the term "palate," signifying both the roof of the mouth and the sense of taste. While the palette is both the board on which the paint is placed and the paint itself, the palate is only juxtaposed to the canvas for gustatory compositions, unless one considers that the palate—as in the sense of taste—is the tongue which generates flavor by crushing the food mass and the taste buds on to the hard roof of the mouth, a rich analogue to the application of paint to canvas. Receptor cells on the tongue are responsible for sensing particular flavors, the primary ones being bitter, sweet, salt, and sour. The stimuli from these cells in combination with saliva and the olfactory sense generate taste. Just as the primary hues generate all others in the color spectrum, the four taste cells blend to create all flavors. Thus <u>the palate is the palette for the chef's creative endeavors</u>. Crushing the tongue against the roof of the mouth drives the food mass into the taste buds, and this clamping or sucking motion intensifies and prolongs the flavor.

However, taste also requires the intervention of the ________________ which must recognize, evaluate, and categorize the stimuli from the mouth and nasal passages. The evaluative quality of taste or the recognition and judgment of flavor can be processed only in the brain, and, as with the visual imagery of painting, the quality of taste is assessed in relationship to a history of tastes, and the pleasure or revulsion generated relates in large part to the familiarity of the flavor. The tasting subject frequently judges the outcome of the experience in opposition to or alliance with previous experiences of the same or similar tastes. This process might be defined as the "semiotics" of taste.

Fill in the blank with the ONE most appropriate word from the passage. Then, explain what the underlined part means.

02 Read the passage and follow the directions. [4 points]

전공B 서술형 10번

The history of Impressionism is indeed inextricably bound up with the quarrels and power struggles that almost immediately threatened the very feasibility of the exhibitions for which, essentially, its members had come together in the first place. From 1874 to 1886 there were eight exhibitions, six of which revealed the artists' __________ of cohesion and shared ambition. In order to share the costs of organizing their exhibitions more widely, they were forced to admit painters who were less talented or more conservative. Moreover, they also had to deal as best they could with the personal ambitions of their members and, although the statutes of 1873 had been carefully drafted so as to give the paintings without a salon and without an audience a real chance, the experience of each exhibition showed that none of them was really ready for this adventure.

From one Impressionist exhibition to the next, we can trace the relations between the different chapels within the group, but also its capacity to generate new sources of dynamism. In 1876, Caillebotte emerged. In 1879, Gauguin was introduced by Pissarro and confirmed by Degas. In 1886 the neo-Impressionists barged in, eating up exhibition space and edging out Impressionism itself. Every new arrival, except for Caillebotte and Mary Cassatt, was greeted by wailing and the gnashing of teeth. But it has to be admitted that these newcomers were born from and because of Impressionism.

But then what do these recruits really matter? As of the late 1870s, the movement was no longer the property of its artists. Already, they were moving away. Cézanne, Renoir, Monet, and even Degas, who continued to promote his little realist school, had already chosen their solitary paths. They wanted no lack of recognition from the Salon. Also, and above all, they wanted one-person exhibitions where their work could be appreciated in and for itself, where visitors would not get lost in comparisons, where critics would not confuse the true Impressionist and true painter with <u>the last-minute guest</u>. The history of Impression would be written by several hands, but above all by individuals.

Fill in the blank with the ONE most appropriate word from the passage, and explain what the underlined part means.

03 Read the passage and follow the directions. [4 points]

전공B 서술형 11번

In the classroom today, there are a growing number of children who are being raised outside their parents' home cultures after moving across geographic boundaries because of their parents' employment. Children in this situation are called "Third Culture Kids" (TCKs). To be categorized as a TCK, a child must spend more than three years outside their passport country during the developmental years, from birth to eighteen years old. Living as a TCK can provide benefits as well as undeniable challenges.

Growing up internationally, TCKs are able to become speakers of multiple languages. Learning a language can be easier if you have daily exposure to it. TCKs attend schools taught in the target language and encounter the language in everyday life. This can help them learn the language more quickly, especially during their formative years. Depending on how much time is spent in a country, the level of fluency can vary, but it would not be unlikely for a TCK to be capable of speaking three or more languages by the end of high school.

Despite this benefit, there is an undeniable challenge that comes along with being a TCK. The multiple shifts in location can lead to a sense of isolation for these children. Having to repeat the process of moving and adjusting to new life circumstances can take a serious toll. Such changes can prevent children from maintaining relationships with those outside their immediate family. Hence, isolation becomes the most common challenge for TCKs.

Given the modern context in which the migration and transnational flow is increasing, understanding TCKs' lives will be a valuable resource for international and global education. It is important that educators support this growing community by maximizing the potential benefits of cross-cultural experiences while helping them navigate the challenges that arise.

Write a summary following the guidelines below.

Guidelines

- Summarize the above passage in one paragraph.
- Provide a topic sentence, two supporting ideas, and a concluding sentence based on the passage.
- Do NOT copy more than FIVE consecutive words from the passage.

2020학년도

01 **Read the passage and follow the directions.** [4 points] 전공A 서술형 8번

According to W. Ury and R. Fisher's best-selling book, you can walk away from any negotiation. The authors purport that by having a good walk-away option (BATNA: Best Alternative to a Negotiated Agreement), you protect yourself from difficult opponents. They advocate walking away from more powerful opponents so you don't give away the store, or at the very least, make a sale that doesn't "make sense."

In theory, this might make sense, but in the world of selling when you haggle with your customers, it is folly.

Telling a salesperson to walk away from the table and kissing off a sale is a bit cavalier for an expert who's never had to make a living by making a quota. For those of us who have spent a significant portion of our careers in sales, we know we would never just up and walk away from a potential sale, no matter how slim the chances are of actually getting the business. That is one of the characteristics that makes salespeople successful: <u>irrational optimism in the face of certain defeat</u>.

Technically, you might have the ability to abort settling on a big sale, but you still have a quota to make and a job to keep.

With that said, however, salespeople are always better dealers when they've already reached their quota. Why? Because they don't need the business. Still, they may indeed walk away from a potential sale, but they always come back as the situation changes.

As a sales manager, I urged my team to have as many potential prospects as possible. I encouraged them to be working on many potential deals, not just because it would help them make quota, but also because it made them tougher negotiators. They were all much better at holding their ground when they didn't feel desperate to have a customer's business.

Here's an important side note:

At times, I get the opportunity to ask about the skills taught in the *Getting to Yes* seminar with people who attended the workshop in the past. I always ask them, "What is the thing you most remember about the Ury and Fisher tenet?" to which I receive the almost universal response: "The thing I remember most is to make sure you know your BATNA."

Even though most cannot recall what the initials stand for, they believe that knowing which options they have if a settlement can't be reached empowers them a bit. I find it curious that the term most remembered from a course designed specifically to improve negotiation skills is one that describes how to walk away from the table—in other words, by refusing to ____________.

Fill in the blank with the ONE most appropriate word from the passage. Then, explain what the underlined part means. Do NOT copy more than FOUR consecutive words from the passage.

02 Read the passage and follow the directions. [4 points]

전공A 서술형 9번

Included in the possible outcomes of culture learning are several not always desirable results, such as alienation from the native culture and marginality. Marginality refers to a situation in which a person, for a variety of reasons (such as race or religion) remains on the outskirts of a social or cultural group. Marginal individuals or groups are isolated, and, in the words of John Lum, their actions "do not reflect well any one culture." Marginality is not necessarily always a(n) ____________ factor. It plays a part in all cultural change; it is part of the lives of children whose parents remain monocultural while they become bicultural. Richard Rodriguez' poignant book *Hunger of Memory* recounts the pains of cultural transition and the agonies of the loss of cultural identity. In anthropology, the marginal person has often been seen as the one most likely to accept change and to be willing to deal with the foreigner (e.g., the anthropologist) who comes along and asks such seemingly stupid questions.

That marginality and mediation are lonely states is also beautifully expressed in an often-quoted passage from the autobiography of Nehru:

I have become a queer mixture of the East and the West, out of place everywhere, at home nowhere. Perhaps my thoughts and approach to life are more akin to what is called Western than Eastern, but India clings to me, as she does to all her children, in innumerable ways; and behind me lie, somewhere in the subconscious, racial memories of a hundred, or whatever the number may be, generations of Brahmans. I cannot get rid of either that past inheritance or my recent acquisitions. They are both part of me, and, though they help me in both the East and the West, they also create in me a negative feeling of spiritual loneliness not only in public activities but in life itself. I am a stranger and alien in the West. I cannot be of it. But in my own country also, sometimes, I have an exile's feeling.

Lum concludes that "marginal people who fall may be rootless or alienated; those who rise may be synthesizers." They may become marginal in all cultures, belonging wholly to none and without cultural identity. On the other hand, they may cross cultural boundaries and leap cultural chasms.

Fill in the blank with the ONE most appropriate word from the passage. Then, explain what the underlined part means. Do NOT copy more than FOUR consecutive words from the passage.

03 **Read the passage and follow the directions.** [4 points] 전공A 서술형 10번

Many contemporary tourists avoid encountering reality directly but thrive on psuedo-events in their tourism experiences thus affecting tourism entrepreneurs and indigenous populations. For one, many tourists prefer to stay in comfortable accomodations, thereby separating themselves from the local people and environment. For instance, sleeping in a hotel filled with the comforts of home may insulate them from the fact that they are in a foreign land. In addition, much of the tourism industry is bolstered by the use of tourist-focused institutions such as museums and shopping centers. The needs of the contemporary tourists have induced entrepreneurs to build tourist attractions for the sole purpose of entertaining visitors. This detracts from the colorful local culture and presents a false view of the indigenous cultures. The other group affected by modern tourism is the local population. These people find themselves learning languages in a contrived way based on the changing tides of tourist groups solely for marketing purposes. Furthermore, when curious visitors do venture outside their cultural bubbles, they enjoy, albeit intrusively, watching locals doing their daily tasks, thereby making them the subject of the tourist gaze. In sum, while tourism is on the rise, the trend is to maintain a distance from the real environment rather than to see the locations for their own values, and this negatively affects tourism entrepreneurs and local people.

Complete the topic sentence in the handout. Do NOT copy more than FOUR consecutive words from the passage.

Handout
Topic sentence : Modern tourists' demands ______________________
____
A. Effects on tourism entrepreneurs • Provide comfortable accommodations • Create tourist-focused entertainment attractions
B. Effects on local populations • Learn tourists' languages • Become the objects of the tourist gaze

____

____

____

____

____

04 Read the passage and follow the directions. [4 points]

전공A 서술형 11번

You can learn a lot about a society by examining who or what it reveres. You can learn even more by studying what it is afraid of, as a new exhibit at the Morgan Library and Museum in New York proves. "Medieval Monsters" takes the visitor on a jaunt through Europe's Middle Ages via its beasties. Artefacts such as illuminated manuscripts and tapestries are adorned with unicorns, dragons, antelopes with forked tails, blemmyes—humanoids with no heads, their faces instead on their chests—and more.

Monsters were often dispatched in the service of a specific ideology. Medieval power brokers used incredible creatures as a medium to display their magnificence: saints, clergymen and kings were depicted as slayers to show that they were extraordinary. King Henry VI's rule over his land was symbolized through heraldry, which featured an antelope with horns thought to be sharp enough to cut down trees. Maps provided another opportunity to wield ____________. A 16th-century plot of Iceland shows the island ringed by various mythological beasts. Their purpose was to scare off competing traders and keep the waterways clear for colonial powers.

Most of the early manuscripts were produced by monks by virtue of their education, and monsters were a medium through which the divine and the unknowable could be visualized. As ships went farther afield in the 15th and 16th centuries, the recurrence of "sea swine" and (1) <u>Leviathan-esque water creatures</u> may reflect an increasing fear of an endless and deadly sea. Demons and the gaping "maw of hell" could illustrate a fear of death, or dying without absolution. Drawings of unicorns, mermaids and sphinxes reveal a sense of wonder about the supernatural.

How do the insights of the exhibition apply to modern monsters, and contemporary Western anxieties? (2) <u>Killer robots</u> point to a fear of indestructible, clever, artificial intelligence-powered computers. Angela Becerra Vidergar, a scholar at Stanford, suggests that the fascination with zombies and the undead in media is one of the creative legacies of the Second World War, when the Holocaust and the use of the atomic bomb changed perceptions about humanity's propensity for mass destruction. Modern art and society are not yet rid of the instincts found in the Morgan's medieval collection.

Fill in the blank with the ONE most appropriate word from the passage. Then, identify ONE common human emotion that (1) and (2) represent, and explain the reason why the identified emotion is represented by (2). Do NOT copy more than FOUR consecutive words from the passage.

05 Read the passage and follow the directions. [4 points]

전공A 서술형 12번

We've come to assume that just about any bug we're saddled with—from strep to staph—can be wiped out with a quick round of antibiotics. But in the U.S. alone, roughly 2 million people every year get infections that can't be treated with antibiotics, and 23,000 of them die as a result. The bacteria to blame are now present in every corner of the planet, according to a landmark report from the World Health Organization (WHO). In some countries, about 50% of people infected with K. pneumoniae or E. coli bacteria won't respond to our most powerful antibiotics, say global health experts. That suggests doctors are increasingly running out of (1) <u>the ammunition</u> they rely on to fight these harmful microbes.

Bacteria have been evolving to resist the drugs designed to kill them since the first antibiotic was discovered in 1928. But our overuse of antibiotics in farming, prescription drugs and antibacterial soaps has supercharged (2) <u>the process</u>. The WHO report was a sober warning of a dire future, but globally, progress is slowly being made.

France used to have the highest rate of antibiotic prescription in Europe, but a government mandate helped lower the number of doctor-issued Rxs by 26% in six years.

In Sweden, regulations to phase out preventive use of antibiotics in agriculture—in which low doses are given to keep animals healthy and plump—cut sales of the drugs for farming by 67% since 1986. The Netherlands and Denmark have also restricted antibiotic use on livestock.

Progress in the U.S. has been slower. The Food and Drug Administration recently tried to encourage farmers to voluntarily reduce antibiotics in farming. The agency is also taking steps to curb use of antibacterials in some consumer goods, requiring manufacturers to prove that antibacterials are better than simple soap and water in keeping germs at bay.

Before antibiotics, something as minor as a cut or a sore throat could be a death sentence. While some ____________ has recently been made in the right direction, some might say that much more needs to be done.

Fill in the blank with the ONE most appropriate word from the passage. Then, specify what the underlined parts (1) and (2) refer to, respectively. Do NOT copy more than THREE consecutive words from the passage.

06 Read the passage and follow the directions. [4 points] 전공B 서술형 9번

What could be better than studying physics under Albert Einstein? A lot, it turns out. While geniuses have done much to help society progress and flourish, perhaps they don't belong in front of the classroom. While logic dictates that the best teachers would be the most capable and accomplished people, there are two other qualities that are more vital than intelligence.

The first quality of effective teachers is that they had to put forth a lot of effort into their studies. While this may seem counterintuitive, it is probably more helpful to be guided by a person who had to work daily to master difficult concepts than by someone for whom learning was a breeze. Students often gravitate toward prodigies like Einstein because their expertise seems so effortless, but that's a mistake. It makes more sense to study under people who had to struggle to become experts because they've gone through the process of building their knowledge one concept at a time.

The next quality is a little more obvious but is often overlooked: being able to explain content clearly. A teacher who has a long list of publications probably isn't going to remember how to methodically explain the basics. In the first university course he taught, Einstein wasn't able to attract much interest in the esoteric subject of thermodynamics: Just three students signed up, and they were all friends of his. The next semester he had to cancel the class after only one student enrolled. This example shows how someone who has inborn genius may not be able to relate to students' ignorance to help them understand abstract concepts.

It's often said that those who can't do teach, yet the reality is that the best doers are often the worst teachers. So, teachers' most important qualities are having had the experience of building their knowledge and having the ability to make content easy to grasp. Being a great physicist doesn't make one a great physics teacher. Rather than taking an introduction to physics class with Einstein, it would be more valuable to learn from his protégé who spent years figuring out how to explain what it would be like to chase a beam of light.

Write a summary following the guidelines below.

Guidelines

- Summarize the above passage in one paragraph.
- Provide a topic sentence, two supporting ideas, and a concluding sentence based on the passage.
- Do NOT copy more than FIVE consecutive words from the passage.

2019학년도

01 **Read the passage and follow the directions.** [2 points] 전공A 기입형 8번

Ancient Easterners saw the world as consisting of continuous substances while ancient Westerners tended to see the world as being composed of discrete objects or separate atoms. Remarkably, it is still the same in the modern era.

In a survey of the values of middle managers, Hampden-Turner and Trompenaars examined whether respondents from both Eastern and Western cultures thought of a company as a system to organize tasks or as an organism coordinating people working together. They asked respondents to choose between the following definitions:

(a) A company is a system designed to perform functions and tasks in an efficient way. People are hired to fulfill these functions with the help of machines and other equipment. They are paid for the tasks they perform.

(b) A company is a group of people working together. The people have social relations with other people and with the organization. The functioning is dependent on these relations.

About 75 percent of Americans chose the first definition, and more than 50 percent of Canadians, Australians, British, Dutch, and Swedes chose that definition. About a third of a group of Japanese and Singaporeans chose it. Thus for the Westerners, especially the Americans and the other people of primarily northern European culture, a company is an atomistic, modular place where people perform their distinctive functions. For the Easterners, a company is an organism where the social relations are an integral part of what holds things together.

Fill in the blank with the ONE most appropriate word from the passage.

Research shows that people from Western cultures tend to see the world in a more atomistic way. This view leads them to see a social institution like a workplace as a system to perform distinctive functions. On the other hand, according to the Easterners' perspective, a company is seen as an interdependent organism. Its function is made possible by ________________ among its members as well as between the members and the organization. Knowledge of such differences can be helpful for intercultural understanding.

____

02 Read the passage and follow the directions. [4 points]

전공A 서술형 13번

There's no shortage of therapies for autism, some of which work well, some not so well. But there is one simple treatment that hasn't been getting the attention it may deserve: time. According to a new study in the *Journal of Child Psychology and Psychiatry*, some children who receive behavioral interventions to treat autism might be able to age out of their symptoms, outgrowing them like last year's shoes.

The idea of maturing out of psychological ills is not new. All 10 personality disorders, for example—including schizoid, which shares features with schizophrenia—can lessen as people age. Some of this may be attributable to patients' learning to manage their symptoms, but it's also possible that the brain, which is still developing into our late 20s, is improving too. "The fact that these things aren't engraved in granite is terribly exciting," says psychologist Mark Lenzenweger of the State University of New York at Binghamton.

There have been hints that <u>this kind of remission</u> might be possible in autism, but previous studies were plagued with questions about whether the children who had apparently shed their autism were properly diagnosed with the disorder in the first place. In the current analysis, a team led by psychologist Deborah Fein of the University of Connecticut looked at 34 people ages 8 to 21 who had been diagnosed with autism but no longer met the criteria for the disorder. It compared them with 44 patients in the same age group who still had symptoms. Both groups had received similar treatments. After the researchers corrected for other variables, the subjects with the better outcomes seemed simply to have matured out of the condition.

"I view it as a landmark kind of study," says Geraldine Dawson, chief science officer for Autism Speaks. Others disagree. It's possible, they say, that some kids just mask their symptoms, imitating healthy behaviors that they come to appreciate as desirable. Still, it's hard to dismiss Fein's work entirely. The 34 subjects whose symptoms had vanished were able to attend school without one-on-one assistance and needed no further social-skills training. Something had to account for that, and maturation, in this research at least, is the best answer.

Describe what the underlined part refers to. Provide TWO pieces of evidence showing that the group of 34 subjects in Fein's work had recovered from autism. Do NOT copy more than THREE consecutive words from the passage.

03 Read the passage and follow the directions. [4 points]

전공B 서술형 5번

Inanimate objects are classified scientifically into three major categories. The goal of all inanimate objects is to resist man and ultimately to defeat him, and the three major classifications are based on the method each object uses to achieve its purpose.

As a general rule, any object capable of breaking down at the moment when it is almost needed will do so. The automobile is typical of the category. With the cunning typical of its breed, the automobile never breaks down while entering a filling station. It waits until it reaches a downtown intersection in the middle of the rush hour. Thus it creates maximum inconvenience, frustration and irritability among its human cargo, thereby reducing its owner's life span.

Many inanimate objects, of course, find it extremely difficult to break down. Keys, for example, are almost totally incapable of breaking down. Therefore, they have had to evolve a different technique for resisting man. They get lost. Science has still not solved the mystery of how they do it, and no man has ever caught one of them in the act of getting lost. The most plausible theory is that they have developed a secret method of locomotion which they are able to conceal the instant a human eye falls upon them.

Scientists have been struck by the fact that things that break down virtually never get lost, while things that get lost hardly ever break down. A furnace, for example, will invariably break down at the depth of the first winter cold wave, but it will never get lost. A woman's purse, which after all does have some inherent capacity for breaking down, hardly ever does. Some persons believe this constitutes evidence that inanimate objects are not entirely hostile to man, and that a negotiated peace is possible.

The third class of objects is the most curious of all. These include such objects as cigarette lighters and flashlights. It is inaccurate, of course, to say that they never work. They work once, usually for the first few hours after being brought home, and then quit. Thereafter, they never work again. In fact, it is widely assumed that they are built for the purpose of not working.

They have truly defeated man by training him never to expect anything of them, and in return they have given man the only peace he receives from inanimate society. He does not expect his cigarette lighter to light or his flashlight to illuminate, and when they don't it does not raise his blood pressure. He cannot attain that ____________ with furnaces and keys, and cars and women's purses as long as he demands that they work for their keep.

Fill in the blank with the ONE most appropriate word from the passage. Then, state THREE methods that inanimate objects use to resist man.

____

____

____

____

____

04 **Read the passage and follow the directions.** [5 points] 전공B 서술형 7번

Melatonin—a hormone naturally produced by the pineal gland—is released when darkness falls, signaling to the body that it is time to rest. While it is well known for its sleep-inducing properties, now, as a result of growing research, scientists know that the substance not only induces sleep but also keeps the brain in order.

One way it does so is as an antidepressant. Seasonal affective disorder is a form of depression common during winter months, thought to be the effect of a mismatch between one's normal sleep cycle and the shifting light-dark cycle. For some people this rhythm mismatch depresses mood. However, this disorder can be readily treated with melatonin. Research has shown that low doses of melatonin along with bright light therapy can realign the sleep-wake cycle and alleviate symptoms of seasonal affective disorder.

Another way it keeps the brain in order is by slowing the cognitive impairment associated with age-related diseases such as Alzheimer's. Amyloid beta and tau proteins are toxic and they build up in patients with this disease, leading to cognitive decline. Melatonin helps to offset the toxic effects of these proteins, but people with Alzheimer's disease produce one fifth the amount of melatonin as healthy young adults. Therefore, melatonin supplements can improve cognitive function in these patients by countering the toxic influence of these two harmful proteins.

These promising newly found effects of this hormone have attracted much attention and have stimulated further research to make humans healthier and happier. What is clear is that melatonin is no longer just an alternative to counting sheep.

Write a summary following the guidelines below.

Guidelines

- Summarize the above passage in one paragraph.
- Provide a topic sentence, two supporting ideas, and a concluding sentence based on the passage.
- Do NOT copy more than FIVE consecutive words from the passage.

2018학년도

01 **Read the passage and follow the directions.** [2 points] 전공A 서술형 2번

From the very beginning of school we make books and reading a constant source of possible failure and public humiliation. When children are little we make them read aloud, before the teacher and other children, so that we can be sure they "know" all the words they are reading. This means that when they don't know a word, they are going to make a mistake, right in front of the whole class. Instantly they are made to realize that they have done something wrong. Perhaps some of the other children will begin to wave their hands and say, "Ooooh! O-o-o-oh!" Perhaps they will just giggle, or nudge each other, or make a face. Perhaps the teacher will say, "Are you sure?" or ask someone else what he thinks. Or perhaps, if the teacher is kind, she will just smile a sweet, sad smile—often one of the most painful punishments a child can suffer in school. In any case, the child who has made the mistake knows he has made it, and feels foolish, stupid, and ashamed, just as any of us would in his shoes.

Before long many children associate books and reading with mistakes, real or feared, and penalties and humiliation. This may not seem sensible, but it is natural. Mark Twain once said that a cat that sat on a hot stove lid would never sit on one again—but it would never sit on a cold one either. As true of ____________ as of cats. If they, so to speak, sit on a hot book a few times, if books cause them humiliation and pain, they are likely to decide that the safest thing to do is to leave all books alone.

Fill in the blank with the ONE most appropriate word from the passage.

02 Read the passage and follow the directions. [4 points]

전공A 서술형 14번

For at least 10,000 years, humans have been manipulating their own brains by drinking alcohol. And for at least the last few decades, researchers have wondered whether alcohol had a positive effect on physical health. Study after study seemed to suggest that people who imbibed one alcoholic beverage per day—a 12-ounce beer, a 6-ounce glass of wine, or a 1.5-ounce shot of spirits—had healthier hearts than did people who abstained from drinking altogether. A drink a day, it seemed, kept the cardiologist away.

Yet the methods in these studies may be flawed. When Kaye Fillmore, a researcher at the University of California, San Francisco, and her team analyzed 54 published studies on how moderate drinking affects the heart, they found that most of the drink-a-day studies had not used random assignment. In studies with random assignment, researchers used coin tosses or the like to decide into which condition—the control group or various experimental groups—each study participant should go. By letting chance dictate who goes into which group, researchers are more likely to end up with truly comparable groups.

Instead of randomly assigning participants to drinking and non-drinking groups, though, 47 of the 54 studies compared people who were already having one drink daily to people who were already teetotaling. Why is this design method a problem? In the United States, where most of these studies took place, many people have a drink once in a while. Usually, people who never drink abstain for a reason, such as religious prohibitions or medical concerns.

In fact, Fillmore and her team found that many of the nondrinkers in these studies were abstaining from alcohol for medical reasons, including advanced age or a history of alcoholism. In other words, the nondrinking groups in most of the studies included more unhealthy people to begin with, compared to the drinking groups. As a result, these studies didn't show that drinking alcohol led to better health. Instead, they showed that better health often leads to a level of alcohol consumption that is moderate.

First, describe the characteristics of the participants in the two groups in 47 of the 54 studies. Second, explain why those 47 studies were flawed in design.

03 Read the passage and follow the directions. [4 points]

전공B 서술형 3번

The act of searching for and finding underground supplies of water using nothing more than a rod is commonly known as "dowsing." Many dowsers in Germany claim that they respond to "earthrays" that emanate from water. These earthrays, say the dowsers, are a subtle form of radiation potentially hazardous to human health. As a result of these claims, the German government in the mid-1980s conducted a 2-year experiment to investigate the possibility that dowsing is a genuine skill.

A group of university physicists in Munich, Germany, were provided a grant of 400,000 marks to conduct the study. Approximately 500 candidate dowsers were recruited to participate in preliminary tests of their skill. To avoid fraudulent claims, the 43 individuals who seemed to be the most successful in the preliminary tests were selected for the final, carefully controlled, experiment.

The researchers set up a 10-meter-long line on the ground floor of a vacant barn, along which a small wagon could be moved. Attached to the wagon was a short length of pipe, perpendicular to the test line, that was connected by hoses to a pump with water. The ________________ along the line for each trial of the experiment was assigned using a computer-generated random number. On the upper floor of the barn, directly above the experimental line, a 10-meter test line was painted. In each trial, a dowser was admitted to this upper level and required, with his or her rod, stick, or other tool of choice, to ascertain where the pipe with water on the ground floor was located.

Over the 2-year experimental period, the 43 dowsers participated in a total of 843 tests. The experiment was "double blind" in that neither the researcher on the top floor nor the dowser knew the ________________, even after a guess was made.

For each trial, an examination of the actual pipe's location (in decimeters from the beginning of the line) and the dowser's guess were recorded. The German physicists from these data concluded in their final report that although most dowsers did not do particularly well in the experiments, "some few dowsers, in particular tests, showed an extraordinarily high rate of correct guesses, which can scarcely if at all be explained as due to chance … a real core of dowser-phenomena can be regarded as empirically proven …."

Fill in the blank with the TWO most appropriate consecutive words from the passage. (Use the SAME consecutive words for both blanks.) Then, write the two factors used to determine the underlined words, "correct guesses."

04 Read the passage and follow the directions. [5 points]

전공B 서술형 7번

As children, many of us were taken to museums. In most cases this was probably with a group of fellow students from our school on a field trip. We were there to learn. The displays were static and the importance of the so-called great works escaped many in attendance. As a result, many adults rarely revisited museums. Museums were only seen as cultural repositories. In the last few decades, however, they have changed their purpose and role in society.

Throughout human history, museums collected the extraordinary as evidence of the past. More recently, they have reevaluated the purpose of their collections and put much more effort into collecting the ordinary and everyday, in recognition of the fact that it is this material which best represents the lives of most people. Such a change in their collections enables museums to show their relevance to people who previously were underrepresented, and thus uninterested in museums.

Museums have started to play a new role in society through their partnerships, as well. It is no longer an option for a museum to remain isolated and aloof. Museums are social constructs and have assumed their place in mainstream contemporary life. They are now networking their value to all sectors of society, not just with traditional allies like the education sector. Political associations and business and community sectors are now included.

In these ways, the institutions that once were just hallowed halls of important objects are now quickly adapting with new attitudes towards what they collect. They also have evolved to interact and work with a variety of members within their communities. Modern museums are reinventing themselves as the center of contemporary culture.

Write a summary following the guidelines below.

Guidelines

- Summarize the above passage in one paragraph.
- Provide a topic sentence, two supporting ideas, and a concluding sentence based on the passage.
- Do NOT copy more than FIVE consecutive words from the passage.

2017학년도

01 **Read the passage and follow the directions.** [2 points] 전공A 서술형 2번

M. Ringelmann, a French agricultural engineer, was one of the first researchers to study the relationship between process loss and group productivity. Ringelmann's questions were practical ones: How many oxen should be yoked in one team? Should you plow a field with two horses or three? Can five men turn a mill crank faster than four? Instead of speculating about the answers to these questions, Ringelmann set up teams of varying sizes and measured their collective power.

Ringelmann's most startling discovery was that workers—including horses, oxen, and men—all become less productive in groups. A group of five writers developing funny skits can easily outperform a single person, just as a team pulling a rope is stronger than a single opponent. But even though a group outperforms an individual, the group does not usually work at maximum efficiency. When Ringelmann had individuals and groups pull on a rope attached to a pressure gauge, groups performed below their theoretical capabilities. If person A and person B could each pull 100 units when they worked alone, could they pull 200 units when they pooled their efforts? No, their output reached only 186. A three-person group did not produce 300 units, but only 255. An eight-person group managed only 392, not 800. Groups certainly outperformed individuals—but as more and more people were added, the group became increasingly inefficient. To honor its discoverer, this tendency is now known as the Ringelmann effect.

Ringelmann identified two key sources of process losses when people worked together. First, Ringelmann believed some of the decline in productivity was caused by motivation losses: People may not work so hard when they are in groups. Second, coordination losses, caused by "the lack of simultaneity of their efforts," also interfere with performance. Even on a simple task, such as rope pulling, people tend to pull and pause at different times, resulting in a failure to reach their full productive potential.

Complete the main idea by filling in the blank with the ONE most appropriate word from the passage.

Groups were found to become more ____________ as group size increased because the potential output that each member could contribute individually was not realized when they participated in groups.

02 Read the passage and follow the directions. [4 points]

전공A 서술형 14번

The early 20th century was not a great time for grocery shoppers. Sure, industrialization meant that more food products were available than ever before, and at lower prices, too. But in the days before the FDA, who knew what those products were really made of? A bottle of ketchup might contain dyed pumpkin, ground ginger might be mixed with bits of tarred rope, and cans labeled "potted chicken" might include no chicken at all.

All those things happened, and worse. Once the public became aware of the extent of the problem, the Pure Food and Drug Act of 1906 was passed. The legislation laid out standards for food safety: You could no longer mix poisonous, dirty, or rotten ingredients into a product. It also stopped outright mislabelling: You could not call something a particular food if it was not that food.

This was going to hurt the bottom line for manufacturers of cheap imitation food, so they came up with a way around the new rules. What if you technically did not say a product was something it was not? What if you are calling a product that is mostly cornstarch *Puddine*, expecting that people will think it is real pudding?

That strategy worked for a while. A "distinctive name" proviso was inserted into the law that allowed clever names. In addition to Puddine (mostly cornstarch), consumers could buy Grape Smack (imitation grape juice) and Bred Spred (a nearly fruit-free sugar-pectin mixture in a jam jar). If buyers thought they were getting pudding, grape juice, and strawberry jam—well, it was not the companies' fault. They did not say their products were those other things.

The courts agreed. In the marvelously titled cases *United States v. 150 Cases of Fruit Puddine, United States v. 24 7/8 Gallons of Smack, and United States v. 15 Cases of Bred Spred*, the distinctive name proviso let the imitators off the hook. But the rules got stricter with the 1938 Food, Drug, and Cosmetic Act, which mandated that products could still bear fanciful names, but if they looked a lot like something they were not, they had to be explicitly labeled a(n) ____________.

Fill in the blank with the ONE most appropriate word from the passage. Then explain why manufacturers started to use so-called 'distinctive names'.

03 Read the passage and follow the directions. [5 points]

전공B 서술형 7번

Have you ever felt overwhelmed trying to do too many things at once? In modern times, hurry, bustle, and agitation have become a regular way of life for many people—so much so that we have embraced a word to describe our efforts to respond to the many pressing demands of our time: multitasking. Used for decades to describe the parallel processing abilities of computers, in the 1990s the term multitasking became shorthand for the human attempt to simultaneously do as many things as possible, as quickly as possible, and with the help of new technologies.

It was originally assumed that multitasking was a useful strategy for increasing productivity. More recently, however, challenges to the presumed advantages of multitasking began to emerge. For example, numerous studies have addressed the sometimes fatal danger of driving and using cell phones or other electronic devices at the same time. As a result, several countries have now made that particular form of multitasking illegal. Researchers have also found that multitasking in the workplace can actually decrease productivity because the constant attention paid to emails, messaging apps, and phone calls temporarily impairs our ability to solve complex problems. Moreover, multitasking may negatively influence how we learn. Even if we learn while multitasking, that learning is likely to be less flexible and more fragmented, so we cannot recall the information as easily. As the research on multitasking implies, perhaps it is time to challenge the assumption that doing more is better.

Write a summary following the guidelines below.

Guidelines

- Summarize the above passage in ONE paragraph.
- Provide a topic sentence, supporting ideas from the passage, and a concluding sentence.
- Do NOT copy more than FIVE consecutive words from the passage.

2016학년도

01 **Read the passage and follow the directions.** [4 points] 전공A 서술형 11번

When it comes to climate, what counts is not only what humans do to reduce the buildup of greenhouse gases, but also how the earth responds. Currently half the carbon we release into the atmosphere gets absorbed by land and sea—much of it by plants, which take in carbon dioxide in the process of photosynthesis.

This cycle has the potential to change at any time. At issue is the balance between two natural phenomena. One is beneficial: as carbon-dioxide levels in the air rise, plants grow more quickly, absorbing more carbon in return. Scientists can measure this in the lab, but they don't know how much more fertile the new, carbon-enhanced environment will be for plants. The other is that as temperatures rise, permafrost, which holds an enormous amount of carbon from long-dead plants, tends to dry out, allowing decay and a release of carbon into the atmosphere. If this phenomenon, called "outgassing," were to kick in, it could inundate the atmosphere with carbon dioxide, perhaps doubling or tripling the effect of the past century of human industry.

Nobody knows for sure what might trigger outgassing, but preventing a global temperature increase of more than 2 degrees Celsius is considered essential. To stay below that limit, the consensus is that we should establish a maximum level of carbon in the atmosphere and do whatever is necessary to stay below it. A few years ago, scientists thought that a doubling of carbon concentrations over preindustrial times, to 550 parts per million, was a reasonable line in the sand; in recent years they've revised that figure downward, to 450 ppm. But reaching that would require a drastic 80 percent cut in emissions by midcentury.

> Meanwhile, observations, though not conclusive, have been pointing in the wrong direction: temperatures are rising quickly at the poles, the north polar ice cap is in retreat, permafrost is showing troubling signs of change, and ocean currents may be weakening the uptake of carbon. As we feel good about driving hybrids and using fluorescent bulbs, our fate may be riding on an obscure contest between __________ and permafrost.

Fill in the blank with ONE word from the passage. Then explain what would happen to the permafrost if global temperature rises by more than 2 degrees Celsius.

___

___

___

___

___

02 Read the passage and follow the directions. [4 points] 전공A 서술형 14번

> A paragraph in the papers of last week recorded the unusual action of a gentleman called Smith (or some such name) who had refused for reasons of conscience to be made a justice of the peace. Smith's case was that the commission was offered to him as a reward for political services, and that this was a method of selecting magistrates of which he did not approve. So he showed his contempt for the system by refusing an honour which most people covet, and earned by this such notoriety as the papers can give. "Portrait of a gentleman who has refused something!" He takes his place in (1) <u>the gallery of the odd</u>.
>
> The subject for essay has frequently been given, "If a million pounds were left to you, how could you do most good with it?" Some say they would endow hospitals, some that they would establish almshouses; there may even be some who would go as far as to build half a Dreadnought. But there would be a more decisive way of doing good than any of these. You might refuse the million pounds. That would be a shock to the systems of the comfortable—a blow struck at the great Money God which would make it totter; a thrust in defence of pride and freedom such as had not been seen before. That would be a moral tonic more needed than all the draughts of your newly endowed hospitals. (2) <u>Will it ever be administered</u>? Well, perhaps when the Declined-with-Thanks club has grown a little stronger.

Write TWO consecutive words from the passage that correspond to the meaning of the underlined words in (1). Then explain the implication of the underlined words in (2).

03 Read the passage and follow the directions. [4 points]

전공B 서술형 4번

"The average Yaleman, Class of '24*, makes $25,111 a year." *Time* magazine reported.

Well, good for him!

But, come to think of it, what does this improbably precise and salubrious figure mean? Is it, as it appears to be, evidence that if you send your boy to Yale you won't have to work in your old age and neither will he? Is this average a mean or is it a median? What kind of sample is it based on? You could lump one Texas oilman with two hundred hungry free-lance writers and report *their* average income as $25,000-odd a year. The arithmetic is impeccable, the figure is convincingly precise.

In just such ways is the secret language of statistics, so appealing in a fact-minded culture, being used to sensationalize, inflate, confuse, and over-simplify. Statistical terms are necessary in reporting the mass data of social and economic trends, business conditions, "opinion" polls, this year's census. But without writers who use the words with honesty and understanding and readers who know what they mean, the result can only be semantic nonsense.

In popular writing on scientific research, the abused statistic is almost crowding out the picture of the white-jacketed hero laboring overtime without time-and-a-half in an ill-lit laboratory. Like the "<u>little dash of powder, little pot of paint</u>," statistics are making many an important fact "look like what she ain't."

* *graduates of 1924*

Write TWO consecutive words corresponding to the underlined words from the passage. Then explain why the average Yaleman's annual income mentioned in the passage could be misleading.

04 Read the passage and follow the directions. [5 points]

전공B 서술형 7번

> Korea continues to expand its role in the global community culturally and economically. The effects are far reaching. Domestic businesses find themselves with new challenges and the public is exposed to a large number of new choices. At the same time, the outpouring of Korean made products, especially in the electronic and automotive industries, has been monumental. Along with these, as is the case with most successful adaptations to globalization, Korea has also found itself, at times inadvertently, shipping out culture, as well. From TV dramas, movies, K-pop, and food, Korean culture is simply what is hot right now, globally. The countries surrounding Korea have embraced everything from Korea. The reasons for all this are complex, to be sure, but it is clear it involved a bit of being in the right place at the right time and a lot of deliberate planning. It is not a coincidence that globalization is successful for Korea. Unlike many countries, it has dealt, and continues to deal, with the challenges and capitalizes on them. That being said, Korea's ongoing successful participation in the global sphere necessitates that it continue to carefully manage its role in globalization so that it can maintain the momentum it has created.

Write a summary following the guidelines below.

Guidelines

- Summarize the above passage in ONE paragraph.
- Provide a topic sentence, supporting evidence from the passage, and a conclusion.
- Do NOT copy more than FIVE consecutive words from the passage.

2015학년도

01 **Read the passage and fill in the blank with ONE word from the passage.** [2 points]

전공A 기입형 1번

A psychology professor spent several decades studying the "fixed mindset entity theory." She refers to people who view talent as a quality they either possess or lack as having a "fixed mindset." People with a "growth mindset," in contrast, enjoy challenges, strive to learn, and consistently see potential to develop new skills.

Now Carol Dweck, the psychology professor, is extending her work on mindset beyond individuals. Can an organization, like an individual, have a fixed or a growth mindset? If so, how can managers help organizations embrace a growth mindset? To explore this issue, she conducted surveys and found that often top management must drive the change; for instance, a new CEO might focus on maximizing employees' potential. Dweck points to one emblematic growth mindset CEO who hired according to "runway," not pedigree, preferring big state university graduates and military veterans to Ivy Leaguers, and spent thousands of hours grooming and coaching employees on his executive team.

As this CEO's example shows, one area in which mindset is especially important is hiring. Fixed mindset organizations reflexively look outside their companies, while growth mindset organizations are likely to hire from within their ranks. "Focusing on __________ is not as effective as looking for people who love challenges, who want to grow, and who want to collaborate," Dweck says. Some companies appear to be making such a shift; these companies have recently begun hiring more people who have proven that they are capable independent learners.

Despite the survey results, not all employees will be happier in growth mindset organizations, Dweck acknowledges. In general, though, the early evidence suggests that organizations focused on employees' capacity for growth will experience significant advantages.

02 Read the passage and follow the directions. [5 points]

전공B 서술형 2번

Scientists made a splash last week when they presented a radical new view of DNA, solving a puzzle that has long gnawed at investigators and shedding light on diseases such as cancer, heart disease, and Alzheimer's. Ever since decoding the human genome, scientists have been perplexed by the long strands of our DNA that appear to do nothing. They called the idle double helixes "junk DNA," thinking they were nothing but leftovers from ill-fitting assembly parts, useless bits of this and that, last season's models.

The days of junk status are now officially over. Working for almost 10 years on a collaborative project, 440 scientists from 32 labs across the globe announced that they have finally figured out just what the silent majority of our DNA does: <u>It's middle management</u>.

It seems these large branches of the DNA family tree—formerly called "junk" but now renamed as "dark matter"—run the factory but don't actually make anything. They're the deciders, the guys with administrative approval to greenlight a project or stop it cold—in this case to determine which genes step forward to produce a protein and which ones remain stalled, waiting for that second chance. And with a million supervisors for every 23,000 genes, a ratio of about 50 to 1, it appears middle management is well staffed.

Though perhaps a bit humbling to discover that our DNA is so bureaucratic, the insight is likely to result in substantial medical benefit. Up to now, therapies have focused on influencing the behavior of the gene itself—sometimes successfully but often not. The problem is that genetic mutations, though somewhat understood for many diseases, have proven difficult to fix. The realization that genes are surrounded by an entourage of promoters and suppressors expands the list of possible targets for intervention considerably. In cystic fibrosis, for example, we've discovered the genetic mutation that causes disease, but we've been unable to repair it. Using the new approach, researchers might defuse not the mutant gene itself but one of the bits of DNA responsible for greenlighting the bad gene's expression.

Describe what the underlined words mean in the above context, and explain why DNA's "middle management" could be the key to future cures.

03 Read the passage and follow the directions. [10 points]

전공B 논술형 1번

> All products may be considered as either disposable or durable. Disposable products are goods made for short-term usage, many even meant to be thrown away after one use. Manufacturing them requires constant development of new designs and the employment of large numbers of workers. This provides ongoing benefits for the growth of the economy. However, this type of production causes a great deal of waste. Some disposable products like plastic bags do not easily decompose and thus have anything but a positive impact on the environment.
>
> Durable products are intended to last for a long time. As such, any given product would be sold less often. However, making products durable requires the support of secondary industries to supply parts and do repairs. This, in turn, establishes long-standing economic advantages. In addition, long-term use of products helps cut emissions of pollutants. As durable products also include less residual waste, landfill expansion is significantly reduced, which makes them a good environmental choice.

How do different types of products affect the economy and the environment? Write a composition following the guidelines below.

Guidelines

- Write TWO paragraphs based on the above passage: one a comparison paragraph regarding the effect on the economy and the other a contrast paragraph on the environment.
- Provide each paragraph with a topic sentence and two supporting pieces of evidence.
- Do NOT copy more than FIVE consecutive words from the passage.

2014학년도

01 **Read the passage and follow the directions.** [2 points] 전공A 기입형 6번

We are born, each of us, with such self-centeredness that only the fact of being babies, and therefore cute, saves us. Growing up is largely a matter of growing out of that condition: we soak in impressions, and as we do so we dethrone ourselves—or at least most of us do—from our original position at the center of the universe. It is like taking off in an airplane: the establishment of identity requires recognizing how relatively small we are in the larger scheme of things. Remember how it felt to have your parents unexpectedly produce a younger sibling, or abandon you to the tender mercies of kindergarten? Or what it was like to enter your first public or private school? Or as a teacher, to confront your first classroom filled with sullen, squirmy, slumbering, solipsistic students? Just as you have cleared one hurdle, another is set before you. Each event diminishes your authority at just the moment at which you think you have become an authority.

If that is what maturity means in human relationships—the arrival at identity by way of relative insignificance—then I would define historical consciousness as the projection of that maturity through time. We understand how much has preceded us, and how unimportant we are in relation to it. We learn our place, and we come to realize that it is not a large one. Even a superficial acquaintance with the existence, through millennia of time, of numberless human beings helps to correct the normal adolescent inclination to relate the world to oneself instead of relating oneself to the world. As historian Geoffrey Elton pointed out, "History teaches those adjustments and insights which help the adolescent to become adult, surely a worthy service in the education of youth."

Complete the main idea by filling in the blank with TWO consecutive words from the passage.

History helps us mature by making us realize the __________ of ourselves in a wider context.

____

02 Read the passage and follow the directions. [3 points] 전공A 서술형 1번

If there is a single most important flaw in the current news style, it is the overwhelming tendency to downplay the big social, economic, or political picture in favor of the human trials, tragedies, and triumphs that sit at the surface of events. For example, instead of focusing on power and process, the media concentrate on the people engaged in political combat over the issues. The reasons for this are numerous, from the journalist's fear that probing analysis will turn off audiences to the relative ease of telling the human-interest side of a story as opposed to explaining deeper causes and effects.

When people are invited to take the news personally, they can find a wide range of private, emotional meanings in it. However, the meanings inspired by personalized news may not add up to the shared critical understandings on which healthy citizen involvement thrives. The focus on personalities encourages a passive spectator attitude among the public. Whether the focus is on sympathetic heroes and victims or hateful scoundrels and culprits, the media preference for personalized human-interest news creates a "can't-see-the-forest-for-the-trees" information bias that makes it difficult to see the big picture that lies beyond the many actors crowding center stage who are caught in the eye of the news camera.

The tendency to personalize the news would be less worrisome if human-interest angles were used to hook audiences into more serious analysis of issues and problems. Almost all great literature and theater, from the Greek dramas to the modern day, use strong characters to promote audience identifications and reactions in order to draw people into thinking about larger moral and social issues. News often stops at the character development stage, however, and leaves the larger lessons and social significance, if there is any, to the imagination of the audience. As a result, the main problem with personalized news is that the focus on personal concerns is seldom linked to more in-depth analysis. What often passes for analysis are opaque news formulas such as "He/She was a reflection of us," a line that was used in the media frenzies that followed the deaths of Britain's Princess Diana and America's John Kennedy, Jr. Even when large portions of the public reject personalized news formulas, the personalization never stops. This systematic tendency to personalize situations is one of the defining biases of news.

Describe the defining characteristic of the current news style, and explain how it differs from the common characteristic of great literature and theater. Do NOT copy more than FIVE consecutive words from the passage.

03 Read the passage and follow the directions. [5 points]

전공B 서술형 1번

The population of a certain species tends to remain relatively stable over long periods of time. After domestic sheep became established on the island of Tasmania in the early nineteenth century, for instance, their population varied irregularly between 1,230,000 and 2,250,000—less than a factor of 2—over nearly a century. We know this because sheep were, and still are, very important to the economy of Tasmania, and their numbers were carefully recorded. In sharp contrast, populations of small, short-lived organisms may fluctuate wildly over many orders of magnitude within short periods. Populations of the green algae and diatoms that make up the phytoplankton may soar and crash over periods of a few days or weeks. These rapid fluctuations overlay changes with longer periods that occur, for example, on a seasonal basis.

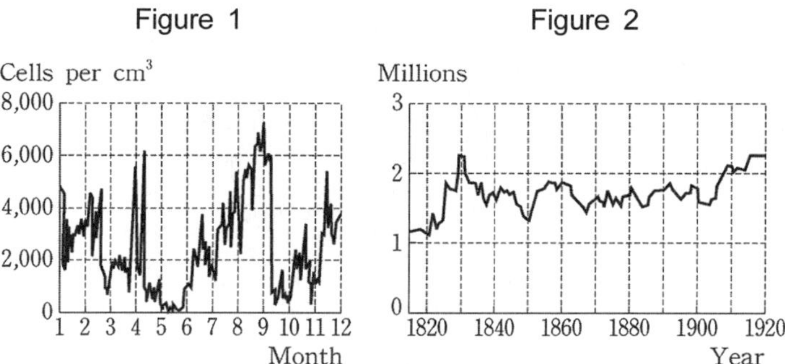

Why do sheep and algae show such disparate fluctuations in population? First of all, sheep and algae differ in their sensitivity to environmental change. Because sheep are larger, they have a greater capacity for homeostasis and better resist the physiological effects of environmental change. Furthermore, the populations of sheep and algae are differentially affected by birth rate fluctuations. Because sheep have a relatively long lifespan, short-term fluctuations in birth rate do not greatly affect the overall population at a given time. Thus, sheep populations possess a high intrinsic stability. On the other hand, the lives of single-celled algal cells span only a few days, so these intrinsically unstable populations turn over rapidly.

** homeostasis : the maintenance of a stable equilibrium*

Identify the figure that represents the fluctuations in sheep population and explain why the sheep population fluctuated the way the figure depicts. Do NOT copy more than FIVE consecutive words from the passage.

04 Read the passage and follow the directions. [10 points] 전공B 논술형 1번

Korea is quickly becoming an aging society. Consequently, we need to prepare so that we can effectively deal with the changes this situation will bring about. Clearly, these changes will have a wide-ranging impact on different facets of the nation. We should consider how we must prepare for the future from both individual and societal perspectives. Below are some of the points to consider within these two main areas.

- **Possible preparation points at the individual level**
  Develop life-long hobbies
  Embrace healthier lifestyles
  Seek financial self-sufficiency

- **Possible preparation points at the societal level**
  Re-examine mandatory retirement ages
  Improve the healthcare system
  Expand the existing pension system

How must we prepare for the future? Choose one preparation point that you think is most important at each level, and write a composition following the guidelines below.

Guidelines

- Write TWO paragraphs, one for each preparation point.
- For each paragraph, include a topic sentence.
- Support each preparation point with two specific reasons.
- Use neat handwriting.

Chapter 02

2013~2009학년도 기출문제

모범답안 및 번역 p.51

2013학년도 1차

01 **Which of the following would best fit in the blanks?** [2 points]

Christopher Austin inched forward on his hands and knees with only a headlamp to light his way. The herpetologist and his assistant were searching Papua New Guinea's damp forest floor for the source of a ___(A)___ mating call coming from the ground foliage. They assumed an insect was projecting the high-pitched chirp, but there was no bug to be found. So the two bagged up some leaves and brought them back to camp. There, they searched each leaf, one by one, until they found the surprising ___(B)___ : not insects but tiny frogs with skin the color of earth, one-third of an inch long. Austin later reported that his find was a new species, *Paedophryne amauensis*, the smallest known vertebrate in the world, measuring a millimeter shorter than the Southeast Asian fish that previously held the record. "One way to evolve a small body size is to never grow up," Austin says. What is the advantage? Their miniature size makes them ideal ___(C)___ for even smaller invertebrates, including the mites that are their prey in the moist leaves of tropical forests.

	(A)	(B)	(C)
①	perceptible	culprits	invertebrates
②	perceptible	convicts	vertebrates
③	mysterious	culprits	predators
④	mysterious	convicts	invertebrates
⑤	perceptible	suspects	victims

02 **Which of the following would the writer most likely agree with?** [2 points]

> The freedom of thought was recently challenged in the case of Charles T. Sell, who claimed, "The court of appeals erred in rejecting the petitioner's argument that allowing the government to administer antipsychotic medication against his will solely to render him competent to stand trial ··· would violate his rights under the Amendments." The Supreme Court ruled, in a 6-3 decision, in favor of Sell. While neuroscience is only beginning to get a handle on brain states, much less mind reading, in Sell's case the government wanted to use pharmacology to force a mental state upon him. Structuring someone's biochemical milieu to render him or her mentally competent is a total dream; antipsychotic medication deals with the symptoms of a disorder, not with the underlying structure. At this point, neuroscience has a long way to go before it can claim that specific chemical manipulations of brain cells produce an explicit state of mind, for neuroscience reads brains, not minds.

① Forced drugging by the government protects Sell's rights.
② The government is allowed to use pharmacology to cure Sell's mental illness.
③ Specific chemical manipulations can help Sell to produce an explicit state of mind.
④ Sell's mind may go beyond what neuroscience can know about his brain.
⑤ Antipsychotic medication can render Sell competent to read his mind.

03 **What would be the best title of the passage?** [1.5 points]

You may argue that music is a purely human manifestation not to be touched by the intrusion of electronic probes. Yet, several successful programs have been written that seem to produce "quite good" musical pieces. One such program was written by Steve Larson, who selected three compositions—one by Johann Sebastian Bach, one by himself, and one by a computer—to be played before an audience. In an outcome somewhat bemusing to Larson, his own composition was judged to have been composed by the computer, while the computer-generated music was judged to be the authentic Bach. At least on a limited basis, computer-generated music fools some of the people some of the time. Another program called Improvisor has been written to emulate a range of styles from that of Bach to those of jazz musicians like Louis Armstrong.

At the present time, computer-generated music seems to be very convincing. The main weakness in these programs, however, is in their ability to create music that is persuasive over a longer period of time, especially among musical specialists who are sensitive to the nuances of specialized types of music. While a novice may be convinced that a computer-generated piece of music was composed by Mozart, a Mozart virtuoso could identify the artificial Mozart. One might be moved to observe that it sounds like Mozart, but it sounds as if he was having a 'bad hair day.' Of course, it is possible that future programs will not only produce Mozart-like compositions, but surpass the talented young Austrian and generate super-Mozart compositions—music that would reincarnate the apotheosis of the boy genius.

① Musical Intelligence: Nature versus Nurture
② Composers: Novices and Virtuosos
③ Marketing via Computer-Generated Music
④ The Achievements of Great Musicians
⑤ The Potential of Machine-Generated Music

04 **What is the main idea of the passage?** [2.5 points]

Why be moral? This question is fundamental for ethics because even if people can figure out what are the right things to do, we can still ask why they would in fact do these things. The traditional philosophical responses to the problem of moral motivation have been rationalist: We should be more moral because it would be irrational to do otherwise. The rationality of morality might derive from *a priori* truths about what is right, or from arguments that it is rational for people to agree with others to be moral.

The philosopher Sean Nichols argues that a major problem for rationalism is that psychopaths, with no impediments in abstract reasoning, nevertheless see nothing wrong in harming other people. Nichols argues convincingly that what is wrong with psychopaths is not their reasoning but their emotions. Psychopathy, whose symptoms include antisocial behavior, lack of guilt, and poverty of emotions, is the result of impairments to emotional learning that derive from disrupted functioning of the amygdala.

According to Nichols, an adequate account of ethical thinking must explain how emotion plays a role in linking moral judgment to motivations, while also allowing a place for reason in moral judgment. His explanation of ethical norms is cultural and historical: Norms are more likely to be preserved in the culture if the norms resonate with our affective systems by prohibiting actions that are likely to elicit negative affect. Norms that prohibit harm to others are virtually ubiquitous across cultures because of this "affective resonance." The adoption of norms enables us to reason about what is right and wrong, but these norms have an emotional underpinning that intrinsically provides a connection between morality and action.

① It is imperative we understand psychopathic behavior.
② Norms which include not harming others are universal.
③ Moral action is linked to emotions as well as reasoning.
④ One major aspect of psychopathy is an intrinsic lack of guilt.
⑤ Acting emotionally must be seen as irrational in all societies.

05 **Which of the following is LEAST likely to be inferred from the passage?** [2 points]

Our belief in insects as adversaries shapes our interactions with them. It has given rise to the regulatory agencies and big-business conglomerates whose goal is to eradicate or control insects. Propaganda generated by these institutions simplifies the complexities of our relationship with the creatures and feeds us hostile images that perpetuate a militaristic stance toward thousands of species. The taproot, however, is our fear.

"I didn't know what it was, so I killed it," is what biologist Ronald Rood heard over and over again when he questioned people who brought him the dead bodies of insects or other unfamiliar creatures to identify. The curiosity natural in a non-threatening situation was absent. They had killed it—just to be safe—to crush the fear invoked by the creature's presence.

A large part of our fear revolves around being bitten. Bug zappers, those glowing fixtures in suburban yards, keep those fears at bay, killing billions of insects each year. One entomologist said that all these devices do is amuse us; they are otherwise ineffective. Fewer than one fourth of the insects killed are the ones with an appetite for blood. Any mirth, however, would be short-lived if we realized that when insects hit the zapper and explode, they spray bacteria and viruses in a radius of at least two meters.

Self-protection may motivate us to stop using bug zappers because compassion for the estimated seventy-one billion nontarget insects that are killed has not. In fact, there is not much that influences our conviction that insects are adversaries. When our experiences do not substantiate our fears, we tend to discount the contradictory evidence. Convinced we are justified and acting realistically, we are quick to defend our aggressive stance and do not even see the opportunities that arise for a different, more positive relationship.

① Some businesses tend to instill the idea that insects are dangerous.
② Fear of insects is one reason why people kill them.
③ The majority of the insects killed by bug zappers do not feed on human blood.
④ Fear of the bacteria and viruses found in insects may stop people from using bug zappers.
⑤ Negative attitudes toward insects are easily changed.

06 **Which of the following is the best order to complete the passage? The first part of the passage is given below.** [2 points]

Do all risks have to be physical? Of course not. There are intellectual risks, too. Unlike a physical risk that challenges the body and involves potential physical harm to it, an intellectual risk challenges the mind and causes a potential disturbance in common beliefs. It is a "thinking" risk.

[A] It was a risk because it challenged people to rethink a certain, long-held belief. The producer took the risk, hoping that the viewers would think again about the utter brutality against slaves. Potentially, the producer stood to lose not only the money he invested, but also his reputation. In this case, taking the intellectual risk paid off. It disturbed then-current views about the human rights of African Americans and helped educate many people about a rarely-talked-about past.

[B] In the mid-1970s, for example, the first miniseries appeared on television. *Roots* was a multi-day series of movies depicting the life of a young African in the 1700s who was kidnapped and brought to the United States as a slave. The series was graphic; it portrayed how slaves were really treated. It made people uncomfortable to watch—even more uncomfortable because they were from a nation that wished to leave the unpleasant history of slavery in the past.

[C] What does an intellectual risk involve? This type of risk forces other people to distrust what they used to believe in. Perhaps it exposes something that has not been considered previously. Perhaps it attempts to stretch intellectual ability. These intellectual risks are similar to physical risks, and a certain sense of satisfaction can take place from such experience.

① [A] – [B] – [C]
② [A] – [C] – [B]
③ [B] – [C] – [A]
④ [C] – [A] – [B]
⑤ [C] – [B] – [A]

2013학년도 2차

Read and follow the directions. [25 points]

A second-year high school teacher wanted to diagnose the strengths and weaknesses of his students' writing ability. He asked the students to write a well-formed paragraph about Ho Chi Minh City, which they had visited on a school trip. The following are two writing samples that particularly attracted his attention.

[Writing Sample 1]

Last year I went to Ho Chi Minh City. It's a fascinating place. It is in Vietnam. It is located on a river. They say it was once an important trading center for the French. French effect was everywhere. You should visit there. I saw many building there. Many of them are built in French style. The famous French architect Gustave Eiffel designed a building there. Some cafe serve French-style bread. Many people, especially the older generations, learned French in school. Rich Vietnamese people still speak French today. Hotels and restaurants also have French food. Typically, Vietnamese people have a baguette, yogurt and orange juice for breakfast. All of those are French. The Vietnamese and the French fought, too. Then French left the country. You can see many museums and monuments. They show the country's long war history. So I think Ho Chi Minh City is a fascinating place to visit.

[Writing Sample 2]

For travelers to Southeast Asia, there is no more fascinating place to visit than Ho Chi Minh City. Due to historical importance as French trading center in Southeast Asia, French culture's influences remain pervasive in this city. For example, many inhabitant, especially older generation, learned French in school and can still speak it very well. Vietnamese elite also continue to speak French today. In addition, many cafe, hotel and restaurant serve French-style pastries, along with French item like asparagus and white potato. Typical Vietnamese breakfast would consist baguette, yogurt and orange juice, which are all French item. French influence's another sign is that many building in the city were built in French style. This can be seen, for example, in Saigon Central Post Office. It has French Gothic style since it was designed and constructed by famous French architect Gustave Eiffel. Numerous museum and monument also document country's long—and often bloody—history of conflict between Vietnamese and French. Although French eventually left country, cultural influences continue. If you are looking for unique city to visit in Southeast Asia, Ho Chi Minh City is excellent choice.

Write three well-formed paragraphs that compare and contrast the two writing samples in terms of content, organization, and language use. First, in one paragraph, discuss the content. Second, in another paragraph, discuss organization (cohesion and coherence). Third, in the last paragraph, discuss language use (i.e., grammar, vocabulary, etc.).

Include the following in each paragraph:
- A topic sentence
- Two key points (similarities and/or differences)
- A supporting example for each key point

2012학년도 1차

01 **What would be the best title of the passage?** [1.5 points]

Although he availed himself of the results of the labours of preceding artists, William Turner nevertheless, from his earliest youth, received his sole inspiration from nature. And yet his art did not lie in the literal transcription of nature. His was not the skill to count the blades of grass, and reproduce, without variation, the exact aspect of the scene before him. Every scene that he has represented is bathed, so to speak, in the mystic poetry of his own imagination. He painted his portrait of the earth not merely as it appeared to him at any one given moment, but with a true comprehension of all its past history, of the earthquakes that had shaken it, the storm-winds that had swept over it, and the loveliness that still clung to it. He has revealed to us this loveliness in all its varying aspects—in its joy and in its sadness, in its brightness and its gloom, in its pensive mood and in its fierce madness, in its love and in its hate, but the portrait, although true in the highest sense, is never directly copied from nature for he painted, like Raphael and all great idealists, from an image or ideal in his own mind. But this ideal was founded on the closest observation and study of the real.

① William Turner and His Predecessors
② Mood Swings in William Turner's Life
③ William Turner: A Painter of Idealized Reality
④ William Turner and Nature Depicted in Precision
⑤ William Turner's Favorite Theme: Return to Nature

02 Which of the following would best fit in the blank? [2 points]

Aristotle, so far as I know, was the first man to proclaim explicitly that man is a rational animal. His reason for this view was one which does not now seem very impressive; it was that some people can do sums. He thought that there are three kinds of soul: the vegetable soul, possessed by all living things, both plants and animals, and concerned only with nourishment and growth: the animal soul, concerned with locomotion, and shared by man with the lower animals; and finally the rational soul, or intellect, which is the Divine mind, but in which men participate to a greater or less degree in proportion to their wisdom. It is in virtue of the intellect that man is a rational animal. The intellect is shown in various ways, but most emphatically by mastery of arithmetic. The Greek system of numerals was very bad, so that the multiplication table was quite difficult, and complicated calculations could only be made by very clever people. Nowadays, however, calculating machines do sums better than even the cleverest people, yet no one contends that these useful instruments are immortal, or work by divine inspiration. As arithmetic has grown easier, it has come to be less respected. The consequence is that, though many philosophers continue to tell us what fine fellows we are, ______________________________.

① we still must depend on our intellect to solve arithmetic
② it is no longer on account of our arithmetical skill that they praise us
③ only the cleverest people have the rational soul to apply arithmetic
④ it is dubious that we are unique in our possession of a rational soul
⑤ there is still room to improve our intellect through the mastery of arithmetic

03 Which of the following is LEAST likely to be inferred from the passage? [2 points]

> The new language of the information sciences has transformed many molecular biologists from scientists to engineers, although they are little aware of the metamorphosis. When molecular biologists speak of mutations and genetic diseases as errors in the code, the implicit assumption is that they should never have existed in the first place, that they are 'bugs,' or mistakes that need to be deprogrammed or corrected. The molecular biologist, in turn, becomes the computing engineer, the writer of codes, continually eliminating errors. This is a dubious and dangerous role when we stop to consider that every human being brings with him or her a number of lethal recessive genes. Do we then come to see ourselves as miswired from the get-go, riddled with errors in our code? If that be the case, against what ideal norm of perfection are we to be measured? If every human being is made up of varying degrees of error, then we search in vain for the norm, the ideal. What makes the new language of molecular biology so subtly chilling is that it risks creating a new archetype, a flawless, errorless, perfect being to which to aspire—a new man and woman, like us, but without the warts and wrinkles, vulnerabilities and frailties, that have defined our essence from the very beginning of our existence.

① The writer thinks that human genes are riddled with errors that need correcting.
② A paradigm used in information sciences has influenced molecular biology.
③ Molecular biologists intend to eliminate lethal recessive genes.
④ The writer views the molecular biological approach to genetic diseases as undermining human beings' perception of themselves.
⑤ The writer is worried that human beings might strive to become what is no longer human.

04 **Which of the following is the best order to complete the passage?** [2 points]

[A] There are few divisions of the book industry with a worse a reputation than business publishing. Hundreds if not thousands of business books come out every year, all with glowing press release and effervescent puffs. Literary editors tend to consign them straight to the bin.

[B] The best books provide an insight into how business revolutionizes the world. Why is the centre of growth shifting from the developed to the developing countries? Why do some companies succeed and others fail? Why are we swapping the white collar for the no-collar workplace? Why do managers say the astonishing things that they say? The answers to these questions lie in the business books that many literary editors so casually toss out.

[C] Understandable but wrong. It is silly to dismiss a whole genre just because so many business books are bad. There are some excellent titles in among the dross: CEO biographies that capture something essential about business, useful prescriptions for restoring companies to health, even self-help books that help make sense of the contradictory pressures of modern corporate life. The average employed person in the West spends more waking time in the office than at home, so it makes no sense to be so dismissive of writers who focus on such an important activity.

[D] This is understandable. An astonishing number are worthless. Celebrity CEOs blow their trumpets, consultants market miracle cures, and self-help gurus promise that you can grow rich by working four hours a week. Wait a few months: the CEOs have been caught with their hands in the till, the miracle cures are poisons, and the self-help gurus bankrupt. What remains is a tangle of jargon-ridden prose.

① [A] – [B] – [D] – [C]
② [A] – [C] – [B] – [D]
③ [A] – [C] – [D] – [B]
④ [A] – [D] – [B] – [C]
⑤ [A] – [D] – [C] – [B]

05 **What is the main idea of the passage?** [2.5 points]

According to economist Vilfredo Pareto, there are four kinds of trades that people can make. First, there are win-win trades, in which both parties gain; in this case it is clear that welfare has gone up. Second, there are trades, in which one party gains, but no one loses, and again welfare has unambiguously gone up. Third, there are trades, in which no gains but someone loses, and in this case welfare has unambiguously gone down. Fourth and finally, there are trades, in which some parties win and some lose, but without the ability to directly measure utility, it is impossible to determine what the net impact is. Pareto argued that since it takes two consenting people to trade and people aren't stupid, they would only engage in trades that were either win-win or at least win-no-lose, both of which raise the total welfare of the participants. These trades later came to be called Pareto superior trades, and Pareto contended that in free markets, people would keep trading until they had exhausted all the Pareto superior trades. At that point trading would stop since any further trades would make someone worse off, and the market reach an equilibrium point that later economists called Pareto optimal. The Pareto optimal is thus the point at which no further trades can be made without making someone worse off. The Pareto optimal is not necessarily the point at which value is maximized for the entire group, as there might be some trades that would harm some people for the benefit of others, but would nonetheless raise the sum total utility of the group. Without a way to precisely measure utilities and a dictator to force trades that reduce the welfare of some for the benefit of others, the Pareto optimal is the best that one can do in a free society.

① Authoritarian government is necessary to achieve utility beyond the Pareto optimal.
② With new ways to measure utility it will be possible to increase the net welfare beyond the Pareto optimal.
③ In any given society, the Pareto optimal is the point at which society reaches the greatest possible welfare.
④ At the Pareto optimal, further trades cannot be made because no parties involved are able to measure utility directly.
⑤ In a society where people are permitted to trade in their own interests, the Pareto optimal is the indicator of maximum welfare.

06 Which of the following is LEAST likely to be inferred from the passage? [2 points]

Analytical, creative, and practical abilities, as measures by our tests, can be viewed as forms of developing expertise. All are useful in various kinds of life tasks. However, conventional tests may unfairly disadvantage those students who do not do well in a fairly narrow range of kinds of expertise. By expanding the range of developing expertise that we measure, we discover that many children not now identified as able have, in fact, developed important kinds of expertise. The abilities that conventional tests measure are important for school and life performance, but they are not the only abilities that are important.

We have conducted studies in which we have measured informal, procedural knowledge in children and adults. We have found in studies with business managers, college professors, elementary school students, salespeople, college students, and general populations that this important aspect of practical intelligence is generally uncorrected with academic intelligence as measures by conventional tests. Moreover, the tests predict performance as well as or better than do tests of intelligence quotients. The lack of correlation between the two kinds of ability tests suggests that the best prediction of job performance will result when both academic and practical intelligence tests are used as predictors. Most recently, we have developed a test of common sense for the workplace that predicts self-ratings of common sense but not self-ratings of various kinds of academic abilities.

① Procedural knowledge is a form of practical intelligence.
② Intelligence quotients can contribute to the prediction of job performance.
③ Conventional tests are not enough to measure the potential of young students.
④ The kinds of developing expertise assessed in conventional tests are different from those assessed in practical intelligence tests.
⑤ Compared to other children, children who have a high level of practical intelligence are less likely to have a high level of academic intelligence.

2012학년도 2차

Read the following and write an essay. [15 points]

[Situation]

School A in a local city has been requiring its students to participate in supervised night self-study. A neighboring school, School B, is also considering implementing the same program. School A's administration conducted a survey of its students to compile a list of pros and cons about the supervised night self-study. School A then passed on the survey's results to School B. School B's principal will ask teachers to consider the results of the student survey and decide whether or not the new policy of supervised night self-study will be beneficial to the students. As a teacher working at School B, take a position for or against the policy by considering the following pros and cons gathered from the survey.

** supervised night self-study : the program in which under a teacher's supervision students study by themselves in the classroom until late at night*

KEY EXPRESSIONS

<Pros>

1. Motivating study environment
2. More effective use of study hours
3. Less money being spent on private education

<Cons>

1. Less free time with friends and family
2. Increased anxiety due to feeling of "have-to-study"
3. Limitation of students' rights to autonomous learning

Compose a well-structured essay indicating your position according to these guidelines:

- Write four paragraphs from 20 to 25 lines.
- Do not copy more than 7 consecutive words from the description of the situation above.
- Include the following:
  - A thesis statement in the introductory paragraph
  - Two key expressions of pros or cons
  - A topic sentence for each body paragraph
  - A supporting example for each key expression in each body paragraph
  - A concluding sentence in the final paragraph

2011학년도 1차

01 **Read the following and answer the question.** [1.5 points]

> A person usually has two reasons for doing a thing: one that sounds good and a real one. The person himself will think of the real reason. You don't need to emphasize that. But all of us, being idealists at heart, like to think of motives that sound good. When the late Lord Northcliffe found a newspaper using a picture of him which he didn't want published, he wrote the editor a letter. But did he say, "Please do not publish that picture of me anymore; I don't like it"? No, he appealed to a nobler motive. He appealed to the respect and love that all of us have for motherhood. He wrote, "Please do not publish that picture of me anymore. My mother doesn't like it." When John D. Rockefeller Jr. wished to stop newspaper photographers from snapping pictures of his children, he too appealed to the nobler motive. He didn't say, "I don't want their pictures published." No, he appealed to the desire, deep in all of us, to refrain from harming children. He said, "You know how it is, boys. You've got children yourselves, some of you. And you know it's not good for youngsters to get too much publicity."

Which of the following would be the best title of the passage?

① An Appeal to a Nobler Motive
② How to Become Well Known
③ The Press's Appeal for Realism
④ The Effects of Publicity on Children
⑤ Keeping Children Out of Harm's Way

02 Read the following and answer the question. [2 points]

It is apparent that all societies, even the most primitive, have ideologies and that these ideologies are an intimate and important part of their culture. Each society regards its central ideologies as sacred and tolerates no questions with respect to them. Indeed, it is a significant sociological fact that the pressure to believe them is frequently stronger than the pressure to conform to the norms of conduct to which they are related. Thus, in all religions sinners may sometimes be "saved," but unbelievers never. The sinner may live a life spotted with infamy, but appropriate penance may absolve him from its consequences. The heretic, on the other hand, may lead a pure and virtuous life, perhaps almost saintly in character, but his conduct will not necessarily save him from damnation. It is pardonable to violate the norms if only one accepts the ideology. It is unpardonable, on the other hand, to reject the ideology no matter how closely one conforms to the norms. In short, ________________________. This sociological fact, evident in every time and society, is a paradox.

Which of the following would best fit in the blank?

① one should behave according to one's needs
② norms are more important than ideologies
③ curiosity is the most condemnable crime
④ violation of norms is unacceptable
⑤ skepticism is more serious than sin

03 **Choose the best order to complete the passage. The first part of the passage is given.** [2.5 points]

Psychology and physiology deal with the explanation of play. They try to determine the nature and significance of play in life. The necessity of play as a function forms the starting point of all research on play.

[A] To each of the "explanations" one might object: "What actually is the fun of playing? Why are crowds roused to frenzy by football matches?" This intensity of, and absorption in, play finds no explanation in biological analysis. Yet, in this intensity and absorption lies the essential aesthetic quality of play.

[B] These explanations are, therefore, only partial solutions to the problem. Most only deal incidentally with the question of what play is and what it means for the player. They attack play with quantitative methods without paying attention to its aesthetic quality.

[C] The numerous attempts to define the biological function of play show striking variations. In one theory, play constitutes a training of the young for serious work later in life. According to another, it serves as an innate urge to exercise a certain faculty. Yet, others regard it as an outlet for harmful impulses.

[D] All these hypotheses assume that play must serve something that is not play, based on some kind of biological purpose. They all inquire into the why of play, without coming nearer to a real understanding of the play-concept.

① [B] − [D] − [A] − [C]
② [C] − [A] − [D] − [B]
③ [C] − [D] − [B] − [A]
④ [D] − [B] − [A] − [C]
⑤ [D] − [B] − [C] − [A]

04 Read the passage and answer the question. [2 points]

"Use it or lose it" is what doctors have been telling people who want to protect their brains from dementia in their golden years. The more active you keep your neural circuits throughout life, the less likely it is that your brain will succumb to dementia or Alzheimer's disease. Or, at least, that is what doctors thought.

In a new study of 1,157 mentally healthy volunteers over age 65, researchers found that while those who remained intellectually stimulated by reading or playing card games were less likely to show symptoms of cognitive decline over a 12-year follow-up, they also showed significantly faster mental deterioration once they were diagnosed with dementia, compared with people who did not engage in mentally stimulating activity.

That is because such activity may allow the brain to compensate for any initial biological changes related to dementia and mask the progression of the disease, say the scientists. The findings imply that while brain exercises can hold off the symptoms of the neurological disorder for a while, they do not address its root cause.

Which of the following is consistent with the findings of the study above?

① Mental activity masks dementia's initial progression.
② Brain exercises and games address dementia's root cause.
③ Reading is the best cerebral activity for mental health.
④ Intellectual activity prevents neurological disorders.
⑤ Brain exercises reverse the progress of dementia.

05 Read the following and answer the question. [2 points]

In the animal kingdom, it is common for males to have ornamentation, like bright feathers, to impress females of their species, but a newly identified species of dancing fly found in the forested regions of Mount Fuji in Japan adds something new to the game of sexual display. The ornamentation, a protrusion shaped like a boxing glove, appears on some males on both legs, some on neither, and many on just one leg.

The researchers describe their finding in the journal *Biology Letters*. "One struggles to explain why they are asymmetric—it could mean that it sticks one leg up in the air to attract females," said Adrian Plant, one of the study's authors. Of the 33 male flies collected, 14 had one ornamented leg, and the others two or none. The fact that so many were asymmetric led the researchers to believe that it was more than a freak of nature.

What does seem clear is that the boxing glove detracts the insect's ability to fly efficiently, which suggests its function is to attract females. Further research is needed, but it is possible that the gloves also contain silk-secreting glands that allow the flies to capture prey and display their catch to potential female partners.

Which of the following correctly describes the ornamentation on the dancing flies found in Japan?

① It functions better when it appears asymmetrically on their body.
② It appears on both males and females of the species.
③ It is found only on one leg among 14% of the collected male flies.
④ It seems to be an obstacle to efficient flight.
⑤ It is proven to be mainly used to capture prey.

06 **Read the following and answer the question.** [2 points]

Why do we view English as if it were a single, monolithic language? The answer to this question basically rests on whether speakers of two languages can understand each other. This criterion, mutual intelligibility, is usually employed to distinguish between two different languages. If there is no mutual intelligibility, they are speakers of two different languages. While discussing mutual intelligibility, we should also consider one-way intelligibility, involving speakers of different, but historically related, languages. For example, speakers of Brazilian Portuguese who do not know Spanish can often understand the forms of Spanish spoken in neighboring countries. The analogous Spanish speakers, however, find Portuguese ___(1)___. Even if one group of speakers can understand another group, they cannot be said to speak the same language unless the second group also understands the first. Hence, the notion of mutual intelligibility is crucial in specifying when two languages are the "same" language.

Notice, however, that applying the notion of mutual intelligibility can be considerably complicated by social and political factors. In China, for example, a northern Chinese speaker of the Beijing dialect (also known as Mandarin) cannot understand the speech of a southern Chinese speaker of Cantonese, and vice versa. For this reason, a linguist might well label Mandarin and Cantonese as ___(2)___ language(s).

Which of the following would best fit in the blanks?

	(1)	(2)
①	totally incomprehensible	the same
②	totally intelligible	distinct
③	largely comprehensible	distinct
④	largely incomprehensible	the same
⑤	largely unintelligible	distinct

2011학년도 2차

One of your students, Minsu Park, has asked you for a letter of recommendation. He is applying to participate in a cultural exchange program that is sponsored by the school boards of Seoul, South Korea and Sydney, Australia. The aim of this program is to foster cultural awareness between the two countries by introducing Korean culture to Australian students, while at the same time allowing Korean students to experience Australian culture. Ten students will be chosen for this program. They will leave Korea on the 10th of next February and return on the 20th. While in Sydney, the students will stay with a host family.

Applicants for this program will be evaluated based on academic performance, relevant extracurricular activities, and personality. You have been Minsu's homeroom teacher for about a year. The table below is a summary of Minsu's merits.

Minsu's Merits	
Academic Performance	• grade point average (GPA) : top 20% of his grade • world history : top 5% of his grade • English : top 3% of his grade with excellent speaking skills
Extracurricular Activities	• practiced Pansori for 5 years • performed Pansori last April at school
Personality	• outgoing • shows leadership

You are to complete the letter of recommendation below according to the following guidelines:

1) The letter will have five paragraphs. The first paragraph is already provided for you. The next three paragraphs should discuss Minsu's merits in terms of his academic performance, extracurricular activities, and personality, respectively. The final paragraph should be a closing paragraph.
2) Throughout the letter, you must maintain the formal tone that was set in the first paragraph.
3) You must give Minsu the strongest recommendation possible.

4) You must include all of the information in the table above and add your own supporting details where needed.
5) The four paragraphs that you write must be between 15 and 20 lines.

02

Write the four paragraphs on the answer sheet. [20 points]

Soo-Yeon Lee
Namhangang High School
1234 Eunsan-dong, Geumgang-si
Chungnam, Korea

November 27th, 2010

Program Coordinator
Seoul-Sydney Cultural Exchange
2-77 Sinmunno 2-ga, Songwol-gil 28
Jongno-gu, Seoul, Korea

Re: Recommendation for Minsu Park

To whom it may concern,

It is with great pleasure that I recommend Minsu Park for the 2010 Seoul-Sydney Cultural Exchange Program. Having known Minsu for about a year as his homeroom teacher, I can say with the utmost certainty that he is an ideal candidate for this program.

Sincerely,
Soo-Yeon Lee

2010학년도 1차

01 **Read the following and answer the question.** [2 points]

There are two words whose meanings reflect our somewhat warped attitudes toward levels of commitment to physical and mental activities. These are the terms *amateur* and *dilettante*. Nowadays, these labels are slightly ___(1)___. An amateur or a dilettante is someone not quite up to par, a person not to be taken very seriously, one whose performance falls short of professional standards. But originally, "amateur," from the Latin verb *amare*, "to love," referred to a person who loved what he was doing. Similarly, a "dilettante," from the Latin *delectare*, "to find delight in," was someone who enjoyed a given activity. The earliest meanings of these words therefore drew attention to experiences rather than ___(2)___. They described the subjective rewards individuals gained from doing things, instead of focusing on how well they were achieving. Nothing illustrates as clearly our changing attitudes toward the value of experience as the fate of these two words. There was a time when it was admirable to be an amateur poet or a dilettante scientist, because it meant that the quality of life could be improved by engaging in such activities. But increasingly the emphasis has been to value behavior over ___(3)___ states; what is admired is success, achievement, the quality of performance rather than the quality of experience.

Which of the following best fits in the blanks above?

	(1)	(2)	(3)
①	derogatory	accomplishments	subjective
②	condescending	failures	ideal
③	cryptic	enjoyment	disorderly
④	conciliatory	accomplishments	emotional
⑤	pejorative	failures	natural

02 Read the following and answer the question. [2 points]

Society regards as true the systems of classification that produce the desired results. The scientific test of "truth," like the social test, is strictly practical, except for the fact that the desired results are more severely limited. The results desired by society may be irrational, superstitious, selfish, or humane, but the results desired by scientists are only that our systems of classification produce predictable results. Classifications determine our attitudes and behavior toward the object or event classified. When lightning was classified as "evidence of divine wrath," no courses of action other than prayer were suggested to prevent one's being struck by lightning. But after Benjamin Franklin classified it as "electricity," a measure of control over it was achieved by the invention of the lightning rod. Certain physical disorders were formerly classified as "demonic possession," and this suggested that we "drive the demons out" by whatever spells and incantations we could think of. The results were uncertain. But when those disorders were classified as "bacillus infections," courses of action were suggested that led to more predictable results. Science seeks only the most generally useful systems of classification; these it regards for the time being, until more useful classifications are invented, as "true."

Which of the following would be the best title of this passage?

① The Importance of Societal Classification
② The Eternity of Scientific Classification
③ The Methodology of Effective Classification
④ The Implications of Different Classification Systems
⑤ Societal Classification as a Measure of Predictability

03 Read the following and answer the question. [2 points]

Like the corporate pursuit of computer technology, profit-motivated biotechnology creates several concerns. First is the concern that only the rich will have access to such life-saving technologies as genetic screening and cloned organs. Such fears are justified, considering that companies have been patenting human life. The obesity gene, the premature aging gene, and the breast cancer gene, for example, have already been patented. These patents result in gene monopolies, which could lead to astronomical patient costs for genetic screening and treatment. A biotechnology industry argues that such patents are the only way to recoup research costs that, in turn, lead to further innovations. The commercialization of technology causes several other concerns, including issues of quality control and the tendency for discoveries to remain closely guarded secrets rather than collaborative efforts. In addition, industry involvement has made government control more difficult because researchers depend less and less on federal funding. Finally, although there is little doubt that profit acts as a catalyst for some scientific discoveries, other less commercially profitable but equally important projects may be ignored.

Which of the following is NOT a concern of the writer about profit-motivated biotechnology?

① The costs of genetic treatment will increase.

② The high costs of earning a patent make it difficult to conduct innovative research.

③ Biotechnology industries might keep their research findings confidential.

④ Researchers' decreasing dependence on federal funding has weakened government control.

⑤ Scientific research might hinge more upon commercial profit than upon its importance.

04 Read the following and answer the question. [2 points]

Over the last decade or so, the central debate in the field of early-childhood education has been between one group that favors what you might call a pre-academic approach to pre-kindergarten and kindergarten and another group that contends that the point of school in those early years is not to prepare for academic study but to allow children to explore the world, learn social skills and have free, unconstrained fun. The pre-academic camp seemed to dominate the debate in the late 1990s, drawing on some emerging research that showed that children's abilities at the beginning of kindergarten were powerful predictors of later success. If a child reached his 5th birthday well behind his peers in measures of cognitive ability, this research showed, he would most likely never catch up. The good news in the research was that if you exposed struggling children to certain intensive reading and math interventions in pre-kindergarten and kindergarten, when their minds were still at their most pliable, you could significantly reduce or even eliminate that lag. And so the answer, to many scholars and policy makers, was clear: ___________. More recently, though, a backlash has been growing against the pre-academic approach among educators and child psychologists who believe that kindergarten should be a garden of delight, not a place of stress and distress.

Which of the following best fits in the blank above?

① there was no time to waste in those early years on the playground
② the solution was a return to ample doses of "unstructured play" in kindergarten
③ children are born with flowering imaginations and a natural instinct for make-believe
④ the real purpose of early-childhood education was to free children from disciplinary rules
⑤ the most important goal of kindergarten was to help children develop social skills

05 Read the following and answer the question. [2 points]

Leonardo da Vinci just became even more prolific. An analysis released last month claims a small portrait once attributed to a 19th-century German artist was actually painted by the Italian master around the year 1500. The surprising revelation is but the latest in a series of cases in which "lost" pieces of artwork were rediscovered through art authentication. But how can experts be so sure that a specific painter is responsible for a work of art?

In the case of the Da Vinci painting, the authentication was based on physical evidence. Using a high-resolution multispectral camera, a Canadian forensic-art expert named Peter Paul Biro was able to identify a faint fingerprint left on the canvas. The print was then matched to one on a known Da Vinci painting hanging in Vatican City. Absent compelling forensic evidence like a fingerprint, the authentication process becomes a bit murkier. In the past, pieces of art have been certified through the combination of factors, including brushstroke patterns and analysis of the artist's signature. A painting's provenance, or its history of ownership, is also important. Being able to trace a portrait back from owner-to-owner over the course of centuries is no small feat, making it one that often lends significant weight to a work's legitimacy.

One recent high-profile case highlighting the difficulties in authenticating a piece of art is a disputed Jackson Pollock painting, purchased for $5 by an ex-trucker in a thrift store. Biro was also involved in that investigation, matching a partial fingerprint on the canvas to a paint can used by Pollock. Despite the forensic evidence, the art community has been reluctant to certify the work because there is no record of the painting's former ownership.

Which of the following is correct according to the passage?

① A Da Vinci painting has recently been attributed to a 19th-century German artist.
② By identifying a fingerprint, Biro recently authenticated a known Da Vinci painting hanging in Vatican City.
③ In the past, pieces of art were often certified through physical evidence like a fingerprint.
④ An ex-trucker has unwittingly sold a Jackson Pollock painting for $5.
⑤ The disputed Pollock painting hasn't been readily certified because of the lack of its provenance.

06 **Choose the best order to complete the passage. The first part of the passage is given below.** [2 points]

In the first half of the 20th century, Gestalt psychology served as the foil to behaviorism.

[A] However, research indicates the importance of preparatory work on a problem and an incubation period, followed by elaboration and other activities, to develop the idea.

[B] In the early studies, animal and human subjects were presented with problems that required a novel solution. Perceptual reorganization of the situation led to a solution. Currently, insight is described as seeing clearly into the heart of a situation or problem through a nonconscious process. Suddenness of a solution sometimes is mentioned as a characteristic.

[C] In addition to the laws of perceptual organization that indicate the factors influencing visual perception, Gestalt psychology introduced the concept of insight.

[D] Maintaining that molar rather than molecular behavior should be studied, the Gestalt psychologists focused on perception in learning. Specifically, organisms respond to sensory wholes rather than specific stimuli, and the organization of the sensory environment influences the organism's perception.

① [B] – [A] – [C] – [D]
② [B] – [C] – [A] – [D]
③ [C] – [A] – [B] – [D]
④ [D] – [B] – [C] – [A]
⑤ [D] – [C] – [B] – [A]

2010학년도 2차

Read the passage below and follow the directions. [20 points]

I've finally figured out the difference between neat people and sloppy people. The distinction is, as always, moral. Neat people are lazier and meaner than sloppy people.

Sloppy people, you see, are not really sloppy. Their sloppiness is merely the unfortunate consequence of their extreme moral rectitude. Sloppy people carry in their mind's eye a heavenly vision, a precise plan, that is so stupendous, so perfect, it can't be achieved in this world or the next.

Sloppy people live in Never-Never land. Someday is their métier. Someday they are planning to alphabetize all their books and set up home catalogues. Someday they will go through their wardrobes and mark certain items for tentative mending and certain items for passing on to relatives of similar shape and size. Someday sloppy people will make family scrapbooks into which they will put newspaper clippings, postcards, locks of hair, and the dried corsage from their senior prom. Someday they will file everything on the surface of their desks, including the cash receipts from coffee purchases at the snack shop. Someday they will sit down and read all of the back issues of *The New Yorker*.

Sloppy people can't bear to part with anything. They give loving attention to every detail. When sloppy people say they're going to tackle the surface of the desk, they really mean it. Not a paper will go unturned; not a rubber band will go unboxed. Four hours or two weeks into the excavation, the desk looks exactly the same, primarily because the sloppy person is meticulously creating new piles of paper with new headings and scrupulously stopping to read all the old book catalogs before he throws them away. A neat person would just bulldoze the desk.

Neat people are bums and clods at heart. They have cavalier attitudes toward possessions, including family heirlooms. Everything is just another dust-catcher to them. If anything collects dust, it's got to go and that's that. Neat people will toy with the idea of throwing the children out of the house just to cut down on the clutter.

Neat people don't care about process. They like results. What they want to do is get the whole thing over with so they can sit down and watch the rasslin' on TV. Neat people operate on two unvarying principles: Never handle any item twice, and throw everything away.

The only thing messy in a neat person's house is the trash can. The minute something comes to a neat person's hand, he will look at it, try to decide if it has immediate use and, finding none, throw it in the trash.

** rasslin' : wrestling*

Summarize the above passage in a well-formed paragraph. Your summary must contain the main idea and all major supporting ideas expressed by the author and must not contain any of your own ideas. Do not copy more than eight consecutive words from the passage.

2009학년도 1차

01 **Read the following and answer the question.** [2 points]

For a long time, up to the 16th century, English had been considered inferior to Latin and not equal to expressing abstract and complex thoughts. It took time for English to establish itself as a recognized medium. It needed to establish a regular and uniform orthographical system and to expand its vocabulary to meet the increased demands caused by the demise of Latin and by developments in science and new discoveries throughout the burgeoning Empire. From the 16th century onwards, English flourished. A large number of classical works were translated into English. They became available to the monolingual middle classes and non-academics in general. William Wyclif's campaign against the use of Latin by the church during the Protestant Reformation did much to assist the establishment of English as the accepted form of communication in all fields. Moreover, given the more widespread use of the printing press, it rapidly became obvious that English-language books sold better, so that market forces (a modern term applicable to this period) did much to strengthen the position of English.

Which of the following is correct according to the passage?

① English had established a standardized spelling system before the 16th century.
② Developments in science and new discoveries caused a revival of Latin.
③ The monolingual middle class could get access to classical works before the 16th century.
④ William Wyclif criticized the use of English by the church.
⑤ The increase in demand for English books contributed to enhancing the status of English.

02 Read the following and answer the question. [2 points]

Human beings did not suddenly become ___(1)___. We have always been desirous of things. We have just not had many of them until quite recently, and, in a few generations, we may return to having fewer and fewer. Still, while they last, we enjoy shopping for things and see both the humor and the truth reflected in the aphoristic "born to shop," "shop 'til you drop," and "when the going gets tough, the tough goes shopping." Department store windows, whether on the city street or inside a mall, did not appear by magic. We enjoy looking through them to another world. It is voyeurism for capitalists. The attraction to the inanimate happens all over the world. Berlin Walls fall because people want things, and they want the culture created by things. China opens its door and not because it wants to ___(2)___, but because it wants to ___(3)___. Our love of things is the cause of the Industrial Revolution, not the consequence.

Which of the following would best fit in each blank above?

	(1)	(2)	(3)
①	materialistic	get out	get things in
②	materialistic	get things out	get out
③	democratic	get out	get things in
④	democratic	get things in	get out
⑤	altruistic	get things in	get out

03 Read the following and answer the question. [2 points]

Acupuncture techniques used in Asia as daily remedies over a long history have now become distant to the general public. A major reason why acupuncture is not widely understood is that it does not demonstrate direct healing effects. An acupuncture needle is just a thin piece of stainless steel without pharmacological properties. Analyzing acupuncture in this way, however, cannot explain its treatment effects. Within an oriental medicine perspective, the acupuncture needle itself does not do the healing—it functions only as a key to activate the healing process of the body. The brain is connected to sensors all over the body, which manage its natural healing processes. When the appropriate signal is received at certain places, the brain initiates healing mechanisms, mostly controlled by hormones. The sensor locations are called response points or acupuncture points. They are gates on our bodies through which energy comes and goes; they also function as energy storage and distribution points. Acupuncture functions as more than just a purely physical input.

Which of the following would be the best title of the passage?

① The History of Acupuncture
② The Flow of Energy in the Body
③ Acupuncture and Modern Medicine
④ The Proper Use of the Acupuncture Needle
⑤ The Healing Process of Acupuncture

04 **Choose the best order to complete the story. The first part of the story is given below.** [2 points]

> Our next-door neighbor Jane loves animals. She has a pet rat and two hamsters. She knocked on our door in the morning. "Is this your cat?" she asked. She was holding an old, thin, ginger cat with a little green collar. "No," we replied. "We've never seen it before. Why?"
>
> [A] "You know that cat?" Jane said, "The ginger one with the green collar? Well, the vet said it was very old and very sick. So he gave it an injection and put it to sleep. It's in cat heaven now. Well, what else could he do? We didn't know whose cat it was."
>
> [B] "I don't think it's very well," Jane said. "I'm going to take it to the vet." We agreed with her idea. She cares about animals a lot. But when we saw her again that evening, she was looking sad.
>
> [C] "How are you getting on in your new home?" one of us asked. "Oh, fine," said Mrs. Johnson, looking happily at her husband and her two young children. "But there's just one problem. Our cat's gone missing."
>
> [D] On Saturday, Jane came for a drink. So did the Johnsons, who moved into a house two doors down the road. We had invited them for a drink last week.

① [A] – [C] – [B] – [D]
② [B] – [A] – [D] – [C]
③ [B] – [D] – [A] – [C]
④ [D] – [B] – [A] – [C]
⑤ [D] – [C] – [A] – [B]

05 Read the following and answer the question. [2 points]

> From an early age, Silva saw the damage that reckless business interests were doing to Brazil's ecosystem. As a child, instead of going to school, she worked in the forest tapping rubber from the trees to help support her ten brothers and sisters. She watched as the bulldozers came for her trees, clearing land for roads that would connect the rain forest with the rest of Brazil. It wasn't just the trees that were devastated—so were the lives of many Brazilians who depended on the rain forest. She organized a group which fought deforestation at the grassroots level. She mobilized the unions of rubber tappers to fight against powerful interest groups. She later moved into the political mainstream, becoming the first rubber tapper in Brazil's Senate. When populist President Lula came to power in 2002, Silva was the obvious choice for Environment Minister. The outsider was in. After six acrimonious years as Brazil's Environment Minister, fighting a losing battle against industrial and political leaders eager to develop the Amazon at any cost, Silva resigned in protest in May. However, ____________________

Which of the following best completes the last sentence?

① Silva remains a lasting symbol of courage for the environment.
② Silva was a victim of the short-term vagaries of politics.
③ the Amazon's ecosystem was doomed to failure.
④ Silva is done fighting for the environment.
⑤ Silva fought against the supporters of the green movement.

2009학년도 2차

Read the statement below and follow the directions. [10 points]

Some people believe that homework is an important component of learning which facilitates further understanding; others think that homework is largely ineffective as a learning aid and may actually diminish a student's interest in learning.

Which view do you agree with? Take a position and defend it. Be sure to follow the guidelines below.

Guidelines

- Write one paragraph, composed of approximately 200 words (20 lines).
- Include a thesis statement and a concluding sentence.
- Use two specific reasons to support your position.
- Explain your reasons as persuasively and convincingly as possible.

2009학년도 6월 모의평가

01 **Read the following and answer the question.** [2.5 points]

At first sight experience seems to bury us under a flood of external objects, pressing upon us with a sharp and importunate reality, calling us out of ourselves in a thousand forms of action. But when reflection begins to play upon those objects, they are dissipated under its influence; the cohesive force seems suspended like some trick of magic; each object is loosed into a group of impressions—color, odor, texture—in the mind of the observer. And if we continue to dwell in thought on this world, not of objects in the solidity with which language invests them, but of ____(1)____, unstable, flickering, inconsistent, which burn and are extinguished with our consciousness of them, it contracts still further: the whole scope of observation is dwarfed into the narrow chamber of the individual mind. ____(2)____, already reduced to a group of impressions, is surrounded for each one of us by that thick wall of personality through which no real voice has ever pierced on its way to us, or from us to hat which we can only conjecture to be without. Every one of those impressions is the impression of the individual in his isolation, each mind keeping as a solitary prisoner its own dream of a world.

Which of the following best fits in each blank above?

	(1)	(2)
①	impressions	Experience
②	impressions	Thought
③	experiences	Thought
④	experiences	Reality
⑤	personalities	Experience

02 Read the following and answer the question. [1.5 points]

When older people can no longer remember names at a cocktail party, they tend to think that their brainpower is declining. But a growing number of studies suggest that this assumption is often wrong. Instead, the research finds, the aging brain is simply taking in more data and trying to sift through a clutter of information, often to its long-term benefit. Some brains do deteriorate with age, as in the case of Alzheimer's disease. But for most aging adults, much of what occurs is a gradually widening focus of attention that makes it more difficult to latch onto just one fact, like a name or telephone number. Although that can be frustrating, it is often useful. It may be that distractibility is not, in fact, a bad thing. It may increase the amount of information available to the conscious mind. For example, in studies where subjects are asked to read passages that are interrupted with unexpected words or phrases, adults 60 and older work much more slowly than college students. Although the students plow through the texts at a consistent speed regardless of what the out-of-place words mean, older people slow down even more when the words are related to the topic at hand. That indicates that they are not just stumbling over the extra information, but are taking it in and processing it.

When both groups are asked the questions to which the out-of-place words are answers, who will do better and why?

① Students respond better because they can read faster.
② Students respond better because they are not distracted.
③ Older people respond better because they retain the extra data.
④ Older people respond worse because their brains decline.
⑤ Older people respond better because they have more time.

03 **The first part of the passage is given below. Reorder [A], [B] and [C] to complete the passage.** [2 points]

Economists are very confident that cost-benefit analysis and diminishing marginal utility are good descriptions of decision-making because there is plenty of evidence that other species also behave in ways consistent with these concepts.

[A] Other species seem to be affected by this diminishing marginal utility principle and become indifferent to marginal units of something that they've recently enjoyed a lot of. Even bacteria seem to display this behavior. So while economists' models of human behavior may seem to ignore some relevant factors, they do take into account some very fundamental and universal behaviors.

[B] Scientists can train birds to peck at one button in order to earn food and another button to earn time on a treadmill. If scientists increase the cost of one of the options by increasing the number of clicks required to get it, the birds respond rationally by not clicking so much on the button for that option. But even more interesting is that they also switch to clicking more on the button for the other option.

[C] The birds seem to understand that they have only a limited number of clicks they can make before they get exhausted, and they allocate clicks between the two options so as to maximize their total utility. Consequently when the relative costs and benefits of the options change, they change their behavior quite rationally in response.

① [C] – [B] – [C]
② [B] – [A] – [C]
③ [B] – [C] – [A]
④ [C] – [A] – [B]
⑤ [C] – [B] – [A]

04 Read the following and answer the question. [2 points]

The debt Singaporeans owe to their 149 year old botanical gardens is as much economic as ecological. In 1888, an eccentric but zealous gardener named Nicholas Ridley cut channels into the bark of several rubber trees grown from seedlings sent from London. He trapped the sap, giving birth to the then British colony's rubber industry. Over the next half century, rubber utterly transformed Singapore, whose sleepy economy had hitherto been dominated by the spice trade. With the advent of the automobile and its insatiable demand for tires, Singapore boomed.

The city-state hasn't looked back since. These days, when its citizens feel like a gentle walk, many of them consider the 63 hectare Botanic Gardens to be one of the very best places of it. Modern amenities abound—every tree, shrub and herb is now meticulously labeled, for example, and the eco-friendly open-air bathrooms are immaculate, thanks to the exertions of its 90 member staff and a generous $5.8 million annual budget. For the roughly three million visitors who stream through the gardens annually, slipping through one of its 10 gates is like slipping into a wilder past. More than any museum or library, the majestic trees, palms and flowers are a reminder of what Singapore once was.

Which of the following is NOT true?

① Rubber trees that grew in the Botanic Gardens are not native to Singapore.
② The auto industry contributed to the economic growth of Singapore.
③ The Botanic Gardens were restored to their state before the rubber industry.
④ The Botanic Gardens provide good sanitary facilities.
⑤ The Botanic Gardens are a famous tourist attraction.

05 Read the following and answer the question. [2 points]

Speak about something you have earned the right to talk about through experience or study. Such speakers never fail to keep the attention of their listeners. I know from experience that speakers are not easily persuaded to accept this point of view—they avoid using personal experiences as too trivial and too restrictive. They would rather soar into the realms of general ideas and philosophical principles, where unfortunately the air is too rarefied for ordinary mortals to breathe. They give us editorials when we are hungry for the news. None of us is averse to listening to editorials, when they are given by someone who has earned the right to editorialize—an editor or publisher of a newspaper. Several years ago, I made a survey of topics that held the attention of listeners in my classes. I found that the topics most approved by the audience were concerned with certain fairly defined areas of one's background. Topics that deal with the family, childhood memories, school days, invariably get attention, because most of us are interested in the way other people met and overcame obstacles in the environment in which they were reared. The point is this: Speak about ________________________.

Which of the following best concludes the passage?

① what you aspire to know and I will be interested in your story
② what others are interested in and you will keep their attention
③ newspaper editorials and you will be appreciated by publishers
④ what life has taught you and I will be your devoted listener
⑤ general ideas or you will lose your audience

06 Read the following and answer the question. [2 points]

The key to understanding Picasso's abstraction of Marie-Therese is to realize that abstractions may not represent whole things but one or another of their less obvious properties. Picasso decided to focus his attention not on his model but on the space she inhabited. It is essential to the interpretation of this picture that we recognize that, unlike most models, Marie-Therese was in motion. Her knitting needles swung back and forth, in and out. Picasso has therefore drawn the curves that her head, hands, elbows, shoulders, and body swept out as they moved through space. It is as if he had attached luminescent markers that left a trace in the air as she moved. The result is a complex picture. Picasso tells us from his realistic portrayals of himself and his model that he could have drawn her realistically if he had wanted to. He did not. There is, his portrait says, another reality that is also Marie-Therese, one that is just as interesting and significantly more unexpected. You are looking, Picasso admonishes us, but you are not seeing. Find the surprising properties hidden behind the obvious ones. See with your mind, not your eyes!

Which of the following would be the best title of the passage?

① Visual Stimulus for Creativity
② The Use of Space in Painting
③ Picasso's Affection for Marie-Therese
④ Abstraction: The Spirit of Modern Art
⑤ How to Interpret Picasso's Abstract Art

Chapter 03

2008~1997학년도 기출문제

모범답안 및 번역 p.82

2008학년도 서울 · 인천

01 **다음 글을 읽고, 글에 드러난 갈등과 시사점을 각각 30자 내외의 우리말로 쓰시오.** [4 points]

The Forest

A small town on the edge of a large, old-growth forest was facing a lot of hardship. The town's main industry, coal mining, was no longer profitable and the industry was shut down. Many of the townspeople lost their jobs and were unable to find new work. One day, a wood-chipping company came to the town. They wanted to open up a factory there. They planned to chop down trees from the forest and transport them to the factory to turn them into wood-chips. The company said that over four thousand jobs would be created by this new industry. The town instantly became divided. In one group were the people who said that if the town did not take up the company's offer, there would be no jobs and the town would die. The other group of people said that it was wrong to chop down an old forest and that the environment would suffer damage that could not be repaired. It was a terrible situation for the people to face. If the town was going to survive, the most beautiful part of it, the forest, would have to be destroyed. However, if the forest was saved, the town would die without an industry. Finally, a group of people in the town decided that there was a third possibility—tourism. They started a business taking groups of tourists into the forest and explaining the history of this beautiful place. The town became a very popular place to visit and soon many jobs were created.

• 갈등 : ______________________________

____

____

• 시사점 : ______________________________

____

____

02 **다음 글을 읽고, 인간의 감정 형성에 관한 세 입장을 가장 잘 나타내는 핵심어를 각각 6자 내외의 우리말로 쓰시오.** [4 points]

Psychological anthropologists have been conducting research on the topic of emotions since the early research of Benedict and Mead, who argued that each culture is unique and that people in various societies have different personalities and consequently, different types of emotions. These different emotions are a result of the unique kind of enculturation that has shaped the individual's personality. In their view, the enculturation process is predominant in creating varying emotions among different societies. In other words, culture determines not only how people think and behave but also how they feel emotionally.

Other early psychological anthropologists focused on universal biological processes that produce similar emotional developments and feelings in people throughout the world. According to this perspective, emotions are seen as instinctive behaviors that stimulate physiological processes in the brain. In other words, if an individual feels "anger," this automatically raises his or her blood pressure and stimulates specific muscle movements. In this view, emotional developments are part of the biology of humans universally, and thus emotions are experienced the same everywhere.

More recently, anthropologists have emphasized an interactionist approach, taking both human universals and cultural variation into account in their studies of emotions. Based on his ethnographic study of three Indonesian groups, Karl Heider concluded that four of the emotions—sadness, anger, happiness, and surprise—tend to be what he classifies as basic cross-cultural emotions. Other emotions, however, such as love, fear, and disgust, appear to vary among these societies. Fear, for example, is mixed with guilt, and feelings of disgust are difficult to translate across cultural boundaries.

- 입장 1 : ______________________
- 입장 2 : ______________________
- 입장 3 : ______________________

03 **Fill in the blank with the most appropriate word from the passage. Change the word form if necessary.** [3 points]

> In my boyhood I never liked to go into London; nor was I content to remain in the suburb of Wimbledon. As often as I could, I took the train with one or other of my brothers into the countryside of Surrey. After thirty or forty minutes we could at last set our eyes upon uninterrupted field and forest, and breathe in the fresh air of God's nature, and rejoice in the freedom of which we were deprived in our London suburb. What I particularly noticed about the roads there were the gardens in front of every house. For the houses didn't immediately front on the roads, as in the centers of towns or cities; but they were set back from the roads with a space for gardens. I noticed two things in particular. One was that no two of them were identical, but each was a work of art in itself. The other was that in each garden there were invariably roses: in other words, they weren't just gardens, but more precisely rose-gardens. Truly, I said to myself, not only in the countryside but even in the city England is a garden—a rose-garden. It wasn't for nothing that Shakespeare called his country "this other Eden, demi-paradise." As for the people, they are indeed a nation, not—as Napoleon contemptuously called them—of shop keepers, but of (   ).

---

04 **Write the best title for the passage. Use all and only the words from the word list.** [3 points]

> Many people begin their criticism with sincere praise followed by the word "but" and ending with a critical statement. For example, in trying to change a child's careless attitude toward studies, we might say, "We're really proud of you, Johnnie, for raising your grades this term. But if you had worked harder on your algebra, the results would have been better." In this case, Johnnie might feel encouraged until he heard the word "but." He might then question the sincerity of the original praise. To him, the praise seemed only to be a contrived lead-in to a critical inference of failure. Credibility would be strained, and we probably would not achieve our objectives of changing Johnnie's attitude toward his studies. This could be easily overcome by changing the word "but" to "and." "We're really proud of you, Johnnie, for raising your grades this term, and by continuing the same conscientious efforts next term, your algebra grade can be up with all the others." Now, Johnnie would accept the praise because there was no follow-up of an inference of failure. We have called his attention to the behavior we wished to change indirectly, and the chances are he will try to live up to our expectations.

Word List

way / behavior / indirect / a(n) / changing / of

____

05 다음 글을 읽고 글의 요지를 25자 내외의 우리말로 쓰시오. [3 points]

Is it better to be loved than feared, or vice versa? I don't doubt that every prince would like to be both; but since it is hard to accommodate these qualities, if you have to make a choice, to be feared is much safer than to be loved. For it is a good general rule about men, that they are ungrateful, fickle, liars and deceivers, fearful of danger and greedy for gain. While you serve their welfare, they are all yours, offering their blood, their belongings, their lives, and their children's lives—so long as the danger is remote. But when the danger is close at hand, they turn against you. Then, any prince who has relied on their words and has made no other preparations will come to grief; because people are less concerned with offending a man who makes himself loved than one who makes himself feared. The reason is that love is a link of obligation which men, because they are rotten, will break any time they think doing so serves their advantage; but fear involves dread of punishment, from which they can never escape. Still, a prince should make himself feared in such a way that, even if he gets no love, he gets no hate either.

2008학년도 전국

01 **다음 글을 읽고 <보기>에 제시된 세 개의 표현을 나열하여 빈칸에 들어갈 가장 적절한 문장을 완성하시오.** [3 points]

The word that has been most cheapened and devalued in our language is "love." We use it for everything—we love our mother, we love our new car, we love ice cream and Mozart and picnics and being left alone. Most people suppose that first we think, and then we find words to express our thoughts. Actually, we think in and with words, and the words we have at our command shape the thoughts they express, rather than the other way around.

For example, we do not love our children in the same way we love our wives or sweethearts. We do not love our country in any sense that we love the color blue or the taste of peppermint or the smell of roses. We do not love God in the way we love our pet cockatoo. Our failure to make these verbal distinctions is more than "a manner of speaking"; it is a manner of conceptualizing, of defining and distinguishing.

(   ). We are spurred to action by slogans and catchwords rather than by the concrete realities they embody.

보기

control and direct   our thoughts   the words we use

02 다음 글을 읽고 <보기>의 모든 표현을 사용하여 빈칸에 들어갈 가장 적절한 문장을 완성하시오. [4 points]

Through socialization humans learn to be effective members of the society, class, region, and family into which they are born, and come to understand the social relations that surround them. Indeed, socialization goes on throughout life and people prove almost infinitely capable of learning and unlearning social roles. For example, the ways a doctor and a patient will interact are largely prescribed in the roles of "doctor" and "patient." Doctors learn their part of the script in medical school. Patients learn theirs in the mass media, or by interacting with doctors. People comc into a world of fairly stable pre-existing relations. In a world they never made, people must learn to play their assigned parts. This top-down theory is more likely to emphasize persistent inequalities of power. Such inequalities favour certain roles and interactions over others. In general, top-down theory fits the observed persistence of social order.

Yet, even under the simplest conditions, interactions are more than a performance of prescribed social roles. People repeatedly meet new situations and create new roles and rules. Whether they realize it or not, people often negotiate social relations from the bottom-up through interaction. It is this negotiation process that creates and re-creates what we call social structure. Creativity is evident in all newly forming ethnic communities and movements to protest social inequality. The resurgence of neighborhoods, networks, and informal communities shows human creativity despite the supposed "death of community." Thus, ( ); and all respond to pressures for change. Socialization influences the forms creativity may take, and the patterns of change that finally emerge.

보기

all social organizations		and	bottom-up
creativity	display	socialization	top-down

03 다음 글을 읽고 빈칸 ①과 ②에 공통으로 들어갈 가장 적절한 한 단어를 <보기>에서 찾아 쓰시오. [3 points]

Although it is obvious that specific languages differ from each other on the surface, if we look closer we find that human languages are surprisingly (①). For instance, all known languages are at a similar level of complexity and detail—there is no such thing as a primitive human language. All languages provide a means for asking questions, making requests, making assertions, and so on. And there is nothing that can be expressed in one language that cannot be expressed in any other. Obviously, one language may have terms not found in another language, but it is always possible to invent new terms to express what we mean: anything we can imagine or think, we can express in any human language.

Turning to more abstract properties, even the formal structures of language are similar: all languages have sentences made up of smaller phrasal units, these units in turn being made up of words, which are themselves made up of sequences of sounds. All of these features of human language are so obvious to us that we may fail to see how surprising it is that languages share them. When linguists use the term *language*, or *natural human language*, they are revealing their belief that at the abstract level, beneath the surface variation, languages are remarkably (②) in form and function, conforming to certain universal principles.

보기

disorderly primitive popular similar indistinguishable

04 **다음 글을 읽고 apartheid를 가장 명확하게 의미하는 두 단어로 이루어진 '어구'를 글에서 찾아 쓰시오.** [4 points]

"I'll cut you down to size yet, my boy," my father shouted after me. "Wait until I send you to the mountain school back in the homelands, where they'll teach you respect. Just you wait and see." I stayed at Granny's a week, and then returned home. My father said nothing, but I sensed that he was planning some sort of retaliation. I was ready for anything. He couldn't whip me as he used to when I was a child, for I was growing stronger and more stubborn every day. We both knew that we were on a collision course. I was set in my ways, he in his. He disparaged education, I extolled it; he believed all that the white man said about him without protesting against racial segregation, I did not; he lived for the moment, I for the future, uncertain as it was. It soon became evident that the reason my father lived for the moment was because he was terrified of the future—terrified of facing the reality that I was on the way to becoming a somebody in a world that regarded him as a nobody, a world that had stripped him of his manhood, of his power to provide. Years of watching him suffer under the double yoke of <u>apartheid</u> and tribalism convinced me that his was a hopeless case, so long as he persisted in clinging to tribal beliefs and letting the white man define his manhood.

---

05 **다음 글을 읽고 글의 요지를 30자 이내의 우리말로 쓰시오.** [4 points]

Many of today's drivers continue to have trouble avoiding collisions, and traffic-safety experts continue to search for ways to make driving safer. After an emphasis on improving the designs of cars and roads in recent years, the auto-safety focus now is reverting to what used to be called "the nut behind the wheel." But it isn't easy to improve the ingrained behavior of drivers, whom some analysts blame for more than 90% of all traffic accidents. The problem is that pinpointing which drivers are to blame for crashes, why accidents happen and how to stop them remains elusive. For example, drivers with the worst accident or violation records do account for more than their share of accidents, but their numbers are relatively few, and they cause only a small percentage of all crashes. The largest part of the traffic-accident problem has been shown to involve lapses by normal drivers rather than errors by just a few problem cases. Changing driver habits is so difficult partly because people just don't take driving seriously.

2007학년도 서울 · 인천

01 **Fill in the blank with one word from the passage below so that it can best fit the passage.** [3 points]

Differences in conventional ways of "framing" can cause confusion and misinterpretation in public settings. For example, "mainstream" American conventions require workers to look busy even if they aren't, but some cultural styles require people to look "cool"—that is, not busy—even if they are. A customer walks into a post office and is pleased to see that there are no other customers before her, and the clerk isn't busy. He's singing to himself, dancing in place, and dawdling with some papers, moving slowly and casually, showing no signs of focused attention. So the customer is annoyed when the clerk makes no move to help her or even to acknowledge her approach.

But the clerk really was doing something important. When he finished, he turned to her and cheerfully served her. If he had displayed toward his task an air of great attention and preoccupation, with focused movements, she would have gotten the metamessage "I am (   )" before she approached and wouldn't have expected immediate service.

---

02 **Fill in the blank with one appropriate word beginning with the two letters 'i' and 'n'.** [3 points]

> Let us consider for a moment what most of the trouble and anxiety which I have referred to is about, and how much it is necessary that we be troubled or, at least, careful. It would be some advantage to live a primitive and frontier life, though in the midst of an outward civilization, if only to learn what are the gross necessaries of life and what methods have been taken to obtain them; or even to look over the old daybooks of the merchants, to see what it was that men most commonly bought at the stores, what they stored, that is, what are the grossest groceries. For the improvements of ages have had but little (in__________) on the essential laws of man's existence; as our skeletons, probably, are not to be distinguished from those of our ancestors.

____

03 **Fill in each blank with one appropriate word from the word list. The same word should be used only once.** [3 points]

> The genetic differences must be minor quantitative variations. The reason is (①). Imagine that two people were really built from fundamentally different designs: either physical designs, like the structure of the lungs, or neurological designs, like the circuitry underlying some cognitive process. Complex organisms require many finely structured parts, which in turn require many genes to build them. But the chromosomes are randomly split, re-joined, and shuffled during the formation of sex cells, and then are paired with other halves at fertilization. If two people really had different designs, their (②) would inherit a jumble of fragments from the genetic blueprints of each. Only if the two designs were extremely similar to begin with could the new combination work. That is why the variation that geneticists tell us about is (③) and kept within narrow limits by natural selection.

Word List

offspring	characteristic	psychological
microscopic	typography	anatomy
quality	circuit	sex

① ______________________

② ______________________

③ ______________________

04 **Read the story below and complete the given statement indicating where Paragraph A should be placed. Write the paragraph number in the bracket.** [3 points]

A shopkeeper walks down the street with the week's takings in his briefcase. Suddenly a thief snatches the bag and drives off.

[1] But then things start to go wrong for the robber. First, the bag makes a loud, high-pitched noise. Then it becomes hot and starts to smoulder, so that the car is soon filled with thick red smoke.

[2] The thief may throw his booty out on to the pavement and escape, coughing. But even without the alarm and smoke from the briefcase, the prize would have been worthless. Another of its defences is to release a red dye over the banknotes, making them worthless.

[3] The S-100 system has two main features—a radio receiver and an alarm—and can be hidden in any lockable non-metallic bag. The owner carries in his pocket a transmitter which sends a continuous signal to the receiver in the bag.

[4] Unless it is brought back to within two metres of the transmitter, after another ten seconds it gives off another signal and the dye is automatically released over the contents of the bag. Then the fireworks start.

[5] The S-100 has already been successful in use. In February two robbers threw a case containing ￡8,000 out of their speeding car.

Paragraph A

The alarm does not go off as long as it receives the signal from within a two-metre radius. If the bag is moved further away for more than ten seconds, the receiver makes a loud noise.

Paragraph A should be placed immediately before paragraph [   ].

2007학년도 전국

01 다음 글을 읽고, <보기>의 단어를 모두 한 번씩 사용하여 맨 끝 문장을 완성하시오. [3 points]

Those who cannot accept change often miss out on many new experiences. These people are afraid of change probably because they think the current level of comfort in their lives will be threatened by the burden of learning and adapting to something new. Due to this fear, new foods, new languages, new cities and new friends are left for others to try. As a matter of fact, however, all these elements, when added to one's life, create opportunities for increased knowledge and experience. Mastering new languages, for example, would ensure one could travel around the world with comfort, and would help to expand one's experience with new cultures. Friendship with new and different people can open one's eyes to different life-styles, which also makes life richer. Challenges with new foods could increase one's interest in new hobbies like cooking and traveling. Undoubtedly, people who fear change will ________________.

보기

themselves	deprive	to	lives
opportunities	their	of	ameliorate

---

02 **다음 (1)과 (2)는 원문을 풀어 쓴 것(paraphrase)이다. (1)에 비해 (2)가 바람직하지 않은 이유를 30자 내외의 우리말로 쓰시오.** [3 points]

원문

Video rental stores started out in the 1970s as locally owned mom-and-pop stores. But these small-scale operations didn't last very long after big national chains emerged and gobbled up most of the local market.

(1)

In the 1970s, video rental stores were frequently small and locally owned. But many of these stores lost their market and went out of business when the huge national chains came to town.

(2)

In the late 1970s, video rental stores were widely successful as small, local businesses, but they couldn't compete with the huge national chains that charged less and drove small stores out of business.

03 다음 글을 읽고, 지시에 따라 답하시오. [3 points]

Of all of the senses that humans possess, sight is the most developed. The structure of human eyes and their placement at the front of the head gives human vision some important capabilities. The eyes of humans can detect and resolve fine detail; they are capable of distinguishing a wide range of colours of the spectrum; and (a) <u>their broad area of binocular overlap</u> permits ready appreciation of the depth of visual fields. These capabilities are part of the universal biological features assigned to *Homo sapiens* in the evolutionary sequence, distinguishing us from other species. Together they form the biological basis for the primacy accorded to sight among human senses. The primacy of vision is evident in many everyday sayings, such as 'Seeing is believing' and 'I wouldn't have believed it if I hadn't seen it with my own eyes.' Seeing provides a certainty that ______(b)______. It is therefore unsurprising that scientific discourse is replete with visual imagery. Science is based on true 'observations' of the world and endeavors to develop objective, 'clear-sighted,' unbiased 'views' of the phenomena that it investigates.

3-1 밑줄 친 (a)의 의미를 우리말로 쓰시오.

____

3-2 <보기>에 주어진 단어를 모두 한 번씩 사용하여 빈칸 (b)를 완성하시오.

보기

sense	capable	other	no	affording	seems	of

____

04 다음 글을 읽고, 지시에 따라 답하시오. [3 points]

Today, marriage and motherhood are coming apart. Remarriage and marriage rates are declining even as the rates of divorce remain stuck at historic highs and childbearing outside marriage becomes more common. Many women see single motherhood as a choice and a right to be exercised if a suitable husband does not come along in time. The vision of the "first stage" feminism of the 1960s and '70s, which held out the model of the career woman unfettered by husband and children, has been accepted by women only in part. Women want to be fettered by children, even to the point of going through grueling infertility treatments or artificial insemination to achieve ____(a)____. But they are increasingly ambivalent about the ties that bind them to a husband and about the necessity of ____(b)____ as a condition of parenthood. As the bearers and nurturers of children and increasingly as the sole breadwinners for families, women continue to be engaged in personally rewarding and socially valuable pursuits. They are able to demonstrate their feminine virtues outside marriage.

4-1 초기 단계 페미니즘에서 추구했던 여성상이 무엇인지 20자 내외의 우리말로 쓰시오.

____

4-2 빈칸 (a)와 (b)에 들어갈 단어를 <보기>에서 찾아 각각 하나씩 쓰시오.

보기

parenthood   divorce   motherhood   marriage

(a) ______________________________

(b) ______________________________

2006학년도 서울 · 인천

01 **Read the passage and follow the directions.**

In talking with people, don't begin by discussing the things on which you differ. Begin by emphasizing the things on which you agree. Get the other person saying "Yes, yes" at the outset. Keep your opponent, if possible, from saying "No." Keep emphasizing, if possible, that you are both striving for the same end and that your only difference is one of method and not of purpose. A "No" response is a most difficult handicap to overcome. When you have said "No," all your pride of personality demands that you remain consistent with yourself. You may later feel that the "No" was ill-advised; nevertheless, there is your precious pride to consider! Once having said a thing, you feel you must stick to it. Hence it is of the very greatest importance that a person ______________________________.

Fill in the blank with ALL and ONLY the words in the box below. [3 points]

affirmative	started	direction	be	in	the	should

____

02 Read the passage and follow the directions.

> If readers are reading to get a general idea of a text, then they can probably skip over a fair number of unknown words as long as those words are not important and thus may be ignored. One strategy to determine if the meaning of an unknown word is necessary to the overall meaning of the sentence is to read the sentence ____(1)____ and see if a general meaning is obtained. Another strategy is to examine the grammatical category of the word. If it is an adjective or an adverb, readers can probably get by without it. If, on the other hand, an unknown word appears several times in a text and seems to be the key to ____(2)____, then that word needs to be dealt with. Nouns and verbs are usually important enough to the basic meaning in the sense that readers cannot get a general idea without knowing what they mean.

Fill in each blank with THREE words in the box below. The word the can be used more than once. [4 points]

idea	general	word	the	without

(1) ______________________________

(2) ______________________________

03 Read the passage and follow the directions.

By the eighteenth century printed materials were so widespread as to bring on fear of a "literacy crisis," a literacy crisis which was the exact opposite of ours in that it involved too much rather than too little reading. There is a continuing, and unresolvable, argument about the actual increase in literacy rates in the eighteenth century. But the leaders of society then certainly feared that reading had become much too widespread, and the dangers of increased reading by the lower classes were much discussed. Locke did not, for example, favor teaching the poor. Those who deplored reading did not simply condemn its effects on morals and politics; they feared it would damage public health. A 1795 tract listed the physical consequences of excessive reading: "susceptibility to colds, headaches, weakening of the eyes, heat rashes, indigestion, melancholy, etc." Reading came to be ______________ in much the same way that too much television viewing in the late twentieth century has become a kind of cultural bogey.

Fill in the blank with ONE word from the passage. [3 points]

____

04 **Read the statement below and follow the directions.** [9 points]

> The human teacher may be replaced by multimedia tools for language learning in the future.

Write a paragraph indicating whether you agree or disagree with the statement. Follow these guidelines.

Guidelines

- Include a topic sentence.
- Support your position with TWO specific reasons.
- Use neat handwriting.
- Use approximately 100 words.

2006학년도 전국

01 **다음 글을 읽고 밑줄 친 otherwise가 가리키는 내용을 본문의 단어만 사용하여 8단어 내외로 빈칸에 쓰시오.** [3 points]

> What is a thesis? It's a viewpoint, a contention. A good thesis, I would argue, is above all *arguable*—that is, not everyone will agree with it. But please understand that it won't necessarily concern a 'right/wrong' issue. Often it will concern whether something is urgent or not urgent, interesting or not interesting, a good way to do something or a not-so-good way to do something, a can-we-achieve-this issue or a can-we-not-achieve-this issue. Whatever position you are taking, it should involve some conviction, preferably bold, that even skeptics will approach with curiosity, if only to see how biased, benighted, or boring you'll prove to be. Your job, of course, is to convince them otherwise! That is always the grand challenge in writing, isn't it: *to bring people around*—to teach them, amuse them, inspire them, goad them, charm them, awaken them, convince them.

Your job, of course, is to convince them that ______________________________.

02 다음 글을 읽고 지시에 따라 답하시오. [4 points]

In my own research, complaints from women about their husbands most often focused not on tangible inequities such as having given up the chance for a career in order to assist her husband in his own, or doing far more than their share of life-support work like cleaning, cooking, social arrangements and errands. Instead, they focused on ___①___ : “He doesn’t listen to me,” “He doesn’t talk to me.” I found that most wives want their husbands to be, first and foremost, conversational partners, but few husbands share this expectation of their wives.

How can women and men have such different impressions of communication in marriage? Why the widespread imbalance in their interests and expectations? Stanford University’s Maccoby reports the results of her own and others’ research showing that children’s development is most influenced by the social structure of peer interactions. Boys and girls tend to ___②___, and their sex-separate groups have different organizational structures and interactive norms. I believe these systematic differences in childhood socialization made talk between women and men like cross-cultural communication.

2-1 **빈칸 ①에 들어갈 알맞은 단어를 본문에서 찾아 1단어로 쓰시오.**

____

2-2 **<보기>의 단어를 모두 한 번씩 사용하여 빈칸 ②를 채워 문장을 완성하시오.**

보기

children	with	of	own	gender	their	play

____

03 다음 글을 읽고, 지시에 따라 답하시오. [4 points]

How do today's meditators achieve a successful meditation? A few simple recommendations are almost universal. ___(a)___, anyone who wants to meditate successfully must set aside a quiet time each day, usually about a half-hour. This must be done consistently, ___(b)___ the results are cumulative and will not appear in a single session. The place you select for meditation also matters. In my own private poll, I found many people who meditate best in an empty church. Perhaps even more often, experienced meditators turn to natural locales—a forest, a lonely shore. Each answers the need to be alone and the need for a feeling of space.

Most important is attitude. All the various techniques of meditation seek to produce a state of openness, inner calm and increased self-awareness. ___(c)___ no one can see into the depths of his mind when it is whirling about like a cyclone. ___(d)___ the seemingly absurd devices of posture and concentration—which are designed as aids to quiet the storm of daily concerns.

빈칸 (a), (b), (c), (d)에 들어갈 적합한 단어를 <보기>에서 찾아 쓰시오. (단, 대·소문자 구분 필요 없음)

보기

finally	first	hence	because	although	but

(a) ______________________

(b) ______________________

(c) ______________________

(d) ______________________

2005학년도 서울 · 인천

01 **Read the passage and follow the directions.** [3 points]

Good writers assume, with a pessimism born of experience, that whatever isn't plainly stated, the reader will invariably misconstrue. They keep in mind that she is, after all, a perfect stranger to their garden of ingenious ideas. In fact, to her, that garden may initially resemble a tangled thicket, if not a tropical rain forest. This being so, their job as a writer is to guide her through, step by step, so that the experience will be quick and memorable. This involves alertly anticipating her moments of confusion and periodically giving her an explanation of where she's headed. The writer's golden rule is the same as the moralists: Do unto others as you would have them do unto you.

Complete the main idea of the passage by filling in the blank with about 10 words.

A good writer's duty ____.

02 Read the passage and follow the directions. [6 points]

The more we learn about the inner workings of the mind, ___(a)___. The world of the mind has been considered very different from that of our bodies. Cut into the body, and blood pours forth. But slice into the brain, and thoughts and emotions do not spill out onto the operating table. The latest mind-body research, ___(1)___, shows that the brain is just another organ, although more complex than the rest. The thoughts and emotions are the result of complex electric and chemical interactions between nerve cells. The feelings of worthlessness that accompany depression are no more than diseases in brain electrochemistry.

Scientists are also learning something else. Not only is the mind like the rest of the body, but the well-being of one is closely connected with that of the other. This makes sense ___(2)___ they share the same systems. What happens in the pancreas or liver can directly affect brain function. Disorders of the brain, conversely, can send out biochemical shock waves that disturb the rest of the body. More and more doctors—and patients—recognize that mental states and physical well-being are closely connected. An unhealthy body can lead to an unhealthy mind, which worsens diseases in the body. Fixing a problem in one place, ___(3)___, can often help the other.

2-1 **Fill in blank (a) with about 15 words including the ones in the box below.** [3 points]

mind, body, different, realize, more

____

2-2 **Fill in blanks (1), (2), and (3) with one word from the box below.** [3 points]

because, besides, therefore, whereas, however, otherwise

(1) ____

(2) ____

(3) ____

03 Read the passage and follow the directions. [3 points]

To understand what a writer is saying, we must understand more than the surface meanings of words; we have to understand the context as well. To grasp the words on a page, we have to know a lot of information that isn't set down on the page. When Putnam says that Americans can be depended upon to distinguish tigers and leopards but not elms and beeches, he assumes that his readers will agree with him because they are culturally literate. He takes it for granted that one literate person knows approximately the same things as another and is aware of the probable limits of the other person's knowledge. That second level of awareness—knowing ____________________—is crucial for effective communication. To know what educated people know about tigers but don't know about elm trees is the sort of cultural knowledge, limited in extent but possessed by all literate people, that must be brought into the open and taught to our children.

Fill in the blank with ALL and ONLY the words in the box below. The word *know* can be used twice.

probably, know, not, and, do, what, others

____

04 **Read the passage and follow the directions.** [3 points]

Two main types of arguments to persuade are rational and emotional. If you are writing an essay against hunting, for example, an emotional appeal might begin as follows: "Every year hundreds of bloodthirsty killers go out and ruthlessly slaughter thousands of innocent, helpless animals." A rational appeal against hunting, on the other hand, might begin as follows: "Every year sportsmen buy their hunting licenses and legally kill the state-allotted limit of animals; however, evidence shows that this practice must be stopped because nature cannot replenish the dwindling animal supply."

Rational arguments are better, especially when writing for an academic audience. In the rational example above, for instance, it would be possible to support your position with the number of licenses issued, the number of animals killed every year, and the estimated decline in animal populations. Emotional arguments work best when writing for an audience that already agrees with your position; however, they are rarely successful in persuading someone who does not already agree. It is best to use emotional arguments very sparingly for an academic audience.

Complete the summary by filling in each blank with ONE word from the passage.

When you write a persuasive essay, it is a good idea to use ___(1)___ arguments for an audience who does not already agree with you but is likely to be persuaded through ___(2)___. On the other hand, use ___(3)___ arguments for a like-minded audience whose feelings you want to appeal to.

(1) ______________________

(2) ______________________

(3) ______________________

2005학년도 전국

01 **다음 글을 읽고, 지시에 따라 답하시오.**

In the United States, it is important to be on time for an appointment, a class, etc. However, this may not be true in all countries. An American professor discovered this difference in a Brazilian university. His first two-hour class was scheduled to begin at 10 a.m. and end at 12 p.m. On the first day, when the professor arrived on time, no one was in the classroom. Many students came after 10 a.m. Several arrived after 10:30 a.m. Two students came after 11 a.m. These students greeted the professor few apologized for their lateness. Were these students being rude? He decided to study the students' behavior.

The professor talked to American and Brazilian students about lateness in both an informal and formal situation: lunch with a friend and attendance in a university class, respectively. He gave them an example and asked them how they would react. If they had a lunch appointment with a friend, the average American student defined lateness as 9 minutes after the agreed time. On the other hand, the average Brazilian students felt the friend was late after 33 minutes.

Unlike students in an American university, neither the teacher nor the students always arrive at the university at the appointed hour in Brazil. Classes begin and end at the scheduled time in the United States. In the Brazilian class, however, few students left the class at noon and many students remained past 12:30 p.m. to discuss the class and asked more questions. The explanation for these differences is complicated. In Brazil, the students believe that a person who usually arrives late is probably successful than a person who is always on time. In fact, Brazilians expect a person with status or prestige to arrive late, while in the United States lateness is usually considered to be disrespectful and unacceptable. Consequently, if a Brazilian is late for an appointment with a North American, the American may misinterpret the reason for the lateness and become angry.

위 글의 요지를 People's로 시작하여 한 문장으로 쓰시오. (단, <보기>의 모든 단어들만 한 번 씩 사용해야 함) [3 points]

보기

among, punctual, towards, being, attitudes, differ, cultures

People's ____.

02 **다음 글의 흐름이 자연스럽게 전개되도록 주어진 문단 뒤에 (A), (B), (C) 순서를 재배열 하시오.** [2 points]

Nothing would be more interesting than to know from historical documents the exact process by which the first man began to lisp his first words, and thus to be rid of all the theories on the origin of speech.

All the religions and mythologies contain stories of language origin. Philosophers through the ages have argued the question. Scholarly works have been written on the subject. Theories of divine origin, evolutionary development, and language as a human invention have all been suggested.

(A) Despite the difficulty of finding scientific evidence, speculations on language origin have provided valuable insights into the nature and development of language, which prompted a scholar to state that "linguistic science cannot refrain forever from asking about the whence (and about the whither) of linguistic evolution."

(B) The difficulties inherent in answering this question are immense. Anthropologists think that the species has existed for at least one million years, and perhaps for as long as five or six million years. But the earliest deciphered written records are barely six thousand years old, dating from the writings of the Sumerians of 4000 B.C. These records appear so late in the history of the development of language that they provide no clue to its origin.

(C) For these reasons, some scholars in the 19th century ridiculed, ignored, and even banned discussions of language origin. In 1886, the Linguistic Society of Paris passed a resolution "outlawing" any papers concerned with this subject.

순서 : (　　　　　) → (　　　　　) → (　　　　　)

03 **다음 대화에서 화자들의 관계를 고려할 때 부적절한 표현을 찾아 쓰고, "I"로 시작하는 4단어의 표현으로 바꾸어 쓰시오. (단, 부정어를 사용한 것은 정답으로 인정하지 않음)** [2 points]

Youngsu : Hello, Minkyung! Have you heard that a new English teacher has come to our school?

Minkyung : Really? Oh, look! Is that lady our new English teacher?

……………………………………………………………

Ms. Brown : (In the classroom) Good morning, everyone. I'm Susan Brown. I'm your new English teacher. I'm delighted to meet you. What I'm like to do today is to show you how to write a résumé.

Youngsu : Say what?

Ms. Brown : Well, I said I'd like to show you how to write a résumé.

(1) 부적절한 표현 : ______________________________

(2) 적절한 표현 : I ______________________________

2004학년도 서울 · 인천

01 **Read the passage and follow the directions.** [3 points]

> Indirectness itself does not reflect powerlessness. It is easy to think of situations where indirectness is the prerogative of those in power. For example, a wealthy couple who know that their servants will do their bidding need not give direct orders, but can simply state wishes: The woman of the house says, "It's chilly in here," and the servant sets about raising the temperature. The man of the house says, "It's dinner time," and the servant sees about having dinner served. Perhaps the ultimate indirectness is ________________ : The hostess rings a bell and the maid brings the next course; or a parent enters the room where children are misbehaving and stands with hands on hips, and the children immediately stop what they're doing.

Fill in the blank in 10 words or so, including ALL the words in the box. You may change their forms, if necessary.

all, something, anything, someone, get, without, say

____

02 Read the passage and follow the directions. [3 points]

In some cultures it is common to use titles when talking to people who are not family or friends. Sometimes these titles show a person's profession. Or they tell us that he or she is older and should be honored. In general, North Americans are not very formal; they are casual. That is true with titles, too. In every day life, titles are not used, except for Doctor (Dr.) for a medical doctor, and sometimes Professor (Prof.) for a university professor. Naturally, Mr. and Mrs., Miss, and the newer form Ms. (pronounced Miz, and used for any woman, married or not) are used sometimes. But people in the United States and Canada are ______________________. In fact, many times even a boss or older person will ask you to use his or her first name or even a nickname.

Fill in the blank in 15 words or so. Use ALL the words in the box.

after, away, so, meeting, right, that, casual

____

03 **Read the passage and follow the directions.** [5 points]

Apologies work the magic in myriad ways. Among the most surprising: Offering an apology can be a way to get someone else to admit fault. For many of us (more women than men), apologies come in pairs and constitute a ritual exchange: I apologize for x, then you apologize for y, and we both consider the matter closed. The apologies are a verbal equivalent of a handshake that marks the settling of a dispute. So if I think you are at fault, one way I can get you to apologize is to utter the first apology myself; this should compel you to do your part and utter the second. For example, if I say, "I'm sorry I blew my stack when you broke the glass; it's only a glass. I overreacted," I expect you to say something like, "That's okay, I'm sorry I broke the glass. I'll try to be more careful."

We compare what they say with what we expected them to say, which is typically based on what we would say. So men tend to overinterpret women's apologies as evidence that they lack self-confidence, because most men don't recognize the ritual nature of women's apologies and don't expect people to apologize when they don't have to.

By the same token, women tend to overinterpret men's not apologizing. The very suggestion that an apology is missing—that the man resisted apologizing—reflects the women's view. She sees a lack because she expects an apology; he sees nothing because he does not expect apologies to pepper conversations.

One reason many men resist apologizing is that it seems superficial, too easy. What really matters with men is not their words they are saying, but their actions they are doing. Another reason many men resist apologizing is that they are more inclined to avoid talking in a way that puts them in a one-down position. Viewed this way, apologizing implies weakness, which others could exploit in the future.

3-1 Compare men's and women's misunderstandings of each other's apologizing behavior, as described in the passage. Use 20 words or so including "while." [2 points]

3-2 Write down TWO reasons why many men resist apologizing, as given in the passage. For each reason, use 20 words or so including "because." [3 points]

04 Read the passage and follow the directions. [6 points]

Did you ever wonder why you're likely to be greeted with a warm smile and "Hi, how are you today?" when you enter a store? Or why the hottest merchandise is on the shoppers' right when they walk in the front door? Or why cookies and candy are often displayed at a child's eye level? These are not just random events, but are based on an actual science involved in watching you buy and trying to make you buy more.

When shoppers first enter a store, they need some space to slow down and get into shopping mode. This area just inside the front door is called the "decompression zone" where they are not supposed to buy anything. Americans tend to go to the right when they enter stores—the same way as they drive—while the British and Japanese tend to move toward the left. Retailers can make millions from this tendency. Thus, store owners put the hottest merchandise just to the right of the "decompression" zone, and then continue this pathway to the right, bringing the customer through the rest of the store. The theory is very simple. Getting us to the rest of the store increases the chances we will buy something.

A consumer habit called "product petting" is another discovery that shopping researchers have made. Shoppers love to touch and pet things, so merchandise has to be within easy reach. They have found that the more we can feel products, the more likely we are to buy them. Once we touch something, we are much more connected to it, and much more interested in buying it. So, shop owners place merchandise within easy reach and encourage customers to touch it, in order to increase sales.

The most famous shopping discovery is the so-called "butt brush." Americans are uncomfortable when other people get too close. They especially dislike having their "butts," or backsides, accidentally brushed. When this happens, particularly in a public setting, people subconsciously say, "I think I'll move along." The solution is simply to provide wider aisles.

4-1 **Complete the following table based on the passage. Use 15 words or so in each cell.** [3 points]

Category	What American shoppers do	What American shop owners do
Decompression Zone	They feel comfortable when given some space before getting into shopping mode.	(1)
Product Petting	They love to touch merchandise.	(2)
Butt Brush	They feel uncomfortable and move along when other people get too close.	They make the aisles of the store wide enough for people to feel comfortable while shopping.

(1) ____________________

(2) ____________________

4-2 **Imagine that in America, a department store frequented mostly by British and Japanese travellers displays the hottest merchandise to the right after they enter the store. Write down a reason, inferred from the passage, for the lower than expected sales volume of this store. (50자 이내의 우리말로 쓰시오.)** [3 points]

____

____

____

05 **The following three graphs show changes in the farm population, the number of farms, and the average farm size. Write a report, following the guidelines.** [7 points]

Guidelines

- Examine each graph in terms of overall trends.
- Compare and contrast the three graphs.
- Draw your own conclusion.
- Use neat handwriting.
- Use approximately **<u>70 WORDS</u>**.

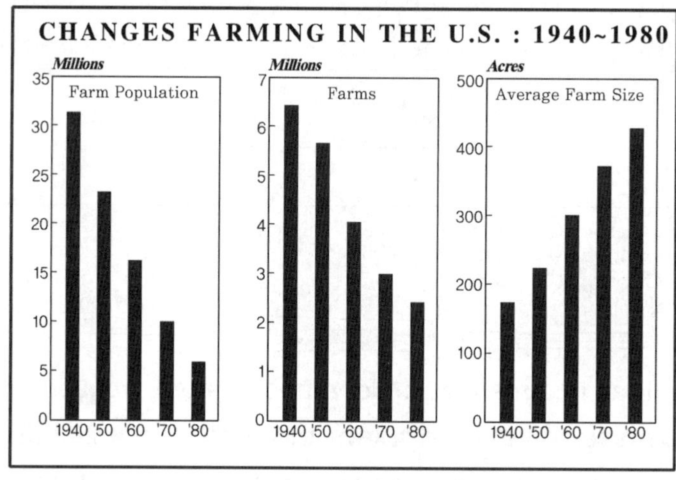

06 Read the passage and follow the directions. [4 points]

Most people have come to realize that to stay healthy they need a balanced diet; they are vitamin conscious, and they understand that their bodies require a variety of foods. But they are much less likely to be aware that a balanced "diet" of activities, with varied outlets for their emotions, is equally important to their well-being. Most important of all is the emotional atmosphere in which one lives while he works or plays. Of course one cannot thrive if this world is full of hatred and anger. But it is equally important to realize that there is no thriving in a sort of neutral world of neither hate nor love. It is not enough simply to hate no one. There is more positive need. It is a basic teaching of psychiatry that we must love or fall ill. Man needs the love and the affectionate "give and take" of true friendship. And, just as a lack of vitamins may, in extreme cases, result in such diseases as scurvy or pellagra, so one who denies himself adequate emotional expression is apt to suffer from what might be called a sort of "psychological scurvy." He surely becomes a victim of chronic fatigue, a weariness of body and mind that no amount of rest will relieve.

Complete the following summary with words from the passage.

People need varied ___(1)___ for emotions as well as a balanced diet for their ___(2)___. Excessive negative emotions are unhealthy, but positive emotions, such as love and friendship, are a requirement. A ___(3)___ of motional expression may lead to a ___(4)___ weariness analogous to illness caused by inadequate diet.

(1) ______________________

(2) ______________________

(3) ______________________

(4) ______________________

07 **Read the passage and follow the directions.** [3 points]

People who deal with me often marvel at my capacity for handling bad news. This wasn't always the case, and though I haven't learned to like bad news, I have learned to deal with it. Bad news is seldom as bad as it first sounds, and most business disasters are rarely as disastrous as they first seem. Over the years I have learned—and am still learning—the importance of patience and how destructive the lack of it can be.

It is still amazing to me how the simple passing of time can totally alter a situation, solve problems, render other problems meaningless, cool down confrontations, and add a whole new perspective. "What goes around comes around" should be tattooed on the chest of every new, hyperactive executive.

What does this have to do with taking an edge? A lot. Part of being opportunistic is waiting, like a cat in a forest, for an opportunity to come along. Learning to wait, learning to be patient, has so many applications and ramifications it is difficult for me to give one or two examples without trivializing its importance. I would say, however, that in our twenty-odd years in business, 90 percent of our successes have involved in some way the need for patience, and 90 percent of our failures have been caused in part by a lack of it.

Write down the advice the writer gives in 15 words or so.

08 Read the passage and follow the directions. [3 points]

> To write about human aggression is a difficult task because the term is used in so many senses. Aggression is one of those words which everyone knows, but which is nevertheless hard to define. As psychologists and psychiatrists use it, it covers a wide range of human behavior. The red-faced infant squalling for the bottle is being aggressive; and so is the judge who awards a thirty-year sentence for robbery. The guard in a concentration camp who tortures his helpless victim is obviously acting aggressively. Less manifestly, but no less certainly, so is the neglected wife who threatens or attempts suicide in order to regain her husband's affection. When a word becomes so diffusely applied that it is used both of the competitive striving of a footballer and also of the bloody violence of a murderer, it ought either to be dropped or else more closely defined. Aggression is a portmanteau term which is fairly bursting at its seams. Yet, until we can more clearly designate and comprehend the various aspects of human behavior which are subsumed under this head, we cannot discard the concept.

위 글의 "human aggression"을 나타내는 구체적인 행위 중 5가지만 본문에서 찾아 우리말로 쓰시오.

(1) ____________________

(2) ____________________

(3) ____________________

(4) ____________________

(5) ____________________

2004학년도 전국

01 **다음 글을 읽고, 밑줄 친 Netspeak에 상응하는 어구를 찾아 그 중 1개만 쓰시오.** [3 points]

> There is no indication of <u>Netspeak</u> replacing or threatening already existing language varieties. On the contrary, the arrival of new, informal, even bizarre forms of language extends the range of our sensitivity to linguistic contrasts. Formal language, and other kinds of informal language, are seen in a new light, by virtue of the existence of Netspeak. An analogy with clothing helps make this point. I remember once owning a very formal shirt and another I used for informal occasions. Then I was given a grotesque creation that I was assured was the latest cool trend in informality; and certainly, the effect was to make my previously informal shirt look really somewhat staid. The new shirt had not destroyed my sense of the value of formal vs. informal contrast in dress behavior; it simply extended it. I was sartorially enriched, with more options available to me. I see the arrival of Netspeak as similarly enriching the range of communicative options available to us.

---

02 **다음 글을 읽고, 밑줄 그은 부분에 공통으로 들어갈 단어를 쓰시오.** [3 points]

> Research shows that there are crucial links between what we say to ourselves and what we accomplish. In addition, our self-talk, the inner conversation we have with ourselves, has a powerful ____________ on our emotional well-being.
>
> Whether we know it or not, we all engage in an early constant subconscious monologue with ourselves. Sometimes we vocalize the monologue aloud, but often it is silent thinking or an internal whisper we are scarcely aware of. Even though such self-talk may be quiet, its ____________ can be enormous. Our behaviour, feelings, sense of self-esteems, and even level of stress are influenced by our inner speech.
>
> Everything we do begins as self-talk. Self-talk shapes our inner attitudes, our attitudes shape our behaviour, and of course our behavior—what we do—shapes the results we get.

---

03 **다음 글을 읽고, <보기>의 단어를 모두 한번만 사용하여 마지막 문장을 완성하시오.** [4 points]

Despite the attention paid within advertising agencies to the whole business of targeting specific groups, there have been some spectacular failures to get it right when companies have tried to go international or global with their products. This has been for a variety of reasons. Sometimes, the brand name of the product has unfortunate associations when translated into other languages. Looking at this area can illustrate how powerful the operation of connotation is—the way in which words can call up associations in our minds. Because of the way we make connections between words and particular ideas, feelings and experiences, brand names are crucial for advertisers. They are very economic, acting as little concentrated capsules of meaning. Where advertisers get it right, readers will do ______________________________.

보기

connotations, the, to, generate, the, work, intended

04 **다음 글을 읽고, 의사 결정에 관한 전개 과정표(Flow Chart)를 만들 때, 밑줄 그은 부분 (1), (2), (3)에 각각 알맞은 단어를 쓰시오.** [3 points]

> To make sure that creative decisions are also practical decisions, organizations need to follow a number of specific practices. Once an idea has been suggested, managers should spend a significant amount of time analyzing its merits. They need, that is, to figure out the costs and the benefits of implementing a new idea or decision.
>
> The next step is to commit resources to the project, assuming of course that the project is feasible. Such a commitment might take the form of funds for research or a line item in the budget. Whatever the form, the goal at this step is to provide the resources that can turn a creative idea into a practical reality.
>
> Finally, the project has to be implemented. It has to be translated into a tangible product or course of action. The key here is to maintain a realistic perspective on what an organization can or cannot expect in the way of a return.

Idea generation	▶	Preliminary ___(1)___	▶	___(2)___ of resources	▶	___(3)___

(1) ______________________

(2) ______________________

(3) ______________________

05 다음 글을 읽고, 밑줄 그은 부분에 알맞은 말을 쓰시오. [3 points]

A 24-year-old woman named Carina visits Dr. Jenkins because she's having trouble sleeping at night. It's been weeks since she slept soundly. The poor woman is exhausted, she can't concentrate at work, and she feels irritated all the time. This morning, Carina's boyfriend got fed up with her grumpiness and suggested that she see Dr. Jenkins.

Carina : Doctor, I don't know what's going on, but it's been weeks since I had a good night's sleep. I don't know what kind of damage this does to my body, but it's definitely damaging my relationship. My boyfriend is very upset!

Dr. Jenkins : Well, Carina, sleep is important. It allows the body to repair itself. During sleep, the immune system is more active, and tissue building reaches a peak.

Carina : So, ______________________________?

Dr. Jenkins : Pills? Let's make medicine a last resort. There are more natural ways to alleviate the problem, and they have no negative side effects. For example, you can cut out caffeine, alcohol and cigarettes. All contribute to sleeplessness.

---

06 **다음 글을 읽고, 예술의 4요소 중에서 밑줄 친 universe가 구체적으로 무엇을 의미하는지 10자 이내의 우리말로 쓰시오.** [3 points]

Four elements in the total situation of a work of art are discriminated and made salient, by one or another synonym, in almost all theories which aim to be comprehensive. First, there is the work, the artistic product itself. And since this is a human product, an artifact, the second common element is the artist. Third, the work is taken to have a subject which, directly or deviously, is derived from existing things—to be about, or signify, or reflect something which either is, or bears relation to, an objective state of affairs. This third element, whether held to consist of people and actions, ideas and feelings, material things and events, or super-sensible essences, has frequently been denoted by that word-of-all-work, 'nature'; but let us use the more neutral and comprehensive term, <u>universe</u>, instead. For the final element we have the audience: the listeners, spectators, or readers to whom the work is addressed, or to whose attention, at any rate, it becomes available.

---

07 **다음 글을 읽고, <보기>에서 알맞은 단어를 골라 <요약문>을 완성하시오.** [3 points]

I have friends who have simplified their grocery shopping by planting a garden. Their entire yearly crop is grown in planters on their front deck. They have fresh tomatoes, peppers, green beans, and others, as well as an extensive herb garden. They are professionals who work long hours. They decided some years ago they'd rather spend time on their deck tending their plants than running to the market every time they need a tomato. As a result, they get a tremendous amount of satisfaction from being the source of much of the produce that goes on their table, not the least of which comes from the fact that it is organically grown. They have also developed an appreciation for plants and nature they might not otherwise have had.

보기

effort, enormous, sell, pollution, raise, simplified

요약문

I have friends who are professionals working long hours. Some years ago, they decided to ___(1)___ a yearly crop with little ___(2)___, instead of buying all the groceries they need. As a result, they get ___(3)___ satisfaction from growing crops and have also developed an appreciation for plants and nature.

(1) ______________________

(2) ______________________

(3) ______________________

08 다음 글을 읽고, 물음에 답하시오. [5 points]

For many years leadership was viewed as a combination of personality traits, such as self-confidence, intelligence, and dependability. A consensus on which traits were most important was difficult to achieve, however, and attention turned to styles of leadership behavior. In the last few decades several styles of leadership have been identified: authoritarian, laissez-faire, and democratic.

The authoritarian leader holds all authority and responsibility, with communication usually moving from top to bottom. This leader assigns workers to specific tasks and expects orderly, precise results. At the other extreme is the laissez-faire leader, who waives responsibility and allows subordinates to work as they choose with a minimum of interference. Communication flows equally among group members. The democratic leader holds final responsibility but also delegates authority to others, who participate in determining work assignments. In this leadership style, communication is active both upward and downward.

Each of these styles has its advantages and disadvantages. For example, democratic leadership can motivate employees to work effectively because it is their decisions that they are implementing. On the other hand, the decision-making process takes time that employees could <u>otherwise</u> be devoting to their tasks. Actually, each of the three leadership styles can be effective.

8-1 위 글의 주제를 본문에 나오는 어구를 사용하여 쓰시오. [2 points]

____

8-2 위 글의 밑줄 친 otherwise를 20자 이내의 우리말로 구체적으로 설명하시오. [3 points]

____

____

____

09 **다음 (A)에 대한 (B)의 요약문에서, (B)의 밑줄 친 부분은 (A)의 내용과 일치하지 않습니다. 한 문장으로 바르게 고쳐 쓰시오.** [4 points]

A

Harold Rose, a retired industrial scientist, has occasionally had dreams which his wife dismisses as chance coincidence; but one is harder to explain away. In 1987 they had been briefly acquainted with Fred Kormet, a well-known painter. They had not subsequently seen or heard of him. Two years later, Harold woke one morning, and because he thought his wife would immediately dismiss the subject of his dream, he impressed her with the fact that he had dreamt that morning, just before waking, that Fred Kormet had died. Two days later his obituary appeared in *The Times*.

When he checked with the director of the art gallery with which the painter was connected, he found that Kormet had died on the morning of the dream.

B

Mr. Rose dreamt that Fred Kormet, a well-known painter whom he had met two years before, had died. Two days later his death notice appeared in the paper and <u>Mr. Rose was told by a painter at the gallery that Mr. Kormet died while working at the place.</u>

10 다음 글을 읽고, 필자의 주장을 한 문장으로 나타낼 때, 밑줄 그은 부분에 알맞은 말을 쓰시오. [4 points]

> The whole aim of good teaching is to turn the young learner, by nature a little copy cat, into an independent, self-propelling creature, who can not merely learn but study—that is, work as his own boss to the limits of his powers. This is to turn pupils into students, and it can be done on any rung of the ladder of learning. When I was a child, the multiplication table was taught from a printed sheet which had to be memorized one "square" at a time—the one's and the two's and so on up to nine. It never occurred to the teacher to show us how the answers could be arrived at also by addition, which we already knew. No one said, "Look, if four times four is sixteen, you ought to be able to figure out, without aid from memory, what five times four is, because that amounts to four more ones added to the sixteen." This would at first have been puzzling, more complicated and difficult than memory work, but once explained and grasped, it would have been an instrument for learning and checking the whole business of multiplication. We could temporarily have dispensed with the teacher and cut loose from the printed material.

필자의 주장

> Show the students how to apply ________________ to a new learning task.

2003학년도 서울

01 **Read the following passage and answer the question.** [3 points]

Some of the most interesting stories to come out of the Klondike Gold Rush focus on the courageous women who risked everything, including their lives, to struggle over the pass and fight for their share of the gold and the glory. One out of every ten Stampeders was a woman. The woman worked just as hard as the men, and faced as many, if not more, hardships. Imagine trying to climb the pass wearing the typically long woman's dress of the time, with a corset making every breath difficult. Many women abandoned their traditional attire in favor of more sensible trousers, and faced the insults of men. In 1897, Belinda Mulroney heard about the Gold Rush and sold her dress shop in Juneau, Alaska. She bought fabric and hot water bottles, and carried them to the Klondike, where she sold her goods at a 600% profit. She stayed on to open a restaurant, hotels, and a construction business. For many, the journey to the Klondike began as a road to riches, ended as a trail of broken dreams, but led Belinda Mulroney on the adventure of a lifetime.

The following is a summary of the passage. Fill in the blanks, choosing the most suitable words from the list.

An interesting feature of the Klondike Gold Rush is that one out of ten Stampeders was a woman. The ① _________ women risked everything and ② _________ extreme hard ship. It happened that, apart from gold-digging, the women went into business and found ③ _________ jobs. They were on a journey into unusual, exciting, and dangerous things throughout their lives.

Word List

rude, confronted, losing, avoided, dauntless, lucrative

02 Read the following passage and answer the question. [3 points]

Imagine that someone at dinner is watching you use the pepper grinder and then utters when you are finished: *Can you pass the pepper*? In this context, the literal question about your ability to pass the pepper is bypassed, because the intended request is so salient. As this example illustrates, many indirect requests are idiomatic. Given the frequent cooccurrence of their surface form and implied meaning, it is not surprising that people activate the implied meaning automatically.

People do not always ignore literal meaning, however. Imagine that someone calls a merchant on the telephone and asks: *Would you mind telling me what time you close tonight*? The merchant could provide two kinds of information in response: First, she could respond to the literal question and state whether she minds providing the information. Second, she could respond to the indirect request and state what time her business closes. If she bypasses the literal meaning and only processes the intended message, then she should not begin her utterance by saying 'yes' or 'no' in response to the literal question. Instead, she should only provide the closing time. If she also processes the literal meaning, though, she may preface the closing time by stating whether she minds providing it.

To test this, H. H. Clark had a research assistant call local merchants and ask them their closing times. He found that <u>the merchants often responded to the literal meaning of the request, as well as to the indirect request</u>. Whether they compute both the literal and implied meaning depends on current circumstances and the nature of the utterance.

Write ONE possible response as indicated in the underlined part.

____

03 **Read the following passage and answer the question.** [4 points]

> ____________________ since it first appeared in a book review in April 27, 1895, describing a woman who "has in her the capacity of fighting her way back to independence." It is the basic proposition that, as Nora put it in Ibsen's *A Dolls's House* a century ago, "Before everything else I'm a human being." It is the simply worded sigh hoisted by a little girl in the 1970 Women's Strike for Equality: "I AM NOT A BARBIE DOLL." Feminism asks the world to recognize at long last that women aren't decorative ornaments, worthy vessels, members of a "special-interest group." They are half of the national population, and just as deserving of rights and opportunities, just as capable of participating in the world's events, as the other half. Feminism's agenda is basic: It asks that women be free to define themselves.

Fill in the blank with the topic statement of the paragraph, including the words in the box. Change their forms if necessary.

change, meaning, feminism

____

04 Read the passage and answer the questions. [5 points]

Today, the most effective way to reach a narrow audience is with a classified ad. Each classification represents a small community of interest: people who want to buy or sell a rug, for example. Tomorrow, the classified ad won't be tied to paper or limited to text. If you're looking for a used car, you will send out a query specifying the price range, model, and features that interest you and will be shown a list of the available cars that match your preferences. Or you will ask a software agent to notify you when a suitable car comes on the market. Car sellers' ads might include links to a picture or a video of the car or even the car's maintenance records, so you can get a sense of what shape it is in.

At first, these benefits of on-line classified ads may not be apparent. On-line classified ads won't be very attractive, because not many people will be using them. But then word-of-mouth from a few satisfied customers will entice more and more users to the service. There will be a positive-feedback loop created as more sellers attract more buyers and vice versa. When a critical mass is achieved, which might be only a year or two after the service is first offered, the information highway's classified advertising service will be transformed ______________________.

4-1 **Write a title that best fits the passage, using FiVE words from the passage above.** [2 points]

____

4-2 **Fill in the blank, using ALL AND ONLY the words in the box.** [3 points]

buyers, the primary, to, together, and, get, way, from, a curiosity, private sellers

____

05 **다음 글을 읽고 제목 "Too Little, Too Late"의 의미를 가장 잘 나타낸 문장을 하나씩 찾아 쓰시오.** [4 points]

Too Little, Too Late

For a year-and-a-half, I had resolved to spend some extended time with my 78-year-old father. I was looking forward to a summer holiday with him on his farm, steeping my children in the pastoral rhythms that shaped my childhood.

For Christmas, I planned to give him a written collection of memories gathered from our extended family. I also anticipated presenting him with a copy of my first book, with the acknowledgements conveying "eternal respect and gratitude" to him and my late mother.

In reality, I had only a couple of hurried visits. Plans were repeatedly postponed. Then in March 1999 my father's hardcover copy of my book was sitting on my desk when the call came: Dad had suffered a stroke. He died eight days later.

My overriding memory of my father is the time he always spent with his children. On our farm, we rode the tractor or did chores side by side. We shared innumerable evenings, watching television or just sitting on the veranda talking. Whenever I ran to my room crying over some childhood scrape, my father always comforted me, a kindness that taught me the power of parental presence.

As my brother, sister and I shouldered the responsibilities of adulthood, Dad applauded all our undertakings. "Live life to the fullest," he would say. "You're making memories."

Taking the lesson of my father's death to heart, I am slowing my pace. Now and then, when I find myself in a peaceful moment, relishing a sweet remark from one of my kids, the fragrance of a wet forest or the beauty of a field of wheat swaying in the wind, the words I wish I had spoken pop into my head: "I'm ready now, Dad. I'm ready to spend some time."

There is, of course, no answer.

① Too Little : ________________________

② Too Late : ________________________

06 **Imagine you are one of the young people in these pictures. Using the pictures as a guide, write a short story describing what you did.** [7 points]

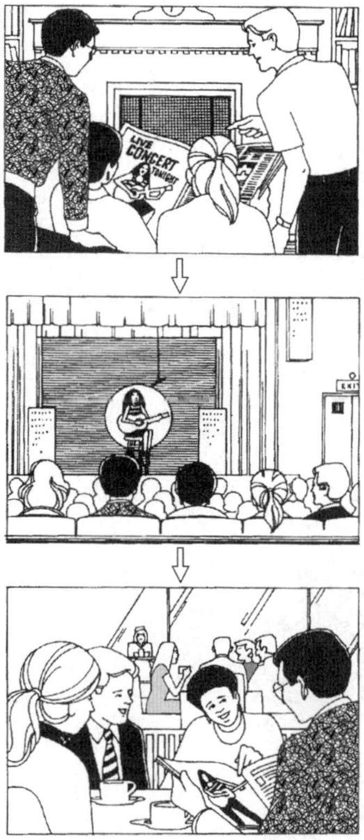

Directions

- Write a sequenced narrative.
- Start with the picture on the top and go through to the picture at the bottom.
- Use neat handwriting.
- Use approximately **70 WORDS**.

2003학년도 전국

01 **다음 글을 읽고, 문맥에 어울리도록 빈칸에 한 단어를 영어로 쓰시오.** [2 points]

Most studies have affirmed the positive effects of friendship, with some exploring whether you're better off having many companions or just one good one. Some studies find that having a wide range of social contacts—belonging to community groups as well as having a network of friends—offers the greatest protection. But others show that most crucial is having even just a few close friends—"the kind of people you can't imagine life without," says psychologist Laura Carstenson. "__________ beats quantity all the time."

02 **TV 시청에 관한 다음 글의 요지를 한 문장의 우리말로 쓰시오.** [4 points]

William Belson, British psychologist studied the television diets and subsequent behavior of 1565 London boys aged 12 to 17. He found cartoon, slapstick or science-fiction violence less harmful at this age; but realistic fictional violence, violence in close personal relationships, and violence "in a good cause" were deadly poison. Heavy viewers were 47 percent more likely to commit acts such as knifing during a school fight, burning another with a cigarette, slashing car tires, burglary and attempted rape. To Belson's surprise, the TV exposure did not seem to change the boys' opinions toward violence but rather seemed to crumble whatever constraints family, church or school had built up. "It is almost as if the boys then tend to let go whatever violent tendencies are in them. It just seems to explode in spontaneous ways."

---

03 다음 광고를 읽고, 광고 내용에 대한 아래 대화의 빈칸 ①과 ②를 영어로 채우시오. [4 points]

Free!
EXPERT HAIRSTYLING

We need volunteers for our statewide hairstyling competition among the top hair stylists of South Dakota.

Friday January 28
Ramada Inn, Rapid City
Free Lunch & Dinner
Free Transportation

The only qualification is long hair, at least 8 inches.

Call toll free
1-800-222-1010
South Dakota Society of Beauticians and Hairstylists
SODASCOBAH

Mike : Jane, have you seen this ad?
Jane : Yeah. It looks great, doesn't it? I called them an hour ago. They'll call back if they want me.
Mike : Oh, they'll want you for sure. I mean you ① ________________.
Jane : I hope so. If I go, I'll get a new hairdo—and have a lot of fun too.
Mike : Yeah, right. When do you think you will leave?
Jane : Well, the competition ② ____________________, so I should be leaving by Thursday.

---

04 **다음 글을 읽고, 주어진 문장이 들어가기에 가장 적절한 곳을 찾아 바로 앞과 뒤의 영어 단어를 각각 쓰시오.** [4 points]

That was the cause of the rattle.

A man had bought a new car, and he was very proud of it. There was only one problem. There was an irritating noise—a rattle—in the front of the car. The man had taken the car to a garage several times, but the mechanics couldn't find anything wrong with it. After several months they found the problem and explained it to him. The man was a non-smoker. He used the ashtray to keep small change for car parks and parking meters. He kept several pounds in the ashtray in 20p and 10p coins. They had not discovered this before, because everytime the man had taken his car to the garage, he had removed the coins from the ashtray. He didn't trust the mechanics—he thought they might steal them. The last time he took the car to the garage he forgot to remove the coins.

앞 : ______________________ 뒤 : ______________________

05 **다음 글을 읽고 주어진 조건에 맞추어 취업 면접 시 할 수 있는 질문을 한 문장의 영어로 쓰시오.** [4 points]

> 조건 1 : "your previous supervisor"를 화제로 삼을 것.
> 조건 2 : 저자가 바람직하다고 생각하는 질문 유형에 맞게 쓸 것.

Deciding whether someone is right for a job is always a little confusing. It's rare for a manager to have all the information he or she needs to make well-informed decisions. But knowing how to ask good questions can make a world of difference. The secret, says psychologist and personnel consultant Kurt Enstein, is understanding the difference between open- ended and close-ended questions. The problem with close-ended questions is that they encourage limited, yes/no answers. Either that or they'll signal to the interviewee what you are hoping to hear. Open-ended questions make no prejudgement, and provide greater insights into the candidate.

---

06 **<보기>에 제시된 단어의 일부를 활용하여, 빈칸 ①과 ②를 완성하시오. 단어는 한 번만 활용하시오.** [6 points]

To see how the mind can shape what we perceive, look at the two pictures below.

What do you see? Each would present you with two distinctly different images. When you look at the first one in one way, you see a vase. Look at it differently and you see two faces. The second picture presents either a beautiful young lady facing away from you or an ugly old woman in profile. How is this possible? The sense data that your eyes take in—the arrangement of lines and shading—remain the same. But you can "shift" the pictures you see. What you "see," then, is the meaning that your mind ① ____________ and your mind can reprocess that data so that they ② ____________.

보기

language, data, different, question, impose,
avoid, represent, same, something, acquisition

① ________________________________

② ________________________________

07 **다음 글을 읽고, 주어진 단어로 시작되는 요약문을 영어로 완성하시오. 단, 연속된 4단어 이상의 본문 표현을 그대로 옮겨 쓰지 마시오.** [5 points]

If human beings paid attention to all the sights, sounds, and smells that besiege them, their ability to codify and recall information would be swamped. Instead, they simplify the information by grouping it into broad verbal categories. For example, human eyes have the extraordinary power to discriminate some ten million colors, but the English language reduces these to no more than four thousand color words, of which only eleven basic terms are commonly used. That is why a driver stops at all traffic lights whose color he categorizes as red, even though the lights vary slightly from one to another in their hues of redness. Categorization allows people to respond to their environment in a way that has great survival value. If they hear a high-pitched sound, they do not enumerate the long list of possible causes of such sounds: a human cry of fear, a scream for help, a policeman's whistle, and so on. Instead they become alert because they have categorized high-pitched sounds as indicators of possible danger.

요약문

Human beings ______________________________.

2002학년도 서울

01 **Read the following passage and answer the questions.** [4 points]

> 1 NEW YORK—Chain reactions are commonplace on Earth. They occur in chemical plants when a single excited molecule prompts its neighbors into a cascade of combination to create plastics.
>
> 2 Now, experts say, a dangerous new kind of chain reaction is getting under way in space, where it threatens to limit mankind's endeavors beyond the planet. For instance, it could put billions of dollars worth of advanced communications and weather satellites at risk of destruction.
>
> 3 The problem is that <u>some orbits near Earth have become junkyards of dead and active satellites, spent rocket stages and billions of bits of whirling debris</u>.
>
> 4 And last week, sensors on the ground detected the breakup of a Russian rocket stage. So far, that event has produced 38 observable bits of debris.
>
> 5 The trashing of the heavens has reached the point where a speeding scrap of metallic refuse could hit a large object, shattering it into hundreds of pieces that repeat and amplify the process in a cascade of destruction. A chain reaction of this sort begins at a point known as the critical density.

1-1 **Which expression is similar to the underlined part of the passage in meaning? Write down your answer, using FIVE words from the passage.** [2 points]

____

1-2 **위 글의 흐름으로 보아 어색한 단락을 찾아 그 번호를 쓰시오.** [2 points]

____

02 Read the following dialogue and answer the questions. [4 points]

> Situation: Minji promised to return a textbook to her American classmate within a day or two, after Xeroxing several pages from it. She held onto it for almost ten days. The following conversation took place between Minji and her classmate when they ran into each other in the hallway.
>
> Kelly : Hi, Minji. I was looking for you.
> Minji : Why?
> Kelly : I'm really upset about the book because I needed it to prepare for last week's class.
> Minji : <u>I have nothing to say</u>.

2-1 민지의 대답에서 밑줄 친 부분이 부적절한 이유를 우리말로 쓰시오. [2 points]

____

____

____

2-2 Write the response that can replace the underlined part of the dialogue. Write TWO sentences that are continuous in their meaning, but not the same. [2 points]

____

____

____

03 **다음 글에서 'psychological warfare'를 이용하는 세 가지 이유를 찾아 각각 15자 내외의 우리말로 요약하시오.** [4 points]

Throughout history, we can find cases when 'psychological warfare,' also called 'public relations war,' was used. For example, in 330 B.C., Alexander the Great used propaganda when his army ran thin after a series of invasions. He ordered the armory to make several oversized armor plates and helmets that would fit a person eight feet tall. He would leave these behind. So, when the enemy ranks saw them, they were led to believe how close they were to fighting 'giants' and considered themselves lucky to have avoided certain death. This ploy, plus stories which Alexander deliberately circulated of his brutality, rarely gave an opposing army enough courage to pursue him.

During World War I, Britain rained down a phenomenal number of leaflets, nine million in all, in 90 varied designs on German trenches. During World War Ⅱ, Joseph Goebbles, the master of mass psychology, used modern media like radio and cinema to let loose his virulent anti-Jewish campaign. Such was their intensity that systematic disinformation since then has become synonymous with his name. The Japanese excelled in their use of radio broadcasts. They used an English-speaking person, Tokyo Rose, to broadcast music and words of discouragement to Allied Soldiers. The Germans used a similar technique against U.S. soldiers.

(1) ______________________________

(2) ______________________________

(3) ______________________________

04 **Read the following passage and answer the questions.** [4 points]

If you had to guess, how would you say mobile phones rate with American teenagers compared with having a boyfriend or girlfriend, or with partying? According to a new survey by a market-research firm, 85 percent of teens say the phone is just as cool. Manufacturers of wireless communications devices and services can read research. They're flocking to offer products to this tech-loving generation, about 31 million in the United States. It's marketing 101: hook them early.

Just as important, companies are latching on to teens because they've earned a reputation for discovering hot new trends long before they hit the mainstream. Teens were among the first to spot the appeal of AOL's Instant Messenger service, for example. And they touched off the peer-to-peer file-sharing revolution, through Napster and streaming digital music. Today the mobile phone is the must-have gadget. Parents are giving phones to their kids in order to keep tabs on them; teens, in turn, use their mobile phones to plan parties on the fly and buy tickets for 'American Pie 2' over the Web. The next trend in Teenville: text appeal. Already a runaway hit among teenagers in Europe and Asia, the habit of sending bursts of text from phone to phone is starting to catch on here.

4-1 **Complete the following sentence with the information from the passage, using 12 words or less.** [2 points]

Just as teenagers prompted a peer-to-peer file-sharing trend on the computer, they ____.

____

4-2 **Write a sentence, using ONLY the given words, to convey the intention of American companies mentioned in the passage. The word 'trends' can be used more than once.** [2 points]

trends, trying, new, companies, forecast, from, are, mainstream, teenagers', to

____

05 Read the following passage and answer the questions. [6 points]

Barbara Jewell spoke in tears today of how her and her son Richard's life have changed, since the Atlanta Journal named him as a suspect in the bombing in the park a month ago. Mrs. Jewell told the reporters that her son has had no real life since then. At a news conference this afternoon Mrs. Jewell said that her son was a prisoner in her home, so that he couldn't either work or lead any type of normal life. She lamented that he only sits and waits for this nightmare to end. She was furious when she said that although her son was not a murderer he had been convicted in the court of public opinion.

Meanwhile, the Jewell family has continued to be besieged by reporters. Mrs. Jewell said that they had taken all privacy away from them. They have rented an apartment which faces her home in order to keep their cameras focused on her home around the clock. They have watched and photographed everything they have done. They wake up to photographers. They can't look out the windows. They can't walk their dogs without being followed down the sidewalk.

Mrs. Jewell said she was not just saddened and hurt by the ordeal, but was also angry.

Suppose that you are Barbara Jewell. You want to send a Letter of Complaint to the Editor. Write the letter by filling in the blanks on the form given.

Dear Editor.

I am writing this letter concerning your report on the bombing in the park a month ago.

(1) ____

____

(2) ____

____

(3) ____

____

(4) ____

____

(5) ____

____

(6) ____

____

I look forward to hearing from you. Thank you.

Sincerely,

2002학년도 전국

01 **다음 글을 읽고, 주어진 철자로 시작되는 단어를 본문에서 찾아 요약문을 완성하시오.** [3 points]

> One of the greatest power imbalances on earth today divides the rich countries from the poor. That unequal distribution of power, which affects the lives of billions of us, will soon be transformed as the new system of creating wealth spreads.
>
> From now on, the world will be split between the fast and the slow. Historically, power has shifted from the slow to the fast. In fast economies, advanced technology speeds production. Yet, this is the least of it. Their pace is determined by the speed of transactions, the time needed to take decisions (especially about investment), the speed with which new ideas are created in laboratories, the velocity of capital flows, and above all the speed with which information and knowledge pulse through the economic system. Fast economies generate wealth—and power—faster than slower ones.

요약문

> Power ① (i   ) around the world will be dependent on the ② (s   ) at which producing goods, money transactions, decision-making, capital flows, and exchange of money and knowledge are made. If a country makes them ③ (f   ), it will become more powerful.

① i ______________________

② s ______________________

③ f ______________________

02 **다음 글에서 Leonids는 무엇의 종류인가를 영어로 쓰시오.** [2 points]

Even veteran stargazers were amazed with the light show that thousands of tiny meteors gave them early Sunday. This year's much-anticipated Leonids shower delighted people around the world who stayed up late or woke up early to see it, including a meteor-watching party of about 75 people atop Mount Wilson, northeast of Los Angeles. Every few seconds at least a bit of space dust burned harmlessly into the atmosphere. The brightest flares left shimmering trails that hung for a few seconds. "I've never seen it like this. I don't recall seeing this many meteors—ever" said Rick Yessayian, a sixth-grade teacher in Montebello who for nine years has helped organize the Mount Wilson party.

---

03 다음 글을 읽고, 물음에 답하시오. [4 points]

The drive to establish ourselves and make our mark in the world is most urgent in our twenties and thirties, and then into our forties. However, by our mid-forties or early fifties people typically reevaluate their goals, because they often come to the radical realization that life is limited. With this acknowledgement of mortality comes a reconsideration of what really matters.

"By mid-life, there are many, many corporate executives and lawyers pulling down <u>seven-figure salaries</u> who wish instead they were doing social work or running a restaurant," says Stephen Rosen, a professional counsellor.

A consultant who has assessed top executives at firms such as General Electric and Mobil Oil tells me that many at mid-life are "highly excited about pet project—being on a school board, running a small business on the side." One highly successful entrepreneur who had started a series of businesses found himself running one he hated: "This company is at the point where it controls me. I'm stuck…. I'm much happier fixing the engine on my boat or something, but not this."

3-1 성공한 사람들이 중년기에 새로운 일을 시작하려는 근원적인 이유를 본문에서 찾아 영어로 쓰시오. [2 points]

3-2 밑줄 친 seven-figure salaries가 무슨 의미인지 구체적으로 쓰시오. [2 points]

04 **다음 글을 읽고, 각 문단의 요지를 우리말로 쓰시오.** [4 points]

1 What do Barbra Streisand, Willard Scott, Sidney Poitier, and Liza Minnelli have in common? All are professional performers, and all admit to being nervous about public speaking. If the pros can feel fear, it's no wonder beginners are sometimes scared speechless. In fact, survey after survey has confirmed that public speaking is the number one fear, so if you're anxious about stepping in front of an audience, you're not alone.

2 Nervousness might make your hands tremble, your mouth feel dry. As bad as these symptoms can be, bear in mind that nerves are a good indicator of your concern for the occasion, the topic, and the audience. If you didn't care, you wouldn't be anxious.

3 Remember also that you'll feel a little less nervous with every speech. Once you see how the audience responds to your first speech, you'll realize that you did better than you feared you would.

4 You can harness your nerves by focusing on what you want to accomplish. In the words of actress Carol Channing, "I don't call it nervousness—I prefer to call it concentration." Like Channing, you can concentrate your efforts on making that all-important connection with your audience, but don't make the mistake of expecting perfection. Put that nervous energy into planning, preparing, and practicing, and you'll be better equipped to face your audience, the first time and every time.

- 문단 1 ______________________________
- 문단 2 ______________________________
- 문단 3 ______________________________
- 문단 4 ______________________________

05 다음 글을 읽고 주어진 문장을 완성하시오. [3 points]

Some products made from non-renewable resources can be reprocessed and used again for their original purpose. This is called recycling. Aluminum, for instance, is a non-renewable resource that can be reprocessed. One hundred used tin cans can make ninety new ones. Recycled aluminum also saves energy.

Nevertheless, less than 10% of consumer goods are recycled. About 20% of the paper used in the United States each year is recycled. If we increased this to 50%, we could save about 100 million trees. Enough energy would be saved to supply 750,000 homes with electricity.

Perhaps the main reason recycling has not become more popular is that it is generally thought to be expensive. Manufacturers consider it cheaper to consume the energy needed to produce goods from virgin materials than to hire the labor necessary to recycle. An aluminum can is worth about one cent in the United States. For that one cent, many people would rather throw the can in the trash than worry about recycling it. However, it takes about 20 times more energy to manufacture a can from raw ore than from recycled scrap metal. If the costs of manufacturing and then dumping the can were considered, the value of recycling would be more readily appreciated.

Fill in the blank with appropriate words.

Recycling is not popular because people believe that ____ⓐ____ than it actually ____ⓑ____.

2001학년도

01 **다음 글을 읽고 물음에 답하시오.** [3 points]

> There are three kinds of book owners. The first has all the standard sets and best-sellers—unread, untouched. The deluded individual could be said to (A) wood pulp and ink, not books. The second has a great many books—a few of them read through, most of them dipped into, but all of them as clean and shiny as the day they were bought. This person would probably like to make books his own, but is restrained by a false respect for (B) <u>their physical appearance</u>. The third has a few books or many—every one of them dog-eared and dilapidated, shaken and loosened by continual use, marked and scribbled in from front to back. This man does (C) books.

1-1 **위의 글의 빈칸 (A), (C)에 공통으로 들어갈 가장 알맞은 단어를 본문에서 찾아 쓰시오.** [2 points]

1-2 **밑줄 친 (B) their physical appearance의 상태를 묘사하는 3단어로 된 어구를 본문에서 찾아 쓰시오.** [1 point]

---

02 **다음 글의 요지를 한 문장으로 표현하려 한다. <보기>에 있는 단어를 그대로 사용하여 문장을 완성하시오.** [2 points]

During the course of three weeks, one group of people repeatedly assessed the severity of a continuing personal problem, such as material troubles or a stubborn weight problem. In addition to completing these ratings at fixed times each day, people in both group took a brisk 10-minute walk. After the walk, chronic personal problems appeared less serious. The walk also increased general optimism. These improvements were small and were not noticeable every day, but after three weeks the difference became obvious.

→ Short walks helped make personal problems ______________________

____

보기

and, optimism, appear, increase, serious, less

03 **밑줄 친 the same misconception이 어떤 생각을 말하는 것인지 가장 잘 묘사한 부분을 본문에서 찾아 쓰시오.** [2 points]

I'm not talking about musicals. Musicals are movies that warn you by saying "Lots of music here. Take it or leave it." I'm talking about regular movies that extend no such courtesy but allow unsuspecting people to come to see them and then assault them with a barrage of unasked-for tunes. There are two major offenders in this category: black movies and movies set in the fifties. Both types of movies are afflicted with <u>the same misconception</u>. They don't know that movies are supposed to be movies. They think that movies are supposed to be records with pictures. They have failed to understand that if God had wanted records to have pictures, he would not have invented television.

---

04 다음 글을 읽고 물음에 답하시오. [3 points]

Neither scholars nor pop sociologists have really got around to charting and diagosing all the changes brought about by air conditioning. Professional observers have for years been preoccupied with the social implications of the automobile and television. Mere glancing analysis suggests that the car and TV, in their most decisive influences on American habits, have been powerfully aided and abetted by air conditioning. The car may have created all those shopping centers in the boondocks, but only (A) has made them attractive to mass clienteles. Similarly, the artificial cooling of the living room undoubtedly helped turn the typical American into a year-round TV addict. Without air conditioning, how many viewers would endure reruns (or even Johnny Carson) on one of those pestilential summer nights that used to send people out to collapse on the lawn or to sleep on the roof?

4-1 **빈칸 (A)에 가장 적당한 표현을 본문에서 찾아 쓰시오.** [1 point]

4-2 **냉방시설이 없다면 사람들이 무덥고 짜증나는 여름밤에 무엇을 할 것이라고 위의 글이 시사하는지 우리말로 기술하시오.** [2 points]

---

05 **밑줄 친 this self-imposed trap이 가리키는 상황이 무엇인지 우리말로 구체적으로 설명하시오.** [2 points]

It's just past noon, late July, and I'm listening to the desperate sounds of a life-or-death struggle going on a few feet away.

There's a small fly burning out the last of its short life's energies in a futile attempt to fly through the glass of the windowpane. The whining wings tell the poignant story of the fly's strategy: *Try harder*.

But it's not working.

The frenzied effort offers no hope for survival. Ironically, the struggle is part of the trap. It is impossible for the fly to try hard enough to succeed at breaking through the glass. Nevertheless, this little insect has staked its life on reaching its goal through raw effort and determination.

This fly is doomed. It will die there on the window-still.

Across the room, ten steps away, the door is open. Ten seconds of flying time and this small creature could reach the outside world it seeks. With only a fraction of the effort now being wasted, it could be free of <u>this self-imposed trap</u>. The breakthrough possibly is there. It would be so easy.

---

06 **밑줄 친 the reverse situation obtains가 무엇을 의미하는지 우리말로 구체적으로 설명하시오.** [2 points]

Because reading demands complex mental manipulations, a reader is required to concentrate far more than a television viewer. An Audio expert notes that "with the electronic media it is openness that counts. Openness permits auditory and visual stimuli more direct access to the brain … someone who is taught to concentrate will fail to perceive many patterns of information conveyed by the electronic stimuli."

It may be that a predisposition toward concentration, acquired, perhaps, through one's reading experiences, makes one an inadequate television watcher. But it seems far more likely that <u>the reverse situation obtains</u>: that a predisposition toward "openness" (which may be understood to mean the opposite of focal concentration), acquired through years of television viewing, has influenced adversely viewers' ability to concentrate, to read, to write clearly—in short, to demonstrate any of the verbal skills a literate society requires.

07 다음 글에서 전체적인 흐름으로 볼 때 어울리지 않는 두 문장을 골라 그 알파벳 기호를 쓰시오. [2 points]

(A) The animals in zoos, isolated from each other and without interaction between species, have become utterly dependent upon their keepers. (B) Consequently most of their responses have been changed. (C) Within limits, the animals are free, but both they and their spectators presume on their close confinement. (D) What was central to their interest has been replaced by a passive waiting for a series of arbitrary outside interventions. (E) The events they perceive occurring around them have become as illusory in terms of their natural responses, as the painted prairies. (F) In zoos animals constitute the living monument to their own disappearance. (G) At the same time this very isolation guarantees their longevity as specimens and facilitates their taxonomic arrangement.*

** taxonomy : the scientific process of classifying living things.*

---

08 **밑줄 친 Balkanization이 이 글에서 어떤 의미로 사용되었는지 글에 제시된 예를 통해서 우리말로 설명하시오.** [2 points]

> The <u>Balkanization</u> of nations is a worldwide phenomenon that the US has not escaped. Regions and localities are less and less willing to incur costs that will primarily help people in other parts of the same country. Consider the development of the coalfields of Wyoming and Montana. There is no question that most of the benefits will accrue* to those living in urban areas in the rest of the country while most of the costs will be imposed on those living in that region. As a result, the local population objects. More coal mining might be good for the US, but it will be bad for local constituents. Therefore, they will impose as many delays and uncertainties as possible.
>
> ** accrue : increase over a period of time*

09 **다음 글을 읽고 물음에 답하시오.** [2 points]

If a problem came up, those with the least illness would look for resources, perhaps do some reading or learning in another way, and then try a solution. If the first one didn't work, they would try another. In contrast, people who reported being frequently ill were more likely to approach problems passively. To give some examples, they would leave it to a spouse to discipline the children or decide where they would go on a weekend evening; they would be uneasy about speaking to the boss when something was wrong at work.

Those with the least illness were also personally committed to a goal of some kind. The goal might be completing a college career, being a better parent, advancing a community activity, or engaging in a hobby. But in any case, these people spent 4-6 hours out of the 168 in a week doing something. I don't mean that everything went well for them during these hours, but rather that the activity had personal significance to them. People who were more prone to illness were, however, quite likely to indicate that they were bored or were unable to find something that interested them.

다음 요약문이 위 글의 내용과 일치하도록 빈칸 (A), (B), (C)에 들어갈 가장 알맞은 단어를 <보기> (A), (B), (C)에서 각각 찾아 답란에 쓰시오.

Those with the least illness are likely to maintain (A) personal control in their lives and to commit themselves to a goal of some kind with a sense of (B) and a sense of meaningful (C) in life.

보기

(A) passive, egoistic, reasonable
(B) humor, challenge, remoteness
(C) participation, meditation, isolation

2000학년도 추가

01 **다음 밑줄 친 곳에 공통으로 들어갈 영어 단어 하나를 쓰시오.** [1 point]

> Neither Adam Smith nor his successors, with a few exceptions, believed that the whole of public activity should be left to the ______________. For one thing, a system depends on a legal framework and a way of enforcing those laws. No one has seriously suggested that the police and the law courts should be run by private concerns for profit. None the less, the recent vogue for privatization suggests that we should push the ______________ philosophy as far as it can go. There are dangers in that approach, dangers which can distort our priorities.

____

02 **다음 <보기>는 아래 글의 내용을 요약한 것이다. 밑줄 친 곳에 들어갈 가장 알맞은 영어 단어 하나를 쓰시오.** [1 point]

보기

> One pleasing outcome of the information age is that more of us can enjoy the good things without spoiling the ___________.

> The future is not gloom. Perhaps economic growth and the 'cultivation' which many former economists think should be the proper purpose of society, are no longer incompatible nowadays. There are interesting possibilities on the horizon. Many of the things for which we will be shopping in future use up much less of our environment. A CD-ROM, for example, which can contain on one disc all of the Encyclopedia Britannica, leaves the forests untouched, takes up less shelf-space in the shops, needs no sweat-shops to produce it and no huge trucks to transport it. Many of the consumer goods of the information age are as environmentally neutral as the computer disc.

03 **다음 글의 ONE UNGROWN-UP GROWNUP은 어떤 사람인지 우리말로 50자 이내로 쓰시오.** [1 point]

> In the home, the child is always being taught. In almost every home, there is always at least ONE UNGROWN-UP GROWNUP who rushes to show Tommy how his new engine works. There is always someone to lift the baby up on a chair when baby wants to examine something on the wall. Every time we show Tommy how his engine works we are stealing from that child the joy of life—the joy of discovery—the joy of overcoming an obstacle. Worse! We make that child come to believe that he is inferior, and must depend on help.

____

____

____

04 **다음 글을 읽고 밑줄 친 부분에 글의 흐름상 가장 알맞은 문장을 영어로 쓰시오.** [2 points]

Language is the principal means whereby we conduct our social lives. When it is used in contexts of communication, it is bound up with culture in multiple and complex ways.

To begin with, the words people utter refer to common experience. They express facts, ideas or events that are communicable because they refer to a stock of knowledge about the world that other people share. Words also reflect their authors' attitudes and beliefs, their point of view, that are also those of others. In both cases, language expresses cultural reality.

But members of a community or social group do not only express experience; they also create experience through language. They give meaning to it through the medium they choose to communicate with one another, for example, speaking on the telephone or face-to-face, writing a letter or sending an e-mail message, reading the newspaper or interpreting a graph or a chart. The way in which people use the spoken, written, or visual medium itself creates meanings that are understandable to the group they belong to, for example, through a speaker's tone of voice, accent, conversational style, gestures and facial expressions. Through all its verbal and non-verbal aspects, language embodies cultural reality.

Finally language is a system of signs that is seen as having itself a cultural value. Speakers identify themselves and others through their use of language; they view their language as a symbol of their social identity. The prohibition of its use is often perceived by its speakers as a rejection of their social group and their culture. Thus we can say that ______________________________.

We shall be dealing with these three aspects of language and culture throughout this book. But first we need to clarify what we mean by culture.

____

05 **다음 글을 읽고 "Table of the Classification of Species"의 빈칸(①~⑥)을 영어로 쓰시오.** [2 points]

The group species is the starting point for classification. Sometimes smaller groups, subspecies, are recognized, but these will not concern us until we discuss evolution. There are many larger groups: genus, family, order, class, phylum, and kingdom.

Let us begin with the first seven species. We belong to the genus Homo and to these more inclusive groups: the family Hominidae, which includes, in addition to Homo, extinct men not of the genus Homo, and the order Primates, which includes also the lemurs, monkeys and apes. The three cats —lion, house cat, and tiger—belong to the genus Felis. In general we can think of a genus as a group of closely related species. The three cats also belong to the family Felidae. Generally a family includes related genera*.

The first seven species, different enough to be put in three orders, are yet alike in many ways. All are covered with hair, they nurse their young with milk, and their red blood cells are without nuclei. Because of these and other resemblances they are combined in a still more inclusive group, Class Mammalia. A class, therefore, is composed of related orders.

** genus의 복수형임*

<Table of the Classification of Species>

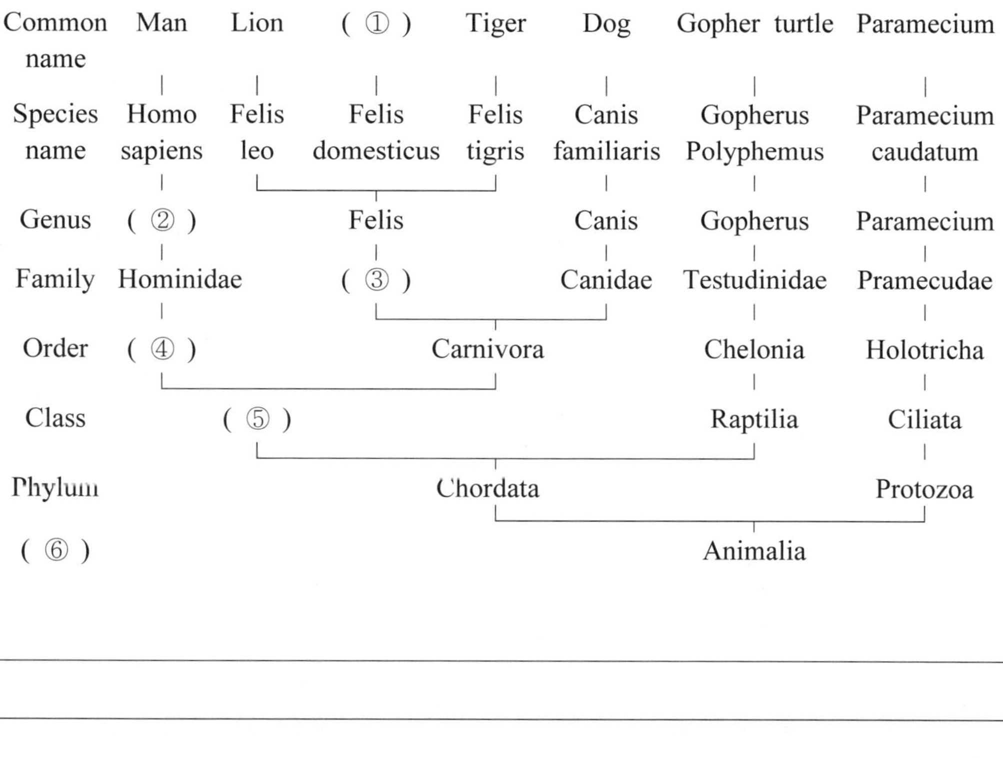
Common name
Man
Lion
(①)
Tiger
Dog
Gopher turtle
Paramecium
Species name
Homo sapiens
Felis leo
Felis domesticus
Felis tigris
Canis familiaris
Gopherus Polyphemus
Paramecium caudatum
Genus
(②)
Felis
Canis
Gopherus
Paramecium
Family
Hominidae
(③)
Canidae
Testudinidae
Pramecudae
Order
(④)
Carnivora
Chelonia
Holotricha
Class
(⑤)
Raptilia
Ciliata
Phylum
Chordata
Protozoa
(⑥)
Animalia

2000학년도

01 **다음 글을 읽고 회사에서 uniform을 입는 이유 세 가지를 우리말로 쓰시오.** [3 points]

> There are a number of reasons why there should not be dress-down days at work. First of all, workplace need to maintain a conscious distinction between the professional and the casual. This distinction is maintained largely by dress. When this distinction vanishes, workers might begin to be more casual with each other, making it difficult to maintain a professional atmosphere. More importantly, casual wear destroys company hierarchy. When the president of the company comes to work wearing khaki pants and a polo shirt, employes are likely to say, "why, he's just one of us." While in "real life" he may indeed be their equal, in the workplace he is not. But the most important reason employees should not be allowed to come to work dressed casually is because it drastically decreases productivity. When people are dressed in their work clothes, they work; when they are dressed casually, the temptation to be casual about getting work done is too great. Employees spend a great deal of time milling about and have a great tendency to cut corners; "Oh, I don't need to proofread again. It's good enough." This attitude in the workplace can not only be dangerous to a company's welfare—it can be deadly.

02 **다음 글의 요지를 두 줄 정도의 우리말로 쓰시오.** [3 points]

A thorough analysis of utopia would involve showing first that it is rooted in the nature of man himself, for it is impossible to understand what it means for man "to have utopia" apart from this fundamental fact.

Any evaluation of utopia must begin with its positive meaning, and the first positive characteristic to be pointed out is its truth—utopia is truth. Why is it truth? Because it expresses man's essence, the inner aim of his existence. Utopia shows what man is essentially and what he should have as telos* of his existence. Every utopia is but one manifestation of what man has as inner aim and what he must have for fulfillment as a person. This definition stresses the social as much as the personal, for it is impossible to understand the one apart from the other. A socially defined utopia loses its truth if it does not at the same time fulfill the person, just as the individually defined utopia loses its truth if it does not at the same time bring fulfillment to society.

* *telos : final purpose*

03 다음 글을 읽고 물음에 답하시오. [4 points]

Like the increasing millions of americans who regularly follow a vigorous exercise program, I know that working out makes me feel good. Moreover, I am convinced it contributes to both my physical and psychological well-being. But there is an added enticement you may not be aware of: keeping healthy may save you insurance dollars as well. How can you trade a pound of flesh for an ounce of cash?

First of all, you must be a standard risk: those with dangerous professions (a stunt man, say) or hobbies (skydiving, for instance) are automatically disqualified. Beyond that, no physical exertion is actually required for the most basic health discount: the nonsmoker's life insurance discount. Because of the medical links between smoking and such major killers as heart disease and lung cancer, insurance companies have been rewarding (   ) with lower rates for twenty years. Today four out of five life insurance company offer discounts averaging from 10 to 15 percent. Smokers are automatically disqualified.

3-1 문맥으로 보아 빈칸에 알맞은 영어 단어를 본문에서 찾아 적절한 형으로 쓰시오. [2 points]

____

3-2 위 글에서 보험료의 불이익을 받는 모든 집단을 우리말로 쓰시오. [2 points]

____

04 **다음 글을 읽고 물음에 답하시오.** [4 points]

When a handful of American scientists installed the first node of a new computer network in the late 60's, they could not know by any chance what phenomenon they had launched. They were set a challenging task to develop and realize a completely new communication system that would be either fully damage-resistant or at least functional even if an essential part of it was in ruins, in case the Third World War started. The scientists did what they had been asked to. By 1972 there were thirty-seven nodes already installed and Advanced Research Projects Agency NET, as the system of the computer nodes was named, was working. Since those "ancient times" during which the network was used only for national academic and military purposes, much of the character of the network has changed. Its today users work in both commercial and non-commercial branches and not just in academic and governmental institutions. Nor is the network only (   ) : it has expanded to many countries around the world, the network has become international and in that way it got its name. People call it Internet.

4-1 **문맥으로 보아 빈칸에 알맞은 영어 단어를 본문에서 찾아 쓰시오.** [2 points]

4-2 **초기의 단순한 컴퓨터 네트워크로 출발한 것이 오늘날 '인터넷'으로 불리게 된 두 가지 요인을 우리말로 쓰시오.** [2 points]

---

05 다음 글을 읽고 물음에 답하시오. [5 points]

The whole subject of happiness has, in my opinion, been treated too solemnly. It had been thought that man cannot be happy without a theory of life. Perhaps those who have been rendered unhappy by a bad theory may need a better theory to help them to recovery, just as you may need a tonic when you have been ill. But when things are normal, a man should be healthy without a tonic and happy without a theory. If a man delights in his wife and children, and finds pleasure in the alternation of day and night, he will be happy whatever his philosophy may be. If, on the other hand, he finds his wife hateful, his children's noise unendurable; if in the daytime he longs for night, and at night sighs for the light of day, then ______(1)______.

Man is an animal, and his happiness depends on his physiology more than he likes to think. This is a humble conclusion, but I cannot make myself disbelieve it. Unhappy businessmen would increase their happiness more by walking six miles every day than by any conceivable change of philosophy. This, incidentally, was the opinion of Jefferson, who on this ground deplored the horse. (2) <u>Language would have failed him</u> if he could have foreseen the motor-car.

5-1 다음 단어들을 이용하여 문맥에 맞게 (1)의 빈칸을 완성하시오. [2 points]

is not, what, a new philosophy, a new exercise, he, but, needs

____

5-2 밑줄 친 (2)를 해석하고, 필자가 그렇게 표현한 이유를 답안지 두 줄 정도의 우리말로 설명하시오. [3 points]

____

____

1999학년도

01 다음 글을 읽고, "recovered" 대신에 "recovering"이라는 표현을 쓰는 이유를 40자 이내의 우리말로 쓰시오. [2 points]

Like addiction, recovery—learning to live without alcohol or drugs—is a process that happens over time. The first two steps are to recognize that there is a problem with alcohol or drugs and to make the decision to give them up. The third step is to actually remove these drugs from the body. This process is called detoxification and should take place under supervision.

People in recovery describe themselves as "recovering" instead of "recovered." This is because the recovery process is ongoing and lifelong. Alcoholism and drug dependence cannot be cured. They can, however, be prevented from progressing further. And people can begin the recovery process at any point on the downward slide into addiction—even before they suffer major losses.

02 다음 글의 밑줄 친 부분이 가리키는 내용을 40자 이내의 우리말로 쓰시오. [2 points]

Conservation is often hampered by social and economic conditions. Poor countries' priorities are often development and education—or simply food, housing and public health—at the expense of the environment. Their economic interests are sometimes combined with conservation programs supported by international organizations. In 1987 the first "debt for nature swap" was arranged. $650,000 worth of Bolivia's national debt was written off against a 160,000-sq-km area of rain forest and savanna. This area is now designated a biosphere reserve: a whole ecosystem with a strictly controlled central zone where no interference is allowed, surrounded by a transition zone in which research is permitted, and finally a buffer zone to protect the ecosystem from encroachment. There are now over 250 worldwide.

03 다음 글을 읽고 물음에 답하시오. [2 points]

One silly question I simply can't stand is "How do you feel?" Usually the question is asked of a man in action—a man on the go, walking along the street, or working up a storm at his desk. So what do you expect him to say? He'll probably say, "Fine, I'm all right," but you've put a bug in his ear—maybe now he's not sure. If you're a good friend, you may have seen something in his face, or his walk, that he overlooked that morning. It starts him worrying a little. First thing you know, he looks in a mirror to see if everything is all right, while you go merrily on your way asking someone else, "How do you feel?"

Every question has its time and place. It's perfectly acceptable, for instance, to ask "How do you feel?" if you're visiting a close friend in the hospital. But if the guy is walking on both legs, hurrying to make a train, or sitting at his desk working, it's no time to ask him that silly question.

When George Bernard Shaw, the famous playwright, was in his eighties, someone asked him "How do you feel?" Shaw put him in his place. "When you reach my age," he said, "either you feel all right or you're dead."

What does the writer argue concerning the use of the question "How do you feel?"? Write your answer in one sentence. Use the word "proper".

04 다음 글을 읽고 물음에 답하시오. [3 points]

FARMERS NO LONGER HAVE COWS, PIGS, CHICKENS, or other animals on their farms; according to the U. S. Department of Agriculture, farmers have "grain-consuming animal units" (which, according to the Tax Reform Act of 1986, are kept in "single-purpose agricultural structures," not pig pens and chicken coops). Attentive observers of the English language also learned recently that the multibillion dollar stock market crash of 1987 was simply a "fourth quarter equity retreat"; that (a) airplanes don't crash, they just have "uncontrolled contact with the ground"; that (b) janitors are really "environmental technicians"; that it was a "diagnostic misadventure of high magnitude" which cause the death of a patient in Philadelphia hospital, not medical malpractice; and that President Reagan wasn't really unconscious while he underwent minor surgery, he was just in a "non-decision-making form." In other words, doublespeak continues to spread as the official language of the public discourse. Doublespeak is a blanket term for language which pretends to communicate but doesn't, language which makes the bad seem good, the negative appear positive, the unpleasant attractive, or at least tolerable. It is language which avoids, shifts, or denies responsibility, language which is at variance with its real or its purported meaning. It is language which conceals or prevents thought. Basic to doublespeak is incongruity, the incongruity between what is said, or left unsaid, and what really is: between the word and the referent, between seem and be, between the essential function of language, communication, and what doublespeak does—mislead, distort, deceive, inflate, circumvent, obfuscate.

4-1 Answer the following question with "yes" or "no": In (a), does the author mean that airplanes don't crash? Then give a reason for your answer according to the passage given. (우리말 100자 이내로 답하시오) [2 points]

____

____

____

4-2 (b)의 janitor가 왜 "environmental technicians"로 불리는지 우리말 50자 이내로 답하시오. [1 point]

____

____

____

05 다음 글을 읽고 물음에 답하시오. [4 points]

Brenda Linson never goes anywhere without an empty spectacles case. It is as vital to her as her purse. Yet, she doesn't wear glasses. The reason she can't do without it is because she can't read and she can't write. If ever she gets into any situation where she might be expected to do either of these things, she fishes around in her bag for the specs case, finds it's empty, and asks the person concerned to do the reading for her. Brenda is now in her late thirties. She's capable and articulate and a few months ago hardly anybody knew she was illiterate. Her husband didn't know and her children didn't know. The children still don't.

She had any number of tactics for concealing <u>her difficulty</u>—for example, never lingering near a phone at work, in case she had to answer it and might be required to write something down. But, in fact, it is easier for illiterates to conceal the truth than the rest of us might imagine. Literacy is so much taken for granted that people simply don't spot the giveaway signs.

It has never been occurred to the children that their mother cannot read. She doesn't read them stories, but then their father doesn't either, so they find nothing surprising in the fact. Similarly they just accept that Dad is the one who writes the sick notes and reads the school reports. Now that the elder boy Tom is quite a proficient reader, Brenda can skillfully get him to read any notes brought home from school simply by asking, "What's that all about, then?"

Brenda's husband never guessed the truth in 10 years of marriage. For one thing he insists on handling all domestic correspondence and bills himself. An importer of Persian carpets, he travels a great deal and so is not around so much to spot the truth. While he's away Brenda copes with any situations, by explaining that she can't do anything until she's discussed it with her husband.

Brenda was very successful in her job until recently. For the last five years she had worked as waitress at an exclusive private club, and had eventually been promoted to head waitress. She kept the thing a secret there too, and got over the practical difficulties somehow.

5-1 **Explain the underlined "her difficulty" in one English sentence.** [1 point]

____

5-2 **The following is part of the summary of the passage. Complete the summary in less than 50 English words.** [3 points]

This article describes the case of Brenda, ______________________

____

____

____

06 다음 글을 읽고, 물음에 영어로 답하시오. [8 points]

The idea that parents shape their children is so ingrained that most people don't even realize it is a testable hypothesis and not a self-evident truth. The hypothesis has now been tested, and the outcome is one of the most surprising in the history of psychology.

Personalities differ in at least five major ways: whether a person is sociable or retiring, whether a person worries constantly or is calm and self-satisfied, whether the person is courteous and trusting or rude and suspicious, whether a person is careful or careless, and whether a person is daring or conforming. Where do these traits come from? If they are genetic, identical twins should share them, even if they were separated at birth, and biological siblings should share them more than adoptive siblings do. If they are a product of socialization by parents, adoptive siblings should share them, and twins and biological siblings should share them more when they grow up in the same home than when they grow up in different homes. Dozens of studies have tested these kinds of predictions on thousands of people in many countries. The studies have looked not only at these personality traits but at actual outcomes in life such as divorce and alcoholism. The results are clear and replicable, and they contain two shockers.

One result has become well known. Much of the variation in personality—about fifty percent—has genetic causes. Identical twins separated at birth are alike; biological siblings raised together are more alike than adopted siblings. That means that the other fifty percent must come from the parents and the home, right? Wrong! Being brought up in one home versus another accounts, at most, for five percent of the differences among people in personality. Identical twins separated at birth are not only similar; they are virtually as similar as identical twins raised together. Adoptive siblings in the same home are not just different; they are about as different as two children plucked from the population at random. The biggest influence that parents have on their children is at the moment of conception.

No one knows where the other forty-five percent of the variation comes from. Perhaps personality is shaped by unique events impinging on the growing brain: how the fetus lay in the womb, how much maternal blood it diverted, how it was squeezed during birth, whether it was dropped on its head or caught certain viruses in the early years. Perhaps personality is shaped by unique experiences, like being chased by a dog or receiving an act of kindness from a teacher. Perhaps the traits of parents and the traits of children interact in complicated ways, so that two children growing up with the same parents really have different environments. One kind of parent may reward a rambunctious child and punish a placid one: another kind of parent may do the opposite. There is no good evidence for these scenarios, and I think two others are more plausible, both of which see personality as an adaptation rooted in the divergence of interests between parents and offspring. One is the child's battle plan for competing with its siblings. The other is the child's battle plan for competing in its peer group.

6-1 **What is this passage about? Write your answer using under 10 words.** [2 points]

____

6-2 **The writer asserts that about fifty percent of personality variation has genetic causes. And in the last paragraph he discusses other forty-five percent. Then, where does the remaining five percent of personality variation come from? Write your answer in one sentence.** [3 points]

____

____

____

6-3 **What are the two scenarios which the writer finds relatively plausible for explaining the forty-five percent of personality variation? Write your answer using under 30 words.** [3 points]

____

____

____

07 다음 글을 읽고 물음에 답하시오. [5 points]

The technological revolution that will prevail for the remainder of this century will create jobs and professions that as little as five years ago were nonexistent. These newly developed markets will demand of workers an understanding of sophisticated technical communications systems as well as an increased technical expertise. By the year 2001 basic skills that once were vital to business will be rendered obsolete. The spot welder on the automobile production line and the field worker on a farm will go the way of the steamboat pilot and the blacksmith. The most significant trend in years to come will be the demise of the blue-collar worker. The American economy will witness the demise as automation and robotics become more prevalent, heralding the rise of the steel-collar worker. Such traditional blue-collar employers as automobile companies have already begun to automate their factories. By contrast, office and service jobs will be abundant, but only for those prepared to improve their technical skills. Again it will be automation that will displace many of the low-skilled and semiskilled workers in the present economy. In fact, the era of the paperless office has already begun. It has been promoted by two principal developments: computers and the explosive growth of telecommunications systems. This office revolution not only has changed how work is done and information is handled but has redefined the function of everyone who works in an office, from the corporate executive down to the lowliest clerk. For the job hunter of 2020, scanning classified ads will be a quick education in how drastically the workplace will have changed. He or she is likely to see openings for such positions as biological historians, biofarming experts, robot trainers, teleconferencing coordinators, to cite but a few.

7-1 **What is the main idea of this passage? Write your answer in about 25 words.** [3 points]

____

____

____

7-2 **What does the underlined "the steel-collar worker" refer to? Write your answer in one or two word(s).** [2 points]

____

1998학년도

01 **다음 글을 읽고 밑줄 친 부분이 가리키는 내용이 무엇인지 70자 정도의 우리말로 쓰시오.**

[3 points]

Anne was expecting an important piece of express mail on the day a severe snowstorm paralyzed the city. The next day she called the post office and asked whether she had any chance of getting her express mail. The man who answered the telephone said, "No, ma'am!" She asked, "Isn't there going to be any delivery of express mail?" He said, peremptorily and with a derisive laugh, "No, ma'am! Whatever is here is going to stay here and whatever isn't isn't. Nothing's coming in or out." His tone was saying that this was obvious. She was getting annoyed. "Well, couldn't I come and get it?" "No!" he snapped, his annoyance reaching a peak. "The post office is closed. The only reason I'm here is because I couldn't get home last night." At that <u>Anne's frustration</u> melted. She said, "Oh, I'm sorry. It's nice of you to answer the phone."

02 다음 글을 읽고 물음에 답하시오. [7 points]

_______ⓐ_______. The conversations which English people hold about the weather, for example, do not as a rule leave the participation any the wiser; only on rare occasions can information be said to have been exchanged. As far as communicating thought is concerned, they get nowhere; are they then quite pointless? No, a little reflection will show that this kind of use of language also has great social value. Most peoples have a feeling that a silent man is a dangerous man. Even if there is nothing to say, one must talk, and conversation puts people at their ease and in harmony with one another. This sociable use of language has been given the name phatic communion. The anthropologist Malinowski invented the term. He said, "It was actuated by the demon of terminological invention." Although he was half in joke, the name has stuck. Malinowski defined it as "a type of speech in which ties of union are created by a mere exchange of words." It enters the everyday experience of everybody, from the most highly civilized to the most primitive, and, far from being useless, this small-talk is essential to human beings getting along together at all.

2-1 다음 단어를 순서대로 이용하여 빈칸 ⓐ에 들어갈 문장을 완성하시오. (<보기>에 주어진 단어는 순서대로 변형 없이 이용하되, 필요하면 다른 어구를 보충할 것) [3 points]

보기

There, some uses, language, which, concerned, communication of thoughts

____

2-2 What is the main idea of the passage? Write your answer using the given words below. [4 points]

phatic, important, getting along

____

03 다음 글을 읽고, 본문에 있는 영어 낱말을 그대로 사용하여 아래 요약문의 빈칸을 채우시오. [6 points]

There is an apparently simple solution to mass unemployment: the shortening of working hours by 10, 15 or 20%. For several reasons such simplicity is more apparent than real. Given the comparatively low level of British wages and salaries, organised labour would not and could not accept wage cuts by the same proportion. Any attempt to create employment for all by such cuts might create social upheaval on a scale larger than that of riots. To pay the same wages for significantly reduced hours to a larger workforce, however, would lower British competitiveness on the world market even further. But even if the world market could absorb more expensive goods—an unlikely assumption anyhow—the attempt could not succeed because of the geographical distribution of unemployment and the mismatch between the skills of the unemployed and the skills required by modern enterprises.

And yet, in the long run the shortening of working hours per day, per year or per lifetime is the most constructive measure if new technologies actually reduce the amount of work required to give the population a respectable standard of living. The psychological benefits of employment are not tied to an eight-hour day or a 40-hour week. They would accrue even in the improbable case for this century that working hours could be halved without lowering the standard of living. In this country as elsewhere a gradual reduction of working hours is actually taking place and there are efforts afoot to cut overtime, one of the few positive aspects of an otherwise dark picture. The immediate impact of such developments will be mostly an improvement in the quality of working life for the employed; it is inevitably a slow way of reducing the number of the unemployed.

요약문

It may seem that if working hours are cut by 10 to 20%, then it will solve the problem of mass unemployment. But organised labour will not accept wage cuts on such a (①). If wage cuts are imposed, it might (②) extremely serious social (③). If hours are cut but (④) and salaries maintained, Britain will be unable to compete in world markets because her (⑤) will be so expensive. Even if Britain's goods could be sold, (⑥) would not fall because of the (⑦) distribution of unemployment and the (⑧) between the skills the (⑨) can offer and the skills required for modern employment.

Shortening working hours has value because we may get (⑩) benefits from employment even when we work less. Cutting (⑪) will improve the quality of working life for the employed but it will slowly reduce the number of the unemployed.

04 다음 글을 읽고 물음에 답하시오. [5 points]

The other complaint wives make about their husbands is (A) “He doesn’t listen to me anymore.” The wives may be right that their husbands aren’t listening, if they don’t value their wives’ telling of problems and secrets to establish rapport. But some of the time men feel unjustly accused: “I was listening.” And some of the time, they’re right. (B) They were. Whether or not someone is listening only that person can really know. But we judge whether or not we think others are listening by signals we can see—not only their verbal responses but also their eye contact and little listening noises like “mhm,” “uh-huh,” and “yeah.” These listening noises give the go-ahead for talk; if they are misplaced along the track, they can quickly derail a chugging conversation. Maltz and Borker also report that women and men have different ways of showing that they’re listening. In the listening role, women make—and expect—more of these noises. So when men are listening to women, they are likely to make too few such noises for the women to feel the men are really listening. And when women are listening to men, making more such listening noises than men expect may give the impression they’re impatient or exaggerating their show of interest.

4-1 **여성들이 밑줄 친 (A)처럼 느끼는 두 가지 이유를 100자 정도의 우리말로 설명하시오.** [3 points]

4-2 **밑줄 친 (B)에서 생략된 말을 영어로 쓰시오.** [2 points]

05 **다음 글을 읽고 물음에 답하시오.** [5 points]

Many of the learning experiences might be enhanced or expanded, or completely new experiences created, when the computer's capabilities are used in concert with other instructional media. As technology increases in both sophistication and affordability, interactive audio and video capabilities will most likely become standard features of basic computer systems. At the present time, however, combining the computer with relevant audio or video features usually involves either very expensive peripheral equipment or a simple noninteractive or not-very-interactive pairing with audio—or videocassettes. As costs decrease, better interactive multimedia applications should become available. Interactive video is already a reality, albeit an expensive one. It features both sound and visual images, and is often used to produce very realistic simulations. Interactive audio, which can recognize, analyze, and manipulate the learner's speech as well as produce synthetic spoken feedback is still in its most rudimentary development stages. In the meantime, valid learning experiences may derive from less complex, more readily available audio capabilities. Speech from cassettes or audiodiskettes may be linked to computer programs, alone or in conjunction with textual or visual displays, to produce listening, speaking, and comprehension activities. During the past two decades, one of the major criticisms of most language laboratory activities has been their emphasis on practice without feedback. Incorporating the computer's feedback capabilities into many of these activities ________(A)________.

5-1 **Rearrange the following group of words so that they can best fit in the blank (A).** [3 points]

instructionally valuable, far more, to emerge, could, permit, learning experiences

____

5-2 **What is the main idea of the passage? Write your answer in about 10 words.** [2 points]

____

____

____

06 **다음 글을 읽고 각 문단의 요지를 완성하시오. (박스 안에 주어진 단어는 순서대로 변형 없이 이용하되, 필요하면 다른 어구를 보충할 것)** [6 points]

[1] Science and technology are getting a bad press these days. Increasingly scornful of the materialism of our culture, young people speak about returning to a simpler, preindustrial, pre-scientific day. They fail to realize that the "good old days" were really the horribly bad old days of ignorance, disease, slavery and death. They fancy themselves in Athens, talking to Socrates, listening to the latest play by Sophocles—never as a slave brutalized in the Athenian silver mines. They imagine themselves as medieval knights on armored chargers—never as starving peasants.

[2] Yet, right down to modern times, the wealth and prosperity of a relative few have been built on the animal-like labor and wretched existence of many—peasants, serfs and slaves. What's more, nothing could be done about it. Slavery and peonage were taken for granted. Not until science became prominent did slavery come to be recognized as a dreadful wrong, to be abolished. It was the scientist, supposedly cold and concerned with things rather than ideals, who brought this about. His investigations made possible the harnessing of the energy of the inanimate world. With steam, electricity and radio beams to do our work for us, there was less need for the comparatively weak and fumbling human muscle—and slavery began to vanish.

[3] Yet, science has helped create problems, too—serious ones. And we must labor to solve them—in the only way history tells us problems have been solved; by science. If we were to turn away now, if a noble young generation abandoned the materialism of an industry, what would happen? Without the machinery of that industry, we would inevitably drift back to slavery.

6-1 **<첫째 문단> Young people tend ______________________________.** [2 points]

think, wrongly, preindustrial, better

____

6-2 **<둘째 문단> Advances in science ______________________________.** [2 points]

possible, free, human beings

____

6-3 **<셋째 문단> We have no choice but to solve the problems _____________.** [2 points]

created, science, help, science

____

1997학년도

01 **다음 글을 읽고 물음에 답하시오.** [3 points]

The Eskimos can speak about snow with a great deal more precision and subtlety than we can in English, but this is not because the Eskimo language (one of those sometimes mis-called 'primitive') is inherently more precise and subtle than English. This does not bring to light a defect in English, a show of unexpected 'primitiveness'. The position is simply and obviously that the Eskimos and the English live in different ＿＿＿＿＿. The English language would be just as rich in terms for different kinds of snow, presumably, if the environments in which English was habitually used made such distinction important. Similarly, we have no reason to doubt that the Eskimo language could be as precise and subtle on the subject of motor manufacture or cricket if these topics formed part of the Eskimos' life. For obvious historical reasons, Englishmen in the nineteenth century could not talk about motorcars with the minute discrimination which is possible today; cars were not a part of their culture. But they had a host of terms for horse-drawn vehicles which send us, puzzled, to a historical dictionary when we are reading Scott or Dickens. How many of us could distinguish between a chaise, a landau, a victoria, a brougham, a coupe, a gig, a diligence, a whisky, a calash, a tilbury, a carriole, a phaeton, and a clarence?

1-1 **Fill in the blank with a suitable word used in the text.** [1 point]

____

1-2 **The modern readers of Scott or Dickens often have to consult a historical dictionary, because ______________.** [2 points]

____

02 다음 글을 읽고 물음에 답하시오. [7 points]

William O'Connor was once a member of the Boston School Committee, in which capacity he made the following remark: "We have no inferior education in our schools. What we have been getting is an inferior type of student." The remark is easy to ridicule, but in a sense it is perfectly sound.

A classroom is a technique for the achievement of certain kinds of learning. It is a workable technique provided that both the teacher and the student have the skill and, particularly, the attitudes that are fundamental to it. Among these, from the student's point of view, are tolerance for <u>delayed gratification</u>, a certain measure of respect for and fear of authority, and a willingness to accommodate one's individual desires to the interests of group cohesion and purpose. These attitudes cannot be taught easily in school because they are a necessary component of the teaching situation itself. Such attitudes must be learned during the years before a child starts schools; that is, in the home.

Without the attitudes that lead to order, the classroom is an entirely impotent technique. Therefore, one possible translation of Mr. O'Connor's remark is "We have a useful technique for educating youth but too many of them have not been provided at home __________________."

2-1 **Rearrange the following group of words so that they can best fit in the blank.** [2 points]

necessary, with, work, for, the attitudes, to, the technique

____

2-2 **밑줄 친 delayed gratification의 의미를 답안지 한 줄 이내로 쓰시오.** [2 points]

____

2-3 **어떤 의미에서 O'Connor의 말이 일리가 있는지, 빈칸 포함 75자 이내의 우리말로 쓰시오.** [3 points]

____

____

____

03 **What is the main idea of the passage? Write down your answer in about 20 words.** [3 points]

The greatest enrichment the scientific culture could give us is a moral one. Among scientists, deep-natured men know that the individual human condition is tragic; for all its triumphs and joys, the essence of it is loneliness and the end death. But what they will not admit is that, because the individual condition is tragic, therefore the social condition must be tragic, too. Because a man must die, that is no excuse for his dying before his time and after a servile life. The impulse behind the scientists drives them to limit the area of tragedy, to take nothing as tragic that can conceivably lie within men's will. The scientists have nothing but contempt for those representatives of the traditional culture who use a deep insight into man's fate to obscure the social truth, just to hang on to a few perks. Dostoevsky sucking up to the Chancellor Pobedonostsev, who thought the only thing wrong with slavery was that there was not enough of it; Ezra Pound broadcasting for the Fascists; Faulkner giving sentimental reasons for treating Negroes as a different species. They are all symptoms of the deepest temptation of the clerks—which is to say: "Because man's condition is tragic, everyone ought to stay in their place, with mine as it happens somewhere near the top." From that particular temptation, made up of defeat, self-indulgence, and moral vanity, the scientific culture is almost totally immune. It is that kind of moral health of the scientists which, in the last few years, the rest of us have needed most.

2S2R

유희태 일반영어 ③ 기출

초판 1쇄 2010년 4월 28일
2판 1쇄 2014년 4월 29일
3판 1쇄 2016년 4월 29일
4판 1쇄 2018년 4월 30일
5판 1쇄 2021년 4월 30일
6판 1쇄 2023년 1월 10일
2쇄 2025년 2월 10일
7판 1쇄 2026년 1월 15일

저자와의
협의하에
인지생략

저자 유희태 **발행인** 박 용 **발행처** (주)박문각출판
표지디자인 박문각 디자인팀
등록 2015. 4. 29. 제2019-000137호
주소 06654 서울시 서초구 효령로 283 서경 B/D
팩스 (02) 584-2927
전화 교재 문의 (02) 6466-7202 동영상 문의 (02) 6466-7201

정 가 38,000원
ISBN 979-11-7519-611-7

유희태 일반영어

2S2R ③ 기출

다음카페_유희태 전공영어
http://cafe.daum.net/YHT2S2R

네이버 블로그_유희태 전공영어
http://blog.naver.com/kmo7740

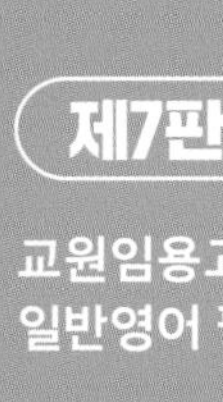

제7판

교원임용고시
일반영어 필독서

임용영어 수험생 대다수가 선택하는
전공영어의 보 통 명 사

- 교원임용고시 전공영어 독보적 전국 1위
  (2025년 예스24 전공영어 부문 박문각 누적 판매량 1위)
- 미국 버클리대학 유희태 박사의 독창적 방법론을 통한 기출분석
- 1997~2026학년도 모든 기출문제와 답안 수록
- 2016~2026학년도 기출문제의 섬세한 분석 제공

유희태 일반영어

2S2R ③ 기출

LSI 영어연구소 유희태 박사 편저

● 모범답안 및 번역

박문각 임용
동영상강의 www.pmg.co.kr

유희태 일반영어

2S2R ③ 기출

제7판

교원임용고시
일반영어 필독서

임용영어 수험생 대다수가 선택하는
전공영어의 보통명사

- 교원임용고시 전공영어 독보적 전국 1위
  (2025년 예스24 전공영어 부문 박문각 누적 판매량 1위)
- 미국 버클리대학 유희태 박사의 독창적 방법론을 통한 기출분석
- 1997~2026학년도 모든 기출문제와 답안 수록
- 2016~2026학년도 기출문제의 섬세한 분석 제공

유희태 일반영어

2S2R ③ 기출

LSI 영어연구소 유희태 박사 편저

● 모범답안 및 번역

박문각 임용 동영상강의 www.pmg.co.kr

Chapter 01 2026~2014학년도 기출문제

본책 p.218

2026학년도

01

하위내용영역	배점	예상정답률
일반영어 A형 서술형	4점	50%

모범답안 The word is "close-up". Second, it means that the close-up forces viewers to perceive the character's unspoken inner feelings, exposing the silent emotional truth that contrasts with the dialogue being spoken aloud.

한글번역

현대 무대는 더 이상 음성 독백을 사용하지 않는다. 그것 없이는 등장인물들이 가장 진실하고 관습에 가장 덜 구속받을 때, 즉 혼자 있을 때 침묵하게 되는데도 말이다. 오늘날 관객은 음성 독백을 용인하지 않는다. 그것이 "부자연스럽다"는 이유에서다. 이제 영화는 우리에게 침묵의 독백을 가져다줬다. 이 침묵의 독백에서 얼굴은 부자연스럽게 보이거나 관객의 반감을 일으키지 않으면서도 가장 미묘한 의미의 뉘앙스를 전달할 수 있다. 이 침묵의 독백에서 고독한 인간의 영혼은 어떤 음성 독백보다 더 솔직하고 거침없는 언어를 찾을 수 있다. 왜냐하면 그것은 본능적으로, 무의식적으로 말하기 때문이다. 얼굴의 언어는 억압되거나 통제될 수 없다. 아무리 훈련되고 습관적으로 위선적인 얼굴이라 해도, 확대된 클로즈업 속에서 우리는 그것이 무언가를 감추고 있다는 것, 거짓말을 하고 있다는 것조차 볼 수 있다. 왜냐하면 그런 것들은 가장된 표정 위에 덧씌워진 고유한 표현을 지니고 있기 때문이다. 말로 거짓말하는 것이 얼굴로 거짓말하는 것보다 훨씬 쉬우며, 영화는 이를 의심의 여지 없이 증명해왔다.

영화에서 얼굴의 무언의 독백은 주인공이 혼자 있지 않을 때도 말한다. 바로 여기에 인간을 묘사하는 새롭고 위대한 기회가 있다. 독백의 시적 의미는 그것이 육체적 고독이 아니라 정신적 고독의 표현이라는 점이다. 그럼에도 무대에서 등장인물은 다른 사람이 없을 때만 독백을 할 수 있다. 설령 그 인물이 거대한 군중 속에 홀로 있을 때 천 배는 더 외로움을 느낄 수 있다고 해도 말이다. 외로움의 독백은 그가 누군가와 들리게 대화하는 중에도 그의 내면에서 백 번이고 목소리를 높일 수 있다. 따라서 가장 깊이 느껴지는 인간의 독백은 그러한 표현을 찾을 수 없었다. 클로즈업은 가장 큰 군중의 한가운데서 등장인물을 끌어올려 그가 실제로 얼마나 고독한지, 이 붐비는 고독 속에서 무엇을 느끼는지 보여줄 수 있기 때문이다.

영화, 특히 유성영화는 타인과 대화하는 등장인물의 말을 얼굴 표정이라는 무언의 움직임과 분리할 수 있다. 그 움직임을 통해 우리는 그러한 대화 한가운데서 무언의 독백을 엿듣게 되고, 이 독백과 들리는 대화 사이의 차이를 깨닫게 된다. 생신의 배우가 실제 무대에서 보여줄 수 있는 것은 기껏해야 그의 말이 진실하지 않다는 것뿐이며, 그러한 대화의 상대가 모든 관객이 볼 수 있는 것을 보지 못한다는 것은 단지 관습일 뿐이다. 그러나 영화의 고립된 클로즈업에서 우리는 아무리 예리한 관찰자인 상대조차 결코 지각하지 못할 얼굴 근육의 미세한 움직임을 통해 영혼의 밑바닥까지 볼 수 있다.

02

하위내용영역	배점	예상정답률
일반영어 B형 서술형	4점	35%

모범답안 The word is "contingent". Second, it means a conceptual model through which humans turn natural events into simple cause-and-effect stories rather than depicting the world's actual, complex workings.

한글번역

과학은 강력한 설명적 서사를 만들어내는 풍부한 원천이다. 예를 들어, 뉴턴은 힘이 어떻게 질량에 가속도를 발생시키는지를 설명했다. 이는 사과가 나무에서 떨어지고 행성이 태양을 도는 방식을 이해하게 해주는 하나의 이야기 구조를 제공한다. 또한 로켓이 달까지 가기 위해 어느 정도의 추진력이 필요한지 판단할 수 있게 해준다. 인과 모델은 공장이나 컴퓨터처럼 복잡한 기계를 설계할 수 있게 하는데, 이러한 기계는 매우 길고 정교한 인과적 연쇄를 기반으로 입력을 우리가 원하는 출력으로 변환한다.

우리가 만들어낸 인과 이야기가 곧 세계가 실제로 작동하는 방식이라고 믿도록 유혹받기 쉽다. 그러나 사실 그것들은, 세계를 다루고 이해하기 편하도록 설명을 구성하는 데 사용하는 하나의 인지적 틀에 불과하다. 예를 들어, 뉴턴의 방정식 $F=ma$는 힘이 가속의 원인이라고 말해주는 것도 아니고, 질량이 힘을 일으킨다고 말해주는 것도 아니다. 우리는 힘을 조건적으로 달라지는 것으로(우리의 선택이나 상황에 따라 달라지는 것으로) 간주하는 경향이 있는데, 힘을 가할지 말지는 종종 우리가 선택할 수 있기 때문이다. 반대로 질량은 우리의 통제를 벗어난 것으로 바라보는 경향이 있다. 그래서 우리는 자연을 의인화해, 자연의 힘이 마치 스스로 질량을 밀어 움직이기로 결정하는 것처럼 상상한다. (반면) 가속이 질량을 만들어내기로 '결심한다'고 상상하는 것은 훨씬 어렵기 때문에 우리는 이야기를 특정 방식으로 구성한다. 우리는 행성의 공전을 중력의 공으로 돌리고, 사과가 떨어지는 일을 중력 탓으로 돌린다.

이렇게 편리하게 자연을 의인화하는 것은 우리로 하여금 자연 세계를 설명하기 위해 서사적 사고 장치를 활용할 수 있게 해준다. 원인과 결과라는 사고방식은 과학이 공학적 목적, 즉 세상을 우리의 편의에 맞게 배열하는 데 사용될 때 특히 효과적이다. 이런 경우 우리는 종종 인과 관계의 '환상'을 실제와 거의 구분되지 않을 정도로 만들 수 있다. 컴퓨터가 그 대표적 예이다. 컴퓨터의 작동 핵심은 입력이 출력을 결정하지만 그 반대는 일어나지 않는다는 점이다. 컴퓨터를 구성하는 부품들은 모두 이러한 일방향적 관계를 만들어내도록 설계됐다. 논리 게이트 같은 이러한 부품들은 조건적 입력을 예측 가능한 출력으로 바꾸도록 특별히 고안됐다. 다시 말해, 컴퓨터의 논리 게이트는 인과 구조를 구성하는 가장 작은 단위가 되도록 만들어진 것이다.

(하지만) 우리가 출력이라고 여기는 요소가 입력이라고 간주하는 요소에 영향을 미치기 시작하면 인과 개념은 무너진다. 양자역학의 역설은 그 대표적 예인데, 여기서는 우리가 어떤 입자를 관측하는 행위만으로도 멀리 떨어진 다른 입자가 다른 상태에 놓이도록 하는 '원인'이 될 수 있다. 물론 여기에는 실제로 역설이 있는 것이 아니라, 단지 그 상황에 맞지 않는 우리식 서사 틀을 억지로 적용하려 할 때 생기는 문제일 뿐이다.

03

하위내용영역	배점	예상정답률
일반영어 B형 서술형	4점	55%

모범답안 While sport offers health and recreational benefits, it poses significant environmental challenges. First, sporting facilities such as golf courses destroy natural landscapes and require excessive chemical use for maintenance. Second, large spectator sports and their stadia generate substantial plastic waste and noise pollution that degrades surrounding areas. In conclusion, therefore, sport organizations must adopt proactive environmental policies to ensure the long-term sustainability of athletic activities.

한글번역

놀이터에서 공을 차는 아이들부터 농구 코트의 스타 선수들에 이르기까지, 스포츠는 어디에나 존재한다. 나이, 성별, 배경과 관계없이 스포츠는 신체 건강을 증진시킬 뿐만 아니라 많은 사람들에게 여가 활동의 출구를 제공하는 중요한 활동이다. 이러한 장점에도 불구하고, 스포츠 분야는 환경에 미치는 부정적 영향으로 인해 압박을 받고 있다.

스포츠 행사 자체가 환경적으로 문제가 되는 것으로 여겨진다. 스포츠 환경의 인공화는 자연과 경관에 여러 방식으로 악영향을 미친다. 예를 들어, 세계 주요 도시들을 둘러싼 녹지대로 골프장이 급속히 확산되는 것은 많은 우려를 증가시킨다. 많은 사람들, 특히 골퍼들은 잘 관리된 골프장을 아름다운 것으로 여기지만, 그것의 개발은 환경적 대가를 수반한다. 골프장이 건설되면서 자연 경관의 일부가 파괴된다. 게다가 골프장을 조성하고 유지하기 위해 엄청난 양의 화학 비료가 토양에 투입된다.

환경에 영향을 미치는 것은 스포츠 활동만이 아니다. 대규모 관중 스포츠와 관련 경기장들은 인접 지역에 문제를 일으킨다. 경기장에서는 군중의 소비와 인근 매점으로부터 병과 음식 용기 등 수만 개의 플라스틱 쓰레기가 발생한다. 더욱이 관중의 도착과 출발로 인한 소음 배출은 그 지역에 많은 부담을 준다. 축구와 럭비의 경우, 관중의 과도한 응원과 증폭된 스피커에서 나오는 큰 음악 소리는 엄청난 양의 소음을 만들어내며, 이는 공공 공간의 스포츠 시설의 환경적인 질을 낮춘다.

종합적으로, 이러한 문제들은 스포츠계에서 지속 가능한 환경을 유지하는 데 우려를 불러일으킨다. 스포츠 단체들은 환경에 미치는 부작용을 줄이기 위한 정책을 추진함으로써 이러한 어려움을 극복하는 데 더 적극적이어야 한다. 이것은 스포츠의 장기적인 생존 가능성과 지속 가능성을 보호할 것이다.

2025학년도

01

하위내용영역	배점	예상정답률
일반영어 A형 서술형	4점	45%

모범답안 The word is "nothing". Second, the underlined phrase means that the ultimate meaning or purpose of our lives—symbolized as the "pearl"—can only be understood at the conclusion of the journey or narrative.

한글번역

"이야기를 한다는 것은 인간에게 먹는 것만큼이나 기본적인 일이다," 리처드 커니는 이렇게 쓴다. "사실 먹는 것보다 더 그렇다(even more basic to human beings than eating is). 음식이 우리를 살게 해준다면, 이야기는 우리 삶을 살 가치 있는 것으로 만들어주기 때문이나." 아니면 살 가치 없게 만들 수도 있기 때문이다(stories are what make our lives not worth living). 우리가 그렇듯이(as we also live on the edge of the abyss), 삶이 벼랑 끝에 있을 때, 존재의 가치와 의미에 대한 근본적인 질문의 대답은 결국 자신이 스스로에게 들려주는 이야기에 크게 좌우된다. 그리고 실패는 우리 존재의 핵심에 자리하고 있기 때문에, 우리가 스스로에게 들려주는 가장 중요한 이야기들, 그리고 우리가 타인에 대해 읽는 이야기들 역시 대부분 실패의 이야기다. 실제로, 그리스 비극에서부터 최신 뉴스 기사에 이르기까지, 어느 이야기든 일정 정도의 실패 없이는 좋은 이야기라 할 수 없다. 그런 이야기들이 우리를 사로잡는다. 로봇의 내면을 누가 읽고 싶겠는가? 실패와 이야기, 이 둘은 친밀한 친구이며 언제나 짝을 이룬다.

그렇기 때문에 우리의 삶이 "완전한 실패였다," "아무 의미가 없다," 또는 "고통을 감수할 가치가 없다"는 관찰(혹은 생각)은, 우리의 존재 여정 중에 많은 이들이 할 수도 있는 관찰이다. 그런데도 대부분의 사람은 그 즉시 삶을 끝내지는 않는다. 그건 용기가 없어서가 아니다 (죽고 싶을 땐 누구든 용기를 낸다). 오히려 그 실패로 가득한 이야기조차 아직 끝나지 않았다는 느낌 때문이다. 우리는 기다리며 지켜보고 싶어 한다(아직 끝나지 않았다고 느끼기 때문에, 우리는 어떻게 되는지 계속 보고 싶어 한다, 즉 아직 '자신의 이야기'의 마지막 페이지가 나오지 않았다는 이야기 감각이, 우리를 살아 있게 만드는 것이란 의미). 그리고 이것은 의미심장하다(많은 것을 말해 준다).

어느 한순간, 우리의 삶이 충만하지 않거나 존재가 무의미하게 느껴질 수는 있다. 하지만 더 깊은 차원에서는 아직 끝나지 않았다는 걸 안다. 우리의 이야기는 아직 끝나지 않았다. 그리고 책이든 영화든, 아니면 자기 자신의 삶이든, 이야기가 끝나기 전에 중단하는 것은 깊은, 본능적인 좌절감을 불러일으킨다. 일단 **그 지점("that point")**에 도달하면, 우리는 더 이상 말할 것이 없다고 결정할 수도 있다. 하지만 이야기가 아직 진행되고 있는 동안 그 이야기를 그만두는 것은 서사에 대한 위반일 뿐만 아니라 자연에 대한 위반이기도 하다. 우리가 그토록 바라왔던 의미는 이야기의 마지막에서야 드러날 수도 있고, 우리는 더 이상 그 계시를 받을 수 있는 곳에 있지 않을 수도 있다. 결국, 우리가 추구해야 할 "진주"는 이야기의 끝에 가서야 발견되는 것이라 쓰여 있다. **(삶의 의미를 찾기 위해서는 끝까지 살아야 한다는 철학적 메시지)**

그렇다면 이야기가 내 삶을 구할 수 있을까? 그렇다. 구할 수 있다. 진실은, 오직 이야기만이 우리의 삶을 구원할 수 있다는 것이다. 단지 우리의 삶만이 아니라, 삶 자체를. 그래서 인생엔 그렇게 많은 이야기들이 있는 것이다. 이야기가 없다면 우리는 아무것도 아닐 것이다.

➕ 보충설명

"that point": 인생의 자연스러운 종착점, 즉 이야기가 완전히 끝나는 순간.

자연스러운 종료 vs 인위적 중단을 구분하고 있다. 이야기가 자연스럽게 완결되는 시점에서는 "더 이상 말할 것이 없다"고 느낄 수 있다. 하지만 이야기가 아직 진행 중일 때 인위적으로 중단하는 것은 다른 차원의 문제로 이중적 위반이 된다.

1. 서사적 위반: 스토리텔링의 기본 원칙 위반 (이야기는 끝까지 들어야 한다.)
2. 자연적 위반: 자연의 법칙이나 질서에 대한 위반 (생명은 자연스럽게 중간에 멈추지 않고 흘러가야 한다.)

핵심 메시지: 인생을 인위적으로 끝내는 것은 단순한 개인적 선택이 아니라, 서사와 자연이라는 더 큰 질서에 대한 근본적 위반이 된다.

02

하위내용영역	배점	예상정답률
일반영어 B형 서술형	4점	45%

모범답안 The word is "scarcity". Second, it means that humans, like cacti in rainforests, are poorly adapted to abundance. Just as cacti struggle with too much water in a rainforest, humans struggle to regulate desires in a world overflowing with resources.
또는, Second, it means that human beings, like cacti in a rainforest, are poorly adapted to their current environment of abundance. Just as cacti struggle with too much water in a rainforest due to their evolution for arid conditions, humans, whose brains are designed for a world of scarcity, face challenges in regulating their behavior and desires in a world overflowing with resources, leading to issues like overconsumption and addiction.
또는, it means that humans, like cacti, evolved to survive in harsh, dry environments (scarcity), but now live in a world of constant excess (abundance), which they are not adapted for. Just as a cactus would suffer in an overly wet climate, modern humans struggle psychologically and physically in a world flooded with pleasure and stimulation. (It highlights the mismatch between our evolutionary design and our current environment.)

한글번역

과학은 우리에게 모든 쾌락에는 대가가 따르고, 그 쾌락에 따라오는 고통은 쾌락보다 더 오래 지속되며, 더 강렬하다고 가르친다.

지속적이고 반복적인 쾌락 자극에 노출되면, 우리는 고통을 견디는 능력이 감소하고, 쾌락을 경험하기 위한 우리의 역치(어떤 자극을 느끼기 시작하는 최소한의 기준)가 증가한다.

즉각적이고 영구적인 기억을 각인시킴으로써, 우리는 원할 때조차도 쾌락과 고통의 교훈을 잊을 수 없다: 평생 지속되는 해마(기억을 담당하는 뇌 부위)의 문신들.

쾌락과 고통을 처리하는 계통발생적으로 매우 오래된 신경 기제(뇌의 작용 체계)는 진화의 전 과정과 여러 종을 통틀어 대부분 그대로 유지돼왔다. 이 기제는 결핍의 세계에 완벽하게 적응돼있다. 쾌락이 없었다면 우리는 먹지도, 마시지도, 번식하지도 않았을 것이다. 고통이 없었다면 우리는 부상이나 죽음으로부터 자신을 보호하지 못했을 것이다. 반복된 쾌락으로 인해 우리의 신경 기준점(쾌락을 느끼는 기준선)이 올라가면, 우리는 끊임없이 더 많은 것을 추구하는 존재가 된다. 지금 가진 것에 결코 만족하지 못하고, 항상 더 많은 것을 찾는.

하지만 바로 여기에 문제가 있다. 궁극적인 탐구자들인 인간은 쾌락은 추구하고 고통은 피하라는 도전에 지나치게 잘 반응해왔다. 그 결과, 우리는 세상을 결핍의 장소에서 압도적인 풍요의 장소로 바꿔 놓았다.

우리의 뇌는 이러한 풍요의 세계를 위해 진화하지 않았다. 앉아서 먹는 만성적인 생활 속에서 당뇨병을 연구하는 톰 피누케인 박사는 이렇게 말했다. "우리는 열대우림 속의 선인장이다(건조한 환경에 맞춰진 선인장이 물이 넘치는 환경에서 오히려 병들 수 있다는 점을 통해, 인간이 지금의 풍요로운 환경에 부적응하고 있음을 비유적으로 표현)."

그 총체적인 결과는 이렇다: 우리는 이제 쾌락을 느끼기 위해 더 많은 보상이 필요하고, 고통을 느끼기 위해서는 더 적은 자극만으로도 충분하다. 이러한 재조정은 개인의 수준에서만이 아니라 국가의 수준에서도 일어나고 있다. 이것은 질문을 불러일으킨다: 우리는 이 새로운 생태계 속에서 어떻게 생존하고 번영할 수 있을까? 우리는 아이들을 어떻게 길러야 할까? 21세기의 주민으로서 우리는 어떤 새로운 사고방식과 행동 양식을 갖춰야 할까?

강박적인 과소비(오늘날 풍요 사회의 핵심 문제 중 하나)를 피하는 법을 우리에게 가장 잘 가르쳐줄 수 있는 이들이 누구겠는가? 바로 그것에 가장 취약한 이들—중독과 싸우는 사람들이다. 수천 년 동안 다양한 문화 속에서 이들은 타락자, 기생충, 추방자, 도덕적 부패를 퍼뜨리는 자로 외면받아 왔다. **하지만 이제 이 중독자들은 우리가 살아가는 이 시대에 완벽하게 들어맞는 지혜를 진화시켜 왔다.("people with addiction have evolved a wisdom perfectly suited to the age we live in now")**

⊕ 보충설명

마지막 문장의 의미

중독자들(중독에 취약한 사람들)은 바로 그 문제의 최전선에서 싸우고 있는 존재이며, 그들이 얻은 생존 지혜는 과소비와 쾌락 추구가 넘쳐나는 지금의 풍요시대에 가장 유의미한 통찰을 제공할 수 있다는 점을 강조한다. 즉, 가장 약했던 자들이야말로, 병든 현재 사회에서 진짜로 살아남는 법을 배운 자들일 수 있다는 역설적인 진리를 말하고 있다.

03

하위내용영역	배점	예상정답률
일반영어 B형 서술형	4점	50%

모범답안 Putting oneself first can offer several advantages, not only for individuals but also for those around them. First, declining unwanted requests, such as avoiding shopping trip where both people might end up feeling unhappy, can reduce stress and improve relationships. Second, prioritizing personal well-being increases happiness, which can positively impact those around us, such as children benefiting from a relaxed parent. In conclusion, it is important to have the confidence to decline requests that feel overly demanding.

한글번역

지나친 이타심은 '거절하지 못하는 것'으로 이어진다. 우리는 무례하게 보이거나, 사람들을 불쾌하게 하거나, 기분 상하게 할까 봐 두려움 속에 살아간다. 어떤 사람은 자신을 먼저 생각하는 것이 이기적인 행동이라고 믿을 수도 있다. 그러나 자신을 먼저 생각하는 것은 실제로 여러 가지 이점을 가져온다.

자신을 우선시한다고 해서 항상 다른 사람의 감정을 완전히 무시할 필요는 없다. 예를 들어, 친구가 당신에게 쇼핑하러 가자고 요청했고, 당신은 그녀를 실망시키고 싶지 않아서 "예스"라고 대답했다. 결과적으로, 당신은 가게에 들어서기도 전에 스트레스를 받게 된다. 그리고 당신은 억지로 따라간 그 쇼핑 내내 스트레스를 받는다. 만약 당신이 "아니"라고 말했다면 결과는 어땠을까? 그녀는 처음에는 다소 섭섭하게 느낄 수 있었겠지만, 짜증 나고 스트레스받은 쇼핑 친구를 참을 필요는 없었을 것이다!

또한, 자신을 우선시하는 것은 주변 사람들의 행복에도 기여할 수 있다. 점점 더 많은 연구들이 사람들이 다른 사람의 필요를 우선시할 때보다 자신을 우선시할 때 더 행복하다고 제시하고 있다. 결과적으로, 그들은 그 행복을 다른 사람들과 나눌 수 있다. 아이들과 시간을 보내는 것이 사치처럼 느껴질 수 있지만, 만약 한 시간의 거품 목욕이 당신이 원하는 것이라면, 아이들은 모든 사람을 위해 무언가를 하려고 애쓰며 자신에게 제대로 된 휴식조차 주지 않는 부모보다 휴식을 취한 부모와 함께 있을 때 훨씬 더 행복할 것이다.

자신을 우선시하지 않으면 결국 자신과 다른 사람들에게 모두 부정적인 힘이 될 수 있다. 장기적으로, 자신을 우선시하는 것은 종종 관련된 모두에게 이익이 된다. 이런 의미에서, 이기심(자신을 우선시하는 것)은—많은 경우—이타적인 행동이 될 수도 있다(while putting yourself first may seem like an act of selfishness, in the long run, it can actually lead to greater benefits for others, making it an act of selflessness). 그러므로, 다음에, 어려운 일을 부탁받을 때 '아니오'라고 말하는 것을 두려워하지 마라.

2024학년도

01

하위내용영역	배점	예상정답률
일반영어 A형 서술형	4점	45%

모범답안 The word is "response". Second, it is because, for tourists who search for authenticity, the grandeur of the natural environment of the Alps, unlike culture, provides an authentic experience beyond human intrusion.

한글번역

관광 연구가 번창하기 시작했지만, 관광과 표현적 문화를 다루는 연구는 상대적으로 드물다. 관광 인류학과 기호학은 관광 산업의 부산물인 이미지 창조 과정을 희생시키면서 이미지 소비자의 역할을 지나치게 강조한다는 점이 지적된다. 나시 말해, 호스드 시회기 연구되긴 했지만, 그들 자신의 표현적 문화 측면에서가 아니라 관광 압력에 대한 그들의 대응 측면에서 더 자주 연구됐다. 관광 예술에 관한 연구에서 줄스-로제트는 장인이 "관광 예술"을 생산하는 사업에 오래 종사할수록, 그는 자신의 문화적 정체성을 만족시키는 미학을 더 발전시켰다는 것을 발견했다. 시장, 관객, 그리고 공연자들의 복잡한 상호작용 속에서, 장인들은 결국 외부에서 부과된 진정성의 개념을 전유했다. [Even though outsiders (tourists, the tourism industry) initially defined what counted as "authentic" local culture, the artisans eventually reclaimed and redefined this concept of authenticity on their own terms.]

딘 맥캐널에 따르면, 관광객은 계속해서 진정성 있는 경험을 찾는다. 이에 대응해 관광 산업은 관광객이 호스트 사회에서 실제로 살아가는 삶을 바라볼 수 있도록 점점 더 교묘한 방법을 사용해 이러한 갈망을 충족시킨다. 그러나 관광객이 일상적인 영역을 얼마나 깊이 들여다볼 수 있든, 관광객이 그것을 보고 있다는 바로 그 사실 때문에 진정성은 여전히 연출된 상태로 남아 있다. 그러나 문화 영역에서 진정성을 찾기가 관광객에게 어렵다면, 어떤 종류의 경험이 가능한가? 베른 고원지대의 인터라켄에서는 알프스의 웅장한 물리적 환경이다. 경관은—문화와 달리—연출될 수 없으며, **대부분의 관광객들은 수많은 인간의 침입—**정성껏 관리된 들판, 재건된 개울, 많은 스키 리프트와 톱니바퀴 철도**—에 대해 생각하지 않는 것을 선호한다("most tourists prefer not to think about the numerous human intrusions")**. 왜냐하면 웅장함을 경험하기 위해선 그들 중 일부의 도움으로만 충분히 가까이 갈 수 있기 때문이다. 자연의 아름다움은 진정한 경험의 인상을 망치기에는 너무 크며, 마을의 호수와 봉우리 사이의 독특한 지리적 위치가 아니었다면 인터라켄에는 아마도 관광객이 없었을 것이다.

⊕ 보충설명

The phrase **"most tourists prefer not to think about the numerous human intrusions"** suggests that tourists generally want to believe they're experiencing untouched, pristine nature, even when the reality is different. The passage points out that, unlike cultural experiences that can be deliberately staged for tourists, landscapes seem to offer an "authentic" natural experience. However, the passage then highlights **the irony** that these seemingly "natural" landscapes often contain many human modifications: "Carefully tended fields" (managed agricultural land); "Rebuilt streams" (waterways that have been engineered); "Ski lifts and cog railways" (transportation infrastructure). The key insight is that tourists rely on these very human interventions to access and enjoy the natural beauty they seek, creating a contradiction: the "authentic" experience of nature is facilitated by human modifications that tourists prefer to ignore.

The passage concludes by noting that Interlaken's appeal depends entirely on its unique geographic location between lakes and mountains—suggesting that despite human interventions, the natural setting remains so impressive that it still provides what tourists perceive as an authentic experience of nature.

In essence, this is pointing out a **cognitive dissonance** in tourism: visitors seek authentic natural experiences while simultaneously benefiting from (and often ignoring) the human interventions that make those experiences accessible.

02

하위내용영역	배점	예상정답률
일반영어 B형 서술형	4점	35%

모범답안 The word is "reliable". Second, it is because when the signalers send honest information, it benefits the natural selection of both honest signalers and receptive opponents by keeping the whole system of communication.

또는, Second, organism signals honestly because the success of dishonest signaling would destruct the whole communication system, which harms the natural selection of both honest signalers and receptive opponents.

한글번역

신호는 일반적으로 수신자라고 불리는 다른 유기체의 행동을 변화시키는 행동이나 구조다. 크렙스와 도킨스는 동물 신호를 "조작자"(신호 발신자)와 "마음-읽기자"(수신자) 사이의 군비 경쟁으로 설명한다. 신호 발신자는 자신의 능력이나 의도에 관한 사적 정보를 가지고 있으며 수신자에게 보낼 신호를 선택한다. 수신자는 행동을 선택해 반응하고, 이익(또는 비용)은 두 개체의 행동에 따라 달라진다. 신호는 음향적, 시각적, 또는 화학적일 수 있으며, 부모에게는 자원 요구사항을, 경쟁자에게는 싸움 능력을, 짝에게는 유전적 능력을 나타낸다.

신호 이론의 중심 원칙은 진화적 균형 상태에서 신호 발신자와 수신자 모두 정보 교환으로부터 이익을 얻어야 한다는 것이다. 만약 수신자가 자신의 반응으로부터 이익을 얻지 못한다면, 자연선택은 신호를 무시하는 수신자를 선호할 것이다. 이 요구사항은 신호가 신뢰할 수 있는 정보를 전달해야 함을 의미한다. 이 아이디어는 동물 의사소통에 관한 이론적, 경험적 연구들을 둘러싼 논쟁의 원천이 돼왔다. 이 논쟁을 이해하기 위해서는 불성실한 신호 전달이 무엇인지 정의해야 한다. 시어시와 노위키는 불성실한 신호 전달에 대한 공식적 정의를 제공했다. 수신자가 신호 발신자로부터 X를 인식하고, 신호 발신자에게 이익이 될 뿐만 아니라 X가 Y를 의미한다면 수신자에게도 이익이 되는 방식으로 반응하지만, Y가 거짓일 때 불성실함이 발생한다. 다시 말해, 불성실한 의사소통은 신호가 신호 발신자의 능력이나 필요와 연결이 끊어질 때 발생한다. 이 정의는 불성실함이 신호 발신자에게 주는 이익을 강조하고 근본적인 질문을 제기한다: 불성실함이 잠재적으로 주목할 만한 보상을 제공하는데, 왜 어떤 유기체는 상대방에게 성실한 신호를 보낼까? 약한 개체가 마치 자기가 강한 것처럼 신호를 보낸다면, 이 약한 개체는 다른 약한 개체들과 일부 강한 개체들이 자원을 (자기에게) 양보하도록 설득할 수 있을 것이다. 이러한 이익 때문에, 불성실한 신호 발신자의 유전자가 개체군 내에서 (널리) 퍼질 수 있다. (이렇게 되면) 결국, 불성실한 개체들의 성공은 전체 의사소통 체계(전체)를 파괴할 것이다. 불성실한 신호 전달 비율이 증가함에 따라, 자연선택(특수한 환경하에서 생존에 적합한 형질을 지닌 개체군이, 그 환경하에서 생존에 부적합한 형질을 지닌 개체군에 비해 '생존'과 '번식'에서 이익을 본다는 이론으로 진화론의 핵심이다. "생물은 자연선택으로 진화한다")은 힘의 신호에 주목하는 수신자보다 그것을 무시하는 수신자를 선호하기 시작할 것이다. 일단 수신자들이 신호를 무시하면, 자연선택은 더 이상 신호 전달에 필요한 구조나 행동을 선호하지 않을 것이다. **개체군이 진화적 균형에 접근함에 따라, 신뢰할 수 있는 신호 전달은 완전히 사라질 것이다. ("As the population approached an evolutionary equilibrium, reliable signaling would disappear altogether.")** (그러나 실제로 이런 일은 현실에선 일어나지 않는다.)

⊕ 보충설명

A signaler sends signal X.
The receiver detects signal X.
The receiver interprets X to mean Y(some quality or information).
The receiver responds in a way that benefits the signaler.
This response would also benefit the receiver if Y were true.
However, Y is actually false.

⇨ This describes a situation where the signaler is being dishonest—sending a signal that conveys false information, yet still gaining benefits from the receiver's response. The receiver acts based on what it thinks the signal means, but is actually being deceived because the signaler doesn't possess the quality or attribute that the signal supposedly indicates. For example, if a weak animal signals as if it were strong, and another animal backs down from confrontation (benefiting the signaler), this would be dishonest if the second animal would only benefit from backing down when facing truly strong opponents.

마지막 문장의 의미

What would happen if dishonesty became prevalent in a signaling system? In this scenario:

① Dishonest signalers initially gain advantages by deceiving receivers.
② As dishonesty spreads, receivers evolve to ignore all signals (both honest and dishonest).
③ When receivers ignore signals, there's no longer any benefit to producing signals.
④ **Natural selection** would then favor individuals who don't waste energy on signaling at all.
⑤ Eventually, the entire signaling system collapses.

The "evolutionary equilibrium" refers to a new stable state where signaling has disappeared completely. This is different from the equilibrium where honest signaling persists.

보충

Evolutionary equilibrium refers to a stable state in an evolving population where natural selection has optimized traits and behaviors to the point where they are unlikely to change significantly over time. In the context of signaling theory, it describes **a situation where the communication system between signalers and receivers has reached a stable balance.**

At evolutionary equilibrium: the signaling strategies have evolved to **a point where neither signalers nor receivers would benefit from changing their behavior**. Both parties are **getting optimal benefits** from the communication exchange.

The system is stable because any deviation (like increased dishonesty) would be selected against.(하단참조) This is similar to how economists describe **market equilibrium**, where supply and demand have balanced and prices **stabilize**.

In a stable signaling system, both signalers and receivers benefit from **honest communication**. If some individuals start being more dishonest (the deviation), several things happen:

① Initially, dishonest signalers might gain advantages (like weak animals pretending to be strong).
② As dishonesty increases, receivers evolve to be more skeptical and start ignoring signals.
③ This skepticism reduces the benefits for dishonest signalers—their deceptive signals no longer work.

④ The reduced effectiveness of dishonest signals means those individuals gain fewer advantages.
⑤ Natural selection then favors honest signalers again, as they can still communicate effectively.

⇨ This process of "**being selected against**" means that dishonest individuals ultimately have lower reproductive success than honest ones, preventing dishonesty from becoming the dominant strategy in the population. The system maintains stability because natural selection continuously works against deviations that would undermine the mutual benefits of honest communication.

03

하위내용영역	배점	예상정답률
일반영어 B형 서술형	4점	55%

모범답안 A digital representation offers two advantages over a physical representation. First, digital representations, unlike traditional representations, can be stored and maintained without information damage for an extended period, since they are a series of numbers. Second, unlike the static analog images of the past, digital images are easy to manipulate, incorporating visual effects with computer programs. In conclusion, while digital representations present advantages, caution is necessary in their use and online sharing.

한글번역

캔버스에 그림을 그릴 때 우리는 순전히 물리적 재현을 창조해낸다. 그러나 휴대폰으로 셀카를 찍을 때, 휴대폰은 디지털 재현을 만들어낸다—즉, 유한한 기호 집합을 사용해 물체를 기록하는 것이다. 휴대폰의 카메라는 우리 얼굴을 작은 셀의 수치적 그리드로 나누고 각각에 숫자를 부여한다. 이 숫자들이 우리 디지털 이미지의 본질을 구성한다. 이 디지털 재현은 더 전통적인 물리적 재현보다 많은 이점을 제공한다.

디지털 표현은 정보의 훼손 없이 오랫동안 저장될 수 있다. 우리의 얼굴을 일련의 숫자로 변환한 후, 이 수치적 버전은 더 이상의 품질 손실 없이 유지되고 전송될 수 있다. 시간이 지남에 따라 품질이 저하되는 부모님의 아날로그 사진들과 달리, 우리 얼굴의 그 이미지는 오랜 기간 동안 동일하게 유지될 것이다.

정적인 것이 아니라, 이 디지털 재현은 조작될 수 있다. 디지털 표현은 시각적 효과를 추가함으로써 밝게 하고 선명하게 할 수 있다. 컴퓨터 프로그램에서는 미소를 추가하거나, 배경의 나무를 지우거나, 심지어 우리 눈의 색을 바꾸는 것도 가능하다. 이것은 확실히 과거의 아날로그 사진에서는 절대 가능하지 않았을 것이다.

디지털 표현은 저장할 수 있고 조작하기 쉽다. 이 두 가지 필수적인 특성이 이점을 제공하는 반면, 그것은 또한 우리가 디지털 재현의 피해자가 될 수도 있다는 것을 의미한다. 알고리즘에 의해 인코딩된 우리 각자의 디지털 재현은 우리가 원하지 않을 때도 온라인에서 떠돌 수 있다. 따라서, 우리가 디지털로 재현된 것을 온라인에 업로드할 때는 주의를 기울여야 한다.

2023학년도

01

하위내용영역	배점	예상정답률
일반영어 A형 서술형	4점	45%

모범답안 The one word is "resilient". Second, it means that the high cognitive reserve of a bilingual person can resist the onset of full-blown Alzheimer's symptoms longer just as strong sandbags postpone the flooding of the river.

한글번역

언어는 뇌 전체의 영역을 활성화하면서 하루 종일 많은 시간을 소비한다. 엘렌 비알리스톡과 연구팀은 이중언어 사용이 인지적 예비력을 증가시킴으로써 노인 환자들의 알츠하이머병 증상의 시작 연령을 지연시킬 수 있나는 이론을 실험했다. 그들의 연구는 단일 언어와 이중언어 환자의 가벼운 인지 장애에서 알츠하이머병으로의 전환 시간을 조사한다. 비알리스톡 박사는 이중언어 사용이 증상들의 시작은 지연시키지만, 일단 진단을 받고 나면, 병이 더 심한 상태에 있기 때문에 알츠하이머병이 정점으로 악화되는 것은 이중언어 사용자가 단일 언어 사용자보다 훨씬 빠르다고 말한다.

모래주머니가 강의 수문을 막고 있다고 상상해보자. 언젠가는 강이 이길 것이다. 모래주머니 둑방의 견고함이 홍수를 지연시키고 있고, 경도인지장애 진단을 받는 그 시점에는 이미 심각한 병리 현상이 있지만, 높은 인지적 예비력 덕분에 기능을 발휘할 수 있었기 때문에 병의 증거가 없었던 것이다. 결국 아무리 (회복탄력이) 강한 사람도 한계가 있다. 그들이 더 이상 저항할 수 없을 때, 수문은 완전히 씻겨나간다. 결과적으로, 그들은 더 빨리 침몰한다.

5년간의 연구에서, 연구원들은 가벼운 인지 장애로 진단받은 158명의 환자들을 추적했다. 이 연구를 위해, 그들은 높은 인지능력을 가진 이중언어 사용자들과 낮은 인지능력을 가진 단일 언어 사용자들로 분류했다. 환자들의 경도인지장애 진단 당시 연령, 교육, 인지 수준을 일치시켰다. 연구원들은 병원의 기억 클리닉에서 6개월 간격의 진찰을 통해 가벼운 인지 장애에서 알츠하이머병으로 진단이 바뀌는 시점을 알아봤다. 초기 진단 후 1.8년이 지난 이중언어 사용자의 전환 시간은 알츠하이머병으로 전환하는 데 2.6년이 걸린 단일 언어 사용자의 전환 시간보다 상당히 빨랐다. 이 같은 차이는 이중언어 환자들이 동일한 수준의 인지기능을 보여줬음에도 불구하고 경도인지장애 진단을 받았을 당시 신경병리증이 단일 언어 환자들보다 더 심각했음을 시사한다.

이러한 결과는 이중언어 사용자가 단일 언어 사용자보다 신경 퇴화를 처리하는 데 더 탄력적이라는 것을 보여주는 증거가 늘어나는 데 기여한다. 그들은 인지적 예비력 때문에 더 높은 수준의 인지 능력을 가동시킬 수 있고, 이는 이들 중 많은 사람들이 신경병증을 더 오래 견딜 것이라는 것을 의미한다. 이 연구는 임상적 한계를 넘어서면 감소가 더 가파르다는 것을 보여줌으로써 새로운 증거를 보태고 있으며, 아마도 이는 뇌에 이미 더 많은 질병이 있기 때문인 것이다.

02

하위내용영역	배점	예상정답률
일반영어 B형 서술형	4점	55%

모범답안 Tunnel vision, which is a common experience where a person's field of vision shrinks as if looking through a tube, has two major causes. First, lacking background knowledge can make learners lose track of the bigger picture. Second, poor reading habits, especially reading too slowly, lead to excessive focus on individual details rather than the whole text. In conclusion, building contextual knowledge and increasing reading speed can effectively cure tunnel vision.

한글번역

터널 비전(앞이 똑바르지 않아 잘 보이지 않는 것; 좁은 시야)은 거의 모든 사람들에게 공통적인 경험이다. 터널 비전을 경험하는 동안, 마치 사람이 튜브나 파이프를 통해 보는 것처럼 세상이 축소되고 시야가 좁아지는 것처럼 보인다. 주의는 한두 개의 작은 세부사항에 집중되고, 맥락은 사라지고, 이해는 매우 어려워진다. 이것은 시각적 자극을 처리하는 뇌의 제한된 능력의 결과이다. 터널 비전은 당신의 마음이 더 큰 시스템의 일부로서 의미가 없는 시각적 정보를 너무 많이 수신할 때 발생한다. 터널 비전의 주요 원인은 다음과 같이 두 가지이다.

일반적인 배경 및 맥락 지식의 부족은 터널 비전의 첫 번째 주요 원인이다. 예체능에 약한 학습자들은 그림을 그리거나 야구 규칙을 기억하려고 할 때 터널 비전에 시달릴 수 있다. 그들의 그림과 야구에 대한 배경 지식의 부족은 비록 그들이 효과적인 학습자일지라도 게임이나 예술 작품의 더 큰 흐름을 놓치게 할 수 있다.

나쁜 독서 습관은 터널 비전의 두 번째 주요 원인이다. 느린 독서는 그러한 나쁜 습관 중 하나다. 속도를 내면 다 이해하지 못할까봐 천천히 읽는 사람들이 많다. 너무 느리게 읽는 것은 뇌가 텍스트의 각각의 작은 특징에 집착하도록 장려하고 터널 비전이 발생하기에 완벽한 상황을 만든다. 그것은 너무 많은 개별 문자와 단어들로 시각 체계를 막는다.

위에서 언급한 바와 같이, 터널 비전은 일반적인 배경 정보 부족 및 잘못된 독서 습관으로 인해 발생할 가능성이 가장 높다. 문맥적 지식이 부족하다면, 학습자는 다른 곳에서라도 지식을 얻어와야 한다. 읽기가 잘 안 된다면, 속도를 높이는 것이 당신의 터널 비전을 고쳐줄 수도 있다.

03

하위내용영역	배점	예상정답률
일반영어 B형 서술형	4점	50%

모범답안 The one word is "knowledge". Second, it means that human beings now passively rely on a computer (automation) instead of working directly (or actively) with tools.

한글번역

자동화는 근본적으로 우리가 행동하거나 생각하는 방식을 바꾼다. 우리가 컴퓨터를 다룰 때, 우리는 종종 오류를 일으키기 쉽게 만드는 두 가지 인지적 질병, 즉 자만심과 편견의 희생양이 된다. 자동화의 안일함은 컴퓨터가 우리를 안전이라는 망상에 빠지게 할 때 발생한다. 기계가 완벽하게 작동하고 발생하는 어떤 문제도 처리할 것이라고 자신하면, 우리는 부주의해진다. 우리는 우리의 일에서 벗어나게 되고, 우리 주변에서 일어나고 있는 일들은 배경으로 희미해진다. 자동화 편향은 모니터를 통해 들어오는 정보의 정확성을 지나치게 신뢰할 때 발생한다. 소프트웨어에 대한 우리의 신뢰는 매우 강해져 우리는 우리 자신의 눈과 귀를 포함한 다른 정보원을 무시하거나 평가절하한다. 컴퓨터가 부정확하거나 불충분한 데이터를 제공할 때, 우리는 오류를 인식하지 못한다. 실제로, 자동화는 우리를 행위자에서 관찰자로 변화시킨다. 그러한 변화는 우리의 삶을 더 쉽게 만들 수도 있지만, 앎(지식)의 발달을 저해할 수도 있다.

캐나다 북부에 위치한 작은 섬 이글루익에서, 이누이트 사냥꾼들은 약 4,000년 동안 그들의 집에서 위험을 무릅쓰고 나와 사냥감을 찾기 위해 수 마일의 얼음과 툰드라를 가로질러 여행했다. 사냥꾼들은 랜드마크가 적고, 눈 형성이 일정한 흐름을 이루며, 밤새 흔적이 사라지는 척박한 북극 지대의 광대한 지역을 탐험했다. 이누이트족이 가장 좋은 길을 발견하던 비범한 방법은 바람, 눈보라 패턴, 별, 조수와의 오랜 투쟁에서 비롯된다. 그러나 이누이트 문화는 지금 변하고 있다. 이글루릭 사냥꾼들은 돌아다니기 위해 컴퓨터로 만든 지도에 의존하기 시작했지만, 사냥 중에 심각한 사고가 발생했다는 보고가 확산됐다. 독자적인 길 찾기 방법을 개발하지 않은 사냥꾼은 특히 GPS 수신기가 고장 나면 쉽게 길을 잃을 수 있다. 위성 지도에 매우 꼼꼼하게 표시된 경로가 숙련된 탐험가라면 피했을 만한 살얼음이나 다른 위험으로 그들을 이끌 수도 있는 것이다. GPS는 이미 변화하는 조건에 대해 직관적으로 적응하는 방식의 저하를 가져왔다.

안다라는 것은 행동을 필요로 하는 것이다: 우리가 현실과 충돌할 때마다, 우리는 세상에 대한 지식을 심화시키고 그것의 더 완전한 일부가 된다. 우리가 어려운 일과 씨름하는 동안, 우리는 우리의 노력의 결과에 대한 기대에 의해 동기 부여를 받을 수도 있지만, 우리를 현재의 우리로 만드는 것은 일 그 자체, 즉 수단이다. 컴퓨터 자동화는 목적과 수단을 괴리시킨다. 그것은 우리가 더 쉽게 원하는 것을 얻게 만들지만, 우리의 욕망을 의미 있게 만드는 바로 그 몸부림으로부터 우리를 분리시킨다. 우리가 쟁기를 몰기보다는 화면을 보는 생명체로 자기 자신을 변화시키면서, 우리는 실존적인 질문에 직면한다: 우리의 본질은 여전히 우리가 아는 것(지식)에 있는 것인가, 아니면 우리는 이제 자신이 욕망하는 것이 무엇인지에 따라 정의되는 존재로 만족하는 것인가? 만약 우리가 스스로 그 질문에 대처하지 않는다면, 우리의 도구들이 기꺼이 우리를 대신해 답을 하려 할 것이다.

2022학년도

01

하위내용영역	배점	예상정답률
일반영어 A형 기입형	4점	45%

모범답안 The word is “deception”. Second, an ink-dummy would not work in the air because the air is not a medium that could support an ink cloud for long enough and the deep sea is too dark for the ink-dummy to be seen.

한글번역

많은 문어, 오징어류는 그들의 포식자로부터 달아나는 데 있어 특별히 효과가 있는 행동을 보이는 것으로 알려져있다. 그들의 내장에는 주머니처럼 생긴 특별한 장기가 있다. 이 주머니 벽에는 멜라닌 색소가 풍부한 갈색 액체나 검정색 액체 — 이것이 먹물이다 — 를 분비하는 샘이 있다. 이 동물들(문어나 오징어류)은 위협을 받으면 먹물주머니를 압축해 항문을 통해 먹물을 분사하는 능력이 있다. 물에 떠다니는 자욱한 먹물은 가상pseudomorph이라 불리는 허구의 오징어를 만들어내는데, 이 가상이 포식자의 주의를 끌어 이 동물들이 포식자로부터 벗어나 안전한 곳으로 달아날 수 있게 해준다. 이러한 속임수는, 가늘고 긴 것들은 가늘고 긴 가상을 만들어내고, 둥근 것들은 둥근 가상을 만들어내기 때문에, 더욱 효과가 있다.

오징어와 문어는 연체동물로, 분류학적으로는 민달팽이와 달팽이의 친척뻘이다(같은 과에 속한다). (하지만) 민달팽이가 달아나면서 자신들의 포식자인 새를 따돌리기 위해 공기중에 가상을 남기려고 먹물을 뿜어대는 것을 상상할 수 있겠는가? 물론 아닐 것이다. 단순한 이유가 있기 때문이다. 즉, 이런 행동 전략은, 동물이 도망갈 수 있을 정도의 충분한 시간 동안 자욱한 먹물 덩어리를 유지할 수 있는 밀도 높은 매개체에 의해 동물이 둘러싸여 있을 때만 효과가 있기 때문이다. 물속에서는 이 전략(가상을 남기려고 먹물을 뿜어대는 것)이 효과가 있지만, 밀도가 낮은 공기중에서는 이 전략은 효과가 없다.

일부 문어와 오징어류는 깊은 바다에 서식한다. 이 깊은 바다는 표면으로부터 빛이 아주 적게 통과하거나 전혀 통과하지 않아 이곳의 바닷물은 항상 잉크처럼 검다. (그렇기 때문에) 거짓 먹물 전략이 여기서는 효과가 없을 것은 명확하다; 그 전략이 (위에서 봤던) 대기 속에서 효과가 없었듯이 말이다. 가상이 물기둥에서 떠다니겠지만, 이러한 속임수가 잉크처럼 검은 배경에서는 성공할 가능성이 거의 없다. 이러한 환경에서, 깊은 바다에 서식하는 헤테로테우티스와 같은 오징어류는 발광잉크를 내뿜는데, 이 발광잉크는 잠재적 포식자를 혼란스럽게 만들어 도망치기에 충분한 시간을 제공하는 순간적인 빛을 만들어낸다고 알려져 있다.

02

하위내용영역	배점	예상정답률
일반영어 B형 서술형	4점	40%

모범답안 The word is "agreement". Second, it means that by revealing their criticisms, the critics themselves will be exposed and their tastes (will be) scrutinized.

한글번역

패션비평은 엄격하고, 명확하게 진술돼야 하며, 역사적으로 풍부한 지식을 지니고 있어야 한다. 패션비평은 지나치게 단순화하거나(현재의 패션비평이 흔히 그렇듯이), 불필요하게 모호해선 안 된다(현재의 예술비평이 흔히 그렇듯이). 패션비평은 활력과 대담성을 찾아내야 하고, 독창적인 것과 파생적인 것을 분별할 줄 알아야 한다. 패션비평은 디자이너가 어떻게 발전해왔는지를—또는 정지 상태에 있는지, 아니면 (심지어) 퇴행하고 있는지—추적하고, 그런 다음 이 디자이너가 이러한 특정한 미적 선택을 하게 된 원인을 파악해 사용된 기술과 재료에 대해 자세히 설명한 뒤에, 최종적으로 비평적 판단을 내려야 한다. 이미 언급했듯이 적절한 판단은 단순한 의견을 넘어선 어떤 것이다. 즉, 그것은 더 넓은 타당성을 목표로 하는 *일리 있고 정당한* 의견이다. 비평은 결코 완전히 객관적일 수는 없다. 비평이 크게 주관적일 수밖에 없는 것은 필연적이다. (왜냐하면) 비평이란 비평가가 검토하고 있는 대상에 대한 것만큼이나 비평가 자신에 대해서도 말하는 것이기 때문이다. 비평문을 쓴다는 것은 필연적으로 결국 비평가 자신을 드러내는 것임을 의미하는 이유도 바로 여기에 있다. 비평문을 쓴다는 것은, (첫째) (비평문을 쓰는) 당신이 현재 정확히 어떻게 처리해야 될 지를 알지 못한다는 것을 받아들이려 애를 쓰고, (둘째) 판단을 내리기 위해 애를 쓰고, (셋째) 비평가 본인의 위신과 바로 그 정체성을 위험에 빠뜨린다는 것을 알면서도, 비평가 본인을 드러내기 위해 애쓰는 것에 관한 것이다. (프랑스 철학자) 피에르 부르디외가 말했듯이, "취향은 분류하며, 취향은 분류하는 사람을 분류한다." 이것은 우리 모두에게 적용될 수 있는 사실이지만, 이 사실은 특히 비평가—이들의 판단은 대중들에 의해 가장 꼼꼼히 검토되기에—의 경우에 더욱 예리하게 적용된다. 진정한 비평문을 쓴다는 것은 스스로를 매번 위험에 처하게 만드는 것이다.

비평가들 간의 불일치는 어떠한가? 그 불일치는 환영받아야 한다. 너무 많은 사람들이 너무 많은 것들에 동의하는 것은 결코 좋은 신호가 아니다. 그것이 의미하는 바는 거의 항상, 우리가 너무 얕게 사고하고 있다는 것이기 때문이다. 비평가 사이의 불일치는 반드시 존재해야만 한다. 예를 들어보면, 두 명의 비평가는 분명히 알렉산드르 헤르치코비치(브라질태생의 세계적 디자이너)와 피비 파일로(영국의 세계적 디자이너) 같은 두 디자이너들의 상대적인 장점에 대해 동의하지 않을 수 있다. 하지만 이 비평가들의 판단에는 상당한 정도의 수렴되는 지점이 있다는 것은 주목할 만하다. 한 비평가는 헤르치코비치를 선호하고 다른 비평가는 파일로를 선호해서, 심지어는 어떤 컬렉션은 정말 아무런 취향이 없는 밋밋한 것이라 말할 수도 있다. 하지만, 만약 그 비평가들 중 한명이, 헤르치코비치나 파일로는 미학적 가치가 없는 디자이너라고 주장한다면 아마도 엄청나게 놀랄 것이다. 그 어떤 진지한 비평가가 이러한 판단을 내릴까? (이런 판단을 하지 않을 것이란 의미). 불일치는 존재한다, 하지만 불일치는 더 큰 일치(동의)를 배경으로 할 때만 가능하다.

03

하위내용영역	배점	예상정답률
일반영어 B형 서술형	4점	50%

모범답안 Doublespeak, which is language used to misrepresent things intentionally, has several forms. The first of doublespeak's forms comes from inflated language. Inflated language occurs when ordinary things and situations are given importance they don't deserve. The second form of doublespeak is jargon. It comes to pass when professional language is used with those outside of a specialized group to add prestige to one's expression. In conclusion, since doublespeak is a common tool used to distort reality, we, thus, should be aware of various forms of doublespeak.

한글번역

대통령의 행정부가 "사용자 수수료"를 통한 "수입 확대"를 제안했을 때 무슨 의미였는가? 번역하자면, "사용자 수수료"를 통한 "수입 확대"는 시민들이 내는 세금을 말하는 것이다. 이것은 이중어법의 예시다. 이중어법은 사물이 실제와 다르게 보이도록 신중하게 설계되고 구성된 언어이며, 여러 형태로 나타난다.

이중어법의 한 형태는 과장된 언어다. 과장된 언어는 평범한 것을 특별하게 보이도록 설계됐다. 가방 제작에 사용된 저렴한 재료는 "정품 모조 가죽"으로, 장신구의 유리 돌은 "진짜 모조 다이아몬드"로 묘사될 수 있다. 이런 종류의 묘사는, 상황을 설명하기 위해서도 사용될 수 있다. 한 무리의 프랑스 관광객에게 에펠탑 방문이 "일생에 단 한 번뿐인 기회"라고 말하는 가이드는 거의 확실히 이중어법을 사용하고 있다, 특히 그 명소가 집에서 멀지 않을 때는 더욱 그렇다. 이런 유형의 언어는 일반적으로 중요하다고 여겨지지 않는 상황과 사물을 마치 중요한 것처럼 인식하도록 해준다.

이중어법의 또 다른 형태는 전문용어다. 전문용어가 이중어법으로 사용되는 경우는 "내부자"가 아닌 사람들에게 전문적인 언어가 사용될 때다. 전문용어의 사용은 특수 집단 내에서 효율적인 의사소통 방법일 수 있다. 그러나 내부자가 아닌 사람들에게 사용될 때, 그 의도는 심오함, 권위, 위신을 부여하기 위한 것일 수 있다. 컴퓨터 기술자가 인터넷 연결 문제가 있는 초보 컴퓨터 사용자에게 "라우터 플러그를 뽑았다가 다시 꽂으세요"라고 말하는 대신 "라우터를 전원 주기해보세요"라고 말하면, 그 기술자는 이중어법을 사용하고 있을 수 있다.

이중어법은 나쁜 것을 좋게, 기본적인 것을 심오하게 만드는 언어다. 위의 예에서 볼 수 있듯이, 이중어법은 우리 삶의 많은 측면에 존재한다. 이중어법의 정의와 형태에 대한 인식을 유지하는 것은 누군가가 우리에게 믿게 하려는 것과 현실 사이를 구별하는 데 도움이 될 수 있다.

2021학년도

01

하위내용영역	배점	예상정답률
일반영어 A형 서술형	4점	35%

모범답안 The word is "brain". Second, the palate is where the flavor from good food is experienced combining input from the four tastes in the same way a painter combines a few colors on a palette into many hues.

한글번역

"Palette"는 입천장과 미각을 나타내는 "palate"와 동음이의어다. Palette는 페인트를 그리는 판자나 페인트 그 자체인 반면, '미각'을 의미하는 palate를 '음식 덩어리와 미뢰를 경구개로 밀어 넣음으로써 맛을 내는 혀'라고 생각하지 않는 한, palate는 미각적인 구성을 위한 캔버스에 견줄 수 있을 뿐이다. 이것은 페인트를 캔버스에 칠하는 것과 상당히 유사하다. 혀의 수용기 세포는 기본적인 쓴맛, 단맛, 짠맛, 신맛과 같은 특정한 맛의 감각을 책임진다. 침과 섞인 이러한 세포들로부터의 자극과 후각의 감각은 맛을 만들어낸다. 주요한 빛깔이 색의 스펙트럼에서 모두 다른 빛깔을 내는 것처럼 네 가지 미각 세포들은 모든 맛을 창조하기 위해서 (맛들을) 섞는다. 그러므로 구개(palate)는 요리사의 창조적인 노력을 위한 팔레트(palette)이다. 혀를 입천장에 대고 뭉갬은 음식 덩어리들을 미각돌기들을 향해서 몰아대는 것이다. 그리고 이러한 꽉 무는 것 혹은 흡입하는 움직임은 맛을 강화하고 연장한다.

그러나 맛은 또한 구강과 비강을 통해 들어오는 자극들을 인식하고 평가하고 분류하는 뇌의 중재가 필요하다. 맛을 평가하는 자질 또는 맛을 인식하고 판단하는 것은 오직 뇌 안에서 이뤄질 수 있다. 그리고 그림의 시각화된 이미지처럼, 맛의 자질은 맛의 역사와 관계돼 평가된다. 유발된 즐거움 또는 혐오감은 많은 부분에서 익숙한 맛과 연관돼있다. 맛봐지는 대상은 흔히 동일하거나 비슷한 맛을 이전에 경험한 것과 연결해 그와 상반된 경험이거나 동질의 경험의 결과로 판단된다. 이러한 과정은 맛의 "기호학"이라고 정의될 수 있을 것이다.

[출전] James Keller(1960－), "Food, Film, and Culture: A Genre Study" (2002)

02

하위내용영역	배점	예상정답률
일반영어 B형 서술형	4점	35%

모범답안 The word is "lack". Second, the underlined part refers to the neo-Impressionists (that joined the movement later and edged out the Impressionists).

한글번역

인상파의 역사는 사실상 전시회의 타당성을 거의 직접적으로 위협했던 다툼과 권력투쟁과 불가분의 관계에 있었는데, 애초에 인상파 화가들은 근본적으로 이 전시회를 위해 모였던 것이었다. 1874년부터 1886년까지, 8개의 전시회가 있었는데 그중 6개는 예술가들 사이의 결합력과 공유된 포부가 부족했음을 보여줬다. 그들의 전시회를 조직하는 데 사용되는 비용을 광범위하게 분산시키기 위해서, 그들은 재능이 부족하거나 더 보수적인 화가들도 받아들일 수밖에 없었다. 게다가, 그들은 구성원들의 개인적인 야망을 최대한 다뤄야만 했다. 또한 1873년의 규정이 살롱에 전시될 수도 없고 관중도 없는 작품들에 기회를 주기 위해 고안됐음에도 불구하고, 각각의 전시회들의 사례는 그들 중 어떤 누구도 이러한 모험에 준비가 되지 않았음을 보여줬다.

한 인상파 전시회에서 다음 인상파 전시회로 넘어가면서, 우리는 그 그룹 내에 있는 서로 다른 종파 사이의 관계뿐만 아니라 새로운 활력의 원천을 만들어내는 역량 또한 추적할 수 있다. 1876년에는 칼리보트가 등장했다. 1979년에는 고갱이 피사로에 의해 소개됐고 드가에 의해 인정받았다. 1886년에는 신(新)인상파 화가들이 나타나서, 전시회 공간을 독차지하고 인상파 자체를 몰아냈다. 칼리보트와 카사트를 제외하고는, 신인상파 화가 한 명이 등장할 때마다, 기존 인상파 화가들은 비통한 마음으로 맞이할 수밖에 없었다. 하지만 새로운 신인 화가들이 인상파로부터, 그리고 인상파 때문에 등장했다는 점은 인정돼야만 한다.

하지만 신인 화가들의 유입이 뭐가 문제인가? 1870년대 후반 이후로 인상파 운동은 더 이상 인상파 예술가들만의 소유물이 아니었다. 이미, 그 예술가들은 떠나가고 있었다. 세잔, 르누아르, 모네, 그리고 심지어 그의 작은 사실주의 학교를 홍보하는 것을 이어가던 드가까지도 이미 고독한 길을 선택했다. 그들은 살롱으로부터 인정받기를 원했다. 또한 무엇보다도, 그들의 작품이 그 자체만으로 감상될 수 있는 단독 전시회를 원했는데, 이러한 형태의 전시회에서 관람객들은 타 작가의 작품과의 비교 속에서 헷갈리지 않을 것이고, 비평가들은 진정한 인상파들과 진정한 화가들을 신인상파 화가들과 혼동하지 않을 것이다. 인상파의 역사는 여러 사람에 의해 쓰였지만, 무엇보다도 개개인에 의해 만들어진 것이라고 볼 수 있다.

[출전] Berenice Morvan, "Impressionists" (2002)

03

하위내용영역	배점	예상정답률
일반영어 B형 서술형	4점	50%

모범답안 Third Culture Kids (TCKs) face their own benefits(advantages) and disadvantages. Regarding the former, TCKs can acquire more languages through daily exposure in their formative, everyday lives with new languages. On the other hand, moving abroad can create isolation and problems in maintaining relationships for TCKs. In conclusion, given current challenging situations, these issues should be accommodated by educators to reap the benefits of their cross-cultural lives with less harm.

한글번역

오늘날 학교에는, 부모님의 직업으로 인해 지리적 경계를 넘어 이사한 후 부모님의 가정문화 밖에서 길러지는 학생들 수가 늘어나고 있다. 이러한 환경 속에 있는 아이들을 "제3문화 아이들"(TCKs)이라고 부른다. TCK로 분류하려면 아이는 출생 후 18세 이전까지의 발달단계 동안 모국 밖에서 3년 이상을 보내야 한다. TCK로 산다는 것은 부인할 수 없는 어려움도 분명 있지만 장점도 있다.

국제적으로 자라나기 때문에, 이들은 다양한 언어를 사용할 수 있다. 일상 속에서 목표 언어에 노출된다면, 언어를 배우는 것 또한 쉬울 것이다. 이들은 목표 언어를 사용하는 학교에 다니고 일상 생활에서 그 언어를 접한다. 이것은 이들이 언어를 더 빠르게 습득할 수 있도록 도와주는데, 특히 형성기에 그렇다. 해당 국가에서 얼마나 많은 시간을 보냈는가에 따라 유창성 정도는 다양하지만 고등학교 졸업 전까지는 적어도 3가지 이상의 언어를 습득할 수 있을 것이다.

이러한 장점에도 불구하고, TCK로서 부인할 수 없는 어려움 또한 존재한다. 많은 거주 변화는 이러한 아이들이 고립감을 느끼게 한다. 새로운 삶의 상황에 적응하고 옮기는 과정을 반복하는 것은 심각한 고통을 수반한다. 이러한 변화는 아이들이 그들의 직계가족 외에 다른 사람들과 관계를 유지하는 것을 어렵게 한다. 그러므로 고립감은 TCK들에게 가장 흔한 어려움이다.

이민과 초국가적인 유입이 증가하는 현대 상황을 고려했을 때, TCK의 삶을 이해하는 것은 국제 교육을 위한 가치 있는 자원이 될 것이다. 교육자들은 이들의 다양한 문화 경험의 잠재적인 이점들을 극대화함과 동시에 발생하는 어려움들을 헤쳐 나갈 수 있도록 도와줌으로써 증가하는 지역공동체를 지원할 필요가 있다.

2020학년도

01

하위내용영역	배점	예상정답률
일반영어 A형 서술형	4점	35%

모범답안 The most appropriate word for the blank is "haggle". Next, the meaning of the underlined is that salespeople can be positive in the face of very slim odds(chances) about making a sale which gives them an advantage.

한글번역

W. Ury와 R. Fisher의 베스트셀러에 따르면, 당신은 어느 협상에서든 자리를 박차고 나와버릴 수 있다. 저자들이 주장하기를 당신은 적절한 자리를 박차고 나와 버릴 선택지를 가지고 있음으로써 (BANTA: Best Alternative to a Negotiated Agreement 협상에 대한 최상의 선택지), 당신은 까다로운 상대편으로부터 스스로를 보호할 수 있다. 저자들은 (당신보다) 더 강력한 상대편을 피해버려서 당신이 상점을 포기하거나, 혹은 정말 최소한, "말도 안 되는" 판매를 하지 않을 것을 주장한다.

이론상으론 이것이 말이 될 수도 있지만, 판매의 세계에서 당신이 손님과 흥정할 때, 이것은 어리석은 짓이다.

할당을 채워서 생계를 유지해야 할 필요가 전혀 없던 전문가가 협상 자리를 박차고 판매를 포기하라고 판매원에게 말해주는 것은 약간 무신경한 짓이다. 경력의 상당 부분을 영업 쪽에서 보낸 우리들로서는, 실제로 사업을 따낼 수 있는 가능성이 얼마나 희박하든지 간에, 가능성이 조금이라도 있는 판매를 떠나버리지는 않을 것을 알고 있다. 이것이 판매원들을 성공하도록 만드는 여러 특성 중 하나이다 : 분명한 패배에 직면해서도 비합리적인 낙관주의를 견지하는 것.

엄밀히 말해, 당신은 큰 판매를 성사시킬 수도 있는 것을 포기할 수 있는 능력이 있을지도 모르지만, 그럼에도 당신에겐 여전히 채워야 할 할당량과 유지해야 할 직업이 있다.

그러나, 그렇긴 하지만, 영업맨들은 이미 그들의 할당량에 도달했을 때 항상 더 뛰어난 딜러가 된다. 왜일까? 왜냐하면 그 판매원들은 영업실적이 더 필요치는 않기 때문이다. 그러나, 그들은 가능성이 있는 판매 건수를 정말로 떠나버릴 수도 있지만, 상황이 변하면 항상 다시 돌아온다.

판매 관리자로서, 나는 나의 팀원들에게 가능한 한 많은 잠재적 고객을 가지고 있도록 요구했다. 나는 팀원들이 많은 잠재 거래건에 착수하도록 독려했는데, 이는 팀원들이 할당량을 채우는 데 도움이 될 뿐 아니라, 팀원들을 더 강한 협상가로 만들기 때문이다. 팀원 모두는 그들이 고객의 사업을 절박하게 가질 필요가 없다고 느꼈을 때 자신의 입장을 훨씬 더 잘 유지했다.

여기에 덧붙일 중요한 말이 있다:

때때로, 나는 "Yes에 도달하기"라는 세미나에서 배웠던 기술들에 대해 이전에 그 워크숍에 참가했던 사람들과 서로 물을 기회를 얻기도 한다. 나는 항상 그들에게 물어보기를, "당신이 Ury와 Fisher의 교리에서 가장 잘 기억하고 있는 것은 무엇인가요?" 이 질문에서 나는 거의 같은 응답을 받는다: "제가 가장 잘 기억하는 것은 제가 BANTA를 알고 있다는 것을 확실히 해 두라는 것입니다."

그 초성들이 무엇을 의미하는지 대부분이 기억해내지 못하더라도, 그 사람들이 믿는 것은 합의가 이뤄질 수 없을 때 그들 자신이 어떤 선택지들을 가지고 있는지 아는 것 자체가 스스로에게 조금 더 힘을 준다는 것이다. 내가 생각하기에 특이한 것은, 대부분의 사람들이 기억하고 있는 용어가 협상 기술을 향상시킬 목적으로 특별히 설계된 강의에서 나왔는데, 이것이 어떻게 협상 테이블을 떠나버리는지 기술하고 있다는 점이다. 즉, 다시 말해, 흥정하기를 거부하기.

[출전] "Negotiating with Tough Customers"

02

하위내용영역	배점	예상정답률
일반영어 A형 서술형	4점	35%

모범답안 The best word for the blank is "negative". Second, the underlined part means marginal people belonging to no one culture and benefiting from being free of cultural impediments. (또는 Second, the meaning of the underlined "synthesizers" is marginal people who cross cultural boundaries without suffering from cultural impediments.)

한글번역

문화 학습에서 가능한 결과에 포함된 몇몇 결과가 항상 바람직한 결과만은 아닌데, 이를테면 토박이 문화로부터의 소외나 주변성과 같은 것이다. 주변성이란 어떤 사람이 (인종이나 종교와 같은) 다양한 이유 때문에 사회적 혹은 문화적 집단의 주변에만 머물게 되는 상황을 일컫는다. 주변적인 개인이나 집단들은 소외되며, 존 럼의 말을 빌리자면, 그들의 행위는 "어떠한 하나의 문화도 제대로 반영하지 않는다." 주변성이 항상 부정적인 요소만은 아니다. 변방성은 모든 문화적 변화에서 일정 역할을 담당한다; 변방성은 자신들이 이중 문화적 특성을 가지는 동안 부모는 단일 문화에 남아있는 아이들의 삶의 일부이다. 리차드 로드리게스의 감동적인 책 ≪기억의 기아≫는 문화 변동에서 발생하는 고통과 문화적 정체성의 상실에서 나오는 고뇌를 말해준다. 인류학에서, 주변인은 종종 변화를 매우 잘 받아들이고, 외지인들과 기꺼이 접촉할 가능성이 높은 사람들이다. 이때, 외지인들(예를 들면 인류학자)은 그 주변인들을 따라온 뒤, 외관상으로 볼 때 바보 같은 질문을 하는 사람들이다.

주변성과 매개가 외로운 특성이라는 것은, 네루의 자서전에서 자주 인용되는 구절에 아름답게 묘사됐있다:

> 나는 모든 곳으로부터 왔으나, 그 어디도 고향이 아닌, 동양과 서양의 이상한 혼합이 됐다. 아마도 삶에 대한 나의 생각들과 접근은 동양보다는 서양이라고 불리는 곳과 더 유사할 것이나, 인도가 그 모든 자손들에게 그러하듯 나에게도 수많은 방식으로 고착돼있다; 그리고 내 뒤에, 백 개의, 혹은 몇 개가 됐든 브라만의 세대들이 가지고 있는 잠재의식적이고, 인종과 관련된 기억들의 그 어딘가에 인도가 놓여있다. 나는 과거의 유산이든 내가 최근에 습득한 것들이든 그 어떤 것도 버릴 수 없다. 이들은 둘 다 나의 일부이며, 비록 이들이 동양에서도 서양에서도 나를 돕지만, 공적인 활동뿐 아니라 삶 그 자체 안에서 영적인 외로움이라는 부정적인 감정 또한 만들어낸다. 나는 서양에서 이방인이자 외지인이다. 나는 서양의 일부가 될 수 없다. 그러나 나의 본국에서 또한, 가끔, 나는 망명인의 기분을 느낀다.

럼은 "추락해버린 주변적 인간은 뿌리가 없고 소외될 수도 있지만; 상승하는 주변적 인간은 여러 가지 것을 합성하는 자가 될 수도 있다."고 결론 내렸다. 주변적 인간들은 모든 문화에서 주변적이 돼, 어떤 문화에도 온전히 속하지 못하고 문화적 정체성이 없게 될 수도 있다. 반면에, 주변적 인간들은 문화적 경계를 넘어서고 문화적 간극을 뛰어넘을 수도 있다.

[출전] "Culture Learning: The Fifth Dimension in the Language Classroom"

03

하위내용영역	배점	예상정답률
영어교육론+일반영어 A형 혼합형	4점	60%

모범답안 have a negative effect on tourism entrepreneurs and the local population.

한글번역

동시대의 많은 여행자들은 현실을 직면하는 것을 피하고, 그 대신 그들의 여행 경험 속에서 가짜 사건들을 즐김으로써 여행 기업과 토속 주민들에 영향을 끼치고 있다. 우선, 많은 여행자들은 편안한 숙소에 머무르는 것을 선호하며, 그럼으로써 지역 사람들과 환경으로부터 자신들을 분리시킨다. 예를 들어, 가정의 편의용품들로 채워진 호텔에서 자는 것은 그들이 이국땅에 있다는 사실로부터 그들을 절연시킨다. 게다가, 많은 여행 산업은 박물관과 쇼핑센터와 같은 관광객 중심 시설의 사용에 의해 더 강화된다. 우리 시대 여행객들의 요구는 기업들이 방문객을 즐겁게 하려는 목적 하나만을 가지고 관광객을 이끌 명소를 짓도록 유도해왔다. 이는 다채로운 지역 문화를 격하시키며 토속 문화에 대한 잘못된 시각을 보여준다. 현대적 관광에 영향을 받는 다른 집단은 지역 주민들이다. 지역 주민들은 오직 시장적 목적만을 위해서 관광객 집단의 경향의 변화에 따라 부자연스러운 방식으로 언어를 배우고 있음을 발견하게 된다. 더불어, 호기심 많은 방문객들이 그들의 문화적 보호막 밖으로 모험을 감행할 때, 그들은, 비록 그것이 방해가 될지라도 지역민들이 일상생활을 영위하는 것을 구경하는 것을 즐김으로써 지역민들을 관광객들 자신의 눈을 통해 대상화하게 된다. 요약하자면, 관광이 상승세인 반면, 그 추세는 지역을 그 고유 가치를 가지고 보기 보다는 실제 환경과 거리를 유지하는 것이며, 이것은 여행 기업과 지역 주민들에게 부정적으로 영향을 미칠 수 있다.

[출전] "Studying the Middle Ages through its monsters"

04

하위내용영역	배점	예상정답률
일반영어 A형 기입형	4점	40%

모범답안 The word that best fits the blank is "power". Next, the common human emotion represented by (1) and (2) is "fear", and the emotion is represented by (2) because of the modern human fear of being harmed by technology. (or because modern human beings fear being harmed by science and technology such as AI.)

한글번역

우리는 한 사회가 누구를, 혹은 어떤 것을 바꿔 놓는지를 유심히 관찰해 그 사회에 대해 많은 것을 배울 수 있다. 그 사회가 무엇을 두려워하는가를 연구하면 그 사회에 대해 훨씬 더 많이 배울 수 있는데, 이는 뉴욕에 있는 모건 도서관 및 박물관의 새 전시회가 증명하는 바와 같다. "중세의 괴물들" 전시회는 야수들을 통해 방문객들로 하여금 유럽의 중세시대로 가는 짧은 여행을 하게 해준다. 오래된 서적과 태피스트리와 같은 유물들은 유니콘, 용, 코르크로 된 꼬리가 달린 영앙, 블레미스—머리가 없고, 대신 얼굴이 가슴에 달려있는 사람처럼 생긴 생명체—등으로 장식돼있다.

괴물들은 종종 특정한 이데올로기에 복무하기 위해 처리된다(죽임을 당한다). 중세의 권력자들은 그들의 장엄함을 보여주려는 매개체로 놀라운 생명체들을 활용했다 : 성인, 성직자, 그리고 왕은 살해자들로 묘사돼 그들이 특별하다는 것을 보여줬다. 헨리 6세가 자신의 영토를 통치하는 것은 가문의 문장으로 상징화됐는데, 이 문장에는 나무도 벨 수 있을 만큼 날카로운 뿔을 가진 영양이 특징적이다. 지도는 권력을 행사하는 또 다른 기회를 제공했다. (예를 들어) 16세기 아이슬란드 지도는 다양한 신비로운 야수로 둘러싸인 섬을 보여준다. 그들 모두의 목적은 경쟁 중인 상인들을 겁주어 쫓아내고 식민 강대국들이 그 수로를 피하도록 하는 데 있었다.

초기의 수고(손으로 쓴 육필원고)들 중 대부분은 수도승들이 그들의 교육을 목적으로 만들었고, 괴물들은 신성한 존재와 불가지의 존재를 시각화하는 매개체였다. 15세기와 16세기 선박이 훨씬 더 멀리까지 떠나갔을 때, "쇠물돼지"와 레비아탄풍 생명체의 재발은 무한하고 위험한 바다에 대해 늘어나는 공포를 반영했다. 악마나 거대한 "지옥의 구렁텅이"는 죽음에 대한 공포나, 혹은 면죄 없이 죽는 것에 대한 공포를 보여줄 수도 있다. 유니콘, 인어와 스핑크스의 그림은 초자연에 대한 경이의 감정을 드러낸다.

이 전시회에 대한 통찰이 현대 괴물, 그리고 현대 서구인의 불안에 어떻게 적용될까? 살인 로봇은 파괴할 수 없고, 똑똑하며, 인공지능으로 작동되는 컴퓨터에 대한 공포를 보여준다. 스탠포드대학의 학자인 앤젤라 비더가는 매체에서 좀비와 완전히 죽지 않는 자들에 매료되는 것은 2차 세계대전이 남긴 가장 창조적인 유산 중 하나로, 이 시기는 홀로코스트와 원자폭탄의 사용이 대량 살상을 향한 인류의 경향성에 관한 인식을 바꿔 놓았던 때이다. 현대 예술과 사회는 아직 모건의 중세 수집품에서 발견되는 본성에서 벗어나지 못하고 있다.

05

하위내용영역	배점	예상정답률
일반영어 A형 서술형	4점	50%

모범답안 The word that best completes the blank is "progress". Second, the underlined in (1) and (2) refer to "antibiotics" and "bacteria evolving against antibiotics", respectively.

한글번역

우리는 연쇄상구균에서 포도상구균에 이르기까지 우리가 다루기 어려워하는 거의 모든 어떤 종류의 병균이라도 항생제의 신속한 투약을 제거할 수 있다고 가정하기에 이르렀다. 그러나 미국에서만 매년 약 2백만 명의 사람들에게 항생제로 처치될 수 없는 감염이 생기며, 그들 중 2만 3천 명이 그 결과 사망한다. 세계보건기구(WHO)의 획기적인 한 보고서에 따르면, 문제의 박테리아는 현재 지구 모든 곳 곳에서 나타난다. 일부 국가들에서, 폐렴간균이나 대장균에 감염된 사람들 중 약 50%가 우리가 가진 가장 강력한 항생제에 반응하지 않을 것이라고 세계의 여러 보건 전문가들은 말한다. 이것이 시사하는 점은 의사들이 이런 해로운 미생물과 싸우기 위해 의존하는 탄약이 점점 더 부족해지고 있다는 것이다.

박테리아는 1928년 첫 항생제가 발견된 이후 그들을 죽이도록 설계된 약에 저항하도록 진화해왔다. 그러나 우리가 농장, 처방 약과 항균비누 따위에서 항생제를 과용하는 것은 (박테리아가 진화하는) 그 과정을 더 가속시켰다. WHO 보고서는 심각한 미래에 대한 진지한 경고였지만, 세계적으로, 진전은 느리게 되고 있다.

프랑스는 과거에 유럽에서 가장 높은 항생제 처방 비율을 가지고 있었으나, 정부의 명령이 의사 발행 처방전의 수를 6년 동안 26%만큼 줄이는 것을 가능케 했다.

스웨덴에서는, 농업에 있어 동물을 건강하고 살찌게 만들기 위해 저용량을 투여하는 예방적인 항생제 사용을 단계적으로 폐지하는 규제가 시행돼, 1986년 이후로 농업용 항생제 판매량을 67% 감소시켰다. 네덜란드와 덴마크 역시 가축에게 사용되는 항생제를 규제해왔다.

미국 내에서 진전은 (다른 나라들보다는) 더 느리다. FDA(미국 식약처)는 최근 농부들이 농업에서 자발적으로 항생제를 줄이도록 독려하려 노력했다. 해당 기관은 또한 제조자들이 항균제가 단순 비누와 물에 비해 세균을 방지하는 데 더 좋다는 것을 증명하도록 요구함으로써, 일부 소비재에 항균 제품을 사용하는 것을 억제하기 위한 조치를 취하고 있다.

항생제가 발견되기 이전에는, 창상이나 인후통과 같은 사소한 것이 사형 선고가 될 수도 있었다. 일부 진전은 최근 옳은 방향으로 되고 있는 반면에, 누군가는 훨씬 더 많은 진보가 이뤄질 필요가 있다고 말할 수도 있다.

[출전] "Man vs Microbe"

06

하위내용영역	배점	예상정답률
일반영어 B형 서술형	4점	50%

모범답안 Geniuses such as Einstein do not necessarily make great teachers due to two important qualities. *(There are two important qualities great teachers have that geniuses such as Einstein may not have.)* The first quality is that non-geniuses have made a lot of effort *(or have struggled)*, unlike geniuses, to build their knowledge and thus are familiar with learning concepts one at a time. Second, effective teachers can explain difficult content clearly as opposed to geniuses, who may not relate enough to the ignorance of students to communicate well, as in Einstein's sparsely-attended lectures. To sum up, looking for a great teacher rather than a genius is recommended.

한글번역

앨버트 아인슈타인 밑에서 물리학을 공부하는 것보다 더 나은 것이 있을 수 있을까? 실제로는, 아주 많은 것들이 있을 수 있다. 천재들이 사회가 진보하고 번영하는 데 도움되는 많은 것을 해 온 것은 사실이지만, 아마도 교단 앞은 그 천재들이 속할 곳은 아니다. 논리에 따르자면 최고의 선생님이란 가장 유능하고 성공한 사람일 수도 있겠지만, 사실, 지능보다 더 중대한 다른 두 가지 자질이 있다.

효과적인 교사의 첫 번째 자질은 교사가 자신의 공부에 정말 많은 노력을 했다는 점이다. 이것은 직관에 어긋나 보이지만, 배우는 것이 식은 죽 먹기였던 사람보다는 어려운 개념을 숙달하기 위해 매일같이 노력해야 했던 사람에게 지도를 받는 것이 아마 더 도움이 될 수 있다. 학생들이 종종 아인슈타인과 같은 영재에게 끌리는 이유는 그 영재들의 전문성이 너무도 수월해 보이기 때문인데, 그러나 그것은 오해이다. 전문가가 되기 위해 분투해야 했던 사람 문하에서 공부하는 것이 더 이치에 맞는데, 이는 그러한 사람들이 그들의 지식을 한 번에 한 개념씩 구축해오는 과정을 거쳐왔기 때문이다.

다음의 자질은, 조금 더 명백하지만 종종 경시되는 것인데, 내용을 명확하게 설명할 수 있는 것이다. (자신의) 출판물의 긴 목록을 가지고 있는 교사는 기초를 어떻게 방법론적으로 설명해야 할지 기억해내지 못할 수도 있다. 아인슈타인은 그가 가르친 첫 번째 대학 강의에서, 열역학의 난해한 주제에 많은 관심을 끌어올 수 없었다: 단지 세 학생만이 등록했고, 그들은 모두 아인슈타인의 친구였다. 그다음 학기에 오직 한 학생만이 등록한 후 아인슈타인은 수업을 취소해야 했다. 이 예시가 보여주는 것은 선천적으로 천재성을 가진 자가 어떻게 학생들의 무지를 이해하지 못해 학생들이 추상적인 개념을 이해할 수 있도록 돕지 못할 수도 있는가이다.

할 수 없는(능력 없는) 자가 가르친다고 종종 일컬어지지만, 현실은 최고로 잘 하는 사람들이 최악의 교사인 경우가 자주 있다. 따라서, 교사의 가장 중요한 자질들은 그들의 지식을 구축하는 경험을 가지고 있는 것과 내용을 파악하기 쉽게 만드는 능력을 가지고 있는 것이다. 위대한 물리학자가 되는 것이 위대한 물리 교사를 만들어 주는 것은 아니다. 아인슈타인에게 물리학 개론 수업을 듣는 것보다는, 광선을 쫓아 가는 것이 무엇과 같을지를 어떻게 설명할지 알아내느라 수년을 쓴 아인슈타인의 제자에게 배우는 것이 더 가치 있을 것이다.

2019학년도

01

하위내용영역	배점	예상정답률
일반영어 A형 기입형	2점	55%

모범답안 relations

한글번역

고대 동양인들은 세계를 연속적인 물질로 구성돼있다고 보는 반면, 고대 서양인들은 세계를 별개의 물체나 분리된 원자로 구성돼있다고 보는 경향이 있었다. 놀랍게도, 그것은 현대에서도 여전히 똑같다.

중간 관리자들의 가치관에 대한 조사에서, 햄든-터너와 트롬펜나르스는 동양과 서양 문화권의 응답자들이 회사를 업무를 조직하는 시스템으로 생각하는지 아니면 함께 일하는 사람들을 조정하는 유기체로 생각하는지 조사했다. 그들은 응답자들에게 다음 정의 중 하나를 선택하도록 요청했다.

(a) 회사는 효율적인 방법으로 기능과 업무를 수행하도록 설계된 시스템이다. 사람들은 기계와 다른 장비들의 도움으로 이러한 기능을 수행하기 위해 고용된다. 그들은 그들이 수행하는 업무에 대해 보수를 받는다.
(b) 회사는 함께 일하는 일군의 사람들이다. 사람들은 다른 사람들과 그리고 조직과 사회적 관계를 가진다. 이러한 관계에 따라 회사의 기능은 달라진다.

미국인의 약 75%가 첫 번째 정의를 선택했고 캐나다인, 호주인, 영국인, 네덜란드인, 스웨덴인 중 50% 이상이 첫 번째 정의를 선택했다. 일본인과 싱가포르인 중 약 3분의 1이 그 정의를 선택했다. 그러므로 서양인들, 특히 미국인과 주로 북유럽 문화의 다른 사람들에게 회사는 사람들이 그들의 독특한 기능을 수행하는 원자적이고 조립식인 장소이다. 동양인에게 회사는 사회적 관계가 여러 상황들을 하나로 묶어주는 것의 필수적인 부분인 유기체이다.

[출전] Richard E. Nisbett, “The Geography of Thought—How Asians and Westerners Think Differently”

02

하위내용영역	배점	예상정답률
일반영어 A형 서술형	4점	50%

모범답안 The underlined part refers to "the improvement of symptoms over time". Second, two pieces of evidence are their ability to attend school without individual assistance and the lack of needing further social-skills coaching(instruction).

한글번역

자폐증의 치료에 관해서라면 그것들의 효과가 좋은 것이든 더딘 것이든 치료 자체엔 부족함은 없는 실정이다. 하지만 이제까지 응당 받아야 할 주목을 받지 못했던 단 하나의 단순한 치료법이 있다면 그것은 바로 '시간'이다. "아동 심리학과 정신의학 전문 저널"에서의 새로운 연구에 따르면, 자폐증 치료를 위해 행동 중재를 받는 아이들은 나이가 듦에 따라 마치 오래된 신발이 맞지 않아 버리게 되는 것처럼 그 자폐 증상들이 소멸될 수 있다고 한다.

나이가 들면서 심리적 질병으로부터 벗어날 수 있다는 아이디어는 새로운 것은 아니다. 조현병을 포함한 모든 10가지 성격장애는 사람들이 나이를 먹음에 따라 완화될 수 있다. 이러한 현상엔 환자들이 자신의 증상을 관리하는 방법을 학습해온 것이 공헌할 수도 있지만, 또한 우리의 뇌가 20대 후반에 들어서도 여전히 발달하는 현상 역시 성격장애가 치료되는 요인이 될 수 있다. "이러한 것들(병들)이 화강암에 새겨져 있지 않다는 사실은 정말 놀랍다."라고 뉴욕주립대 빙햄튼 캠퍼스 소속 심리학자 마크 렌젠웨거가 말한다.

이렇게 (시간의 흐름에 따라) 자폐증의 차도를 보이는 것이 가능할 거라는 징후들은 존재해왔다. 하지만 이전의 연구들은 자폐증에서 명백히 치료된 아이들이 애초에 그 질병에 관해 적절히 진단을 받았는가에 관한 물음에 시달려야 했다. 최근의 연구에서는, 커넥티컷 대학교의 심리학자 데보라 페인이 이끄는 팀이 과거에 자폐증을 진단 받았지만 더이상 질병의 기준을 충족하지 않는 8~21세 나이의 34명을 관찰했다. 그 팀은 그 연구 결과를 아직 자폐증 증상을 가지고 있는 같은 나이대 그룹의 44명의 것과 비교했다. 양 그룹은 모두 비슷한 방식의 치료를 받았다. 연구원들이 다른 변수들을 바로 잡은 이후에, 더 나은 결과를 얻은 피실험자들은 단순하게도 병의 상태가 좋아진 것으로 나타났다.

"난 이 연구를 역사적으로 획기적인 연구라고 생각한다"라고 오티즘 스픽스의 수석 과학담당관인 제럴다인 도슨은 말한다. 그리고 어떤 이들은 동의하지 않는다. 그들에 따르면 어떤 아이들은 그저 자신들의 증상을 숨기고 그들이 바람직하다고 깨닫게 된 건강한 행동을 모방하며 지낼 수도 있다는 것이다. 그럼에도 불구하고 페인의 연구 결과를 완전히 부정하기는 어렵다. 자폐증상이 사라져버린 34명의 피실험자들은 1대1 도움 없이도 학교에 갈 수 있었고, 더 이상의 사교 능력 훈련을 필요로 하지 않았기 때문이다. 무엇인가는 이러한 현상을 설명해야만 했고, 적어도 이 연구에서는 시간에 따른 '성숙'이 최선의 답이다.

[출전] "Aging Out of Autism—A new study suggests symptoms can fade with time" *TIME* (Feb, 2013)

03

하위내용영역	배점	예상정답률
일반영어 B형 서술형	4점	50%

모범답안 The word for the blank is "peace". Next, the three methods that inanimate objects use to resist man are breaking down when needed, getting lost, and working for just the first few hours.

한글번역

무생물들은 과학적으로 크게 세 가지 범주로 분류된다. 모든 무생물체들의 목표는 인간에게 저항하고 궁극적으로 인간을 굴복시키는 것이다. 그리고 세 가지 주된 분류체계는 각 물체들이 목적을 달성하기 위해 사용하는 방법에 근거를 둔다.

일반적으로, 필요할 때 고장 날 수 있는 모든 물체는, 우리 인간이 필요로 하는 그 순간 바로 고장 나는 경향이 있다. 자동차가 이런 범주의 전형적인 부류이다. 그런 교활한 전형적 종자인, 자동차는 주유소에 들어가는 동안에는 절대 고장나지 않는다. 자동차는 러시아워 중에 시내 교차로에 들어설 때까지 기다린다. 이런 식으로 자동차는 운전자들에게 극도의 불편함과 좌절 그리고 짜증을 야기해 자신의 주인의 생명을 단축시킨다.

물론 많은 무생물체들은 고장 나는 것이 극도로 어렵다는 것을 알게 된다. 예를 들어, 열쇠들은 완전히 고장 나는 것은 거의 불가능하다. 따라서 그들은 인간에게 저항하기 위한 다른 기술을 진화시켜야만 했다. 그것들은 분실된다. 과학은 여전히 어떻게 그것들이 그렇게 하는지에 대한 미스터리를 풀지 못했다. 그리고 어떤 인간도 분실되는 행동 중에 그것들을 발견하지 못했다. 가장 그럴듯한 이론은 그것들이 인간의 눈이 자기들에게로 향하자마자, 그것들은 스스로를 은폐할 수 있는 비밀스러운 이동 방법을 개발했다는 것이다.

과학자들은 고장 나는 것들은 사실상 결코 잃어버려지지 않는 반면에 분실되는 것들은 거의 고장 나지 않는다는 사실을 깨닫게 됐다. 예를 들면, 용광로는 첫 겨울 한파가 절정인 때 항상 고장 나곤 하지만, 결코 분실되지는 않는 경향이 있다. 여성용 지갑은 결국 고장 나는 어떤 내재적인 능력을 갖고 있지만, 거의 그러지는 않는다. 어떤 사람들은 이것이 무생물체들이 인간에게 완전히 적대적이지는 않다는 증거가 된다고 생각하면서, 협상된 평화가 가능하다고 믿는다.

세 번째 부류의 물체들은 모든 것 가운데 가장 별난 것이다. 이것들은 담배 라이터와 손전등과 같은 것을 포함한다. 물론 이것들이 결코 작동하지 않는다고 말하는 것은 부정확하다. 그것들은 한 번은 작동하는데 대체로 집으로 데려온 지 첫 몇 시간 동안이다. 그리고는 멈춘다. 그러고는 절대 다시는 작동하지 않는다. 사실, 널리 가정되는 바로는 그것들이 작동하지 않기 위해서 만들어졌다는 것이다.

이런 물건들은 인간이 자신들에게 어떤 기대도 하지 않도록 사람을 훈련시키는 것으로 굴복시킨다. 그리고 그에 대한 보답으로 이 물건들은 자신들의 사회로부터 인간이 받을 수 있는 유일한 평화를 준다. 인간은 자신의 담배 라이터가 불을 붙이거나 손전등이 빛을 비출 거라고 기대하지 않고, 그것들이 그렇게 하지 않을 때, 인간은 자신의 혈압을 올리지 않는다. 그가 그것들을 보유하기 위해 그것들로 하여금 작동하도록 요구하는 한, 인간은 용광로, 열쇠, 자동차 그리고 여성용 지갑으로부터 그런 평화를 얻을 수 없다.

[출전] Russell Baker(1925－), "The Plot Against People," *The New York Times* (June, 1968)

04

하위내용영역	배점	예상정답률
일반영어 B형 서술형	5점	45%

모범답안 Melatonin has important benefits for the brain's health as well as inducing sleep. First, it acts as an antidepressant, helping to combat seasonal affective disorder, which is a kind of depression, when given along with light therapy. Also, melatonin can aid in countering the effects of mental decline in Alzheimer's patients by offsetting toxins caused by harmful proteins such as amyloid beta and tau. In conclusion, given these promising effects, further research on melatonin's other health benefits has been stimulated.

한글번역

송과샘(좌우 대뇌 반구 사이 제3뇌실에 있는 내분비 기관)에 의해 자연적으로 생성되는 호르몬인 멜라토닌은 어둠이 내려올 때 몸에 쉴 시간이라고 신호를 보내주며 분출된다. 이것은 잠을 유도하는 특성으로 잘 알려져 있지만, 연구가 늘어나면서 지금 과학자들은 멜라토닌이 잠을 유도하는 것뿐 아니라 두뇌를 잘 유지시키는 데 도움이 된다는 것을 안다.

멜라토닌이 두뇌를 잘 유지하는 한 가지 방법은 항우울제로서다. 계절성 정서 장애는 보통의 수면 주기와 바뀌는 낮과 밤의 주기 간에 부조화의 영향으로 여겨지는 겨울 동안 흔한 우울증의 한 형태이다. 몇몇의 사람에게 이러한 주기의 부조화는 그들을 우울하게 만든다. 하지만, 이러한 장애는 멜라토닌으로 손쉽게 치료될 수 있다. 연구는 밝은 광 치료와 함께 소량의 멜라토닌이 수면 및 각성 주기를 재편성하고 계절성 정서 장애의 증상을 완화할 수 있다고 보여주고 있다.

멜라토닌이 두뇌를 잘 유지시키는 다른 방법은 알츠하이머와 같이 나이와 관련된 질병과 연관돼있는 인지 손상을 둔화시킴으로써다. 아밀로이드 베타와 T 단백질은 독성이 있는데, 이것들은 이러한 질병을 가지고 있는 환자들 안에서 쌓이고, 인지능력 감소를 초래한다. 멜라토닌은 이러한 단백질의 유해한 효과를 상쇄시키는 것을 돕지만, 알츠하이머 질병을 지닌 사람들은 건강하고 젊은 사람들이 생성하는 멜라토닌의 양의 5분의 1만을 생성한다. 그래서, 멜라토닌 공급은 이러한 두 가지 해로운 단백질의 독소적 영향을 상쇄시킴으로써 알츠하이머 환자들의 인지 기능을 증진시킬 수 있다.

멜라토닌의 이러한 새롭게 발견된 유망한 효과들은 많은 주목을 받고 있고, 사람들을 더욱 건강하고 행복하게 만들기 위한 추가 연구를 자극하고 있다. 확실한 것은 멜라토닌이 더 이상 단순히 양을 세는 것(주—서양에선 잠이 안 올 때 머릿속으로 양을 셈으로써 잠을 자려 노력함)의 대안은 아니라는 것이다.

2018학년도

01

하위내용영역	배점	예상정답률
일반영어 A형 기입형	2점	60%

모범답안 children

한글번역

우리는 아주 이른 학창 시절에서부터 책과 독서를 끊임없는 실패와 남들 앞에서 창피를 당하게 만드는 것이 되도록 만든다. 아이들이 어릴 때, 우리는 읽는 단어를 전부 알고 있는지 확인하기 위해 교사와 다른 아이들 앞에서 그 아이들에게 소리 내서 책을 읽게 한다. 이는 아이들이 한 단어라도 모르면 학급의 모든 아이들이 지켜보고 있는 가운데 실수를 할 것임을 의미한다. 이렇게 되면 즉시 그 아이들은 자신이 무언가를 잘못했다는 것을 깨닫는다. 어떤 아이들은 손을 흔들며 야유를 할 것이고, 다른 어떤 아이들은 단순히 낄낄거리거나, 서로를 툭툭 치거나, 얼굴을 찌푸릴 것이다. 어쩌면 교사는 "너 그것 확신하니?"라고 묻거나 다른 아이에게 어떻게 생각하는지 다시 질문할 것이다. 혹은 그 선생이 괜찮은 사람이라면, 그녀는 부드럽고도 슬픈 미소만을 지을 것이다. 이것은 학생이 학교에서 겪을 수 있는 처벌 중에 가장 고통스러운 처벌일 것이다. 어찌됐든, 실수를 저지른 학생은 자신이 실수를 했다는 것을 알 것이며, 누구든 그의 입장이 되면 그렇겠듯이 자신이 바보 같고 어리석고 부끄러울 것이다.

곧 많은 아이들이 책과 독서를, 실제로 그렇든 아니면 무서워서든, 실수나 처벌, 그리고 창피함과 연관 짓는다. 이는 합리적이라고 말하기는 어렵지만 자연스러운 일이다. 마크 트웨인은 뜨거운 솥뚜껑 위에 앉아본 고양이는 다시는 그 위에 앉지 않지만, 또한 차가운 솥뚜껑 위에도 앉지 않는다고 말한 적이 있다. 고양이에게 적용되듯이 아이들에게도 그러하다. 말하자면, 아이들이 뜨거운 책 위에 몇 번 앉아 봤다면, 책이 그들에게 창피함과 고통을 안겨준다면, 그들은 책을 멀리하는 것이 가장 좋다는 결론에 다다를 것이다.

02

하위내용영역	배점	예상정답률
일반영어 A형 서술형	4점	45%

모범답안 The characteristics of the two groups in 47 of the 54 studies are that one group already imbibed*(had)* a drink a day and the other already abstained before the study began, without being randomly assigned to do so. Second, these studies are problematic*(flawed; imperfect)* because the reason the latter group abstained was often because of medical conditions, meaning that those non-drinkers were in poor health from the start *(and not because of their non-drinking during the course of the given study).*

한글번역

적어도 지난 10,000년 동안, 인간은 음주를 통해 그들 자신의 뇌를 조작해왔다. 그리고 적어도 지난 수십 년 동안, 연구원들은 술이 인간의 육체 건강에 긍정적인 영향을 끼칠지에 대해 연구해왔다. 여러 연구들에 따르면, 하루에 술 한 잔, 즉 맥주 12온스, 와인 6온스, 혹은 1.5온스의 증류주 한 진을 마시는 사람들이 완전히 술을 절제하고 있는 사람들보다 더 건강한 심장을 가지고 있을 수 있다고 암시하는 것처럼 보인다. 하루에 한 잔의 술을 마시면 심장병 전문의를 만날 일이 없다는 것이다.

하지만 이런 연구원들의 접근 방식은 틀렸을 수 있다. 샌프란시스코 캘리포니아 대학교의 연구원인 캐이 필모어와 그녀의 팀은 적절한 음주가 심장에 미치는 영향을 다룬 54개의 출간된 논문을 분석했는데, 그들은 그 논문들 중 대부분이 무작위할당(무선할당) 방법을 사용하지 않았다는 사실을 밝혀냈다. 무선할당 방법이 사용된 연구에서는 연구자들이 동전을 던지거나 참가자가 통제집단과 실험집단 중 어떤 쪽에 배속될지 고르게 하는 식의 방법을 썼다. 누가 어떤 집단에 들어갈지를 우연에 맡김으로써 연구자들은 진정한 비교 가능한 집단을 만들어 낼 수 있었던 것이다.

참가자들을 음주 집단과 비음주 집단으로 임의로 배정하는 대신, 54개 중 47개의 연구는 음주를 전혀 하지 않는 사람들과 하루에 한 잔의 음주를 하는 사람들을 비교했다. 왜 이런 연구 설계가 문제가 되는가? 이러한 연구의 대부분은 미국에서 이뤄졌다. 미국에서는 많은 사람들이 어쩌다 한 번씩 술을 먹는 것은 흔한 일이다. 보통 술을 절대 마시지 않는 사람들은 종교적인 금기나 건강상의 염려와 같은 이유 때문에 술을 마시지 않는다.

필모어와 그녀의 팀은 이런 연구들에서 비음주 그룹 중 대부분은 고령이나 알코올 중독 이력 등의 의학적인 문제 때문에 음주를 멀리하고 있다는 사실을 발견했다. 즉, 대부분의 연구 안의 비음주 그룹은 음주 그룹에 비해 원래부터 건강이 좋지 않았던 사람들을 포함했던 것이다. 결과적으로 이 연구들은 음주가 건강에 도움이 되는지를 밝혀내지 못했다. 대신에 필모어와 그녀의 팀은 더 나은 건강상태가 자주 적절한 음주로 이어진다는 사실을 밝혀냈다.

03

하위내용영역	배점	예상정답률
일반영어 B형 서술형	4점	35%

모범답안 The appropriate words are "pipe's location". Second, the two factors used to determine "correct guesses" were the pipe's location and the dowser's guess, which were checked against each other.

한글번역

오직 막대 하나를 사용해서 지하수 자원을 찾고 발견하는 행위를 흔히 '다우징(수맥 찾기)'이라고 말한다. 독일의 많은 다우저(다우징 막대로 점치는 사람)들은 본인들이 물에서 나오는 '땅 속 방사선'에 반응하는 것이라고 주장한다. 그 다우저들은 이런 방사선이 인간의 건강에 잠재적으로 위험한 방사선의 미묘한 형태라고 말한다. 이러한 주장들의 결과로 1980년대 중반 독일 정부는 다우징이 진정한 기술이 맞는지 그 가능성을 조사하기 위해 2년간의 실험을 진행했다.

연구를 진행하기 위해 독일 뮌헨에 있는 대학 물리학자들로 이루어진 한 집단에게 40만 마르크의 연구비가 제공됐다. 약 500명의 다우저들이 다우징 기술 관련 예비 실험에 참가하기 위해 모집됐다. 부정한 주장을 방지하기 위해 신중히 설계된 최종 실험에는 예비 실험에서 가장 성공률이 높았던 43명이 투입됐다.

연구원들은 비어 있는 헛간의 1층 바닥에 작은 수레 하나가 따라 움직일 수 있는 10m 길이의 선을 설치했다. 짧은 길이의 파이프가 그 테스트 선에 수직 방향으로 호스를 통해 물 펌프에 연결된 채 수레에 붙여졌다. 실험에서 각각의 시도를 위한 라인에 걸친 파이프의 위치는 컴퓨터로 생성된 임의의 수로 배정됐다. 헛간의 위층에는 실험 선의 바로 위 위치에 10m의 테스트 선이 그려졌다. 각 시도에서 다우저는 이 위층에 배치돼 본인의 막대나 스틱, 또는 선택한 다른 도구로 1층 바닥에 물 펌프에 연결된 파이프가 어디에 위치해 있는지 알아내도록 요구됐다.

2년 동안의 실험 기간 동안 43명의 다우저들은 총 843번의 테스트에 참여했다. 꼭대기 층에 있는 연구원이나 다우저 둘 모두 추측이 행해진 다음에도 파이프의 위치를 모른다는 점에서 실험은 '이중은폐'였다.

각 시도에서 실제 파이프의 위치[선의 시작점에서부터 데시미터(1/10미터) 단위로]와 다우저의 추측이 기록됐다. 이 데이터를 통해 독일 물리학자들은 최종 보고서에서 대부분의 다우저들이 실험에서 특출나게 잘한 것은 아니지만, "소수의 확률에 기대기에는 설명하기 힘들 정도로 정답률이 높은 사람들이 있었으며 이들을 통해 다우저 현상은 경험적으로 증명됐다고 할 수 있다"고 말했다.

04

하위내용영역	배점	예상정답률
일반영어 B형 서술형	5점	55%

모범답안 Museums have recently transformed their aims and functions in society. First, museums now collect more ordinary objects instead of special or rare items to better portray common living in the past. In addition to this, museums have begun to partner with allies*(sectors)* beyond the narrow educational sphere, reaching out to political, business, and community institutes. Through these changes, modern museums have adapted themselves to be a crucial part of contemporary culture.

한글번역

우리는 어린 시절에 박물관에 가보게 된다. 대부분의 경우 이런 경험은 학교에서 또래 친구들과 같이 현장 학습을 가는 경우일 것이다. 우리는 배움을 위해 그곳으로 갔다. 전시품들은 정적이었고 소위 말하는 위대한 작품들의 중요성은 많은 이들의 이목을 끌지 못했다. 결과적으로, 많은 성인들은 거의 박물관에 재방문하지 않았다. 그저 박물관들은 문화 지장소로 여겨졌다. 그러나 최근 몇십 년 동안 박물관은 사회에서의 그들의 목적과 역할을 바꿔오고 있다.

인류의 역사 속에서 박물관들은 과거를 보여주는 증거로서 예외적인 것들을 수집해왔다. 최근 들어서 박물관들은 그들이 수집하는 작품들의 목적에 대해 다시 평가하고, 평범하고 일상적인 것들을 모으는 것에 더 많은 노력을 쏟고 있다. 이렇게 하는 것은 대다수의 사람들의 삶을 가장 잘 드러내 보여주는 것이 바로 이런 수집품들이라는 것을 인식했기 때문이다. 이러한 수집품에 대한 변화는 전에는 과소평가됐던 사람들, 따라서 박물관에 별 관심이 없던 사람들과의 연관성을 보여주게 한다.

박물관은 협업을 통해 사회에서 새로운 역할을 하기도 한다. 박물관의 입장에서는 홀로 고립되는 것은 더 이상 선택지에 없다. 박물관은 사회 구조의 일부분이고 현대인의 삶의 주류에 자신을 위치시켰다. 그들은 자신의 가치를 교육 분야와 같이 전통적인 영역뿐 아니라 사회 전 영역과 연결시키고 있는 것이다. 이제는 정치적 연계와 기업과 지역의 분야도 포함돼있는 것이다.

이러한 방식으로, 한때 단지 중요한 물건들이 있는 텅 빈 복도였던 기관(박물관)이 이제는 그들이 수집한 것들에 맞춰 새로운 자세로 적응하고 있다. 박물관은 또한 공동체 안에서 다양한 구성원들과 상호 교류하고 작업하기 위해 진화해 왔다. 현대 박물관들은 현대 문화의 중심으로 스스로를 재창조하고 있는 중이다.

2017학년도

01

하위내용영역	배점	예상정답률
일반영어 A형 기입형	2점	65%

모범답안 inefficient

한글번역

프랑스의 농업 기술자인 M. 링겔만은 과정에서의 손실과 그룹(집단)의 생산성 간의 관계를 연구한 최초의 연구원들 중 한 사람이다. 링겔만의 의문은 실용적인 것들이었는데 다음과 같은 것들이었다. 한 팀에 몇 마리의 소에게 멍에를 씌워야 하는가? 두 마리 혹은 세 마리의 말로 밭을 갈아야 하는가? 다섯 명의 남자가 네 명의 남자보다 방앗간 크랭크를 더 빨리 돌릴 수 있을까? 질문들에 대한 답을 (단순히 머릿속에서) 추측하는 것 대신에 링겔만은 다양한 크기의 팀을 만들었고 그들의 집단적 힘을 측정했다.

링겔만의 가장 놀라운 발견은 말, 소 그리고 사람을 포함한 모든 일꾼들이 집단으로는 효과가 덜하다는 것이었다. 재미있는 촌극을 개발한 다섯 명의 작가로 이뤄진 집단은 한 작가가 한 것보다 더 뛰어난 성취를 보였는데, 이것은 밧줄을 잡아당기는 집단이 단 한 명의 상대보다 강한 것과 마찬가지 이치이다. 하지만, 집단이 개인을 능가함에도 불구하고 집단은 최고로 효율적으로 일하지는 않는다. 링겔만이 개인과 집단이 압력 게이지에 부착된 줄을 당기도록 했을 때, 집단은 그들이 이론적으로 가능한 능력보다 부족하게 일을 했다. 만약 A라는 사람과 B라는 사람이 혼자서 일할 때 각각 100단위를 잡아당길 수 있다면, 그들이 그들의 노력을 모았을 때 200단위를 잡아당길 수 있을까? 그들의 생산량은 겨우 186단위밖에 되지 않았다. 세 명으로 구성된 집단은 300단위를 산출하지 못했고 단지 255단위만을 산출했다. 여덟 명으로 구성된 집단은 800단위가 아닌 단 392단위만 해냈다. 확실히 집단은 개인을 능가하지만, 사람이 추가되면 될수록 집단은 상당히 비효율적이게 된다. 이러한 경향은 지금 링겔만 효과로 알려져있다. 이것의 발견자를 기리기 위해서이다.

링겔만은 사람들이 함께 일을 할 때 일어나는 과정의 손실에 있어서 두 가지 중요한 원천을 알아봤다. 첫째로, 링겔만은 생산성의 저하 중 일부는 동기 손실로 인해 발생한다고 믿었다. 즉, 사람들은 집단 내에 있을 때 일을 매우 열심히는 하지 않을 가능성이 있다는 것이다. 둘째로, 노력의 동시성 부족에서 기인한 협동 손실은 수행에 방해가 된다. 심지어 줄 잡아당기기와 같은 단순한 과제에 있어서도 사람들은 서로 다른 타이밍에 잡아당기고 멈추는 경향이 있어서 최대로 끌어낼 수 있는 잠재적 생산성에 도달하는 데 실패한다는 것이다.

02

하위내용영역	배점	예상정답률
일반영어 A형 서술형	4점	40%

모범답안 The appropriate word for the blank is imitation. Second, manufacturers began using 'distinctive names' in order to give the impression that imitation foods were the actual real items to consumers, without breaking the Drug Act of 1906.

한글번역

20세기 초반이 식료품 쇼핑객들에게 좋은 시절은 아니었다. 물론, 산업화는 그 이전보다 식료품을 더 싼 가격으로 더욱더 많이 구할 수 있다는 것을 의미했다. 하지만 FDA 설립 이전에는, 그 제품이 실제로 무엇으로 만들어졌는지 알 수가 없었다. 케첩 한 병에는 염색된 호박이 들어있을 수도 있고, 다진 생강에는 약간의 타르를 칠한 밧줄 일부가 섞여 있을 수도 있으며, '저장된 닭고기'라 상표가 붙은 캔들은 닭고기를 전혀 포함하고 있지 않을 수도 있다.

이러한 모든 일들이 발생했고, 더 심각하기도 했다. 일단 대중들이 그 문제의 정도를 인식하게 되자, 식품위생과 약품에 관한 법이 1906년에 통과됐다. 그 법은 식품 안전에 대한 기준을 제시했는데 독성이 있고, 더럽고, 또는 부패한 재료들을 식품에 더 이상 섞을 수 없다는 것이었다. 또한 잘못된 라벨을 붙이는 것을 막았는데, 어떤 특정한 식품이 그 식품이 아니라면, 제품에 그 이름을 쓸 수 없었다.

그것은 값싼 모조식품을 생산하는 사람들의 이익에 타격을 줄 것이었고, 그래서 그들은 새로운 규칙을 피해갈 방법을 고안해냈다. 만약 엄밀히 따져서 그것이 아닌 어떠한 것으로 식품을 부르지 않는다면 어떻게 될까? 만약 사람들이 이것을 진짜 푸딩으로 생각할 것이라고 기대하면서, 대부분이 옥수수 녹말가루인 한 식품을 푸딘(Puddine)이라고 부른다면 어떻게 될까?

이런 전략은 잠시는 효과가 있었다. '독특한 이름'에 대한 단서가 기발한 이름들을 허용하는 법에 삽입됐다. Puddine(대부분 옥수수전분) 뿐만 아니라, 소비자들은 Grape Smack(모조 포도 주스)과 Bred Spred(잼 병에 담긴 과일이 거의 없는 당-펙틴)를 구입할 수 있었다. 구매자들이 푸딩, 포도 주스, 그리고 딸기 잼을 구입하고 있는 중이라고 생각했다면, 글쎄, 그것은 그 회사의 잘못이 아니었다. 왜냐하면, 그들은 그들의 제품이 그 다른 것(즉 원래의 정통의 것)들이라고 말하지 않았기 때문이다.

법원은 동의했다. 기묘하게 이름 붙여진 소송들, 즉 미국 대 150개의 Fruit Puddine, 미국 대 24와 7/8갤런의 Smack, 그리고 미국 대 15개의 Bred Spred에서, 독특한 이름에 대한 단서는 그 모방 기업들에게 처벌을 면하게 해줬다. 하지만 그 규칙은 1938년 식품과 약품 및 화장품에 관한 법(FDCA)으로 더 엄격해졌는데, 그 법은 식품들이 계속해서 공상적인 이름을 가질 수 있도록 했지만, 만약 식품들이 그것들이 아닌 어떤 것과 매우 유사하게 보인다면, 그것들은 모조식품이라는 상표가 드러나게 붙여져야 한다고 명령했다.

03

하위내용영역	배점	예상정답률
일반영어 B형 서술형	5점	45%

모범답안 Multitasking, which is motivated by the desire to fulfill many demands simultaneously, has been shown to (be ineffective and) have many problems as opposed to conventional thinking. It increases the danger in driving, reduces productivity in the workplace, and has a negative effect on the way people learn. Given these negative factors, multitasking should not be recommended.

한글번역

한 번에 너무 많은 일을 동시에 해보려고 시도하다가 압도당한 느낌을 받은 적이 있는가? 현대에는 서두름, 부산스러움, 그리고 동요가 많은 사람들에게 삶의 일상적 방식이 돼왔다. 그런데 그런 것이 많은 사람들에게 너무나 삶의 일상적 방식이 돼서, 우리 시대의 많은 거절할 수 없는 요구사항들에 대응하기 위해 우리는 하나의 용어를 받아들였는데, 그것은 다중작업이다. 컴퓨터의 병행처리 능력을 묘사하기 위해 수십 년 동안 사용되던 다중작업이라는 용어는 1990년대 동시적으로 가능한 많은 것들을, 가능한 빠르게, 그리고 새로운 기술의 도움으로 하려는 인간의 시도를 일컫는 약칭이 됐다.

다중작업은 원래는 생산성을 향상시키는 데 유용한 전략으로 추정됐다. 그러나 보다 최근에 들어서는 다중작업에 대해 당연하게 여겨지는 장점들에 대한 이의 제기가 생겨나기 시작했다. 예를 들어, 많은 연구들은 운전 중 핸드폰이나 다른 전자기기들을 동시에 사용하는 것의 치명적인 위험성에 대해 말해왔다. 그 결과, 몇몇 국가에서는 다중작업의 특정한 형태를 불법화했다. 연구자들은 또한 직장에서의 다중작업이 실제로 생산성을 감소시킨다는 것을 발견했는데, 그 이유는 이메일, 전자통신 앱, 전화에 기울여지는 끊임없는 주의가 복잡한 문제를 해결하기 위한 우리의 능력을 손상시키기 때문이다. 게다가, 다중작업은 우리가 어떻게 배우는지에 대해 부정적으로 영향을 끼칠지도 모른다. 우리가 다중작업 중에 무언가 배울지라도, 그 학습은 덜 유연하고 더 파편적일 것으로 예상되고, 그렇기 때문에 우리는 그 정보를 쉽게 기억해 낼 수 없다. 다중작업에 관한 연구가 암시해주는 것처럼, 아마도 이제는 더 많이 하는 것이 더 좋다는 가정에 이의를 제기할 때가 아닌가 싶다.

2016학년도

01

하위내용영역	배점	예상정답률
일반영어 A형 서술형	4점	35%

모범답안 The proper word for the blank is "plants". A rise of 2 degrees in global temperatures would (is predicted to) cause permafrost to dry out and release carbon emissions in a process called "outgassing".

어휘

at issue 논쟁 중인, 쟁점이 되는
buildup 축적
carbon concentration 탄소 농도
carbon dioxide 이산화탄소
count 중요하다
drastic 과감한, 극단적인, 대폭적인
fertile 비옥한
fluorescent bulb 형광등
greenhouse gas 온실가스
in return 답례로; 대신에
inundate 범람시키다; 감당 못할 정도로 보내다
kick in 나타나다, 시작되다
line in the sand 어떠한 것이 더 이상 진행하지 않을 정도를 넘는 시점(a point beyond which one will proceed no further)
midcentury 금세기 중반
permafrost 영구동토층
photosynthesis 광합성
potential 가능성; 잠재력
release into ~속으로 방출하다
ride on ~에 달려 있다
take in ~을 흡수하다
trigger 촉발시키다
when it comes to ~에 관한 한(= as for)

한글번역

기후에 관해 볼 때, 인간이 온실가스가 축적되는 것을 줄이기 위해 하는 일뿐만 아니라, 어떻게 지구가 반응하는지도 중요한 점이다. 현재, 우리가 대기로 배출하는 탄소의 절반은 대지와 바다, 주로 광합성 과정에 이산화탄소를 흡수하는 식물들에 의해 흡수된다.

이러한 주기는 언제든지 바뀔 가능성이 있다. 쟁점은 두 자연 현상 간의 균형이다. 한 가지는 이롭다. 공기 중에 이산화탄소 농도가 높아지면, 식물은 더 많은 이산화탄소를 흡수하면서 더 빠르게 자라게 된다. 과학자들은 이것을 실험실에서 측정할 수 있지만, 그들은 새롭고, 탄소가 증가된 환경이 식물에게 얼마나 더 많이 비옥할지는 모른다. 나머지 하나는 기온이 올라감에 따라, 오래전에 죽은 식물로부터 엄청난 양의 탄소를 품고 있는 영구동토층이 고갈되는 것(즉 얼음이 녹는 것)인데, 이렇게 되면 썩은 식물과 탄소가 대기 속으로 방출되게 된다. '가스분출'이라 불리는 이런 현상이 시작되면, 대기를 이산화탄소로 범람시킬 것인데, 아마도 인간 산업(인간이 산업을 하면서 배출한 이산화탄소)의 지난 (수)세기보다 두 배, 또는 세 배 더 많은 결과를 가져올 것이다.

아무도 어떤 것이 가스분출을 촉발시키는지 확실히 알지는 못하지만, 섭씨 2도 이상으로 지구의 기온상승을 막는 것은 필수적이라고 여겨진다. 그 한계 아래에 머물기 위해, 합의안은 우리가 대기 중에 있는 탄소의 최대 수위를 설정하고, 그 아래 수준을 유지하기 위해 필요한 어떠한 것이든 해야 한다는 것이다. 몇 년 전, 과학자들은 산업화 시기 이전보다 탄소 농도를 두 배로 만드는 것인, 550ppm까지 정도가 상황을 유지시키는 타당한 수준이라 생각했다. (하지만) 최근에 그들은 450ppm까지 그 수치를 아래로 수정했다. 그러나 그 목표치에 도달하려면, 금세기 중반까지 방출량의 80%나 되는 대폭적인 삭감이 필요할 것이다.

한편, 관측 기록은 비록 이것이 결정적이진 않지만, (현재 우리가) 틀린 방향으로 가고 있다는 것을 보여주고 있다. 극지방에서 기온은 급격하게 올라가고 있고, 북극의 만년설은 후퇴 중이고(사라지는 중이고), 영구동토층은 변화의 골치 아픈 신호를 보여주고 있으며, 해류는 탄소의 흡수를 약하게 만들고 있을지 모른다는 것이다. 우리가 하이브리드 자동차를 타는 것과 형광 전구를 사용하는 것에 대한 느낌이 좋다고 하더라도, 우리의 운명은 식물과 영구동토층 간의 모호한 경쟁에 달려 있을지 모른다.

[출전] "Global Warming Is Out of Control", *Newsweek* (Aug 14, 2009)

02

하위내용영역	배점	예상정답률
일반영어 A형 서술형	4점	35%

모범답안 The two words corresponding to the underlined words in (1) are "Declined-with-Thanks club". Second, the implication of the underlined words in (2) is that these surprising refusals to participate in gifted money or power would give a spiritual cure to the system that is more helpful than the medical cure of a newly-created hospital. However, the writer is skeptical of the possibility that people would refuse rewards.

해설 밑줄 친 부분이 지칭하는 것을 구체적으로 설명한 뒤 저자가 그것을 통해 말하려 하는 바를 명확하게 서술해야 한다.

한글번역

지난주 신문들의 한 단락은 스미스라던가 혹은 그와 유사한 이름의 한 신사가 양심상의 이유로 치안판사직을 거절한 흔하지 않은 행위에 대해 보도했다. 스미스의 경우는, 정치적으로 봉사한 것에 대한 보상으로 그 직위가 그에게 주어졌는데, 이런 식으로 치안판사가 뽑히는 방식은 그가 용납할 수 없는 방식이었다. 그래서 그는 대부분의 사람들이 갈망하는 명예를 거절함으로써 그런 시스템에 대한 경멸을 드러냈고, 그는 신문기사가 줄 수 있는 악명을 얻게 되었다, '어마어마한 것을 거절한 신사의 초상'이라는. 그는 괴짜들의 모임 안에서 자신의 자리를 잡게 됐다.

"만약 너에게 백만 파운드가 상속된다면 그 돈을 가지고 가장 좋은 일을 어떻게 할 것 같니?"라는 에세이의 주제는 빈번하게 제시돼왔다. 몇몇 사람들은 병원에 그 돈을 기증한다고 말하거나 또한 몇몇은 빈민 구호소를 설립할 것이라고 말한다. 심지어 일종의 드레드노트(전함)의 절반 정도를 만들기까지 한다는 사람도 몇몇 있다. 그러나 위에 제시된 어느 것들보다도, 좋은 일을 할 수 있는 훨씬 결단력이 있는 방법이 있다. 바로 그것은 백만 달러 상속을 포기하는 것이다. 그것은 편안함을 추구하는 시스템에 충격을 가하는 것이고, 그 충격은 위대한 돈의 신을 강타해서 휘청거리게 만들 수 있는 것이고, 이전에는 볼 수 없었던 형태의 자긍심과 자유를 방어하는 타격이다. 그것은 최근에 기증한 병원에서 나오는 모든 약들보다도 더욱 필요한 우리 사회의 도덕적인 강장제가 될 가능성이 있다. 과연 그것(도덕적인 강장제)이 주어질 수 있을까? 글쎄, 아마도 '고맙다고 말하면서 (돈을) 거절하는 모임'이 점점 더 힘을 얻게 될 때 가능할 것 같다.

[출전] Alan Milne, "Declined with Thanks" from *Not That It Matters* (1921)

03

하위내용영역	배점	예상정답률
일반영어 B형 서술형	4점	40%

모범답안 The corresponding two words are "abused statistic". Second, the "average Yaleman" statistic could be misleading because if just one graduate became a multimillionaire among hundreds of impoverished graduates, it would raise the group average and could create the notion that the whole group is doing well.

어휘

confuse 혼란시키다
dash 소량
impeccable 오류 없는(= perfect)
lump … with ~ …을 ~과 같은 범주에 두다
median 중간값, 중앙치
paint (색조) 화장
salubrious (몸 마음의) 건강에 유익한
crowd out 몰아내다
ill-lit 희미한, 어두침침한
improbably 있음직하지 않게; 개연성이 낮게
mean 평균치
odd 대략의
powder (얼굴) 분칠; 분
time and-a-half 50%의 초과근무수당; 1.5배

한글번역

타임지는 평균적인 예일대생인 1924년 졸업생이 연간 25,111달러를 번다고 보도했다.
음, 그 사람 참 대단하네!
그러나 생각해보자면 이 있음직하지 않게 정확하고 유익한 통계가 의미하는 바가 무엇일까? 그 통계가 나타내다시피 당신이 자식을 예일대에 보내면 당신은 노년기에 일할 필요 없고 당신의 아들도 일할 필요가 없을 것이라는 증거인가? 이는 보통 평균인가 아님 중앙치인가? 이 통계가 어떤 종류의 표본에 기반하고 있는가? 당신은 텍사스에 사는 한 석유 사업가를 200명의 굶주리는 프리랜서 작가들과 같은 집단에 묶을 수 있고 그들의 평균 소득을 연간 대략 25,000달러로 보도할 수 있다. 계산이 결점이 없으면 통계는 납득할 수 있게 정확하다.
통계학의 비밀스러운 언어는 이런 방식들로 사실지향적 문화권에서 굉장히 매혹적이다. 이는 과장하고, 부풀리고, 혼란스럽게 하고, 과도하게 단순화하는 데 사용된다. 통계학적 용어들은 사회와 경제 경향, 비즈니스 상황, '견해' 통계, 올해의 인구조사 등 대량의 데이터를 보도함에 필수적이다. 그러나 정직함과 이해를 가지고 통계학 단어를 사용하는 작가나 통계학적 용어들이 의미하는 바를 아는 독자들 없이는, 결과는 의미적으로 이치에 맞지 않게 될 뿐이다.
과학 연구에 관한 대중적 글에서, 오용되는 통계는 어두침침한 실험실에서 50%의 초과근무수당도 없이 야근을 하는 하얀 재킷을 입은 영웅의 사진을 거의 몰아내고 있다. "소량의 분칠과 약간의 화장"처럼 통계는 많은 중요한 사실들을 "사실이 원래 보여야 하는 모습이 아니게 보이게끔" 꾸며내고 있다.

[출전] Darrell Huff, *How to Lie with Statistics* (1954)

04

하위내용영역	배점	예상정답률
일반영어 B형 서술형	5점	50%

모범답안 Korea has been continuously increasing its participation in the global community, both in terms of culture and business, through good fortune and planning. The interest in Korean products from overseas has seen a huge increase, especially regarding electronics and automotive industries. Likewise, the Korean cultural contents such as television programming, music, and cuisine, has become fashionable outside of Korea and inspired further export. Thus, Korea can continue to flourish if it controls its place and growth on the global stage.

어휘

a bit of 다소
capitalize on ~을 이용하다
far reaching 광범위하게 영향을 미치는, 지대한 영향을 가져올
find themselves with + n 명사(n)에 놓여 있다
monumental 기념비적인
as is the case with ~에는 흔히 있는 일이지만
outpouring 분출, 쏟아져 나옴
inadvertently 의도치 않게, 우연히
necessitate ~을 필요로 하다

한글번역

한국은 문화적으로나 경제적으로 계속해서 국제사회에서의 역할을 확장하고 있다. 이 영향은 매우 광범위하다. 국내 사업들은 새로운 도전에 놓여 있고, 대중은 수많은 새로운 선택에 노출돼 있다. 동시에, 특히 전자 및 자동차 산업에서 한국산 상품의 분출은 기념비적이다. 이러한 경향과 더불어, 세계화에 대한 가장 성공적인 적응의 사례로서 한국은 의도치는 않았겠지만 문화까지도 수출하고 있다. TV 드라마, 영화, 한국 가요, 음식에 이르기까지 한국 문화는 그야말로 세계적으로 인기가 있다. 한국 주위의 국가들은 한국으로부터 나오는 모든 것을 받아들이고 있다. 이러한 모든 것들에 대한 원인은 물론 간단히 설명될 것은 아니지만, 적절한 시점에 적절한 위치라는 약간의 원인, 그리고 의도적인 계획이라는 상당한 원인이 포함돼있음이 분명하다. 한국의 세계화가 성공한 것은 우연의 일치가 아니다. 많은 국가들과는 달리, 한국은 난관에 도전해왔고, 계속해서 도전하고 있으며 그 고비를 기회로 삼았다. 비록 이렇다 할지라도, 한국의 계속되는 국제사회로의 성공적인 참여는 한국이 세계화 속에서 자신의 역할을 신중하게 관리해 그간 쌓아 온 세계화의 속도를 유지하는 것을 필요로 한다.

2015학년도

01

하위내용영역	배점	예상정답률
일반영어 A형 기입형	2점	50%

모범답안 pedigree

해설 임용고시에서 단골로 출제되는 빈칸에 올바른 어휘를 집어넣는 유형의 문제이다. 이 유형의 문제는 단순히 독해가 된다고 해서 풀리지는 않는다. 글의 전체 맥락과 핵심어를 찾고 이를 바탕으로 추론할 줄 알아야 풀 수 있다. 많은 수험생들이 이 문제의 답을 talent로 골랐다. 왜 그랬을까? 빈칸에 talent가 들어간다고 해서 완전히 틀린 것은 아니기 때문이다. 하지만 항상 답은 하나밖에 없다는 걸 명심해야 한다. 이 문제를 푸는 키워드는 'hire'이다. 따라서 빈칸에 들어갈 것은 이 키워드에 연관되어 있어야 한다. 따라서 맨 앞에 있는 talent가 아니라 두 번째 문단에 있는 'runway'와 'pedigree' 둘 중 하나인데 'not as effective as'가 나와 있으니 당연히 둘 중 'pedigree'가 빈칸에 답으로 들어가야 한다.

TIP 무조건 많이 읽는 이른바 '독해력'만을 늘리는 것은 한계가 있다. 논리적으로 글을 읽고 분석할 줄 아는 능력을 길러야 한다. 글을 읽고 반드시 소리 내어 요약해보자. 논리력이 놀랍게 증강될 것이다.

어휘

coach 지도하다
entity 실체
grooming 훈련시키기; 손질, 단장
pedigree 혈통; 족보
reflexively 자동적으로; 반사적으로
embrace 포용하다, 수용하다
executive team 임원진; 경영진
mindset 사고방식
rank 구성원들

한글번역

한 심리학 교수가 '고정된 사고방식 이론'을 연구하는 데 수십 년을 보냈다. 그녀는 재능을 그들이 가지거나 부족한 자질로 보는 사람들을 고정된 사고방식을 가진 것으로 간주한다. '성장적 사고방식'을 갖춘 사람들은 대조적으로 도전을 즐기고, 배우려고 노력하고, 계속 새로운 기술을 발전시킬 잠재력을 찾는다.

그 심리학 교수인 캐럴 드웩은 그녀의 사고방식에 대한 연구를 개인들을 넘어 확장시키고 있다. 개인과 마찬가지로 조직도 고정된 혹은 성장적 사고방식을 가질 수 있을까? 만약 그렇다면 어떻게 하면 관리자들은 자신들의 조직이 성장적 사고방식을 수용하도록 할 수 있을까? 이 문제를 탐구하기 위해 그녀는 설문조사를 수행했고, 최고경영자가 자주 변화를 이끌어야 한다는 것을 발견했다. 예를 들어, 새로운 회사 대표는 노동자들의 잠재력을 극대화하는 문제에 집중할 수도 있다. 드웩은 성장적 사고방식을 지닌 최고경영자로 상징성이 있는 한 인물에 주목했다. 이 최고경영자는 규모가 큰 주립대학 졸업생이나 참전 군인을 아이비리그 출신들보다 더 선호해 채용했는데, 이것은 혈통이 아닌 '능력'에 따른 것이었다. 또한 그는 수천 시간을 임원진 내에 있는 직원들을 훈련시키고 지도하는 데 사용했다.

이 최고경영자의 사례가 보여주듯이, 사고방식이 특히나 중요한 한 분야는 채용 부문이다. 고정된 사고방식을 지닌 조직들은 자동적으로 그들의 회사 바깥을 본다. 반면에 성장적 사고방식을 지닌 조직들은 그들의 회사 내에 있는 구성원들 안에서 채용한다. 드웩은 말한다. "혈통에 집중하는 것은 도전을 사랑하고, 성장하기 원하고, 협력하기 원하는 사람을 찾는 데 효과적이지 못하다." 몇몇 회사는 이와 같은 변혁을 진행 중인 것으로 보인다. 이러한 회사들은 최근에 유능하고 독립적인 학습자라 판명된 사람들을 더 고용하기 시작했다.

조사 결과에도 불구하고, 모든 노동자들이 성장적 사고방식을 지향하는 조직에서 더 행복한 것은 아니라고 드웩은 인정한다. 하지만, 일반적으로, 앞선 증거는 성장을 위한 노동자들의 능력에 초점을 둔 조직들이 상당한 이점을 경험할 것이라는 점을 시사해준다.

[출전] "How Companies Can Profit from a 'Growth Mindset'" from *Harvard Business Review* (Nov. 2014)

02

하위내용영역	배점	예상정답률
일반영어 B형 서술형	5점	35%

모범답안 First, the underlined words mean that "junk DNA" makes administrative decisions to have other DNA either work or not, just like a middle manager of a factory. This realization expands the possibility to cure diseases caused by genetic mutation because now it is possible for researchers not to examine the bad gene itself but to intervene those "supervisors," or the middle managers which decide the behavior of the bad gene. Its number is a lot more than that of the gene; thus, the possibility of cure is far more increased.

해설 2015학년도 시험에서 전공 A형 서술형 3번 문학 문제와 더불어 지문과 답안 쓰기 모두에서 가장 어려운 문제였던 것 같다. 심지어 노량진 강사들의 답안 중에서조차 고개를 갸우뚱하게 만드는 답안이 있기도 했다. 지문 내용이 과학에 관련된 것이다 보니 우선 '독해가 되었다고' 생각했지만 그것의 구체적 내용이 내 것으로 와닿지 않는, 마치 거울에 햇빛이 반사되는 것처럼 툭툭 내용이 튕겨나가 버리는 문제였다. 내용의 이해도 어려웠지만 그것의 답을 영어로 옮기는 과정 또한 만만한 것이 아니었다. 그러다 보니 본문에 있는 것을 그대로 가져다 써놓고 맞는 답이라 생각하는 경우도 생기게 되었다.

TIP 출제자가 요구하는 것이 무엇인지를 정확하게 꿰뚫어 지문 안에서 실현시키는 고도의 논리력과 그것을 나의 표현으로 만들 줄 아는 영어 작문 실력이 동시에 필요하다. 매일 이런 유형의 문제를 1문제씩 풀어본다. 먼저, 본문에 있는 표현 그대로 답안을 적어놓는다. 그런 다음, 그것을 패러프레이즈한다. 하루에 50자 정도 글을 쓰는 연습을 꾸준히 해보자.

어휘

be well staffed 보조인력이 충분하다
decode 해독하다
double helix 이중나선구조
fix 고치다; 치료하다
gnaw at (오랫동안) ~를 괴롭히다
humbling 겸손한; 변변치 않은; 실망스러운(비하하는)
junk 쓰레기
middle management 중간관리자
shed light on ~을 비추다, 밝히다, 해명하다
cystic fibrosis (선천성) 낭포성 섬유증
defuse (폭탄 뇌관을) 제거하다; 진정시키다
entourage 수행단
genetic mutation 유전적 돌연변이
greenlight ~을 허락하다; 청신호
intervention 개입
make a splash 많은 관심을 모으다; 깜짝 놀라게 하다
perplex 당황하게 하다
stalled 정지된

한글번역

지난 주 과학자들은 연구자들을 오랫동안 괴롭혀왔던 수수께끼를 풀고, 암, 심장병, 알츠하이머와 같은 질병을 밝히는 DNA에 관한 혁신적인 새로운 관점을 보여주면서 세상을 깜짝 놀라게 했다. 인간 유전체를 해독한 이래로, 과학자들은 아무것도 하지 않는 것처럼 보이는 우리 DNA의 긴 선에 의해 당황해왔다. 그들은 이 게으른 이중나선구조를 그저 안 맞는 조립 구조로부터 떨어져 나온 잔재물, 지난 시즌 모델인 이것저것의 쓸모없는 조각들이라 생각하면서 '쓰레기 DNA'라고 불렀다.

쓸모없는 지위의 날들은 이제 공식적으로 끝났다. 거의 10년 동안 공동 프로젝트에 일해오면서, 전 세계의 32개의 연구실의 440명의 과학자들은 그들이 마침내 침묵하던 다수의 DNA가 무엇을 하는지 밝혔다고 발표했다: 그것은 중간 관리자이다.

전에는 '쓰레기'로 불렸지만, 지금은 '암흑물질'로 개명된 이 DNA 족보의 큰 가지들은 공장 운영은 하지만, 실제로는 아무것도 만들지 않는 것처럼 보인다. 그들은 프로젝트를 승인할지, 그것을 멈춰서 차갑게(죽게) 만들지를 결정하는 자들이다. 이 경우에는 어떠한 유전자가 단백질을 만들기 위해서 더 나아갈지, 어떤 것이 두 번째 기회를 기다리며 정지된 상태로 남을지 결정하는 것이다. 그리고 23,000개의 모든 유전자에 백만 개의 감독자들이 있는데, 이것의 비율은 약 50대 1의 비율이며, 이것이 의미하는 바는 중간 관리자층에 대한 보조 인력이 잘 갖춰져 있는 것처럼 보인다는 것이다.

우리의 DNA가 매우 관료적이라는 것을 아는 것은 약간은 실망스러운 것일지라도, 이 통찰력은 의학적으로 상당히 도움이 될 것 같다. 지금까지 치료는, 가끔은 성공적이었으나 자주는 그렇지 않았던, 유전자 자체의 행동에 영향을 주는 것에 초점을 맞춰 왔다. 문제는, 많은 질병들 때문에 어느 정도 이해는 되지만, 유전적 돌연변이를 고친다는 것은 쉽지 않다는 점이다. 유전자들이 촉진하는 자와 진압하는 자의 수행단에 의해 둘러싸여 있다는 것을 아는 것은 (의료적) 개입을 위한 가능한 목표물의 목록을 상당히 확장한다. 예를 들어, 선천성 낭포성 섬유증에서, 우리는 질병을 유발하는 유전적 돌연변이를 발견했지만 그것을 고치는 것은 가능하지 않았다. 새로운 접근법을 사용하면, 연구원들은 돌연변이 유전자 자체가 아닌, 나쁜 유전자의 발현을 승인하는 것에 책임이 있는 DNA 파편 중 하나를 제거하는 것이 가능할지 모른다.

[출전] "Junk DNA Redeemed" from *Newsweek* (Sep 10, 2012)

03

하위내용영역	배점	예상정답률
일반영어 B형 논술형	10점	50%

모범답안 Disposable products and durable goods are both beneficial to the economy. To begin with, since people use disposable goods for a very short time or even only once, manufacturing them promotes innovation of designs and large employment of the industry. Consequently, it is conducive to economic growth. Durable products also serve long-standing economic substantiality because they require the development of the secondary industry providing the supply of parts and repairs necessary for long-term use of products.

On the other hand, disposable products and durable products have different impacts on the environment. First, disposable products harm the environment because they generate much waste some of which is hard to decompose. In contrast, durable products help preservation of the environment. They reduce pollution, residual waste and landfill to bury the waste. In short, durable goods are environmentally friendly while disposable products damage the environment.

TIP 일주일에 1~2개 정도 이런 유형의 문제를 풀어본다. 단 조심할 것은, 다음 해에도 이와 유사한 유형이 또 나올 것이란 근거는 없기 때문에 다른 유형의 논술 문제도 접해보는 것이 중요하다.

어휘

as such 이렇듯이
disposable 1회용의
landfill expansion 쓰레기 매립장 확대
residual 잔량의, 잔여
decompose 분해되다
in turn 결국
long-standing 오래된, 오래 지속되는

한글번역

모든 상품은 일회용 상품 또는 오래 사용 가능한 상품으로 여겨질 수 있다. 일회용 상품은 짧은 기간 동안 사용하도록 만들어진 것이고, 많은 경우 정말로 한 번 사용하고 버리도록 의도된 것이다. 일회용 상품을 제조하는 것은 새로운 디자인에 대한 계속되는 발전과 많은 노동자의 고용이 요구된다. 이는 경제 성장에 계속적인 이점을 제공한다. 그러나 이러한 종류의 상품은 막대한 낭비를 야기할 수 있다. 비닐봉지와 같은 몇몇 일회용 상품은 쉽게 분해되지 않으며, 그 결과 환경에 어떠한 긍정적인 영향도 미치지 않는다.

내구성 있는 상품은 오래 유지되도록 의도된 상품이다. 이렇듯이 어떤 특정한 상품은 덜 자주 팔릴 것이다. 그러나, 내구성 있는 상품을 제조하는 것은 부품을 제공하거나 수리하는 것에 대한 2차 산업의 지원이 요구된다. 결국에는 이것은 오래 지속되는 경제적인 이점을 만들어낸다. 게다가, 상품을 오래 사용하는 것은 대기오염의 방출을 줄이는 것에 기여한다. 내구성 있는 상품이 또한 잔여 폐기물을 줄일 수 있으므로, 쓰레기 매립장 확대는 상당히 줄어들고 이러한 것은 좋은 환경적인 선택을 하도록 만든다.

2014학년도

01

하위내용영역	배점	예상정답률
일반영어 A형 기입형	2점	60%

모범답안 relative insignificance

어휘

acquaintance 아는 사람, 지인, 면식, (약간의) 친분
correct 교정하다; 고치다
cute 귀여운, 매력적인, 약삭빠른
dethrone (왕을) 퇴위시키다, 권좌에서 몰아내다
grow out of ~로부터 벗어나다
grow up 성장하다, 철이 들다, 서서히 생겨나다
hurdle (경기용) 허들, 장애, 난관
inclination (~하려는) 의향, 성향
maturity 성숙함, 원숙함, 성인임, 성숙한 상태, 만기
mercy 자비, 고마운 일
millennia (특히 예수 탄생을 기준으로 그 전후의) 천년, 새로운 천년이 시작되는 시기
numberless 수없이 많은
precede ~에 앞서다, ~ 앞에 가다
scheme 계획, 제도, 책략
self-centeredness 자기 본위, 자주성
sibling (한 명의) 형제자매
slumbering 잠, 수면
soak in ~에 적시다
solipsistic 유아론적인
squirmy 꿈틀거리는, 꼼지락거리는; 우물쭈물하는
sullen 뚱한, 시무룩한, 음침한, 침울한
superficial 깊이 없는, 얄팍한, 피상적인, 깊지 않은, 표피상의, (진지성·중요성이 없이) 가벼운, 표면의, 표면에 드러난
taking off 제거, 치우기, 이륙, 이수, 이함, 출발, 흉내
unexpectedly 뜻밖에, 예상외로, 갑자기, 돌연

한글번역

우리는, 우리 각자는, 너무나 강한 자기중심성을 가지고 세상에 태어나기 때문에 단지 아기라는, 따라서 귀엽다는 사실만이 우리를 구원한다. 성장이라는 것은 대체로 그와 같은 상태에서 벗어나는 문제이다. 우리는 그럼으로써 우리의 원래 자리인 세계의 중심으로부터 우리 자신을 퇴위시킨다. 아니 적어도 우리 중 대부분이 그렇게 한다. 그것은 비행기 안에서 이륙하는 것과 같다. 정체성의 확립은 사물의 방대한 계획에서 우리가 얼마나 비교적으로 작은지를 알아차리는 것을 필요로 한다. 당신의 부모님이 예상치 못하게 어린 동생을 낳고, 당신을 유치원의 자비심에 내버려 둘 때의 심정을 기억해봐라. 아니면 첫 공립이나 사립학교로 입학할 때는 어떠했는가? 아님 교사로서, 시무룩하고, 꿈틀거리고, 잠을 자고, 자기중심적인 학생들로 가득 찬 첫 교실을 마주했을 때는 어땠는가? 하나의 장애물을 극복했듯이, 다른 장애물이 당신 앞에 놓여 있다. 각 사건은 당신이 권위자가 됐다고 생각하는 바로 그 순간에 당신의 권위를 약화시킨다.

만약 그것이 인간관계에서 원숙함이 의미하는 것이라면—상대적 하찮음의 인식을 통해 정체성에 도달하는 것—나는 역사적인 자각을 시간을 통한 원숙미의 투영이라고 정의할 것이다. 우리는 우리 앞에 얼마나 많은 것이 있으며, 그것에 비하면 우리 자신이 얼마나 하찮은지를 이해한다. 우리는 우리의 위치를 배우고, 그것이 크지 않다는 것을 깨닫게 된다. 수천 년에 걸쳐 존재해 온 셀 수 없이 수많은 사람들에 대해 피상적으로나마 아는 것만으로도, 보통 청소년기에 세계를 자신에게로 연관 짓는 경향에서, 자신을 세계로 연관 짓도록 수정하는 데 도움을 줄 수 있다. 역사학자인 제프리 엘튼은 "역사는 청소년에서 성인이 되기를 돕는 그러한 적응과 통찰력을 가르치고, 이것은 젊은이들의 교육에서 확실히 가치 있는 서비스이다"라고 지적했다.

02

하위내용영역	배점	예상정답률
일반영어 A형 서술형	3점	50%

모범답안 The current news tends to neglect the big institutional aspects and to personalize serious issues and problems. Second, the current news style is different from great literature and theater in that the latter employs strong characters to make the audience think about larger moral and social situations in critical terms whereas the former rarely makes people engage in serious social issues because of its systematic tendency to personalize social, economic, and political situations.

어휘

angle 관점; 각도, 각, 기울기
bias 편견, 편향
big picture 큰 그림(사회의 전반적 상황)
"can't-see-the-forest-for-the-trees" 나무만 보고 숲을 보지 못하다
culprit 범인, (문제를 일으킨) 장본인
defining 결정적인
downplay 경시하다, 대단치 않게 생각하다
ease 완화, 편함
hook 고리, 걸이; 바늘
involvement 관련, 관여, 개입, 연루, 몰두, 열중, 연애
numerous 많은
opaque 불투명한; 불분명한
overwhelming 압도적인, 너무도 강력한, 저항하기 힘든
personalize 개인적인 것으로 국한시키다
probe 캐묻다, 조사하다
promote 촉진하다, 홍보하다, 승진시키다
scoundrel (비열한) 악당
tendency 성향, 기질; 경향, 동향, 추세
trial 재판, 공판
turn off 신경을 끄다
what passes for ~라 여겨지는 것
worrisome 걱정스럽게 만드는, 걱정스러운

한글번역

최근 뉴스 형태에서 단 하나 가장 중요한 결점이 있다면 그것은 뉴스가 사건들의 표면에 있는 인간의 재판, 비극 그리고 대성공을 선호하기 때문에, 큰 사회적, 경제적, 그리고 정치적 상황을 경시하는 압도적인 경향성을 띈다는 것이다. 예를 들면, 권력과 과정에 초점을 맞추는 대신 매체는 그 이슈에 관해 정치적 싸움에 연루된 사람들에게 집중한다. 이에 대한 이유들은 무수히 많은데, 면밀한 분석이 청중들의 관심을 끄게 만들 거라는 기자의 공포감부터 시작해, 심오한 원인과 결과를 설명하는 것과는 반대로 어떤 이야기의 흥미를 불러일으키는 면을 말하는 것이 상대적으로 편하기 때문이다.

사람들이 뉴스를 개인적으로 받아들이도록 요청됐을 때, 그들은 넓은 범위의 사적이고, 감정적인 의미들을 그 뉴스 안에서 찾을 수 있다. 하지만, 개인화된 뉴스에서 영감을 받은 의미들은 건강한 시민들의 참여가 넘쳐나게 하는 공유되는 비판적 이해에 도움이 되지 않는다. 인물에 대한 초점은 대중들 사이에서 수동적인 방관자 태도를 부추긴다. 그 초점이 동정어린 주인공들과 희생자들에 있든지 아니면 혐오스러운 악당들과 범죄자들에 있든지 간에, 개인화된 흥미를 불러일으킬 만한 뉴스에 대한 매체의 선호도는 "나무들 때문에 숲을 보지 못하는" 정보 편파를 만들고, 이것은 뉴스 카메라의 시선에 잡힌 무대 중앙에 북적거리는 많은 배우들 너머에 있는 큰 그림을 보기 어렵게 만든다.

만약 독자의 흥미를 불러일으키는 관점이 독자들로 하여금 이슈와 문제들에 대한 더 진중한 분석을 요구하도록 사용된다면 뉴스를 개인화하는 추세가 덜 우려될 것이다. 고대 그리스 희곡부터 현재까지 대부분 위대한 문학과 연극은 사람들이 더욱 큰 도덕적이고 사회적인 문제들에 대해 생각하도록 이끌기 위해 청중의 인지 발견과 반응을 촉진하는 강한 캐릭터를 사용한다. 하지만, 뉴스는 종종 캐릭터 개발 단계에서 멈추고, 더 큰 교훈과 사회적 의의를—(별로 없을 것 같지만) 만약 그것이 있다고 한다면—청중들의 상상에 남겨둔다. 결과적으로, 개인화시킨 뉴스의 주요 문제는 개인 문제에 대한 초점이 결코 더 심도 있는 분석으로 연결되지 않는다는 점이다. 종종 분석으로 여겨지는 것은 불분명한 판에 박힌 뉴스 문구들인데, "그/그녀는 우리의 반영이었다"와 같은 것들이다. 이 말은 영국 왕자빈이었던 다이애나와 미국의 존 케네디 주니어의 죽음 뒤에 나온 매체들의 광란에서 사용됐다. 심지어 다수의 대중이 개인화된 뉴스의 판에 박힌 공식을 거부했을 때도, 개인화는 결코 멈추지 않는다. 객관적 상황을 개인화하려는 이 조직적인 경향성은 뉴스의 결정적인 편향 중 하나다.

03

하위내용영역	배점	예상정답률
일반영어 B형 서술형	5점	50%

모범답안 Figure 2 represents the fluctuations in sheep population, which shows stable status over a hundred years. The lesser fluctuations of the population of sheep are due to their larger size and longer lifespan (which make them less affected by changes in environment and birth rate respectively).

어휘

a factor of 2 2배만큼
crash over 와르르 전복하다
disparate 서로 전혀 다른, 이질적인
fluctuate 변동을 거듭하다
fluctuation (방향・위치・상황의) 변동, 오르내림; 파동, 동요, (유전)개체 변이(cf. mutation)
homeostasis 항상성
overlay (무엇이 표면에 안전히) 덮어씌우다
rapid 빠른(짧은 시간 내에 이뤄지는)
algae 조류
diatoms 규조류
figure (특히 공식적인 자료로 제시되는) 수치
turn over 몸(자세)을 뒤집다, 뒤집히다
orders of magnitude (수학) 자릿수
population 인구, 주민, 개체 수
soar (가치・물가 등이) 급증하다, 치솟다

한글번역

특정한 종의 개체 수는 장기간 동안 상대적으로 안정되게 유지되는 경향이 있다. 예를 들면, 19세기 초에 사육용 양이 태즈메이니아섬에 정착하게 된 이후로 그 개체의 수는 거의 한 세기 동안 1,230,000에서 2,250,000으로, 2배보다는 작고 불규칙하게 변화했다. 이것을 우리가 아는 이유는 양이 태즈메이니아의 경제에 매우 중요했고, 여전히 중요해서 그들의 수가 철저하게 기록됐기 때문이다. 확연히 대조적으로, 작으며 짧은 생명을 지닌 유기체들은 짧은 기간 동안에 많은 자릿수를 왔다 갔다 할 정도로 개체 수 변동이 크기도 하다. 식물성 플랑크톤을 구성하는 녹조와 돌말의 수는 며칠이나 몇 주 동안 급증하거나 추락할지도 모른다. 이러한 급격한 변동은 더 긴 시간 동안, 예를 들면 계절 단위로, 일어나는 변화들을 가릴 수 있다.

왜 양과 조류는 개체 수에 있어서 그렇게 다른 변화를 보여주는 것일까? 우선, 양과 조류는 환경 변화에 대한 민감성부터가 다르다. 양은 더 크기 때문에 항상성에 대한 더 큰 능력을 가지고 있고 환경적 변화로 인한 생리적 영향을 더 잘 견딜 수 있다. 게다가, 양과 조류의 수는 출생률 변동에 의해 다르게 영향을 받는다. 양은 비교적 긴 수명을 지니고 있기 때문에 출생 비율의 단기간 변동은 주어진 기간 내의 전반적인 개체 수에 큰 영향을 미치지 않는다. 그러므로 양의 개체 수는 높은 내부적 안정성을 가진다. 반면, 단세포로 된 조류의 세포들의 삶은 단지 며칠 정도만 지속되므로 내부적으로 불안정한 개체 수는 빠른 속도로 변화한다.

04

하위내용영역	배점	예상정답률
일반영어 B형 논술형	10점	55%

모범답안 It is inevitable that Korea becomes an aging society. Koreans are required to prepare in order to effectively deal with their longer life expectancies. In terms of the individual level, people in Korea should embrace healthier lifestyles for the following two reasons. First off, healthy living not only improves one into old age but also improves the outlook and effectivity of the individual through their whole life. This means a better outlook, improved mental health and physical ability. A second reason to pursue health-oriented lifestyles is that keep one away from unhealthy excesses or vices. Bad habits such as smoking or excessive drinking are detrimental to the individual.
To meet the needs of a larger elder population, Korea should develop its pension system. First, by creating an expanded safety net for senior citizens, we would see alleviation on the pressures placed onto younger generations to support their parents and grandparents. This will have a positive effect on the whole. Secondly, an expanded pension system would mean retirees can leave the workforce and give employment to the young while caring for the elderly. In these two ways an expanded relief system can address this tough issue of Korean aging well.

어휘

aging 노화, 늙어 가는, 노화하는
facet 측면, 양상, (보석의 깍인) 면
consequently 그 결과, 따라서
wide-ranging 광범한, 폭넓은

한글번역

한국은 빠르게 노령화 사회가 되고 있다. 결과적으로, 우리는 이러한 상황이 유발하게 될 변화에 효과적으로 대처할 수 있도록 준비해야 한다. 분명히, 이러한 변화들은 국가의 각기 다른 측면에 광범위한 영향을 끼칠 것이다. 우리는 개인적 그리고 사회적 관점에서 미래에 어떻게 대비해야 하는지 고려해야 한다. 아래의 내용은 이러한 두 가지 주요 범위 내에 고려해야 할 몇 가지 요점들이다.

- **개인적 차원에서 준비할 수 있는 사항**
  평생 취미를 발전시킨다.
  더 건강한 생활방식을 받아들인다.
  재정적인 자급자족을 추구한다.
- **사회적 차원에서 준비할 수 있는 사항**
  의무적 퇴직 연령을 재검토한다.
  건강관리 시스템을 향상시킨다.
  기존의 연금 시스템을 확장한다.

Chapter 02 2013~2009학년도 기출문제

본책 p.306

2013학년도 1차

01 모범답안 ③

어휘

bag up 자루에 넣다
chirp 짹짹거리다
convict 기결수; 유죄를 선고하다, 유죄 판결을 내리다
culprint 장본인, 범인
foliage 나뭇잎
vertebrate 척추동물
headlamp 머리나 헬멧에 장착하는 조명구; (자동차의) 전조등
herpetologist 파충류 학자
inch forward 조금씩 조금씩 전진하다
invertebrate 무척추동물
miniature 작은
mite 진드기
perceptible (규모·정도 등이) 감지할 수 있는
predator 포식자
projecting 돌출한, 툭 튀어나온
suspect 용의자; (확실하지는 않지만 특히 좋지 않은 일이 있다고·있을 것으로) 의심하다

한글번역

크리스토퍼 오스틴은 그의 길을 밝히기 위해 오직 전조등만 들고 손과 무릎을 이용해 천천히 전진했다. 그 파충류 학자와 그의 조교는 낙엽으로부터 들리는 신비한 짝짓기 음성의 근원지를 찾기 위해 파푸아 뉴기니의 축축한 숲 바닥을 수색했다. 그들은 곤충이 높은 음조의 울림을 멀리 퍼뜨리고 있다고 가정했으나, 거기에는 어떤 곤충도 발견되지 않았다. 그래서 두 사람은 일부 나뭇잎을 가방에 싸서 캠프로 가지고 왔다. 거기서, 그들은 그 놀라운 장본인을 찾을 때까지 각 나뭇잎을 하나씩 살폈다. 그것은 곤충이 아닌 흙 색깔의 삼 분의 일 인치 크기의 작은 개구리였다. 오스틴은 그가 찾은 것이 페도프라이네 아마우엔시스라는 새로운 종이라고 이후에 발표했다. 이것은 이전에 기록을 보유하고 있던 남부 아시아 물고기보다 일 밀리미터 더 작아서, 세상에서 가장 작은 척추동물이다. 오스틴은 "작은 몸집으로 진화하는 방법은 아예 성장하지 않는 것입니다."라고 말했다. 무엇이 이득일까? 그 개구리들의 초소형 크기는 심지어 열대림의 가장 축축한 나뭇잎들에 있는 그들의 먹이인 진드기를 포함한 더 작은 무척추동물에게 그들이 이상적인 포식자가 되게 한다.

02 모범답안 ④

어휘

administer 주다; 관리하다, (공정하게) 집행하다
antipsychotic 항정신성의
biochemical 생화학의, 생화학적인
competent ~할 수 있는; 유능한; 능숙한
court of appeal 항소법원(2심법원)
err 실수를 범하다
explicit 분명한, 명쾌한, 솔직한, 터놓고 말하는, 명백한; 노골적인
get a handle on ~을 이해하다(= comprehend)
have a long way to go (목표를 달성하려면) 아직 멀었다
mental state 정신상태
milieu (사회적) 환경
neuroscience 신경과학
petitioner 진정인, 신청인, 탄원하는 사람
pharmacology 약리학; 약물(학)
render (어떤 상태가 되게) 만들다
stand trial 재판을 받다
underlying (겉으로 잘 드러나지는 않지만) 근본적인; 기저의

한글번역

사상의 자유는 최근에 찰스 T. 셀의 사례에 의해 도전받았는데, 그는 다음과 같이 주장했다. "그 항소법원이 청원자의 주장, 즉 정부가 항정신성 약물을 환자의 의지에 반해 오로지 재판에 설 수 있도록 하기 위해 투여하도록 허락한 것은 수정헌법이 보장하는 개인의 권리를 침해하는 것이라는 주장을 기각한 것은 잘못이다." 대법원은 6대 3으로 셀에게 유리한 판결을 내렸다. 신경과학이 마음을 읽기는커녕 뇌의 상태에 대해서도 이제 막 이해하기 시작한 단계일 뿐임에도, 셀의 경우는, 정부가 그에게 어떤 정신 상태를 강요하기 위해 약물을 사용하기를 원했다. 누군가를 정신적으로 능력 있게 하기 위해서 그의 생화학적 환경을 조직하는 것은 완전히 꿈일 따름이다. 항정신성약은 이상 증세를 다루는 것이지 기저구조를 다루는 것이 아니다. 이 시점에서, 신경과학은 뇌를 읽는 것이지 마음을 읽는 것이 아니므로, 뇌세포들의 특정 화학물질 조작이 명확한 정신적 상태를 만든다고 신경과학이 주장할 수 있을 때까지는 아직 멀었다.

03 모범답안 ⑤

어휘

apotheosis 절정, 극치, (누구의 인생이나 사회생활에서) 절정기, 신격화
authentic 진본인, 진짜인, 정확한, 진짜와 꼭 같게 만든, 모사한
bemuse 멍하게 만들다, 어리벙벙하게 하다; 생각에 잠기게 하다
composition 작품; 작곡; 구성 요소들, 구성
convincing 설득력 있는, (승리 등이) 확실한
emulate 모방하다(= imitate)
generate 발생시키다, 만들어 내다
bad hair day 만사가 잘 안 풀리는 날
intrusion (개인 사생활 등에 대한) 침범
novice 초보자
nuance (의미 · 소리 · 색상 · 감정상의) 미묘한 차이, 뉘앙스
reincarnate 환생시키다
surpass 능가하다, 뛰어넘다
talented (타고난) 재능이 있는
virtuoso 대가(maestro)

한글번역

당신은 음악이 전자탐침기의 침입에 영향을 받지 않는 순수한 인간의 표현이라고 수상할지도 모른다. 하지만, '꽤 훌륭한' 곡들을 생산해내는 것처럼 보이는 여러 성공한 프로그램들이 만들어져왔다. 그런 프로그램이 관중들 앞에서 연주될 세 개의 작품—하나는 바흐에 의해, 또 다른 하나는 자기 자신에 의해, 그리고 나머지 하나는 컴퓨터에 의해서 작곡됐다—을 선별한 스티브 라르손에 의해 만들어졌다. 라르손을 다소 어리벙벙하게 만든 결과는, 그가 작곡한 곡이 컴퓨터에 의해 생성됐다고 판단됐고, 반면 컴퓨터가 생성한 음악은 정통 바흐의 곡이라고 판단된 것이다. 적어도 제한적으로, 컴퓨터에서 생성된 음악은 가끔 몇몇 사람들을 속인다. 임프로바이저라고 불리는 또 다른 프로그램은 바흐부터 루이 암스트롱과 같은 재즈 뮤지션의 음악의 다양한 스타일을 모방하기 위해 쓰였다.

현재, 컴퓨터에서 생성된 음악은 매우 설득력 있어 보인다. 그러나 이러한 프로그램들의 주된 약점은, 특히 전문화된 음악의 미묘한 차이에도 예민한 음악 전문가들 사이에서, 장기간에 걸쳐 설득력 있는 음악을 만들어내는 그들의 능력에 있다. 초보자는 컴퓨터가 생성한 음악을 모차르트에 의해 작곡됐다고 확신할지도 모르지만, 모차르트 대가는 가짜 모차르트를 판별해낼 수 있다. 누군가는 이 음악이 모차르트의 것 같다고 마음이 움직일지 모르겠지만, 그 소리는 모차르트가 '컨디션이 안 좋은 날'을 겪는 것처럼 들린다. 물론, 미래의 프로그램들은 모차르트 같은 작품을 생산하는 것뿐만 아니라, 그 재능 있는 젊은 오스트리아인을 능가해 그 천재 소년의 절정기를 재현할 더 대단한–모차르트 작품을 만들어낼 것이다.

04 모범답안 ③

어휘

a priori 선험적인; 연역적인
amygdala 편도체
disrupted 손상된(= damaged)
fundamental 근본적인, 핵심적인, 필수적인
impediment 장애(물)
prohibit (특히 법으로) 금지하다, ~하지 못하게 하다
reasoning 추리, 추론
underpinning 근거; 받침대, 토대
adoption 채택
antisocial 반사회적인
elicit (정보 · 반응을 어렵게) 끌어내다
impairment (to) ~의 손상; 장애
intrinsically 내재적으로
psychopathy 정신병, 정신병질
resonate with ~와 공명하다; ~로 가득 차다

한글번역

왜 도덕적으로 살아야 하는가? 이 질문은 윤리학에서 근본적인 것인데, 왜냐하면 사람들이 어떤 행동이 옳은 일인지는 알 수 있어도, 왜 사람들이 사실상 그러한 일들을 하는지에 대해 여전히 물을 수 있기 때문이다. 도덕적 동기의 문제에 대한 전통적인 철학적 대답은 합리주의였다: 우리는 더 도덕적이어야 하는데, 그것은 그와 다르게 행동하는 것이 비이성적이기 때문이다. 도덕의 합리성은 무엇이 옳은지에 대한 선험적 진리로부터, 또는 사람들이 도덕적이기 위해 다른 이들과 의견을 같이하는 것이 이성적이라는 주장들로부터 나오는 듯하다.

철학자 션 니콜스는 합리주의의 중대한 문제는 사이코패스들이, 추상적 추론에 장애가 없음에도 불구하고 타인에게 해를 끼치는 행동에 아무런 잘못이 없다고 여기는 것이라고 주장한다. 니콜스는 사이코패스의 잘못된 점이 그들의 추론에 있는 것이 아니라 그들의 정서에 있다고 설득력 있게 주장한다. 반사회적 행동, 죄책감 결여, 감정의 메마름과 같은 증세를 포함하는 사이코패스는 소뇌에 있는 편도체의 오작동에서 비롯된 정서 학습 장애의 결과이다.

니콜스에 의하면, 도덕적 사고에 대한 적절한 설명은 어떻게 감정이, 도덕적 판단에 이성적인 사고를 허용하면서, 도덕적 판단을 동기에 연결시키는 역할을 하는지 설명해야 한다. 그의 윤리적 규범에 대한 설명은 문화적이고 역사적이다. 만약 부정적인 정서를 불러일으킬 만한 행동을 금지함으로써, 그 규범들이 우리의 정서체계를 반영한다면, 그 규범들은 문화 안에서 보존될 확률이 높다. 타인에게 해를 끼치는 것을 금지하는 규범은 이 "정서적 공명" 때문에 사실상 전 문화에 걸쳐 존재한다. 규범들의 채택은 우리로 하여금 무엇이 옳고 그른지에 대해 생각할 수 있게 하지만, 이러한 규범들은 본질적으로 도덕과 행동 사이에 연결고리를 제공하는 정서적 토대를 가지고 있다.

05 모범답안 ⑤

어휘

adversary (언쟁 · 전투에서) 상대방, 적수
appetite for ~에의 욕구
conglomerate (거대) 복합 기업, 대기업
fixture 설비
glowing 백열(작열)하는, 빨갛게 단
ineffective 무익한
invoke (법 · 규칙 등을) 들먹이다, 적용하다
keep ~ at bay ~의 접근을 막다
militaristic 군국주의(자)의
mirth (유쾌한 · 즐거운) 웃음소리, 즐거움
perpetuate 영구화하다, 영속시키다
zapper 해충 박멸 장치
propaganda (정치 지도자 · 정당 등에 대한 허위 · 과장된) 선전
revolve around (관심 · 주제가) ~을 중심으로 삼다(돌아가다)
substantiate 입증하다
taproot (식물의) 곧은 뿌리

한글번역

곤충을 적으로 여기는 우리의 생각이 우리와 곤충들과의 상호작용을 형성한다. 이것은 곤충을 박멸하거나 통제하는 것을 목표로 하는 규제기관과 거대한 대기업들을 생기게 했다. 이러한 기관들에 의해 만들어진 허위 선전은 우리와 곤충들의 관계의 복잡성을 단순화시키고, 수천 종을 향해 군국주의적인 자세를 영속시키는 적대적 이미지를 우리에게 제공한다. 하지만, 그것의 뿌리는 우리의 두려움이다.

"나는 그게 뭔지 몰라서 죽였어"는 생물학자인 로날드 루드가 곤충이나 무엇인지 모르는 낯선 생물의 시체를 가지고 온 사람들에게 물었을 때마다 듣고 또 들은 말이다. 위협적이지 않은 상황에서 나오는 자연스러운 호기심은 부재했다. 그들은 그 생물체의 존재에 의해 일어난 두려움을 없애버리기 위해 그냥 안전하기 위해 그것을 죽인 것이다.

우리가 가지고 있는 두려움의 큰 부분은 물린다는 것을 중심으로 한다. 살충장치, 교외의 마당에서 타오르고 있는 설치물은 매년 수십억 마리의 곤충을 죽이며 두려움의 접근을 막았다. 한 곤충학자는 이러한 모든 장치들이 하는 일은 우리를 즐겁게 하는 것뿐이라고 말한다. 다른 면에서 보면 이 장치들은 비효과적이다. 살충되는 곤충들의 4분의 1보다 적은 수가 흡혈을 한다. 그러나, 만약 곤충이 살충장치에 닿으면 폭발해, 박테리아와 바이러스를 적어도 반경 2미터 내로 뿌린다는 것을 우리가 아는 순간, 어떠한 즐거움도 오래 가지 못할 것이다.

목표가 아닌데도 죽임을 당하는 710억 마리로 추정되는 곤충들에 대한 연민은 그러지 못했으므로, 자기방위야말로 우리로 하여금 살충장치를 그만 사용하도록 동기를 부여할지도 모른다. 사실상, 곤충들이 적이라는 우리의 신념에 영향을 줄 수 있는 것은 별로 많지 않다. 우리의 경험이 우리의 두려움을 뒷받침하지 않을 때, 우린 그 모순적 증거를 무시하는 경향이 있다. 우리가 정당화되고 현실적으로 행동한다는 것을 확신하며, 우리는 자신의 공격적 자세를 재빨리 옹호하고, 색다르고 더 긍정적 관계를 일으키는 기회들은 보지도 않을 것이다.

06 모범답안 ⑤

어휘

challenge 도전; 이의를 제기하다, 도전 의식을 북돋우다
disturb 교란시키다; 불안하게 만들다
long-held 오랫동안 간직해 온
pay off 성공하다; 성과를 거두다
risk ~의 위험을 무릅쓰다

한글번역

모든 위험들은 신체적이어야 하는 건가? 물론 아니다. 지적인 위험들도 존재한다. 신체에 도전하고 잠재적으로 신체적 피해를 수반하는 신체적 위험과는 달리, 지적 위험은 정신에 도전하고 공통된 신념의 잠정적 혼란을 야기한다. 이것은 '사고의' 위험이다.

[C] 정신적인 위험은 무엇을 수반하는가? 이런 유형의 위험은 다른 사람들로 하여금 그들이 평소 믿어오던 것들을 불신하게끔 강요한다. 이것은 아마도 이전에는 고려되지 않았던 것을 폭로하는 것일 수도 있다. 아마도 그것은 지적능력을 발휘하려는 시도로 볼 수도 있다. 이러한 지적 위험은 신체적 위험과 비슷하며, 그러한 경험으로부터 특정한 만족감이 발생할 수 있다.

[B] 예를 들면, 1970년대 중반에 첫 번째 미니시리즈들이 텔레비전에 방영됐다. <뿌리>는 1700년대에 납치돼 미국에 노예로 팔려간 젊은 아프리카인의 삶을 묘사한 수일간의 영화 시리즈였다. 그 시리즈는 생생했다. 노예들이 정말로 어떻게 다뤄졌는지를 묘사했다. 이것은 시청하는 사람들을 불편하게 만들었다. 불쾌한 노예 역사를 과거에 남기기를 원하는 나라의 국민이었기에 훨씬 더 불편했다.

[A] 이것은 사람들에게 어떤, 오랫동안 지켜왔던 믿음을 재고하도록 도전하므로 위험하다. 프로듀서는 노예들에게 가한 완전히 야만적인 행위에 대해 시청자가 다시 생각하기를 바라면서, 위험을 무릅썼다. 잠재적으로, 그 프로듀서는 투자한 돈뿐만 아니라, 그의 명성까지도 잃을 처지였다. 이 경우에는, 지적인 위험을 감수한 것은 성공적이었다. 그 영화는 아프리카계 미국인의 인권에 대한 당시의 관점을 교란시켰고, 거의 언급되지 않았던 과거에 대해 많은 이들을 교육시키는 데 도움을 줬다.

2013학년도 2차

모범답안 Even though Writing Sample 1 and Writing Sample 2 have exactly the same topic of visiting Ho Chi Minh City, the two writings contrast one another greatly in terms of content, organization, and language use. First of all, WS 2 contains elaborated description of the city's rich history and culture to provide in-depth information to the reader. Contrary to this, WS 1's information is short and fails to explain the reasons for writing the sentence. For example, WS 1 states that "older generations" learned "French in school," but fails to explain further why this information is pertinent. In WS 2, however, the writer describes how the older generation "can speak it very well" and how the elite also continues to "speak French today."

In terms of organization, WS 1's information is scattered, whereas WS 2 shows coherence and cohesion. Regarding coherence, WS 1 jumps from the topics of buildings to food, then to language, and then back to food. In contrast, WS 2 moves in progression from culture to food, then to history, and clearly points out how these are all intertwined and related to one another. Addressing cohesion, WS 1 doesn't use cohesive indicators to show examples or changes in subject area like WS 2 does with "for example", "in addition."

Lastly, WS 2 contains more varied and educated vocabulary in comparison to WS 1. Not only that, but in WS 1 the sentences are short and lack style, stating, "the Vietnamese and the French fought, too." In WS 2, the same information is presented using sophisticated language and elaborated content, such as, "[numerous] museum and monument also document country's long—and often bloody—history of conflict between Vietnamese and French"(sic). Therefore, when reviewing the two writing samples, it is clear that WS 2 is the far better written piece in content, organization, and language use.

2012학년도 1차

01 모범답안 ③

어휘

blade 날
fierce 사나운, 험악한
portrait 묘사; 초상화
cling to ~을 고수하다
pensive 깊은 생각에 잠긴, 수심 어린
transcription 글로 옮김, 수기, 문자화

한글번역

비록 그는 앞선 예술가들의 노동의 결과물들을 활용했지만, 그럼에도 불구하고 윌리엄 터너는 그의 유년시절부터 자연으로부터 자신의 유일한 영감을 얻었다. 하지만 그의 예술은 자연을 있는 그대로 옮기는 것에 있지 않았다. 그의 예술은 풀잎의 개수를 센다던가, 변형 없이 자신의 앞에 놓인 장면의 정확한 양상을 재현하는 기술에 있지 않았다. 그가 재현했던 모든 장면들은, 말하자면, 그의 고유한 상상의 신비로운 시에 휩싸여 있다. 그는 대지를 묘사할 때 그 대지가 어떤 주어진 한 순간에 보이는 대로만 그리는 것이 아니라, 그 대지의 지나간 과거 역사와 그 대지를 흔들어대던 지진, 대지를 압도했던 폭풍우, 그리고 여전히 대지에 있는 사랑스러움 등에 대한 진실한 이해를 가지고 그렸다. 그는 우리에게 즐거움과 슬픔, 밝음과 어둠, 수심어린 분위기와 강렬한 광기, 사랑과 미움과 같은 모든 다양한 측면에서의 사랑스러움을 드러내왔다. 그의 묘사는 최고조로 사실적이었지만, 그의 그림은 자연으로부터 그대로 복사된 것이 아니었는데, 그것은 그가, 라파엘로와 모든 위대한 이상주의자들이 그랬던 것처럼, 그 자신의 마음속 이미지나 이상으로부터 온 것이었기 때문이다. 하지만, 이러한 이상은 가장 면밀한 관찰과 실제에 대한 탐구에 기반을 두고 있다.

02 모범답안 ②

어휘

arithmetic 수체계; 산술, 계산
emphatically 강조하여, 힘차게
in virtue of ~의 덕분에(= because of)
jargon-ridden (못 알아들을) 전문용어로 가득 찬
proclaim 선언하다, 선포하다
do a sum 산수를 하다
in proportion to ~에 비례하여
intellect 지적능력
locomotion 운동(이동)능력
to a greater or less degree 다소간에

한글번역

내가 알기로 아리스토텔레스는 인간이 이성적인 동물이라고 명백히 선언한 첫 번째 인물이었다. 이러한 관점에 대한 근거는 지금에 와서는 많이 인상 깊어 보이지 않는데, 그 이유는 그가 제시한 근거가 어떤 사람들은 계산할 줄 안다는 점이기 때문이다. 그는 세 가지 종류의 영혼이 존재한다고 생각했다. 동, 식물을 포함한 살아 있는 모든 것들에 의해 소유되고 오로지 생장과 영양분에만 관심을 두는 식물의 영혼, 이동에 관심을 두고 인간이나 하등동물에 의해 공유되는 동물의 영혼, 그리고 마지막으로 신성한 정신인 이성적인 영혼, 즉 지적능력이 있는데, 인간은 그들 자신의 지혜에 비례해 여기에 다소간에 참여한다. 이 지적능력의 미덕 안에서 인간은 이성적인 동물이다. 지적능력은 다양한 경로를 통해 드러나지만, 가장 두드러지게는 산술적 계산의 통달에서 드러난다. 그리스의 숫자 체계는 굉장히 열악해서 구구단은 오로지 매우 총명한 사람들만 할 수 있는 굉장히 어렵고 복잡한 계산이었다. 그러나 오늘날에는 계산기가 가장 총명한 사람들보다도 더 계산을 잘하지만, 아무도 이 유용한 도구가 불멸의 것이며, 신의 영감에 의해 작동한다고 주장하지는 않는다. 산술이 더 쉬워짐에 따라, 이것은 덜 높이 평가받게 되었다. 그 결과로, 많은 철학자들이 우리가 어떤 괜찮은 이들인지를 계속적으로 말해줄지라도, 그 철학자들이 우리를 높이 평가하는 것이 더 이상 우리가 지니고 있는 산술적 능력 때문은 아니다.

03 모범답안 ①

어휘

archetype 원형
bring 지니고 있다(= carry)
deprogram 신념을 버리게 하다, 눈뜨게 하다; (악습에 젖은) 사람을 재교육하다
dubious 의심스러운, 미심쩍은
from the get-go 처음부터
lethal 치명적인
miswired 잘못 연결된
mutation 돌연변이
risk -ing 위험하게도 ~을 하려 하다
wart 사마귀
be riddled with ~로 (특히 나쁜 것이) 가득하다
chilling 등골이 서늘한
frailty 노쇠함, 허약함
in turn 결국; 차례차례
metamorphosis 탈바꿈, 변형, 변태
molecular 분자의, 분자로 된, 분자에 의한
recessive 열성의
vulnerability 취약성

한글번역

정보과학의 새로운 언어는 분자생물학자들을 과학자에서 엔지니어로 변모시켰다. 비록 많은 분자생물학자들이 그런 변모에 대해 거의 알지 못하지만. 분자생물학자들이 돌연변이와 유전적인 질병들을 코드의 오류라고 말할 때, 그것이 내포하고 있는 의미는 그들이 처음부터 존재하지 말았어야 한다는 것과 그들은 재 프로그램화되거나 수정돼야 하는 '오류'이거나 실수라는 것이다. 분자생물학자들은 지속적으로 오류들을 제거하며 결국 컴퓨터 엔지니어, 코드 입력자가 된다. 모든 인간이 많은 수의 치명적 열성인자를 지니고 있다는 것을 고려해본다면, 이것은 의심스럽고 위험한 역할이다. 그렇다면 우리는 우리 자신을 처음부터 코드 내에 오류로 가득 차 있는, 잘못 설계된 것으로 보아야 하는가? 만일 그렇다면, 어떠한 이상적인 완벽한 기준에 맞춰 우리를 평가해야 할까? 만일 모든 인류가 다양한 정도의 오류들로 구성돼있다면, 우리가 그 이상적인 기준을 찾는 것은 헛된 일이다. 분자생물학의 새 언어를 그토록 미묘하게 등골이 서늘하게 만드는 것은, 그것이 위험을 무릅쓰고 새로운 원형, 즉, 결점도 없고 오류도 없는 완벽한 존재를 만들어내려고 하는 것이다. 이것은 우리가 열망하는 것으로 우리처럼 새로운 남성과 여성이지만, 우리 인간이 존재하기 시작할 때부터 우리의 본질을 정의해온 사마귀, 주름, 취약성이나 노쇠함이 없다.

04 모범답안 ⑤

어휘

book industry 출판업
come out 나오다
consign ~을 (어디에) 놓다
contradictory 모순되는
corporate life 집단생활; 회사생활
dismiss (고려할 가치가 없다고) 묵살하다
dismissive 무시(멸시)하는
division 분과
dross 싸구려 (물건들), 찌꺼기
effervescent 거품이 이는; 열광하는
guru 구루(힌두교 · 시크교의 스승이나 지도자), (비격식)전문가, 권위자
jargon (특정 분야의 전문 · 특수) 용어
no-collar 정장이 아닌 캐주얼로 출근하는 정보산업의 고급인력
press release 대언론 공식발표
puff 과대광고
reputation 평판, 명성
swap A for B A를 B로 교환하다
till 돈 서랍
toss out ~을 밖으로 던져버리다

한글번역

[A] 출판 산업의 여러 갈래 가운데 경영서 출판보다 악명 높은 것은 거의 없다. 해마다, 비록 수천은 아니지만, 수백 개의 경영서들이 출간되는데, 삐까뻔쩍한 대언론 공식 발표라던가 거품 가득한 과장 광고와 함께 나온다. 문학 편집자들은 그 출판물들을 쓰레기통으로 직행시키곤 한다.

[D] 이렇게 하는 것은 이해할 만한 일이다. 놀라울 정도의 많은 출판물이 쓸모가 없다. 유명한 최고경영자들은 자화자찬을 하고, 회사의 고문들은 기적의 회생법을 선전하고, 자기계발 전문가들은 당신이 일주일에 네 시간을 일하면서 부유해질 수 있음을 약속한다. 몇 달 기다려 보자. 그 최고경영자들은 공금에 손을 댄 죄로 붙잡히고, 기적의 회생법은 독이었으며, 자기계발 전문가들은 파산한다. 남아 있는 것은 전문 용어로 들끓는 산문들의 뒤엉킨 혼란일 뿐이다.

[C] (이렇게 주장하는 것이) 이해는 가지만 맞는 것은 아니다. 너무 많은 경영도서들이 엉망이라 해서 그 전체 장르 자체를 없애버리는 것은 어리석은 짓이다. 쓰레기 (같은 책) 가운데서도 몇몇 특출한 도서들이 있다. 사업에 관한 정수를 담아놓은 최고경영자들의 자서전, 회생해가는 회사들을 위한 처방전이라든지, 심지어 현대 회사생활의 모순된 압력들을 이해하는 데 도움이 되는 자기계발서들이 그것이다. 서양의 평균적인 고용 노동자들은 집보다 일터에서 더 많은 시간을 보내므로, 이런 중요한 활동들에 초점을 맞추는 작가들을 무시하는 것은 이치에 맞지 않다.

[B] 최고의 책들은 어떻게 비즈니스가 세상을 혁신시키는지에 관한 통찰력을 제공한다. 왜 성장의 중심이 선진국에서 개발도상국으로 넘어갔을까? 왜 어떤 회사들은 성공하고 어떤 회사들은 실패할까? 왜 우리는 화이트컬러를 노 컬러(정장이 아닌 캐주얼로 출근하는 정보산업의 고급인력) 직장으로 교체하고 있을까? 왜 관리자들은 놀라운 것들에 관해 말할까? 이러한 질문들에 대한 대답들은 문학 편집자들이 무심코 던져버리는 비즈니스 도서에 존재한다.

05 모범답안 ⑤

어휘

consenting 동의하는
equilibrium 평형 상태, (마음의) 평정
net impact 최종 충격
worse off 경제적으로 곤란한
Pareto optimal 파레토 최적(다른 사람이 불리해지지 않고는 어느 누구도 유리해질 수 없는 상황)
party 당사자
sum total 총계액
unambiguously 분명하게
utility 효용성(욕구만족도)

한글번역

경제학자 빌프레도 파레토에 의하면, 사람들이 할 수 있는 네 가지 종류의 무역이 있다. 첫 번째로 양쪽 당사자가 모두 이익을 얻는 윈윈 무역이 있다. 이 경우에 복지가 증가하는 것은 명확하다. 두 번째로 한쪽 당사자만 이익을 보고, 아무도 손해를 보지 않으며, 복지는 분명히 증가하는 무역이 있다. 세 번째, 아무도 이익을 얻지 못하지만, 누군가는 손해를 보는 무역이 있는데, 이 경우에는 복지가 분명히 감소한다. 네 번째이자 마지막으로, 어떤 당사자는 이익을 얻고 몇몇은 손해를 보는 무역이 있다. 하지만 직접적으로 효용성을 측정할 수 있는 능력 없이는, 최종적 영향이 어떠한지 결정하는 것은 불가능하다. 파레토는 무역을 진행하기 위해서는 두 명의 합의된 사람들이 필요하고, 사람들은 멍청하지 않기 때문에, 그 사람들이 윈윈 무역이나 적어도 한쪽이 이득을 얻고 손해를 보는 사람이 없는 무역에만 참여하려고 하며, 이 두 가지 형태의 무역은 그 무역 참여자들의 전체적인 복지를 증가시킨다고 주장했다. 이러한 무역은 이후에 '파레토 개선'이라고 불렸고, 파레토는 자유 시장에서 사람들이 모든 파레토 개선을 다 소진할 때까지 무역을 유지한다고 주장했다. 그 (소진) 시점에서 무역은 어떤 이를 더 빈곤하게 만들지 않고는 이루어질 수 없기 때문에 무역이 중지하게 되는데, 이때 시장은 이후 경제학자들이 '파레토 최적'이라고 부르는 평형 상태에 도달하게 된다. 그러므로 파레토 최적은 누군가를 손해 보게 만들지 않고는 더 이상의 무역이 이루어질 수 없는 시점을 말한다. 누군가의 이익을 위해 다른 이들에게 해를 끼쳐야 하는 무역이 있을 수 있으므로 파레토 최적은 그 전체 그룹에게 이익이 꼭 극대화되는 시점은 아니지만, 그럼에도 불구하고 그 그룹의 총 효용성의 합은 증가한다. 효용성을 정확하게 측정하는 방법이나 누군가의 이익을 위해 다른 이의 복지를 차감하는 무역을 강행하는 독재자가 없다면, 파레토 최적은 누군가가 자유 사회에서 할 수 있는 최선의 것이다.

06 모범답안 ⑤

어휘

conduct 수행하다
do well 잘 하다
intelligence quotient 지능지수
practical ability 응용력
quotient (나눗셈에서) 몫
unfairly 불공평하게, 편파적으로, 교활하게, 부정하게
correlation 연관성, 상관관계
expertise 전문성
measures 방안, 방법, 조치
predictor 예측 변수
self-rating 자기평가

한글번역

우리의 시험에 의해 측정되는 분석력, 창의력, 그리고 응용력은 전문성 개발의 여러 형태로 볼 수 있다. 그 모든 능력들이 삶의 다양한 과제에서 유용하다. 하지만, 관습적인 시험들은 매우 좁은 범위의 전문분야에서 잘하지 못하는 학생들에게 불공평하게 불이익을 줄 수도 있다. 우리가 측정하는 전문성 개발의 범위를 확장시킴으로써, 지금은 재능이 있다고 확인되지 않은 많은 아이들이, 사실상 중요한 종류의 전문성을 발달시켰다는 것을 발견할 수 있다. 전통적인 시험들이 평가하는 능력들은 학교와 인생의 수행능력에서 중요하지만, 그 능력들만 중요한 것은 아니다.

우리는 아이들과 어른들에게 비공식적이고, 절차적인 지식들을 측정하는 연구들을 진행해왔다. 기업의 운영자, 대학 교수, 초등학교 학생들, 판매원, 대학생들, 그리고 일반인들에 대한 연구들을 통해 우리는 이 실용적 지식의 중요한 측면이 일반적으로 전통적 시험들에서 평가되는 학업적 지능과 상관관계가 없음을 발견했다. 게다가, 이 (실용적 지식의) 검사들은 지능지수(IQ) 검사만큼이나 혹은 그것보다 더 잘 수행능력을 예측한다. 두 가지 능력 검사 간의 비 상관관계는 학업적 그리고 실용적 지식 검사 모두가 예측 변수로 사용될 때, 직업적 수행능력을 가장 잘 예측할 것을 시사해준다. 가장 최근에, 우리는 직장에 대한 상식의 자가 진단을 예측하지만 다양한 학문적 능력에 대한 자가 진단은 포함하지 않는 상식 평가를 개발했다.

2012학년도 2차

모범답안 a. Cons

Our school is now considering adopting a mandatory, supervised self-study program. This program will entice some but we should deny it on the grounds of: negative impact on students of an increased workload and the limitations on their freedoms and rights.

To begin with, the increased workload can cause additional stress physically and psychologically on the students. Clearly, Korean students have little time to keep up with demanding school schedules and homework, and adding more to this might be "the straw that breaks the camel's back." In terms of mental health, with additional studying will mean schoolwork occupies most of their waking hours, surveyed students in this program show "increased anxiety" due to their study-heavy schedules.

The other key issue is the imposition this program creates on students' freedoms and rights. Every student should have the "rights to autonomous learning," to choose or not. Students might instead opt to spend more time with their family or friends, which is just as important for a student's well-being and society. Extending respect and independence to the student is important for their development; they must learn to work under their own direction. Likewise, giving them choice imbues them with a sense of power or control over their own destiny, which is a fundamental desire of all individuals.

In conclusion, entertaining new projects is part of our responsibility, but in this case, we can be certain that more is not always better, and for the sake of student health and freedom, we must refrain from this program.

b. Pros

Our school is now considering adopting a mandatory, supervised self-study program. This program should be adopted because of the following merits: an increased focus on studying and the easing of economic burden.

The required study hours will be a benefit because they have been proven more "effective." In a survey of this type of program, this is what students had to say. Leaving students to their own devices, unsupervised, or under the control of institutes outside the government school system are naturally less-ideal approaches.

Another key point for today's world is the economic reality of this school program. In preparation for better education, the private education sector has become bloated and invasive, playing on parent's hopes for their children. If schools themselves provided this additional support it would mean "less money" flowing in the direction of profiteering academics. Many parents will breathe easier if this burden is lifted.

In conclusion, designing for better education is our mandate, and in order to reach this we should employ the more efficient and financially-beneficial required study hours after school.

2011학년도 1차

01 모범답안 ①

어휘

appeal to ~에 호소하다
refrain from ~을 삼가다(참다)
youngster 청소년, 아이
publicity 매스컴의 관심(주목)
snap 사진을 찍다

한글번역

한 사람이 어떤 일을 하는 데는 보통 두 가지 이유가 있다. 바로 듣기 좋은 이유와 진짜 이유이다. 그 사람 스스로는 진짜 이유를 머리에 떠올릴 것이다. 당신은 그것을 굳이 강조할 필요가 없다. 그러나 내심 이상주의자로서 우리 모두는 듣기 좋은 이유들을 생각하고 싶어 한다. 고인이 된 노스클리프 경은 그가 게재되지 않길 원했던 그의 사진을 사용하는 신문을 발견했을 때, 편집장에게 편지를 썼다. 허나 그가 "제발 나의 사진을 더 이상 싣지 마시오, 나는 그 사진을 좋아하지 않소."라고 말했을까? 아니다, 그는 더 숭고한 이유에 호소했다. 그는 누구나 가지고 있는 어머니에 대한 존경과 사랑에 호소했다. 그는 "제발 나의 사진을 더 이상 싣지 마시오. 나의 어머니가 그 사진을 좋아하지 않소."라고 편지를 썼다. 존 록펠러 주니어는 신문 사진기자들이 그의 아이들의 사진을 찍는 것을 막고 싶었을 때, "아이들의 사진이 게재되는 것을 바라지 않습니다."라고 말하지 않았다. 그는 아이들이 다치지 않길 바라는 우리 모두에게 내재된 강렬한 소망에 호소했다. 그는 "당신들도 어떠할지 알 겁니다. 당신들 중 누군가도 아이들이 있을 거예요. 그리고 아이들에게 너무 많은 매스컴의 관심이 좋지 않다는 것도 아실 겁니다."라고 말했다.

02 모범답안 ⑤

어휘

absolve 사면하다
conform (규칙·법 등에) 따르다
intimate 사적인
penance 속죄
saintly 성스러운
tolerate 용인하다
virtuous 도덕적인
apparent 분명한
damnation 지옥살이, 지옥으로 보냄
norm 규범
sacred 신성한
sinner 죄인
unpardonable 용서할 수 없는, 변명의 여지가 없는

한글번역

모든 사회들과 심지어 가장 원시적 사회조차도 이념들을 가지고 있으며, 그 이념들이 그들 문화의 친밀하고 중요한 부분이라는 사실은 분명하다. 각 사회는 자신들의 중심 이념을 신성시 여기고 이것과 관련한 어떤 의문도 용인하지 않는다. 실제로, 그런 이념들을 믿도록 하는 압력이 그들이 관련한 행동에 대한 규범에 순응하도록 하는 압박보다 더 강할 때가 많다는 것은 중요한 사회학적인 사실이다. 그래서 모든 종교에서 죄인들은 때때로 '구원'되지만, 그것을 믿지 않는 자들은 절대 구원되지 않는다. 그 죄인들은 악명으로 더럽혀진 삶을 살지도 모르지만, 적절한 속죄가 그의 죄를 사면해줄지도 모른다. 반면, 이단자는 순수하고 도덕적인 인생을, 아마도 거의 성자처럼 살았을 수도 있겠지만, 그의 품행이 지옥살이로부터 그를 꼭 구제해줄 수는 없다. 한 사람이 그 이념을 받아들였을 경우에만, 규범들을 어기는 것을 용서받을 수가 있다. 반면에, 얼마나 규범에 잘 순응했는지와 관계없이 이념을 거부하는 것은 용서받을 수가 없다. 한마디로 말해서, 회의주의는 죄보다 더 심각하다. 모든 시대와 사회에서 자명한 이 사회학적 사실은 모순적이다.

03 모범답안 ③

어휘

frenzy 격분, 격앙, 광포
outlet (감정, 생각, 에너지의 바람직한) 발산(배출) 수단, 직판점(전문 매장)
physiology 생리학, 생리 **quantitative** 양적인

한글번역

심리학과 생리학은 (운동) 경기에 관한 설명을 다룬다. 그들은 삶에서 차지하는 경기의 중요성과 본질을 결정하려 노력한다. 기능 면에서의 경기의 필요성은, 경기에 관련한 모든 연구들의 시작점을 형성한다.

[C] 경기의 생물학적 기능을 정의하려는 수많은 시도들은 놀라울 정도로 다양하다. 한 이론에서, 운동 경기는 이후에 인생에서 진지한 일을 하기 위해 젊은이를 훈련시키는 것을 포함한다. 다른 이론에 따르면, 경기는 어떠한 기능을 연마하기 위한 내재적 욕구로 작용한다고 말한다. 그러나 또 다른 분석들은 경기를 해로운 충동에 대한 분출구로 여긴다.

[D] 이러한 모든 가설들은 어떤 종류의 생물학적인 목적에 근거해 운동 경기가 경기 자체가 아닌 어떤 역할을 한다고 추정한다. 그들은 경기의 개념에 대한 진정한 이해에 도달하지 않은 채, 경기의 이유를 조사한다.

[B] 그러므로, 이 설명들은 문제에 관한 부분적인 해결책들일 뿐이다. 대다수는 오직 경기가 무엇인지 그리고 그것이 선수들에게 어떤 의미인지에 관한 질문을 부수적으로 다룰 뿐이다. 그들은 경기의 심미적 특성에 대해 주의를 기울이지 않고 그저 운동 경기를 양적 방법으로 공격한다.

[A] 그 각각의 설명에 대해 누군가는 이의를 제기할지도 모른다: "무엇이 실제로 경기를 재미있게 하는가? 왜 관중들은 축구 시합에 의해 미친 듯이 광분하는가?" 운동 경기의 이런 강렬함과 흡입력은 생물학적 분석을 통해 그 설명을 찾을 수는 없다. 그러나 이러한 강렬함과 흡입력은 운동 경기의 본질적인 미적 특성과 관련돼있다.

04 모범답안 ①

어휘

address ~을 다루다; 처리하다
dementia 치매
deterioration 악화, (가치의) 하락, 저하; 퇴보, 의미의 하락
disorder 엉망, 어수선함, 난동, (신체 기능의) 장애
hold off 시작하지 않다, 미루다(연기하다)
mask 감추다
neurological 신경의; 신경학의

한글번역

"사용하거나, 잃거나"는 의사들이 노년기에 치매로부터 뇌를 보호하고 싶어 하는 사람들에게 해왔던 말이다. 인생에 걸쳐서 신경회로를 더 활발하게 유지할수록, 당신의 뇌는 치매나 알츠하이머병을 앓게 될 확률이 줄어들게 된다. 아니, 적어도, 이것이 의사들의 생각이다.

65세 이상의 정신적으로 건강한 1,157명의 지원자들을 대상으로 한 새로운 연구에서, 연구원들은 12년의 관찰 결과 독서나 카드 게임 등으로 인해 지적으로 자극을 받아온 자들이 인지적 감퇴 증세를 보일 확률이 적었고, 그들은 또한 한번 치매 진단을 받은 이후 정신적 자극과 관련된 활동을 하지 않은 사람들에 비해 상당히 더 빠르게 정신 황폐를 보였다는 것을 발견했다.

이것은 이러한 활동이 뇌로 하여금 치매와 관련한 초기의 생체적 변화를 보상하게 해주고 그 질병의 경과를 감춰줄지도 모르기 때문이라고 과학자들은 말한다. 이러한 연구 결과들은 뇌 운동이 신경 질환의 증상을 한동안 미뤄줄 수는 있지만, 그 질환의 근본적 원인을 처리하지는 못한다는 것을 보여준다.

05 모범답안 ④

어휘

constitute ~이 되는 것으로 여겨지다; 구성하다
protrusion 돌출, 돌출부
detract 주의를 딴 데로 돌리다, (가치·중요성·명성 등을) 감하다, 손상시키다, 비방하다
freak 기이한 것
impress 깊은 인상을 주다, 감명을 주다
ornamentation 장식
ornamented (글자체가) 화려한, 장식체의

한글번역

동물의 왕국에서 수컷이 같은 종의 암컷을 유혹하기 위해 밝은 빛의 깃털 같은 장식물을 가지고 있는 것은 공통적이지만, 일본 후지산 조림 지역에서 새롭게 발견된 춤추는 파리는 성적 과시행동의 게임에 새로운 정보를 추가한다. 권투장갑처럼 튀어나온 모양의 이 장식은 어떤 수컷엔 두 다리 모두에 달려 있고 어떤 수컷엔 아예 달려 있지 않으며, 대다수는 한쪽의 다리에만 달려 있다.

연구원들은 그들의 이와 같은 발견을 '바이올로지 레터스'라는 저널에서 설명했다. "저는 왜 그 장식들이 비대칭인지 설명하기 위해 노력합니다. 그것은 암컷들을 유혹하기 위해 한 다리를 공중으로 든다는 의미일 수도 있습니다."라고 그 연구의 저자 중 한 명인, 애드리언 플랜트가 말했다. 수집된 33마리의 수컷 파리 중에 14마리는 하나의 다리에만 장식물이 달려 있었고, 나머지는 두 개이거나 아예 달려 있지 않았다. 많은 파리의 장식물이 불균형하다는 사실로 하여금 연구원들은 이 현상이 단순히 자연에서 발생하는 기이한 일만은 아니라는 것을 믿게 됐다.

분명해보이는 것은, 그 권투장갑이 그 곤충이 효율적으로 날 수 있는 능력을 손상시킨다는 것이며, 이것은 그 권투장갑의 기능이 암컷을 유혹하기 위한 것임을 암시한다. 더 많은 연구가 필요하겠지만, 그 장갑들은 먹이를 잡아서 그들이 잡은 것을 미래의 암컷 파트너에게 과시하기 위한 실크 분비선을 가지고 있을 수도 있다.

06 모범답안 ⑤

어휘

analogous 유사한
incomprehensible 이해할 수 없는
unintelligible 이해할 수 없는
distinct 확실한; 서로 다른
monolithic 획일적인; 단일체의; 하나의 암석으로 된

한글번역

왜 우리는 영어를 마치 하나의, 획일적인 언어인 것처럼 보는 것인가? 이 질문에 대한 답은 두 언어의 화자들이 서로 이해할 수 있는지 없는지에 기본적으로 기초한다. 상호 명료성이란 기준은 보통 다른 두 개 언어 사이를 구분하기 위해 사용된다. 만약 상호 명료성이 없다면, 두 개의 다른 언어를 사용하는 화자들이 있는 것이다. 상호 명료성에 대해 논하는 동안, 다르지만 역사적으로는 관련된 언어들의 화자들을 의미하는 일방향적 명료성을 고려해야 한다. 예를 들면, 스페인어를 모르는 브라질계 포르투갈인들은 이웃 나라에서 사용되는 스페인어의 형태를 종종 이해할 수 있다. 그러나 유사한 스페인어 화자들은 포르투갈어가 대체로 이해하기 어렵다고 생각한다. 비록 한 그룹의 화자들이 다른 그룹을 이해할 수 있다고 하더라도, 그 두 번째 그룹도 이 그룹을 이해할 수 있지 않는 한, 같은 언어를 말한다고 할 수 없다. 그러므로 상호 명료성이라는 개념은 두 언어가 같은 언어라고 규정짓는 데 매우 중요하다.

그러나, 상호 명료성이라는 개념을 적용하는 것은 사회적, 정치적 요소에 의해 상당히 복잡해질 수 있다는 것을 주목하라. 예를 들어, 중국에서는 북쪽의 북경 사투리(북경어라고도 알려져 있는) 화자들이 남쪽의 광둥어를 사용하는 중국인들의 말을 이해하지 못하고, 그 반대로도 그렇다. 이러한 이유로, 언어학자들은 북경어와 광둥어를 서로 다른 언어라고 꼬리표를 붙일지도 모른다.

2011학년도 2차

모범답안 Minsu has demonstrated admirable and highly-competitive achievement in terms of score academic achievement. He is ranked in the top 20 percent of our student body in terms of his overall GPA. Notably, for World History, he performed among the top 5%. In addition, with regard to performance in English courses, he was in the top 3%, with excellent speaking ability. His excellent understanding of the outside world and language ability make him highly fit for this short cultural exchange program.

In addition, outside of the normal course load, Minsu has been pursuing Pansori, which is traditional Korean monologue opera. For over five years now he has been involved in the study and practice of Pansori. In fact, last year, in April, he performed live on campus. Suggesting my humble opinion, you will get a great asset to introduce traditional Korean culture to Australian students by choosing Minsu in your program.

It is also important to note his stellar personal qualities as well. I have to say that I've always found Minsu to be outgoing with those around him. He has also proven himself assertive in terms of taking the lead among his peers. I have no doubt that Minsu will get the most out of this cultural exchange program using his active and outgoing personality.

In summation, Minsu is a stellar student and the ideal candidate for consideration in your cultural exchange program. As addressed above, he has performed well, kept reaching beyond his studies and proven himself a positive student to communicate with.

2010학년도 1차

01 모범답안 ①

어휘

achieve 성취하다
dilettante 호사가
fall short of A A가 부족한
increasingly 점점
physical 신체적
reflect 반영하다
commitment 헌신
engage 참여하다
improve 향상시키다
performance 수행; 성취
professional 전문적인
warp 왜곡하다

한글번역

신체적 그리고 정신적 활동에 헌신하는 수준에 대한 다소 왜곡된 태도를 반영하는 두 가지 단어가 있다. 그 용어들은 '아마추어'와 '딜레탕트(호사가)'이다. 오늘날 이 용어들을 붙이는 것은 다소 경멸스러운 것이 됐다. 아마추어와 딜레탕트는 기준치에 아직 미치지 못한 사람, 매우 진지하게 받아들여지지 않은 사람, 수행능력이 전문적 기준에서 떨어지는 사람을 의미한다. 그러나 원래 '아마추어'란 용어는 '사랑하다'라는 뜻의 amare라는 라틴 동사에서 유래돼, 자신이 사랑하는 일을 하는 사람을 의미했다. 마찬가지로 딜레탕트는 라틴어 delectare, '즐거움을 찾다'로부터 유래해 어떤 주어진 활동을 즐기는 사람을 의미했다. 따라서 원래 이러한 단어들의 의미는 성취라기보다는 경험들에 초점이 맞춰져 있다. 이 단어들은 그들이 얼마나 잘 성취했는지에 포커스를 맞추는 대신에, 어떤 일을 함으로써 개개인이 얻는 주관적인 보상을 묘사했다. 그 어떤 것도 이러한 두 단어의 운명만큼 경험의 가치에 대한 우리의 변화하는 태도를 명확하게 설명할 수 없다. 한때는 아마추어 시인과 딜레탕트 과학자가 되기를 소망하는 시기가 있었는데, 이것은 그런 활동에 참여함으로써 인생의 질이 향상된다는 것을 의미했기 때문이다. 그러나 점점 주관적 상태보다는 행동을 가치 있게 여기게 됐고, 경험의 질보다는 성공, 성취, 수행의 질이 더 각광받는 것이 됐다.

02 모범답안 ④

어휘

bacillus infection 세균 감염
classification 분류
drive out ~을 몰아내다
humane 인도적인
superstitious 미신적인
control over ~을 통제하다
demonic possession 귀신 들림
electricity rod(lightening rod) 피뢰침
incantation (마술) 주문
wrath 분노, 노여움

한글번역

사회(공동체)는 (자신들이) 원하는 결과를 생산해내는 분류체계를 사실이라 간주한다. '사실'에 대한 과학적 검증은 사회적 검증과 마찬가지로 상당히 실용적이지만, 차이는 과학적 검증은 원하는 결과가 사회적 검증보다 훨씬 제한적이란 사실이다. 사회(공동체)가 바라는 결과는 비합리적이고, 미신적이고, 이기적이며, 또는 인간적이지만, 과학자들이 바라는 결과는 우리의 분류체계가 예측 가능한 결과를 만들어내는 것뿐이다. 분류는 분류된 대상이나 사건에 대한 우리들의 태도나 행동을 결정한다. 번개가 '신의 분노의 증거'라 분류됐을 땐, 번개를 맞지 않기 위해 우리가 취해야 할 행동양식은 기도밖에는 없게 된다. 하지만 벤자민 프랭클린이 번개를 '전기'라 분류한 이후로 번개를 컨트롤하는 조치는 피뢰침의 발명에 의해 해결됐다. 몇몇 육체적 질병은 예전엔 '악령에 사로잡힌' 것으로 분류됐기에, 따라서 여기에 적합한 조치는 우리가 생각할 수 있는 모든 주문을 통해서 악령을 몰아내는 것이었다. 그 결과는 불확실한 것이었다. 하지만, 그런 질병이 '세균 감염'으로 분류됐을 때, 더욱 예측 가능한 결과를 만들어내는 행동조치가 제안됐다. 과학은 가장 일반적으로 유용한 분류체계만을 추구한다: 더욱 유용한 분류가 나올 때까지는, 당분간 과학은 가장 일반적으로 유용한 그 분류체계를 '사실'로 간주한다.

03 모범답안 ②

어휘

astronomical 천문학적인
catalyst 촉매, 기폭제
genetic screening 유전자 스크리닝(개인의 유전적 질병의 발견과 예방을 위한 조사)
monopoly 독점
patent 특허; 특허를 얻다
premature 조숙한
pursuit 추구
recoup 보상하다, 변상하다

한글번역

컴퓨터 기술에 대한 기업의 추구처럼, 이익에 고무된 생명공학은 여러 우려를 만든다. 첫 번째 우려는, 오직 부자만이 유전자 검사나 복제 장기 등과 같은 사람의 생명을 살릴 수 있는 기술에 접근할 수 있다는 점이다. 기업들이 인간의 생명을 특허내고 있는 것을 고려하면, 그런 두려움은 정당화된다. 예를 들어, 비만 유전자, 조숙한 노화 유전자와 유방암 유전자는 이미 특허가 됐다. 이들 특허는 유전자 검사와 처방을 위한 천문학적인 환자 비용을 야기시킬 수 있는 유전자 독점으로 귀착된다. 생명공학 산업은 그와 같은 특허가 보다 더 나아간 혁신을 이끌어내는 연구 비용을 메우는 유일한 방법이라고 주장한다. 기술의 상업화는 품질 관리라는 문제와, 협조적인 노력보다는 오히려 발견들을 철저히 비밀에 부치려는 경향성을 포함한 여러 다른 우려들을 일으킨다. 게다가, 기업의 개입은 연구원들이 연방 자금 조달에 점점 더 적게 의존하기 때문에 정부 통제를 더욱 어렵게 했다. 마지막으로, 이익이 몇 가지 과학적인 발견을 위한 촉매로 작동하는 것이 거의 확실할지라도, 상업적으로 돈이 덜 되기는 하지만 마찬가지로 중요한 다른 프로젝트는 묵살될 가능성이 있다.

04 모범답안 ①

어휘

cognitive 인식의
distress 괴로움; 괴롭히다, 고통스럽게 하다
eliminate 제거하다
intensive 집중적인
kindergarten 유치원
predictor 예측 변수
struggle 투쟁하다, 몸부림치다
contend 주장하다
dominate 지배하다
explore 탐구하다
intervention (타국의 내정 등에 대한) 개입, (내정) 간섭
measure 측정하다
social skill 사회성
unconstrained 구속받지 않은

한글번역

지난 십여 년 동안, 유아교육 분야에서 중점적인 논쟁이 두 가지 그룹 사이에서 벌어졌는데, 그 하나는 유아원이나 유치원이 선행 학습 접근방식을 택해야 한다는 입장이고, 다른 하나는 그렇게 이른 나이의 학교의 초점은 학습을 준비시키는 것이 아니라, 아이들이 세계를 탐험하고, 사회성을 배우며, 자유롭고 구속받지 않은 즐거움을 누리는 것이라는 입장이다. 선행 학습 접근방식 진영은 유치원 초기의 아이들 능력이 이후의 성공에 대한 강력한 예측 지표라는 것을 보여준 연구를 근거로 1990년대 후반에 이 논쟁을 주도했다. 만약 한 어린이가 다른 동료들보다 인지능력이 많이 뒤처진 채로 5번째 생일을 맞이한다면, 그 어린이는 거의 다른 동료들을 따라잡지 못할 것임을 이 연구가 보여줬다. 이 연구에서 얻은 좋은 소식은 만약 당신이 힘겹게 공부하는 어린이들을 유아원이나 유치원에서의 집중적인 독해나 수학 보충수업들에 노출시킨다면, 아이들의 정신이 여전히 가장 유연한 상태에 있을 때, 다른 학생들과의 격차를 큰 폭으로 줄이거나 심지어 제거할 수도 있다는 사실이다. 이리하여 많은 학자들과 정책 입안자들에게 정답은 분명했다. 즉, 그 초창기의 시기를 운동장에서 놀면서 시간을 낭비할 겨를이 없다는 것이다. 하지만 더 최근에 유치원이 압박과 고통의 장소가 아닌 기쁨의 정원이 돼야 한다고 믿는 교육자들과 유아심리학자들 사이에서 선행 학습 접근법에 반대하는 반발이 거세지고 있다.

05 모범답안 ⑤

어휘

attribute to A (결과를 A로) 돌리다
canvas 화폭(화폭 등을 만드는 데 쓰이는 질긴 천)
disputed 논란이 된
high-resolution 고해상도의, 고화질의
provenance 기원, 출처
release 발표하다
authentication (진품임을) 입증; 인증
claim 주장하다
evidence 증거
prolific 다작하는
rediscover 재발견하다
revelation 폭로(된 사실)

한글번역

레오나르도 다 빈치는 훨씬 더 다작한 셈이 되었다. 지난달에 나온 한 분석은 한때 19세기 독일 예술가의 것으로 추정되던 작은 초상화가 실제로는 1500년 무렵 이탈리아의 장인에 의해 그려졌다고 주장했다. 그 놀라운 폭로는 '잃어버린' 작품들이 예술 감정을 통해 재발견됐던 일련의 사례들 중에 가장 최근의 것일 뿐이다. 그러나 전문가들은 어떻게 한 예술 작품이 특정 화가의 것이라고 그렇게 확신할 수 있는 것일까?

다 빈치 그림의 경우, 감정은 물리적인 증거에 기초했다. 고해상도 다중스펙트럼 카메라를 이용해서, 피터 폴 비로라는 캐나다 법정의 예술 전문가는 화폭 좌측에 희미한 지문을 발견할 수 있었다. 그 지문은 바티칸시에 걸려 있는 다 빈치의 것으로 알려진 그림에 있는 지문과 일치했다. 지문과 같은 강력한 법적 증거 없이는, 감정 과정은 미궁으로 빠진다. 과거에는 미술 작품이 붓놀림 형태나 예술가의 자필 서명의 분석을 포함한 다양한 요소들의 종합을 통해 입증되었다. 그림의 기원이나 그 소유권의 역사 또한 중요하다. 수 세기에 걸쳐 초상화의 소유권이 어디에서 어디로 옮겨갔는지 추적하는 일은 쉬운 일이 아니며, 그것은 작품의 적법성에 무게를 실어주기도 한다.

예술 작품 감정의 어려움을 강조하는 최근의 한 명백한 경우는 중고품 할인매장에서 전 트럭 운전사에 의해 5달러에 구매된 논란의 잭슨 폴록 그림이다. 비로 역시 캔버스 위의 부분적인 지문을 폴록에 의해 사용된 페인트와 대조하면서 그 사건에 연관됐다. 법의학적인 증거에도 불구하고, 미술 협회는 그 그림의 이전 소유자에 대한 기록이 없다는 이유로 그 작품을 입증하는 것을 꺼려왔다.

06 모범답안 ⑤

어휘

perception 지각　　serve as a foil to ~의 조연 역할을 하다

한글번역

20세기 전반기에, 게슈탈트 심리학은 행동주의의 조연 역할을 했다.

[D] 분자행동보다는 몰행동을 연구해야 한다고 주장하면서, 게슈탈트 심리학자들은 학습에서의 지각에 관심을 기울였다. (그들의 주장에 따르면) 구체적으로, 유기체들은 특정한 자극보다는 감각 전체에 반응하며, 감각환경의 (전체적) 조직이 (각각의) 유기체의 지각에 영향을 미친다.

[C] 시지각에 영향을 미치는 요인들을 가리키는 지각 체제화의 법칙 이외에도, 게슈탈트 심리학은 통찰이라는 개념을 도입했다.

[B] 초기 연구들에서는, 동물과 인간 연구 대상자들에게 새로운 해결책을 요구하는 질문(문제)들이 제시됐다. (어떤) 상황을 지각적으로 재구조화하는 것이 해결책을 만들어냈다. 현재, 통찰은 무의식적인 과정을 통해 상황이나 문제의 핵심을 분명하게 보는 것으로 표현된다. 해결책의 돌연함은 하나의 특징으로서 때때로 언급되기도 한다.

[A] 하지만, 연구는 아이디어를 생산하기 위해 문제에 대한 준비 작업과 잠복기, 그 이후엔 노력과 또 다른 활동들의 중요성을 시사한다.

2010학년도 2차

모범답안 The narrator tells the reader that sloppy people have higher ethical standards than neat people. Sloppy people are so upright and concerned with such high and perfect standards that they are impossible to realize. Also, the sloppy so attentively plan for everything that things are hard to be accomplished. Their desks and wardrobes are meant to be cleaned and the family scrapbooks will be made someday; however, the unfortunate result is it is unlikely to be fulfilled soon and things are the same. On the other hand, neat people are lazy and mean and insensitively throw away things around them simply to make a clean result. They only believe in use values ignoring the importance of process and caring.

어휘

bulldoze 불도저로 밀다, 강력히 밀고나가다
cavalier 무신경한
excavation 발굴
mending 수선
métier 직업, 전문 분야
part with ~을 주다
rectitude 정직
sloppy 엉성한, 대충의, 헐렁한
tackle 씨름하다, 맞서다, 달려들다
toy with (재미 삼아) ~을 잠시 생각해보다
bum 보잘 것 없는 사람
clod 돌머리
mean 인색한
meticulously 꼼꼼하게
Never-Never land 꿈의 낙원
prom (고등학교 졸업 등의) 무도회
scrupulously 용의주도하게
stupendous 거대한, 어마어마한
tentative 잠정적인
wardrobe 옷장

한글번역

나는 마침내 깔끔한 사람과 엉성한 사람의 차이점을 알아냈다. 깔끔한 사람과 엉성한 사람의 구별은 늘 그랬던 것처럼 도덕적인 것이다. 깔끔한 사람은 대충 지내는 사람보다 더 게으르기도 하고, 인색하기도 하다.

엉성한 사람은 보이는 것처럼 실제로 그렇게 엉성하지 않다. 그들의 엉성함은 단지 너무나 도덕적으로 정직한 나머지 발생하는 유감스러운 결과이다. 엉성한 사람은 너무 거대하고 너무 완벽해 이 세상이나 다음 세상에서는 성취될 수 없는 치밀한 계획인 하늘의 이상을 마음속에 지니고 있다.

엉성한 사람은 모든 좋은 것들이 존재하는 꿈의 나라에 살고 있다. 언젠가라는 말은 그들의 전문 분야이다. 언젠가 그들은 집에 있는 모든 책들을 알파벳 순서로 정리하고, 옷을 분류할 것이다. 언젠가 엉성한 사람들은 옷장을 살피고, 잠정적인 수선을 위해 특정 옷에 표시하며, 어떤 옷들은 비슷한 체격의 친척에게 전달해줄 것이다. 언젠가 엉성한 사람들은 신문을 오려낸 것, 엽서, 머리카락 뭉치, 졸업 무도회에서 받은 꽃 장식을 말린 것으로 가족 스크랩북을 만들 것이다. 언젠가 간식을 파는 가게에서 커피를 사고 받은 영수증을 포함해 책상 위에 있는 모든 것을 보관하고자 정리할 것이다. 언젠가 그들은 자리에 앉아 지난 호의 '더 뉴요커'를 모두 읽을 것이다.

엉성한 사람들은 차마 어떠한 것을 내어줄 수 없다. 그들은 모든 사소한 것에 집중하는 것을 매우 좋아한다. 엉성한 사람들이 그들이 책상 표면에 맞설 것이라고 말한다면, 그들은 정말로 그것을 의미한다. 종이는 뒤집어지지 않을 것이고, 고무 밴드는 상자에서 꺼내지지 않을 것이다. 발굴하는 데만 4시간 또는 2주가 걸리는데, 책상은 정말로 이전과 똑같다. 왜냐하면 우선 엉성한 사람들은 꼼꼼하게 새로운 표제로 새로운 종이 더미를 만들어내고 용의주도하게 오래된 책 카탈로그를 버리기 전에 그것을 읽기 위해 청소를 멈추기 때문이다. 깔끔한 사람들은 책상을 단지 불도저로 밀고 나간다.

깔끔한 사람은 마음속으로는 보잘것없는 사람이고 돌머리이다. 깔끔한 사람은 가족 가보를 포함해, 소유에 있어서 무신경하다. 모든 것은 그들에게 먼지를 빨아들이는 또 하나의 것일 뿐이다. 어떤 것이 먼지를 모으기만 한다면, 그것은 없어져야 하는 것이고 그것으로 끝이다. 깔끔한 사람은 단지 잡동사니를 치우기 위해 어린 아이들을 집 밖으로 내보내는 건 어떨까 하는 생각도 잠시 해볼 것이다.

깔끔 떠는 사람들은 과정에 대해서는 신경 쓰지 않는다. 그들은 결과만 좋아한다. 깔끔한 사람이 원하는 것은 모든 것을 끝내버려서 그들이 앉을 수 있고 텔레비전으로 레슬링 경기를 보는 것이다. 깔끔한 사람들은 두 개의 불변의 원칙으로 작동한다. 첫 번째는 어떤 물건이라도 두 번 쓰지 않는다는 것이고, 두 번째는 모든 것을 버려버린다는 것이다.

깔끔한 사람의 집에 있는 지저분한 것이라고는 오직 쓰레기통뿐이다. 어떠한 물건이 깔끔 떠는 사람의 손에 닿자마자, 그는 그것을 볼 것이고, 즉시 이것을 사용할 수 있을지 아닐지 결정한 후에, 사용할 수 없는 것이라고 판단하면 바로 쓰레기통에 버려버릴 것이다.

2009학년도 1차

01 모범답안 ⑤

어휘

burgeoning (인구 등이) 급증하는; 급성장하는
medium 수단
Protestant (개)신교도
flourish 번창하다
monolingual 하나의 언어(단일어)를 사용하는
Reformation 종교개혁

한글번역

16세기까지 오랜 시간 동안, 영어는 라틴어보다 열등하며, 추상적이고 복합적인 사상들을 표현하기에 적합하지 않다고 여겨졌다. 영어가 인정받는 표현 수단으로 자리 잡는 데는 시간이 걸렸다. 영어는 규칙적이고 일관적인 철자 시스템을 구축할 필요가 있었고, 라틴어의 종말과 과학의 발전, 그리고 급성장하는 제국의 도처에 새로운 발견들에 의해 급증하는 수요를 충족하기 위해 어휘도 확장해야 했다. 16세기 이후로부터 계속 영어는 번성했다. 많은 양의 고전 작품들이 영어로 번역됐다. 그 책들은 단일어를 사용하는 중산층과 비 학문 영역에서도 이용 가능해졌다. 종교 개혁 시기에 교회의 라틴어 사용을 반대한 윌리엄 위클리프의 운동은 영어가 모든 영역에 걸쳐 통용되는 의사소통 수단으로 자리 잡는 데 큰 도움을 줬다. 또한, 인쇄기의 광범위한 사용으로, 영어로 된 책들이 더 잘 팔린다는 사실이 명백해졌고, 그리하여 시장의 힘(이 시기에 적용될 수 있는 현대적 용어)이 영어의 지위를 강화하는 데 많은 역할을 했다.

02 모범답안 ①

어휘

aphoristic 경구적인, 금언적인
be desirous of ~을 바라다, 갈망하다
voyeurism (for) (~을 향한) 관음증
attraction 끌림
inanimate 생명이 없는

한글번역

인류가 갑자기 물질주의적으로 변한 것은 아니다. 우리는 항상 물질들을 소망해왔다. 우린 단지 매우 최근까지는 많은 물질들을 소유하지 못했을 뿐이며 지금부터 몇 세대 안에 우리는 점점 적고 더 적은 물질을 소유하는 상황으로 다시 돌아갈지도 모른다. 하지만, 여전히 물질들이 남아 있는 동안은, 우리는 물건을 사는 것을 즐기며, 격언적인 "쇼핑하기 위해 태어나다," "지쳐 쓰러질 때까지 쇼핑하다" 혹은 "상황이 어려워지면, 강인한 사람들은 쇼핑하러 간다."에 반영된 유머와 진실 모두를 본다. 도시의 거리이든 쇼핑몰의 내부이든, 백화점 창문은 마술에 의해 나타나지 않았다. 우리는 그 너머로 다른 세상을 보는 것을 즐긴다. 이것은 자본가들을 향한 관음증이다. 이 생명 없는 것에 대한 끌림은 전 세계적으로 발생한다. 사람들이 물질을 원했기 때문에 베를린 장벽이 무너졌고, 그들은 물질에 의해 세워진 문화를 원했다. 중국이 문을 개방한 이유는 (세계에) 나오고 싶었기 때문이 아니라 (물질들을) 안으로 들이고 싶어서였다. 우리의 물질에 대한 사랑은 산업혁명의 원동력이었지, 그 결과물이 아니었다.

03 모범답안 ⑤

어휘

activate 촉진하다, 활성화시키다
healing effect 치료 효과
pharmacological 약학적, 약물의
remedy 치료법
acupuncture 침술
initiate 시작하다
property 특성

한글번역

오랜 역사에 걸쳐 일상적인 치료법으로 아시아에서 사용돼 온 침술은 이제 일반 대중과는 거리가 멀게 됐다. 침술이 널리 알려지지 못했던 주 요인은 직접적인 치료 효과를 보이지 않았기 때문이다. 침술에 쓰이는 침은 약물적 특성이 없는 그저 얇은 스테인리스 철 조각에 불과하다. 그러나 이런 식으로 침술을 분석하는 것으로는 침의 치료 효과를 설명할 수 없다. 동양 의학의 관점에서는, 침술에 쓰이는 침 그 자체는 치료를 하지 못한다. 침은 단지 신체의 치료 과정을 활성화시켜주는 열쇠로 작용하는 것이다. 뇌는 몸의 모든 곳에 걸쳐 있는 감각을 감지하는 부분들과 연결돼있는데 이 감각 감지 부분들이 자연스러운 치료 과정을 이끌어준다. 적절한 신호가 어떤 특정 장소에 도달하면 뇌는 주로 호르몬에 의해 조절되는 치료 메커니즘을 시행한다. 이 감각을 감지하는 부분의 위치가 반응 지점 혹은 침술 지점으로 불린다. 우리 몸에서 그것들은 에너지가 오고 가는 문과 같다. 또한, 그 감각 감지 부분들은 에너지 창고나 분배 지점으로서의 기능을 한다. 침은 단지 순수한 물리적 입력 이상의 역할을 하는 것이다.

04 모범답안 ②

어휘

a ginger cat 적갈색 고양이
vet 수의사(veterinarian)
injection 주사

한글번역

우리의 옆집 이웃 제인은 동물들을 사랑한다. 그녀는 애완용 쥐 한 마리와 두 마리의 햄스터를 가지고 있다. 그녀는 아침에 우리 집 문을 두드렸다. "이거 당신 고양이예요?" 그녀가 물었다. 그녀는 늙고, 말랐으며, 초록색 작은 목걸이를 한 적갈색의 고양이 한 마리를 안고 있었다. "아니요."라고 우리는 대답했다. "우린 얘를 이전에 본 적도 없어요. 왜 그러시죠?"

[B] "난 얘가 건강한 것 같지 않아요." 제인이 말했다. "나는 고양이를 수의사에게 데려갈 거예요." 우리는 그녀의 생각에 동의했다. 그녀는 동물들을 끔찍이 아꼈다. 하지만 우리가 그녀를 저녁에 다시 보았을 때, 그녀는 슬퍼 보였다.

[A] "당신 그 고양이를 알죠?" 제인이 말했다. "초록색 목걸이를 한 연한 적갈색인 고양이요? 글쎄요, 수의사가 말하길 그 고양이는 굉장히 늙고 아프다고 했어요. 그래서 그 의사가 주사를 놓아서 그 고양이를 안락사시켰어요. 그 고양인 지금 하늘나라에 있겠죠. 음, 그 의사가 할 수 있는 일이 뭐가 더 있었겠어요? 우리는 그게 누구 고양이인지도 몰랐다구요."

[D] 토요일에, 제인은 술 한 잔을 마시러 왔다. 길 아래쪽 방향 두 번지 옆의 집으로 이사한 존슨 씨 일가도 함께 왔다. 우리는 지난주 그들을 술자리에 초대했었다.

[C] "새로운 집에서 살 만한가요?" 우리 중 하나가 질문했다. "아, 괜찮아요." 존슨 여사가 남편과 두 아이들을 행복하게 바라보며 대답했다. "하지만 문제가 하나 있어요. 우리 고양이가 사라졌거든요."

05 모범답안 ①

어휘

acrimonious 폭언이 오가는, 험악한
deforestation 삼림 벌채
grassroot 풀뿌리
losing battle 승산 없는 싸움
reckless 무모한, 신중하지 못한; 난폭한
vagary 변화; 변덕
clear (땅을) 개간하다; 쫓아내다
devastate (한 장소나 지역을) 완전히 파괴하다
in protest 항의(의 표시)로
mobilize (사람들을) 동원하다
resign 사임하다

한글번역

초창기부터, 실바는 무분별한 사업 간 이해관계가 브라질 생태계에 끼친 해악을 봤다. 학교에 가는 대신에 어릴 적부터 그녀는 열 명의 동생들을 뒷바라지하기 위해 숲에서 나무로부터 고무 수액을 뽑아내는 일을 했다. 그녀는 불도저들이 그녀의 나무 때문에 찾아와, 열대우림과 나머지 브라질 땅을 잇는 길을 만들기 위해 땅을 개간하는 것을 봤다. 황폐화된 것은 단지 나무들만이 아니었다. 열대우림에 의존해 살아가던 많은 브라질 사람들의 삶 또한 앗아갔다. 그녀는 풀뿌리 기반의 산림 파괴에 대항하는 단체를 설립했다. 그녀는 강력한 이해관계 단체들에 대항하기 위해 고무 채취공 협동조합을 동원했다. 그녀는 이후에 정당으로 들어갔고, 브라질의 최초 고무 채취공 출신 상원의원이 됐다. 포퓰리스트 대통령인 룰라가 2002년 정권을 장악했을 때, 실바는 명백한 환경부 장관 후보였다. 아웃사이더가 입성한 것이다. 브라질 환경부 장관으로서 어떤 수를 써서라도 아마존을 개발하고 싶어 하는 산업, 정치계 지도자들과 승산 없는 싸움을 하는 혹독한 6년 이후에, 실바는 5월에 항의의 의미로 사임했다. 그러나 실바는 환경 보호에 대한 용기의 상징으로 영원히 남아 있다.

2009학년도 2차

모범답안 As a long-standing pillar of most education systems, homework is an important element for students, and helps to encourage self-activation and improving time management. First, in terms of self-activation, homework distinguishes itself from classwork in that the student must rely on their own motivation and problem solving abilities to finish a given set of tasks to complete homework. This helps prepare students for some of the challenges of college or adult work tasks which often require this self-leading ability. Secondly, regarding time management, students need to create their own framework within all school assignments as well as social or personal obligations to get homework finished. Learning to manage one's own schedule in this way is an invaluable ability that should start developing in school.

2009학년도 6월 모의평가

01 모범답안 ①

어휘

conjecture 추측하다
contract 수축하다
dissipate 흩어지다; 사라지다
importunate 성가시게 조르는
invest A with B A에게 B를 부여하다
personality 개성

한글번역

언뜻 처음 볼 때는 경험이 우리를 외적 대상들의 홍수 속에 묻어버리고, 날카롭고 끈질긴 현실로 내리누르고, 행동의 수많은 형태들로 우리를 우리 자신에게서 불러내는 것처럼 보인다. 하지만 생각(심사숙고)이 그러한 대상들에게 작용되기 시작할 때, 그 대상들은 생각의 영향하에 소멸되는데, 그 응집력은 어떤 속임수나 마술처럼 중단된 것처럼 보이며, 각각의 대상은 관찰자의 마음속 색깔, 냄새, 촉감 같은 일단의 인상들 속으로 느슨히 들어간다. 그리고 만약 우리가 언어가 부여한 견고한 대상들의 세계가 아닌, 불안정하고, 깜빡거리고, 일관성 없고, 우리의 의식 속에서 불타오른 뒤 꺼져버리는 인상들의 세계에 대한 생각 속에 계속 머무르게 된다면, 사고는 훨씬 더 축소되게 된다. 관찰의 전 영역은 각 개인의 마음이라는 좁은 방 속으로 쪼그라들기 때문이다. 이미 일단의 인상들로 축소된 경험은 개성이라는 두꺼운 벽에 의해 둘러싸이게 된다. 그런데 어떠한 진정한 목소리도 이 개성을 뚫고 우리에게 도달한 적이 없고, 또는 우리로부터 우리가 오직 존재하지 않는 것이라 추측하는 것으로 도달한 적도 없다. 그러한 인상들 모두 고립된 개개인의 인상이며, 각각의 마음은 세상에 대한 그 자신만의 꿈을 고독한 죄수처럼 간직하고 있다.

02 모범답안 ③

어휘

at hand 당면한
latch onto ~을 꼭 붙잡다
out-of-place 부적절한
plow through 애써서 나아가다
sift through ~을 체로 걸러내다; 꼼꼼하게 살펴 추려내다

한글번역

나이 든 사람들은 칵테일파티에서 만난 사람의 이름을 더 이상 기억하지 못할 때, 자신들의 지능이 감퇴하고 있다고 생각하는 경향이 있다. 그러나 점점 더 많은 수의 연구들은 이러한 가정이 종종 틀렸다고 주장한다. 대신, 연구에 따르면, 나이 든 뇌는 그저 더 많은 데이터를 받아들여, 그 많은 뭉텅이 정보를 체로 걸러내려고 노력하는 중인데, 이것은 종종 장기적으로는 이로운 것이다. (물론) 일부 뇌는 실제로 나이가 들어감에 따라 악화되기도 하는데, 알츠하이머병과 같은 경우가 그렇다. 하지만 나이 든 사람들에게 실제로 일어나는 대부분의 것은 주의 집중의 초점이 점점 넓어지는 것인데, 이것이 이름이나 전화번호 등과 같은 어떤 단순한 한 가지의 사실을 꼭 붙잡고 있는 것을 어렵게 만든다. 이러한 현상들이 절망스럽게 보일지라도, 이것은 종종 유용하다. 산만함은 사실 나쁜 것이 아닐지도 모른다. 이것은 의식 속에서 이용 가능한 정보의 양이 증가하는 것일 수 있다. 예를 들어, 피실험자가 예기치 못한 단어들 또는 구들이 글을 읽는 데 방해하는 글을 읽도록 하는 연구에서, 60세 이상의 성인들은 대학생들보다 더 천천히 글을 읽었다. 그 학생들이 그 부적절한 단어들이 의미하는 것에 상관없이 일정한 속도를 보이며 글을 애써 읽어나가는 반면에, 나이 든 성인들은 그 단어들이 당면한 주제와 연관될 때에는 읽는 속도를 훨씬 더 늦췄다. 이러한 연구는 나이 든 성인들이 단순히 추가적인 정보 앞에서 휘청거리는 것이 아니라 (오히려) 그것을 받아들여 처리한다는 것을 보여준다.

03 모범답안 ③

어휘

cost-benefit analysis 비용편익분석
decision-making 의사결정
description 지표
diminishing marginal utility 한계효용체감

한글번역

경제학자들은 비용편익분석과 한계효용체감이 의사결정의 유용한 지표라는 것에 대해 매우 확신한다. 왜냐하면 다른 종들 또한 이러한 개념들과 일맥상통하게 행동한다는 수많은 증거들이 있기 때문이다.

[B] 과학자들은 새들이 음식을 얻게 되는 버튼을 쪼거나, 쳇바퀴에서 시간을 벌기 위해 다른 버튼을 쪼도록 훈련시킬 수 있다. 만약 과학자들이 보상을 얻기 위해 필요한 클릭의 횟수를 증가시키는 것으로 선택지들 중 하나의 비용을 증가시킨다면, 그 새들은 그 선택지와 관련된 버튼을 많이 클릭하지 않는 식으로 합리적인 반응을 보일 것이다. 그러나 더욱 인상적인 것은 그들은 또한 다른 선택지와 관련된 버튼을 더 많이 클릭하도록 바뀐다는 것이다.

[C] 그 새들은 지쳐버리기 전에 그들이 할 수 있는 클릭의 수가 아주 제한적이라는 사실을 이해하고 있는 것처럼 보이고, 그 새들은 총 효용을 극대화할 수 있도록 두 가지 선택지 사이에서 클릭의 수를 할당한다. 결과적으로 선택지의 상대적인 비용과 편익이 변한다면, 그 새들은 반응으로써 자신들의 행동을 상당히 합리적으로 변화시킨다.

[A] 다른 종들은 이러한 한계효용체감의 원리의 영향을 받은 것처럼 보이고, 그들이 최근에 상당히 향유했던 한계효용에는 무관심해졌다. 오죽하면 박테리아조차도 이러한 행동을 보이는 것 같았다. 그래서 인간의 행동에 관한 경제학자들의 모델이 몇몇 유의미한 요소들을 무시하는 것처럼 보일지도 모르지만, 그 모델들은 몇몇 매우 근본적이고 보편적인 행동들을 설명해낸다.

04 모범답안 ③

어휘

cut channel 수로를 개통시키다
give birth to ~을 낳다
majestic 위풍당당한
owe debt to ~에게 빚을 지다
reminder 상기시키는 것
sap 수액
seedling 묘목
slip through ~을 지나가다(통과시키다)(= pass through)
stream 줄을 지어 이동하다; 흘러나오다(들어오다)
trap 구멍을 뚫어 ~의 즙을 받다; 수도꼭지

한글번역

싱가포르 사람들이 그들의 149년 된 식물원에 진 빚은 생태학적인 것만큼이나 경제적인 것이다. 1888년에, 기이하지만 열성적인 정원사였던 니콜라스 리들리는 런던에서 보내진 묘목에서 자란 여러 그루의 고무나무 껍질에 수로를 개통시켰다. 그는 구멍을 뚫어 수액을 받았고, 이것이 그 당시 영국 식민지였던 싱가포르의 고무 산업을 탄생시켰다. 다음 반세기 동안, 고무는 향신료 무역에 의해 지배돼 왔던 생기 없던 싱가포르의 경제를 완전히 바꿨다. 싱가포르는 자동차의 출현과 타이어에 대한 끝없는 요구와 함께 호황을 누렸다.

그 도시국가는 그 이후 뒤를 돌아보지 않았다. 요즘 싱가포르 시민들이 가볍게 산책할 때, 많은 시민들은 63헥타르의 식물원이 싱가포르에서 가볍게 산책하기에 가장 좋은 장소 중 하나라고 여긴다. 현대적 편의시설들은 아주 풍부하다. 예를 들면 모든 나무, 관목 그리고 허브는 현재 자세하게 구분돼있고, 90명의 구성원들의 노력과 넉넉한 580만 달러의 연간 예산 덕분에 친환경적인 야외 화장실은 아주 깔끔하다. 매년 그 정원을 찾아오는 3백만 명 가량 되는 방문자들에게는, 이 정원의 10개의 문 중 하나로 통과하는 것은 마치 더 야생적이었던 과거로 들어가는 것과 같다. 어떠한 박물관이나 도서관보다도, 위풍당당한 나무나 야자수, 그리고 꽃들은 싱가포르가 한때 어떠한 곳이었는지를 상기시켜준다.

05 모범답안 ④

어휘

averse (to) ~을 싫어하는
defined 이해하기 쉬운; 구체적인
editorialize (사실을 보도하지 않고) 사견을 표하다; 사설을 쓰다
never fail to ~하는 데 실패하지 않다
soar into 날아(솟아)오르다
speaker 연사

한글번역

당신이 경험과 연구를 통해 말할 권리를 얻은 것에 대해 연설하라. 이러한 연사는 청중을 집중하게 하는 데 있어 결코 실패하지 않는다. 나는 경험으로부터 연사들이 이런 관점을 쉽게 받아들이려 하지 않는다는 것을 안다. 연사들은 개인적 경험은 너무 사소하고 제한적이어서 사용하지 않으려 한다. 그들은 오히려 일반적인 생각과 철학적 원리들의 영역으로 솟구친다. 운이 없게도 그곳은 산소가 너무 희박해서 평범한 사람은 숨 쉴 수 없는 곳이다. 그들은 우리가 뉴스를 갈망할 때 사설을 준다. 우리 중 그 누구도, 사설을 쓸 수 있는 권리가 있는 사람, 즉 신문의 편집인이나 발행인에 의한 사설을 듣는 것을 싫어하지 않는다. 몇 년 전 나는 수업에서 청중의 주의를 사로잡는 주제들에 대한 조사를 했다. (그 조사를 통해) 나는 다음과 같은 것을 알게 됐다. 청중들에 의해 가장 괜찮다고 인정받은 주제들은 청중들의 자신의 배경지식 분야와 관련이 있는 구체적인 것이었다는 것을. 가족, 어린 시절의 기억, 학창시절을 다루는 주제들은 언제나 주목을 얻는다. 왜냐하면 우리 대부분은 다른 사람들이 자라면서, 그들이 부딪힌 장애와 그 장애를 극복하는 방법에 관심이 있기 때문이다. 요점은 이것이다. 삶이 당신에게 가르친 것을 말하라, 그러면 나는 당신의 헌신적인 청자가 될 것이다.

06 모범답안 ⑤

어휘

abstraction 추상
inhabit ~에 거주하다
sweep out (미끄러지듯) 움직이다; 휩쓸고 지나가다
admonish 강하게 충고하다; 책망하다
luminescent 발광하는

한글번역

마리아 테레지아에 대한 피카소의 추상을 이해하는 데 중요한 핵심은 추상들이 전체를 재현하는 것이 아니라 한두 가지의 덜 명백한 특징들을 재현한다는 것을 깨닫는 것이다. 피카소는 그의 모델이 아니라 그녀가 살고 있는 공간에 그의 관심을 집중하기로 했다. 이 그림을 해석하는 데 있어 다른 대부분의 모델들과 다르게 마리아 테레지아가 움직이고 있었다는 것을 인지하는 것은 중요하다. 그녀의 뜨개질 바늘은 앞뒤로, 안팎으로 움직이고 있었다. 그래서 피카소는 그녀의 머리, 손, 팔꿈치, 어깨 그리고 몸이 쓸고 있는 곡선들을 그것들이 공간속에서 움직였던 대로 그렸다. 그것은 마치 그가 그녀가 움직일 때마다 공기 중에 흔적을 남기는 발광 표시들을 붙여놓은 것 같다. 그 결과는 복잡한 그림이다. 피카소는 만일 자신이 원했었다면 그녀를 실제적으로 그릴 수 있었음을 피카소 자신과 모델들에 대한 실제적인 묘사를 통해서 우리에게 말해준다. 그는 그러지 않았다. 피카소의 초상은 마리아 테레지아에게는 또 다른 실제가 있다고 말한다. 그것은 (눈에 보이는) 원래의 실제와 마찬가지로 흥미롭고, 심지어 그것보다 더 의미심장하게도 예상을 벗어나는 것이다. 피카소는 우리에게 강력히 충고한다. 우리는 보고 있지만(그냥 눈으로만 보는 것), 보고 있는 게(사물의 본질을 인식하며) 아니라고. 분명한 것들 뒤에 숨겨져있는 놀라운 특징들을 찾아라. 눈이 아닌 마음으로 보라!

Chapter 03

2008~1997학년도 기출문제

본책 p.350

2008학년도 서울 · 인천

01 모범답안

• 갈등 : Some people want the factory to come in town which would provide new jobs while others are opposed to the opinion because it would ruin the enviornment.

• 시사점 : There can be some solutions which satisfy the needs of both (conflicting) parties.

어휘

chipping 조각, 단편
instantly 즉각, 즉시
chop (음식 재료를 토막으로) 썰다, (장작 같은 것을) 패다
profitable 수익성이 있는

한글번역

크고 오래된 숲 가장자리에 있는 한 작은 마을은 많은 어려움을 마주하고 있었다. 그 마을의 주된 산업인 탄광업이 더 이상 이윤을 남기지 못하고 문을 닫았기 때문이다. 많은 마을 사람들은 직장을 잃었고 새로운 일을 찾지 못했다. 어느 날, 한 목재 칩 공장이 마을에 들어섰다. 그들은 그곳에서 공장을 개업하고 싶어 했다. 그들은 숲에서 나무를 베어 그 나무들을 목재 칩으로 만드는 공장으로 운송할 계획이었다. 이 회사는 이 새로운 산업에 의해 4천 개 이상의 일자리를 창출할 것이라고 언급했다. 순식간에 그 마을은 의견이 나뉘었다. 한 그룹은 만약 그 회사의 사업 제안을 받아들이지 않는다면 일자리가 없을 것이고 이 마을은 사라질 것이라고 주장하는 사람들이었다. 다른 그룹 사람들은 오래된 숲을 벌목하는 것은 그릇된 일이고 환경은 그로 인해 회복될 수 없는 손상을 겪게 될 것이라고 주장했다. 마을 사람들이 마주하기에 이것은 너무 끔찍한 상황이었다. 마을이 살아남게 된다면, 그 마을 중 가장 아름다운 곳인 숲은 파괴될 수밖에 없다. 하지만, 그 숲이 보존된다면, 이 마을은 산업없이 소멸할 것이다. 마침내, 마을에 있는 한 무리의 사람들은 세 번째 가능한 대안이 있다고 결단했는데 바로 관광업이었다. 그들은 여행객들 무리를 숲으로 안내해 그 아름다운 장소의 역사를 설명하는 사업을 개시했다. 그 마을은 매우 유명한 여행 장소가 됐고 곧이어 많은 일자리가 창출됐다.

02 모범답안

• 입장 1 : unique kind of enculturation (Different culture shapes different types of emotions.)

• 입장 2 : Emotions are instinctive resulting from universal biological processes.

• 입장 3 : Humans have both the cross-cultural and culture-specific emotions.

어휘

anthropologist 인류학자
conduct (특정한 활동을) 하다
personality 개성
predominant 우세한
psychological 심리적인
argue 논쟁하다
enculturation 문화화, 문화 적응
perspective 관점
process 과정
take A into account A를 고려하다

한글번역

각 문화는 고유하며 다양한 사회의 사람들은 각기 다른 성격과, 그 결과로 다른 유형의 감정을 지니게 된다고 주장한 베네딕트와 미드의 초기 연구 이후로, 심리 인류학자들은 감정에 대한 주제를 연구해왔다. 이러한 다양한 감정들은 개개인의 성격을 형성해 온 독특한 종류의 문화화의 결과이다. 그들의 관점에서, 문화화 과정은 서로 다른 사회 사이에서 각기 다른 감정들을 생성해내는 데 있어서 지배적이다. 다시 말해서, 문화가 사람들이 어떻게 사고하고 행동하는지 뿐만 아니라 그들이 감정적으로 어떻게 느끼는지도 결정한다는 것이다.

다른 초기 심리 인류학자들은 전 세계에 걸쳐 비슷한 정서적 발달과 감정을 생산해내는 보편적인 생물학적 처리 과정에 관심을 기울였다. 이 관점에 따르면, 감정은 뇌에 있는 생리 작용을 자극하는 본능적인 활동으로 여겨진다. 다시 말해서, 한 개인이 '화'를 느낀다면, 이것은 자동적으로 그 사람의 혈압을 상승시키고 특정 근육의 움직임을 유발한다. 이 관점에서 정서 발달은 보편적인 인간 생물 작용의 일부분이며, 그리하여 감정은 모든 곳에서 똑같이 경험된다.

더욱 최근에, 인류학자들은 인간의 보편적 특성들과 문화적 변화 두 가지 모두를 그들의 정서 관련 연구들 안에 고려하면서 상호주의적 접근법을 강조해왔다. 칼 하이더는 세 개의 인도네시아인 그룹의 인류학적 연구를 근거로 해, 슬픔, 분노, 행복, 그리고 놀람의 네 가지 감정들이 그가 기초 비교문화적 감정이라고 분류한 감정이 되는 경향이 있다고 결론을 내렸다. 하지만, 사랑, 공포, 혐오와 같은 다른 감정들은 사회 간에 다양하게 나타나는 것으로 보인다. 예를 들어, 공포는 죄책감과 섞여 나타나고, 혐오감은 다른 문화 간에 서로 소통되기 어려운 부분이 있다.

03 모범답안 gardeners

어휘

be content to v 기꺼이 ~하다
contemptuously 경멸적으로, 거만하게
invariably 변함없이, 언제나
remain 계속 ~이다
uninterrupted 중단되지 않는; 연속된
boyhood 어린 시절
deprive (물건을) 빼앗다, (권리 등의 행사를) 허용치 않다
not for nothing 충분한 이유가 있는
suburb 교외

한글번역

소년 시절에 나는 런던에 가는 것을 결코 좋아하지 않았고, 윔블던의 교외에 남아 있는 것도 역시 만족스럽지 않았다. 나는 할 수 있는 한 자주, 나의 형제 중 이 사람이나 저 사람과 함께 서리의 전원 지역으로 가는 기차를 탔다. 삼사십 분 뒤에 우리는 마침내 뻥 뚫린 들판과 숲을 볼 수 있었고, 신이 주신 자연의 상쾌한 공기 안에서 숨 쉬고, 우리가 런던 교외에서 박탈당했던 자유를 만끽했다. 내가 그곳에 있는 길에 대해 특별히 알아차렸던 점은 모든 집 앞에 정원이 있었다는 점이다. 그 집들은 시내나 도시 중심지처럼 바로 앞에 길이 놓여 있지 않기 때문에, 길로부터 정원이 있을 공간을 두고 뒤로 물러나 위치해있었다. 나는 두 가지 특별한 점을 알아차렸다. 한 가지는 그 정원들 중 어떤 정원도 같지 않았고, 각각의 정원이 그 자체로 예술 작품이었다는 점이다. 또 다른 한 가지는 각 정원 안에는 하나같이 장미들이 있었다는 점이다. 즉, 그것들은 단순한 정원이 아니라, 더 정확하게 장미 정원이었다. 정말로, 나는 내 자신에게 전원 지역뿐만 아니라 심지어 영국 도시에도 정원, 장미 정원이 있다고 중얼거렸다. 셰익스피어가 그의 국가를 "이 또 다른 에덴 동산, 작은 천국"이라고 부른 데는 이유가 있었다. 영국 국민과 관련해서, 그들은 참으로 하나 된 국민이며, 나폴레옹이 경멸적으로 불렀듯이 상점 주인들이 아니고, 정원사들이다.

04 모범답안 An Indirect Way of Changing Behavior

어휘

algebra 대수학
contrived 억지로 꾸민 듯한; 부자연스러운
encourage 격려하다
live up to one's expectations 기대에 부응하다
statement 성명, 진술, 서술
conscientious 양심적인, 성실한
credibility 신뢰성
inference 추론
sincerity 성실, 정직; 표리가 없음
strain 부담, 중압감

한글번역

많은 사람들은 비판을 할 때 진심어린 칭찬과 그에 뒤따르는 '그러나'라는 단어로 시작해 비판적인 내용으로 끝을 낸다. 예를 들면, 한 아이의 학업에 대한 무심한 태도를 바꾸기 위해 노력할 때, "우린 네가 이번 학기에 성적을 올려서 정말 자랑스럽단다, 조니. 그러나 만약 네가 대수학을 더 열심히 공부했었다면, 그 결과는 더욱 좋았을 거야."라고 우리는 말할지도 모른다. 이런 경우, 조니는 '그러나'라는 말을 듣기 전까진 고무돼있었을 것이다. 그런 이후에, 그는 본래 칭찬의 진설성에 대해 의구심을 가지게 될 것이다. 그에게 그 칭찬은 실패에 대한 비판적인 추론으로 향하는 억지로 꾸며진 도입부일 뿐이었다. 진실성은 한계에 이를 것이고, 우리는 아마 조니의 학업에 대한 태도를 바꾸기 위한 목적들을 달성할 수 없을지도 모른다. 이것은 '그러나'라는 단어를 '그리고'로 바꾸면 쉽게 극복될 수 있다. "우린 네가 이번 학기에 성적을 올렸기 때문에 자랑스럽단다, 조니. 그리고 다음 학기에도 이렇게 성실히 노력을 계속한다면, 너의 대수학 성적도 다른 과목들만큼 오를 수 있을 거야." 이번엔 실패에 대한 추론이 없었으므로, 조니는 그 칭찬을 받아들일 것이다. 우리는 우리가 바꾸기 원하는 행동에 그의 주의를 간접적인 방법으로 맞췄고, 그는 우리의 기대에 부응하려고 노력할 것이다.

05 모범답안 A prince should be feared rather than loved but he should escape being hated.

어휘

accommodate 충분한 공간을 제공하다; 담다, 받아들이다
belongings 소유물
fickle 변덕스러운
ungrateful 감사할 줄 모르는, 배은망덕한
come to grief 실패로 끝나다; 사고를 당하다
obligation 의무

한글번역

사랑을 받는 대상이 되는 것이 두려움의 대상이 되는 것보다 나을까 아니면 그 반대일까? 나는 모든 군주들이 두 가지 모두 되고 싶어 할 거라 생각한다. 하지만, 이 가치들을 모두 받아들이는 것은 힘들기 때문에 만약 당신이 둘 중 하나를 선택해야 한다면, 두려움을 받는 것이 사랑을 받는 것보다 훨씬 안전하다. 왜냐하면 사람이 은혜를 모르고, 변덕이 심하며, 거짓말쟁이이고 사기꾼이며 위험을 무서워하고 이익에 대한 욕심이 많다는 것은 매우 타당한 일반원칙이기 때문이다. 당신이 그들의 복지에 기여하는 동안에는, 그들은 모두 당신의 것이고, 그들의 피와 소유물, 그들의 생명과 그 아이들의 생명까지도 바칠 것이다. 단 위험이 멀리 있는 한에만 그렇다. 하지만 위험이 가까이 오게 되면, 그들은 당신에게서 등을 돌린다. 그러면 그들의 약속에만 의존했고 다른 준비는 전혀 해두지 않았던 왕들은 슬픔에 빠지게 된다. 왜냐하면 사람들은 자기 자신을 두려움의 대상이 되도록 만드는 사람보다 자기 자신을 사랑받도록 만드는 사람을 불쾌하게 만드는 것을 더 개의치 않아 하기 때문이다. 그 이유는 사랑이란 사람들이 타락해, 의무를 깨버리는 것이 그들에게 이익을 가져다 줄 것이라 판단하는 순간 언제든 깨버릴 의무의 연결고리이기 때문이다. 하지만 두려움은 그들이 절대 벗어날 수 없는 처벌의 두려움을 포함한다. 그러나 왕은 다음과 같은 방식으로 스스로가 두려운 존재가 돼야 한다. 사랑은 받지 못하더라도 증오도 받지 않는 방식으로 말이다.

2008학년도 전국

01 모범답안 The words we use control and direct our thoughts.

어휘

catchword 선전문구
cheapen 격이 떨어지다
cockatoo 앵무새
devalue 평가절하하다
spur 박차를 가하다; ~의 원동력이 되다

한글번역

우리의 언어 중 가장 격이 떨어지고 저평가된 단어는 '사랑'이다. 우리는 모든 면에서 '사랑'이라는 단어를 사용한다. 우리는 우리의 어머니를 사랑하고, 새 차를 사랑하고, 아이스크림, 모차르트, 소풍 그리고 혼자 시간을 보내는 것을 사랑한다. 대부분의 사람들은 우리가 먼저 생각하고 그 후에 이러한 생각을 표현할 말을 찾는다고 간주한다. 그러나 사실상 우리는 말과 함께 그리고 말 속에서 생각하고, 우리의 통제하에 있는 말들이 표현하고자 하는 사고를 형성하는 것이지 그 반대는 아니다.

예를 들면 다음과 같다. 우리는 부인과 애인을 사랑하는 방식과 동일하게 우리의 자식들을 사랑하는 것은 아니다. 우리가 파란색, 혹은 페퍼민트 맛 또는 장미의 향기를 사랑하는 것처럼 우리의 나라를 사랑하는 것도 아니다. 또 우리가 우리의 애완조 앵무새를 사랑하는 방식과 동일하게 하나님을 사랑하는 것은 아니다. 이러한 언어적 구별을 하는 것에 있어 우리의 실패는 단순히 '말하는 방식'에 국한되지 않는다. 우리의 실패는 개념화, 정의 그리고 구분의 문제인 것이다.

우리가 사용하는 말이 우리의 사고를 통제하고 지휘한다. 우리는 현실이 구현하고 있는 실제보다 슬로건이나 선전 문구에 의해 행동을 하게 된다.

02 모범답안 All social organizations display top-down socialization and bottom-up creativity.

어휘

emerge (어둠 속이나 숨어 있던 곳에서) 나오다, 모습을 드러내다
ethnic 민족(종족)의
infinitely 대단히
performance 수행
persistent 끈질긴, 집요한
prescribed 미리 정해진, 규정된
resurgence (활동의) 재기, 부활
social relation 사회적 관계
socialization 사회화
unlearn 잊다(= forget)

한글번역

사회화를 통해 인간은 사회, 계층, 지역, 그리고 그들이 태어난 가족의 효과적인 구성원이 되기 위해 학습하고, 주변에 존재하는 사회적 관계들을 이해하게 된다. 사실상, 사회화는 평생에 걸쳐서 계속되고 사람들은 사회적 역할을 무한히 배우고 망각할 수 있는 능력이 있다는 것을 증명한다. 예를 들어, 의사와 환자가 상호작용하는 방법은 '의사'와 '환자'로서의 역할로 인해 규정될 수 있다. 의사들은 대본 안에서의 본인 역할을 의과대학에서 습득하게 된다. 환자들은 매스컴을 통해 그들의 역할을 배우거나 의사들과 직접 소통을 하면서 파악하게 된다. 사람들은 안정적이며 이미 구축된 관계들 속으로 들어가게 된다. 그들이 만들지 않은 세계 속에서 사람들은 그들에게 할당된 역할을 수행하는 것을 배워야만 한다. 이러한 하향식 이론은 지속적인 권력의 불평등을 강조하게 될 가능성이 높다. 그러한 불평등은 다른 것에 비해 특정 역할과 상호작용 형태를 지지한다. 일반적으로, 하향식 이론은 관찰되는 사회체제의 지속성에 들어맞는다.

그러나 심지어 가장 단순한 상황에서도, 상호작용은 정해진 사회적 역할을 수행하는 것 그 이상을 의미한다. 사람들은 계속해서 새로운 상황을 맞닥뜨리면서 새로운 역할 및 규칙들을 창조한다. 그들이 알고 하든지 아니든지 간에, 사람들은 종종 상향식 방법으로 상호작용을 통해 사회관계를 협의하는 경우가 있다. 이것이 바로 우리가 사회구조라고 부르는 것을 창조하고 재창조하는 협상 과정이다. 독창성은 새로이 형성되는 모든 민족 공동체와 사회적 불평등에 저항하려는 운동들에서 명백히 보여진다. '공동체 소멸'에 대한 예측에도 불구하고, 이웃과 네트워크 그리고 비공식 공동체들의 부활은 인간의 독창성을 보여준다. 그러므로 모든 사회 조직 단체는 하향식 사회화와 상향식 독창성을 보여준다. 그리고 모든 사람들은 변화에 대한 압박에 부응한다. 사회화는 독창성이 취하는 형태와, 마지막에 일어날 수 있는 변화의 형태들에 영향을 미친다.

03 모범답안 similar

어휘

assertion 주장
conform to ~에 부합하다, 따르다
property 속성

한글번역

비록 특정 언어들이 표면적으로는 서로 명백히 다를지라도, 자세히 들여다보면 인간의 언어들은 놀라울 만큼 비슷하다는 점을 알 수 있다. 예를 들어, 알려진 모든 언어들은 복잡성과 세부성에 있어 비슷한 수준에 있다. 원시적인 인간 언어 따위는 존재하지 않는다. 모든 언어들은 질문하고, 요청하고, 주장하기 위한 수단을 제공한다. 그리고 어떤 언어에서는 표현되지만, 다른 언어에서는 표현될 수 없는 것은 존재하지 않는다. 물론, 한 언어가 다른 언어에서는 찾을 수 없는 용어를 가지고 있을 수는 있지만, 우리의 의도를 표현하기 위한 새로운 용어를 개발하는 것은 언제나 가능하다. 우리가 상상하고 생각할 수 있는 그 어떤 것이라도, 우리는 어떠한 인간 언어로도 표현 가능하다.

더 추상적인 특성들을 살펴보자면, 언어의 공식적인 구조들조차도 서로 비슷하다. 모든 언어들은 작은 구 단위로 문장을 구성하고, 이러한 단위들은 단어들이 모여 구성되며, 또 단어는 소리의 연속으로 구성된다. 이러한 인간 언어의 모든 특성들은 너무 당연하게 여겨져서 우리는 언어들이 그러한 특성들을 공유한다는 놀라움을 알아차리는 데 실패하기도 한다. 언어학자들이 언어나 본질적 인간 언어라는 단어를 사용할 때, 언어의 표면적인 변화 아래의 추상적 차원에서 언어들이 특정 보편적인 원리들에 순응하면서 형태나 기능 면에서 놀라울 정도로 비슷하다는 믿음을 드러내고 있는 것이다.

04 모범답안 racial segregation

어휘

apartheid 아파르트헤이트(예전 남아프리카공화국의 인종차별 정책)
be on a collision course 극한 충돌이 일어날 상황에 놓여 있다
collision course 충돌 침로(노선); [비유] (의견 등의) 충돌이 예상되는 상황
cut A down to size A에게 자기 수준을 알게 해주다(A의 콧대를 꺾다)
disparage 비난하다
extol 극찬하다
homelands 고향; 조국; (남아프리카 공화국의) 흑인 자치구역
manhood 남성성
nobody 아무것도 아닌 존재
retaliation 보복
set 굳어지다; 결정하다; 정착하다
somebody 중요한 존재
tribalism 부족(중심)주의

한글번역

"네 콧대를 꺾어주마, 아들," 내 뒤에서 아버지가 소리를 치셨다. "너를 고향에 있는 산악학교로 다시 보낼 때까지 기다리고 있어라. 그곳에서 너에게 존경이라는 것을 가르칠 것이다. 너는 그저 기다리고 지켜보고만 있어라." 나는 할머니 집에 일주일을 머문 후 집으로 돌아왔다. 아버지는 아무 말씀도 하지 않으셨지만 나는 그가 일종의 보복 같은 것을 계획하고 있다는 사실을 알 수 있었다. 나는 어떤 것에도 준비가 돼있었다. 아버지는 내가 어렸을 때 하곤 했던 것처럼 나를 때리지 못하셨는데 그 이유는 내가 자라면서 매일 매일 더욱 고집이 세지고 더욱 강해졌기 때문이다. 우리 둘 다 우리끼리 극한 충돌이 예상되는 상황이라는 것을 알고 있었다. 나는 내가 사는 방식으로 정착했고, 그는 그의 방식대로 살았다. 그는 교육을 헐뜯었고 나는 극찬했다; 아버지는 백인이 말한 모든 것들을 인종차별에 대한 저항 없이 믿었고, 나는 그러지 않았다. 그는 순간을 위해 살았고, 나는 불확실하지만 그러한 미래를 위해 살았다. 아버지가 순간을 위해 산 이유가 미래에 대한 두려움 때문이라는 것이 곧 명백해졌다. 또한 그는 그가 아무것도 아닌 걸로 취급되는 세상이자 그에게서 남성성, 공급능력을 빼앗아가버린 세상에서 내가 중요한 존재가 되어가는 중인 현실을 직면하는 것을 두려워했다. 아파르트헤이트(예전 남아프리카공화국의 인종차별 정책)와 부족 중심주의라는 이중 멍에로 그가 수년간 고통 받는 것을 지켜보면서, 나는 아버지가 부족의 신념에 매달리고 백인이 그의 남성성을 정의하게 내버려 두는 한은 아버지의 경우는 절망적인 상황이라는 데 확신을 얻었다.

05 모범답안 Drivers' habits account for the majority of accidents and are hard to change.

어휘

account for (부분; 비율을) 차지하다
revert to ~로 되돌아가다; 복귀하다
lapse 과실; 실수(= error)

한글번역

오늘날의 많은 운전자들은 충돌사고를 피하는 데 계속 어려움을 겪고 있으며, 교통 안전 전문가들은 계속해서 운전을 더 안전하게 만들 여러 방법을 탐색하고 있다. 자동차와 도로의 설계를 개선하는 것에 대한 최근 수년간의 강조 이후에, 자동차 안전의 초점은 이제 소위 '운전대 뒤의 폭군'이라 불리는 것으로 되돌아가고 있다. 그러나 운전자의 고착된 행동을 개선하는 것은 쉽지 않은데, 몇몇 분석가들은 모든 교통사고의 90%가 넘는 사례를 이 운전자들의 탓으로 돌린다. 어떤 운전자들이 충돌에 책임이 있는가, 왜 사고들이 발생하며, 그런 사고들을 어떻게 멈추는가를 특정해내는 것이 어렵다는 점에 문제가 있다. 예를 들어, 최악의 사고나 최악의 위반 기록을 가지고 있는 운전자들이 사고에서 (다른 사람들보다) 더 많은 비중을 차지하고 있는 것은 맞지만, 그런 운전자들의 수는 상대적으로 적고, 이들이 차지하는 비율은 모든 충돌 가운데서 매우 적다. 교통사고 문제에서 가장 많은 부분은 (위와 같은 부류처럼) 매우 적은 사례들이 일으키는 잘못에 있기보다는, 평범한 운전자들이 범하는 과실에 있다고 보여진다. 운전 습관을 바꾸는 것은 매우 어려운데, 부분적인 이유로는 사람들이 운전을 진지하게 받아들이지 않기 때문이다.

2007학년도 서울 · 인천

01 모범답안 busy

어휘

cheerfully 기꺼이, 기분 좋게, 쾌활하게
mainstream 주류, 대세
conventional 관습적인, 관례적인
misinterpretation 오해, 오역

한글번역

'framing(틀 잡기)'이라는 관례적 방법들이 갖는 차이는 공공의 영역에서 혼란과 오해를 일으킬 수 있다. 예를 들어, '주된' 미국식 관례는 노동자들이 심지어 그렇지 않더라도 바쁘게 보이는 것을 요구한다. 하지만 어떤 문화 양식에서는 사람들이 심지어 바쁘더라도 바쁘지 않게, 즉 '멋지게' 보이는 것을 요구한다. 고객이 우체국에 들어갔는데 자기 앞에 다른 고객들이 없고 직원이 바쁘지 않은 것을 보게 되면 매우 좋아한다. 직원은 혼자 노래하고, 자리에서 춤추고, 신문을 보며 빈둥거리고, 느리고 무심한 듯 움직이며, 집중하며 관심을 두는 표시를 내지 않는다. 그래서 고객은 직원이 그녀를 돕기 위해 움직이지 않거나, 심지어는 그녀의 접근을 알아차리지조차 못할 때는 짜증이 나게 된다.

그러나 직원은 실제로 중요한 일을 하고 있었다. 그는 일이 끝났을 때 그녀에게로 향해 기꺼이 그녀를 도왔다. 만일 그가 자신의 일에 몰두돼 관심을 두고 정신이 팔려 있는 모습을 보였다면, 그녀는 다가서기 전에 '나는 바쁘다'라는 이면의 메시지를 알아채고 즉각적인 도움을 기대하지 않았을 것이다.

02 모범답안 influence

어휘

frontier 변경의, 변경 개척지의
necessaries 필수품
primitive 원시의
gross 총(= total)
outward 외적인
skeleton 골격, 뼈대

한글번역

잠시 내가 지금까지 언급해 온 근심과 걱정의 대부분이 무엇에 관한 것이고, 또 우리가 어느 정도로 걱정을 하거나 또는 적어도 신경은 써야 할 것인가에 대해 살펴보기로 하자. 인간 생활에서 으뜸가는 필수품들이 무엇이며, 이것을 얻기 위해 어떤 방법들을 취해 왔는지를 알기 위해 문명의 한가운데서나마 원시적이고 개척자적인 생활을 해보는 것은 꽤 도움이 될 것이다. 또는 상인들의 옛 장부를 들여다보고 사람들이 가게에서 가장 많이 사간 것이 무엇이며, 가게에서 가장 많이 소비되는 식료품과 잡화로는 어떤 물건들이 있었는지 알아봐도 좋을 것이다. 왜냐면 아무리 사회가 발전했어도 인간 생존의 기본 법칙에는 별다른 영향을 주지 못했기 때문이며, 그것은 우리의 골격이 우리 조상의 골격과 별 차이가 없는 것과 같다.

03 모범답안 ① sex ② offspring ③ microscopic

어휘

be paired with ~와 병행되다
circuitry 회로
genetic blueprint 유전자 구성(청사진)
microscopic 미세한; 현미경으로 봐야만 보이는
quantitative 양적인
underlie ~의 기초가 되다
within narrow limits 좁은 범위 내에서
chromosome (생물) 염색체
fertilization 수정
jumble 뒤범벅이 된 것, 허섭스레기
neurological 신경학상의, 신경의
shuffle 섞다
variation 변종, 변이; 변수

한글번역

유전적 차이는 적은 양적 변수임에 틀림없다. 그 이유는 성별이다. 두 사람이 실제로 근본적으로 다른 디자인에 의해 이뤄졌다고 생각해보자. 폐의 구조와 같은 신체적 디자인 혹은 인지 과정상의 회로와 같은 신경학적 디자인이 그렇다. 복잡한 유기체는 많은 정밀한 구조적 부분을 필요로 하며, 그 부분들은 또 그것을 쌓아올릴 많은 유전자를 요한다. 하지만 염색체는 성의 형성 과정에서 임의적으로 분리되고, 재연결되며, 섞인다. 그리고는 수정 시에 다른 반쪽과 쌍을 이루게 된다. 만일 두 사람이 정말로 다른 디자인을 가졌다면 그들의 후손들은 각각의 유전 지도에서 뒤섞인 조각들을 물려받을 것이다. 두 개의 디자인은, 처음부터, 극도로 비슷할 경우에만 새로운 조합이 가능할 것이다. 이것은 곧 유전학자들이 우리에게 말하는 변수가 미시적이고 자연 선택의 좁은 범위 내에서 유지되는 이유이다.

04 모범답안 [4]

어휘

banknote 지폐, 은행권
briefcase (가죽) 서류 가방
in use 쓰이고 있는
radius 반지름, 반경
snatch 잡아채다, 낚아채다
transmitter 송신기
booty 노획물, 훔친 물건
dye 염색제, 염료
lockable 열쇠로 잠글 수 있는, 자물쇠가 달린
smoulder 타다
takings 매상; 매출액

한글번역

한 가게 주인이 그 주에 번 돈을 가방에 가지고 걸어간다. 갑자기 도둑이 가방을 낚아채 운전해 도망간다.

[1] 하지만 그때 강도에게 일이 꼬이기 시작한다. 먼저 가방이 아주 크고 시끄러운 소음을 낸다. 그리고 가방이 뜨거워지며 타기 시작한다. 그래서 차가 곧 짙고 붉은 연기로 가득 찬다.

[2] 도둑은 자신이 훔친 물건을 도로에 던지고 기침을 하며 도망할 것이다. 하지만 가방에서 나는 경보와 연기가 없었더라도 그 훔친 돈은 가치가 없었을 것이다. 또 다른 방어 장치는 지폐에 붉은 염료를 흘려 못쓰게 만드는 것이다.

[3] S-100 시스템은 두 가지 주된 특징, 즉 무선 수신기와 경보 장치를 가지고 있으며, 자물쇠가 달린 어떤 비금속 가방에도 숨길 수 있다. 주인은 주머니에 무선 송신기를 지니고 있어 이것이 가방에 있는 수신기에 계속적인 신호를 보낸다.

[A] 경보는 2미터 반경 내에서 신호를 받는 한 울리지 않는다. 가방이 10초 이상 멀리 있게 되면 수신기가 큰 소리를 낸다.

[4] 그것을 송신기와 2미터 내에 다시 가져가지 않으면 10초 후에 다른 신호를 보내고 염료가 자동적으로 가방의 내용물에 방출된다. 그리고 소각되기 시작한다.

[5] S-100은 이미 실제 사용에서 성공을 거둬 왔다. 2월에 두 명의 강도가 8000파운드가 든 가방을 자신들의 달리던 자동차 밖으로 던져버렸다.

2007학년도 전국

01 모범답안 deprive themselves of opportunities to ameliorate their lives

어휘

ameliorate 개선하다
ensure 보장하다
open one's eye to ~에 눈을 뜨다
deprive A of B A에게서 B를 빼앗다
miss out on ~을 놓치다; 누락시키다
undoubtedly 의심할 여지 없이, 확실히

한글번역

변화를 받아들일 수 없는 사람들은 많은 새로운 경험을 종종 놓치곤 한다. 이러한 사람들은 아마도 그들이 새로운 어떤 것을 배우고 적응하는 부담감에 의해 그들 삶에서 현재의 안락한 수준이 위협받을 것이라 생각하기 때문에 변화를 두려워한다. 이러한 두려움으로 인해 새로운 음식, 새로운 언어, 새로운 도시 그리고 새로운 친구들은 다른 사람들이 시도하도록 남겨진다. 그러나 사실 이러한 모든 요소들은 한 사람의 인생에 더해질 때 지식과 경험을 늘려가는 기회를 제공한다. 예를 들어 새로운 언어를 정복하는 것은 세계를 편하게 여행할 수 있도록 보장해 줄 수 있고, 새로운 문화에 대한 스스로의 경험을 늘려가도록 도와줄 것이다. 새롭고 다양한 사람들과의 우정은 새로운 생활 방식에 대해 눈을 뜨게 하고 또 삶을 풍요롭게 한다. 새로운 음식에 대한 도전은 요리나 여행과 같은 새로운 취미에 대한 스스로의 관심을 늘려줄 것이다. 의심할 여지 없이 변화를 두려워하는 사람들은 삶을 개선할 수 있는 기회를 스스로 박탈시키는 것이다.

02 모범답안 원문에 없는 비디오 가게의 성공 정도와 파산의 이유를 썼고 시기도 부정확하게 기술하여 원래의 글과 의미가 달라졌다. (원문에 없는 내용을 더하여 의미를 변화시켰다.)

어휘

go out of business 폐업하다
gobble up ~을 눈 깜짝할 사이에 잡아먹다, 집어삼키다
mom-and-pop store 구멍가게, 소규모 자영업체

한글번역

비디오 대여점은 지역적으로 소유되는 구멍가게의 형태로 1970년대에 나타나기 시작했다. 그러나 이러한 소규모의 사업체는 거대한 전국적인 체인점이 나타나서 대부분의 지역 시장을 집어삼키고 난 후, 그리 오래가지 못했다.

(1) 1970년대에 비디오 대여점은 흔히 소규모로 그리고 지역적으로 소유됐다. 그러나 이러한 가게들 중 많은 가게가, 거대한 전국적인 체인점이 마을에 들어오자, 그들의 시장을 잃고 폐업했다.
(2) 1970년대 후반, 비디오 대여점은 작은 규모와 지역 사업으로 대단히 성공적이었으나, 그들은 더 적은 요금을 부과하며 소규모 상점을 폐업하도록 하는 거대한 전국적인 체인점과는 경쟁할 수가 없었다.

03 모범답안

3-1 두 눈의 시야가 겹치기 때문에 생기는 넓은 시야

3-2 no other sense seems capable of affording

어휘

accord ~을 부여하다, 주다
afford 제공하다
binocular overlap 양안 중첩
clear-sighted 명석한, 판단력이 있는
endeavor 노력하다, 시도하다
fine 작은, 세밀한
placement 배치, 설치
primacy 최고, 으뜸
replete with ~로 가득한, ~로 충만한
spectrum 스펙트럼, 빛 띠

한글번역

인간이 지니고 있는 모든 감각 중에서 시각이 가장 발달돼있다. 인간 눈의 구조와 머리의 앞부분에 위치한 눈의 배치는 인간의 시력에 있어 몇 가지 중요한 능력을 가능케 한다. 인간의 눈은 아주 세밀한 부분을 찾아내고 분석할 수 있는데, 인간의 눈은 광범위한 색깔 스펙트럼을 구별할 수 있으며 넓은 범위의 양안 중첩은 시야의 깊이 있는 감상을 가능케 해준다. 이러한 능력은 진화적인 과정에서 *호모 사피엔스*에게 부여된 다른 종으로부터 인간을 구별하게 해주는 보편적인 생물학적 특징의 일부분이다. 이와 함께 능력들은 인간 감각들 중 가장 으뜸이라는 지위를 시각에게 부여했던 생물학적 토대를 형성한다. 시각의 우수성은 '백문이 불여일견'이나 '만약 내가 내 눈으로 보지 못했었더라면, 나는 믿지 못했을 것이다'와 같은 많은 일상의 격언에서 명백하게 나타난다. 본다는 것은 어떤 다른 감각도 제공해주지 못하는 확실성을 제공해준다. 따라서 과학적인 담론이 시각적 이미지로 가득한 것은 놀라운 일이 아니다. 과학은 세계에 대한 사실적 '관찰'에 토대를 두고 있고, 조사하고자 하는 현상에 대한 객관적이고, '명석하고', 편견 없는 '관점'을 발전시키려 노력한다.

04 모범답안

4-1 남편과 자녀의 속박을 받지 않고 직업을 가진 여성

4-2 (a) motherhood (b) marriage

어휘

ambivalent 양가적인
bearer 출산자
come along 생기다, 나타나다
even as ~할 때조차도
fetter 속박, 구속하다
grueling 호된, 엄한, 힘든
hold out ~을 제공하다, 제시하다
unfettered 제한, 구속받지 않는
artificial insemination 인공 수정
breadwinner 생계비를 버는 사람, 가장
come apart 분리되다
exercise (권리, 권력 등을) 행사하다
go through (something) ~을 거치다, 겪다
historic 역사에 남을 만한, 역사적인
infertility 불임

한글번역

오늘날, 결혼과 모성은 분리돼있다. 이혼율이 역사에 남을 정도로 높은 수치에 고정돼있고 혼외 자식의 양육이 훨씬 더 흔해지고 있는 이 순간, 재혼율 및 혼인율은 감소하고 있다. 많은 여성이 미혼모가 되는 것을 하나의 선택 및 적절한 남편감이 적시에 동반되지 않는다면 발휘될 수 있는 하나의 권리로서 바라본다. 남편과 아이에 의해 구속받지 않는 직장 여성의 모델을 제시해줬던, 1960년대와 1970년대의 '제1기' 페미니즘적 시각은 오직 여성들 일부에게만 받아들여져 오고 있었다. 심지어 여성들은 어머니가 되기 위해 호된 불임 치료나 인공 수정까지 감안할 정도로 아이들에 의해 구속받고자 한다. 그러나 그들은 점차 그들을 남편에게 묶어두는 구속들과 부모가 된다는 것의 조건으로서 결혼의 필요성에 대해 양가적인 감정을 갖기 시작한다. 임신이 가능한 사람이자 아이들의 양육자들로서 그리고 점차적으로 가족을 위한 유일한 가장으로서, 여성은 개인적으로 보람 있고 사회적으로 귀중한 일들에 계속해서 종사하고 있다. 그들은 결혼 이외에도 그들의 여성적인 미덕들을 증명해낼 수 있다.

2006학년도 서울 · 인천

01 모범답안 should be started in the affirmative direction

어휘

consistent with ~와 일관된, 한결같은
outset 착수, 시초, 발단
strive for ~을 얻으려 노력하다, 애쓰다
ill-advised 경솔한
precious 소중한, 귀중한

한글번역

사람들과 대화할 때, 의견이 다르다는 것을 논하면서 시작하지 말라. 당신이 동의하는 것을 강조하면서 시작하라. 다른 사람이 처음에 '맞아, 맞아'라고 말하게 하라. 가능하면 당신의 상대방이 '아니'라고 말하지 못하게 하라. 가능하면 당신이 같은 목적을 향해 노력하고 있으며 유일한 차이는 방법이지 목적이 아님을 강조하라. '아니'라는 대답은 가장 극복하기 힘든 장애이다. 당신이 '아니'라고 말할 때, 당신의 모든 인격의 자존심이 당신 자신과 일관성을 유지하도록 요구한다. 당신은 후에 '아니'라는 대답이 경솔했다는 것을 느낄 수도 있다. 그럼에도 고려해야 할 당신의 소중한 자존심이 있다! 일단 한 가지를 말했다면 당신은 그것을 고수해야 한다고 느낀다. 따라서 사람이 긍정적인 방향에서 시작하는 것이 가장 중요한 것이다.

02 모범답안 (1) without the word (2) the general idea

어휘

fair 상당한, 꽤 많은
in the sense that ~라는 의미에서
get by 지나가다; 그럭저럭 해 나가다
skip over 건너뛰어 읽다

한글번역

독자들이 텍스트에 대한 일반적 생각을 얻기 위해 독서하고 있다면, 그들은 그 단어들이 중요하지 않고 그래서 무시될 수 있다면 아마 어느 정도의 모르는 단어는 그냥 넘겨 버릴 수 있을 것이다. 모르는 단어의 의미가 문장 전체의 의미를 이해하는 데 필요한지 아닌지 결정하는 한 가지 전략은 문장을 그 단어 없이 읽은 후, 전반적 의미가 얻어지는지 보는 것이다. 다른 전략은 그 단어의 문법적 분류를 점검하는 것이다. 만약 그것이 형용사나 부사라면, 독자들은 아마 그 단어 없이도 지나칠 수 있다. 다른 한편으로 모르는 단어가 한 텍스트에서 여러 번 나타나고 전반적인 생각의 열쇠인 듯하면, 그 단어는 찾아볼 필요가 있다. 명사와 동사는 그것의 의미를 모르고서는 독자가 전반적인 생각을 이해할 수 없다는 의미에서 충분한 중요성을 갖는다.

03 모범답안 feared

어휘

bogey 두려운 것
deplore 비탄하다, 후회하다, 비난하다
indigestion 소화불량
literacy 문해력(글을 읽고 쓸 줄 아는 능력)
public health 공중위생, 공공보건
tract 소논문, 소책자
bring on ~을 야기시키다
heat rash 땀띠
literacy rate 식자율
melancholy 우울증
susceptibility 민감, 감수성, 감염되기 쉬움

한글번역

18세기에 이르러 인쇄 자료는 아주 널리 보급돼 '문해능력의 위기'에 대한 두려움을 가져올 정도였다. 문해능력의 위기는 너무 적은 독서량보다는 너무 많은 독서량과 관련이 있다는 점에서 우리가 말하는 문해능력과는 정반대였다. 18세기에 글을 읽고 쓸 줄 아는 사람들의 비율이 실제 증가했는지에 대한 계속되고 해결되지 않는 논쟁이 있다. 하지만 그 당시 사회의 지도자들은 독서의 과도한 보급을 확실히 두려워했고, 하층 계급의 독서가 증가함으로써 생길 위험이 많이 논의됐다. 예를 들어 로크는 가난한 사람들을 가르치는 것에 호의적이지 않았다. 독서를 비난하는 사람들은 단지 독서의 도덕적, 정치적 영향을 비난하는 것만이 아니었다. 그들은 독서가 공중 보건을 해칠 것을 두려워했다. 1795년 논문은 과도한 독서의 신체적 영향들을 나열하고 있다. 이는 '감기, 두통, 시력 약화, 땀띠, 소화불량, 우울증 등에 걸리기 쉽다'는 것이었다. 독서는 20세기 후반 너무 과도한 텔레비전 시청이 일종의 문화적 불안이 되는 것과 아주 똑같은 방식으로 위험한 것이 됐다.

04 모범답안 In the future multimedia tools for language learning will not replace the human teacher for the following two reasons: cultural context and subtle nuance the language has. First, in terms of cultural context, language reflects the culture where it originates. The same words could have different connotations according to the culture. Multimedia tools may have difficulty in teaching the cultural context reflected in the language. Second, regarding the subtle nuance language has, multimedia tools cannot deliver the subtlety in the language. Even the same expression can be used differently in different contexts. In addition, the similar expressions could have different meanings. Only the human teacher can teach these subtleties the language has.

한글번역

미래에 언어 학습을 위해서 인간 교사는 멀티미디어로 대체될 수 있다.

2006학년도 전국

01 모범답안 you are not biased, benighted, or boring

한글번역

논지란 무엇인가? 그것은 관점이고 논쟁이다. 본인은 좋은 논지란 그 무엇보다 논쟁의 소지가 있는, 즉, 모두가 동의하지는 않는 것이라고 주장하는 바이다. 하지만 그렇다고 해서 논지가 꼭 '옳고/그름'의 문제에 관심을 두는 것은 아니라는 걸 이해하길 바란다. 종종 논지는 무엇이 시급한지 아닌지, 흥미로운지 아닌지, 무언가를 하기에 좋은 방법인지 아닌지, 우리가 이 사안을 달성할 수 있는지 없는지와 관련이 있기도 하다. 당신이 어떤 입장을 취하든 간에, 논지는 가급적이면 대담한 확신을 가지고 있어야 하며, 그런 경우 회의론자들조차 당신이 얼마나 편향되고, 미개하며, 따분한 모습을 드러내는지 보기 위해서라도 호기심을 가지고 다가올 것이다. 당신의 과제는 물론 (위에서 말한 그런 부정적인 것에 대해) 그렇지 않다고 그들을 납득시키는 것이다. 이는 글을 쓰는 데 있어서 항상 거대한 도전과제이다. 그렇지 않은가? 사람들을 불러모아 그들을 가르치고, 즐겁게 해주고, 영감을 주고, 들뜨게 하고, 매료시키고, 깨우침을 주고, 납득시키는 것 말이다.

02 모범답안

2-1 communication

2-2 play with children of their own gender

한글번역

내가 실행한 연구에서, 여성들이 그들의 남편에 대해 갖고 있는 불평은 대다수가 눈에 보이는 불평등한 것, 즉 남편을 돕기 위해 자신의 경력을 포기한 것이라든가 또는 청소, 요리, 사교 모임 준비, 심부름과 같은 생활을 지원해주는 일에서 자신들이 훨씬 더 많이 하는 것 따위에 초점을 둔 것은 아니었다. 대신에, 여성들은 의사소통에 초점을 뒀다. "남편은 내 말을 들으려 하지 않아요." "남편은 나와 말하기 싫어해요." 나는 대부분의 아내들은 자신의 남편이 다른 무엇보다도 자신들의 대화의 파트너가 되기를 원하지만, 남편들은 아내의 이런 기대감을 나누려 하지 않는다는 것을 발견했다.

어떻게 여성과 남성은 결혼생활에서 이렇게 대화에 대해 서로 다른 견해를 지니고 있을까? 그들의 관심과 기대가 그렇게 많이 다른 이유는 무엇일까? 스탠포드 대학의 마코비는 자신과 다른 학자들의 연구 결과를 발표했는데, 그것은 아이들의 발달이 대부분 또래 상호작용의 사회적 구조에 의해 영향을 받는다는 것이었다. 소년과 소녀는 그들 자신과 같은 성별의 아이들과 노는 경향이 있고, 분리된 성별 그룹은 다른 그룹과는 다른 조직 구조와 상호작용 기준을 가지고 있다. 나는 이러한 어린 시절의 사회화에서 발생되는 체계적인 차이가 여성과 남성 사이의 대화를 서로 다른 문화 간의 의사소통을 하는 것처럼(서로 이해가 잘 안 될 정도로) 만들었다고 믿는다.

03 모범답안 (a) first (b) because (c) but (d) hence

어휘

answer ~에 부합하다
cyclone 사이클론(폭풍)
posture 자세
cumulative 축적되는, 누적되는
meditator 묵상가, 명상가
set aside 확보하다, 챙겨두다

한글번역

오늘날의 명상가들은 어떻게 성공적인 명상을 할 수 있는가? 몇 가지 간단한 추천이 거의 보편적이다. 먼저, 성공적으로 명상을 하기를 원하는 이들은 보통 약 30분간의 조용한 시간을 확보해야 한다. 그 결과는 누적적이고 한 번만으로는 나타나지 않으므로, 이것을 지속적으로 유지해야 한다. 명상을 위해 당신이 고르는 장소 또한 중요하다. 내 개인적인 여론조사에 의하면, 많은 사람들이 빈 교회에서 최고의 명상을 한다. 아마도 더 빈번히, 숙련된 명상가들은 자연적인 장소, 즉 숲이나 쓸쓸한 바닷가로 발길을 돌린다. 이 각각의 장소는 혼자 있을 필요와 공간감에 대한 필요에 부합한다.

가장 중요한 것은 태도이다. 모든 다양한 명상 기술들은 개방감, 내적인 평정, 증진된 자아의식 상태를 만들어내는 것을 추구한다. 그러나 한 사람의 마음이 마치 폭풍처럼 소용돌이칠 때, 그 누구도 그 마음의 깊이를 볼 수 없다. 따라서 겉보기에 터무니없어 보이는 자세와 집중의 방법들이 일상에 대한 걱정의 소용돌이를 잠재우도록 돕기 위해 고안됐다.

2005학년도 서울 · 인천

01 모범답안 is to give readers an explanation of where they are headed. (또는 is to state his ideas plainly to readers)

어휘

entangled 뒤엉킨; 얼기설기 얽힌
ingenious 기발한, 독창적인
keep in mind ~을 명심하다
rain forest 우림
golden rule 황금률(행동의 기본 원리)
invariably 언제나; 변함(예외)없이
misconstrue ~을 오해하다
thicket 덤불; 잡목 숲

한글번역

훌륭한 작가들은, 경험에서 생긴 염세주의로 인해, 분명하게 명시되지 않은 것은 무엇이든지 독자가 분명히 오해할 것이라 가정한다. 그들은 결국 그녀(독자)가 그들의 독창적 생각이란 정원에 완전한 이방인이란 사실을 염두에 두고 있다. 사실 그녀에게 그 정원은 처음에는 얼기설기 얽힌 잡목 숲 같은 것이다. 열대 우림은 아니라도 말이다. 이러하기에 작가로서 그들의 일은 그녀를 한 걸음씩 인도해 그 경험이 이해가 쉽고, 기억할 만한 것이 되게 하는 것이다. 이는 기민하게 그녀가 혼란스러워하는 순간을 예상하고 그녀가 향하는 곳에 대한 설명을 주기적으로 해주는 것과 관계있다. 작가의 황금률은 윤리주의자의 그것과 같다. 다른 사람이 당신에게 하기 원하는 대로 그 사람에게 하라.

02 모범답안

2-1 the more we realize the mind is not different from the body

2-2 (1) however (2) because (3) therefore

어휘

accompany 동반하다, 동행하다
electrochemistry 전기 화학
no more than 단지 ~에 지나지 않는
spill out 쏟아져 나오다
biochemical 생화학의
liver 간
pancreas 췌장
worthlessness 가치없음

한글번역

우리가 정신의 내적 작용에 대해 더 많이 알면 알수록, 정신과 육체가 서로 다르지 않다는 것을 알 수 있다. 정신의 세계는 우리 육체의 세계와는 매우 다른 것으로 생각돼왔다. 신체에 상해를 가해보라. 그러면 피가 솟아오를 것이다. 하지만 뇌를 잘라 들어가보라. 그러면 생각과 감정이 수술대로 흘러나오진 않을 것이다. 그러나 최근 정신-육체에 관한 연구는 뇌가 다른 기관보다 더 복잡하기는 하지만 단지 하나의 신체 기관일 뿐이라는 것을 보여준다. 생각과 감정은 신경 세포 사이의 복잡한 전기적, 화학적 상호작용의 결과이다. 우울증을 가져오는 무가치의 감정들은 뇌 전기 화학에서 생긴 질병일 뿐이다.

과학자들은 또한 다른 것도 알아가고 있다. 정신이 나머지 신체와 같을 뿐 아니라, 정신의 안녕이 육체의 안녕과 밀접하게 연결됐다는 점이다. 이는 그것들이 같은 체계를 공유하기 때문이다. 췌장이나 간에서 발생한 일은 직접적으로 뇌에 영향을 미칠 수 있다. 뇌의 무질서는 반대로 나머지 신체 기관을 괴롭히는 생화학적 충격파를 내보낼 수 있다. 더욱더 많은 의사들, 그리고 환자들은 정신 상태와 육체적 안녕이 밀접하게 연결됐다는 사실을 인식하고 있다. 건강하지 못한 육체는 건강하지 못한 정신을 낳을 수 있고, 이 건강하지 못한 정신은 또 육체의 질병을 악화시킨다. 그러므로 한곳에서 생긴 문제를 고치는 것은 종종 다른 곳을 도울 수 있다.

03 모범답안 what others probably know and do not know

어휘

A be depended on to B A가 B하리라 믿어도 된다
bring A into the open A를 공표하다, 밝히다
grasp 완전히 이해하다
set something down ~을 적다
beech 너도밤나무
elm 느릅나무
leopard 표범
take it for granted A A를 당연히 여기다

한글번역

작가가 말하고자 하는 바를 이해하기 위해 우리는 단어의 표면적 의미 그 이상을 이해해야만 하고, 마찬가지로 맥락을 이해해야만 한다. 한 페이지에 있는 단어들을 이해하기 위해, 우리는 해당 페이지에 적혀 있지 않은 많은 정보를 알고 있어야 한다. 퍼트넘이 미국인이 느릅나무와 너도밤나무는 구별하지 못하지만 호랑이와 표범은 구별한다고 믿을 수 있다고 말할 때, 그는 독자들이 교양이 있기 때문에 자신의 의견에 동의할 것이라고 생각했다. 그는 한 명의 교양 있는 사람은 다른 사람과 거의 동일한 것을 알고 있으며, 다른 사람의 지식의 한계를 인지한다는 것을 당연시 여겼다. 인식의 두 번째 단계는 다른 이들이 아마도 알고 있을 것과 모르고 있을 것을 아는 것으로, 이는 효과적인 의사소통에 결정적이다. 교육받은 사람들이 호랑이에 대해서 알지만 느릅나무에 대해서 모른다는 것을 아는 것은 일종의 문화적 지식인데, 그 (지식의) 범위는 세한적이지만 교양 있는 사람들 누구나 가지고 있으며, 그것은 반드시 공표돼 우리 아이들에게 가르쳐져야 한다.

04 모범답안 (1) rational (2) evidence (3) emotional

어휘

bloodthirsty 피에 굶주린
like-minded 생각이 비슷한
ruthlessly 무자비하게, 가차 없이
sparingly 드물게
dwindle 줄어들다
replenish 보충하다
slaughter 학살하다
sportsman 사냥꾼(= a hunter)

한글번역

설득을 위한 논쟁의 두 가지 주요 유형은 이성적인 것과 감정적인 것이다. 만약 예를 들어 당신이 사냥을 반대하는 글을 쓴다면, 감정적인 호소는 다음과 같이 시작될지도 모른다. "매해 수백 명의 피에 굶주린 살인자들이 사냥에 나가 수천의 무고하고 힘없는 동물들을 가차 없이 학살하고 있다." 반면에 사냥에 반대하는 이성적인 호소는 다음과 같이 시작될지도 모른다. "매해 사냥꾼들은 사냥 자격증을 구입하고 합법적으로 주가 허용한 제한만큼의 동물들을 죽인다. 하지만, 증거에 의하면 자연이 감소하는 동물의 공급을 다시 보충할 수 없기 때문에 이러한 관행은 중지돼야 한다."

특히 학자들을 대상으로 글을 쓸 때는 이성적인 논쟁이 더 효과적이다. 예를 들어 위의 이성적인 예에서, 발행된 자격증의 수, 매해 사냥한 동물들의 수, 그리고 측정된 동물 개체 수의 감소로 당신의 견해를 뒷받침할 수 있을 것이다. 감정적인 논쟁은 이미 당신의 의견에 동의한 청중들을 위해 글을 쓸 때 가장 효과적이다. 허나 이러한 논쟁은 이미 동의하지 않는 사람들을 설득하는 데는 성공적이기 어렵다. 학자들에게는 감정적인 논쟁을 아주 드물게 사용하는 것이 최선이다.

2005학년도 전국

01 모범답안 attitudes towards being punctual differ among cultures

어휘

appointment 약속	attendance 출석
misinterpret 잘못 해석하다	prestige 위신, 명망

한글번역

미국에서 약속, 수업 시간 등을 지키는 것은 중요하다. 그러나 이것은 모든 나라에서 다 그런 것은 아니다. 한 미국인 교수는 브라질의 한 대학에서 이 차이를 발견했다. 그의 첫 2시간 수업은 10시에 시작해 12시에 끝나는 것으로 정해졌다. 첫날, 교수가 시간에 맞춰 도착했을 때 교실에는 아무도 없었다. 많은 학생들은 10시가 넘어서 들어왔다. 몇몇은 10시 30분이 지나서야 도착했다. 두 학생은 11시 이후에 들어왔다. 이 학생들은 교수에게 인사했지만, 지각에 대해 사과하는 학생은 거의 없었다. 이 학생들은 무례했던 것인가? 그는 이 학생들의 행태를 연구하기로 했다.

이 교수는 공적인 상황과 그렇지 않은 상황 모두에서 지각하는 것에 대해 미국인 학생과 브라질 학생에게 이야기해봤다. 즉 대학 수업에 출석할 때와 친구와 식사할 때 각각의 경우에 대해서 말이다. 그는 학생들에게 예를 주고 어떻게 반응하는지 물었다. 그들이 친구와 점심 약속이 있다면, 보통 미국인 학생은 동의한 시간보다 9분 정도 늦는 것을 지각으로 정의했다. 한편 평균적인 브라질 학생은 33분이 늦으면 지각했다고 느꼈다.

미국의 대학생들과 달리, 브라질에서는 선생이나 학생들 중 그 누구도 약속된 시간에 늘 나타나지는 않는다. 미국에서 수업은 계획된 대로 시작하고 끝난다. 하지만 브라질의 교실에서는, 정오에 교실을 떠나는 학생은 거의 없고 12시 30분이 지나도 많은 학생들이 남아 수업에 대해 토론하고 더 많은 질문을 한다. 이러한 차이에 대해 설명하는 것은 복잡하다. 브라질에서, 학생들은 보통 늦게 도착하는 사람은 아마도 항상 시간을 지키는 사람보다 더 성공적일 것이라 믿는다. 사실 브라질 사람들은 지위와 명성을 가진 사람이 늦게 도착할 것이라 기대한다. 반면에 미국에서는 지각이 대체로 예의 없고 받아들일 수 없는 것으로 간주된다. 결과적으로 브라질 사람들이 북미인과의 약속에 늦는다면 미국인은 지각의 이유를 잘못 해석해 화를 낼 수도 있다.

02 모범답안 B－C－A

어휘

anthropologist 인류학자
decipher 해독하다, 번역하다
lisp 더듬더듬 말하다, 혀 짧은 소리로 말하다
outlaw 불법화하다
resolution 결단, 결의
scholarly 학구적인, 학문적인
whither (고어) 어디, 장소
be rid of ~을 면하다; 제거하다
immense 거대한, 매우 큰
mythology 신화
refrain from ~을 삼가다
ridicule 조롱하다
whence 출처, 유래, 기원

한글번역

최초의 인간이 처음으로 단어를 더듬듯이 말하기 시작했던 정확한 과정을 역사적 자료에서 알아내서 언어의 기원에 대한 모든 이론을 없애버리는 것보다 흥미로운 일은 없을 것이다.

모든 종교와 신화는 언어의 기원에 대한 이야기를 담고 있다. 여러 시대에 걸쳐 철학자들은 이 문제에 대해 논쟁해왔다. 학술 서적들은 이 주제에 관해 쓰여 왔다. 신성한 유래, 진화적인 발전, 그리고 인간의 발명품으로서의 언어에 관한 이론이 모두 제시돼왔다.

(B) 이 질문에 답하는 것에 내포돼있는 어려움은 상당하다. 인류학자들은 이 (인간이란) 종이 적어도 백만 년, 아마도 5~6백만 년 동안이나 오래 존재해왔다고 생각한다. 하지만 최초의 해독된 문자 기록은 기원전 4000년의 수메르인의 저술에서 유래된 기껏해야 6000년 된 기록이다. 이 기록은 언어의 발전사에서 너무나 늦게 나타나 언어의 기원에 대한 단서를 제공해주지는 못한다.

(C) 이러한 이유로 19세기에 몇몇 학자들은 언어의 기원에 대한 논의를 조롱하고, 무시하고, 심지어는 금지하기까지 했다. 1886년 파리의 언어 학회는 이 주제에 관한 어떤 논문도 '불법'으로 정하는 결정을 통과시켰다.

(A) 과학적 증거를 찾아내는 어려움에도 불구하고, 언어 기원에 대한 추론은 언어의 특성과 발전에 대한 가치 있는 통찰을 제공해왔다. 그리고 이러한 통찰로 인해 한 학자는 "언어학은 영원히 언어학적 진화의 유래에 대해 (그리고 그 행선지에 대해) 묻지 않을 수 없다"고 말하기에 이르렀다.

03 모범답안 (1) Say what? (2) (I) beg your pardon?

한글번역

영수 : 안녕 민경아! 우리 학교에 영어 선생님이 새로 오신 것 들었어?
민경 : 정말? 저기 봐! 저 여자 분이 우리 새로 온 영어 선생님이야?
Ms. Brown : (교실 안에서) 여러분, 좋은 아침이에요. 저는 수전 브라운이에요. 여러분의 새로운 영어 선생님이에요. 만나서 반가워요. 오늘 제가 수업에서 하려는 것은 여러분에게 이력서를 쓰는 방법을 알려주는 것이에요.
영수 : 뭐라고요?
Ms. Brown : 음, 여러분에게 이력서를 쓰는 방법을 알려주려고 한다고요.

2004학년도 서울 · 인천

01 모범답안 getting someone to do something without saying anything at all

어휘

bidding 명령
maid 하녀, 하인
prerogative 특권, 특혜
set about ~을 시작하다

한글번역

간접성 그 자체가 무력함을 반영하는 것은 아니다. 간접성은 권력을 가진 자들의 특권이라고 생각되기 쉽다. 예를 들어 하인들이 그들의 명령을 따를 것이라 알고 있는 부자 부부는 직접 명령할 필요가 없고, 단순히 그들의 요구사항을 말하면 된다. 집주인 여자가 말한다. "이곳이 쌀쌀하네." 그러면 하인은 온도를 높이도록 한다. 집안의 가장이 "저녁 시간이다"라고 말하면 하인은 저녁이 준비되도록 한다. 아마 궁극적인 간접언행은 아무 말도 하지 않고 누군가가 무언가를 하도록 하는 것이다. 그러니까 안주인이 벨을 울리면 하녀가 다음 코스 요리를 가져온다거나, 혹은 아이들이 버릇없이 굴어 부모가 방에 들어와 두 손을 허리춤에 대고 서 있으면 아이들은 즉시 그들이 하고 있는 것을 멈추는 것처럼 말이다.

02 모범답안 so casual that they are inclined not to use titles right away after meeting

어휘

casual 격식을 차리지 않는
formal 공식적인, 형식적인
title 칭호, 작위, 직함

한글번역

어떤 문화권에서는 가족이나 친구가 아닌 사람들에게 말할 때 호칭을 사용하는 것이 일반적이다. 때로 이러한 호칭은 사람의 직업을 나타낸다. 또는 그것들은 그 사람이 나이가 더 많아 존중받아야 하는 것을 우리에게 말해준다. 일반적으로 북미인들은 형식적이지 않다. 즉 격식을 차리지 않는다. 이것은 또한 호칭에 있어서도 마찬가지이다. 일상생활에서 호칭은 병원 의사에게 사용되는 '닥터'와 때때로 대학교 교수에게 사용되는 '프로페서'를 제외하고는 사용되지 않는다. 자연스레, 미스터, 미세스, 미스, 그리고 새로운 형태로 미즈(미즈로 발음하며 결혼과 상관없이 아무 여성에게나 사용된다)가 때때로 사용된다. 그러나 미국인이나 캐나다인들은 격식을 차리지 않아 미팅 직후 직함을 사용하지 않는 경향이 있다. 사실 많은 경우 심지어 상사나 연장자가 당신에게 이름 혹은 별명(약칭)을 사용하도록 요청할 것이다.

03 모범답안

3-1 Men tend to overinterpret women's apologies as evidence that they lack self-confidence while women tend to overinterpret the man's reluctance to apologize.

3-2 Many men resist apologizing because they tend to regard their actions as more important than their words. They also resist apologizing because they think that apologizing implies weakness, which others could exploit in the future.

어휘

constitute ~로 이루어지다; ~이 되다; ~을 구성하다
exploit (부당하게) 이용하다
overinterpret 지나친 해석
resist 저항하다
superficial 가벼운
dispute 논쟁, 논의
myriad 무수한
pepper 첨가하다
ritual 의식적인 절차
token 표시, 징표

한글번역

사과는 수많은 방법으로 마술을 부릴 수 있다. 그중 가장 놀라운 마술은 사과를 하는 것이 누군가로 하여금 잘못을 인정하게끔 하는 방법이 될 수 있다는 것이다. 우리 중 많은 이들에게 (남성보다는 여성들이 더 많이), 사과는 양쪽에서 이뤄지고, 이것은 의례적인 대화를 구성한다. 내가 x에 대해 사과를 하면, 너는 y에 대해 사과를 하고, 그리고 우리 모두는 그 일이 종결된 것으로 간주한다. 사과는 분쟁에 대한 해결을 나타내는 악수와 동일한 구두적 방법이다. 그래서 만약 당신이 잘못을 저질렀을 때, 당신이 사과하게끔 하는 한 가지 방법은 내가 첫 번째로 사과를 하는 것이다. 이것은 당신으로 하여금 당신의 맡은 역할을 해 두 번째 발화를 하게 만든다. 예를 들어, 내가 "네가 유리를 깼을 때 내가 너무 심하게 화를 내서 미안해. 그냥 유리일 뿐인데. 내가 너무 과잉 반응했네"라고 말을 한다면, 나는 당신이 "괜찮아, 내가 유리를 깨서 미안하지. 더 조심하도록 할게"라는 말을 하기를 기대한다.

우리는 상대방이 하기를 기대하는 말과 그들이 실제로 하는 말을 비교하는데, 이것은 일반적으로 우리가 무슨 말을 하느냐에 달려 있다. 그래서 남자들은 여성의 사과를 자신감이 결여된 증거라고 과도한 해석을 하는 경향이 있는데, 이것은 대부분 남성들이 여성이 하는 사과의 의례적인 본성을 알아차리지 못하고, 또한 사람들에게 그들이 사과할 필요가 없을 때 사과하는 것을 기대하지 않기 때문이다.

마찬가지로, 여성은 남성들이 사과하지 않는 것에 대해 과잉 해석을 하는 경향이 있다. 사과가 없다고, 즉 저 사람이 사과하기를 거부한다고 의견을 제기하는 것은 여성의 관점을 반영한다. 여성은 사과를 기대하기 때문에 그러한 결여를 발견하는 것이다. 남성은 대화를 맛깔나게 하기 위해 사과한다는 기대가 없으므로 그 결여를 보지 못한다.

많은 남자들이 사과하기에 저항하는 한 가지 이유는 그것이 피상적이고, 너무 쉬워 보이기 때문이다. 남성들에게 중요한 것은 그들이 하는 말이 아니라, 그들이 하는 행동인 것이다. 남성들이 사과를 거부하는 또 다른 이유는 그들은 자신이 한 단계 낮아보이도록 말하는 것을 피하는 경향이 있기 때문이다. 이러한 관점에서, 사과는 미래에 다른 사람들에게 이용당할 수 있는 약점을 의미한다.

04 모범답안

4-1 (1) They put the hottest merchandise just to the right of the 'decompression-zone'.
(2) They place merchandise within easy reach.

4-2 영국인과 일본인은 백화점 입구에 들어서서 왼쪽으로 이동해가는 경향이 있다. 따라서 천천히 움직이는 구매를 압박하지 않는 지역(decompression-zone)의 왼쪽에 상품을 배열해서 왼쪽으로 계속 쇼핑 이동을 지속시켜야 하지만, 오른쪽에 배치했기 때문에 구매 기회가 감소될 수 있다.

어휘

brush 스치다
connect 연결하다
decompression 감압, 느긋해짐
get into ~를 시작하다
move along (특히 다른 사람에게 공간을 만들어 주기 위해) 움직이다(비키다)
pet 어루만지다
retailer 소매상

한글번역

상점에 들어갈 때 왜 따뜻한 미소와 "안녕하세요, 오늘 하루는 어떠셨나요?"라는 말로 당신을 반기는지에 대해서 궁금했던 적이 있는가? 또는 쇼핑객이 정문을 들어섰을 때 왜 가장 인기 있는 상품이 오른쪽에 위치하는지에 대해서는? 아니면 왜 과자나 사탕이 보통 어린아이의 눈높이에 맞춰 전시됐는지에 대해서는? 이러한 것들은 그냥 무작위하게 일어나는 일들이 아니고, 당신이 구매하는 것을 관찰하고 더 많이 구매하게끔 유도하는 데 관련된 실제 과학을 바탕으로 한다.

쇼핑객들이 상점에 처음 들어갔을 때, 그들은 느긋해지고 쇼핑 모드로 들어갈 약간의 여유가 필요하다. 정문 바로 안쪽에 있는 이 공간은, 쇼핑객들이 아무것도 사지 않는 '감압 지대'라 불린다. 미국인들은 가게에 들어서면 그들이 운전할 때처럼 오른쪽으로 가려는 경향이 있고, 반면 영국인들과 일본인들은 왼쪽으로 가려는 경향이 있다. 소매상들은 이러한 경향을 활용해 수익을 올린다. 그래서 상점주들은 '감압 지대'의 바로 오른쪽에 가장 인기 있는 상품을 진열하고, 이런 식으로 통로의 오른쪽에 진열을 계속해, 고객이 상점의 나머지 부분까지 돌게 만든다. 이 이론은 매우 간단하다. 우리로 하여금 상점의 나머지 부분을 돌게 하는 것은 우리가 무언가를 구매할 확률을 증가시키는 것이다.

쇼핑 연구자들이 또 발견한 고객의 습관은 '상품 만지기'이다. 쇼핑객들은 물건들을 건드리거나 만지는 것을 좋아하므로 상품들은 손이 닿기 쉬운 곳에 있어야 한다. 연구자들이 발견한 것은 우리가 상품에 대해 더 느낄수록, 그 상품을 구매할 확률이 높다는 것이다. 일단 우리가 무언가를 건드리면, 그것에 더 연관되고, 그것을 구매하려는 관심이 더 높아진다. 그래서 상점주들은 매상을 올리기 위해 손이 닿기 쉬운 곳에 상품을 진열하고 고객으로 하여금 상품을 만져보게끔 부추긴다.

쇼핑에 관련한 가장 유명한 발견은 소위 '부딪힘 효과'라고 불리는 것이다. 미국인들은 다른 사람들이 너무 가까이에 있는 것을 불편하게 여긴다. 그들은 특히 '엉덩이'나 그들 뒤편이 잘못 부딪히는 것을 싫어한다. 이러한 일이 발생하면, 특히 공공장소에서, 사람들은 "나는 움직여서 비켜줘야겠다"고 무의식적으로 말한다. 그것에 관한 해결책은 간단하게도 더 넓은 통로를 제공하는 것이다.

05 모범답안 In terms of overall trends, the farm population and the number of farms tend to decrease while the average farm size shows a tendency to increase. Also, the range of decrease in the farm population is wider than that of the number of farms per decade. In conclusion, we can say that there is a growing tendency that the smaller number of farmers cultivate the larger size of farmland than before.

06 모범답안 (1) outlets (2) bodies (3) lack (4) chronic

어휘

affectionate 애정이 넘치는
chronic fatigue 만성피로
pellagra 니코틴산 병리 증후군
scurvy 괴혈병
weariness 피로, 권태
be apt to ~하는 경향이 있다
no amount of 아무리 많은 ~도 (소용없을 것이다)
psychiatry 정신의학
thrive 번창하다, 잘 자라다

한글번역

대부분의 사람들은 건강하기 위해 균형 잡힌 식이요법이 필요하다는 것을 깨닫고 있다. 그들은 비타민을 의식하며 그들의 몸이 다양한 음식을 요구한다는 것을 이해한다. 하지만 그들의 감정을 다양하게 분출하는 균형 잡힌 활동 '요법'이 그들의 행복에 똑같이 중요하다는 점은 잘 모르고 있는 듯하다. 무엇보다 가장 중요한 것은 사람이 일을 하거나 노는 동안 살아가는 정서적 분위기다. 물론 이 세상이 증오와 분노로 가득 차 있다면 우리는 잘 될 수 없다. 하지만 증오도 사랑도 아닌 일종의 중립적 세계에 발전이 없다는 것을 깨닫는 것도 더불어 중요하다. 단순히 아무도 미워하지 않는 것으로는 충분하지 않다. 보다 긍정적인 필요가 존재한다. 우리가 사랑하거나 아파야 한다는 것은 정신 의학의 기본적인 가르침이다. 인간은 사랑과 진정한 우정이 담긴 애정 어린 '주고받기'가 필요하다. 그리고 극단적인 경우에 비타민 결핍이 괴혈병이나 펠라그라와 같은 질병을 가져올 수 있듯이, 적절한 감정 표현을 스스로 부정하는 사람은 일종의 '심리학적 괴혈병'이라 불릴 수 있는 것으로 고생하는 경향이 있다. 그런 사람은 확실히 고질적 피로의 희생자, 곧 어떤 휴식으로도 진정되지 않을 몸과 마음의 피로에 시달리게 된다.

07 모범답안 Learn the importance of patience to handle problems, which are rarely as catastrophic as they seem.

어휘

capacity 능력
ramification 결과; 분기
marvel at ~에 놀라다

한글번역

나를 대하는 사람들은 종종 나쁜 소식에 대처하는 나의 능력에 놀란다. 항상 이런 것은 아니었다. 그리고 내가 나쁜 소식을 좋아하도록 배워왔던 것은 아니지만 나는 그것에 대처하는 법을 배워왔다. 나쁜 소식을 처음에 들을 때만큼 나쁜 경우는 거의 없다. 그리고 대부분의 사업 실패도 처음 보기만큼 파괴적인 것은 거의 없다. 여러 해 동안 나는 인내의 중요성과 인내의 결여가 얼마나 파괴적일 수 있는지 배워왔고 또 아직도 배우고 있는 중이다.

어떻게 단순히 시간을 보내는 것이 상황을 완전히 바꾸고, 문제를 해결하며, 다른 문제를 의미 없게 만들어버리는지, 또 대립을 완화시키고 전혀 새로운 관점을 더할 수 있는지는 아직도 나에겐 놀라운 일이다. "남에게 한 대로 되받는다"라는 말은 활동 과잉의 모든 새내기 임원의 가슴에 새겨야 한다.

이것이 일에서 우위를 점하는 것과 무슨 관계가 있는가? 무척 많다. 운에 맡기는 것 중의 하나는 숲속의 고양이같이 기회가 오기를 기다리는 것이다. 기다림을 배우는 것, 즉 인내를 배우는 것은 너무나 많은 적용(과정)과 결과들을 낳기에 그 중요성을 간과하지 않고 한두 가지 예로 설명하기란 내겐 어렵다. 그러나 우리의 20여 년 사업 가운데, 우리 성공의 90퍼센트는 어느 정도의 인내를 필요로 해왔다. 그리고 우리 실패의 90퍼센트는 부분적으로 그것이 부족해서 생겨난 것들이다.

08 모범답안 다음 중 5가지를 쓰면 맞는다.

(1) 아기가 얼굴이 벌게지도록 우유병을 달라고 소리 지르는 행위
(2) 판사가 강도짓에 대해 30년 징역형을 선고하는 행위
(3) 수용소에서 경비원이 무기력한 희생자(수용자)들을 고문하는 행위
(4) 방치된 아내가 남편의 애정을 되찾기 위해 자살을 위협하거나 시도하는 행위
(5) 살인자의 선혈 낭자한 폭력 행위
(6) 풋볼 선수가 격심하게 경쟁하는 행위

어휘

aggression 공격성; 침략
bottle (우유)병
burst at the seams 넘치도록 꽉 들어차다; 솔기가 터지다
concentration camp 강제 수용소
diffusely 산만하게, 장황하게; 널리
manifestly 명백히, 분명하게
portmanteau 대형 여행가방; 여러 가지로 이루어진
robbery 강도
squall 악을 쓰며 울다; 돌풍
subsume 포함하다, 포괄하다
torture 고문하다
under this head 이와 관련하여, 이 항목에

한글번역

인간 공격성에 관해 기술하는 것은 어려운 과제인데, 왜냐하면 그 용어가 다양한 의미로 사용되기 때문이다. 공격성은 모든 사람들이 알고 있는 단어 중에 하나지만, 그럼에도 불구하고 정의하기는 어렵다. 심리학자와 정신과 의사가 그 용어를 사용할 때는, 인간 행동의 넓은 범위를 포괄한다. 우유병을 달라며 악쓰는 얼굴이 붉어진 아기는 공격적으로 행동하고 있는 것이다. 그리고 강도에게 30년 형을 내린 재판관 또한 그러하다. 강제 수용소에서 힘없는 피해자를 고문하는 보초들은 명백히 공격적으로 행동하는 것이다. 남편의 애정을 다시 얻기 위해 위협하거나 자살을 시도하는 방치된 부인 또한 덜 명백하지만 크게 다를 바 없이 확실히 공격적인 행동을 하는 것이다. 공격성이라는 단어가 너무 널리 적용돼서, 축구에서 경쟁적인 분투를 하는 축구선수와 살인자의 잔인한 폭력성에 둘 다 사용될 때, 둘 중에 하나를 빼버려야 하거나, 아니면 더 자세히 정의돼야 한다. 공격성은 솔기가 터져버린 대형 여행가방 같은 용어이다. 하지만, 우리가 이와 관련된 포괄되는 인간 행동의 다양한 양상들을 더 명백하게 표기하고 이해할 수 있을 때까지, 이 개념을 버릴 수가 없다.

2004학년도 전국

01 모범답안 다음 중 하나를 쓰면 맞는다.

① new, informal, even bizarre forms of language
② a grotesque creation
③ the latest cool trend in informality
④ the new shirt

어휘

assure 확신하다
grotesque 기괴한, 터무니없는
owning 자신의
staid 고루한
enrich 풍부하게 하다
indication 표시, 암시
sartorially 의복으로
virtue 선, 미덕, 장점

한글번역

인터넷 은어가 이미 존재하는 언어의 다양성을 대체하거나 위협하고 있다는 어떠한 증거도 없다. 반대로, 새롭고, 일상적이며 심지어 희한한 형태의 이 언어는 우리로 하여금 언어적 대조성들에 관한 민감도를 확대시킨다. 격식적인 언어, 그리고 일상적 언어의 다른 종류들은, 인터넷 은어의 존재 덕분에 새로운 관점에서 관찰된다. 의복에 대한 비유는 이러한 주장을 돕는다. 나는 한때 매우 포멀한 셔츠와 일상적인 경우에 입었던 다른 셔츠를 가지고 있었던 것으로 기억한다. 그리고 나서 나는 일상복으로는 그 당시 가장 최신의 멋진 트렌드라고 확신했던 기괴한 창조물을 받았고; 확실히, 그 효과로 내가 이전에 가지고 있던 일상용 셔츠가 다소 구식으로 보였다. 그 새로운 셔츠는 내가 옷 입는 행동양식에서 격식적이거나 일상적이라는 가치의 대립에 대한 나의 감각을 무너뜨린 것은 아니다. 그것은 내 감각을 단순히 확장했을 뿐이다. 나는 더 많은 선택권을 가지며 의복과 관련해 더 풍요로워진 것이다. 유사하게 나는 인터넷 은어의 도래가 우리로 하여금 사용할 수 있는 의사소통 방법의 범위를 더 풍요롭게 하는 것이라고 바라본다.

02 모범답안 influence (or impact)

어휘

aware of ~을 깨달은
monologue 독백
subconscious 무의식적인
constant 계속적인
scarcely 거의

한글번역

연구는 우리가 우리 스스로에게 하는 말과 우리가 성취하는 것이 중요한 관련성이 있다고 보여준다. 게다가 자기대화나, 우리 자신과의 내면의 대화들은, 정신 건강에도 강력한 영향을 미친다.

우리가 알고 있든지 아니든지 간에, 우리는 모두 우리 자신과 거의 지속적으로 무의식적인 독백을 한다. 가끔 우리는 독백을 크게 소리 내서 표현하기도 하지만, 자기대화는 주로 조용히 생각하거나 우리가 거의 의식하지 못하는 내적인 속삭임이다. 비록 이러한 자기대화는 조용할지라도 그 영향력은 엄청나다. 우리의 행동, 감정, 자존감, 그리고 심지어 스트레스 레벨까지도 우리의 내적 독백에 의해 영향 받는다.

우리가 행하는 모든 일은 자기대화로 시작한다. 자기대화는 우리의 내적 태도를 형성하고, 태도는 행동을 형성하며, 그리고 당연히 행동, 즉 우리가 하는 일이 우리가 얻는 결과를 형성한다.

03 모범답안 the work to generate the intended connotations

어휘

association 연상
connotation 언외의 의미, 함축
spectacular 극적인, 장관을 이루는
call up ~을 불러내다, ~을 생각나게 하다
get it right 올바르게 이해시키다

한글번역

목표로 하는 특정 그룹의 모든 사업에 대해 광고 대행사 내에서 갖는 관심에도 불구하고, 회사들은 그들 제품을 가지고 국제화 혹은 세계화하려 할 때, 상품을 이해시키는 데 있어서 극적인 실패를 해왔다. 이는 다양한 이유에서였다. 때때로 상품의 브랜드명이 다른 언어로 번역될 때 좋지 않은 의미를 갖기도 한다. 이런 영역을 들여다보면 언어의 함축성이 얼마나 강력한지, 즉 단어가 우리의 마음속에 연상을 불러일으키는 방식을 설명할 수 있다. 우리가 단어와 어떤 특정한 생각, 감정 그리고 경험을 연관시키는 방식 때문에, 광고업자들에게 브랜드 이름은 아주 중요하다. 그것은 매우 경제적이며 의미가 집약된 작은 캡슐 역할을 한다. 광고업자들이 이것을 제대로 하면, 독자들은 의도된 의미를 생성하기 시작할 것이다.

04 모범답안 (1) analysis (2) Commitment (3) Implementation

어휘

commitment 투입, 책무, 헌신
return 수익
line item 품목
tangible 분명한, 분명히 실재하는

한글번역

창의적인 결정이 동시에 실용적인 결정이라는 것을 확실히 하기 위해 조직은 수많은 특정한 관행들을 따라야 한다. 일단 방안이 제시되고 나면, 경영자들은 그 방안의 장점들을 분석하는 데 굉장한 시간을 소비해야 한다. 즉, 그들은 새로운 방안이나 결정을 실행하는 데 드는 비용과 이점들을 파악할 필요가 있다.

그 다음 단계는 물론 그 기획이 실행 가능하다는 가정하에, 자원을 기획에 투입하는 일이다. 그러한 투입은 연구 지원비 혹은 예산에 있는 품목을 지원하는 형태를 띨지도 모른다. 형태가 무엇이든 간에, 이 단계에서의 목표는 창의적인 방안을 실질적인 현실로 바꿀 수 있는 자원을 제공하는 것이다.

마지막으로, 기획은 반드시 실행돼야 한다. 기획은 분명히 실재하는 상품 또는 행동 방침으로 바뀌어야만 한다. 이 단계에서의 핵심은 사업체가 수익에 대해 기대할 수 있거나 기대할 수 없는 것에 실제적인 관점을 가져야 한다는 것이다.

05 모범답안 should I take some pills

어휘

alleviate (문제, 질병 등을) 완화하다
grumpiness 심술궂음
fed up with ~에 진저리가 나다
tissue 세포 조직

한글번역

카리나라는 이름의 24살 여성은 불면증으로 인해 닥터 젠킨스를 방문한다. 그녀가 잠을 제대로 자본 지는 몇 주가 돼간다. 이 가여운 여성은 지쳤고, 일에 집중하지 못하고 항상 짜증을 느낀다. 오늘 아침, 카리나의 남자친구는 그녀의 짜증에 지쳐서 닥터 젠킨스를 방문하는 것을 제안했다.

카리나 : 의사 선생님, 제가 잠을 제대로 자본지 몇 주가 다 돼가는데, 도대체 무슨 일인지 모르겠어요. 제 몸에 이게 어떠한 해를 끼치는지는 모르겠지만, 제 관계를 망치고 있는 것은 분명해요. 제 남자친구가 너무 열이 받아 있어요.

닥터 젠킨스 : 음, 카리나, 잠은 중요하죠. 수면은 몸이 자가 치유를 할 수 있게 해요. 수면 중에는, 면역 체계가 더욱 활발해지고, 세포 조직 형성이 최고치에 다다르게 돼요.

카리나 : 그래서 제가 약을 먹어야 할까요?

닥터 젠킨스 : 약이라고요? 약은 마지막 수단으로 둡시다. 문제를 완화하기 위한 더 자연스러운 방법들이 있는데, 이것들은 부작용도 없죠. 예를 들어 카페인, 술, 담배를 끊는 거예요. 이 모든 것들이 불면증의 원인이죠.

06 모범답안 (예술작품의 토대가 되는) 사물의 객관적 상태인 자연

어휘

affair 문제, 일
artifact 인공품, 가공품
at any rate 적어도
be taken to ~을 취하게 되다
denote 나타내다
deviously 우회적으로
neutral 중립적인
super-sensible 초감각적인
of-all-work 모든 것을 흡수하는(= all absorbing); 잡일하는
salient 중요한
signify 의미하다

한글번역

포괄적이고자 하는 거의 모든 이론에서, 예술작품의 전체 상황에 존재하는 네 가지 요소는 한 가지 혹은 다른 동의어에 의해 구별되고 중요하게 도드라진다. 첫 번째로, 예술적 산물 그 자체인 작품이 있다. 그리고 이것이 인간의 작품이자 인공품이므로, 두 번째 공통적인 요소는 예술가이다. 세 번째로, 예술작품은 직접적이든 우회적이든지 간에, 존재하는 것들로부터 얻은 주제를 갖게 돼있다. 즉, 작품은 문제들의 객관적 상태 혹은 그것과 어떤 관계를 갖는 것을 내용으로 하거나, 의미화하거나, 반영한다. 이러한 세 번째 요소는, 사람과 행동, 생각과 감정, 물질적인 것과 사건들, 또는 초감각적 존재들로 구성돼있다고 여겨지건 간에, 모든 것을 나타내는 단어인 '자연'으로 빈번히 표현돼왔다. 그러나 이 요소는 우리로 하여금 더 중의적이고 포괄적인 용어인 '우주'라는 용어를 대신 사용하게끔 한다. 마지막 요소로는 관객이 있다. 그 작품이 전달되는 청자, 관중, 또는 독자들, 즉, 그들의 관심에 대해, 여하튼, 작품은 이용 가능하다.

07 모범답안 (1) raise (2) effort (3) enormous

어휘

extensive 광범위한
front deck 앞마당
not the least of 적지 않은(= not the smallest of) cf. not the least 조금도 없는
produce 농산물
tending 관리

한글번역

내 친구들 중에는 뜰에 나무를 심어서 장 보는 것을 간소화한 이들이 있다. 그들 대부분의 일 년치 곡식은 앞 테라스 화분에서 자란다. 친구들은 커다란 허브 정원뿐 아니라 신선한 토마토, 고추, 완두콩, 그리고 그 외 다른 것들도 가지고 있다. 그들은 오랜 시간 동안 일하는 전문가들이다. 몇 년 전에 그들은 토마토 한 개가 필요할 때마다 시장으로 달려가는 것보다 그들의 테라스에서 작물을 돌보는 데 시간을 보내는 것이 낫다고 결단을 내렸다. 결과적으로, 그들은 그들 식탁에 올라가는 많은 양의 농산물들의 원천이 되는 것에 대해 엄청난 만족감을 얻었고, 그 농작물들이 유기농으로 길러진다는 사실로부터 오는 만족감도 적지 않았다. 그들에게는 다른 방식으로는 얻지 못했을 식물과 자연에 대한 감사함이 생겼다.

08 모범답안

8-1 several styles of leadership

8-2 의사결정 과정에 참여하여 소통을 행하지 않으면

어휘

authoritarian 독재적인
delegate 대표로 세우다, 위임하다
laissez-faire 자유방임주의의
consensus 일치, 조화, 대다수의 의견
dependability 신뢰성
waive (권리 주장 등을) 버리다, 포기하다

한글번역

수년 동안, 리더십은 자신감, 지능, 그리고 신뢰성과 같은 개인적인 특성의 조합으로 여겨졌다. 어떠한 특성이 가장 중요한지에 대한 의견 일치를 달성하기는 어려웠으나, 관심은 리더십 행동 유형으로 전환됐다. 지난 수십 년 동안, 독재적 유형, 자유방임주의 유형, 민주적인 유형 등 여러 유형의 리더십이 밝혀졌다.

독재적 지도자는 위에서 아래 방향의 의사소통을 하면서 모든 권위와 책임을 쥔다. 이러한 지도자는 사람들에게 특정 과업을 부여하고 규칙적이고 정확한 결과를 기대한다. 다른 극단에 있는 자유방임주의적 지도자는 책임을 포기하고, 하급자들에게 그들이 선택한 대로 간섭을 최소한으로 받으며 일하는 것을 허용한다. 의사소통은 집단 구성원들에게 평등하게 전달된다. 민주적인 리더는 최종 책임을 맡을 뿐 아니라 작업 배당을 결정하는 데 참여하는 구성원들에게 권한을 위임한다. 이러한 리더십 유형에서, 의사소통은 위, 아래 모든 방향으로 활발하다.

각각의 이런 유형은 장, 단점을 가지고 있다. 예를 들어, 민주적인 유형에서 고용인들이 실행하는 일들은 그들의 결정사항이므로, 고용인들이 더 효과적으로 일하도록 동기부여를 할 수 있다. 반면, 그 의사결정 과정은 시간이 소요되는데, 이것은 다른 유형에서는 과업에 전념하는 데 사용될 수 있는 시간이다. 사실상, 이 각각의 세 가지 리더십 유형은 효과적일 수 있다.

09 모범답안 Mr. Rose was told by a director at the gallery that Mr. Kormet died on the morning of the dream.

어휘

be acquainted with ~와 친분이 있다
coincidence 우연의 일치
dismiss 묵살하다, 일축하다
obituary 사망기사
subsequently 그 뒤로

한글번역

[A] 은퇴한 산업과학자 해롤드 로즈는 그의 부인이 우연의 일치로 일축해버리는 꿈들을 가끔씩 꿔왔다. 그러나 그 중 하나는 더 설명하기가 어려웠다. 1987년에 그들은 유명한 화가인 프레드 코밋과 잠시 친분이 있어 왔다. 그 뒤로는 그를 보지도 그에 대한 소식을 듣지도 못했다. 2년 후, 어느 날 아침 해롤드는 일어나서, 부인이 그가 꾼 꿈 내용을 그 자리에서 무시해버릴 것이라고 생각했기 때문에, 부인에게 자신이 프레드 코밋이 죽는 꿈을 깨어나기 바로 직전에 꿨다는 사실을 이해시키려 했다. 이틀 후에 그의 사망 기사가 타임스지에 기고됐다.
코밋이 연관된 미술관의 관장에게 확인해 본 후, 그는 프레드 코밋이 자신이 꿈을 꾼 그 아침에 죽었다는 사실을 알 수 있었다.

[B] 로즈 씨는 그가 2년 전에 만났던 유명한 화가인 프레드 코밋이 죽는 꿈을 꿨다. 이틀 후 그의 사망 소식이 신문에 기고됐고, 로즈 씨는 갤러리에서 한 화가로부터 프레드 코밋이 갤러리에서 일을 하던 중 사망했다는 사실을 듣게 됐다.

10 모범답안 their previous knowledge

어휘

by nature 본질적으로, 태생적으로
self-propelling 자기추진력이 있는
cut loose ~의 영향에서 벗어나다; 풀려나다, 자유로워지다
dispense with 없애다, 생략하다
rung (사다리의) 가로대; 단계

한글번역

훌륭한 가르침의 총체적 목적은 본래 작은 흉내쟁이인 어린 학습자를 독립적이고 자기 주도적인 존재, 곧 단순히 배우는 것뿐 아니라 공부하는 존재로 바꾸는 것이다. 이것은 자기 삶의 주인으로서 자기 능력의 한계에 이르도록 노력하는 존재로 바꿔 가는 것이다. 이것은 어린 아동을 어엿한 학생(공부하는 사람)으로 바꾸는 것이다. 그리고 이것은 배움이라는 사다리의 모든 단계에서 이뤄질 수 있다. 나는 어렸을 때, 구구단을 한 번에 "한 단"씩, 즉 일단, 이단씩 해서 구단까지 암기해야 하는 유인물로 배웠다. 선생님은 우리가 이미 알고 있는 덧셈으로도 어떻게 그 답에 도달할 수 있는지 알려줄 수 있다는 생각을 전혀 하지 못했다. 아무도 "자, 4 곱하기 4가 16이라면 너희들은 기억력의 도움을 받지 않고 5 곱하기 4는 무엇인지 생각해낼 수 있어야 한다. 16에 4를 더한 수가 될 테니까 말이다"라고 설명해주지는 않았다. 이것은 처음에 혼란스럽고, 암기 방식보다 복잡하고 어려울지도 모르지만 일단 설명을 듣고 (원리) 파악을 하게 되면 곱하기의 모든 것을 배우고 점검하는 도구가 됐을 것이다. 우리는 잠시 선생님 없이 배우며 유인물에서 자유로워질 수도 있었을 것이다.

2003학년도 서울

01 모범답안 ① dauntless ② confronted ③ lucrative

어휘

hot water bottle 뜨거운 물주머니(고무로 납작하게 만들어 겨울에 침대 안을 따뜻하게 하는 데 씀)
in favor of ~에 찬성(지지)하여
pass 험난한 (산)길을 건너는 것
struggle over ~을 두고 싸우다
trail 여정
one out of every ten 10명 중 1명
stampeder 우르르 도망치는 데 끼는 사람
traditional attire 전통 의상

한글번역

클론다이크 골드러쉬에서 나온 가장 흥미로운 이야기 중 일부는 용감한 여인들에 관한 것이다. 이 여인들은 험난한 (산)길을 건너기 위한 고투와 자기 몫의 금과 영광을 위한 투쟁에 모든 것을 걸었다. 심지어 자기 목숨까지도 말이다. 금광을 향한 경쟁에 참여한 열 명 중 하나가 여자였다. 이 여인들은 남자들만큼 열심히 일했고, 그 이상은 아니라 하더라도 그들만큼의 많은 역경에 직면했다. 그 시대의 전형적인 긴 여성 드레스에 숨쉬기 힘들 정도로 조이는 코르셋을 입고 (높은 곳에) 오르려 하는 것을 상상해보시라. 많은 여인들은 보다 실용적인 바지를 선호해 전통 의상을 버렸는데, 남성들의 모욕에 직면해야만 했다. 1897년 벨린다 멀로니는 골드러쉬에 대한 이야기를 듣고 알라스카주 주노에 있던 그녀의 옷가게를 정리했다. 그녀는 옷감과 뜨거운 물병을 사서 그것을 클론다이크까지 가져갔다. 거기서 그녀는 6배의 이윤을 남기고 제품을 팔았다. 그녀는 계속 머무르며 식당, 호텔, 건설회사 등을 열었다. 많은 이들에게 클론다이크로의 여정은 부를 향한 길로 시작해 깨져버린 꿈의 길로 끝나고 마는 것이었지만, 벨린다 멀로니에겐 인생을 건 모험으로 이끌었다.

02 모범답안 "Not at all, we close at 9."

어휘

nature 종류; 유형

한글번역

상상해봐라. 저녁 식사 자리에서 누군가가 당신이 후추 분쇄기를 사용하는 것을 지켜보고 나서 당신이 그것을 끝마쳤을 때, '후추 좀 건네주시겠어요?'라고 말한다고. 이러한 문맥에서 후추를 건넬 수 있는 당신의 능력에 대한 글자 그대로의 질문은 우회된다. 왜냐하면 의도된 요구가 너무 명백하기 때문이다. 이 예시가 보여주듯, 많은 간접적인 요구들은 숙어적이다. 동시발생하는 빈번한 표면적인 형태와 의도된 의미를 고려했을 때, 사람들이 반사적으로 암시적인 의미를 활성화하는 것은 놀랍지 않다.

그러나, 사람들이 항상 글자 그대로의 의미를 무시하는 것은 아니다. 누군가가 전화로 상인과 이야기하면서 오늘 밤 몇 시에 가게 문을 닫으시는지 알 수 있을까요?라고 물어본다고 생각해봐라. 그 상인은 아마 대답으로 두 가지 종류의 정보를 제공할 수 있을 것이다. 첫 번째로, 그녀는 글자 그대로의 질문에 대한 대답을 할 수 있을 것이고, 그 정보를 제공하기를 꺼리는지 꺼리지 않는지를 말할 수 있을 것이다. 두 번째로, 그녀는 간접적인 요구에 대한 답을 할 수 있을 것이고, 그녀의 일이 언제 끝나는지에 대한 시간을 말할 것이다. 만약 그녀가 문자 그대로의 의미를 건너뛰고 오직 의도된 메시지만 처리한다면, 그녀는 문자 그대로의 질문에 대한 답으로 그녀의 발화를 '네', 혹은 '아니요'로 시작하지 않을 것이다. 대신에 그녀는 오직 닫는 시간에 대한 정보만 제공할 것이다. 비록 그녀가 문자 그대로의 의미를 받아들여 처리한다고 해도, 그녀는 아마 그녀가 그것을 꺼리는지에 대한 정보를 제공하는 것으로 닫는 시간에 대한 말문을 열 것이다.

이것을 시험하기 위해, H. H. 클락은 조교에게 그 지역의 상인들에게 전화해 그들에게 가게 문을 닫는 시간이 언제인지 묻도록 시켰다. 그는 상인들이 보통 간접적인 의미뿐만 아니라, 문자 그대로의 의미에도 답한다는 것을 발견했다. 그들이 문자 그대로의 의미와 암시된 의미 모두를 계산할지 말지는 그 당시의 환경과 발화의 종류와 관련이 있다.

03 모범답안 The meaning of the word "feminism" has not really changed

어휘

agenda 의제
at long last 오랜 시간이 흐른 뒤, 마침내
hoist 들어 올리다, 끌어올리다
ornament 장식품, 장신구
proposition 명제
special interest group 특별 이익 집단(자신들의 특별한 이익을 위해 정부 등에 압력을 행사하는 단체)
strike 파업
vessel 그릇, 용기, 통

한글번역

1895년 4월 27일 한 서평에서 페미니즘이란 말이 처음 등장했는데, 그 리뷰에서는 '독립적으로 자신의 길을 찾아가는 능력을 자기 안에 가지고 있는' 여성을 묘사하고 있다. 그 후로도 페미니즘의 의미는 실제로 변화하지 않았다. 한 세기 전에 입센의 ≪인형의 집≫에서 노라가 말한 대로 "다른 모든 것 이전에 나는 인간이다"라는 것이 (페미니즘의) 기본적 명제이다. 페미니즘은 1970년 '평등을 위한 여성 파업'에서 한 어린 소녀가 들고 있던 팻말에 쓰여 있던 "나는 바비인형이 아니다"라는 간결한 외침으로도 표현된다. 페미니즘은 여성이 치장을 위한 장식물도, 가치 있는 그릇도, '특별 이익 집단'도 아니라는 것을 마침내 세계가 인지하기를 요구한다. 그들은 국가 인구의 절반을 이루며, 다른 절반(남자)만큼 당연히 권리와 기회를 누릴 자격이 있고, 그만큼 또 세계에서 벌어지는 일들에 참여할 능력이 있다. 페미니즘의 의제는 간단하다. 페미니즘은 여성이 자기 스스로를 정의내릴 수 있어야만 한다고 요구한다.

04 모범답안

4-1 Benefits of On-line Classified Ads

4-2 from a curiosity to the primary way private sellers and buyers get together

어휘

classified ad 안내 광고
loop 고리, 순환; 고리 모양을 만들다
query 문의, 의문, 물음표, 의문을 제기하다
entice 유도하다, 유인하다
maintenance 유지, 지속; 생활비

한글번역

오늘날, 제한된 관객에게 다가갈 수 있는 가장 효율적인 방법은 안내광고다. 예컨대 깔개를 사거나 팔고 싶어 하는 사람들처럼, 각 항목은 작은 관심 집단을 나타낸다. 미래에도 안내광고는 종이에 구애받지 않을 것이고 문서로 제한되지도 않을 것이다. 만약 당신이 중고차를 찾는다면 당신은 관심 있는 가격대와 모델 특징 등을 구체적으로 묻는 질문을 보낼 것이고 그러면 당신의 선호도에 맞는 구입 가능한 자동차의 목록을 보게 될 것이다. 혹은 당신은 소프트웨어 대리인에게 요청해 적당한 자동차가 시장에 언제 나오는지 당신에게 알려달라고 할 것이다. 자동차 판매광고는 자동차의 사진이나 비디오 그리고 심지어는 자동차의 관리 기록과 관련된 링크도 포함돼 자동차가 어떤 상태인지 알 수 있을 것이다.

처음에는 이러한 온라인 안내광고의 장점은 분명하지 않을 수 있다. 온라인 안내광고는 그다지 매력적이지 않을 것이다. 왜냐하면 많은 사람들이 그것을 이용하지 않을 것이기 때문이다. 하지만 소수의 만족한 고객들의 입으로 전해진 소문이 더욱더 많은 사용자를 이 서비스로 끌어들일 것이다. 보다 많은 판매자들이 더 많은 구매자를 끌어들이거나 혹은 그 반대의 경우처럼 긍정적인 의견의 고리가 만들어질 것이다. 서비스가 처음 개시되고 1, 2년이 지나 충분한 양이 달성되면 정보 고속도로의 안내광고 서비스는 처음에는 호기심이지만 이후에는 개인 구매자와 판매자를 함께 모이게 만드는 주요한 방법으로 바뀔 것이다.

05 모범답안

① I had only a couple of hurried visits.
② There is, of course, no answer.

어휘

overriding 다른 무엇보다 더 중요한, 최우선시되는
pastoral 목가적인
pop into 불쑥 들르다
relish (어떤 것을 대단히) 즐기다(좋아하다)
scrape 곤경
shoulder 짊어지다
side by side 함께
steep 담그다, 적시다; 깊이 스며들게 하다; 열중(몰두)시키다
stroke 뇌졸중 발작
take ~ to heart ~을 마음에 새기다
to the fullest 최대한으로
undertaking 일

한글번역

1년 반 동안, 나는 78세의 아버지와 더 많은 시간을 함께 보내기로 결심해왔다. 내 아이들이 내 어린 시절을 형성한 목가적인 리듬에 흠뻑 빠지게 하면서, 아버지의 농장에서 아버지와 함께할 여름 휴가를 고대하고 있었다.

크리스마스에, 나는 우리 대가족에 관련한 추억을 글로 기술한 수집본을 아버지에게 드리기로 계획했다. 또한 아버지와 돌아가신 어머니에 대한 영원한 존경과 감사를 전하는 감사의 글이 실린 내 첫 번째 저서를 아버지께 드리기로 했다.

현실에서는, 나는 오로지 몇 번의 짧은 방문만을 했다. 계획들은 계속해서 연기됐다. 그리고 난 후 1999년 3월 그 전화를 받았을 때, 아버지께 드릴 두꺼운 표지의 내 저서가 책상에 놓여 있었다. 아버지는 뇌졸중으로 쓰러지셨다. 그리고 8일 후에 세상을 떠나셨다.

아버지에 대한 나의 가장 큰 기억은 아버지가 항상 우리들과 시간을 함께 보내셨다는 점이다. 우리 농장에서, 우린 트랙터를 타거나 함께 집안일을 도왔다. 우린 텔레비전을 보거나 베란다에서 앉아 이야기를 나누며 셀 수 없이 많은 밤을 함께 보냈다. 내가 어린 시절 곤경에 빠져 울면서 내 방으로 달려갈 때마다, 아버지는 나를 달래주셨고, 그 다정함은 나에게 부모란 존재의 힘을 가르쳐줬다.

남동생, 여동생, 그리고 내가 성인의 책임들을 짊어지면서, 아버지는 우리가 하는 모든 일에 대해 칭찬을 해주셨다. "인생은 최대한 열심히 살아야 한다."고 그는 이야기했다. "너희들은 지금 추억들을 만들어 나가고 있단다."

아버지의 죽음으로 얻은 교훈을 마음속 깊이 새기면서 나는 삶의 속도를 낮추고 있다. 가끔, 내 자식들 중 한 아이가 사랑스러운 말을 하거나, 젖은 숲의 향기, 바람에 흔들리는 밀밭의 아름다움을 즐기고 있을 때, 나는 내 자신이 평화로운 순간에 있다는 것을 깨닫게 되고, 내 머릿속에 내가 이전에 말했어야 할 말들이 떠오른다. "저는 이제 준비됐어요. 아버지, 이제 저는 시간을 보낼 준비가 됐어요."

물론 어떤 대답도 돌아오지 않았다.

06 모범답안 Our classmates found from a newspaper that a live guitar concert would be held in the university auditorium. We purchased the concert tickets so that we would not miss this good opportunity. The auditorium was full of enthusiastic audiences, most of whom were college students. We enjoyed the performance very much. After the concert, we went to the university restaurant to have a meal. While having a meal, we talked about the singer of the concert.

2003학년도 전국

01 모범답안 Quality

어휘

a network of friends 교우 관계(인적 네트워크, 인맥)
affirm 단언하다
beat 이기다, 통제하다
a wide range of 광범위한; 다양한
be better off 더 낫다

한글번역

대다수의 연구들이 우정의 긍정적 효과에 대해 단언해주고 있는데, 그중 어떤 연구는 많은 친구를 갖는 것이 나은지 아니면 좋은 친구 한 명이 나은지를 연구해왔다. 어떤 연구는, 교우관계를 갖는 것뿐 아니라 공동체 그룹에 속하는 것과 같은, 광범위한 사회적 관계를 갖는 것이 가장 큰 보호망을 제공해 준다고 주장한다. 하지만 다른 연구는 단지 가까운 소수의 몇몇 친구를 갖는 것이 가장 중요한 것이라고 한다. 심리학자 로라 카스텐슨은 이와 같은 친구들을 "그들 없는 인생은 상상할 수도 없는 그런 부류의 사람들"이라고 말한다. "질이 항상 양을 이긴다."

02 모범답안 Television diets are shown to reduce the positive constraints from violence that family, church and school build.

어휘

television diet 텔레비전 시청을 많이 하는 것

한글번역

영국 심리학자인 윌리엄 벨슨은 1565명의 12세에서 17세에 이르는 런던 소년들의 많은 텔레비전 시청과 차후에 이어지는 행동들을 연구했다. 그는 만화나 슬랩스틱 또는 공상과학 소설의 폭력성이 이 나이 또래에 덜 해롭다는 것을 발견했다. 하지만 사실적인 가공의 폭력성, 가까운 관계에서의 폭력, 그리고 좋은 명분의 폭력은 극도로 해로웠다. 골수 시청자들은 학내 싸움에서 칼을 휘두르는 것, 다른 사람을 담배로 지지는 것, 차의 타이어를 칼로 찢는 것, 강도질, 그리고 강간미수 등과 같은 일을 일으킬 가능성이 47퍼센트나 더 높았다. 놀랍게도, TV에 노출되는 것은 폭력에 대한 그 소년들의 생각들을 바꾸는 것이 아니라 오히려 가족, 교회 또한 학교가 형성해 놓았던 모든 제약들을 산산조각나게 하는 것처럼 보였다. "그것은 마치 그 아이들이 그들 내면에 있던, 그것이 어떤 폭력적인 경향을 갖는 것이든 관계없이 모든 폭력적인 것을 풀어내려고 하는 것 같았다. 그것은 그저 자연발생적인 방식들로 폭발하는 것처럼 보였다."

03 모범답안

① have long hair enough to satisfy the requirement they suggested
② will be held on Friday

한글번역

무료로 제공되는 전문가 헤어스타일링!
사우스다코다주 최고의 헤어디자이너들이 펼치는 국내 헤어스타일링 대회에 나갈 지원자(헤어 모델)를 모집합니다.
1월 28일 금요일
래피드 시티의 라마다 인에서
점심 및 저녁 제공(식대 제공)
교통비 지급
모델 지원 자격 조건은 최소 8인치 이상의 긴 머리입니다.
무료전화
1-800-222-1010
미용사 및 헤어디자이너 사우스다코다 협회

마이크 : 제인, 그 광고 봤어?
제인 : 응, 완전 좋지, 안 그래? 나 한 시간 전에 거기에 전화했어. 내가 괜찮다 싶으면 다시 전화하겠지.
마이크 : 응, 걔네는 분명히 너한테 다시 전화할 거야. 그러니까 내 말은 그들이 제시한 조건을 만족할 만큼 네가 긴 머리를 가지고 있다는 거야.
제인 : 그랬으면 좋겠다. 만약 내가 가게 되면, 나는 새로운 머리 손질법도 얻고 엄청 재밌을 것 같아.
마이크 : 맞아. 넌 언제쯤 갈 생각이야?
제인 : 글쎄, 대회가 금요일에 열리니까 목요일까지는 출발을 해야 되겠지.

04 모범답안 앞 : coins, 뒤 : They

한글번역

한 남성이 새 차를 샀고 그는 그것에 대해 굉장히 자랑스러웠다. 그러나 유일한 한 가지 문제가 있었다. 차 앞에서 달그락거리는 짜증나는 소리였다. 그 남자는 몇 번씩이나 정비소에 차를 가지고 갔지만 정비공들은 그 차에서 잘못된 어떤 것도 찾아내지 못했다. 몇 달 후에, 정비공들은 문제를 찾아냈고 그에게 그 문제를 설명해줬다. 그 남자는 비흡연자였다. 그는 주차장이나 주차미터기에 사용할 잔돈을 모아두려고 재떨이를 사용했다. 그는 재떨이에 20파운드와 10파운드짜리 동전들로 약간의 돈을 뒀다. 이것이 달그락거림의 원인이었다. 정비공들은 이전에는 이러한 사실을 발견하지 못했다. 왜냐하면 그 남자가 차고에 그의 차를 가져왔을 때마다 그는 재떨이에서 동전을 치워버렸기 때문이었다. 그는 정비공들을 믿지 않았는데 그들이 동전들을 훔칠지도 모른다고 생각했기 때문이었다. 지난번 그가 정비소에 차를 가지고 갔을 때 그는 동전 치우는 것을 잊어버렸다.

05 모범답안 What do you think of your previous supervisor?

한글번역

누군가가 어떤 직업에 적합한지 아닌지를 결정하는 것은 항상 약간은 혼란스럽다. 관리자에게 있어서 올바른 정보에 입각한 결정들을 내리는 데 필요한 모든 정보를 지니고 있는 것은 드물다. 하지만 좋은 질문을 하는 법을 아는 것은 천양지차의 차이를 만들어낼 수 있다. 심리학자이면서 인사 컨설턴트인 커트 엔스타인에 따르면 이 비밀(좋은 질문을 하는 법)은 개방형 질문과 폐쇄형 질문 간의 차이점을 이해하는 것이다. 폐쇄형 질문의 문제점은 제한된 예, 아니오 답변을 권장하는 것이다. 제한된 예, 아니오 답변을 권장하는 것이나 폐쇄형 질문은 당신이 듣고 싶어 하는 것이 무엇인지 면담자에게 알릴 것이다. 개방형 질문은 속단하지 않으며 지원자에 대한 더 깊은 통찰력을 제공한다.

06 모범답안

① impose on the same data
② represent something different

어휘

arrangement 배열
in profile 옆모습의
reprocess 재처리하다
face away 외면하다
perceive 감지하다, 인지하다

한글번역

어떻게 마음이 우리가 인지하는 것을 구체화하는지 알아보려면 아래 두 그림을 봐라.

당신은 무엇을 보는가? 각 그림은 당신에게 두 가지 아주 다른 이미지를 제공할 것이다. 한 방식으로 첫 사진을 볼 때 당신은 화병을 볼 것이다. 그 사진을 다른 방식으로 보면 당신은 두 얼굴을 볼 것이다. 두 번째 사진은 당신으로부터 얼굴을 돌린 아름다운 젊은 여성 혹은 추하고 늙은 여성의 옆모습을 나타낸다. 어떻게 이것이 가능한가? 당신의 눈으로 받아들인 감각 자료, 즉 선과 음영의 배열은 같다. 하지만 당신은 당신이 보는 그림을 '바꿀' 수 있다. 당신이 '보는' 것은 당신의 마음이 동일한 데이터에 부여하는 의미다. 그리고 당신의 마음은 그 자료를 재처리할 수 있고 그래서 그것들은 뭔가 다른 것을 표시한다.

07 모범답안 use categorization to simplify information and operate practically (better survive)

한글번역

만일 인간이 자신들을 둘러싼 모든 풍경, 소리 그리고 냄새에 집중한다면, 정보를 체계화하고 기억해내는 그들의 능력은 정신없이 바빠지게 될 것이다. 대신, 그들은 넓은 언어적 범주로 정보를 나눔으로써 정보를 단순화한다. 예를 들어, 사람의 눈은 약 천만 개의 색을 구분하는 어마어마한 능력을 가지고 있지만, 영어는 이것들을 단지 4천 개 정도의 색 단어들로 줄여버렸는데, 이 가운데 단 11개의 기본 단어들만이 통상적으로 쓰이고 있다. 이것이 비록 그 신호등마다 빨강의 색조가 약간씩 다름에도 불구하고 운전자가 그가 빨강으로 분류한 색의 모든 신호등에서 멈추는 이유이다. 범주화는 사람들이 생존하는 데 상당히 도움되는 방식으로 자신들의 환경에 대응하는 것을 가능케 해준다. 만일 사람들이 고주파 소리를 듣는다면, 그들은 그와 같은 소리들이 날 가능성이 있는 원인들의 긴 리스트를 열거할 수 없을 것이다. 사람들의 공포에 찬 울음, 도움을 청하는 비명, 경찰의 호루라기 소리 등이 있다. 대신에 그들은 경각심을 갖게 되는데, 그들이 고주파 소리를 일어날 수 있는 위험의 지표로서 범주화했기 때문이다.

2002학년도 서울

01 모범답안

1-1 the trashing of the heavens

1-2 ④

어휘

amplify 증폭시키다
chain reaction 연쇄반응
junkyard 고물 쌓아두는 곳
molecule 분자
scarp 급경사, 벼랑
cascade 쏟아지는 것, 풍성하게 늘어진 것, 작은 폭포
debris 잔해, 쓰레기
metallic 금속의
orbit 궤도
whirling 소용돌이치는, 선회하는

한글번역

① 뉴욕-연쇄반응은 지구에서 아주 흔한 일이다. 연쇄반응들은 화학 공장에서 단일의 활성화된 분자가 플라스틱을 만드는 조합의 연속에서 주변의 것들을 촉발할 때 일어난다.
② 오늘날, 전문가들은 위험한, 새로운 종류의 연쇄반응이 우주에서 일어나고 있으며, 그것이 인류가 지구의 범위를 넘고자 하는 노력을 제한하려는 위협을 가한다고 설명하고 있다. 예를 들어, 그 연쇄반응은 수십억 달러 가치의 진보된 통신기구과 기상위성들을 위기와 파괴에 이르게 할 수 있다.
③ 문제는 지구 주변의 몇몇 궤도들이 죽었거나 활동하는 인공위성들, 사용된 로켓 단들, 수십억 개의 소용돌이치는 잔해들의 고물 창고가 돼버린 것이다.
④ 그리고 지난주, 땅에 있는 센서들이 러시아 로켓 단의 붕괴를 감지했다. 지금까지, 이 사건은 38개의 관찰 가능한 파편 부스러기들을 생성했다.
⑤ 하늘이 쓰레기장이 돼가는 일은 금속 찌꺼기가 속도를 내며 움직일 때 큰 물체와 충돌해 그 물체를 수백 개의 파편으로 부술 수 있는 지경에 이르렀으며, 이 과정은 파괴의 홍수 속에서 계속해서 반복되고 더 증폭된다. 이러한 종류의 연쇄반응은 임계 밀도로 알려진 시점에서 시작한다.

02 모범답안

2-1 민지는 '할 말이 없다. 유구무언이다.'를 의도한 것 같다. 하지만 '더 말하고 싶지 않다.'는 무례한 대답이 된다.

2-2 I'm sorry. I'll return it as soon as possible.

한글번역

[상황] 민지는 교과서 몇 페이지를 복사한 후 하루 이틀 내에 그녀의 미국인 급우에게 교과서를 돌려주기로 약속했다. 그녀는 교과서를 거의 열흘이나 가지고 있었다. 다음의 대화는 복도에서 서로 우연히 만났을 때, 민지와 민지의 급우 사이에서 일어나는 대화이다.

켈리 : 안녕 민지야. 널 찾고 있었어.
민지 : 왜?
켈리 : 네가 돌려주지 않은 책 때문에 화가 나. 왜냐하면 지난 주 수업을 준비하는 데 책이 필요했기 때문이야.
민지 : 내가 할 말이 없구나.

03 모범답안

(1) Exaggeration of the size and brutality of one's force
(2) Disinformation transmission
(3) Discouraging enemy's morale by using their own language or people
[또는 The three reasons psychological warfare is used are to exaggerate the size and brutality of a force, to transmit disinformation, and to speak in the enemy's language with demoralizing(discouraging) words.]

어휘

armor 갑옷, 철갑
brutality 잔인성, 야만성, 무자비
leaflet 광고나 선전용 전단
poly 계책, 술책
rain down ~에 비 오듯 쏟아지다
trench 전장의 참호, 도랑
armory 무기고
disinformation 허위정보
phenomenal 경이적인, 경탄스러운
psychological warfare 심리전, 신경전
run thin 줄어들다
virulent 악성의, 치명적인

한글번역

역사를 돌아봤을 때, 우리는 '선전 전쟁'이라고도 불리는 '심리전'이 사용되는 사례들을 찾을 수 있다. 예를 들어, 기원전 330년에 알렉산더 대왕은 일련의 침략들로부터 그의 군인 수가 줄어들고 있을 때 선전을 사용했다. 그는 키가 8피트 되는 사람에게 맞을 큰 갑옷과 투구를 만들라고 무기고에 명령했다. 알렉산더 대왕은 이러한 큰 갑옷과 투구들을 뒤에 남기고 가곤 했다. 그래서 적군들의 고위층이 그 갑옷과 투구들을 봤을 때, 그들이 '거인들'하고 싸울 뻔했고, 그들 자신이 확실한 죽음으로부터 피할 수 있었음에 운이 좋았다고 여기게 만들었다. 이러한 술책은, 알렉산더 대왕이 고의적으로 그의 무자비함을 유포했던 이야기들과 더불어, 적군에게 그를 추격하기에 충분한 용기를 좀처럼 허용하지 않았다.

제1차 세계대전 동안, 브리튼섬은 모두 합쳐 9백만 개라는 경이로운 수의 선전용 전단을 90가지 다양한 디자인으로 독일군 참호에 쏟아냈다. 제 2차 세계대전 동안에는, 대중 심리학의 대가인 조셉 괴벨스가 치명적인 반 유대인 캠페인을 내보내기 위해 라디오나 영화 같은 현대 미디어를 사용했다. 그때 이후로 조직적인 허위정보를 그의 이름과 동일시할 정도로, 그 효과는 강력했다. 일본 사람들은 라디오 방송의 사용을 가속화했다. 일본 사람들은 연합군을 낙담시키는 음악과 문구를 방송하기 위해 영어로 말할 수 있는 사람인 도쿄 로즈를 이용했다. 독일인들은 미군에 대항하기 위해 이와 비슷한 전략을 사용했다.

04 모범답안

4-1 are making a new trend: sending a burst of text by mobile phones

4-2 Companies are trying to forecast mainstream trends from teenagers' new trends.

어휘

catch on 인기를 얻다
flock to ~로 모여들다
keep tabs on ~을 예의 주시하다
on the fly (비격식) 대충 그때그때 봐가며, 비행기에서
reputation 평판, 명성
touch off 유발하다, 촉발하다
compared with ~와 비교해서
gadget 도구, 장치
latch on to ~에 달라붙다
rate ~의 등급(순위)을 매기다; 평가되다, 평가하다
runaway hit 대히트

한글번역

만약 추측해야 한다면, 미국 청소년들에게 휴대폰이 남자친구나 여자친구를 갖는 것이나 파티를 하는 것에 비교해 어떻게 평가될 것이라고 당신은 말할 수 있는가? 시장조사 업체의 새로운 설문조사에 의하면, 청소년의 85%가 휴대폰이 그것들만큼이나 끝내준다고 말했다. 무선 통신 기계 제조업체와 서비스 업체는 연구를 읽을 수 있다. 그들은 미국의 삼천 백만 명 정도 되는 기술을 사랑하는 세대에게 제품들을 제공하기 위해 떼를 지어 몰려들고 있다. '그들을 빨리 낚아라'는 마케팅의 기본 원리이다.

마찬가지로 중요하게도, 회사들은 십대들에 딱 달라붙는다. 왜냐하면, 십대들은 새로운 유행이 주류 시장에 히트치기 훨씬 전에 그런 경향들을 빨리 발견한다는 평판이 있기 때문이다. 예를 들어, 청소년들은 AOL의 즉석 메신저 서비스의 매력을 첫 번째로 발견했다. 그리고 청소년들은 피어 투 피어식(P2P 방식)의 파일 공유 혁명을 냅스터와 디지털 음악 스트리밍을 통해 촉발했다. 오늘날 휴대폰은 필수적인 도구이다. 부모님들은 아이들을 예의 주시하기 위해 아이들에게 휴대폰을 준다. 청소년들은 결국 대충 그때그때 봐가며 파티를 계획하기 위해, 그리고 '아메리칸 파이 2' 티켓을 웹에서 구매하기 위해 휴대폰을 이용한다. 10대들의 세상에서 다음 트렌드는 문자로 어필하는 것이다. 핸드폰에서 핸드폰으로 폭풍 문자를 보내는 습관은 이미 유럽과 아시아의 청소년들 사이에서 걷잡을 수 없을 정도의 히트를 쳤고 이제 미국에서도 유행하기 시작했다.

05 모범답안

(1) As a result, the unfair media focus on my son and our family has robbed us of all privacy.
(2) In fact, reporters have even rented an apartment facing ours.
(3) They do this so they can watch and photograph every little thing we do.
(4) You must understand that, because of this awful situation, we wake up to the scrutiny of the press.
(5) We are even no longer able to look out the windows of our own home; can you imagine what that is like?
(6) We are even followed when we walk our dogs.

어휘

around the clock 24시간 내내
down the sidewalk 인도를 따라
ordeal 시련
take … away from ~ ~로부터 …를 빼앗다
wake up to ~을 의식하게 되다
besiege 포위하다, 에워싸다
name A as B A를 B로 선정하다, 여기다
sit and wait 가만히 기다리다
the court of public opinion 여론 법정

한글번역

바바라 주얼은 오늘, 애틀랜타 저널이 그녀의 아들 리처드를 한 달 전 공원 폭탄테러 용의자로 지명한 이래로 그녀와 리처드의 삶이 어떻게 바뀌었는지에 대해 눈물을 흘리며 말했다. 주얼 부인은 기자에게 그녀의 아들은 그날 이래로 일상생활을 하지 못하고 있다고 말했다. 그날 오후 기자회견에서, 주얼 부인은 그녀의 아들은 집에서조차 수감자였고, 그 결과 그는 일을 하지도 평범한 삶을 지내지도 못했다고 말했다. 그녀는 그가 오로지 이 악몽이 끝나기만을 앉아서 기다리는 것에 대해 애통해했다. 그녀는 아들이 살인자가 아님에도 불구하고, 여론 재판에서 유죄를 받았었다는 것을 말할 때 분노했다.

한편, 주얼 가족은 기자들에게 계속 둘러싸였다. 주얼 부인은 그들이 기자들에게 모든 사생활을 빼앗겨왔다고 말했다. 기자들은 24시간 내내 그들의 카메라로 그녀의 집을 주시하기 위해, 그녀의 집과 마주보는 곳에 방을 빌리기도 했다. 기자들은 그들 모자가 해왔던 모든 것을 보고 사진을 찍어 왔다. 그들 모자는 파파라치들을 의식하게 됐다. 창문 밖을 쳐다볼 수도 없었다. 그들은 보도를 따라 미행하는 사람들 없이 강아지를 산책시킬 수도 없었다.

주얼 부인은 자신이 이 시련을 통해 슬프고 상처 입었을 뿐만 아니라, 화가 났다고 말했다.

2002학년도 전국

01 모범답안 ① (i)mbalances ② (s)peed ③ (f)aster

어휘

distribution 분배
split between ~끼리 나누다
transaction 거래
velocity 속도
imbalance 불균형
spread 확산
unequal 불공정한

한글번역

오늘날 지구상에서 가장 강력한 권력의 불균형은 부국과 빈국을 나눈다. 권력의 불평등한 분배는 수십억 인구의 삶에 영향을 미치고 부의 분배를 창조하는 새로운 구조로 변화될 것이다.

이제 세상은 급진 경제시장과 부진한 경제시장으로 나뉘게 될 것이다. 역사적으로 봤을 때, 권력은 후자에서 전자로 옮겨갔다. 급진 경제시장에서 진보기술은 생산을 가속화한다. 그러나 이는 별것 아니다. 그들의 속도는 매매의 속도, 결정하는 데 필요한 시간(특히 투자에 필요한 시간), 실험실에서 새로운 아이디어가 생성되는 시간, 자본 흐름의 속도, 그리고 무엇보다도 경제구조 내에서 정보와 지식의 흐름의 속도에 의해 결정된다. 급진 경제시장은 부진한 경제시장보다 부와 권력을 더 빠르게 창출한다.

02 모범답안 meteor(s) [또는 shooting star(s)]

어휘

atop 꼭대기에
meteor 유성
stargazer 천문학자
Leonids 사자자리의 유성군
shimmer 희미하게 빛나다

한글번역

심지어 베테랑 천문학자들도 이른 일요일에 수천 개의 작은 유성들이 보여주는 빛의 쇼를 놀라워했다. 올해 가장 기대됐던 사자자리 유성우는 유성들을 보기 위해 로스앤젤레스 북동쪽에 윌슨 산꼭대기에 모인 약 75명의 사람들을 포함해, 그것을 보기 위해 밤을 새거나 일찍 일어난 전 세계 사람들을 즐겁게 해줬다. 몇 초마다 적어도 소량의 우주먼지가 대기에서 무해하게 타올랐다. 가장 밝게 빛났던 불꽃은 몇 초 동안 걸려 희미하게 빛나는 자취를 남겼다. "저는 이 같은 광경은 본 적이 없었어요. 이런 많은 유성들을 본 적이 없어요."라고 9년 동안 윌슨 산 모임을 조직하는 데 도움을 준 몬테벨로의 6학년 교사 릭 예세얀이 말했다.

03 모범답안

3-1 It is because they begin to realize that life is of temporal limits, and want to be engaged in what gives them something more meaningful in life.
(또는 Because they begin to realize the human mortality, and to reconsider what really matters.)

3-2 일곱 자릿수의 봉급, 즉 수백만 불의 수입

어휘

be stuck 움쭉 못하다; 꼼짝도 못 하다; 강요당하다
on the side 부업으로
pet project 특히 좋아하는 사업
radical 근본적인
make one's mark 이름을 떨치다
or something ~ 등등
pull down (많은 돈을) 벌어들이다
school board 학교 이사회; 교육위원회

한글번역

스스로를 확립하고, 세상에 이름을 떨치려 노력하는 것은 20대와 30대에 매우 중요하다. 그런 다음 우리는 40대로 넘어간다. 그러나 40대 중반 또는 50대 초반이 되면 사람들은 목표를 재평가하곤 한다. 왜냐하면 그들은 종종 인생은 유한하다는 근본적인 깨달음을 얻기 때문이다. 인간은 죽을 수밖에 없다는 것에 대한 각성과 함께 진짜로 중요한 것에 대한 재고가 생긴다.

"중년에, 사회복지 업무나 식당을 운영하고 싶어 하는 수백만 불을 벌어들이는 회사 중역들과 변호사들이 많다."라고 전문 상담가 스티븐 로즌은 말한다.

제네럴 일렉트릭이나 모빌 오일과 같은 회사에서 최고 간부를 평가해온 한 컨설턴트는 중년의 다수는 자신들이 특히 좋아하는 일, 즉 학교 이사회 또는 부업으로 자영업을 운영하는 일들에 매우 열성적이라 말했다. 여러 사업들에서 크게 성공한 한 사업가는 자신이 싫어했었던 사업을 운영한다는 것을 알게 됐다: "이 회사는 나를 통제하는 수준에까지 이르렀지요. 나는 꼼짝도 못해요…. 보트나 다른 뭔가의 엔진을 고치는 것에서 나는 더욱 더 행복함을 느껴요."

04 모범답안

- 문단 [1] 대중 연설에서의 두려움은 누구에게나 있는 일이다.
- 문단 [2] 초조함은 연설과 주제, 그리고 청중에 집중하고 있다는 지표이다.
- 문단 [3] 연설 횟수를 더할수록 덜 초조해진다.
- 문단 [4] 신경을 지나치게 쓰는 대신 목표에 집중하는 것이 두려움 해소에 도움이 된다.

어휘

be equipped to ~할 능력이 있다
harness 이용하다
speechless 말을 못하는
bear in mind 명심하다
professional performer 예능인

한글번역

1 바브라 스트라이샌드, 윌러드 스콧, 시드니 포이티어와 리자 밀레니는 어떤 공통점을 가지고 있는가? 그들은 모두 예능인이며, 공개 연설에 불안감을 느낀다고 말하는 사람들이다. 장점이 두려움을 느낄 수 있는 것이라면, 초보자들이 말을 못하는 두려움을 느끼는 것은 놀라운 일이 아니다. 실은 여러 차례의 설문은 공개 연설이 1위의 두려움의 원인이라는 것을 보여준다. 따라서 대중 앞에 나서는 것을 불안해한다면 당신은 혼자가 아니다.

2 긴장감은 손을 떨게 하고, 입술을 마르게 만든다. 비록 이러한 증상은 나쁜 것이지만, 불안은 행사, 주제나 관중에 대한 걱정의 좋은 지표라는 것을 명심해라. 신경을 쓰지 않는다면, 불안해할 필요가 없다.

3 연설을 할 때마다 긴장감을 덜 느끼게 된다는 것을 또한 기억하라. 일단 당신의 첫 번째 말에 대중이 어떻게 반응하는지를 본다면, 당신이 두려워했던 것보다 더 잘 해냈다는 것을 깨닫게 될 것이다.

4 당신이 무엇을 성취하고 싶은지에 집중함으로써, 불안을 이용할 수 있다. 여배우 캐럴 채닝은 "나는 긴장감이라고 부르는 대신 집중이라 부르는 것을 선호한다."고 말한다. 그녀처럼 당신은 관중과 소통하는 데 전력을 다할 수 있다. 그러나 완벽을 기대하는 실수를 하지는 말라. 초조한 에너지를 계획하고, 준비하고, 연습하는 데 쏟는다면, 관중과 처음, 매번 만날 때마다 더 잘 준비돼있을 것이다.

05 모범답안

ⓐ it would be expensive

ⓑ costs

한글번역

재생 불가능한 자원으로 만들어진 몇 가지 생산품들은 재가공될 수 있으며 원래 목적대로 다시 사용될 수 있다. 이것은 재활용이라 불린다. 예를 들어, 알루미늄은 재가공될 수 있는 재생 불가능한 자원이다. 100개의 깡통에 쓰인 알루미늄으로 90개의 새 깡통을 만들어 낼 수 있다. 재활용된 알루미늄 또한 에너지를 절약한다.

그럼에도 불구하고, 10%보다 적은 소비재들이 재활용된다. 매년 미국에서 쓰인 종이 중 약 20%가 재활용된다. 만약 우리가 이것을 50%로 올린다면, 우리는 약 1억 그루의 나무를 절약할 수 있다. 750,000가구에 전기를 공급할 만큼의 충분한 에너지가 절약되는 것이다.

재활용이 더 대중적이지 못한 주된 이유는 아마 비용이 많이 든다는 일반적인 생각 때문이다. 생산업자들은 원자재에서 생산품을 만들어내는 데 필요한 에너지를 소비하는 것이 재활용을 하는 데 필요한 노동자들을 고용하는 것보다 더 싸다고 생각한다. 알루미늄 깡통 하나는 미국에서 약 1센트의 가치를 지닌다. 많은 사람들은 그 1센트를 위해 재활용에 대해 염려하기보단 쓰레기통에 깡통을 버릴 것이다. 그러나 원자재로 하나의 깡통을 생산하는 것이 재활용된 고철을 생산하는 것보다 약 20배 많은 에너지가 소모된다. 깡통을 생산하고 폐기하는 데 쓰이는 비용을 생각해본다면, 재활용의 가치는 기꺼이 더 높이 평가될 것이다.

2001학년도

01 모범답안

1-1 own

1-2 clean and shiny

어휘

deluded 속임을 당한
dip into 부분적으로 읽다
restrain 저지하다
wood pulp 목재 펄프
dilapidated 다 허물어져 가는
dog-eared 책장 모서리가 접힌
scribble 갈겨쓰다

한글번역

책을 소유하는 사람들에는 세 부류가 있다. 첫 번째 사람들은 모든 권위 있는 전집과 베스트셀러를 읽지도 않고 손도 대지 않은 채 소유하고 있다. 이런 호도된 개인은 책이 아니라 목재 펄프와 잉크를 소유하고 있다고 말할 수 있을 것이다. 두 번째 부류는 아주 많은 책을 소유한 사람들인데 그 많은 책 가운데 일부는 끝까지 읽은 것이고, 대부분 책은 약간 읽다 만 경우이다. 하지만 그 모든 책들은 바로 산 것처럼 깨끗하고 윤이 난다. 이런 사람은 아마도 책을 소유하기는 하지만 책의 외양에 대한 그릇된 존경심에 사로잡혀있다. 세 번째 부류는 몇 권 또는 많은 책을 갖고 있는데, 그 책들 모두는 지속적으로 사용됨으로써 귀퉁이가 너덜너덜하고 닳아 해졌고 책장의 처음부터 끝까지 표시가 돼있거나 지저분하게 적혀 있다. 이 사람이야말로 진정 책을 소유하는 사람이다.

02 모범답안 appear less serious and increase optimism

한글번역

3주의 코스를 진행하는 동안, 한 그룹의 사람들은 계속해서 물질적 고통이라든가 변하지 않는 몸무게에 대한 문제와 같은, 개인적 문제의 심각성에 대해 반복적으로 평가했다. 이러한 평가들을 매일 정해진 시간 안에 끝내고, 두 그룹의 사람들은 10분의 상쾌한 산책을 했다. 그 산책 이후, 만성적이던 개인적 문제들이 덜 심각한 것처럼 보였다. 그 산책은 또한 전반적으로 낙관적인 생각을 증대시켰다. 이런 개선점들은 매일매일로 본다면 작고 주목할 만한 것이 아니었지만, 3주 뒤에는 그 차이가 명확하게 나타났다.

03 모범답안 movies are supposed to be records with pictures

어휘

a barrage of ~이 빗발치는
be afflicted with ~에 시달리다
offender 범죄자
unsuspecting 의심하지 않는
assault 공격하다; 폭행하다
extend 주다; 연장하다
unasked-for 부탁받지 않은

한글번역

나는 뮤지컬에 관해 이야기하려는 것이 아니다. 뮤지컬은 다음과 같이 말함으로써 당신에게 경고하는 영화다. "여기엔 음악이 있다. 그것을 보든지 아니면 떠나라." 내가 말하는 영화는 그러한 예의도 제공하지 않은 채 아무런 의심 없이 영화를 보러 온 관객들로 하여금 그것들을 보게 한 뒤 요구받지도 않은 곡조로 그들을 공격하는 정규 영화들이다. 이런 범주에는 두 주요한 죄인들이 있다. 흑인 영화와 50년대 영화가 그것이다. 두 가지 유형의 영화는 동일한 오해에 시달리고 있다. 그들은 영화가 영화여야 한다는 것을 모르고 있다. 그들은 영화를 그림이 있는 기록물로 여긴다. 그러니 그들은 다음과 같은 사실을 이해할 리 없다. 즉, 만일 하느님이 기록물에 그림(사진)이 있기를 원했다면 텔레비전을 발명하지 않았을 거라는 사실을 이해하지 못하는 것이다.

04 모범답안

4-1 air conditioning

4-2 집 밖으로 나가 잔디밭에 나뒹굴거나 지붕 위에서 잠을 잠

어휘

aid and abet (범행을) 방조하다
clientele 모든 고객들
get around to ~까지도 하다
pestilential 지독히 성가신
boondocks 벽지, 오지
decisive 결정적인
Johnny Carson 조니 카슨(미국 인기 토크쇼 진행자)
preoccupied with ~에 집착하는

한글번역

사실, 학자든 대중 사회학자이든 그 어느 누구도 진정으로 에어컨에 의해 초래된 모든 변화를 명시적으로 기술해서 진단하려는 노력을 하지 않았다. 하지만 전문적인 관찰자들은 수년 동안 자동차와 텔레비전의 사회적 의미를 파악하는 데 몰두해왔다. 단지 대충 살펴보기만 해도, 미국인의 습관에 결정적인 영향을 끼치고 있는 차와 텔레비전은 에어컨의 도움을 크게 받는다는 것을 알 수 있다. 차가 오지에 그 많은 쇼핑센터들을 세웠을지는 몰라도, 그 쇼핑센터들이 다수의 고객들을 유혹하게끔 만드는 것은 오직 에어컨뿐이다. 마찬가지로, 거실을 인공적으로 시원하게 만드는 것은 의심의 여지 없이 전형적인 미국인들이 일 년 내내 TV 중독자가 되는 것에 일조했다. 냉방이 안 된다면, 텔레비전의 재방송(설사 조니 카슨 쇼라고 할지라도)을 볼 사람이 몇이나 되겠는가? 사람들로 하여금 밖으로 나가서 잔디밭에 나뒹굴게 하거나 지붕 위에서 잠자게 하는 끔찍한 여름밤에 말이다.

05 모범답안 파리는 무모한 일인 줄 알면서도 본인의 노력으로 극복해 보려 했지만, 오히려 그 노력의 대가가 자신의 죽음으로 이어지는 결과를 빚는다. 여기서 this self-imposed trap은 가까운 곳에 문이 열려 있음에도 자신의 노력만으로 창을 깨고 밖으로 나가고자 한 파리가 스스로 만든 무덤의 덫을 의미한다.

어휘

a fraction of ~의 일부분
determination 각오; 투지
futile 헛된
poignant 가슴 아픈, 저미는
self-imposed 자진해서 하는
whining 윙윙거리는
breakthrough 돌파구
frenzied 광분한
life-or-death 생사가 걸린, 목숨을 건
raw 날것의
stake on (생명, 돈) ~에 걸다
windowpane 창유리

한글번역

7월 하순 경, 막 정오가 지난 때다. 나는 몇 피트 떨어진 곳에서 벌어지고 있던 필사적인 사생결단의 싸움 소리를 듣고 있다.

파리 한 마리가 있는데, 자신의 짧은 생명의 마지막 에너지를 유리창의 유리를 뚫고 날아가려는 헛된 시도로 소진하고 있다. 윙윙거리는 날개는 파리의 전략에 대한 통렬한 이야기를 들려준다: 그 전략이란, '더욱 더 열심히 하라'는 것이다.

하지만 그것은 소용이 없다.

그 격렬한 노력은 생존에 대한 어떠한 희망도 주지 못한다. 역설적이게도, 그 노력은 함정의 일부이다. 그 파리가 유리창을 뚫고 가는 것을 성공할 정도로 열심히 노력하는 것은 불가능하다. 그럼에도 불구하고, 이 작은 곤충은 있는 그대로의 노력과 각오로 그 목표를 달성하는 데 목숨을 걸었다.

그 파리의 운은 다했다. 그 파리는 그 창턱에서 죽을 것이다.

방을 가로질러 열 걸음만 가면 문이 열려 있다. 10초만 날아갔다면 이 작은 생명체는 그가 바라던 대로 바깥 세상에 도달할 수 있었을 것이다. 낭비된 노력의 일부만으로도, 그는 스스로 만든 무덤에서 벗어날 수 있었을 것이다. 돌파구는 바로 거기 있을 것이다. 그것은 아주 쉬웠을 것이다.

06 모범답안 전자매체로 인해 초래되는 개방성으로의 성향은 집중하기, 읽기, 쓰기 등의 능력을 떨어뜨리게 된다.

어휘

access to ~에의 접근
inadequate 부적합한
adversely 반대로
predisposition 성향

한글번역

읽기는 복잡한 정신적 조작을 요구하기 때문에 읽는 사람은 텔레비전을 보는 사람보다 훨씬 더 많은 것에 집중하는 것이 필요하다. 한 청각 전문가는 "전자 매체에서 중요한 것은 개방성(openness)이다. 개방성은 청각적인 자극과 시각적인 자극이 뇌에 더 직접적으로 접근하게 한다. … 집중하도록 훈련된 사람은 전자 매체에 의한 자극이 가져다주는 많은 정보 유형을 인식하지 못하게 될 것이다."라고 지적하기도 했다.

아마도, 독서 경험에 의해 후천적으로 습득된 집중하려는 성향이, 사람을 부적합한 텔레비전 시청자로 만드는 것일지도 모른다. 하지만 훨씬 더 개연성이 높은 것은, 그 반대의 상황도 널리 생길 수 있다는 점이다. 즉, '개방성'(여기서 개방성이란 집중의 반대로 이해해도 좋을 듯하다)으로의 성향은, 이 또한 수년간에 걸친 텔레비전 시청을 통해 습득될 수 있는데, 오히려 이것이 시청자의 능력들, 즉 집중하고 읽고 명료하게 쓰는 능력들, 간단히 말해 탈문맹 사회가 요구하는 언어적 기능들 중 어떤 것이라도 명확히 보여줄 수 있는 능력에 불리한 영향을 끼칠 수 있다는 점이다.

07 모범답안 C, F

한글번역

(A) 동물원에서 다른 종 사이의 교류 없이 서로로부터 격리된 동물들은 완전히 그들의 사육사들에게 의존하게 돼왔다. (B) 결과적으로 그들 대부분의 반응들은 바뀌었다. (C) 제한된 범위 내에서 동물들은 자유롭지만, 그 동물들과 그들을 보는 구경꾼들 둘 다 그 동물들의 갇힌 상황을 이용해왔다. (D) 동물들의 중심적 관심사는 일련의 자의적인 외부의 개입을 수동적으로 기다리는 것으로 대체됐다. (E) 자신들의 주위에서 일어나는, 그들이 인지하는 사건들은, 동물들의 자연스런 반응의 관점에서 볼 때, (실제 자연이 아니라) 그림으로 그린 대초원과 같은 환상에 불과해져버렸다. (F) 동물원에서 동물들은 그들 자신의 소멸이라는 살아 있는 기념비를 만들어낸다. (G) 그와 동시에 이러한 심한 격리는 시료로서의 그들의 수명을 보장하며, 그들의 분류체계의 정립을 가속화한다.

08 모범답안 와이오밍주나 몬태나주의 석탄 광산 개발은 미국 전체로 보면 이익이 되지만 지역 주민들에게는 희생을 강요하는 것이 된다. 이와 같이 국가의 이익(national interests)과 지역의 이익(local interests)이 상충하게 될 때 지역 주민은 지역의 이익을 선택하게 되는 현상을 가리킨다.

어휘

accrue 축적되다	constituent 주민; 유권자; 구성 성분
impose on 부과하다, 주제넘게 나서다	incur (좋지 않은 상황)을 초래하다
nation 국민	uncertainty 반신반의

한글번역

국민들의 분열(Balkanization)은 미국도 피한 적 없는 전 세계적인 현상이다. 지역들과 지방자치단체들은 주로 같은 나라의 다른 지역 사람들에게 도움을 주지만 자신들이 손해 보는 일을 별로 하지 않으려 한다. (미국의) 와이오밍주와 몬태나주의 탄광 개발을 예로 들어보자. 그 (개발) 이익의 대부분은 미국 나머지 지역의 도회지역 거주자들에게 돌아가는 반면, 그 대가 대부분은 그 지역 거주자들에게 돌아갈 것임은 의문의 여지가 없다. 결과적으로 지역 주민들은 반대를 하게 된다. 더 많은 채탄을 하는 것은 미국에는 좋을지 모른다. 그러나 지역 주민들에게는 좋지 않다. 그러므로 그들은 가능한 한 채탄 작업을 지연시키고 반신반의를 표할 것이다.

09 모범답안 (A) reasonable (B) challenge (C) participation

한글번역

문제가 나타나는 경우 질환이 거의 없는 사람들은 방책을 찾아서 아마도 다른 방식으로 뭔가를 읽거나 배운다. 그러고 나서 해결책을 시도한다. 첫 번째 해결책이 효과가 없으면 또 다른 시도를 한다. 반대로 자주 아픈 사람들은 문제에 대해 수동적으로 접근할 가능성이 더욱 크다. 몇 가지 예를 들어 보면, 그들은 아이들을 가르치는 일이나 주말 저녁에 어디로 외출을 할 것인가 하는 결정을 배우자에게 맡길 것이다. 또 그들은 작업장에서 뭔가가 잘못됐을 때 상급자에게 말하는 것에 대해 불편해할 것이다.

아픈 데가 없는 사람들은 또한 개인적으로 어떤 종류의 목표에 몰두한다. 그 목표는 학업을 마치는 일일 수 있다. 또한 좋은 부모가 되는 일, 공동체 활동을 발전시키는 것, 취미를 즐기는 것 등이 포함된다. 그러나 어떤 경우든, 이 사람들은 일주일의 168시간 중 4~6시간을 뭔가 가치 있는 일을 하는 데 쓴다. 그렇다고 이런 시간 동안 모든 것이 잘된다는 걸 의미하지는 않는다. 오히려 그 활동이 그들에게 개인적 의미가 있다는 말이다. 하지만, 걸핏하면 아픈 사람들은 쉽게 지겨워하고, 그들의 흥미를 끄는 뭔가 가치 있는 것을 발견 못 할 가능성이 크다.

2000학년도 추가

01 모범답안 market

어휘

enforce (법률 등을) 집행, 시행하다
privatization 민영화, 사유화
vogue 유행
with an exception ~는 제외하고

한글번역

아담 스미스와 그 후계자 누구도, 물론 몇몇 예외는 있지만, 공공 활동 전부가 시장에 맡겨져야 한다고 믿지 않았다. 한 가지 예로, (시장) 체계는 법률적 틀과 그 법을 시행하는 방법에 의존한다. 또 어느 누구도 경찰과 법원이 이익을 위한 사적 이해관계에 의해 운영돼야 한다고 진정으로 암시하지 않았다. 그럼에도 불구하고, 민영화로 치닫는 최근의 유행은 우리가 가능한 한 그러한 시장 철학을 추구해야 함을 암시하고 있다. 하지만 그러한 접근에는 위험이 도사리고 있는데, 즉 우리의 우선권을 왜곡할 위험성이다.

02 모범답안 environment

어휘

cultivation 연마; (기술 등의) 함양; 관계 구축; 경작
incompatible 양립할 수 없는
on the horizon 곧 일어날 듯한
shelf-space 선반 공간(소매점에서 어떤 상품 종류가 점하는 선반의 면적)
sweat-shop 노동력 착취의 현장
use up ~을 다 써버리다

한글번역

미래는 어둡지 않다. 아마도 경제 성장과, 이전의 많은 경제인들이 사회의 적절한 목적이어야 한다고 생각했던 '개발'은 더 이상 양립 불가능한 것이 아니다. 흥미 있는 가능성이 부각되고 있다. 미래에 우리가 구매하게 될 많은 것들이 우리 환경을 훨씬 더 고갈시키지 않을 것이다. 가령 CD-ROM은 한 장의 디스크에 브리태니커 백과사전 전부를 담을 수 있는데, 이것은 삼림을 미개발 상태로 보존하며, 점포에서의 진열 공간도 별로 필요로 하지 않는다. 또 이것은 생산을 위한 노동력을 착취하는 공장도 필요치 않으며 그것을 운송하는 데 필요한 거대한 트럭도 필요하지 않다. 정보시대의 많은 소비재는 컴퓨터 디스크처럼 환경 중립적이다.

03 모범답안 아이에게 모든 것을 다 가르쳐 줌으로써 아이한테서 스스로 학습할 수 있는 기회를 빼앗아버리는, 사실은 가장 비교육적인 사람

어휘

grown-up 어른　　overcome an obstacle 장애를 극복하다

한글번역

가정에서 어린이는 언제나 배운다. 거의 모든 가정에 적어도 한 명의 '어른이 아닌 어른'이 있는데, 그는 토미(아이)에게 그의 새로 만든 엔진이 어떻게 작동하는지를 보여주기 위해 안달이 난 어른이다. 어린이가 벽에 뭔가가 있는지를 조사해보려고 할 때면 어김없이 그 아이를 의자 위에 올려주는 사람들이 있다. 우리가 토미(아이)에게 그의 엔진이 어떻게 작동하는지를 보여줄 때마다, 우리는 그 아이한테서 삶의 기쁨, 즉 발견의 기쁨을 빼앗는 셈이다. 다시 말해, 장애물을 극복하는 기쁨을 빼앗아버리는 결과가 돼버린다. 더욱 나쁜 결과가 있다! 그 아이로 하여금 그가 열등하므로 도움을 요청해야 한다고 믿게 만드는 것이다.

04 모범답안 language represents cultural reality

어휘

bound up with ~와 밀접한 관계가 있는　　embody ~을 상징하다, 포함하다

한글번역

언어는 우리가 사회생활을 영위하는 주요한 수단이다. 의사소통의 맥락에서 사용될 때, 언어는 문화와 아주 복잡하게 결부돼있다.

우선, 사람들이 발화하는 단어는 공통의 경험을 나타낸다. 그것들은 다른 사람들이 공유하고 있는, 세계에 관한 풍부한 지식을 나타내기 때문에 의사소통이 가능한 사실과 관념 및 사건을 표현한다. 또한 단어는 그 작가의 태도와 신념, 관점을 반영하는데, 이것들은 또한 다른 사람들과 공유하는 것들이기도 하다. 둘 다의 경우에, 언어는 문화적 실재를 표현한다.

그런데 어떤 공동체나 사회집단의 구성원들은 언어를 통해 경험을 표현할 뿐만 아니라 또한 언어를 통해 경험을 창조하기도 한다. 구성원들은 다른 사람들과 의사소통을 하기 위해 선택하는 매체, 가령 전화통화, 얼굴로 마주보며 이야기하기, 편지 쓰기, 전자우편에 의한 메시지, 신문 읽기, 그래프나 차트 해석하기 등을 통해 그 경험에 의미를 부여한다. 사람들이 구어나 문어 또는 시각매체 자체를 사용하는 방식이 소속 집단의 사람들이 이해할 수 있는 의미를 창조하는 것이다. 사람들이 이해할 수 있다는 것은 화자의 음색, 억양, 대화 양식, 몸짓 및 얼굴 표정 등을 통해 이해할 수 있다는 의미다. 언어는 그 모든 언어적 또는 비언어적 측면을 통해 문화적 실재를 구현한다.

마지막으로 언어는 그 자체가 문화적 가치를 지니고 있는 것으로 여겨지는 기호체계이다. 화자는 그들이 언어를 사용함으로써 자신과 타인을 확인한다. 그들은 언어를 그들의 사회적 동질성의 상징으로 이해한다. 언어 사용을 금지한다는 것은 그들 문화 집단과 문화를 거부하는 것으로 인식된다. 따라서 우리는 언어가 문화적 실재를 상징한다고 말할 수 있다.

우리는 이 책에서 언어와 문화의 이 세 가지 측면을 다루려 한다. 하지만 먼저 우리는 문화가 무엇을 의미하는지를 명확히 할 필요가 있다.

05 모범답안 ① Cat ② Homo ③ Felidae ④ Primates ⑤ Mammalia ⑥ Kingdom

어휘

be composed of ~로 구성되어 있다
inclusive ~이 포함된
nuclei nucleus의 복수
resemblance 유사함

한글번역

종(種)이라는 집단은 분류를 위한 출발점이다. 때때로 더 작은 집단과 하위 집단을 생각할 수도 있지만 이것들은 진화를 논할 때까지는 우리의 관심사가 아니다. 더 큰 집단이 많이 있다. 가령 속(genus), 과(family), 목(order), 강(class), 문(phylum), 계(kingdom) 등이 그것들이다.

처음의 일곱 종부터 시작해보자. 우리는 Homo속에 속한다. 또 더 많은 넓은 집단에 속한다: Hominidae과에 속하는데 이것은 Homo 이외에도 Homo속은 아니지만 현존하지 않는 인간도 여기에 속한다. 또 Primates목에는 또한 여우원숭이, 원숭이 및 유인원이 있다. 고양잇과에 속하는 세 종류, 사자, 고양이 및 호랑이는 Felis속에 속한다. 일반적으로 우리는 속을 더 밀접한 관계의 종의 집단으로 본다. 세 종류의 고양이 또한 Felidae과에 속한다. 일반적으로 과는 서로 관계가 있는 속들로 구성된다.

처음 일곱 가지 종은 세 가지 목으로 분류할 정도로 매우 다른데, 여러 면에서 아주 똑같다. 모두가 털이 있으며 새끼를 젖으로 기르며 적혈구에는 핵이 없다. 이러한 유사성 이외의 다른 유사성 때문에 그 종들은 훨씬 더 광범위한 집단으로 분류된다. 즉, Mammalia강이 된다. 그러므로 강은 관련이 있는 목으로 구성된다.

2000학년도

01 모범답안 이유 1: to maintain a conscious distinction between the professional and the casual; or professional atmosphere
이유 2: to keep company hierarchy
이유 3: to increase productivity

한글번역

직장에서 간편복을 입어서는 안 되는 많은 이유가 있다. 우선, 직장에서는 직업적인 것과 일상적인 것 사이를 의식적으로 구별할 필요가 있다. 이러한 구별은 주로 복장에 의해 유지된다. 이러한 구별이 사라지게 되면, 작업자들은 서로 더 일상적이 되기 시작할지도 모른다. 즉, 업무적인 분위기를 유지하는 것이 어려워지는 것이다. 더욱 중요한 것은, 일상복은 회사의 위계질서를 해친다. 회사의 회장이 카키 바지와 폴로셔츠를 입고 일하러 오게 되면 종업원들은 다음과 같이 말할 것이다. "정말이지, 그는 단지 우리 가운데 하나가 아닌가?" '실제 생활'에서 그는 실로 종업원들과 동등하지만 작업장에서는 그렇지 않다. 그러나 종업원들이 직장에서 일상복으로 작업하는 것이 허용돼서는 안 되는 가장 중요한 이유는 그것이 생산성을 철저하게 떨어뜨리기 때문이다. 사람들은 작업복을 입고 있을 때 일을 하게 된다. 반면 사람들이 일상복을 입고 일을 할 때, 일이 끝날 무렵이면 일상적인 분위기로 돌아가려는 유혹이 대단히 커지게 된다. 종업원들은 많은 시간을 이것저것을 생각하는 데 보내게 되고 안이한 방법으로 일을 끝내려는 성향을 두드러지게 보이게 된다. "아, 난 다시 그 일을 꼼꼼하게 확인할 필요가 없어. 그것이면 충분해"라고 생각하면서. 직장에서의 이러한 태도는 회사의 복지에 위험이 될 뿐만 아니라 치명적일 수도 있다.

02 모범답안 Utopia, which expresses a human being's essence, can be truth only when it emphasizes not only the personal but also the social.

한글번역

유토피아를 철저하게 분석하게 되면 유토피아가 인간 자체의 본성에 깊이 관여하고 있다는 사실을 알게 될 것이다. 왜냐하면, 이러한 기본적인 사실을 별개로 '인간이 유토피아를 갖는다'는 게 무엇인지 이해하는 것은 불가능하기 때문이다.

유토피아를 평가하는 것이 무엇이 됐든 그것은 유토피아에 대한 긍정적인 의미로 시작할 것임에 틀림없다. 또 지적해야 할 그 첫 번째 긍정적인 특징은 그것이 진리라는 것이다. 즉, 유토피아는 진리라는 사실이다. 왜 그것이 진리인가? 유토피아는 인간의 본질 즉, 그의 존재의 내적인 목적을 표현하기 때문이다. 유토피아는 인간이 본질적으로 무엇인지 또 인간이 그 존재의 궁극적 목적으로 무엇을 가져야 하는지를 보여준다. 모든 유토피아는 단지 인간이 내적인 목적으로 무엇을 가져야 하는지 그리고 인간으로서의 성취를 위해 무엇을 가져야 하는지를 단 한 가지로 보여주고 있다. 이러한 정의는 개인적인 것은 물론이려니와 사회적인 것을 강조하고 있다. 왜냐하면, 사회적인 것을 개인적인 것과 별개로 해서 이해한다는 것은 불가능하기 때문이다. 개인적으로 정의된 유토피아가 만약 사회에 만족감을 가져올 수 없으면 진리를 상실하듯이, 사회적으로 정의된 유토피아가 만약 개인을 만족시키지 못하면 진리를 상실하게 된다.

03 모범답안

3-1 nonsmokers

3-2 safe professions, safe hobbyists, nonsmokers

한글번역

규칙적으로 아주 활동적인 운동 프로그램을 따라가는 수백만의 미국인들과 같이, 나는 운동하는 것이 나의 기분을 좋게 한다는 것을 알고 있다. 게다가, 나는 이 프로그램이 나의 신체적이며 정신적인 건강에 도움이 된다고 또한 확신한다. 하지만, 여기에는 당신이 알아차리지 못한 더한 매력이 있다. 건강함을 유지한다는 것은 당신이 보험료를 절약하는 데 또한 한몫할 것이라는 점이다. 어떻게 당신이 살점 1파운드를 현금 1온스와 바꿀 수 있을까?

첫째로, 당신은 일반적인 위험성을 가진 사람이어야만 한다. 즉, 위험한 직업들(말하자면, 스턴트맨)이나 취미들(예를 들어 스카이다이빙)을 가진 사람들은 자동적으로 자격미달이 된다. 가장 기본적인 건강과 관련된 할인에 대해서는 어떠한 신체적인 노력도 그 이상 실제로 요구되진 않는다. 즉, 비흡연자의 생명 보험료 할인처럼 말이다. 이러한 흡연과 주요 사망 질병 요인인 심장병과 폐암의 의학적 연결고리 때문에 보험회사들은 비흡연자에게 20여 년 동안 낮은 비율의 보상을 해왔다. 오늘날 다섯 개 가운데 네 개의 생명 보험 회사는 평균 10에서 15%의 할인을 제공한다. 흡연자들은 자동적으로 자격미달이 된다.

04 모범답안

4-1 national

4-2 첫째, 국내적으로는 공공기관뿐만 아니라 상업적 및 비상업적 단체의 컴퓨터들 사이에 네트워크가 이루어짐. 둘째, 국제적으로 국가 간의 컴퓨터 사이에 네트워크가 형성됨

어휘

damage-resistant 외적 손상에 강한
handful of 한 움큼
not ~ by any chance 결코
functional 가동하는; 작동하는
node 단말장치의 접속점

한글번역

1960년대 후반 소수의 미국 과학자들이 최초의 새로운 컴퓨터 네트워크의 연결점을 설치했을 때, 그들은 자기들이 무슨 현상을 시작했는지 전혀 알 수가 없었다. 그들에게 도전적인 과업이 주어졌는데 그 과업이란, 완전히 새로운 통신 체계를 개발해 구현하는 것이었다. 이것은 3차 대전이 발발하는 경우에 비록 그 핵심부가 파괴되더라도 완전히 손상을 입지 않거나, 아니면 적어도 어느 정도는 가동되는 것이어야 했다. 과학자들은 그들에게 요구됐던 일을 해냈다. 1972년경에는 이미 37개의 접속점이 설치됐고, (미 국방부 산하) 고등연구계획국의 네트워크가 작동하고 있었다. 그 '고대 시대' 이래로, 그때는 그 네트워크가 단지 국내의 학술 및 군사 목적으로 사용됐는데, 네트워크의 많은 특성이 변화됐다. 오늘날 그 네트워크를 사용하는 사람들은 상업적 및 비상업적인 영역에서 사용하고 있다. 꼭 학술 및 정보기관에서만 작업을 하는 것은 아니다. 그 네트워크는 국내적인 것만은 아니다. 오히려 그것은 전 세계의 많은 국가로 확대돼 그 네트워크는 국제적인 것이 됐다. 또 그런 식으로 해서 그 이름을 얻게 됐다. 사람들은 그것을 인터넷이라 한다.

05 모범답안

5-1 what he needs is not a new philosophy but a new exercise

5-2 Jefferson, who deplored the horse on the grounds that people did not walk (exercise) because of the animal, would have been struck dumb with amazement. (be struck dumb with amazement = 기가 차서 말문이 막히다)

한글번역

행복이라는 전체 주제는 내가 보기엔, 지나치게 거창하게 취급돼왔다. 인간은 생에 관한 이론이 없으면 행복할 수 없는 것으로 생각돼왔다. 아마도 나쁜 이론에 의해 불행하게 된 사람들은 그들이 회복하는 데 도움을 줄 더 나은 이론을 필요로 할지도 모른다. 마치 당신이 아플 때는 강장제를 필요로 하듯이 말이다. 모든 게 정상일 때, 인간은 강장제 없이도 건강할 수 있으며 이론 없이도 행복할 수 있다. 만일 누군가가 아내와 아이들을 보고 즐거워한다면, 또 밤낮이 바뀌는 데서 즐거움을 발견한다면 그는 그의 철학이 무엇이든지 간에 행복할 것이다. 한편으로는, 만일 그가 자신의 아내가 밉다는 사실을 발견하거나 아이들의 시끄러운 소리를 견딜 수 없다는 것을 확인하게 되면, 또 낮에는 밤을 그리워하고 밤에는 낮의 햇빛을 한숨지으며 그리워한다면, 그러면 그는 새로운 철학이 필요한 것이 아니라 새로운 운동이 필요한 것이다.

인간은 동물이므로 그의 행복은 자기가 생각하는 것 이상으로 생리학에 달려 있다. 이것은 보잘것없는 결론이지만 나는 그것을 믿지 않을 수 없다. 불행한 사무직 종사자들은 철학의 변화를 생각하기보다는 날마다 6마일을 걷게 되면 더 행복할 것이다. 우연히도 이것은 제퍼슨의 생각이기도 했는데, 그는 이러한 사실에 근거해 그 말을 한탄했던 것이다. 그가 만일 자동차를 예견했더라면 할 말을 잃었을 것이다.

1999학년도

01 모범답안 알코올이나 마약 중독은 완치될 수 있는 것이 아니라 평생 꾸준히 치유해야 하기 때문에

어휘

detoxification 알코올(마약) 중독치료
ongoing 계속 진행 중인
take place under ~하에 두다
on the downward slide 내리막길로
over time 시간이 흐르면서

한글번역

회복은 술이나 마약 없이도 생활할 수 있게 되는 것으로, 중독과 마찬가지로, 오랜 시간에 걸쳐 나타나는 과정이다. 처음 두 단계는 술이나 마약에 어떤 문제가 있음을 인식한 다음 그것들을 끊으려고 결심하는 것이다. 세 번째 단계는 실제로 이러한 마약 성분을 인체에서 제거하는 것이다. 이 과정은 해독과정이라 불리며, 감시하에 실시되야 한다.

회복 중인 사람들은 자신들을 '회복됐다'라고 하는 대신에 '회복 중'이라고 말한다. 이는 회복 과정이 계속 진행 중이며 장기간에 걸친 과정이기 때문이다. 즉, 알코올과 마약에의 의존은 치료될 수 있는 게 아니다. 다만, 더 진행하는 과정을 막을 수 있을 뿐이다. 그래서 사람들은 중독으로 내리닫는 중의 어느 지점에서도 회복의 과정을 시작할 수 있다. 심지어 치명적인 손상을 입기 전에라도 회복 과정을 시작할 수 있는 것이다.

02 모범답안 The meaning of the underlined part is that international organizations will relieve debt in exchange for countries conserving land.

어휘

at the expense of ~의 비용으로, ~를 희생해가며
biosphere 생물권
encroachment 잠식, 침략
write off 빚을 탕감하다
be combined with ~와 결합되다
designate 지명하다, 지적하다
hamper 방해하다

한글번역

보존은 사회적 및 경제적 상황에 의해 종종 방해를 받는다. 가난한 나라는 환경을 희생시켜서 흔히 개발과 교육에 우선권을 둔다. 또는 단순히 식량, 주택 및 공중보건에 우선권이 있다. 그런데 그들 나라의 경제적 이익이 때로는 국제기구의 지원을 받는 보존 계획과 결합되는 경우가 있다. 이를테면, 1987년에 최초의 '빚과 자원의 교환'이라는 보존 프로그램이 마련됐다. 이 계획에 따라, 육십오만 달러의 볼리비아 국가 채무를 탕감해 준 적이 있는데 그 대가는 천육백만 평방킬로미터의 열대 우림과 사바나 지역을 보존하는 것이었다. 이 지역은 이제 생물 보존지역으로 지정됐다. 이 지역은 완벽한 생태계로서 어떤 개입도 허용되지 않는 중앙의 엄격 통제구역이 있는데, 이 지역은 연구가 허용되는 전이지역으로 둘러싸여있다. 또 환경개발로부터 그 생태계를 보호하기 위한 완충지역이 가장 바깥에 자리 잡고 있다. 이는 현재 전 세계적으로 250곳이 넘는다.

03 모범답안 The question "How do you feel?" should be used at a proper time and place. (또는 The question "How do you feel?" should be used in a proper situation.)

한글번역

내가 견딜 수 없는 바보 같은 질문 하나는 "How do you feel?"이다. 보통 이 질문은 일을 하고 있는 사람들을 대상으로 한다. 이를테면, 업무를 수행 중인 사람들, 거리를 걷고 있는 사람들 아니면 책상에서 열심히 일하고 있는 사람들을 대상으로 한다. 그래서 그가 무슨 말을 하기를 기대한단 말인가? 아마도 그는 "Fine. I'm all right."라고 말할 것이지만, 당신은 그의 귀에 도청장치를 심은 셈이다. 어쩌면 이제 그는 확신하지 못할 수도 있다. 만일 당신이 좋은 친구라면 그날 아침에 그 친구가 아침에 놓쳤던 뭔가를 그의 얼굴이나 걸음에서 봤을 것이다. 그것이 그를 약간 불안하게 하기 시작한다. 당신은, 그가 모든 게 잘 돼있는지를 확인하기 위해 거울을 들여다본다는 것을 첫 번째로 알게 될 것이다. 그러는 동안에 당신은 유쾌하게 갈 길을 가게 될 것이다. 누군가에게 또 "How do you feel?"이라고 물으면서.

모든 질문은 때와 장소가 있다. 가령, "How do you feel?"과 같은 질문도 만일 당신이 병원에 입원해 있는 한 친구를 방문하고 있다면 더없이 좋게 받아들여질 만한 것이다. 하지만 그 친구가 두 다리로 걸어가면서 기차를 타려고 서두르고 있다면, 또는 책상에 일을 하면서 앉아 있다면 그에게 그 어리석은 질문을 할 때는 아니다.

유명한 극작가인 버나드 쇼가 여든이 넘었을 때, 어떤 사람이 "How do you feel?"이라고 물었다. 쇼는 그 사람을 자신의 입장에 두고, "자네가 내 나이가 되면 모든 게 괜찮다고 느끼거나 아니면 죽었을 것일세."라고 말했다.

04 모범답안

4-1 No. The comment is a doublespeak which distorts the truth and makes the disastrous situation acceptable.

4-2 The term "environment technicians" makes the janitorial job more positive and attractive than it actually is.

한글번역

농장에는 더 이상 소나 돼지, 닭 또는 다른 동물이 없다. 미국 농무부에 따르면, 농부들은 '곡식을 소비하는 동물 단위들'을 가지고 있다(1986년 세제 개혁법에 따르면 그 단위들은 돼지 축사나 닭장이 아닌 '단일 목적의 농업용 구조물'에서만 길러야 되는 것들이다). 영어를 주의 깊게 관찰하는 사람들은 최근에, 1987년의 수십억 달러의 주식시장 붕괴가 단순히 '4/4분기의 주가 하락'이라는 사실을 알게 됐다. 또 비행기는 추락하지 않았다. 비행기가 다만 '지상과 통제를 벗어난 접촉'을 했을 뿐이라는 사실도 듣게 됐다. 또 '문지기야말로 진정으로 환경 기술자들이다', 필라델피아 병원에서 환자 사망의 원인은 진료 과실이 아니라 '매우 중대한 진단 사고'이다. 레이건 대통령이 간단한 수술을 받는 중에 정말로 의식을 잃은 것은 아니며, 다만 '결정을 내리지 못하는 상태'에 있는 것이다 등등의 말을 듣게 됐다. 달리 말하면, 이중화법은 공공 담화라는 공식적인 언어로 계속 확산되고 있다. 이중화법은 의사전달을 하는 것 같아 보이지만 의사전달을 하지 않는 언어에 대한 포괄적인 용어다. 다시 말해, 나쁜 것을 좋게 보이도록 하는 언어이며, 부정적인 것을 긍정적인 것으로, 싫어하는 것을 매력적인 것으로 또는 적어도 견딜 만한 것으로 만드는 언어를 말한다. 그것은 책임을 회피하고 바꾸며 부인하는 언어이다. 즉, 실제 의미나 의도된 의미와 일치하지 않는 언어이다. 그것은 생각을 감추거나 가로막는 언어이다. 이중화법의 기본은 불일치다. 말한 것 또는 말하지 않은 것과 실제로 말한 것 사이의 불일치가 기본인 것이다. 또 단어와 지시 대상, 보이는 것과 실제로 그런 것, 언어의 본질적 기능인 의사소통과 이중화법이 전달하는 것과의 불일치가 그것이다. 이중화법이 전달하는 것이란, 오도, 왜곡, 기만, 과장, 우회 표현, 판단을 흐리게 하기 등이다.

05 모범답안

5-1 She is illiterate. (또는 She cannot read and write.)

5-2 a married woman in her late thirties who cannot read and write. By employing a number of tactics, she has so far managed to hide her difficulty from the people she works with and even from her family.

한글번역

브렌다 린슨은 안경이 없는 빈 안경집 없이는 어디도 가지 않는다. 안경집은 그녀에게 지갑만큼 중요하다. 하지만 그녀는 안경을 끼지 않는다. 그녀가 안경 없이 지낼 수 없는 이유는 그녀가 읽고 쓸 수 없기 때문이다. 만일 그녀가 읽거나 쓰거나 하는 일이 예상되는 어떤 상황에 빠진다면 안경집을 찾아 가방을 뒤진다. 안경이 없을 경우, 그녀는 관계된 사람에게 그녀를 위해 읽어달라고 요청한다. 브렌다는 이제 30대 후반이다. 그녀는 능력이 있으며, 매사에 분명하다. 또 몇 달 전까지 그녀가 읽고 쓰는 능력이 없다는 사실을 안 사람은 거의 없었다. 그녀의 남편도 몰랐고 아이들도 몰랐다. 아이들은 지금도 모른다.

그녀는 자신의 어려움을 숨기기 위한 꽤 많은 방안을 갖고 있다. 예를 들면, 무언가에 대답을 하고 그것을 받아 적어야 하는 경우가 있을라치면, 작업 시간에 전화기 주변을 맴도는 일을 아예 하지 않는다든가 하는 등이다. 하지만, 사실 글을 읽지 못하는 사람이 그것을 감추는 것은 우리가 생각하는 것보다 더 쉽다. 글 읽는 능력이 있다는 것은 아주 당연한 것으로 여겨지기 때문에 사람들은 그것을 드러내는 징후를 발견하지 못한다.

어머니가 읽을 수 없다는 사실을 아이들은 꿈에도 생각하지 않았다. 그녀는 아이들에게 책을 읽어주지 않는다. 하지만 그 경우 아버지 또한 그렇게 읽어주지 않는다. 그래서 아이들은 그 사실(어머니가 책을 읽어주지 않는 사실)이 전혀 놀랍지 않은 것이다. 마찬가지로 그 아이들은 병결증명서를 쓰고 성적표를 읽는 사람은 아버지임을 받아들인다. 큰 아이 톰은 글을 아주 능숙하게 읽으므로 브렌다는 교묘하게 그로 하여금 학교에서 집으로 오는 모든 통지문을 읽게 한다. 단순히 "근데 그거 뭐에 관한 거니?"라고 물음으로써 읽게 하는 것이다.

브렌다의 남편은 결혼한 지 10년이 지났지만 그 사실을 전혀 모른다. 한 가지 이유는 그는 모든 집안의 서신과 계산서 등을 자신이 직접 다뤄야 한다고 주장하기 때문이다. 페르시아 카펫 수입업자인 그는 여행을 아주 많이 한다. 그래서 그 사실을 발견할 가망은 별로 없다. 남편이 떠나 있는 동안에 브렌다는 그 어떤 상황이라도 헤쳐 나간다. 다음과 같이 설명함으로써 그렇게 한다. 즉, 남편과 상의할 때까지는 어떤 것도 할 수 없다고 설명해 그 상황을 극복하는 것이다.

브렌다는 최근까지 그녀의 일에 성공적이었다. 지난 5년 동안 그녀는 한 고급 개인 클럽에서 점원으로 일했다. 그리고 마침내 급사장으로까지 승진했다. 그녀는 그 일을 그곳에서도 여전히 비밀로 했으며, 어떻게든 현실에서 겪는 어려움을 극복했다.

06 모범답안

6-1 What happens to cause differences between children's personality traits?

6-2 The writer asserts that the remaining 5% of personality variation stems from the home in which the individual is raised.

6-3 The two scenarios the writer presents that could plausibly explain the 45% of personality variation in a child are the battle plans they develop for competing with siblings and also the battle plans they develop for competing within their peer group.

어휘

at random 무작위로
ingrained 몸에 깊게 밴
plausible 타당한 것 같은
rambunctious 난폭한, 사나운
retiring 내성적인
impinge (나쁜) 영향을 주다
placid 차분한, 얌전한
pluck from ~을 잡아 뽑다
replicable 반복 가능한
self-evident 자명한

한글번역

부모가 그들 아이들을 형성한다는 생각은 아주 뿌리 깊이 박혀 있어서 대부분의 사람들은 그것이 검증 대상이 될 수 있는 가설이며 또 자명한 진리가 아닐 거라는 사실을 깨닫지 못하고 있다. 그 가설이 이제 검증 대상이 됐다. 그 결과는 심리학사에서 가장 놀라운 것 가운데 하나이다.

성격은 적어도 다섯 가지 주요 방식에서 다르다. 어떤 개인이 사교적인가 은둔적인가, 지속적으로 걱정을 하는 편인가 평안하며 자기만족형인가, 예의바르고 신뢰를 주는 형인가 아니면 거칠고 의심이 가는 형인가, 사려 깊은 형인가 아니면 부주의한 형인가, 도전적인가 아니면 순응형인가 하는 것 등이다. 이러한 특성들은 어디에서 비롯되는가? 그것들이 유전적이라면 일란성 쌍둥이는, 비록 그들이 태어나면서 바로 헤어졌다 하더라도, 그러한 특징을 공유해야만 한다. 또 생물학적 형제자매는 입양된 형제자매들보다 더 많은 특성을 공유해야 할 것이다. 만일 그 특성들이 부모의 사회화(교육)의 산물이라면 입양된 형제자매가 그 특성들을 공유해야 한다. 쌍둥이와 생물학적 형제자매는 그들이 다른 집에서 자랐을 때보다 같은 집에서 성장했을 때 더 많은 특성을 공유해야 한다. 많은 연구가 많은 나라의 수천 명의 사람들을 근거로 해서 이런 종류의 예측을 검증했다. 그 연구들은 그 인성적 특성뿐만 아니라 이혼과 알콜 중독 같은 삶의 실제적 결과에도 주목했다. 그 결과는 분명하고 실험을 다시 한다 하더라도 같은 결과가 나오며, 두 가지 충격적인 것을 포함하고 있다.

한 결과는 아주 잘 알려져 있다. 인성의 많은 변인은, 즉 약 50% 정도는 유전적인 것이 원인이다. 태어나면서 헤어진 일란성 쌍둥이는 똑같고, 함께 자란 생물학적 형제자매는 입양된 형제자매보다 더 닮았다. 이것이 의미하는 바는, 다른 50%는 부모와 가정이 그 원인이 돼야 한다는 것인데, 맞는가? 그렇지 않다! 한 가정에서 자란 경우와 다른 가정에서 자란 경우를 비교해보면 사람들의 인성적 차이를 기껏해야 5% 설명할 수 있다. 태어나면서 헤어진 일란성 쌍둥이는 닮았을 뿐 아니라, 그들은 실제로 같이 자란 일란성 쌍둥이만큼이나 닮았다. 입양된 형제자매는 다를 뿐만 아니라, 임의로 추출된 두 어린이만큼이나 달랐다. 아이들에게 부모가 미치는 가장 큰 영향은 임신 순간이다.

변인의 다른 45%가 어디에 기인하는지 어느 누구도 모른다. 아마도 인성은 성장하는 뇌에 영향을 끼치는 특정한 사건에 의해 형성되는 것 같다. 즉, 태아가 어떻게 자궁에 놓이는지, 태아가 얼마나 많이 엄마의 혈액흐름을 바꾸는지, 태아가 출산을 하는 동안 어떻게 압박을 받는지, 태아가 머리로 떨어지는지, 태아가 초기에 어떤 바이러스에 감염되는지 등이 그러한 사건에 포함될 것이다. 아마도 인성은 그런 특유한 경험에 의해 형성되는 것 같다. 가령, 개에 의해 쫓기는 경험, 교사로부터 친절한 행동을 받은 경험 등이 될 것이다. 아마도 부모의 인성적 특성과 아이들의 인성적 특성이 아주 복잡하게 상호작용하므로 한 부모 밑에서 자란 두 아이라지만 실제로는 다른 환경이 될 수가 있을 것이다. 부모의 한쪽은 제멋대로인 아이에게 보상을 하고 조용한 아이에게는 벌을 주는 경우가 있을 수 있고, 또 다른 쪽 부모는 그 반대의 행동을 하는 경우가 있을 수 있다. 하지만 이러한 시나리오에 대한 충분한 증거는 없다. 내 생각에는 두 가지 다른 경우가 더 설득력 있어 보인다. 왜냐하면 두 경우 다 인성을 부모와 아이들 사이의 이해관계 차이에 뿌리를 둔 적응이라고 보기 때문이다. 한 경우는, 형제자매들과의 경쟁을 위한 전략이 되고, 다른 한 경우는 또래집단에서의 경쟁을 위한 전략이 된다.

07 모범답안

7-1 The technical revolution will cause unexpected changes in jobs in the future, and therefore we have to make full preparations for getting new jobs.

7-2 robots (또는 the robot)

한글번역

남은 금세기 동안 확산될 기술 혁명은 5년 전까지만 해도 존재하지 않던 직업을 만들어 낼 것이다. 이 새롭게 발달된 시장은 노동자들에게 늘어만 가는 전문기술뿐만 아니라 복잡한 기술 커뮤니케이션 시스템을 이해할 것을 요구하고 있다. 2001년경에는 한때 산업에 중요했던 기본 기술들이 쓸모없는 것이 되고 말 것이다. 자동차 생산라인의 점용접공들과 농장의 현장 노동자들은 기선의 도선사들과 대장장이의 전철을 밟을 것이다. 가까운 미래에 가장 중요한 경향은 현장 근로자(블루칼라)의 몰락이 될 것이다. 따라서 미국 경제는 자동화와 로봇학이 확산됨에 따라 그러한 몰락을 목격하게 될 것이다. 이는 스틸칼라 노동자의 등장을 예고하는 것이다. 자동차 회사처럼 전통적 현장 근로자를 고용했던 회사들은 이미 공장을 자동화하기 시작했다. 이와는 달리, 사무직과 서비스직은 더 늘어날 것이다. 하지만 그것도 자신들의 기술을 향상시키기 위해 준비하는 사람들에게만 해당될 것이다. 다시 말해, 현재 경제 구조에서 많은 비숙련 및 준숙련 근로자들을 대체시키게 될 것은 바로 자동화가 될 것이다. 사실, 종이 없는 사무실의 시대가 이미 시작됐다. 그것은 두 가지 주요한 발달에 의해 촉진되고 있는데, 바로 컴퓨터와 급격하게 성장하는 원거리 통신 시스템이 그 촉진역을 맡고 있다. 이러한 사무실 혁명은 작업 방식과 정보 처리 방식을 변화시켰을 뿐만 아니라, 위로는 기업의 중역에서 아래로는 최하층의 점원에 이르기까지 사무실 직원의 기능도 재편해왔다. 2020년에 직업을 구하려는 사람에게 구인구직 광고를 살피는 것은 작업장이 얼마나 철저히 변화될 것인지에 대해 빠른 교육이 될 것이다. 그 사람은 조금만 열거하겠지만, 생물 역사학자, 생명농업 전문가, 로봇 훈련사, 원거리회의 코디네이터 등과 같은 직업에 대한 기회를 발견할 수 있을 것이다.

1998학년도

01 모범답안 Anne이 우체국의 당연한 서비스뿐만 아니라 자신이 직접 나서서 처리하겠다는 말에도 불구하고 우체국 직원에게 모든 것이 거절당했을 때 겪은 좌절감

어휘

derisive 조롱하는
paralyze 마비시키다
peremptorily 독단적으로

한글번역

극심한 눈보라가 그 도시를 마비시켰던 어느 날 앤은 중요한 속달 우편 하나를 기다리고 있었다. 그 다음 날 그녀는 우체국으로 전화를 걸어서 그것을 받을 수 있는지 아닌지를 물었다. 그 전화를 받았던 남자는, "부인, 안 됩니다"라고 대답했다. 그녀는 "속달 우편이 배달될 수 없을까요?"라고 물었다. 그는, 거만하고 비웃듯이, "부인, 안 됩니다. 여기에 있는 것은 무엇이든지 여기에 머물러야 합니다. 그 어떤 것도 안 됩니다. 어떤 것도 드나들 수가 없습니다"라고 말했다. 그의 목소리는 이러한 사실이 분명함을 말해주고 있었다. 그녀는 점점 조바심이 났다. 그녀는 "제가 가서 가져올 수는 없을까요?"라고 말했다. 그가 "안 됩니다"라고 잘라 말했으며 그의 조바심도 극도에 이르렀다. "우체국은 폐쇄됐어요. 제가 여기에 있는 단 한 가지 이유는 어젯밤에 집에 가지 못했기 때문이죠"라고 그 남자가 말했다. 그제야 앤의 좌절감이 해소됐다. 그녀는 "정말 죄송하군요. 전화에 응해주셔서 감사합니다"라고 말했다.

02 모범답안

2-1 There are some uses of language which is not concerned with communication of thoughts

2-2 Phatic communion has an important role in getting along together.

한글번역

사고의 전달과는 관련 없이 사용되는 언어의 용법이 있다. 예를 들면, 영국인들이 날씨에 대해 이어가는 대화는 대체로 참여자들을 더 현명하게 만들지는 않는다. 또 아주 드문 경우에만 정보가 교환됐다고 말할 수 있을 것이다. 사고의 전달에 관한 한, 그 대화는 아무런 효과도 없다. 그러면 이런 언어 사용이 아주 무의미한 것일까? 아니다. 조금만 생각해봐도 그런 유의 언어 사용 또한 대단한 사회적 가치가 있음을 알 수 있다. 대부분의 사람들은 침묵을 지키는 사람은 위험한 사람이라는 느낌을 갖는다. 그래서 우리는 심지어 할 말이 없는 경우라 할지라도 말을 해야 하며, 대화는 사람들을 편안하게 하며 서로 조화를 이루게 한다. 이러한 사교적인 언어 사용을 의례적 언어(phatic communion)라고 부른다. 인류학자 말리노프스키가 그 용어를 만들었다. 그는, "그것은 용어 창안의 귀재에 의해 활성화됐다"라고 말했다. 비록 그 말이 절반은 농담이라 하더라도 어쨌든 그 용어는 받아들여졌다. 말리노프스키는 그것을 "단순히 단어를 주고받기만 해도 (서로 간에) 결속이 만들어지는 유형의 말"이라 정의했다. 이러한 대화는 가장 고도로 문명화된 사람들부터 가장 원시적인 사람들에 이르기까지 모든 사람들의 일상적인 경험이 되고 있다. 이러한 사소한 대화는, 소용이 없기는커녕, 인간이 서로 함께 지내게 되는 데 없어서는 안 되는 것이다.

03 모범답안 ① scale ② create ③ upheaval ④ wages ⑤ goods ⑥ unemployment ⑦ geographical ⑧ mismatch ⑨ unemployed ⑩ psychological ⑪ (working) hours

어휘

accrue 누적되다, 축적되다
given ~을 고려할 때
afoot 계획 중인, 진행 중인
improbable 사실 있을 것 같지 않은

한글번역

대량 실업에 대한 매우 간단한 해결책이 있다. 그것은 작업시간을 10%나 15% 아니면 20% 줄이는 것이다. 몇 가지 이유로 인해 그러한 단순성은 겉보기만 그렇지 실제로는 그렇지도 않다. 상대적으로 낮은 영국의 임금과 급여를 고려할 때, 조직화된 노조는 동일한 비율의 임금 삭감을 받아들일 수도 없고 받아들이려고 하지도 않을 것이다. 작업시간 단축으로 고용을 늘리려는 시도는 폭풍보다 더 큰 규모로 사회적 격변을 일으킬지도 모른다. 그러한 삭감된 작업시간에 대해 동일한 임금을 대규모 노동력에 지불한다면 세계 시장에서 영국의 경쟁력을 더욱 떨어뜨릴 것이다. 세계 시장이 더 비싼 물건을 받아들인다 하더라도(가능성이 별로 없는 가성이기는 하지만) 실업의 지리적인 분포와, 실업자의 기술과 현대 기업이 요구하는 기술의 격차 때문에 그러한 시도는 성공하지 못할 것이다.

그런데, 결국에는 새로운 기술이 실제로 사람들에게 상당한 생활수준을 제공하는 데 필요한 작업시간을 단축한다면, 일일 작업시간이나 연간 작업시간 또는 평생 작업시간의 단축은 가장 건설적인 대책이 될 것이다. 고용의 심리적인 이점은 단순히 하루 8시간 또는 주 40시간에 있지 않다. 그런 이점들은 금세기 동안 아주 드문 경우의 부산물일 수 있다. 그 드문 경우란, (금세기 우리가 경험한바) 생활수준이 저하되지 않고서도 작업 시간이 절반으로 줄어들 수 있다는 경우를 말한다. 다른 나라에서와 마찬가지로 우리나라에서도, 실제로 점진적인 노동시간 단축이 나타나고 있어 과잉 시간을 줄이려는 노력이 진행 중이다. 이는 다른 모든 어두운 상황에서 몇몇 긍정적 측면 중 하나이다. 그러한 전개의 직접적인 영향은 대체로 직원들의 작업 생활의 질 개선으로 나타날 것이다. 따라서 작업 시간 단축은 불가피한 것으로 실업자 수를 줄이는 심사숙고한 대안이 될 것이다.

04 모범답안

4-1 It is because their husbands do not send enough signals such as listening noises which make wives feel that they are really listening.

4-2 listening

한글번역

아내들이 남편들에 대해 하는 다른 불평은, "그가 내 말을 도무지 듣고 있지 않다"는 것이다. 남편들이 친밀한 관계를 쌓기 위해 문제나 비밀을 털어놓는 아내를 무시한다면 아내들의 말이 맞을 것이다. 하지만 어떤 경우에는 남편들은 부당하게 비난받고 있다는 느낌을 가질 것이다. 실제로 "그는 듣고 있었기" 때문이다. 그래서 어떤 때는 그 남편들이 옳다. 그들은 듣고 있었다. 누군가가 듣고 있는지 아닌지는 그 사람만 알 수 있다. 하지만 우리 생각에 다른 사람이 듣고 있는지 아닌지는 우리가 보는 신호에 의해 확인된다. 그 신호는 언어적 반응일 수도 있고 또한 시선 접촉이나 "음"이나 "어" 또는 "응"과 같은 작은 소음일 수도 있다. 이러한 듣기 반응 소리(listening noises)는 대화를 위한 활력을 준다. 그런데 그 소리들을 잘못 내게 되면 진행되는 대화를 즉각 방해할 수 있다. 몰츠와 보커는 또한 여성과 남성이 듣고 있다는 것을 나타내는 방식이 다름을 보고하고 있다. 듣기 역할에서, 여성은 더 많은 소리를 내고 또 기대한다. 그래서 남성들이 여성들의 말을 들을 때, 남성들은 소리를 너무 적게 내 여성들이 느끼기에는 남성들이 실제로 듣고 있지 않는 것처럼 보일 수 있을 것 같다. 또 여성들이 남성들의 말을 들을 때, 여성들은 남성들이 생각하는 것보다 더 많은 소리를 내게 되므로 남성들에게 자신들이 조급하거나 과장되게 관심을 보여준다는 인상을 줄 수도 있다.

05 모범답안

5-1 could permit far more instructionally valuable learning experiences to emerge

5-2 Improving computer's capabilities will provide better learning experiences for language learners.

한글번역

컴퓨터의 능력이 다른 교육 매체와 결합돼 사용될 때 많은 학습 경험을 제고하거나 넓힐 수 있으며 또는 전혀 새로운 경험을 할 수도 있을 것이다. 기술이 정교함과 구입 가능성 두 가지 모든 면에서 발달함에 따라, 양방향 오디오 및 비디오 능력이 컴퓨터의 표준 사양이 될 것이 틀림없다. 하지만, 현재는 컴퓨터를 해당 음향 및 영상적 기능과 결합한다는 것은 아주 비싼 주변기기를 포함한다거나 또는 단순한 비양방향 또는 거의 양방향 기능이 없는 음향 및 영상기기를 결합한다는 것을 의미한다. 하지만 가격이 떨어짐에 따라, 더 좋은 양방향 멀티미디어 애플리케이션을 구입할 수 있을 것이다. 양방향 비디오는 이미 현실이 됐다. 비록 값이 비싸긴 해도 말이다. 그것은 음성과 영상 이미지를 지원한다는 것이 특징이다. 또 그것은 때로는 아주 실감나는 모의실험을 제작하는 데도 사용된다. 양방향 오디오는 인공 음성 피드백을 하는 것은 물론이거니와 학습자의 말을 인식해 분석하고 조정하는 능력이 있으나 여전히 아직 완전히 초보적인 발전 단계에 머무르고 있다. 한편, 덜 복잡하고 더 쉽게 이용할 수 있는 오디오 기능에서, 유효한 학습 경험을 도출할 수 있다. 카세트 또는 오디오디스켓에서 들려오는 말은 컴퓨터 프로그램들과 결합될 수 있는데, 이는 독자적일 수도 있고 아니면 텍스트 디스플레이 또는 시각용 디스플레이와 결합하는 경우가 있을 수 있다. 이는 결과적으로 듣기, 말하기 및 이해 활동을 지원하게 될 것이다. 지난 20년 동안, 대부분의 어학 실습실 활동에 주요한 비판 중 하나는 그 활동이 피드백 없이 연습만을 강조한다는 것이었다. 컴퓨터 능력을 이러한 피드백 능력과 결합하게 되면 교육적으로 훨씬 더 가치 있는 학습 경험을 할 수 있을 것이다.

06 모범답안

6-1 to think wrongly that preindustrial days were better than today

6-2 made it possible to free human beings from slavery

6-3 created by science with the help of science

한글번역

[1] 오늘날 과학과 기술은 부당한 평가를 받고 있다. 젊은이들은 점점 우리 문화가 물질주의적이라고 비웃으면서, 더 단순하고 산업이전 및 과학이전인 시대로 돌아갈 것을 주장하고 있다. 하지만 그들은 그 '좋은 옛날'이 무지와 질병과 노예와 죽음이라는 끔찍하도록 나쁜 과거였다는 것을 깨닫지 못하고 있다. 그들은 자신들이 아테네에 있다고 상상하는데, 소크라테스에게 말을 걸며, 소포클레스의 최신 희곡을 들으면서 말이다. 그들은 자신들이 아테네 은광에서 짐승처럼 된 노예라고는 전혀 상상도 하지 않고 있는 것이다. 또 그들은 자신들을 중세의 중무장한 군마에 올라탄 기사라고 생각할지언정 굶주린 소작농이라고는 조금도 생각하지 않는다.

[2] 그런데, 근대로 내려오면서, 상대적 소수의 부와 번영은 많은 사람들(농민, 농노 및 노예)의 동물 같은 노동과 비참한 생활에 바탕을 두고 이뤄졌다. 더욱이, 그러한 노동과 생존에 관한 어떤 것도 이뤄질 수 없었다. 노예제도는 당연한 것으로 여겨졌다. 과학이 부각되고 나서야 비로소 노예제도가 아주 잘못된 것으로 간주돼 폐지되기에 이르렀다. 추정컨대 냉철하고, 이상보다는 현실적인 것에 관심을 가졌던 그 과학자야말로 이러한 결과(노예제 폐지)를 가져온 사람들이었다. 다시 말해, 과학자의 연구에 힘입어 무생물 세계(즉, 기계)의 에너지를 이용할 수 있게 됐다. 증기와 증기 및 방사선이 인간을 대신해 일을 하게 됨으로써, 비교적 약하고 어설픈 인간의 근육이 그다지 필요치 않게 됐고 이에 노예제도가 사라지게 됐다.

[3] 하지만, 과학은 또한 문제들, 아주 심각한 문제들을 야기하는 데 일조했다. 그래서 우리는 그 문제들을 해결하기 위해 노력을 해야 하는데, 그것은 역사가 우리에게 보여줬던 문제 해결의 방식이어야 한다. 즉, (과학에 의해 야기된 문제이므로) 과학에 의해야 한다. 우리가 다시 옛날로 돌아가려고 한다면, 또 고귀한 젊은이 세대가 산업의 물질주의를 포기한다면, 어떻게 될 것인가? 그 산업의 기계가 없다면 우리는 불가피하게 노예 상태로 떠밀려 되돌아가게 될 것이다.

1997학년도

01 모범답안

1-1 environments

1-2 they have no share of culture, or environment with the people back then (또는 horse-drawn vehicles are not a part of their culture)

한글번역

에스키모어는 눈에 대해 우리가 영어로 할 수 있는 것보다 아주 더 정밀하고 더 섬세하게 말할 수 있다. 하지만, 이러한 사실은 에스키모어(때때로는 '원시적'이라고 불리는 것들 가운데 하나인데)가 내재적으로 영어보다 더 정밀하고 더 섬세하기 때문이 아니다. 또, 이러한 사실이 영어에 결점이 있다는 것을 보여주거나 예기치 않은 '원시성'을 보여주는 것은 아니다. 그러한 입장은 단순하고 분명하게도 에스키모 사람들과 영국 사람들이 다른 환경에서 살고 있다는 사실을 보여준다. 짐작건대, 만일 영어가 일상적으로 사용됐던 환경에서 (눈에 대한) 그러한 구별이 중요한 것이라면, 영어는 다른 종류의 눈에 대한 용어(어휘)에서 에스키모어와 마찬가지로 풍부할 것이다. 마찬가지로, 자동차 생산이나 크리켓 등의 주제가 에스키모인의 생활의 일부가 됐다고 가정해보면, 에스키모어 역시 그러한 것들에 대한 주제에 관해 (영어만큼) 정밀하고 섬세할 수 있다고 상상하는 것은 당연하다. 몇 가지 분명한 역사적 이유로 인해, 19세기 영국인들은 자동차에 대해, 오늘날 우리가 하는 세세한 구별을 하면서 말을 할 수 없었다. 왜냐하면 자동차가 그들 문화의 일부가 아니었기 때문이다. 하지만 그들은 말이 끄는 탈것에 대해서는 많은 용어가 있었다. 우리가 스코트나 디킨슨의 책을 읽다가 그 '말이 끄는 탈것'이라는 단어들을 만나면, 우리는 당황하면서 역사 사전을 뒤지러 갈 것이다. 우리들 가운데 얼마나 많은 사람들이 마차, 랜도 마차, 빅토리아 마차, 사륜마차, 쿠페형 마차, 이륜마차, 승합 마차, 경 이륜마차, 이륜 포장마차, 지붕 없는 이륜마차, 썰매, 쌍두 사륜마차, 4인승 사륜마차를 구별할 수 있겠는가?

02 모범답안

2-1 with the attitudes necessary for the technique to work

2-2 일의 성취 다음에 오는 만족이란 기다림이 필요한데, 여기서 delayed gratification의 의미는 시간적으로 한참 뒤에 오는, 즉 '지연된 결과에 대한 만족'이다.

2-3 태도는 교육 상황 자체의 필수적 구성요소이므로, 태도는 학교에서 쉽게 가르칠 수 없다. 태도 교육은 가정에서 이루어져야 한다.

어휘

capacity (공식적인) 지위(역할), 자격; 능력
impotent 무력한
gratification 만족감, 희열
provided that ~한다면

한글번역

윌리엄 오코너는 한때 보스턴 학교 위원회의 위원이었는데, 그런 그가 위원 자격으로 다음과 같은 말을 했다. "우리 학교에는 열등한 교육이란 없다. 우리가 받아들이는 것은 열등한 유형의 학생이다." 이 말은 쉽사리 웃을 수 있겠지만, 어떤 의미에서는 아주 타당하다.

교실 수업은 특정한 종류의 학습을 성취하기 위한 기술이다. 교사와 학생 모두가 지닌 기술과 특히, 그 기술에 기본이 되는 태도가 있으면, 그것은 실행될 수 있는 기술이 된다. 학생의 입장에서 보면, 이런 태도 가운데 만족 지연에 대한 인내와, 권위에 대한 어느 정도의 존경이나 경외가 포함되며, 또 자기 개인의 욕구를 집단의 결속과 목적을 위해 기꺼이 맞추는 것도 포함된다. 이러한 태도는 학교에서는 쉽게 배울 수 있는 게 아니다. 태도는 교육 상황 자체가 필요로 하는 구성요소이기 때문이다. 따라서 그러한 태도는 어린이가 학교에 다니기 시작하기 전 몇 년 동안 학습돼야 한다. 즉, 집에서 학습돼야 하는 것이다.

질서에 부응하는 그러한 태도가 없다면, 교실 수업은 완전히 제 기능을 못하는 기술이 되고 말 것이다. 따라서 오코너가 말한 것에 대한 한 가지 가능성 있는 해석은 "우리 학교는 젊은이를 교육하기 위한 유용한 기술을 보유하고 있다. 하지만 그 많은 학생들은 가정에서 그 기술이 작동하기 위해 필요한 태도를 배우지 못했다"는 것이다.

03 모범답안 The scientific culture(or The scientists), as opposed to (people who represent) the traditional culture that obscure(s) the social and moral truth, possess(es) a special kind of moral authority.

한글번역

과학 문명이 우리에게 제공할 수 있는 최대의 풍요로움은 도덕적 풍요로움이다. 과학자들 중 사려 깊은 사람들은 개인의 조건이 비극적이라는 것을 알고 있다. 즉, 그러한 조건이 화려하고 즐거운 것이라고 하더라도, 그것의 본질은 외로움이며 최종적으로는 죽음이다. 하지만, 그 과학자들은 개인의 조건이 비극적이라고 해서 사회적 조건 역시 그래야 한다는 사실은 인정하려 들지 않는다. 또 인간이 반드시 죽어야 한다고 해서, 그러한 사실이 그가 때가 되기 전에 죽는다거나 또는 노예 같은 삶을 살다가 죽어야 한다는 것에 대한 구실은 되지 못한다. 과학자들의 심리 기저에 있는 그러한 (현실을 방관하지 않으려는) 충동이 과학자들로 하여금 그 비극의 영역을 줄이도록 하고 있다. 즉, 생각하기에 따라 인간의 의지 안에 놓여 있을 수 있는 그 어떤 것도 비극적인 것으로 간주되지 않도록 하고 있다. 그 과학자들은 이러한 사회적 진실을 흐리기 위해 인간에 대한 깊은 통찰력을 이용하거나 적은 이익에 매달렸던 전통 문화의 대표자들을 경멸한다. 가령, 도스토예프스키는 대법관인 포브도노체브에게 아부를 했는데, 그는 노예제도에 유일한 잘못된 것이 있다면 그것이 충분하지 않다는 사실에 있다고 생각한 사람이었다. 또 에즈라 파운드는 파시즘 정권을 위해 방송을 했고, 포크너는 흑인들을 다른 종으로 대우하는 것에 대한 구실을 제공했다. 이러한 사실 모두는 성직자들의 가장 뿌리 깊은 유혹의 징후인 것이다. 말인즉, "인간의 조건이 비극적이기 때문에, 모든 사람은 자신의 자리에 있어야 한다. 어쩌다 보니 내 자리가 꼭대기에 가까운 어딘가에 있듯이." 하지만 과학 문명은 패배와 방종 및 도덕적 공허에서 비롯된 그 특별한 유혹으로부터 거의 완전히 자유롭다. 최근 몇 년 동안 나머지 우리가 가장 필요로 하는 것은 다름 아닌 바로 그러한 종류의 과학자들의 도덕적 건강성이다.

2S2R

유희태 일반영어 ③ 기출

● 모범답안 및 번역

초판 1쇄 2010년 4월 28일
2판 1쇄 2014년 4월 29일
3판 1쇄 2016년 4월 29일
4판 1쇄 2018년 4월 30일
5판 1쇄 2021년 4월 30일
6판 1쇄 2023년 1월 10일
2쇄 2025년 2월 10일
7판 1쇄 2026년 1월 15일

저자와의
협의하에
인지생략

저자 유희태 **발행인** 박 용 **발행처** (주)박문각출판
표지디자인 박문각 디자인팀
등록 2015. 4. 29. 제2019-000137호
주소 06654 서울시 서초구 효령로 283 서경 B/D
팩스 (02) 584-2927
전화 교재 문의 (02) 6466-7202 동영상 문의 (02) 6466-7201

ISBN 979-11-7519-611-7